Mastering

Lync™ Server 2010

Nathan Winters

Keith Hanna

John Wiley & Sons, Inc.

Acquisitions Editor: Agatha Kim
Development Editor: Jim Compton
Technical Editors: Ilse Van Criekinge and Harold Wong
Production Editor: Eric Charbonneau
Copy Editor: Kathy Grider-Carlysle
Editorial Manager: Pete Gaughan
Production Manager: Tim Tate
Vice President and Executive Group Publisher: Richard Swadley
Vice President and Publisher: Neil Edde
Book Designers: Maureen Forys and Judy Fung
Proofreader: Jen Larsen, Word One New York
Indexer: Ted Laux
Project Coordinator, Cover: Katherine Crocker
Cover Designer: Ryan Sneed
Cover Image: © Thomas Northcut / Digital Vision/ Getty Images

ISBN: 978-1-118-08953-8 (pbk.)
ISBN: 978-1-118-22350-5 (ebk.)
ISBN: 978-1-118-23322-1 (ebk.)
ISBN: 978-1-118-26172-9 (ebk.)

Library of Congress Control Number: 2011945002

10 9 8 7 6 5 4 3 2 1

Dear Reader,

Thank you for choosing *Mastering Lync Server 2010*. This book is part of a family of premium-quality Sybex books, all of which are written by outstanding authors who combine practical experience with a gift for teaching.

Sybex was founded in 1976. More than 30 years later, we're still committed to producing consistently exceptional books. With each of our titles, we're working hard to set a new standard for the industry. From the paper we print on, to the authors we work with, our goal is to bring you the best books available.

I hope you see all that reflected in these pages. I'd be very interested to hear your comments and get your feedback on how we're doing. Feel free to let me know what you think about this or any other Sybex book by sending me an email at `nedde@wiley.com`. If you think you've found a technical error in this book, please visit `http://sybex.custhelp.com`. Customer feedback is critical to our efforts at Sybex.

Best regards,

Neil Edde
Vice President and Publisher
Sybex, an Imprint of Wiley

This book is dedicated to my wife, Elizabeth. Your love, patience, and encouragement constantly amaze me and help me to take on challenges such as this!
—Nathan Winters

I'd like to dedicate this book to my wonderful family—my wife, Sharon, for giving me the encouragement (and space!) to keep going (not just on this book, but always!), to my daughter, Rosie, for always being right, and to my son, Jamie, who after 22 months has finally mastered the art of walking! We make a great team.
—Keith Hanna

Acknowledgments

As you can imagine (and I know for certain!), writing a book is no simple task. It is something, however, which I had been looking to do for a few years, and with the release of Lync 2010 the opportunity presented itself. How the opportunity came about is something I would like to describe, as it will let me pay tribute to one of the people who has inspired me most throughout my career and without whom, I'm far less likely to have written this book.

Mark Minasi has been the author of the Sybex *Mastering Windows* series since 1994. I first read his *Mastering Windows 2000* when studying for my MCSE and as a result joined his online forum. I ended up moderating the Exchange section and over time became a Microsoft Exchange MVP. For the last five years, we have had a forum get-together in Virginia, USA. At the inaugural event in 2005, I gave my first technical presentation, which I later turned into an article for *Windows IT Pro,* kick-starting my writing career. At the last event, in 2010, I met Agatha Kim, the acquisitions editor for Sybex. We got to talking and the idea for this book was born.

Of course, to write such a book while maintaining a day job and some semblance of a personal life would have been impossible without help. To that end I asked Keith Hanna, a friend and colleague working for Microsoft in the United Kingdom, to coauthor with me. Keith has been a massive support. He not only has written half of the book, but has also shared his considerable technical knowledge of Lync with me, given guidance, and sounded the occasional rallying call when needed. Without him, this book would not exist.

Throughout the process, we have been supported, guided, and cajoled by a superb team at Sybex. Agatha helped shape the book, paring us down from some 30-plus chapters to the much more manageable and focused 19 that you see here. Jim Compton, our developmental editor, was constantly available to help ensure a standard tone for the book, to correct our sometimes ingenious uses of grammar, and to get the formatting right for Sybex. Of course, no technical book can be released without thorough cross-checking, and for that we are very grateful to Ilse Van Criekinge, our technical editor, who spent many hours going through the material replicating our examples to ensure technical accuracy. Finally, Eric Charbonneau and the copy editing team at Sybex did a wonderful job tightening up the content and laying it out as you see it today.

Outside of the Sybex team, there have also been many supporting participants. Adam Gent, Principal Microsoft Consultant for Enghouse Interactive, was kind enough to write a couple of chapters around his specialist expertise. I would also like to acknowledge support from Joanne Warden from Microsoft Consulting Services, Russ Kirk from Grey Convergence, and Matt Hurst from NET Quintum, who all contributed their significant expertise to one or more sections. Joanne, in particular, was also a great help, reading and giving directional advice about several chapters.

My thanks go to all involved in helping to create this book.

—Nathan Winters

In addition to the Sybex team (who I think chased me more than Nathan!), special thanks from me to Nathan for allowing me to help in this creation. Little did I know when he offered to buy me a coffee he had so much bigger plans! I am honored to have been asked to help with this, although since that day I do view any emails from him with deeper suspicion than they perhaps deserve.

It has been an extremely interesting (and mostly enjoyable!) journey over the past year since we started talking about this venture. Keeping with the journey aspect, my portions of this book were written/reviewed/rewritten in various countries across the world—nine at last count—and I know I would have struggled with it were it not for all those hours spent in airports and hotels with nothing else to do!

Special mention and thanks go to my technical mentors at Microsoft. There have been many who have helped, but only two who have "officially" held the *Mentor* title! They are Mark Fugatt, who despite my insistence on being an Exchange engineer started me down the path of Live Communications Server in my early days (I'll never forget his advice: "Never write a book." Sorry, Mark!); and Thomas Binder, who has guided me since the release of Office Communications Server 2007 R2 (what he doesn't know about Edge servers isn't worth knowing).

There are many other people I'd like to thank within Microsoft, and I think listing their names would double the length of the book! Specifically, the community around LCS/OCS and Lync, the Microsoft Certified Master community and the *original* COE team—guys (and gals), you have helped me many times (and continue to do so); hopefully, I can continue to be a member of these valuable communities.

My advice to others: If you work for Microsoft, join these communities; they're invaluable. If you don't, join your local UC user group. These guys reach out via the user groups, or Tech Ed. Catch up with these people; they don't bite!

—*Keith Hanna*

About the Authors

Nathan Winters has worked in IT since graduating from the Royal College of Music (RCM) in 2003, where he studied the clarinet! His first job was at the RCM, migrating from Exchange 5.5 and Windows NT4 to Exchange and Windows Server 2003. Nathan has since worked in a variety of roles for Microsoft partners, including consultancy and practice management. He now works for Microsoft UK as a Unified Communications Technical Specialist. Before joining Microsoft, Nathan was active in the UK technical community, running the Exchange user group (MMMUG) and writing numerous articles for *Windows IT Pro* magazine and the `MSExchange.org` website, among others. He was awarded a Microsoft MVP between 2006 and 2011. On the rare occasions when he is not working, he enjoys wildlife photography and badminton.

Keith Hanna started university life at Sheffield University studying software engineering, but finished by graduating from Queen's University, Belfast, in computer science. His first "real" job was with Lucas Aerospace as a software developer working on aircraft engine control systems—it wasn't rocket science, but it was close! Moving to England from Ireland, Keith helped to design and deploy a communications system for the emergency services, but found his calling in Windows-based application design and support, eventually making his way to Microsoft, where he has been for over five years, working in a number of roles from engineer to consultant, and as this book goes to print, he is about to embark on a new role in service delivery. He has contributed several articles to TechNet as well as several chapters in the *Lync 2010 Resource Kit*. He has written training courses for OCS R2 and Lync, as well as exam questions. He is a Microsoft Certified Master. He's not aware of any life outside work, and he will be keen to discover if such a thing exists now that the book is finished.

Contents at a Glance

Contents

Introduction

This book is the first time the Sybex *Mastering* series has touched on the subject of Microsoft's Unified Communications (UC) platform. With the release of Lync 2010, we are into the third generation of a platform that provides a comprehensive set of functionality, which has placed it in the top right of the Gartner Magic Quadrant for UC in 2011.

Lync is a new name for the platform, a fact that suggests the way in which the product has had a complete makeover. While there is an upgrade path from earlier versions of Office Communications Server 2007 and 2007 R2 (described in Chapter 7), there is a massive amount of new functionality in Lync, for both client and server. With this in mind, we set out to reinforce any prior knowledge you might have of the server platform, but not to assume any, and thereby take you on a journey from the key fundamentals of Lync all the way through deployment to how best to integrate Lync with third-party systems.

We have attempted to ensure that you can gain insight into real-world environments both through the use of lab systems that represent those that might be found in an enterprise network and also through the use of real-world case studies that highlight examples of our day-to-day experience as consultants to some of the world's largest organizations.

What You Need to Run Lync Server 2010

As you read through this book, you will find that there are a range of components that all come together to make Lync function. These include the Lync Server software, Lync client, and the supporting technology from Microsoft Windows Server 2008 R2 and Microsoft SQL Server 2008 R2. Of course, there are additional pieces that can be integrated, such as gateway devices, telephone devices, and software components such as Exchange and SharePoint.

With this much complexity, you may be wondering how on Earth you are going to be able to get started with learning Lync. In addition to all the components, you will find when looking at the published minimum system requirements for Lync that the main front-end (or Standard Edition) servers require a minimum of 16GB of RAM and eight CPU cores. We cover all this in depth in Chapter 5, but no doubt you will think that is rather a challenge for a lab. Well, don't worry! It is perfectly possible to set up a very capable lab system on a single machine. In fact, while writing this book, we ran our numerous lab systems on a variety of hardware, ranging from Dell desktops with 16GB of RAM and a pair of fast hard drives for the virtual machines to Dell Tower server hardware with 24GB and four hard drives. All in all, this is equipment that is well within the reach of any enterprise looking to get up to speed with Lync and something that anyone studying IT as they learn for their career can get hold of for not ridiculous sums.

Within the constraints of the hardware mentioned, we created our labs using Microsoft Hyper-V technology to virtualize many machines. The labs ranged from two machines covering a domain controller and a single Lync server all the way up to the migration lab, which had both OCS and Lync installed with full external communication and mediation servers for connectivity to the PSTN, where we were running ten servers on our single piece of hardware. So while for production use you must take care to size things according to best practice, in the lab you can learn a great deal with a single server, Hyper-V, some public IP addresses, public certificates, and a SIP trunk—which are all readily available for affordable amounts of money.

What's Inside

This book is arranged in six main sections, with a couple of appendixes. The six main areas focus on key elements that help build your knowledge of Lync, starting with fundamentals that get you up to speed. We then move through getting your first Lync system up and running to administrating your system. At that point, the book takes a deep look into using Lync as your telephony platform, before moving on to cover how to integrate Lync into other systems, and we then finish with a look a Lync mobile clients. The appendices wrap up the Bottom Line learning entries from the book and conclude by taking a step back from the technical elements to discuss changes Lync may require to your business and how to make sure you have a successful implementation.

When first picking up a new book, people frequently jump straight to a chapter that answers some immediate need or interest. We have attempted to build concepts throughout this book, with most of the later chapters making the assumption that you are familiar with the previous material. We have, of course, referenced that earlier material wherever possible in case you need to brush up, but as a general recommendation, we suggest that if you're new to Lync, you will have the most success by reading through the chapters in order.

Part 1: Fundamentals

This section covers the background information that will help you understand what makes Lync tick.

- **Chapter 1: What's in Lync?** This chapter runs through Lync from top to bottom, covering key concepts, features, and where Lync sits in the history of real-time communication products from Microsoft.
- **Chapter 2: Standards and Protocols.** Like any technical product, Lync is underpinned by numerous protocols and standards that enable it to operate and interoperate with other platforms. This chapter focuses in particular on SIP, which enables the majority of Lync communications.
- **Chapter 3: Security.** Security is front of mind for all administrators these days. In this chapter, we outline the threats to Lync and explain its architecture in a security-focused manner that will enable you to discuss requirements with your security team. We also cover some of the administrative practices needed to help you administrate Lync securely.
- **Chapter 4: Clients.** Without clients, any server product would be pretty useless! In this chapter, we look at the clients available on a PC, Mac, browser, and telephone, and we dive deep into how the clients connect to Lync.

Part 2: Getting Lync Up and Running

This section is where you actually get hands-on with Lync. We cover planning and sizing and then both the installation and upgrade processes.

- **Chapter 5: Planning Your Deployment.** While we are all keen to dive in and start playing with the nuts and bolts, planning is essential to ensure you achieve what is required. This chapter shows you how to plan utilizing the available tools and it helps you understand the Lync prerequisites, enabling you to choose which hardware to use and whether virtualization will work for you.
- **Chapter 6: Installation.** By the end of this chapter, you should have installed your first Lync system. We take you through from preparing your underlying server OS, through to publishing Lync to the Internet with all the steps in between!
- **Chapter 7: Migration and Upgrades.** Lync is the latest in a line of real-time communications products from Microsoft. This chapter shows you how to get from the earlier Office Communications Server 2007 or 2007 R2 to Lync.

Part 3: Administration

Having planned and installed Lync in the previous section, we now move on to look at administration. These chapters cover PowerShell, explain Admin roles and policies, and even look at troubleshooting.

- **Chapter 8: Introduction to PowerShell and the Lync Management Shell.** PowerShell is what underpins the whole management interface of Lync. In this chapter, you learn what PowerShell is, how to use it, and more importantly how to work with Lync using PowerShell.
- **Chapter 9: Role-Based Access Control.** Role-Based Access Control (RBAC) changes the granularity and ease with which an administrator can be granted permissions required for their job and only their job, allowing specific delegation of functionality to groups of people. This chapter shows you how Lync implements RBAC and how to use it to implement secure administration of Lync.
- **Chapter 10: User Administration.** Having looked at PowerShell and RBAC, the two main concepts underpinning administration, in this chapter, we show how to manage users, enabling, disabling, and configuring them both individually and through policy, to use the Lync features they require.
- **Chapter 11: Archiving and Monitoring.** Lync enables communication, and in many organizations communications must be archived. This chapter covers how Lync does this with the archiving role. It also covers the way in which you can inspect the communication passing through Lync, not only for quality but also more traditionally, showing who spoke with whom. Finally, we also cover how to monitor the Lync service as a whole using System Center Operations Manager (SCOM).
- **Chapter 12: Troubleshooting.** As with any system, there will be times where things don't work as they should. This chapter works through key troubleshooting concepts and then looks at the tools available in Lync and how to use them when trouble strikes.

Part 4: Voice

Lync is the first product from Microsoft that can truly claim to be a full-fledged telephony system (PBX). This section focuses on using Lync as your PBX, taking you from basic phone calls through to complex automated call distribution systems.

- **Chapter 13: Getting Started with Voice.** Lync provides all the capability needed to be a large enterprise telephony platform. This chapter introduces you to the world of the PBX. It covers the features available in Lync and the architecture that supports them.
- **Chapter 14: Call Admission Control.** One of the biggest considerations when utilizing data networks for audio and video communication is bandwidth usage. Call Admission Control enables you to map out your network and protect it from overuse. This chapter shows you how to do this with Lync.
- **Chapter 15: E911 and Location Information Services (LIS).** Especially in North America, the ability to locate where a phone call is being made from and to provide that information to the emergency services is mandatory. This chapter discusses how to provide this functionality with Lync; it also shows how those outside of North America can use this innovative technology.
- **Chapter 16: Extended Voice Functionality.** Lync can do far more than just basic phone calls. This chapter looks at how to implement your own audio-conferencing bridge, how to set up your own mini call center or help desk, and how to deal with other voice scenarios, such as the need to park calls for others to pick up and to deal with calls to people who have left your company.

Part 5: Integration

One of the huge benefits of Lync being a software platform is that it is very easy to extend and integrate with other systems. This section covers that extensibility looking at the way Lync integrates with both other Microsoft and non-Microsoft products.

- **Chapter 17: Exchange, SharePoint, and Group Chat.** While Lync by itself contains a huge amount of technology, it is enhanced even further through tight integration with other Microsoft products. This chapter covers the provision of voice mail and presence integration with Exchange, and presence integration and workflow with SharePoint. We also look at Group Chat, a Lync component that provides subject-based persistent real-time communications.
- **Chapter 18: Third-Party Integration.** In this chapter, we cover Lync as it sits at the center of a unified communications system. We cover integration with third-party PBXs, gateways (including the deployment of Survivable Branch Appliances), and video conferencing systems. We look at extending Lync with third-party software and show how to deploy the XMPP gateway to allow communication with a wide range of IM clouds, including Jabber and Google.

Part 6: Mobile Devices

- **Chapter 19: Mobile Devices.** The final chapter of this book covers the very latest additions to Lync. In the Lync Server 2010 Mobility Services update, following Cumulative Update 4 (CU4), released late in 2011, Microsoft provided new capabilities and clients, which enabled the use of Lync on all major brands of mobile devices, including Android, Windows Phone, Symbian, and iOS. This chapter covers the new clients and the supporting server components.

Appendices

There are two appendices. The first covers all the learning points from throughout the book, and the second discusses how to successfully adopt Lync in your organization.

- **Appendix A: The Bottom Line.** Throughout the book, the Bottom Line section appears at the end of each chapter. It asks relevant questions to help test your understanding of the material in that chapter. This appendix covers all those questions and includes the answers so you can verify yours.
- **Appendix B: Adoption.** While this book has focused on the technology that is Lync, there is another major aspect to utilizing Lync: how do you get Lync adopted in your organization? Without a proper plan and a great team that includes people ranging from very senior personnel to those using the technology every day, you may not have great success deploying Lync. This appendix discusses some of the key elements that come together to enable a business to successfully adopt Lync.

The Mastering Series

The *Mastering* series from Sybex provides outstanding instruction for readers with intermediate and advanced skills in the form of top-notch training and development for those already working in their field and clear, serious education for those aspiring to become pros. Every *Mastering* book includes:

- Real-World Scenarios, ranging from case studies to interviews that show how the tool, technique, or knowledge presented is applied in actual practice.
- Skill-based instruction, with chapters organized around real tasks rather than abstract concepts or subjects.
- Self-review test questions, so you can be certain you're equipped to do the job right.

Conventions Used in This Book

Before you set off into the world of Lync described in this book, there is one final piece of information that we want you to know.

Throughout the book, we used various methods to describe things. In particular, we had many discussions about how best to describe the tools used to administer Lync. As you will see, there are two main interfaces. A web-based control panel called Lync Server Control Panel (LSCP) and a command-line shell called the Lync Server Management Shell (LSMS), which is PowerShell-based. In the book, we used the terms Control Panel and LSCP interchangeably to describe the Lync Server Control Panel, and PowerShell to describe the Lync Server Management Shell. Please don't confuse this use of PowerShell with the standard Microsoft PowerShell shell, which is installed on Windows Server 2008 R2 by default. When working with Lync, unless explicitly stated otherwise, you should be using the Lync Server Management Shell.

How to Contact the Authors

We welcome feedback from you about this book. Obviously, it's always nice to get messages about what you liked about the book, but we also welcome suggestions for improvements we could make in future editions. You can reach Nathan by writing to `nathan@clarinathan.co.uk`, and you can reach Keith at `hannakeith@hotmail.com`. If you are looking for information about future articles or speaking engagements, visit Nathan's blog: `www.nathanwinters.co.uk`.

Sybex strives to keep you supplied with the latest tools and information you need for your work. Please check their website at `www.sybex.com/go/masteringlyncserver`, where we'll post additional content and updates that supplement this book should the need arise.

Fundamentals

Chapter 1

What's in Lync?

Lync Server 2010 is the latest in the line of the Communications Server platforms from Microsoft. The platform originally started with Live Communications Server 2003 (some would say with Exchange Conference Server 2000) and continued through Live Communications Server 2005, Office Communications Server (OCS) 2007, and finally Office Communication Server 2007 R2. This latest version extends the voice capabilities even further than those introduced with Office Communications Server 2007.

After finishing this chapter, you will be able to:

- Describe the features of the client
- Describe the features of the server
- Describe the voice features

Understanding the Lync 2010 Client

As an administrator, the first thing you'll see is the Setup tool; however, the users will see the client. Therefore, understanding what the client can and will provide is important for administrators trying to sell the business justification. It is also important in terms of what policies will need to be configured to enable (or disable) features. Lync 2010 is so much more than a simple instant messaging (IM) tool or a phone, and treating it as either end of the messaging scale will impact the way you deploy it to users. Some of the additional training capabilities freely provided by Microsoft are covered in Appendix A, "The Bottom Line."

One of the most obvious changes with Lync 2010, compared to previous versions, is the removal (or rather incorporation) of the conferencing client, Live Meeting. Almost all communications are now handled within the one client; the exception is the Lync 2010 Group Chat client, which is still a separate downloadable client and server application.

With the 2010 edition, Lync has had a facelift; new features such as user photos have been added and it is more user friendly. As part of this makeover, the Lync 2010 client is focused around three themes:

- Connect
- Communicate
- Collaborate

Figure 1.1 shows the client when first logged in.

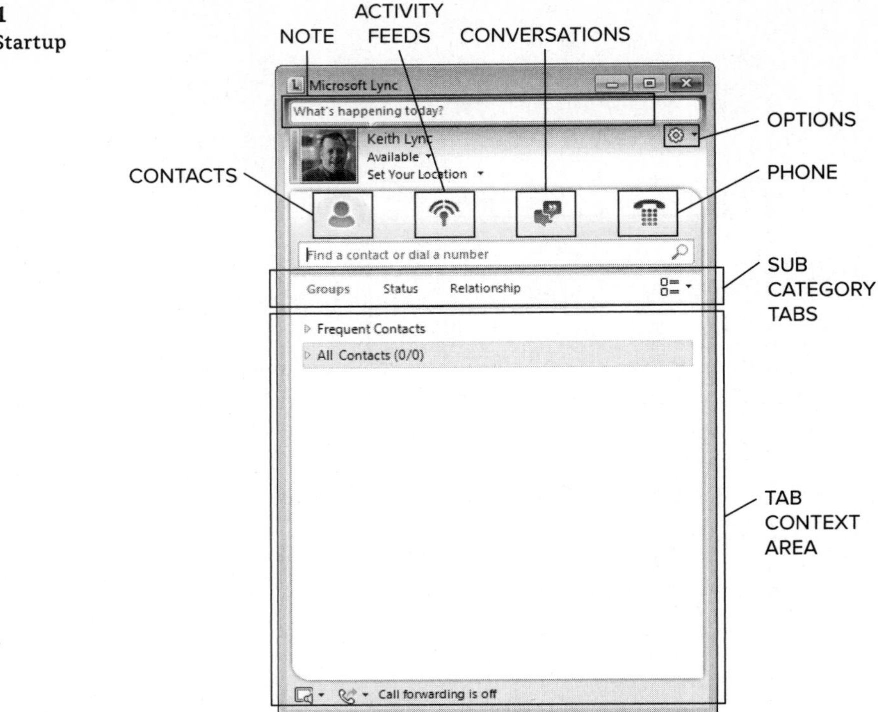

FIGURE 1.1
The Client Startup screen

Connecting via the Lync 2010 Client

In order to communicate and collaborate, Lync client users need to be able to locate and connect to each other on the network. Over time, users will build their own contacts list (sometimes called a ***buddy list***); however, they need to find other users to be able to create and add to the list. The basic search functionality from previous versions has been retained and has been expanded to include integration and key-skills searching within SharePoint 2010, as well as the expected Address Book search. Also new within Lync 2010 is the ability to remove the Address Book download capability and provide only an online web-based search function. Figure 1.2 shows the Client Search bar and results window when data has been entered into the search bar.

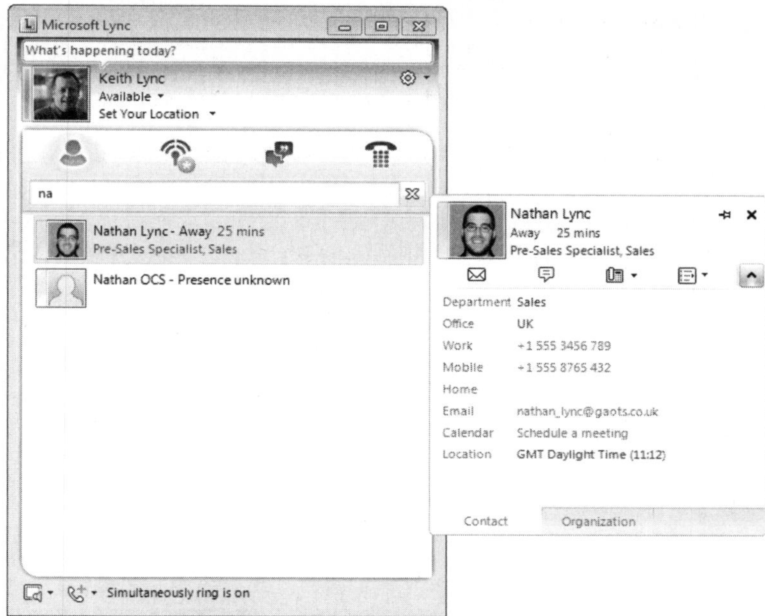

FIGURE 1.2
The Client Search Bar and Results Window

From these results, the User Properties box is extended to provide a lot more contextual information:

- Department
- Office
- Work number
- Mobile number
- Home number
- Alias
- Calendar information
- Location information

This ***contact card*** provides a consistent Lync 2010 client interface across all the integrated applications, such as Office and SharePoint. Connecting from other applications preserves context; if you start a conversation from an Outlook email, both the subject and the priority are carried across to the conversation windows and; the document title is transferred from SharePoint. The contact card now includes the ability to provide location information, giving users a way to quickly establish where people are currently, which can help them determine whether personal contact or a video call is the more appropriate type of communication. The location information also provides the local time for the user, which can be extremely useful when people are spread across multiple geographies.

You can search across the following locations:

- Lync contacts
- Active Directory
- Outlook contacts (including suggested contacts)

Searching allows you to easily establish availability and identity—the extended contact card provides more information to help identify the correct recipient—and quickly establish contact using any modality. In addition to searching by name, the SharePoint integration allows you to search by skills (or keywords) to help identify the correct person.

As mentioned, the capability to add contacts (or *buddies*) and group them is retained; in fact, it is expanded to include an auto-populated Frequent Contacts group. This group is automatically populated with your ten most-frequent contacts, which are weighted based on modality. For example, someone you regularly call is going to be placed higher in the list than someone you IM. You'll learn about other automatically created groups later in this chapter.

The Contacts tab, which is the default, contains a number of subtabs that provide different views (shown in Figure 1.3).

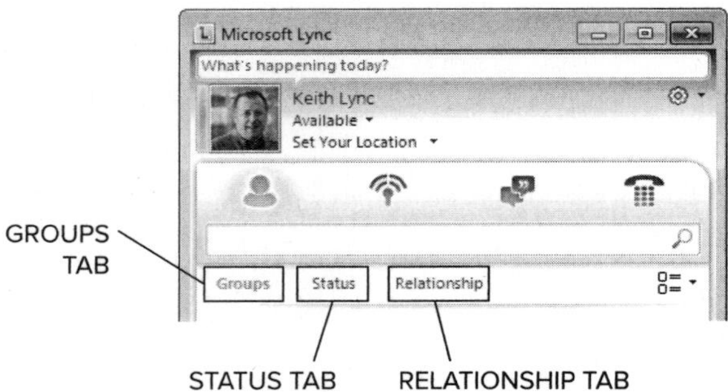

FIGURE 1.3
The Contacts tab

Groups This is probably the most frequently used subtab; it is where you can find all the contacts sorted alphabetically, but also grouped together in user-defined groups.

Status Under this subtab, all the contacts are sorted by availability, under the following groups:

- Away (includes Off Work)
- Unknown
- Unavailable
- Online (includes Busy, In a Meeting, and Do Not Disturb)

Relationships Here, you can manage the permissions assigned to each contact. The default categories are:

Friends and Family This relationship must be assigned manually. It provides the following setting:

- "Share all my contact information except meeting details."

Workgroup This relationship must be assigned manually. It provides the following setting:

- "Share all my contact information except Home and Other phone; contact can interrupt Do Not Disturb status."

Colleagues Any users from within the same Lync organization (or OCS if in coexistence) are automatically placed within this group and receive the following setting:

- "Share all my contact information except Home, Other, and Mobile phone, and meeting details."

External Contacts Any external (federated) users are placed within this group by default and receive the following setting:

- "Share only my name, title, email address, company, and picture."

Blocked Contacts This relationship must be manually assigned and provides the following setting:

- "Share only my name and email address; blocked contacts can't reach me via Lync."

Auto-Assign Relationship This has only one option:

- "Reset this privacy relationship to the Lync default."

Social Networking

The Lync 2010 client provides an Activity Feeds tab, where users can quickly view updates from all their contacts or simply their frequent contacts. Figure 1.4 shows a sample of the Activity Feeds tab.

Figure 1.4
The Activity Feeds tab

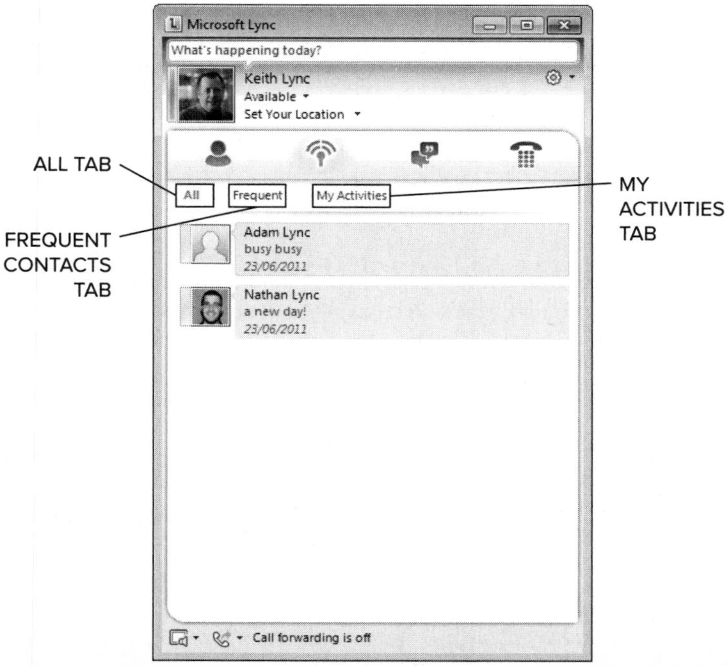

Here you can see updates such as changes to the Note field as well as changes in AD items, including photo, desk location, and job title changes. Finally, out-of-office responses are also included in this view. This information is also provided in each user's contact card; however, this view provides an at-a-glance view of the changes.

There is also a tab showing My Activities, which allows a user to see what information is being provided to others from their own data.

Users can enable or disable this functionality.

Communicating via the Lync 2010 Client

As mentioned in the previous section, the Lync 2010 contact card lets users quickly and easily establish any modality from any integrated application (see Figure 1.5). In particular, Lync 2010 allows users to receive phone calls on any device (including non-Lync devices) as well as manage their own (and potentially other users') communications easily and more effectively than before.

FIGURE 1.5
The contact card

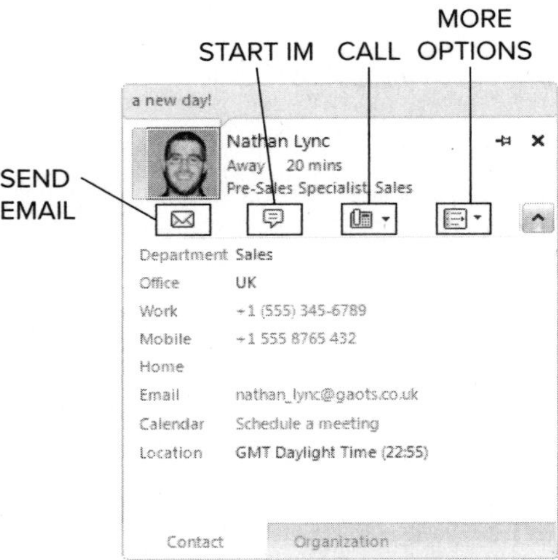

The final button (telephone icon) provides a single page for telecom interaction (see Figure 1.6), so users can make calls (from a dial-pad) and display and listen to voicemails. The dial-pad operates exactly as you would expect; for example, press and hold 1 to call your voicemail. The voicemail section allows quick and easy access to voicemails stored in your inbox.

FIGURE 1.6
The dial-pad

VOICEMAIL DISPLAY

The voicemail display within the Lync 2010 client is not as fully featured as the voicemail integration from within Outlook. Lync 2010 allows only basic integration, providing the name of the user (or phone number display, if caller ID could not be matched to a contact), a Play button, and the Lync 2010 interaction options allowing the call to be responded to from the client (using any modality).

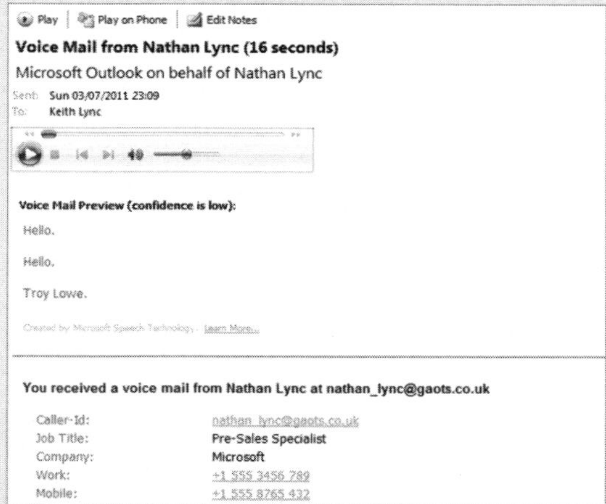

Outlook (2007 or higher) provides additional capability such as Notes, Play-on-Phone, and fully integrated media controls for playback. Exchange 2010 also provides speech-to-text translation, which will be displayed in Outlook only.

Video Calling

As with Office Communications Server 2007 R2, high definition is supported for peer-to-peer video only; however, the conferencing default codec has been changed to VGA (Video Graphics Array) with Lync, rather than CIF (Common Interchange Format). In addition to the higher resolution provided by this default codec, the Lync 2010 client also supports direct integration with the Microsoft RoundTable devices, providing a panoramic video strip when used in calls.

The video screen can be detached from the client and viewed in a separate window, which can be extremely useful for users who have multiple monitors because the video channel can be displayed on a separate display from the main conference window, allowing a more true-life experience.

Device Management

New device management functionality allows the Lync client to intelligently select the appropriate device for your calls. Even changing devices within a call is much easier. The Audio and Video Tuning Wizard is no longer required; you simply use a drop-down menu with all the devices listed and select a new one to transfer the call to the selected device immediately with no further interaction. Devices can even be added mid-call and the audio (or video) directed to the newly added device.

Audio and video device management and tuning is still possible from within the Options page from the Tools menu; however, doing so is now an optional task, whereas previously it was required every time a device was inserted.

The call-forwarding and team-call settings can now be managed with a single click in the main client window, shown in Figure 1.7.

FIGURE 1.7
Making a call forwarding selection

MANAGING COMMUNICATIONS

The Conversations tab provides a single location where you can keep track of ongoing communications. From this tab, it is easy to bring up previous conversations, assuming this information has been stored in Outlook (or more accurately, Exchange). Figure 1.8 shows this tab with content.

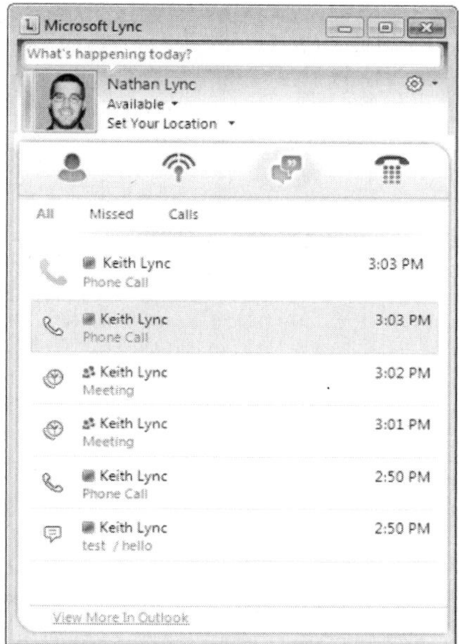

FIGURE 1.8
The Conversations tab

Each entry contains the history of the interaction, including all attendees and the modalities in use. Conversations can be resumed from this tab, and they will include the information from the previous conversation if it is still available. From the user's perspective, this will look like a continuation of the previous conversation.

A private line can be enabled for a user, in addition to their primary line, and is the equivalent of an incoming-only line. A user can have only a single private line, and when enabled, it is associated with the same Session Initiation Protocol (SIP) address (that is, the user does not get a second SIP address). It is an unlisted number and does not appear within any address books or Active Directory. The Private Line function provides a user with the ability to give out a number that will always get through; any Do Not Disturb or delegated-call scenarios are ignored by an incoming private line, and a different style of ***toast*** (the name given to the pop-up notification for any incoming communications) will appear, indicating an incoming call on the private line.

Lync 2010 provides an easy method to initiate calls on behalf of others. Once you are configured as a ***delegate*** for someone (as an assistant might be for a boss), additional options are provided for making calls.

In the delegated-call scenario, incoming calls are displayed on the client for both the delegate and the boss, enabling the delegate to handle any call on the boss's behalf. On the incoming toast, the availability of the boss is also displayed, allowing the delegate to quickly evaluate whether or not to pick up the call.

When added as a delegate, the user receives a notification indicating who added them. As shown in Figure 1.9, additional groups are also created, showing who the user's delegates are as well as those for whom they act as a delegate.

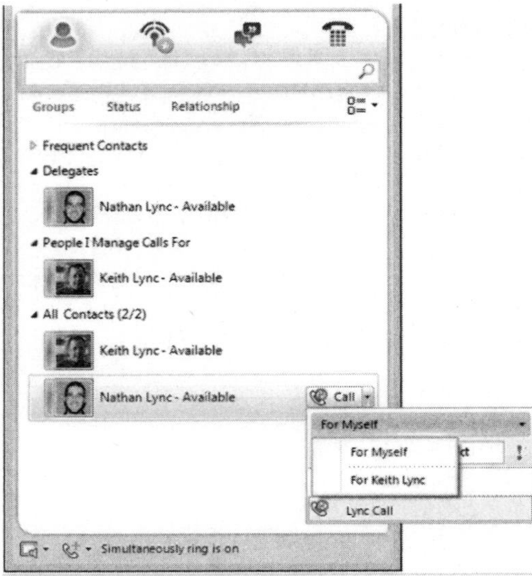

FIGURE 1.9
Delegation groups

When a user is designated as a delegate of someone, they can also place calls on their behalf, as shown in Figure 1.9.

Figure 1.10 shows the additional information added to the toast when a call is for someone who has delegates. If the delegate picks up the call, the toast will change to briefly show who picked up the call and an email message will be sent.

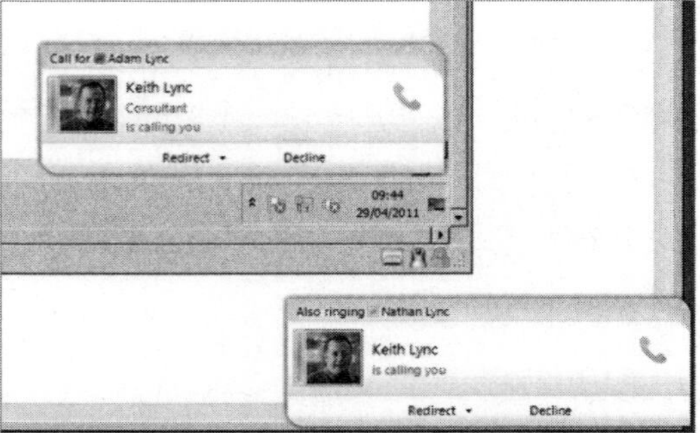

FIGURE 1.10
The toast received for an incoming call

Collaboration via the Lync 2010 Client

As mentioned earlier, previous versions of the Microsoft communications platform provided a separate client targeted for group collaboration: Live Meeting. This provided an interface whereby large groups could "meet" and collaborate on shared content (desktop or documents). Also, an additional add-in client, the Conferencing Add-In for Microsoft Office Outlook, was required to provide integration with Outlook, allowing meetings to be scheduled from the Outlook client.

Within Lync 2010, both the additional Live Meeting client and the Conferencing Add-In for Outlook have been removed, simplifying not only the installation process but also the user interaction. All functionality from within the Live Meeting client is included in the Lync 2010 client. The single installation package includes the Online Meeting Add-In for Microsoft Lync 2010, which provides the online meeting capability previously provided via the separate installation of the Conferencing Add-In for Outlook.

In some cases, it was difficult for users to understand which client was the correct one to use to join meetings or conferences; consolidating the features into the single client removes any scope for this confusion.

The Online Meeting Add-In for Microsoft Lync 2010 provides a single-click approach to creating a meeting. The user no longer needs to decide whether a meeting will be audio only or whether it will require desktop sharing; the client dynamically adapts and provides the needed resources from the server.

Other collaboration highlights include:

- The sharing model within Lync 2010 provides a flexible approach to sharing individual applications, screens, or the full desktop, as well as enabling the coediting of a document opened from SharePoint.
- Meetings now include a *lobby*, where users can wait to join a meeting. Previously users could only enter the conference directly or have their call dropped if the conference had not started or they were not permitted to join.
- Presenting PowerPoint sessions enables an Asynchronous Viewing mode, allowing other presenters to navigate through the content and review it.
- Dial-in conferencing supports the use of DTMF (touch-tone) commands for control of the conference, as well as providing voice announcements of attendees.
- Web-based access to conferences is provided on the platforms shown in Table 1.1.

TABLE 1.1: Web-Based Access Supported by Lync Client 2010

OS	IE 8	IE 7	IE 6	FIREFOX 3.X	SAFARI 5.*x*	SAFARI 6.*x*
Windows 7	Yes	Yes		Yes		
Windows Vista	Yes	Yes		Yes		
Windows XP	Yes	Yes	Yes	Yes		
Windows Server 2008 R2	Yes	Yes				
Windows Server 2003 (except IA-64)	Yes	Yes	Yes			
Windows Server 2000			Yes	Yes		
Mac OS 10.4.8+					Yes	Yes

Understanding Lync Server 2010

Customer feedback played a large role in driving the changes implemented in Lync Server 2010. Some of the issues admins brought to Microsoft's attention in previous versions include:

- There was no common store for configuration items, which could be found in Active Directory and SQL Server as well as in individual server metabases or WMI.
- There were no methods to validate configuration changes prior to deployment.
- MMC (Microsoft Management Console) was becoming complex.
- Automation was difficult.
- Deploying certificates correctly the first time was complicated.
- There was no "proper" support for virtualization.
- Multiple-site deployments required too many servers.

When the changes to address these issues (and more) were wrapped together, the result was the new functionality and management provided in Lync Server 2010.

Managing Lync Server 2010

Lync Server 2010 provides a completely new interface compared to any of the previous communications platforms. Gone is the MMC interface used to navigate and manage the configuration of Live Communications Server and Office Communications Server. (Well, the MMC interface is almost gone. The new Topology Builder application is the only application to continue to use it.) Replacing it is a combination of PowerShell and a Silverlight-based Control Panel application.

Following the lead of Exchange Server and other applications, Microsoft has built Lync Server 2010 on a base of PowerShell, which you can learn more about in Chapter 8, "PowerShell and LMS." When carrying out configuration requests, Lync Server's Silverlight-based Control Panel interfaces directly to PowerShell.

Lync Server 2010 also builds on Exchange Server's introduction of Role-Based Access Control (RBAC), allowing separate disparate groups to manage separate areas of the application such as users or telephony. Chapter 9, "RBAC," covers the topic in detail.

Topology Builder

You'll learn how to use Topology Builder in Chapter 5, "Planning Your Deployment," where we'll define the architecture and overall topology of the environment. The actual configuration of policies and implementation, however, is carried out using either PowerShell or the Control Panel application (in some cases, configuration items are available only in PowerShell). As you'll see, Topology Builder provides the first checkpoint for the topology and ensures configuration consistency; it will not allow configuration items to be removed if they are still in use.

The Topology Builder also consolidates all the information required for a generating a certificate. It ensures that any additional Subject Alternate Name (SAN) entries are included as required, ensuring that when the Setup program for a server gets to the Certificate Wizard, all the information is already in place. Additional user input and control over the certificate template used is provided using this wizard. The Edge server consolidates the external facing requirements from three separate certificates in previous versions to a single external certificate in Lync 2010.

Central Management Store

The multiple configuration stores from previous versions have been replaced with the *Central Management Store*. It is the sole location for all the configuration data for the deployment and operation of Lync Server 2010. Combining all the various configuration stores into a single Central Management Store means there is only a single point of failure, which is this database. Replicating this database to all servers in the environment results in the following benefits:

- Mitigates the single point of failure
- Allows servers to continue operating without access to Active Directory
- Removes reliance on Active Directory schema changes
- Provides consistency in server configuration (especially the Edge server)

The Central Management Store is stored within SQL Server (in a Standard Edition deployment, this is SQL Express) and can be made highly available by the use of a clustered SQL Server.

The Central Management Store operates in a master/replica state. In the event of a catastrophic loss of the Central Management Store, a replica can be promoted to be the master database. During an outage of the master database, no changes can be made to the environment; however, Lync Server 2010 will continue to operate based on the configuration at the time of loss (this also includes server restarts).

Central Management Store Replicas

During a server-role installation, a local copy of SQL Express is installed, and the Central Management Store is replicated to this database. The instance is called RTCLOCAL. This occurs on all server roles installed, including the Edge server.

Some companies are wary about proliferating SQL Express throughout the environment, mostly in the wake of the SQL Slammer virus and similar attacks. (In January 2003, the SQL Slammer virus impacted over 75,000 systems within 10 minutes, causing a large denial of service and Internet slowdown.)

By introducing these additional databases, Lync Server 2010 gives the admin more to manage and patch (if required). In addition, because the configuration information is replicated to the perimeter network on the Edge servers, availability of the configuration is at greater risk if the Edge servers are compromised.

The advantages provided by the local database replication, as well as the measures taken to protect them (e.g., encryption), outweigh the risks involved in most cases.

Many large financial service companies have already deployed Lync Server 2010 Edge servers. If there were significant risk of compromise, they'd be the first to provide feedback!

DNS LOAD BALANCING

Lync Server 2010 introduces DNS load balancing as a method to provide connection-based resilience to both clients and server interactions. DNS load balancing provides functionality only for SIP-based traffic.

Using DNS load balancing reduces the configuration requirements of a hardware load balancer (at the cost of creating a few additional DNS entries), allowing the hardware load balancer to focus on load-balancing HTTP traffic (a job for which it is much better suited).

For example, Table 1.2 shows the configuration required when using hardware to load balance a pool of three Front-End servers.

TABLE 1.2: DNS Records Required When Using Hardware Load Balancing

ITEM	DNS FQDN	DNS A RECORD
Pool VIP	`Lyncpool.company.com`	192.168.0.1
Front End	`FE1.company.com`	192.168.0.2
Front End	`FE2.company.com`	192.168.0.3
Front End	`FE3.company.com`	192.168.0.4

Table 1.3 shows the configuration required when using DNS load balancing on the same pool of three Front-End servers.

TABLE 1.3: DNS Records Required When Using DNS Load Balancing

ITEM	DNS FQDN	DNS A RECORD
Web VIP	`Lyncweb.company.com`	192.168.0.1
Pool	`Lyncpool.company.com`	192.168.0.2
Pool	`Lyncpool.company.com`	192.168.0.3
Pool	`Lyncpool.company.com`	192.168.0.4
Front End	`FE1.company.com`	192.168.0.2
Front End	`FE2.company.com`	192.168.0.3
Front End	`FE3.company.com`	192.168.0.4

Figure 1.11 diagrams the process through which a client will connect when using DNS load balancing. It is important to note that this is only for the first connection; once connected, the client will cache the server name and IP address for subsequent connections.

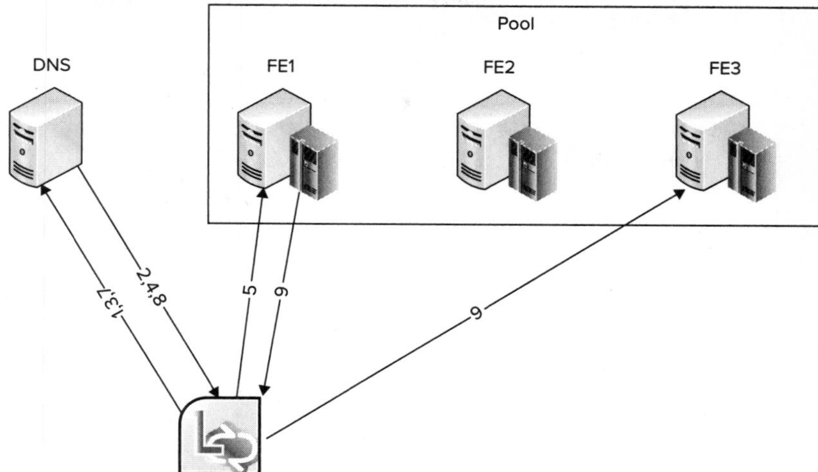

FIGURE 1.11
The client connection process

The following steps correspond to the numbered links in Figure 1.11, and describe the actions within each communications step:

1. The client queries DNS for the service record (SRV). (A service that was published using Domain Name System (DNS) can be discovered through its SRV record. Its SRV record includes information such as protocol, port, priority, and weight in the single record entry.)
2. The DNS server returns the SRV record pointing to the pool Fully Qualified Domain Name (FQDN).
3. The client queries DNS for the pool FQDN.
4. The DNS server returns the IP addresses of pool members.
5. The client connects to a randomly selected IP address from the list returned by the DNS server.
6. If this server is not the home server for the client, the server returns the home server name.
7. The client queries DNS for the address of the home server.
8. DNS returns the IP address of the home server.
9. The client connects to the server and registers the user.

INSTALLABLE SERVER ROLES

Lync Server 2010 introduces a number of new server roles, but more importantly it restructures the existing roles, allowing organizations to consolidate resources by combining various roles onto a single server deployment. Chapter 6, "Installation," covers the steps required to define and install each role.

Office Communication Server 2007 introduced the concept of an *expanded topology*, whereby a single pool could be separated into its constituent parts: web services, conferencing, and front ends. The move to a 64-bit deployment with Office Communications Server 2007 R2 allowed this topology to disappear (it was still supported, although not recommended), due to the capability of the 64-bit hardware to address more memory resources and make them available to the application. Lync Server 2010 provides the capability to do either, depending on the deployment needs. When the user count is greater than 10,000 in a pool, Microsoft recommends separation of the Audio/Video Conferencing Multipoint Control Unit (MCU) to a separate server/pool.

Virtualization is now fully supported for all server roles (except the Survivable Branch Appliance), and more detail is provided in Chapter 5.

The server roles provided in Lync Server 2010 are:

- Front End
- Back End
- Edge
- Director
- Mediation
- Monitoring
- Archiving
- Audio/Video Conferencing
- Survivable Branch Appliance
- Survivable Branch Server

The next sections describe these roles in detail.

Front End

The Front-End server provides the connection point for the client. It is responsible for all registration, via the Registrar service, and routing requests for clients. Because of this routing responsibility, all clients belonging to the same user must register on the same Front-End server. In addition, the Front-End server also holds all the conference MCUs:

- Web
- App sharing
- IM
- Audio/Video (unless separated)

The Front-End server is also home to the web component services, such as Address Book, Group Expansion, Control Panel, and Reach, the Silverlight application that provides web-based access to conferences.

High availability is achieved by the deployment of multiple (up to ten) Front-End servers into a single pool and the utilization of hardware (with or without DNS) load balancing.

Back End

The Back-End role is the SQL Server database, which provides both conference capability and contact/buddy lists. In deployments that also configure the built-in voice applications (Response Groups, Call Park, and Dial-In Conferencing), their data is also stored within this SQL Server. The Central Management Store is also stored in the Back-End role.

High availability is achieved by deploying SQL Server in an Active/Passive cluster, using Microsoft Cluster Services.

> **STANDARD EDITION SERVER**
>
> The Standard Edition server combines both the Front-End and Back-End roles into a single package. In this scenario only, the Back-End role is stored within a SQL Express database. High availability is not possible with Standard Edition.

Edge

The Edge role is deployed within the perimeter network and provides remote capability to Lync Server 2010. Remote capability is defined as:

- Remote access
- Federation with other organizations
- Public Internet Connectivity (PIC) federation with Windows Live, Yahoo!, and AOL

In addition, the Edge server provides a method to reroute calls via the Internet if insufficient internal bandwidth is available. In this case, an Edge server (or pool) is required at each location.

Multiple Edge servers may also be deployed to localize Internet conference traffic. For this purpose, each Edge server (or pool) is associated with an internal Front-End pool, and users homed on the Front-End pool use their locally defined Edge server for all traffic except SIP. SIP traffic (including federation) will only travel via a single Edge location.

High availability of the Edge environment is achieved with the deployment of multiple Edge servers in a single location. High availability of the federation functionality (including PIC) requires the use of a hardware load balancer and is only available in a single location.

Director

The Director role performs authentication, and is recommended when you are also deploying an Edge server. You should use the Director role to perform authentication when you are deploying an Edge server. The Director role provides a stop-off point for all external traffic. By placing this function at the first point of authentication, you ensure that all (any) malicious traffic is intercepted here, rather than a Front-End (where internal clients may be impacted). When an Edge server is used, the Director server is configured as the next hop and proxies the external traffic to its final destination. Figure 1.12 shows a typical Director placement.

FIGURE 1.12
A typical Director architecture

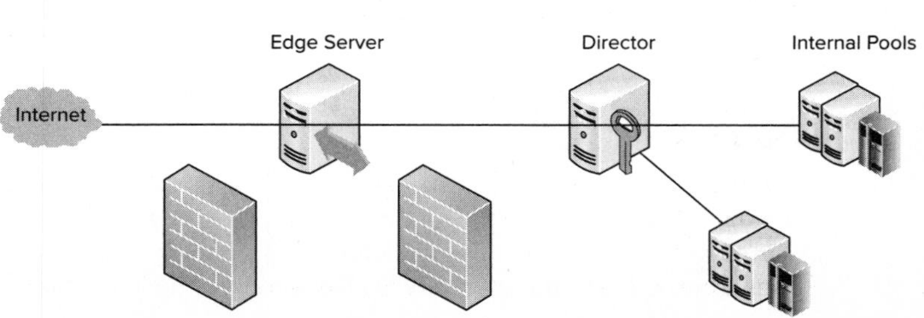

When used for internal traffic, the Director is defined as the result of the DNS SRV query for automatic login and, in this scenario, will redirect traffic to the correct home pool. With the additional support for multiple DNS SRV records, this requirement is redundant within the internal infrastructure.

Unlike the Office Communications Server versions, Lync Server 2010 makes the Director a defined role, not a normal pool with its features disabled.

High availability of the Director role is provided by deploying multiple servers and using DNS (or hardware) load balancing.

AUTHENTICATION MODES

Like previous versions of the platform, Lync Server 2010 supports both NTLM (NT LAN Manager) and Kerberos authentication modes. Traditionally, Kerberos was the preferred authentication method for internal client connections, and NTLM was used for external (remote user) access because the client could not receive a Kerberos ticket when it wasn't connected to the domain.

Lync Server 2010 allows clients to log in without access to Active Directory, so NTLM or Kerberos authentication is not required. Instead, a certificate is downloaded to the client upon first successful login (via either NTLM or Kerberos, so those tools are still required).

This certificate is provided by the Web Services component of the Front-End server. By default, it is valid for 180 days, but the time is configurable. The certificate is valid only for sign-in to Lync Server 2010.

A copy of the certificate is shown here. As you can see, the certificate is issued by Communications Server, and further investigation will show it can be used only for client authentication.

Mediation

The Mediation role is the interface into the public switched telephone network (PSTN). Typically, it is used in conjunction with a media gateway device, allowing an interface either into an existing PBX (private branch exchange) or directly to the PSTN. The latter configuration, known as *SIP trunking*, is now becoming more prevalent; it allows the Mediation server to connect directly to the PBX or PSTN without the need for an additional hardware media gateway device.

With previous versions of the Communications Server platform, the Mediation server was used to transcode the codec used internally (typically, RTAudio) into the codec used by the media gateway, whether it was PBX or PSTN (typically, G711). Lync 2010 introduced the concept of *media bypass*, whereby the client can communicate using G711 directly to the media gateway or PBX, alleviating the need for the transcoding to occur, thus removing the need for transcoding by the Mediation role. Media bypass to the PSTN is not possible, as there is no termination point to which the client can connect.

By removing (or at worst reducing) the need for transcoding on the Mediation role, media bypass reduces the tasks carried out by this role, which means that less powerful hardware can be used to run this role. This, in turn, allows for collocation of the Mediation role with a Front-End role, reducing the server footprint required.

Office Communications Server 2007 (both versions) had a one-to-one ratio of Mediation servers to media gateways; Lync Server 2010 removes this requirement and supports a many-to-many ratio.

High availability of the Mediation role is provided by deployment of multiple servers. Certain configuration options may perform better with or even require the hardware load balancing.

Monitoring

The Monitoring role provides the capability to capture both Quality of Experience and Call Detail Record information objects about all the calls in the environment.

This information is stored in a SQL Server database and evaluated using the provided SQL Reporting Services report pack, which contains almost 50 built-in reports. Additional reports may be created using SQL Reporting Services Report Builder.

High availability of the monitoring role is not yet available; however, the SQL Server database may be stored on a SQL Server cluster. SQL Reporting Services is not cluster-aware and may not be clustered; however, that limitation impacts only the generation of the reports, not the data capture.

Archiving

The Archiving role provides a capture of all IM traffic and records any file transfers (filename and location, not content) occurring in the environment.

This information, like that captured by the Monitoring role, is stored within a SQL Server database. However, it should be noted that there are no additional compliance checks on this database; it is a store only.

Again, like the Monitoring role, Archiving does not yet support high availability, but the SQL Server database may be stored on a SQL Server cluster, providing high availability for the data.

Audio/Video Conferencing

In large environments (greater than 10,000 users in a pool), Microsoft recommends putting the Audio/Video conferencing MCU on a separate server to improve performance (of both the A/V MCU and also the remaining Front-End servers).

A single A/V conferencing pool may be defined per central site (as defined in Topology Builder), and multiple Enterprise Edition pools within this central site can share this A/V MCU resource.

High availability is provided by deployment of multiple servers within a pool. There is no limit to the number of A/V servers within a single A/V pool; however, a maximum of five Enterprise Edition pools can leverage a single A/V pool.

Survivable Branch Appliance (SBA)

The Survivable Branch Appliance is a hardware device provided by one of five hardware vendors:

- Audiocodes
- Dialogic
- Ferrari
- HP
- NET

All support for these devices is provided by the hardware vendor directly.

The SBA is an all-in-one device that provides some of the functionality of a pool (specifically, registrar and routing) as well as having a colocated Mediation role and media gateway. The function of this device is to continue to provide local service to users in the event of a wide area network (WAN) or pool outage in the central location.

Users are provided local calling functionality via the device, but they rely on a central pool for conference and contact/buddy list information. In the event of a WAN or pool outage, the local PSTN breakout will continue to operate, allowing both incoming and outgoing calls. However, contact/buddy list information and access to conferencing will be unavailable, and the client will go into ***Survivable mode***. Figure 1.13 shows the client feedback when in Survivable mode, and as with OCS 2007 R2, any calls currently in progress will continue. Upon restoration of the failed service (network or server), the client will return to normal operations automatically.

FIGURE 1.13 The client display in Survivable mode

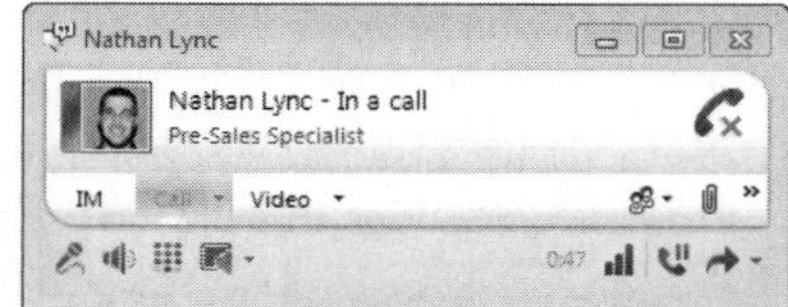

A Survivable Branch Appliance may only be a primary registrar and must be configured with a backup central pool.

High availability is provided by the backup central pool.

Survivable Branch Server

The Survivable Branch Server provides similar functionality to a Survivable Branch Appliance, except that it includes no media gateway. This option is typically used in locations that already have a media gateway deployed. For example, an OCS 2007 was previously deployed, and the cost of replacement cannot be justified.

Like a Survivable Branch Appliance, the Survivable Branch Server may only be a primary registrar, and must be configured with a backup central pool.

High availability is provided by the backup central pool.

Additional Server Roles (Separate Downloads)

All the previously listed server roles are provided as part of the Lync Server 2010 media. In addition to these included roles, the following roles are available as additional downloads:

- Group Chat
- XMPP Gateway
- Web Scheduler

Group Chat

Group chat functionality has not changed significantly since its introduction with OCS 2007 R2. Both the server and client have been given a facelift and made to look like part of the application; however, little has changed under the covers.

The Group Chat role provides chat rooms (or channels) where chat is persistent and searchable, enabling users to continue conversations over days or weeks. Users can also restart their client (following a reboot, for example) and go back to a conversation and be proactively alerted to conversations they missed while logged out.

XMPP Gateway

The XMPP Gateway has not changed since Office Communications Server 2007 R2, and indeed the download is the same. This application gateway is deployed alongside an Edge server and provides interaction with XMPP-compatible applications such as Google Talk.

Web Scheduler

The Web Scheduler role provides an alternative method to schedule conferences; typically, it is used when a customer is not using the Outlook add-in, perhaps because the customer uses Outlook Web Access or a non-Exchange email solution such as Notes or a hosted solution such as Gmail.

The Web Scheduler must be installed on a server running Lync's Web Components features (that is, any Front-End server) and must be integrated with an SMTP server to enable conference invitations to be sent via email.

To summarize the expanded set of server roles, the improvements made by the investment in functionality such as media bypass, as well as the supported colocation options (shown in Table 1.4), lead to a potentially massive reduction in the number of servers required. If you then factor in the full support for virtualization across all modalities, the result should be a significant savings in terms of both direct server purchase costs and indirect operating costs.

TABLE 1.4: SUPPORTED LYNC SERVER 2010 C-LOCATION DEPLOYMENTS

SERVER ROLE	COLOCATED ROLES	NOTES
Enterprise Edition front end	A/V Conferencing Mediation	
Back-End database of Front-End pool	Archiving Monitoring Database instance for Archiving Database instance for Monitoring	
Mediation	None	The Mediation server may be colocated with the Front-End pool.
A/V Conferencing	None	The A/V Conferencing server may be colocated with the Front-End pool.
Monitoring	Archiving Database for Monitoring Database for Archiving Back-End database for a Front-End pool Other SQL Server databases Standard Edition	For performance and tuning reasons, best results will be achieved if the Monitoring and Archiving databases are in their own separate instances. Standard Edition is not supported in production; it is for testing only. A file store can also be colocated here.
Archiving	Archiving Database for Monitoring Database for Archiving Back-End database for a Front-End pool Other SQL Server databases Standard Edition	For performance and tuning reasons, best results will be achieved if the Monitoring and Archiving databases are in their own separate instances. Standard Edition is not supported in production; it is for testing only. A file store can also be colocated here.
Director	None	
Edge	None	
Survivable Branch Appliance	Mediation Media Gateway	
Survivable Branch Server	Mediation	No gateway is included in a Survivable Branch Server.

Server Role	Colocated Roles	Notes
Trusted Application servers	None	
Exchange Unified Messaging	None	Exchange Server roles may be colocated with each other, but not with Lync Server 2010 roles.
Reverse Proxy	None	Reverse proxy may be colocated with other server applications as detailed in the reverse proxy support guidelines; however, no Lync Server 2010 roles may be colocated.

Automation Capabilities

Lync Server 2010 is built from the ground up on PowerShell. This new architecture provides significantly easier scripting and automation capability than previous versions, which relied on Windows Management Instrumentation (WMI) for most (but not all) configuration options. You can find more information about the use of PowerShell for Lync 2010 in Chapter 8.

Understanding the Voice Capabilities

Since the release of Office Communications Server 2007 back in October 2007, Microsoft has been relentlessly developing and pushing the voice capabilities of OCS. Lync Server 2010 takes them to the next level and in most cases fills the gaps from previous versions.

There are still areas in which Lync Server 2010 does not completely address the functionality provided by a traditional PBX. Many of these functions, however, are being made redundant as people move to new ways of communication. One example is ring-back. On a PBX, if you call a number and it is busy, you can enter a DTMF code to tell the PBX to call you back when the line becomes free. It can be argued that the use of presence information in OCS/Lync 2010 removes this requirement (if the ***callee*** is busy initially, the call will not be placed) and provides the capability to notify of presence changes.

The focus points for Lync Server 2010 voice capabilities are:

Resiliency By introducing the concept of a backup registrar and by increasing the scope of the multidatacenter (Metropolitan) pool scenarios supported to include all modalities, Lync Server 2010 expands the resiliency options provided by Office Communications Server 2007 R2.

The backup registrar continues to provide telephony functionality in the event of a failure to the primary registrar. The Lync 2010 client will register to the primary registrar when available; however, in the event that either the network connection to the primary registrar or the registrar itself fails, the client (following a configurable timeout) will register to the backup registrar and enter Survivable mode. As mentioned previously, this mode provides only telephony functionality and limited search capability for other users; all centralized services are lost, including conferencing, contact/buddy lists, and voice applications.

Any pool type (Enterprise or Standard) can act as a backup registrar to any other pool and to a Survivable Branch Appliance (or Server). The Survivable Branch Appliance (or Server) can only be designated as a primary registrar. When you are configuring backup registrars, you need to consider the server specification and overall capacity of the backup registrar, taking into account a potential failure of the primary registrar and the total number of users who could then be homed in on the backup registrar.

The Metropolitan scenario consists of a single pool stretched between two datacenters. This scenario was first introduced with OCS 2007 R2, and places extremely stringent requirements on the network between the datacenters (providing a SQL geo-cluster). In return for the complexity of this approach, the benefit is returned with no loss of functionality in the event of a datacenter failure. The configurations for voice applications (Response Groups, Call Park, and Conferencing) are stored in the single pool; with the resiliency provided by the SQL geo-cluster, this is available to the remaining servers in the surviving datacenter.

Call Admission Control Call Admission Control (CAC) is the capability to manage the number of Lync 2010 calls being placed on the network at any time. It is covered in detail in Chapter 14.

Call Park Call Park is the capability to place a call into a parked location for pickup (typically by another person) on another device or even location. Call Park is frequently used in conjunction with paging systems. A call will be received by an operator and put into an ***orbit***. Then a notification will go out on the paging system/intercom; the call can then be retrieved from orbit simply by dialing the orbit number. Hospitals and manufacturing plants typically use this feature; everyone has heard something like "Call for Dr. Smith on 1234."

Media Bypass The introduction of media bypass in Lync Server 2010 (and client) reduces the role of the Mediation server, which is no longer involved in the transcoding of the codecs, because both the client and the gateway are talking to each other with a common codec (typically, G711). As mentioned, removing this transcoding requirement from the mediation role also means there no longer needs to be one Mediation server per media gateway, allowing a single mediation role to support and control multiple media gateways.

Removing the extra hop of a Mediation server has the side benefit of improving voice quality (because the media traffic has a shorter path to travel) and also removes another potential point of failure.

Enhanced 911 Enhanced 911 is the provision of location-based information when calling emergency services within North America. E911 is covered in detail in Chapter 15, "E911 and LIS."

Analog Device Management Although Lync Server 2010 does not directly support and manage analog devices themselves, it does control the signaling information and, as such, can provide controls to restrict the class of service to which the devices have access (for example, you can choose not to permit international dialing and you can place similar restrictions). The device is connected to the environment via a media gateway, and Lync Server 2010 does not interfere in the media stream, only the signaling. Not being involved in the media stream allows fax machines to also benefit from this management.

Call Detail Records can be captured for all these analog devices because the signaling is controlled from the Lync Server 2010 servers.

Private Line As mentioned previously, the Private Line functionality is a means to assign a second number to a user. Incoming calls to this Private Line number do not follow any delegation rules (or other routing options, such as Do Not Disturb or Call Forward) and will always go through to the recipient. This function is for incoming calls only. The incoming toast, which has a different ring tone associated with it, can be seen in Figure 1.14.

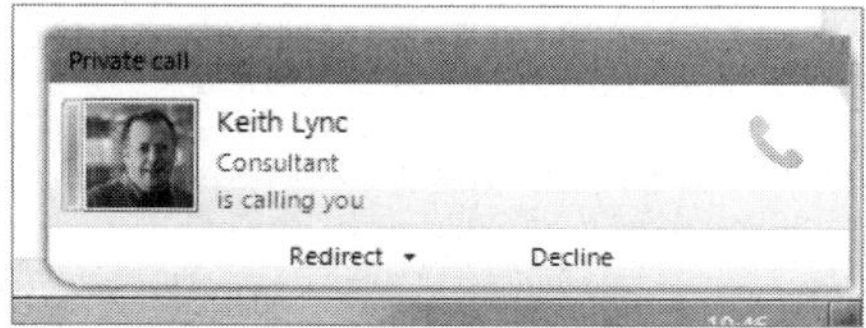

FIGURE 1.14
Private line toast

Routing Changes Lync Server 2010 makes significant changes to the number normalization and outgoing caller ID capability from OCS 2007 R2. Outbound normalization is now possible and can be defined centrally on a per-route (or per-gateway) basis; this allows simplified administration of the media gateways, especially in a global deployment where, perhaps, the same media gateway model (or indeed manufacturer) cannot be used in every country.

Caller ID can be managed on a per-user or per-group basis to suppress or alter the calling party number data presented. This feature is automatically overridden for the simultaneous-ringing scenario, where when the call is forwarded to a mobile device, you want to present the originator number.

Common Area Phones ***Common area phones*** are Lync 2010 Phone Edition devices that are deployed in a communal area such as a lobby. Figure 1.15 shows a Polycom common area phone.

FIGURE 1.15
Polycom CX600 common area phone

Lync Server 2010 provides the capability to manage these devices, even though they are not associated with a user and no one is logged onto them to use.

The ability to control the functions of these common devices ensures that they cannot be misused (e.g., by placing international calls).

In addition to these functionality changes, the portfolio of devices has been significantly increased, with additional device partners on both the end user and media gateway sides.

A number of additional certification programs have been launched for each of these areas:

Open Interoperability Program The Open Interoperability Program is an interoperability testing and certification program not managed by Microsoft. Any devices (not limited to user devices, but also gateways and services such as SIP trunks) qualified through this program are fully supported for interoperability with Lync Server 2010. To learn more, visit:

`http://technet.microsoft.com/en-us/lync/gg131938`

Optimized for Lync 2010 The Optimized For program ensures that devices "just work" on installation — meaning there is no user configuration required, they simply need to be plugged in — and provide high-quality audio/video user experience. These devices are built and tested following the Lync 2010 specifications, and they are created by global partners at the Certified or Gold Certified level. To learn more, visit:

`http://technet.microsoft.com/en-us/lync/gg278164`

Other Compatible IP Phones This program is designed for IP phones based on the publicly available Windows protocols and the Microsoft Office protocols documentation. As with the Optimized For program, they are created by global Certified or Gold Certified partners. To learn more, visit:

`http://technet.microsoft.com/en-us/lync/gg278176.aspx`

Software and Hardware Load Balancers These applications and appliances are tested by the vendor and reviewed by Microsoft to meet Lync Server 2010 requirements. To learn more, visit:

`http://technet.microsoft.com/en-us/lync/gg269419`

Understanding the Unified Communications Managed API Capabilities

The Microsoft approach to Unified Communications is to remove the islands of legacy technology—the voicemail solution that doesn't integrate with the switchboard solution, and so on—to provide one identity and one mailbox from which all capabilities can be taken.

Microsoft provides the familiarity of both the platform and the infrastructure to build new applications, ensuring that they can fully integrate across the environment.

Lync Server 2010 provides extensibility and interoperability by building on the two pillars of development:

- .NET
- Web services

By building on the Lync Server 2010 infrastructure, developers know they already have an enterprise-class platform; by using the .NET framework and the Web Services layer, they have an easily extensible foundation, which can be developed using skills they already have.

Lync Server 2010 allows the creation of presence-aware (known as ***Communications-Enabled Business Process,*** **or** ***CEBP***) applications; this allows the applications to react and make decisions based on the presence of users in the environment, providing notifications or alerts as needed, in the modality required.

Presence can be embedded in already-developed applications, or the Lync 2010 client can be expanded to include the conversation window to show rich context on both sides of the conversation.

Unwrapping the SDK

The Lync Server 2010 SDK allows four scenarios for which developers might need to customize a deployment:

- To integrate with existing line-of-business applications
- To provide contextual conversations
- To add custom applications to the client
- To completely customize the client UI

Developers can utilize the Visual Studio Windows Presentation Foundation and Silverlight controls to quickly add Lync 2010 functionality (drag-and-drop controls) into internal applications; this can include functionality such as docking the conversation windows within the application itself.

Deploying the Lync 2010 client and (hopefully!) using it as the main collaboration toolset doesn't mean you're stuck with the feature set provided. ***Application launch links*** can be sent within conversations, allowing data to be shared in third-party applications; you can see this in the continuation of subject and priority messages started from Outlook. These links also enable developers to extend the menu functionality of both contact cards and the client itself.

An important point with application launch links is that no code is registered on the receiver side; the client simply calls out to existing installed applications. A current example of this functionality is sending of hyperlinks, where clicking the link does nothing other than open the web browser with the address listed in the link; no additional code is executed.

Even scenarios where the client is completely customized are supported; the Lync 2010 controls can be retemplated in Expression Blend.

It should be noted that the Lync 2010 client is still required to be installed in all of these scenarios (with the exception of the web services development); however, it is possible to run the client in UISuppressionMode, whereby only the features from the customized user interface (UI) are presented to a user and all the interaction is behind the scenes.

Further investigation into the customization and development of applications is beyond the scope of this book. See ***Professional Unified Communications Development with Microsoft Lync Server 2010***, by George Durzi and Michael Greenlee (Wiley, 2011) for more information about developing custom applications.

The Bottom Line

Describe the features of the client. The Lync 2010 client is designed to achieve three core goals: connect, communicate, and collaborate. This new client makes it is much easier to find people and verify identity, initiate communications (typically, with a single click), and collaborate with full-blown information sharing. Device integration and call management have been greatly simplified, removing the need to run through wizards constantly.

Master It You are assembling a new product-development team. The new product will be similar to a previously released product, and you want to ask members of the previous team for guidance. How can you find people associated with the previous product team?

Describe the features of the server. Lync Server 2010 provides most of the server roles included in Office Communications Server and introduces the Survivable Branch Appliance (or Server) to help in the high-availability scenarios. The management approach has changed through the introduction of the Topology Builder application and Role-Based Access Control to limit administrative access to defined users and scopes as required. PowerShell and Silverlight combine to provide the day-to-day administration of the environment.

Master It When deploying high availability, which of the following roles can be a primary registrar?

- Audio/Video Conferencing
- Director
- Enterprise Edition Front-End
- Standard Edition Front-End
- Survivable Branch Appliance
- Survivable Branch Server

Describe the voice features. Significant investment and development has gone into Lync Server 2010's voice feature set. The new set has allowed it to become a match for a large portion of the PBX workload and, in many cases, a viable replacement for a PBX.

New functions (such as Private Line, Call Admission Control, Call Park, E911, and Common Area Phones) provide welcome additions to the user experience. By contrast, behind-the-scenes features (such as Media Bypass, routing improvements, resiliency improvements, and analog device management) provide a more integrated and available solution for the administrator, while they help reduce the number of servers required.

Master It As the network and telephony administrator for your company, you want to invest in SIP trunks rather than legacy PBX-style PSTN connectivity using media gateways.

How should you configure media bypass and deploy mediation servers?

Chapter 2

Standards and Protocols

Any platform that needs to interoperate with other platforms will rely on standards, and a communications platform is no different in that respect. Lync Server 2010 uses the Session Initiation Protocol (SIP) standard to provide its backbone, and it builds on that backbone by extending SIP to accommodate additional functionality.

Regardless of whether communication is conducted via the public telephone network using voice or via the Internet with other instant messaging products, you need to know the limitations of the protocols used and understand where interface gateways will be needed to extend beyond the edges of the Lync Server 2010 infrastructure. (Communication may include other organizations running Lync Server 2010 and using federation.)

This chapter introduces the history behind the signaling that led to the introduction of SIP. While the protocol itself is interesting, understanding the background network infrastructure will help you design and troubleshoot Lync Server 2010.

In this chapter, you will learn to:

- Understand the basics of SIP for signaling
- Understand how SIP has been extended to provide additional functionality for Lync Server 2010
- Identify additional protocols used by Lync Server 2010

Understanding SIP's Origins

Before the Internet (yes, there was a time when there was no Internet), the only real-time communication was via the public telephone network. This network was extremely easy to use (pick up the phone and dial) and highly reliable, and communications were understandable at both ends (it was just talk). The system was based on a circuit-switched network.

Circuit-Switched Networks

At some time in their youth, most people have played with a tin-cans-on-a-string communications system (see Figure 2.1). The tin-can system essentially is a basic, circuit-switched network. It's extremely basic, as there is only a single circuit—and even adding one more user requires significant investment because two additional lines are needed so that everyone can talk to each other. With this type of system, complex signaling isn't needed. Each endpoint is connected to only one other endpoint; therefore, when one endpoint is picked up, the users immediately know where the communication is going.

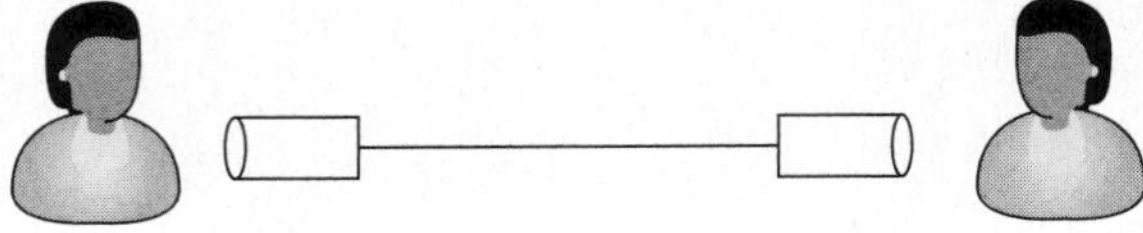

FIGURE 2.1
A primitive communication system

Adding a third person would require two more lines (one for each existing endpoint); adding a fourth person would require three additional lines; a fifth, four more lines; and so on. With this system, any individual must have the number of lines coming to them equivalent to the total number of people in the system minus one. This type of basic system can very quickly become unmanageable.

The solution to this management nightmare was the *switch*. All endpoints terminated at the switch (in a star or hub-and-spoke topology), and it is the responsibility of the switch to determine (or *route*) the call from one endpoint to another. In the early telephony days, the routing was performed by a human switchboard operator who physically connected the two endpoints with a patch cable. Figure 2.2 depicts a manual switchboard.

FIGURE 2.2
A manual switchboard

As technology improved and automation became more prevalent, the endpoints acquired dialing capability and were allocated unique identifiers (extension numbers). A termination endpoint could be signaled simply by dialing the extension number.

Building up to today's larger, modern telephony infrastructure, these switches were connected to each other (they were beginning to be known as *exchanges*), and this allowed for a wider distribution of calls.

Each exchange was allocated a routing number. By first dialing the routing number of the exchange, followed by the extension of the endpoint, a call could be routed from one location to another. Of course, in the early days, this was achieved by calling the operator and asking her to perform the routing manually.

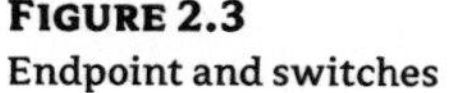

FIGURE 2.3
Endpoint and switches

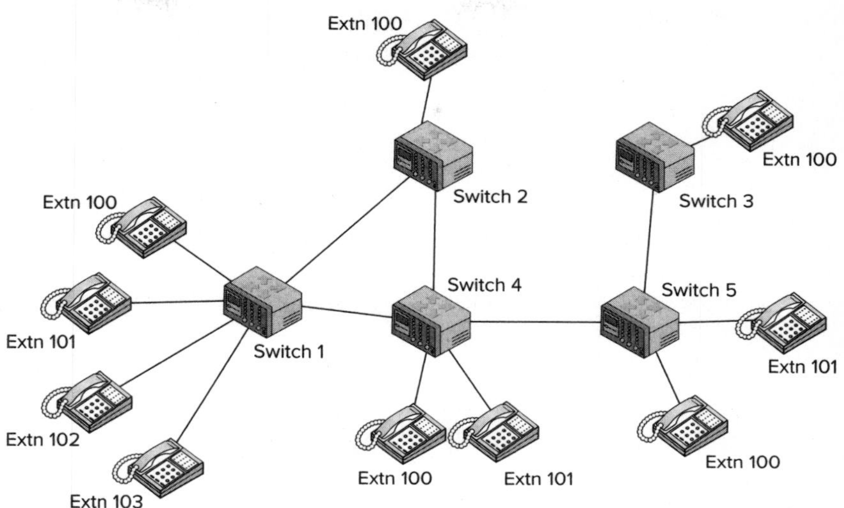

In the rudimentary example shown in Figure 2.3, if you are using Ext 100, connected to Switch 1, you dial only the extension number to reach another internal (connected to the same switch) extension number. However, simply dialing the extension number will not work when you need to reach an extension at another location (switch)—especially when the extensions are duplicates of local extensions—because you will be connected to the local extension on the same switch.

This is where the routing number comes into play. To connect to Switch 5, Extension 101, for example, you could dial 5101. You need to ensure that there is no numerical overlap as there could be when you are dialing to Switch 1. This is where the concept of dialing a specific number (typically, 9 or 0) for an "outside line" comes into play. When the switch sees this outside line number first, it knows to route the following digits away from the internal extensions.

This concept of endpoint/exchange numbering and routing has expanded to include national and international routing as well, and it has led to the national and international numbering plans that are so familiar to everyone making telephone calls today.

Pros and Cons of Circuit Switching

Circuit switching is so-called because to establish a connection from one point to the other, a *circuit* is created, which is in effect a dedicated connection between endpoints—think back to our piece of string between the two cans.

Once this *circuit* has been established, the system is very fast. There are no more decisions to be made or content to be inspected; it is simply forwarded to the destination (or, on a switch basis, to the next interface).

This dedicated path is perfect for analog transmissions because there is no (or, more accurately, an extremely small) delay between the sending and receiving of the signal. However, there is a delay with the establishment of the path before any transmission can occur.

Once the path is in place, it will stay in use until closed down, even if transmission has stopped. This results in wasted capacity and, although it has not had a big impact in voice transmissions, it has much bigger implications when the move is made to digital transmissions where speed of transmission is much greater than the speed of interpretation, resulting in idle time on the transmission path.

Circuit-Switched Signaling

Outside of the tin-cans-on a string scenario, signaling information needs to be provided along with a call. As you can see from Figure 2.4, any transmission type is built of at least two parts, signaling and data (there may be more than one data channel).

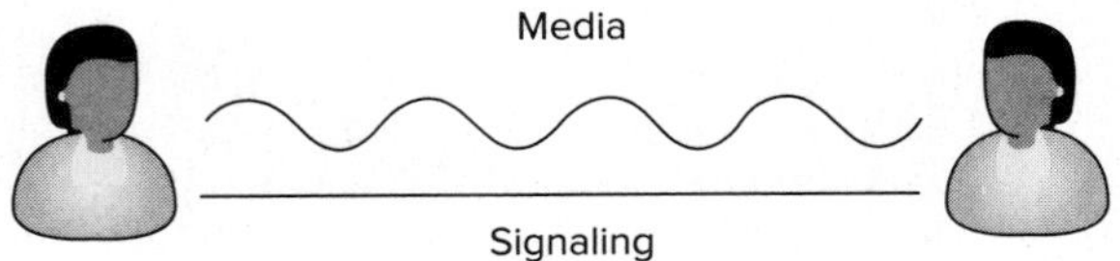

Figure 2.4
Separation of signaling and media

In the basic scenario, this signaling will establish the call in the first place, and then stop it when finished. More advanced signaling provides additional features, such as placing the call on hold or transferring the call to another endpoint. For these more advanced features to work, the signaling needs to be parallel to the actual transmission—you couldn't put a call on hold if you had to hang up first!

Early signaling simply completed an electrical current when the receiver was picked up. The operator saw a light being lit on the switchboard and connected to that endpoint; once the operator understood the target, he used a patch cable to connect the caller to the called party. Although manual switchboards were still around into the eighties, they obviously made way for automated switching systems.

Frequency Division Multiplexing (FDM) allowed multiple calls to be provisioned across a single wire connection, but it also required a new method of signaling. The solution to this was *in-band* signaling, using the same connection for both the signaling and the data transmission.

FDM is extremely expensive to operate, requiring the use of analog filters tuned to specific frequencies to allow continued operations.

Digital Transmission

With the advent of digital transmission in the early sixties, signaling needed to evolve even more. Digital signals are comprised of discrete 0s and 1s (represented in the system as changes of voltage), whereas analog signals are acoustic and must be translated to digital for transmission, and then translated back to analog—sound—at the receiving end to be heard. Many different *codecs* (coder-decoders) are available to do this. Modems (modulator-demodulators) were used to connect to the early Internet; they provided a service similar to codecs except in reverse, converting the digital computer signal to an analog signal suitable for transmission on the telephone network. In actual effect, the telephone network was converting the message back to digital for transmission.

Pros and Cons of Digital Transmissions

The first advantage to digital transmission is that digital equipment is extremely cheap (relatively speaking) because it uses computers rather than the electromechanical valves in analog switching, resulting in less required maintenance.

Second, quality is much higher with digital transmission. The data is either a 1 or a 0; there are no "in-between" values, and any corrective measure required in a digital signal results in retransmission (newer digital protocols include built-in error correction mechanisms). To have digital data travel farther, it is repeated; conversely, to have analog data transmitted farther, it is amplified. Amplification will increase the signal strength, which will also include any interference (or noise). Repetition will simply repeat the clean signal, meaning it is effectively a new signal.

Of course, there are also downsides to digital. The signal must be processed, resulting in a delay while the transformation takes place. Naturally, this occurs twice—once at each end. Additionally, delays are introduced through the switching and signaling mechanisms. Typically, for voice transmissions, a delay higher than 250ms round trip will make it difficult to follow a conversation. Individually, delays are likely to be negligible, but in a badly designed network with multiple congested hops, they will be major factors.

Digital Signaling

Digital transmissions are typically *bursty*; the transmission and idle times have peaks (and consequently an average data rate). Because the data did not flow at a steady stream, a new signaling method, known as Time Division Multiplexing (TDM), was introduced to address the associated issues. TDM, like FDM, allows multiple signals to be transmitted across a single line, but each connection is given a specific time slot during which it is allowed to transmit. Compared with FDM, TDM allows significantly higher bandwidth (number of connections) on the same cable.

TDM requires the use of buffers in the switches, ensuring that the data is stored ready for transmission when the relevant time slot becomes available (time slots always transmit in the same order, 1, 2, 3, 4, and so on; once finished, they restart again).

Early transmissions were 64Kbps channels, which exactly matched the output rate of the telephony codecs. Increases to the amount of data that could be sent meant that more options were made available for sending that data. Bits could discretely define letters, words, and sentences, allowing rules to be easily built around a signal—for example, the signaling command to place a call on hold could now be defined as *HOLD*, making it easily understood by people troubleshooting.

Signaling between switches (exchanges) is known as *trunk* signaling, and signaling between an endpoint and the switch is known as *access* signaling, as illustrated in Figure 2.5.

Figure 2.5
Switch Signaling Types

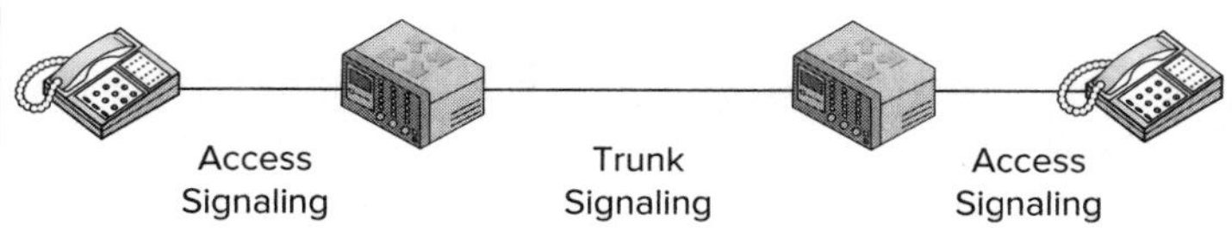

Access Signaling

Initially, access signaling consisted simply of on/off-hook requesting a dial tone (or hanging up). It has progressed to include pulse signaling, or commonly now Dual Tone Multi-Frequency (DTMF) tones used for signaling. Standard tones have been defined (typically, per-country or region) to indicate busy, call waiting, and other common states to the user.

Digital Subscriber Signaling System No. 1 (DSS1), which is used in Europe and elsewhere, is an example of an Access Signaling protocol.

Trunk Signaling

The trunk signaling used between switches is either Channel Associated Signaling (CAS) or Common Channel Signaling (CCS). The difference between these two methods is that in CAS the signaling travels the same path as the data, and in CCS there may be a completely separate signaling path. The CAS data path takes up a single channel; in European systems this is typically channel 16 in a 32-channel link. The CCS separate signaling path allows a signaling network to be completely separate from the data network.

CCS allows advanced network features, such as toll-free calling, to be implemented. For example, a toll-free number on the network translates into the actual number required (seamlessly to a user); this is achieved by the separation of the signaling to allow this number translation/lookup functionality.

SS6 and SS7 are the two main CCS methods in use, and they provide access to supplementary services such as call forwarding; typically, these supplementary services are implemented differently from one telecom provider to another, so the signaling boundary tends to be at the provider level—that is, the specific code used to enable call forwarding is different on Verizon than on AT&T. Typically, these codes are difficult to remember unless frequently used. This is an area where the user interface within the Lync 2010 communicator client excels, by removing this complexity from the user; you simply point and click.

Circuit-switched networks work on the principle that the intelligence is in the network, rather than the endpoint, meaning that the availability of the network nodes is critical, which implies that added expenses will be accrued to ensure that the network nodes are always available.

Packet-Switched Networks

Packet-switched networks work on the assumption that the intelligence is in the endpoint, and the network is purely a routing mechanism. The Internet is the largest public packet-switched network in the world. As mentioned before, data networks are bursty, going from busy to idle to busy. Using dedicated circuits to handle this type of traffic wastes resources. By separating the data into sections (packets) and transmitting them separately, you can better utilize resources by mixing packets from multiple sources being sent to multiple destinations through the same resources. The result is a smoother distribution of data. Each packet is tagged with the destination address in the header and sent to the first network node (router). The router analyzes the packet header to determine the route (the next network node) and forwards the packet to this intermediate point. This process is repeated until the packet arrives at its destination, where the packet header is removed and the data remains. (This description is somewhat simplified, but the outlines should be clear.)

Some of the routers may be visible to route analysis, but with *virtual circuits* many more routers may be hidden behind the physical route. *Virtual circuits* can appear similar to a circuit-switched network because they seem to provide a point-to-point link (remember the string from the tin cans?) between two networks. Virtual circuits can be permanent connections or temporary, where the first packet will establish the link and the final one will disconnect it.

Pros and Cons of Virtual Circuits

Virtual circuits can be beneficial because they ensure that all packets travel the same path. This means that all traffic is likely to suffer the same delays due to the underlying network conditions, resulting in all traffic being treated equally. However, this consistency comes at a cost: the network will need more resources to ensure that the state is kept.

Like circuit-switched networks, virtual circuits must be established, a task that has an associated delay; and interruptions to the network nodes in the underlying infrastructure will result in interruption to the virtual circuit, requiring a new one to be established. Additionally, if a virtual circuit cannot be established end-to-end, the connection will not be established.

Without the virtual circuit overhead, packets are dynamically rerouted in the event of infrastructure problems, possibly introducing delays or even packet loss.

Pros and Cons of Packet Switching

The use of packet switching provides efficiency to the network, allowing better utilization of the available bandwidth by sharing resources. It also allows differing rates of bandwidth between networks. Routers naturally buffer incoming data, so the outgoing data rate may differ from the incoming; this allows multiple networks of differing speeds to be joined and still communicate with each other.

Packet-switching infrastructure is much cheaper than circuit-switching infrastructure; simply put, the packet-switched infrastructure reads the packet header and forwards it as appropriate, whereas a circuit-switched infrastructure must keep the state of all packets (resulting in more resource overhead, which results in more expense).

However, the delay introduced by analyzing every packet is a weakness compared to circuit switching, in which once a connection is established, the data is simply switched from one circuit to another. Compounded with this delay is the queue delay introduced while the packet is being received and waiting to be transmitted. Later, you'll see that this can be mitigated by assigning priorities to packets; but in busy networks, queues can still introduce significant delay.

Finally, every packet has a header attached, adding to the data to be transmitted. The actual impact here depends on the overall packet size, as the headers will typically be the same size, resulting in greater overhead if smaller packet sizes are used.

Early packet-switched networks were based on X.25 (for the access signaling) and X.75 (for the trunk signaling). The Internet is based on Internet Protocol (IP), defined in Request For Comment (RFC) 791.

REQUESTS FOR COMMENT (RFCS)

RFCs are memos published by the Internet Engineering Task Force (IETF) that describe methods and innovations applicable to the working of the Internet and Internet-type systems.

RFCs started as a document circulated among the early pioneers of the Internet (ARPANET) in 1969. As each document was circulated and feedback generated, it eventually became a standard ensuring the interoperability and communications on the Internet as we know it today. Indeed, the RFC process continues to develop new standards. Although not all RFCs become standards, they will be designated as one of the following:

- Informational
- Experimental
- Best Current Practice
- Standards Track
- Historic

The *Standards Track* can be further broken down into these categories:

- Proposed Standard
- Draft Standard
- Internet Standard

Each RFC is uniquely identified by its number and within it may refer to previous RFCs to expand or even deprecate that piece of work.

Later in this chapter, you'll see that SIP itself is a combination of multiple RFCs, some of which are still in the draft stage.

Not all RFCs are serious documents; almost every year since 1989 (and first appearing in 1978), April 1 has seen at least one humorous RFC released. (Indeed, we suspect that some tangled networks are genuine implementations of RFC 1149, A Standard for the Transmission of IP Datagrams on Avian Carriers, or Internet by homing pigeon.)

In addition, RFCS can be found here:

```
www.rfc-editor.org/rfc.html
```

As described there, the IP layer traffic travels on top of many different types of underlying infrastructure, and by leveraging IP as the common infrastructure platform, endpoints can easily communicate with various applications and services. Chapter 5, "Planning Your Deployment," discusses the additional network services that Lync Server 2010 relies on; the use of the common IP networking stack allows these services to interoperate easily.

The main IP network relies on the assumption that intelligent endpoints run the applications, and a dumb network is simply routing the packets to their destination. Current-generation IP routers can obviously provide much more functionality than simple routing, such as packet inspection and firewalls; however, the principle of the dumb network remains!

The Internet Protocol makes the network almost stateless; that is, the state of each packet is not stored, only the state of routes. By doing so, it allows high availability to be achieved, because there are multiple routes to a destination. In the event of a failure on one circuit, traffic is simply rerouted to another. For example, what would you do if you encountered road maintenance on your commute to work? You would take a different route to the same destination, of course. However, taking a different route would be much more difficult by train than by car. Provision of multiple paths is much easier (and cheaper) than trying to ensure that equipment is always available. IP is considered to be layer 3 in the standard 7 layer Open Systems Interconnection (OSI) network model, illustrated in Figure 2.6. Each layer in the OSI model can request services only from the layer below it. The contents of the layer above become the *payload* of the lower layer and are encapsulated with headers (and/or footers), enabling onward routing to the final destination.

FIGURE 2.6
OSI Network layer model

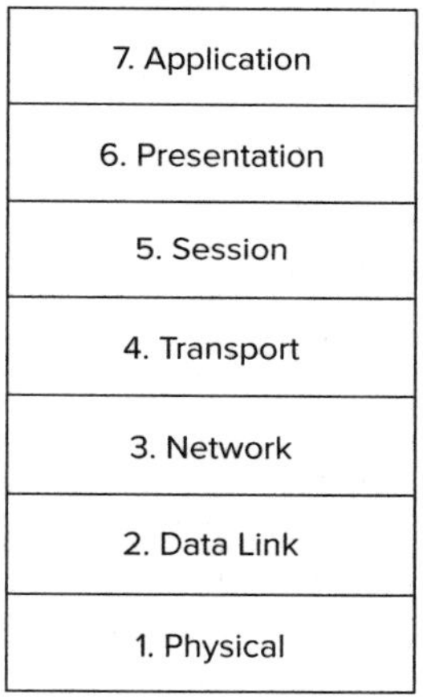

7. Application
6. Presentation
5. Session
4. Transport
3. Network
2. Data Link
1. Physical

At the destination, the reverse occurs, where each layer will inspect and remove the headers/footers and pass the data up to the layer above it.

Some named protocol definitions comprise more than one layer; for example, Ethernet is both layer 1 and 2.

Examples of each layer:

- Physical cable layout, pins, voltages, and so on
- Physical addressing, such as MAC address
- Routing protocols, logical addressing, such as X.25
- Flow control and reliability functionality, such TCP and UDP
- Full-duplex or half-duplex
- Establishment of context, such as XML
- Synchronization of communications and establishment of resources, such as SIP

TRANSPORT LAYER PROTOCOLS

The two transport layer protocols we are interested in are Transport Control Protocol (TCP), RFC 768 and User Datagram Protocol (UDP), RFC 793. The difference between them is that TCP provides a reliable (or connection-oriented) connection. The traffic is acknowledged, and if any packets are not received or errors encountered, they will be retransmitted. The delay introduces an additional overhead to be considered. UDP is considered to use a *fire-and-forget* (or connectionless) approach, meaning that it only cares about transmitting the data. If it gets there, great; but if it doesn't, the data is not retransmitted. There is no guarantee of delivery. Both TCP and UDP require the use of *port numbers* in addition to the IP address to route traffic correctly.

Consider the postal service analogy: You want to send a birthday card (packet) to a friend. For the birthday card to be correctly delivered, it would need a postal/zip code (consider this the IP address) and a house number (the port). Now, suppose you want to send some cash in the birthday card. You would then want to make sure the card was delivered, so you would require proof of delivery, such as a registered letter. This is equivalent to TCP. On the other hand, if you aren't sending cash, you don't really care as much to confirm delivery; this is UDP.

REAL-TIME DATA

Real-time (or very near real-time) transmission is required for two-way audio and video communications, and as such imposes different engineering considerations than non-real-time communications. For example, a delay of minutes when sending an email is typically not significant, whereas a delay of even a second or two can make a conversation (audio or video) unbearable.

As previously mentioned, delay can occur at many points throughout the transmission of audio (or video) data; this delay is normally measured in milliseconds. At a certain point, traffic received can be delayed so much that it is no longer useful and the delay can no longer be ignored.

Both UDP and TCP provide mechanisms to ensure that packets arrive in the correct order when they are received. These ordering mechanisms only guarantee that the packets are replayed in the correct order, not that they appear on time. Packets that arrive late are ignored; however, there are mechanisms within Lync that attempt to cover up these missing packets, as discussed in the codec section later in this chapter.

When packets are received out of order, the effect is called *jitter*; and the amount of jitter can differ based on many factors, such as the devices used for encoding, as well as the routers and switches in the network path. The amount of jitter is not necessarily the same for both endpoints involved in a call.

THE JITTER BUFFER

With the Real-time Transport Protocol (RTP), RFC 1889, a jitter buffer is used to attempt to reduce the delay introduced by the different processing required in transmission (if the delay time exceeds the size of the jitter buffer, packets will be lost). The receiving system buffers the incoming data to allow some delay, resulting in the appearance of no delay to the user listening (or watching), as the stream will appear to have a continuous playback. Figure 2.7 shows the impact of the jitter buffer as traffic is sent, received, and played back.

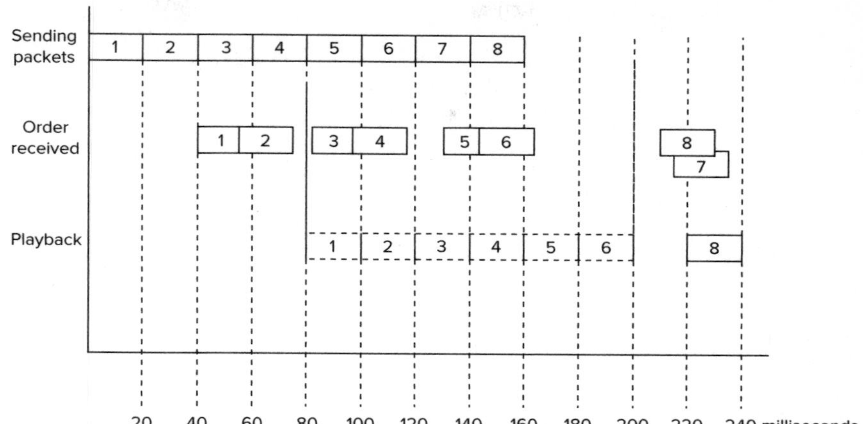

FIGURE 2.7
The operation of the jitter buffer

From this example, you can see that the packets are sent in an orderly fashion; however, some delays are incurred through the transmission. Packets 2, 4, and 6 are beginning to be received before the previous packet has finished and packet 7 actually arrives after packet 8.

The jitter buffer allows a way to store these packets until the correct time for them to be played back. Unfortunately, packet 7 arrives after it is due to be played, so it is useless to us. Dealing with this is where the codecs may differ in approach—some may replay the previous packet, others may attempt to "guess" what the packet contained. Remember that individually, these packets are only 20ms in duration, so they are extremely difficult to detect by the human ear.

The jitter buffer size may change throughout the course of a call (this is automatic), but is likely to be around 40ms in most cases for Lync Server 2010.

Synchronization of Traffic

Until now we've mentioned audio and video separately, but have not considered that each is actually a separate media stream in its own right. This provides an additional level of complexity, because you have to ensure the audio and video are synchronized—after all, they were when they were captured at the sender endpoint. However, because they are two separate streams, there is no guarantee that the traffic has followed the same route from source to destination, and indeed Lync Server 2010 provides the capability to prioritize each traffic stream (modality) separately.

Real-time Transport Control Protocol (RTCP), RFC 1889, is used to associate the timestamps of the data packets with the actual time points in the session. RTCP is also used to track the quality of the RTP transmission, measuring the number of lost packets, total delays, and jitter.

Quality of Service

Being able to prioritize traffic on a network allows you to guarantee a level of traffic delivery. In a busy network, it's a good idea to prioritize voice traffic over file copy traffic, thereby ensuring that the network routers keep any delays to the voice traffic to an absolute minimum. This will result in a longer time to copy a file, but it will at least allow an understandable conversation.

There are two methods to enable Quality of Service (QoS) on a network:

- Integrated Services, RFC 1633
- Differentiated Services, RFC 2475

Lync Server 2010 supports only the use of Differentiated Services, by marking packets using a Differentiated Services Control Point (DSCP)—effectively, an additional flag in the packet header.

Lync Server 2010 allows you to apply a different packet marker to each modality, as shown in Table 2.1.

TABLE 2.1: Default DSCP Marking per Modality

MEDIA TYPE	DEFAULT PER-HOP BEHAVIOR	QUEUING AND DROPPING	NOTES
Audio	EF	Priority Queue	Low loss, low latency, low jitter, assured bandwidth. Pair with WAN Bandwidth Policies on constrained links.
Video	AF41	BW Queue + DSCP WRED	Class 4. Low drop priority. Pair with WAN Bandwidth Policies on constrained links.
SIP Signaling	CS3	BW Queue	Class 3. Bandwidth allocation should be sufficient to avoid drops.
App Sharing	AF21	BW Queue + DSCP WRED	Class 2. Low drop priority. Pair with end-user policy caps.
File Transfer	AF11	BW Queue + DSCP WRED	Class 1. Low drop priority. Pair with end-user policy caps.

The Default Per-Hop Behavior column indicates the DSCP tag applied to the packet (a numeric value provides further differentiation where listed):

- EF: Expedited Forwarding, RFC 2598
- AF: Assured Forwarding, RFC 2597
- CS: Class
- Numeric value: when associated with the same DSCP text, a higher value indicates a higher priority.

It is important to understand that when QoS is used on a network, the same configuration must be on all routers and switches in the path of the traffic; otherwise, the correct priority will fail to be applied at one (or more) hops, thereby introducing unwanted delay.

Session Description Protocol

Session Description Protocol (SDP – RFC 2327) provides the information required to enable a media session to be encoded for transmission; it also provides the receiving endpoint with the information required to decode. In many cases, SDP is used to notify users of upcoming Internet broadcasts (webcasts).

It provides the ability to negotiate information such as IP and port addresses, media codecs used, and authentication, and it can be extended further to future needs through the a= information lines.

The SDP syntax is text-based and consists of lines of human-readable text, providing an easy-to-understand view for troubleshooting. A sample session (taken from the RFC document) is shown here:

```
v=0
o=mhandley 2890844526 2890842807 IN IP4 126.16.64.4
s=SDP Seminar
i=A Seminar on the session description protocol
u=http://www.cs.ucl.ac.uk/staff/M.Handley/sdp.03.ps
e=mjh@isi.edu (Mark Handley)
c=IN IP4 224.2.17.12/127
t=2873397496 2873404696
a=recvonly
m=audio 49170 RTP/AVP 0
m=video 51372 RTP/AVP 31
m=application 32416
```

From this sample, you can immediately discern (or at least make an educated guess at) some of the values of this media stream before even knowing what the field identifiers are. Some of these values include:

- Subject: `s=SDP Seminar`
- Information: `I = A Seminar on the session description protocol`
- Email: `e=mjh@isi.edu (Mark Handley)`
- Media: `m=audio/m=video/m=application`

The following values taken from the RFC show the valid session description identifiers for SDP; for further descriptions of the fields, see the RFC document (any value marked * is optional):

```
v= (protocol version)
o= (owner/creator and session identifier).
s= (session name)
i=* (session information)
u=* (URI of description)
```

```
e=* (email address)
p=* (phone number)
c=* (connection information - not required if included in all media)
b=* (bandwidth information)
z=* (time zone adjustments)
k=* (encryption key)
a=* (zero or more session attribute lines)
t= (time the session is active)
r=* (zero or more repeat times)
m= (media name and transport address)
i=* (media title)
c=* (connection information - optional if included at session-level)
b=* (bandwidth information)
k=* (encryption key)
a=* (zero or more media attribute lines)
```

The Session Initiation Protocol in Depth

What is commonly referred to as Session Initiation Protocol (SIP) is more accurately known as SIPv2. The first version (SIPv1) was submitted to the Internet Engineering Task Force (IETF) as a draft standard for session establishment and was called *Session Invitation Protocol*. Its job was done once the users joined the session, relying on something like SDP to continue control of the established session. SIPv1, which was created by Mark Handley and Eve Schooler, was UDP-based.

At the same time, another draft standard, *Simple Conference Invitation Protocol (SCIP)*, was also submitted to the IETF by Henning Schulzrinne. SCIP used an approach similar to Hypertext Transfer Protocol (HTTP) for communication and defined a new method to continue the session controls. SCIP was based on TCP.

The outcome of these two proposals was SIPv2, which is based on HTTP but able to use both UDP and TCP. For the remainder of this book, we'll use *SIP* to refer to SIPv2.

RFC 2543 describes the basics of SIP; however, a number of extensions have been defined in other RFCs. In the following list, the values in parentheses indicate the SIP message defined in the RFC:

- RFC 2976 (INFO)
- RFC 3261 (ACK, BYE, CANCEL, INVITE, OPTIONS, REGISTER)
- RFC 3262 (PRACK)
- RFC 3265 (SUBSCRIBE, NOTIFY)
- RFC 3311 (UPDATE)
- RFC 3428 (MESSAGE)
- RFC 3515 (REFER)
- RFC 3903 (PUBLISH)

Each of these extensions shows how flexible SIP is with its ability to operate with early implementations while bringing new functionality to bear where possible. The flip side of this extensibility is that it can be difficult to fully define which version of SIP is actually implemented by an application. Later, you'll learn how you can query an application (or endpoint) to see what is supported.

In addition, Microsoft has provided extensions to the Lync Server 2010 implementation of SIP in the form of message headers, which are all prefixed with `ms-`. These extensions, which we'll discuss shortly, are supported only within Lync Server 2010. Although some of them may become standard in a future version, they do not provide any interoperability with other systems at this point.

From this point on, we will focus on the Microsoft implementation of SIPv2 and the architecture within Lync Server 2010; if you want a wider understanding, please refer to the RFC documentation.

Using SIP

In its basic form, SIP is used to create, modify, and end individual sessions between users (or a user and a server). Let's say Nathan wants to call Keith. At a high level, SIP would begin this process with an `INVITE` message and finish with a `BYE` message. However, prior to the `INVITE`, both Nathan and Keith would have to issue `REGISTER` messages to the server, providing the address information for the client on which they are logged in. During the message exchange, there are likely to be several `ACK` messages and possibly more `INVITE` messages if the call were to change from one device to another, or additional functionality were added (such as video or desktop sharing).

SIP is a request-and-response protocol similar to HTTP (on which it is based), meaning that for every request sent out, a response is expected; and within these responses are human-readable *reason phrases*. As you might expect, the response codes are similar to HTTP codes and many will be familiar—for example, 404 - Not Found.

Table 2.2 shows the response classes and some common examples.

TABLE 2.2: SIP Responses

RANGE	RESPONSE CLASS	EXAMPLES
100–199	Informational	100 - Trying 180 - Ringing
200–299	Success	200 - OK
300–399	Redirection	301 - Moved permanently 302 - Moved temporarily
400–499	Client error	401 - Unauthorized 404 - Not found
500–599	Server error	500 - Internal server error 502 - Bad gateway
600–699	Global error	600 - Busy everywhere

The SIP requests each have a different purpose (some are paired) and, as mentioned previously, have been implemented through many additional extensions and new RFCs. We'll look at each of them in turn now.

`INVITE` The `INVITE` message is the initiation of a SIP session, an invitation from one user to another (or more) to begin a communications method. This will proceed any modality, and indeed changing modalities will require additional `INVITE`s to be sent for each modality. The SDP carried in the `INVITE` will detail the actual session modality information, and further communications will establish the connection points for the session.

Figure 2.8 shows the `INVITE` message in the ladder diagram commonly used to illustrate SIP flows.

FIGURE 2.8
An `INVITE` ladder diagram

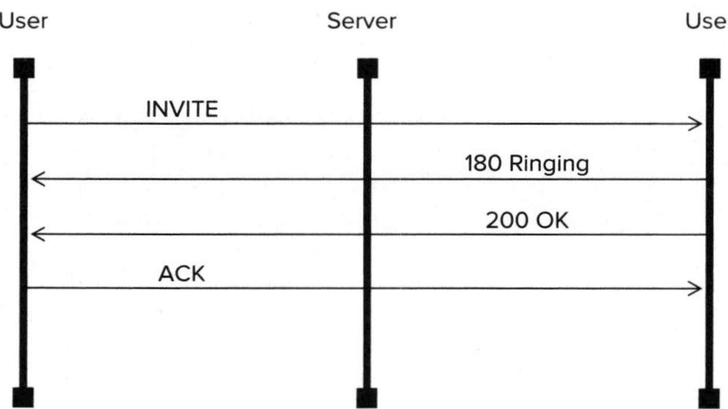

The `180 Ringing` response shown here is an informational response, and there is no expectation or guarantee of informational responses being received. When the remote user accepts the request, a `200 - OK` response is sent.

INFORMATIONAL RESPONSES

The SIP protocol defines that there is no guarantee of Informational responses being received and that connections using it should not rely on such data. However, when TCP is used as the transport, as the Microsoft implementation does, there is a guaranteed response; and Microsoft has included additional useful troubleshooting information in these responses. These additional headers are prefixed with `ms-` (for example, `ms-received-port` and `ms-received-cid`).

`ACK` The `ACK` shown in Figure 2.8 is the acknowledgement of the `INVITE` from the *initiating* user. It is required because the `INVITE` message may take longer than expected to receive a response. `INVITE` is the initiation of a session; and at this point the location of the recipient endpoints are not known, and the user may not be nearby, resulting in a delay in the acceptance of the call.

In a scenario with multiple receiving endpoints (forking), multiple responses will be received, and each response needs to be acknowledged. This is partly a remainder from the initial SIPv1 implementation, in which the expectation was to use UDP, an unreliable transport protocol.

An ACK message also allows additional information to be sent within its SDP.

CANCEL The CANCEL message is used to cancel any pending INVITEs. As you can see in Figure 2.9, a CANCEL message is acknowledged through the separate cancelation message (487 - Transaction Cancelled); this is to accommodate the case where the 200 - OK response and the CANCEL happen to cross paths on the network. Finally, even though the INVITE is cancelled, an ACK message is sent to acknowledge the 200 - OK response.

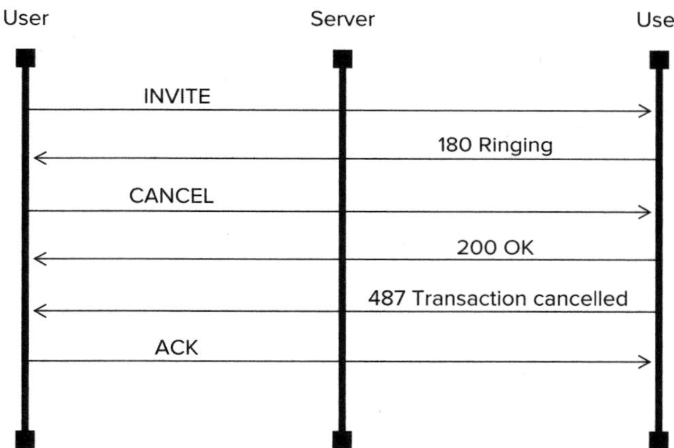

FIGURE 2.9
A CANCEL ladder diagram

BYE A BYE message is used to disconnect an established session. Figure 2.10 shows the SIP ladder diagram including the BYE.

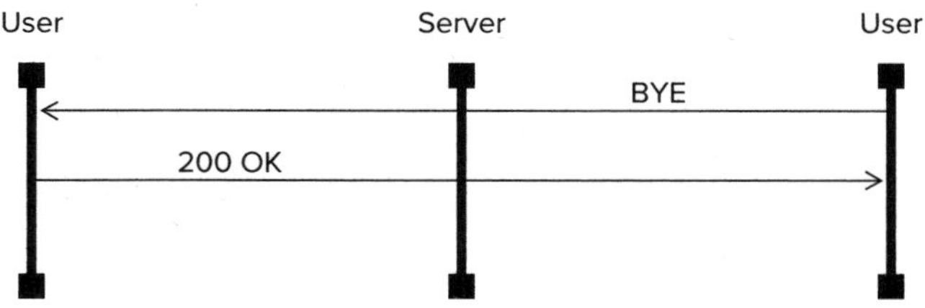

FIGURE 2.10
A BYE ladder diagram

REGISTER A REGISTER is used to inform the server of the location of a user endpoint. Lync Server 2010 supports Multiple Points of Presence (MPoP), and this requires each endpoint to uniquely provide its location (IP address) so that follow-up messages (INVITE, SUBSCRIBE, or OPTION) can be directed to each endpoint on which the user is logged in. Figure 2.11 shows a ladder diagram for REGISTER.

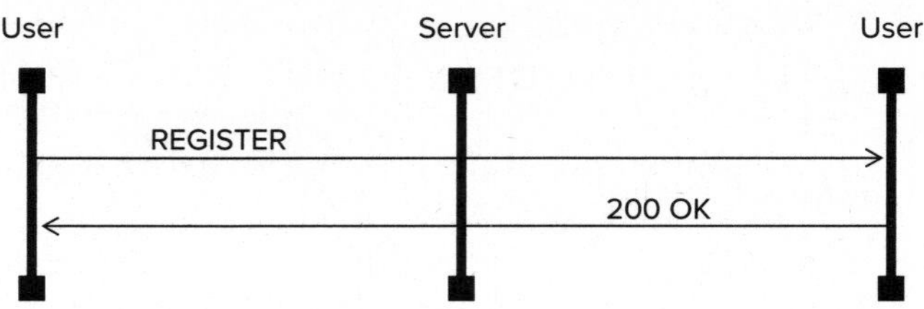

FIGURE 2.11
A REGISTER ladder diagram

OPTIONS `OPTIONS` messages provide the capability to query an endpoint (including a server) for the functionality it supports. This is how different SIP applications can still function with differing implementations of the SIP standard. Figure 2.12 shows the ladder diagram, and in this case the `200 - OK` response will include the data of the capabilities provided.

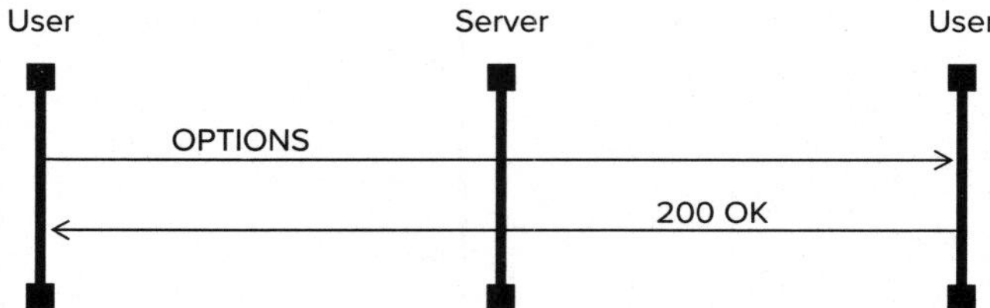

FIGURE 2.12
An OPTIONS ladder diagram

SIP Protocol Formatting

SIP messages are transmitted in human-readable format; however, this means they are required to follow strict formatting to ensure functionality.

For a request, this format is as follows:

- Request line
- Several header lines
- Empty line
- Message body

Similarly, a response consists of:

- Status line
- Several header lines
- Empty line
- Message body

The request line is comprised of the request, request URI, and finally the version, as shown here:

```
INVITE sip:nathan_lync@gaots.co.uk SIP/2.0
```

The response line consists of simply the version, response code, and reason phrase:

```
SIP/2.0 180 Ringing
```

There are many available header lines, and some of the more interesting standard ones are listed here:

- `Accept`
- `Alert-info`
- `Authorization`
- `Call-ID`
- `Contact`
- `Content-length`
- `Content-type`
- `Cseq`
- `Date`
- `Encryption`
- `Error-Info`
- `From`
- `In-reply-to`
- `Max-forwards`
- `Record-Route`
- `Route`
- `Server`
- `Subject`
- `Supported`
- `Timestamp`
- `To`
- `User-agent`
- `Via`

However, headers can be extended, and, as mentioned, Microsoft has added many customized headers, all beginning with `ms-`. It's worth looking at some of the more useful headers in more detail. Understanding them will dramatically help you when troubleshooting (see Chapter 12 for more about troubleshooting). Here are a few of the standard headers explained:

`Call-ID` The `Call-ID` header is unique for each SIP session; it allows the flow of a single session to be monitored across several servers and indeed different systems, ensuring consistency and ease of troubleshooting.

If an original call is transferred, the `Call-ID` header is changed; and if multiple calls are merged, a new `Call-ID` header is also generated.

`Contact` The `Contact` header is similar to the `From` header except that it contains the specific IP address and port information for which the user/endpoint can be contacted. This becomes extremely useful when you're dealing with a forked session, which will be delivered to multiple endpoints; you can uniquely identify each one.

`Cseq` The Command Sequence (`Cseq`) header is used to keep track of individual requests within a session. For example, the first `INVITE` will be:

```
Cseq: 1 INVITE
```

The corresponding `200 - OK` response will include this `Cseq` value also. If the session is modified to include additional modalities, the next `INVITE` will be:

```
Cseq: 2 INVITE
```

(and it will have a corresponding `200 - OK` response). If there are any delays in the first `200 - OK` response, the `Cseq` value will indicate which `INVITE` is being referenced.

The `ACK` message will always have the same `Cseq` value as the `INVITE` to which it corresponds, as will any `CANCEL` request. Other request messages will have an incremented `Cseq` value.

`From` This header is the SIP URI for the user sending the message, similar to the From field in an email.

`Record-Route/Route/Via` These three headers indicate the routing through which the SIP message has traversed in terms of SIP proxy servers. The `Record-Route` header indicates a proxy server that must remain in the return route. This may be for security reasons, where a specific path is required.

The `Route` header provides the return path, without forcing a specific route hop-by-hop.

The `Via` header is used to detect routing loops; it stores each proxy that has handled the request, as shown in this example:

```
Via: SIP/2.0/TLS 192.168.3.106:61382;received=192.168.3.10;ms-received-
port=63942;ms-received-cid=57738800
Record-Route: <sip:se.gaots.local:5061;transport=tls;ms-
fe=se.gaots.local;lr;received=192.168.3.10;ms-received-cid=4FCF2601>
Record-Route: <sip:fed.gaots.co.uk:443;transport=tls;opaque=state:Ci
.D57738800;lr;ms-route-sig=hhekkICd-Rvcsd8OF--J6yJgk7YJjn8ihOWzOXIb_
dEi4gL9pjnDiCAQAA>
```

`To` This header is the SIP URI for the recipient of the message, similar to the To field in an email.

Providing Presence

So far you've seen how to `REGISTER` your endpoints and `INVITE` sessions. However, you haven't looked at one of the key features of Lync Server 2010 (and previous versions), which is also implemented via SIP—presence.

Presence in the user sense is the availability and willingness of a user to communicate. Technically, it is the functionality behind knowing how available or how busy a user is. When a user is logged in with multiple sessions, a level of aggregation is provided so that other users will see only the result of this presence, not each individual state. The two SIP messages SUBSCRIBE and NOTIFY are used to indicate this functionality.

NOTIFY is used to update the presence state of an endpoint to the server, and within Lync Server 2010 an aggregation script runs to provide a final updated result of the user's presence based on this change.

For example, assume a user is logged in on both a laptop and a Lync 2010 Phone Edition device. If the user picks up the phone and dials a number, the status of the phone device becomes *busy* (or more accurately *in a call*); at the same time, the user is no longer using the laptop Lync 2010 client, so this client changes to *away*. Any other users who have this user in their own Buddy list will simply see the status to be *in a call*; there is no indication of the second client (on the laptop) and certainly no indication of the user being *away*. The Lync Server 2010 server is responsible for this aggregation of presence from all the endpoints and provision of the data out to other users. In fact, the Lync 2010 client will show *In a Call* as the aggregated presence update will also feedback to the user.

For a user to receive presence updates of contacts (buddies), they must be added to the *Contacts list* on the client (see Chapter 4, "Client Access"). The background SIP message used by the Lync 2010 client is SUBSCRIBE. This message contains the SIP URI of the user whose presence is to be added to the Contacts list.

For presence information outside the Lync 2010 client, an ad hoc request is created for a single view of presence; this is typically the case for email messages or SharePoint sites where the users involved are not necessarily on the Contacts list.

Upon login to the Lync 2010 client and download of the Contacts list from the server, a *batch subscription* is requested for all the users listed in the Contacts list. A batch subscription also sets up a request for permanent updates to any of the presence states of the contacts on the Contacts list.

Figure 2.13 shows the ladder view when multiple users log in, change state, and subscribe to presence. Notice that the users also subscribe to their own presence state.

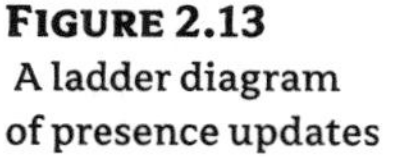

FIGURE 2.13
A ladder diagram of presence updates

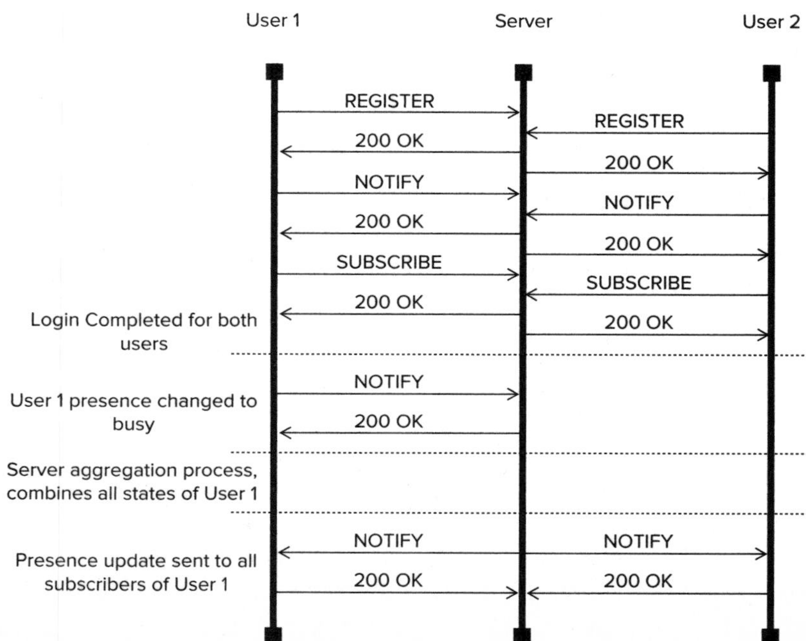

Sending an Instant Message

After presence updates, sending instant messages is probably the second most popular of Lync Server 2010's SIP features.

Once you have identified the user you want to send a message to, the new IM window will open so that you can type the message. At this point, in the background you will have already logged in (`REGISTER`) and received the presence status of the user (`SUBSCRIBE`, `NOTIFY`). Not surprisingly, the `MESSAGE` request is used to process the sending and receiving of IMs.

The content (SDP) of the `MESSAGE` is not visible within the logs of the Lync 2010 client (or server) for privacy reasons. Figure 2.14 shows the SIP message exchange process in ladder format.

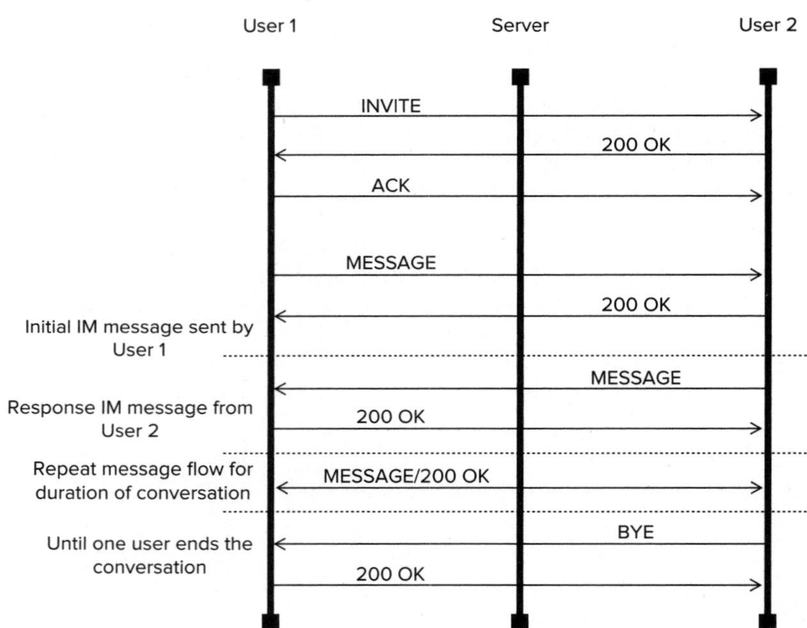

FIGURE 2.14
A ladder diagram for sending an IM

Understanding Lync 2010 Codecs and Standards

So far we've looked at SIP's background and how SIP is used to provide the IM and presence functionality in Lync Server 2010. Obviously, Lync Server 2010 (like Office Communications Server 2007 and R2) extends the client functionality beyond IM and presence to include peer-to-peer desktop sharing, voice, and video, as well as conferencing versions of all of these. These features are not just for internal communication; the Edge server provides the same client functionality to remote users in a secure way. All of these extensions to SIP are implemented in Lync using the codecs we'll discuss next.

Call Admission Control (CAC) can be used to control which codecs are available for communications between endpoints; for more information, see Chapter 14, "Call Admission Control."

Using the Voice Codecs

Prior to Lync Server 2010, the default codec was Real-Time Audio (RTAudio); now the preferred codec is G711. From the session setup perspective, the codec used is irrelevant because it is negotiated (via the SDP content) in the initial `INVITE`, as shown in the following example log.

```
CSeq: 1 INVITE
Contact: <sip:keith_lync@gaots.co.uk;opaque=user:epid:rKqM2mMJqV2mDOKToUtijwAA;gruu>
User-Agent: UCCAPI/4.0.7577.314 OC/4.0.7577.314 (Microsoft Lync 2010)
Supported: ms-dialog-route-set-update
Ms-Conversation-ID: AcyDJ2+hW2+XFkopTdeZrXulwA41yA==
Supported: timer
Supported: histinfo
Supported: ms-safe-transfer
Supported: ms-sender
Supported: ms-early-media
Supported: 100rel
ms-keep-alive: UAC;hop-hop=yes
Allow: INVITE, BYE, ACK, CANCEL, INFO, UPDATE, REFER, NOTIFY, BENOTIFY, OPTIONS
ms-subnet: 192.168.0.0
Accept-Language: en-US
ms-endpoint-location-data: NetworkScope;ms-media-location-type=Intranet
P-Preferred-Identity: <sip:keith_lync@gaots.co.uk>
Supported: replaces
Supported: ms-conf-invite
Proxy-Authorization: Kerberos qop="auth", realm="SIP Communications Service",
opaque="4E502AF5", targetname="sip/se.goats.local", crand="2257d26a", cnum="12",
response="040400ffffffffff000000000000000005c49a725aa9918f694cf4cec"
Content-Type: multipart/alternative;boundary="----=_NextPart_000_0006_01CC832F
.D19DE7F0"
Content-Length: 3304

------=_NextPart_000_0006_01CC832F.D19DE7F0
Content-Type: application/sdp
Content-Transfer-Encoding: 7bit
Content-ID: <4a9a5f370140470a9bd92a02c4c0f7f2@gaots.co.uk>
Content-Disposition: session; handling=optional; ms-proxy-2007fallback

v=0
o=- 0 0 IN IP4 192.168.0.10
s=session
c=IN IP4 192.168.0.10
b=CT:99980
```

```
t=0 0
m=audio 4680 RTP/SAVP 114 9 112 111 0 8 116 115 4 97 13 118 101
a=candidate:UgthpTzpXdxzN80OUm7KdqW+4eLzS6ekVGT899b5Tts 1 1azIPAGwsoG5ed3FKOQ/Lg
UDP 0.830 172.23.24.236 13646
a=candidate:UgthpTzpXdxzN80OUm7KdqW+4eLzS6ekVGT899b5Tts 2 1azIPAGwsoG5ed3FKOQ/Lg
UDP 0.830 172.23.24.236 13647
a=candidate:33hmkNOOYZHHwWb36Z7XdlW7zI9q1DD8i+HMP054xiI 1 49feTBWu+huGWNQFxBbGWA
UDP 0.840 192.168.0.10 4680
a=candidate:33hmkNOOYZHHwWb36Z7XdlW7zI9q1DD8i+HMP054xiI 2 49feTBWu+huGWNQFxBbGWA
UDP 0.840 192.168.0.10 4681
a=cryptoscale:1 client AES_CM_128_HMAC_SHA1_80 inline:ShWUCidF5aWY6EWHAXrWULrPZYJ
DN8d6cEUDhP39|2^31|1:1
a=crypto:2 AES_CM_128_HMAC_SHA1_80 inline:UuMge3Oy0ozckMdHhNYpGQGDIcixnEyU0+Q2JN
qy|2^31|1:1
a=crypto:3 AES_CM_128_HMAC_SHA1_80 inline:903WFSguPZMR/SPKb+dzLtX+5oH1jzuTVlGrGS
6k|2^31
a=maxptime:200
a=rtpmap:114 x-msrta/16000
a=fmtp:114 bitrate=29000
a=rtpmap:9 G722/8000
a=rtpmap:112 G7221/16000
a=fmtp:112 bitrate=24000
a=rtpmap:111 SIREN/16000
a=fmtp:111 bitrate=16000
a=rtpmap:0 PCMU/8000
a=rtpmap:8 PCMA/8000
a=rtpmap:116 AAL2-G726-32/8000
a=rtpmap:115 x-msrta/8000
a=fmtp:115 bitrate=11800
a=rtpmap:4 G723/8000
a=rtpmap:97 RED/8000
a=rtpmap:13 CN/8000
a=rtpmap:118 CN/16000
a=rtpmap:101 telephone-event/8000
a=fmtp:101 0-16
a=encryption:required
```

Here, you can see the `a=rtpmap` entries, listing each of the different codecs available; the value after the codec name is the sample rate used, so there may be multiple entries for the same codec, but different sample rates (for example, `a=rtpmap:114 x-msrta/16000` and `a=rtpmap:115 x-msrta/8000`).

The line

```
m=audio 4680 RTP/SAVP 114 9 112 111 0 8 116 115 4 97 13 118 101
```

shows the order in which the codecs are negotiated, with each number corresponding directly to the number immediately after the `a=rtpmap` designator. You may notice that the first codec in the list is RTAudio with a sample rate of 16000; although Lync prefers to use the G711 codec, it will only do so once it has confirmed there is suitable bandwidth, and so the first codec negotiation attempt will be RTAudio.

The actual workings of the codec are the interesting parts, and we'll look at how generic codecs operate in the Lync Server 2010 environment.

We've already discussed how the media stream is negotiated via the SDP and is separate from the signaling. Lync Server 2010 includes healing capability to allow recovery from the loss of packets, using Forward Error Correction (FEC). FEC is dynamic, so it will be in effect only when problems are detected on the network.

For example, consider the sound wave shown in Figure 2.15.

FIGURE 2.15
Input audio wave

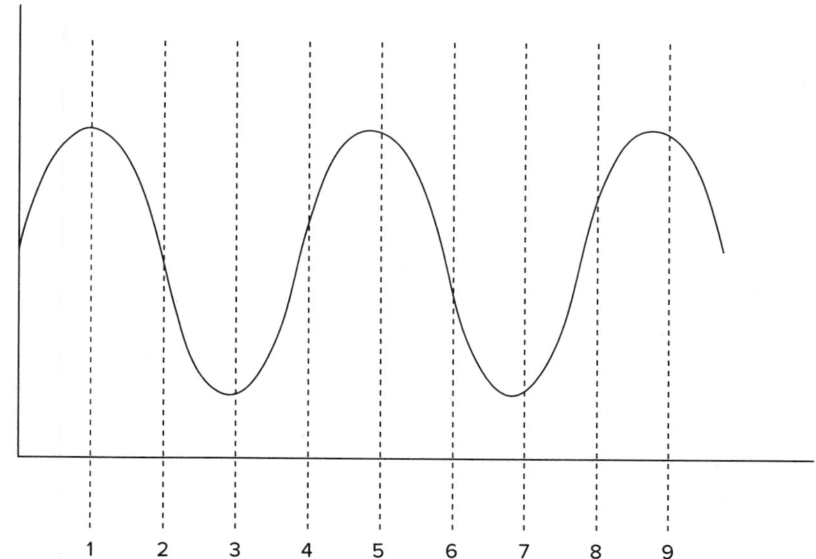

The Lync 2010 client will sample the input, in this example at a rate assumed to be 20ms per packet; and it will output the data in a number of packets to be sent across the network (Figure 2.16).

FIGURE 2.16
Sampled data for packetization

1	2	3	4	5	6	7	8	9

Now suppose that a problem occurs on the network, resulting in packet loss, and some of the data is lost. At this point, the endpoints will be aware of the packet loss and implement FEC on the audio stream. This means that another copy (compressed) of the previous packet will be sent with each actual packet (Figure 2.17).

FIGURE 2.17
Sampled data for packetization with FEC

2|1	3|2	4|3	5|6	6|5	7|6	8|7

This will result in additional data on the network; however, it compensates well for packet loss and allows the codec to "heal" the data into a more usable form. Figure 2.18 shows a comparison with and without FEC, assuming packet loss of packets 4 and 5.

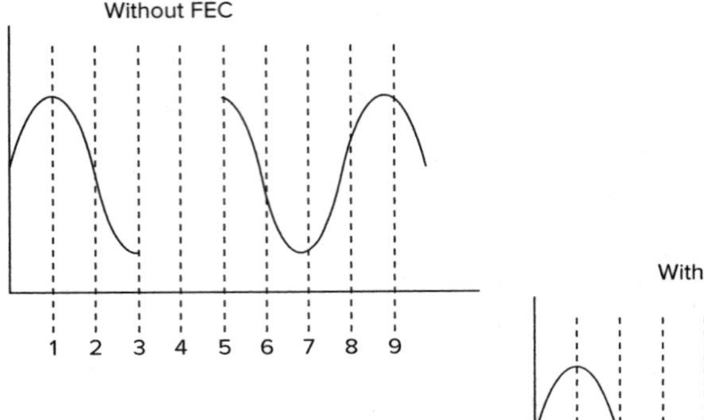

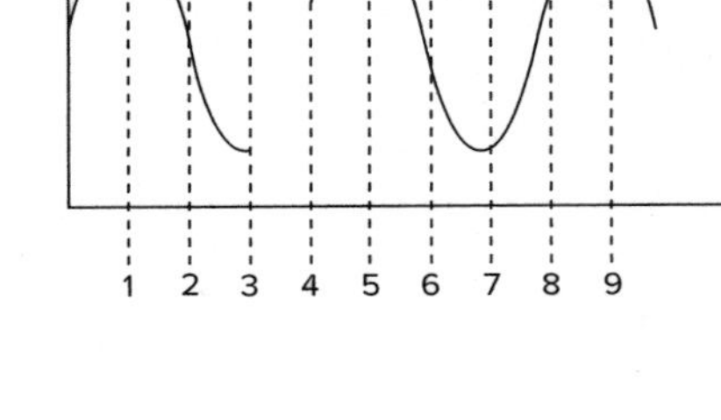

FIGURE 2.18
Received audio wave after packet loss (top); after packet loss using FEC (bottom)

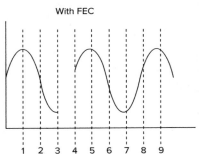

Losing two consecutive packets with FEC means that the healing capability has to try to recover 40ms worth of data; on the other hand, using FEC means that you actually have the information for the second packet, thereby reducing the amount of data the healing algorithm needs to repair.

USING THE VIDEO CODECS

The video codecs have not changed significantly with the introduction of Lync Server 2010, with the exception that the default video for conferences is now Video Graphics Array (VGA) instead of Common Interchange Format (CIF). High definition is supported only in peer-to-peer calls.

Lync Server 2010 uses compressed video to reduce the amount of data required to be transferred over the network. The video codec is negotiated in the same way as the audio, via the SDP associated with the `INVITE`. Here's a sample log:

```
CSeq: 1 INVITE
<shortened for brevity, but would include the same audio details as the previous
example>
```

```
m=video 51140 RTP/SAVP 121 34
a=x-caps:121 263:1280:720:30.0:1500000:1;4359:640:480:30.0:600000:1;8455:352:288:
15.0:250000:1;12551:176:144:15.0:180000:1
a=x-caps:34 262:352:288:15.0:250000:1;4358:176:144:15.0:180000:1
<candidate information removed for brevity>
a=rtcp:53646
a=rtpmap:121 x-rtvc1/90000
a=rtpmap:34 H263/90000
a=encryption:required
```

In this case, you can see the `m=video 51140 RTP/SAVP 121 34` line, listing only two codecs and translating via their relevant `rtpmap` entries, results in these being RTVideo (`x-rtcv1`) and H263.

The additional `a=x-caps` line provides the encapsulation details for each codec (as with audio, the number is the identifier). This `x-caps` line definition has the following format for each video quality contained within the protocol:

```
port:width:height:framerate:bitrate;
```

Therefore, the entry:

```
a=x-caps:121 263:1280:720:30.0:1500000:1;4359:640:480:30.0:600000:1;8455:352:288:
15.0:250000:1;12551:176:144:15.0:180000:1
```

corresponds to the following quality definitions: 720p;VGA;CIF;QCIF.

Lost frames are simply ignored, as the next frame will provide more info, and frames appearing out of order are useless to the picture. But because some frames are dependent upon others, this approach can lead to a "stuttering" or "artifact" effect in the playback. Figure 2.19 shows a typical sample for a conference video codec using a frame rate of 30 frames per second.

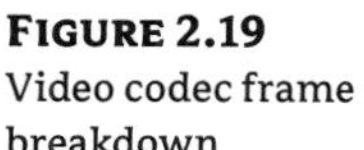

FIGURE 2.19
Video codec frame breakdown

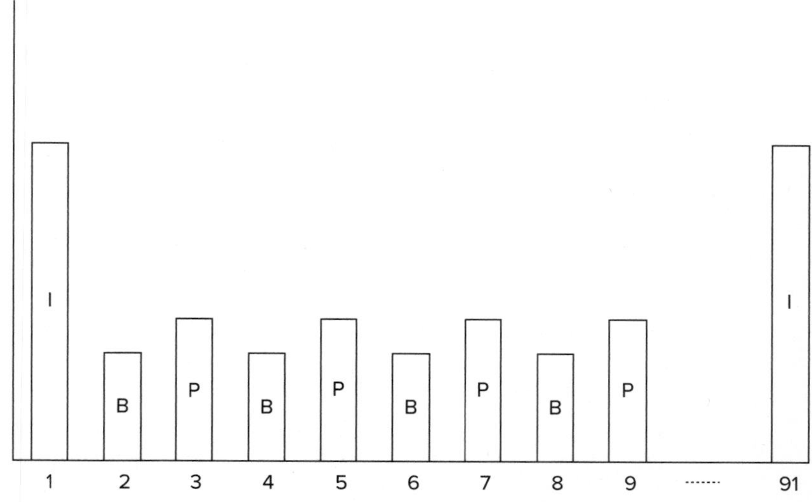

Each full sample will begin and end with an *I-frame* (Intra-coded picture), which appears every 4 seconds for peer-to-peer video and every 3 seconds for conferences; the period between I-frames is known as the Group of Pictures (GoP). No compression is available with this frame.

Within the full sample period is a combination of *P-frames* (Predicted picture) and *B-frames* (Bi-predictive picture). Each of these P-frames and B-frames contain only changes from the previous frame, with the B-frame also containing changes from the *next* frame.

Figure 2.20 shows the content within an I-frame and a P-frame (the dotted line represents the removal of content). Here, the P-frame predicts that the character will next raise her arms. It describes only their new position and the deletion of the old.

FIGURE 2.20
I-frame versus P-frame

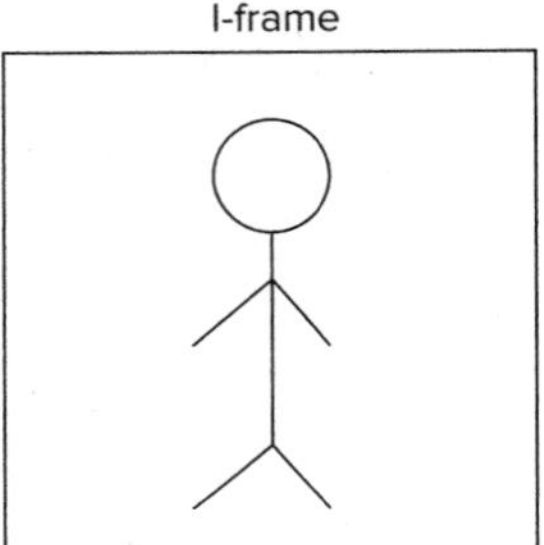

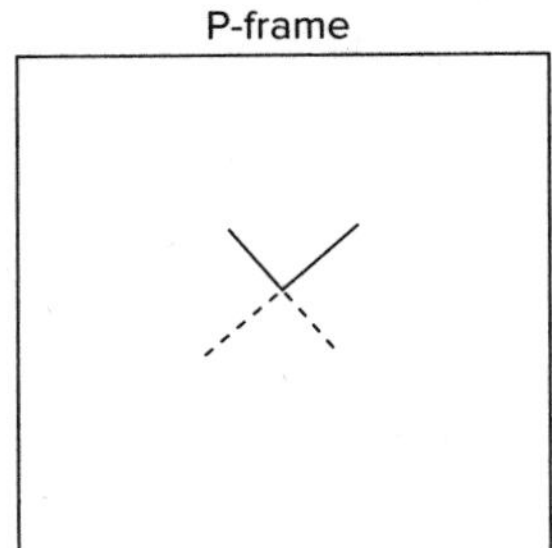

An individual frame loss will not have a massive impact; however, depending on the specific type of frame lost, it may lead to a pause or some ghosting of images, in which a frame has been dropped and some updated information has been missed (such as an artifact not being removed).

A packet loss will cause an artifact to appear until the next same type or larger frame. For example, an I-frame is the largest frame, and losing it will cause a problem until the next I-frame. On the other hand, losing a P-frame will result in a problem until the next P-frame or I-frame (whichever occurs first).

Using Desktop Sharing

Desktop sharing uses Remote Desktop Protocol (RDP) as its media stream. The Desktop Sharing function has been improved dramatically in Lync 2010, providing users more control; they can now specify individual applications for sharing, individual screens, or the full desktop.

From the communications perspective, Lync only leverages the RDP protocol, and uses SIP as the signaling method, as it does with all other communication functions. Apart from permissions and workstation configuration, there is nothing specifically different between an RDP session within the Lync 2010 client and a direct RDP session.

Connecting Remotely

During the session establishment process of the `INVITE`, the SDP will carry information of the IP address on which the client can be reached. This will always be the direct interface address from the client, as the clients will always try to connect peer-to-peer.

This scenario fits perfectly into an enterprise environment, where all clients share a network (likely via a WAN connection) and can be directly reached. However, it doesn't work as well when firewalls have been implemented, and even less so when clients are connecting via the Internet.

The solution to this is the Edge server, which will act as a SIP proxy server, but also as a media termination point. Where clients previously connected directly to each other, they can now use the Edge server to provide a common termination point to exchange media.

The establishment of this termination point is a multistep process:

1. Log in to the Front End server using SIP via the Edge server (as a proxy).
2. Request the Media Relay Authentication Service (MRAS) credentials via the front-end server.
3. Request the Edge endpoint details.
4. Send the `INVITE` to another user, populating the SDP with Edge endpoint details.
5. Negotiate which endpoint to use for media communications.
6. Begin the session.

When an endpoint is located remotely, it can be directly connected to the Internet or connected behind a Network Address Translation (NAT) device, effectively hiding its direct IP address (Figure 2.21).

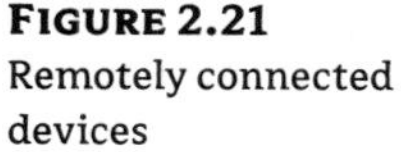

FIGURE 2.21
Remotely connected devices

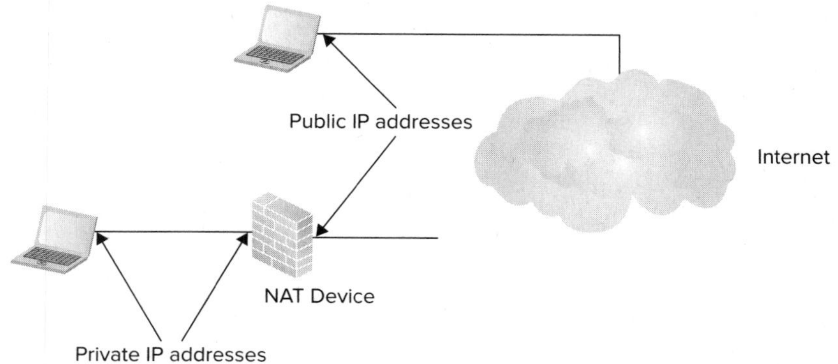

Even though the endpoint may be behind a NAT device, it will not automatically be aware of that and will continue to include its local IP address in the SDP exchange. If it is behind a NAT device, it needs to have a method to determine that, and also to determine the actual IP address (and port) to use on the Edge server.

This is where Internet Connectivity Establishment (ICE), RFC4091, 5245/Session Traversal Utilities for NAT (STUN), RFC 3489, and 5389/Traversal Using Relay NAT (TURN), RFC 5766 come into play. All of them provide methods to overcome the problem of hidden IP addresses with NAT when using media connectivity.

Simply put, using STUN and TURN methods allows the endpoint to identify addresses via the Edge server; STUN provides a reflexive address (on the NAT device), and TURN provides a relay (on the Edge server). Figure 2.22 shows this in detail.

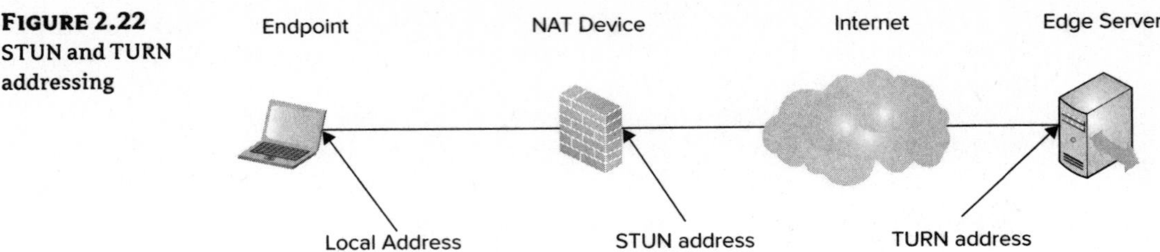

FIGURE 2.22
STUN and TURN addressing

Once the endpoint has identified its own available addresses, it can populate the SDP and begin negotiating which address to communicate.

Once the SDPs have been exchanged, the negotiation of connection addresses will begin and follow this order:

1. UDP direct
2. UDP NAT (STUN)
3. UDP Relay (TURN)
4. TCP Relay (TURN)

Once bidirectional connectivity is established, the `INVITE` is stopped and reissued, this time including only the valid address information. From here the session will begin as normal.

The Bottom Line

Understand the basics of SIP for signaling. SIP originates from an extensive background of telephony signaling. Although knowing that background is not strictly required for Lync administration, understanding how we have gotten to where we are today will help you overcome some of the challenges you'll face when integrating with legacy telephony environments.

Master It For what is a jitter buffer used?

Understand how SIP has been extended providing additional functionality for Lync Server 2010. In its plainest form, SIP provides session-based signaling; however, with some of the extensions for SIP, you can extend this session-based signaling approach to incorporate additional functionality within the SIP request itself, such as IM and presence information.

Master It Assuming a user is not yet logged in, describe the SIP requests required to log in and establish an IM session with another user.

Identify additional protocols used by Lync Server 2010. Lync Server 2010 uses many different protocols for its various modalities as needed by the user. It can also tie many of these modalities together providing an integrated solution running on top of SIP. Microsoft has also been able to successfully (and securely) extend this functionality to the Internet.

Master It When negotiating the address to be used for an externally connected endpoint, which order is preferred for the media session?

Chapter 3

Security

In today's world, where security breaches are all too common, the ability to secure your Lync Server 2010 deployment is critical. In particular, your key focus should be protecting external access to Lync. The Lync Edge role and its supporting components deliver the ability to communicate with close to a billion people worldwide. However, the possibility of communicating with that many people entails risk. When correctly configured, Lync's design will help you mitigate that risk.

Of course, its various core capabilities provide security. For example, Lync encrypts all its communications, both the signaling and the media, which means that as a platform it can be used in highly secure environments where systems that leave the media unencrypted on the wire would be less useful. With Lync, there is no need to implement another security system, such as IP Security (IPsec), just to secure media traffic. The authentication mechanisms available constitute another key element to securing Lync. While the standard username and password options are used for several clients (the PC-based ones), PIN and extension authentication underpinned by certificate authentication are used on all the new Lync IP Phone edition devices.

Finally, many Lync policies enable you as an administrator to run a secure platform. Chapter 10, "User Administration," covers policies in depth; this chapter covers security-based policy topics. For example, you'll learn how to determine PIN policies, you'll learn about the length and complexity of the PIN, and you'll learn how to define who can federate with external parties.

In this chapter, you will learn to:

- Secure external access
- Understand core security
- Provide security administratively

Securing External Access

One of Lync's most exciting features is its ability to provide communication functionality not only to users within your network, but to those outside it, whether they are employees working from home or while mobile, or perhaps partners, or even the general public. Lync makes it possible to communicate with literally millions of people worldwide through a variety of networks, including Windows Live, Yahoo!, Google, and AOL. Table 3.1 summarizes the available types of communication based on the different types of external users.

TABLE 3.1: Communication Types Available to Different Types of External Users

Scenario	Remote User	Federated User	Public IM Connectivity/Interop	Anonymous User
Presence	Yes	Yes	Yes	No
Instant messaging (IM) peer-to-peer	Yes	Yes	Yes	No
IM conferencing	Yes	Yes	No	Yes
Collaboration	Yes	Yes	No	Yes
A/V peer-to-peer	Yes	Yes	Yes, if using the latest version of Windows Live Messenger	No
A/V conferencing	Yes	Yes	No	Yes
File transfer	Yes	Yes	No	No

Using AV with Windows Live Messenger

If you require audio/video (AV) to work with Live Messenger, you must use the latest Live Messenger client and alter the encryption policy used by Lync from `required` to `supported`. You can do that using the following command from the Lync Server Management Shell (LSMS), also known simply as PowerShell. PowerShell will be covered in depth in Chapter 8, "PowerShell and LMS."

```
Set-CsMediaConfiguration Global -EncryptionLevel
```

When this command is issued, Lync will no longer insist on encrypting all media traffic; it's needed because the Live Messenger cloud can't perform encryption. Lync will try to negotiate encryption, but if that fails it will fall back to unencrypted media.

Finally, to enable AV with cloud providers, you must use the following command:

```
Set-CsExternalAccessPolicy Global -EnablePublicCloudAccess $true
-EnablePublicCloudAudioVideoAccess $true
```

This code will alter the Global CsExternalAccessPolicy to allow AV to the Cloud (PIC). Of course, the external access policy can also be configured through Lync Server Control Panel (LSCP).

All of this communication potential can send security professionals running scared! Think about opening up all that traffic through firewalls…and what about information leakage?

If you look closely, you will see that the way Lync has been designed combined with the best practices for its deployment will go a long way toward mitigating the risks of broad communication. Clearly, though, you need to get your security guys to understand that. The next few sections will help you do so!

Edge Security Components

Like other elements of Lync architecture, the way you provide external access offers choices—but not as many as back in the Office Communications Server (OCS) 2007 days, when it was possible to have a whole range of different roles split onto different servers. Now with Lync, all the Edge roles are consolidated onto a single Edge server. Your main choice is whether to have one or many of these servers and, if there will be many, how to load balance them to provide high availability. There are three traditional topologies that allow you to provide external access: Single Consolidated Edge, Scaled Consolidated Edge with DNS Load Balancing, and Scaled Consolidated Edge with Hardware Load Balancing.

Of course, the Edge server is not the only element that comes into play to provide external access to Lync functionality; there are also many supporting components, which are detailed throughout the chapter.

The Edge Server

The Single Consolidated Edge model takes all the Edge roles, Access Edge, AV Edge, and Web Conferencing Edge, and runs them on a server. This provides all the external access capabilities of Lync in a single box. Each of these roles provides specific security capabilities and has specific requirements. In particular, each requires certificates that have the correct name entries to be provided and firewalls to be configured with the relevant ports open.

The Access Edge role is a specially designed proxy concerned with passing Session Initiation Protocol (SIP) signaling traffic. It is a routing solution in that two Network Interface Cards (NICs) are used and traffic is terminated on the way into the external NIC and then reestablished through the internal NIC on the way out. This creates a barrier between external and internal components. The Access Edge role doesn't carry out authentication, and so it is not required to be a member of the Active Directory (AD). Remote user authentication traffic is passed through to the next internal hop, either the Director pool or the front-end pool, which, being a member of AD, carries out the authentication.

The Web Conferencing Edge is a proxy for PSOM (Persistent Shared Object Model) traffic. This protocol is used to provide access to conferencing content such as slides, whiteboards, and poll pages shared between internal and external users. It works in conjunction with the Access Edge for SIP session setup and the reverse proxy for slide/attachment content downloads.

The AV Edge is where Lync implements the Interactive Connectivity Establishment (ICE) protocol, which provides the ability to enable media traffic to traverse a Network Address Translation (NAT) environment. In Lync Server 2010, the AV Edge role also provides the ability to allow file transfers through NAT via the Edge server, whereas in previous OCS versions clients had to set up a routable session directly between them for transfers to work.

The key benefits of combining these three roles into a consolidated Edge server are simplicity and fewer hardware requirements. As mentioned, each Edge server will have two NICs, one of which is on the external side of the DMZ (demilitarized zone) and the other on the internal side. The external NIC will require three IP addresses assigned to it, one for each of the Edge roles. This will equate to three separate URLs, one for each role. The internal interface requires a single IP on a different subnet that is routable from the internal LAN.

USING A SINGLE EXTERNAL IP ADDRESS

Although it is possible to use a single IP address on the external Edge interface, doing so is not recommended because it would require the ports to be reconfigured on which each Edge role listens. By default, Lync was designed (where possible) to require only well-known ports, such as TCP/443, to be opened. Therefore, this port is required by all the Edge roles, and so having a single IP only would cause clashes as these ports overlapped. You would, therefore, have to change to other ports, thereby complicating deployment and making the system harder to understand for other administrators who might not be aware of the changes.

As mentioned, four IP addresses and, therefore, four URLs will be on each Edge server. When you're setting up Edge servers, choose these URLs carefully. For example, if OCS is already deployed, you must consider the URLs already in use. The Lync Edge role should use new URLs so it can be deployed side by side. For more information about these options, see Chapter 7, "Upgrades and Migrations." The specifics of topology are discussed later in this chapter.

When you are deploying Edge servers, another key consideration is where they will be deployed. If you have a single Central site, the choice is simple because the Edge server will be there; however, once you scale out to several Central sites, perhaps in a global deployment, you need to consider how best to route external traffic. Keep in mind that there is only one path to the external world for all federation traffic for a particular SIP domain. As discussed in the Domain Name System (DNS) section later, a specific SRV DNS record is needed for federation, and it can point only to one Fully Qualified Domain Name (FQDN)—namely that of the Access Edge, which provides the route for federation traffic. Either this would be a Virtual IP (VIP) on a Hardware Load Balancer (HLB) device or load balancing would be provided through DNS Load Balancing, as discussed later in the chapter. Other Edge traffic (based on the nature of its content, such as real-time audio) is probably better off being localized to where the front-end pool is. In such cases, you can have multiple Edge pools, each defined as the next hop for their respective Front End or Director pools.

THE DIRECTOR

The Director role in Lync is now a full-fledged role in its own right. Prior to Lync, the Director was a modified front-end server that had to be manually customized by turning off certain services; it was, however, still possible to accidently end up with users homed to the Director. In Lync, this is no longer possible. The Director role provides user authentication and redirects users to a front-end server in their home pool. The ability to provide authentication and redirection means that the Director is essentially an additional layer sitting between the Edge servers and the front-end servers and is, therefore, in the path of external users coming through the Edge servers to the internal front-end servers. This functionality provides a range of benefits. First, in Lync organizations with multiple pools deployed in a central site, the Director is configured as the first point of contact for users who are signing in. This means that all user registration/authentication requests first arrive at the Director, which can then authenticate and route the traffic to the relevant Lync front-end-server pool rather than having the front-end servers burdened with all this traffic when they could be providing resources for all the other functions they support. The second area where the Director role comes into play is in providing a stop-gap between external users and the front-end servers. As traffic is passed on from the

Edge to the Director, it is the Director that does the authentication. Therefore, if your Lync system were to be subjected to an externally sourced Denial of Service (DoS) attack, where large quantities of malformed authentication traffic were blasted at your Edge, the Director would take the brunt of the attack, rather than the front-end servers that serve the internal users. Admittedly, external users would no longer be able to gain access, but internal users who were already logged onto the system would be able to continue working.

Like many of the other Lync roles, the Director can be installed either as a standalone server or as a pool of Directors that have some form of load balancing. As with the Edge and front-end servers, this load balancing can either be DNS Load Balancing or Hardware Load Balancing, about which you'll learn more shortly.

The Reverse Proxy

While the Edge server and the Director provide access to the SIP and media facilities within Lync, another type of remote access is required by Lync clients. This is the requirement for access to the various web-based elements provided by Lync through IIS websites. The role of the reverse proxy is to publish the required URLs on the front end and Director servers. The process by which it does so is discussed in depth in Chapter 6, "Installation."

The external access to web services allows remote users to connect to meetings or dial-in conferences using simple URLs, to download meeting content when in a conference, to expand distribution groups, to obtain a user-based certificate for client certificate–based authentication, to download files from the Address Book server, submit queries to the Address Book Web Query service, and to obtain updates to client and device software.

Table 3.2 shows the URLs that are published through the reverse proxy and describes the certificates that are needed.

Table 3.2: URLs That Must Be Published Through the Reverse Proxy

Role/Subject Name	Used to Publish	Subject Name Syntax Example
External Web Services/ FQDN of the front-end pool	Address Book files Distribution Group Expansion Conference content Device update files	`Se01webext.gaots.co.uk`
External WebServices/ FQDN of the Director pool	Address Book files Distribution Group Expansion Conference content Device update files	`Directorwebext.gaots.co.uk`
Simple URL/AdminFQDN	AdminFQDN is not published externally. It is only used internally.	N/A
Simple URL/DialinFQDN	Dial-in Conferencing information	`dialin.gaots.co.uk`
Simple URL/MeetFQDN	Meeting URL	`meet.gaots.co.uk`

Multiple areas of functionality are listed in the "used to publish" column of Table 3.2; however, best practice is to publish them all using a single rule in TMG (Forefront Threat Management Gateway 2010), which uses the `FQDN/*` in the Paths field.

> **PUBLISHING HTTP EXTERNALLY**
>
> You may notice that the bulk of external connections come over HTTPS. However, HTTP is still required for device updates to work.

One of the elements published is the *simple URL*. Simple URLs are a method of making the URL used in conferencing a lot easier for end users to understand. Where there is a Director pool in place, the URLs are published on the Director, as this gives a single point of ingress to the network. You can configure the simple URLs in a variety of ways. You should consider this configuration carefully during your planning phase; once the URLs are set, changing them will require rerunning setup on the front-end server and can also require certificate changes. You will need three simple URLs: the Meet URL, the Dial-in URL, and the Admin URL. The Admin URL is optional, but it simplifies internal access to the Lync Control Panel. It is never published externally. One thing to be aware of is that the Meet URL is set per supported SIP domain, while only one Admin and Dial-in URL are needed per organization. The following three examples demonstrate different ways you can configure your simple URLs.

The simplest option is to have a dedicated simple URL for each site:

```
https://meet.gaots.co.uk
https://dialin.gaots.co.uk
https://admin.gaots.co.uk
```

You will need additional Meet URLs for any additional SIP domains:

```
https://meet.anotherdomain.co.uk
```

This method requires a significant number of certificates or subject alternative names to support each URL and many different DNS entries.

In the next option, the simple URL is essentially presented as a virtual directory under the external web services URL. This is called the *shared simple URL* syntax:

```
https://directorwebext.gaots.co.uk/meet/
https://directorwebext.gaots.co.uk/dialin/
https://directorwebext.gaots.co.uk/admin/
```

Here you benefit from using the same base URL as the external web services and, therefore, the same DNS records and certificate. Were you to want support for additional SIP domains, you would need another URL, again only for the Meet URL. For example:

```
https://directorwebext.anotherdomain.co.uk/meet/
```

Finally, to make the most efficient use of URLs, you can tweak the shared format, as shown here:

```
https://directorwebext.gaots.co.uk/gaotscouk/meet/
https://directorwebext.gaots.co.uk/anotherdomain/meet/
https://directorwebext.gaots.co.uk/dialin/
https://directorwebext.gaots.co.uk/admin/
```

This technique uses the least number of certificates or subject alternative names and DNS entries and is, therefore, the simplest to configure and most cost effective.

Now that you've seen the various types of simple URLs, here's a summary of when you would use each one:

Format	**Used For**
Shared	Single pool deployments
	Multiple pool deployments where each pool shares global simple URLs
	Multiple pool deployments where each pool has dedicated simple URLs and public certificate cost is an issue (you can save one certificate per pool by using shared simple URLs)
Dedicated	Multiple pool deployments where each pool has dedicated simple URLs
	Deployments where you do not want to potentially display internal server names externally

When the reverse proxy publishes sites, it actually breaks the traffic from the external source, inspects it, and then sends it to the internal server. This process has two elements with specific requirements. First, one important step during this process is for the reverse proxy to translate incoming requests on the public ports 80 and 443 to internal requests for the Lync external websites on ports 8080 and 4443. Second, certificates are used to terminate the encrypted traffic and then send it on again also encrypted. Externally, these should be trusted certificates from a public CA. The reverse proxy uses them to identify itself externally. When re-encrypting the traffic to pass on to the internal server, it uses the certificates on the front end or the Directors, which come from the internal CA. If this is not possible because the reverse proxy cannot trust additional internal CAs, then you need to set up the external web services site on the Lync servers with trusted public certificates.

In Table 3.2, you can see that both the Director and the front-end pools have external web URLs that must be published. The Director must be published because it plays a role in web ticket authentication, about which you'll learn more later. The front end must be published because the URLs of the front end are sent in-band to the client for operations such as Distribution Group Expansion.

High Availability

Because all the Edge roles are provided on a single server, making them highly available is a simple case of adding more Edge servers. Of course, when you do this, you need some way to balance and route the traffic between the different Edge servers accordingly, so that they can present a single identity. In Lync, you have two ways of doing this: DNS Load Balancing and Hardware Load Balancing (HLB). Both have advantages and disadvantages. In a migration or when you need to communicate externally with earlier versions of OCS, using an HLB is still the way to go.

In OCS, it was a challenge to set up HLB devices correctly to support both the web and SIP traffic that needed to be load balanced. In order to simplify the LB requirements, DNS load balancing was introduced in Lync. Another benefit is that DNS LB supports the *server draining* feature, which allows a server to be prepared for shutdown by not accepting any new connections but still allowing existing ones to come to a natural conclusion.

HLB does not provide the application layer mechanisms required to support the server draining feature.

The simplicity of DNS load balancing comes from the fact that it is application-based and uses client intelligence to determine which traffic can and can't be load-balanced. Each front-end server in a pool registers its FQDN as an A record in DNS, and then the pool FQDN is configured in DNS to return each of the front-end IP addresses. The client then has the ability to order them and try them as required until it is signed in. When you're using an HLB device to load balance the internal NIC of the Edge server, you must ensure that traffic to the Web Conferencing Edge role is not load balanced, even though the rest of the traffic to the other two Edge roles should be load balanced. When using DNS load balancing, another benefit of the client intelligence is that the Lync client knows how to handle the traffic flow and setup is simpler.

Another key consideration is compatibility. Although DNS load balancing is simpler to set up, you must ensure that the clients and third parties to which you will be connecting can use the new method. As mentioned, DNS load balancing requires intelligence in the client. For example, the RTM version of Exchange 2010 Unified Messaging (UM) doesn't understand DNS load balancing; therefore, if you provide remote access to UM, you could end up with remote users always hitting a single server. If that single server were down, no redundancy would kick in. Also, clients from OCS don't understand DNS load balancing, which must be considered in a migration, as discussed in Chapter 7. When referring to things specifically related to the Edge role, Public Internet Connectivity (PIC) providers, Extensible Messaging, Presence Protocol (XMPP) clouds (covered in Chapter 18, "Third-Party Integration"), and older OCS networks as federated partners all have issues with DNS load balancing. All in all, you may find DNS load balancing useful inside the network; however, for external communication, you may still need to use an HLB.

Of course, you may not realize that whatever you do, HLB devices are still required to implement high availability. They are, however, required only for the HTTP and HTTPS traffic unless you need some of the elements listed earlier, which are not possible with DNS load balancing. This is because the web traffic is stateful and, therefore, the session must be maintained between a single client and server. Currently, there is no way to build this technology into the client (essentially the browser), unlike the way it is built into the Lync client for the other traffic streams.

Mixing LB Types

You cannot mix and match load-balancing methods on the internal and external interfaces of the Edge server.

The traditional option for making the web service and reverse proxy components highly available requires an HLB device in front of an array of reverse proxies. If using Forefront Threat Management Gateway 2010 (TMG), however, you may also be able to use an array with WNLB performing the LB. For the external web services URLs on the Director and front end, you would publish a single URL on the reverse proxy that would equate to a VIP on an HLB device in front of the Director and front-end pools.

GETTING THE RIGHT LOAD BALANCER

Given that so many load balancer devices are available, it is important to make sure you follow proper procedures and use one that is certified by Microsoft for use with Lync. To find out which models are certified, see this TechNet article:

`http://technet.microsoft.com/en-us/lync/gg269419.aspx`

CERTIFICATES

Certificates play an important role in publishing Lync externally. They help establish trust between the client and server so that the client knows it is talking to the correct server and not one that is spoofing its identity. Certificates are used on both interfaces of the Edge server. On the external interface, a public certificate authority (CA) trusted certificate is needed to identify all three roles. Another change in Lync is that a single, public trusted certificate can now be used for all these roles, as long as it has the right names. Getting the names on the certificate correct is critical. Thankfully, the Certificate Wizard introduced in Lync helps you do this, as shown in Chapter 6.

The subject of the external certificate is the Access Edge name. The subject name should also be the first Subject Alternative Name (SAN), and then further SANs should be used to include the other required URLs, such as the FQDN of the Web Conferencing Edge. When running the wizard, you may notice that the AV Edge FQDN is not included on the certificate. This is because it doesn't need the name to use the certificate for encryption. This saves you the cost of an additional SAN.

For client autoconfiguration to work, the SANs should contain the `sip.`*`domainname`*`.com` URL for each SIP domain supported, as this is one of the failback URLs used by the clients. See Chapter 4, "Client Access," to learn more.

As a rule, you should create the external certificate with an exportable private key. This is a requirement if you are running a pool of servers, because the certificate used for the AV Edge authentication on the external interface must be the same on each server in the pool. It is also needed if you create the certificate request on a server other than where it will be used.

You must also take into account that certificates are required on the reverse proxy. This is covered in depth in Chapter 6, where you will configure these components. Briefly, the reverse proxy needs a certificate to identify all the websites it must publish. The certificate should come from a trusted CA. This certificate should cover the simple URLs and the external web services URLs, which are published as described in "The Reverse Proxy" section. The certificates you require will vary depending on your defined topology. If you split out simple URLs, each will need to be published with a certificate. If not, and the simple URLs all point to a single central location, then the URLs can be published via the standard URL used for external web services for that location. For example, you would publish `meet.gaots.co.uk` with a certificate that has the same subject name, rather than using the `se01webext.gaots.co.uk/meet` version, which could be published using the same external certificate at the reverse proxy.

DNS Entries

Of course, all of the components just described are useless unless you can locate them, which is where DNS comes in. Lync uses two types of DNS entries, the A record and the SRV record, and is generally deployed in a *split-brain* DNS implementation where the same zones are configured internally as well as externally but have different entries to give different results based on where the query originates. For example, for autoconfiguration of Lync clients to work, you would configure `_sipinternaltls._tcp.gaots.co.uk` to point to `se01.gaots.co.uk` internally, whereas externally you would configure `_sip._tls.gaots.co.uk` to point to `accessedge.gaots.co.uk`.

With this configuration, you need to make sure that the machines in your network resolve the correct addresses. In particular, it is important to consider where the Edge servers point for DNS. Essentially, they can point either internally or to external-facing DNS servers. Either way, what is really important is that they can resolve the correct addresses for queries. You may, therefore, find that a combination of DNS and HOSTS file entries are needed. It is important to note that internal clients and servers must resolve the external address for the AV Edge service.

The Lync Edge server should resolve as follows:

FQDN	Expected Behavior
`Accessedge.gaots.co.uk`	Public IP of Access Edge (or VIP)
`sip.gaots.co.uk`	Public IP of Access Edge (or VIP)
`webconf.gaots.co.uk`	Public IP of Web Conferencing Edge (or VIP)
`avedge.gaots.co.uk`	Public IP of AV Edge server (or VIP)
`se01.gaots.local`	Private IP of front-end server (or VIP)

A computer on the internal network should resolve as follows:

FQDN	Expected Behavior
`av.gaots.co.uk`	Public IP of AV Edge server (or VIP)
`edge01.gaots.local`	Internal IP of Edge server

The Lync front-end server should resolve as follows:

FQDN	Expected Behavior
`av.gaots.co.uk`	Public IP of AV Edge server (or VIP)
`edge01.gaots.local`	Internal IP of Edge server

A computer outside your network should resolve from external DNS as follows:

FQDN	Expected Behavior
`Accessedge.gaots.co.uk`	Public IP of Access Edge (or VIP)
`sip.gaots.co.uk`	Public IP of Access Edge (or VIP)
`webconf.gaots.co.uk`	Public IP of Web Conferencing Edge (or VIP)
`avedge.gaots.co.uk`	Public IP of AV Edge server (or VIP)
`se01.gaots.local`	Not resolved (internal only record)

As long as the resolution laid out here is possible, Lync will work correctly.

Of course, there are scenarios where split-brain DNS simply isn't possible. For example, suppose your internal AD domain is not the same as your external presence, such as `gaots.local` rather than `gaots.co.uk`. In this case, you would need to either create a zone internally for `gaots.co.uk` and populate it with entries for your external resources, or use another type of Lync client autoconfiguration, as described in Chapter 4. The problem here is that you might not be able to create an internal zone matching your external zone, because you might have hundreds of entries in the external `gaots.co.uk` zone that you don't want to have to transpose to the internal zone and continue to keep up to date.

In that case, what can be done? Well, you can create something called a *pin-point zone.* This internally created zone is essentially the specific SRV record we wanted to create in the `gaots.co.uk` zone you were not allowed or were unable to create. To create it, you must use the command line because the Windows DNS server GUI doesn't allow you to create pin-point zones. Therefore, open `CMD.exe` as an administrator on your DNS server and run the following commands:

```
dnscmd . /zoneadd _sipinternaltls._tcp.gaots.co.uk. /dsprimary
dnscmd . /recordadd _sipinternaltls._tcp.gaots.co.uk. @ SRV 0 0 5061
se01.gaots.co.uk.
dnscmd . /zoneadd se01.gaots.co.uk. /dsprimary
dnscmd . /recordadd se01.gaots.co.uk. @ A 192.168.1.223
```

Note that if you were performing DNS load balancing, you would need to add the additional A records for each Front End. For example:

```
dnscmd . /zoneadd _sipinternaltls._tcp.gaots.co.uk. /dsprimary
dnscmd . /recordadd _sipinternaltls._tcp.gaots.co.uk. @ SRV 0 0 5061
eepool01.gaots.co.uk.
dnscmd . /zoneadd eepool01.gaots.co.uk. /dsprimary
dnscmd . /recordadd fe01.gaots.co.uk. @ A 192.168.1.223
dnscmd . /recordadd fe02.gaots.co.uk. @ A 192.168.1.224
dnscmd . /recordadd fe03.gaots.co.uk. @ A 192.168.1.225
```

Firewalls

Given the extent of external communication that Lync allows through use of machines in the DMZ, it is not surprising that firewalls come into play. In a Lync deployment, the recommended route is to have two firewalls as part of the topology. There should be a front firewall that sits between the Internet connection router and the Lync DMZ subnet. There should then also be a back firewall, which sits between the Lync DMZ subnet and the LAN. This means that there is a routed connection between the LAN and the DMZ and the Internet, and it ensures that all external traffic passes through two firewalls before entering the LAN. This configuration is shown in Figure 3.1.

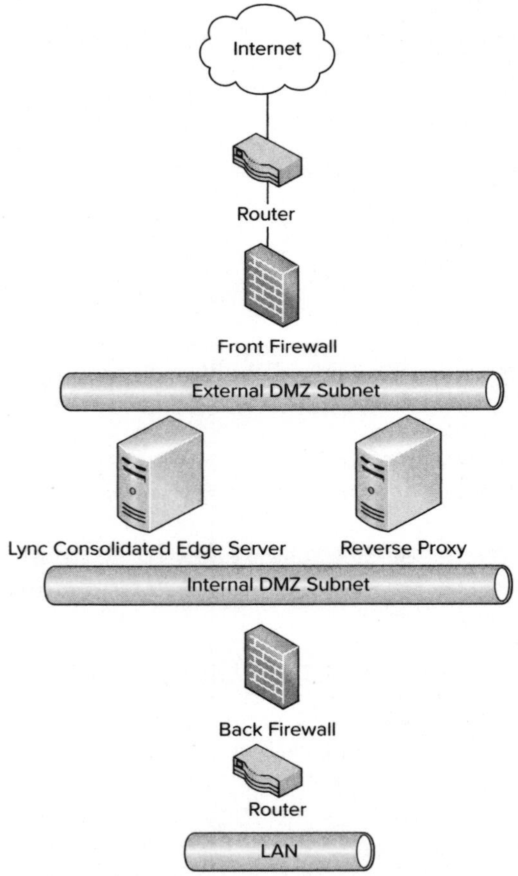

FIGURE 3.1
The Lync Edge Network layout

After you establish the location of firewalls, you must look at what holes need to be poked in them. As with any product that communicates using TCP/IP or UDP/IP, Lync requires specific firewall ports to be open. The improved Lync is much more frugal with the ports that need to be opened, especially if you are talking only to other Lync systems externally.

Real World Scenario

DEALING WITH THREE-TIERED NETWORKS

In Figure 3.1, you can see that Lync is essentially a two-tiered system. The Edge server sits in the first tier in a DMZ and is exposed to the Internet, while the LAN containing the front-end servers is on the second tier. Throughout our consulting experience, we sometimes come across organizations that operate systems where there is a middle tier between the DMZ and LAN. These organizations are commonly in highly secure or regulated industries such as financial services.

This causes problems for Lync. The issue is that Lync has no out-of-the box way of working in these networks. The Edge would have to be in the middle tier and, therefore, the Internet would have to be opened into that tier (not supported by the organization in question), or the front end would have to be moved to the middle tier with the Edge in the first tier (DMZ). Again, having LAN-based servers with all their AD requirements in the middle tier was not supported in such cases.

Fortunately for these installations, a company called Sipera has come up with a range of gateway devices that can act as a super proxy for all traffic destined for a Lync Edge server. The gateway device sits in the first tier (DMZ), allowing the Lync Edge to sit in the middle tier and the front end to sit securely in the third tier (LAN). For more information, check out:

`www.sipera.com/company/`

As an example, the following series of figures illustrate an enterprise perimeter network configuration in which Lync is deployed with a single Consolidated Edge server and the ports that need to be opened for Lync to work externally. Figure 3.2 shows the Reverse Proxy server and its external and internal connections. Figure 3.3 shows the external Internet port connections to the Consolidated Edge server, and Figure 3.4 shows the internal network connections. This configuration forms the basis of the ports needed even when load balancing is introduced.

Note that a range of ports is required for the AV Edge server role. If you look closely, you may also notice that the Access Edge role is enabled for port 53 outbound to resolve DNS. If instead you allow DNS resolution to the internal DNS servers, port TCP & UDP 53 access for DNS queries would be needed through the other side of the DMZ network via the back firewall.

Because the AV Edge role has the most complex port requirements (and possibly the most concerning security), it is worth exploring those requirements in more detail. Another reason this is worth doing is that while the external ports required by the other external services stay the same no matter who you are communicating with or how, the AV Edge requirements can change—for example, if you talk with an OCS 2007 system rather than a Lync system. These requirements are detailed in Table 3.3.

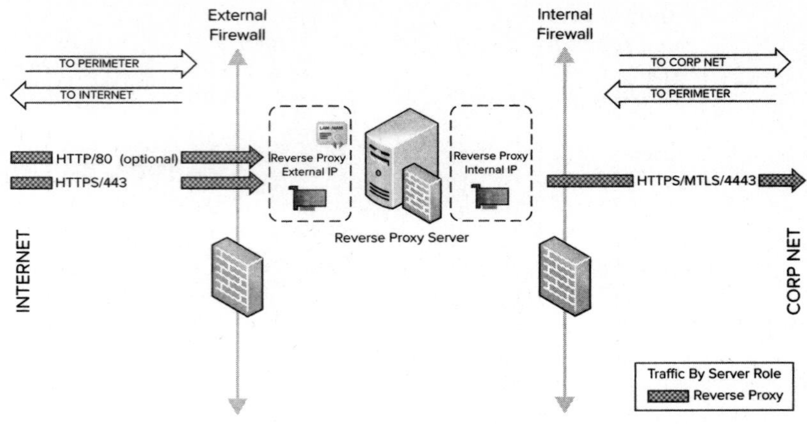

FIGURE 3.2
The Reverse Proxy server and its required connections

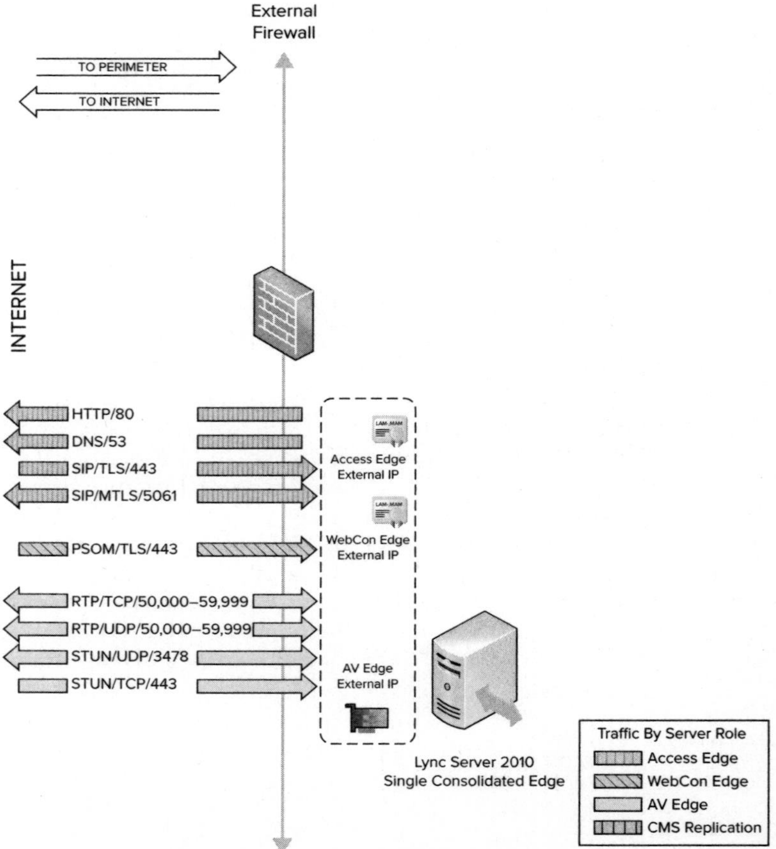

FIGURE 3.3
Internet connections with the Lync Server 2010 Consolidated Edge server

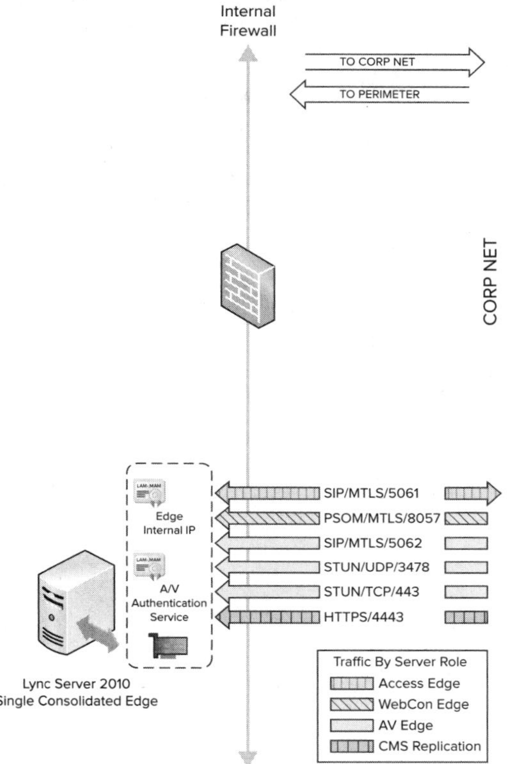

FIGURE 3.4
Internal corporate network connections with the Lync Server 2010 Consolidated Edge server

TABLE 3.3: Ports Required Under Different Circumstances by the AV Edge Role

FEDERATION WITH	FEATURE	TCP/443	UDP/3478	RTP/UDP 50,000–59,999	RTP/TCP 50,000–59,999
Windows Live Messenger 5.0	Point to Point Audio/Video (A/V)	Open in	Open in and out	Not open	Open in
Lync Server 2010	Lync Server 2010	Open in	Open in and out	Not open	Open in
Lync Server 2010	Application sharing/desktop sharing	Open in	Open in and out	Not open	Open in
Lync Server 2010	File transfer	Open in	Open in and out	Not open	Open in
Office Communications Server 2007 R2	A/V	Open in	Open in and out	Not open	Open in

TABLE 3.3: *(CONTINUED)*

FEDERATION WITH	FEATURE	TCP/443	UDP/3478	RTP/UDP 50,000–59,999	RTP/TCP 50,000–59,999
Office Communications Server 2007 R2	Desktop sharing	Open in	Open in and out	Open in and out	Open in and out
Office Communications Server 2007 R2	File transfer	N/A	N/A	N/A	N/A
Office Communications Server 2007	A/V	Open in	Open in	Open in and out	Open in and out
Office Communications Server 2007	Desktop sharing	N/A	N/A	N/A	N/A
Office Communications Server 2007	File transfer	N/A	N/A	N/A	N/A

As you can see, generally it is best practice to open the range TCP 50000–59999 from the AV Edge interface outbound to any remote hosts, as this allows the widest level of communication. UDP 50000–59999 is required only if you need to communicate with those on OCS 2007. It is required both inbound and outbound. The requirements for opening large port ranges have significantly improved since the early days of OCS. If you don't need the ability to talk to partners running OCS 2007, only three ports require opening inbound: TCP 5061 for SIP traffic, TCP 443 for a variety of traffic (this port is usually open for other services anyway), and UDP 3478, which is for STUN traffic, which provides external access to AV traffic.

Support for NAT on the Edge interfaces has been a long-running topic for OCS administrators. When OCS 2007 first shipped, administrators were faced with the need for large numbers of externally routable IP addresses. NAT was not supported for all interfaces (in particular the AV Edge interface/IP address). OCS 2007 R2 improved matters by allowing all the Edge interfaces to sit behind a NAT device (whether a router or firewall), but only in the single consolidated Edge server mode. Now in Lync 2010, NAT can be used for all external Edge server interfaces, including Scaled Consolidated mode. NAT is still not supported on the internal Edge interface. This must be routable from the internal LAN.

To implement NAT on the Edge interfaces, some specific requirements must be met, in particular for the AV Edge address. These requirements cover how the destination and source addresses of the IP packets are modified when passing through the NAT device. Essentially, the principle is that traffic coming from the outside (that is, the Internet) should have its destination address in the packet header changed, and traffic coming from the inside should have its source address in the IP header changed. This means that both types of traffic maintain a return path; the outside traffic maintains its source, and the internal traffic changes its source. If the internal traffic did not change its source, then return traffic would try to reach the internal NAT address, which would not be routable from the Internet.

Running Lync with Firewalls on Your Internal Network

It is not uncommon to find networks on which Lync needs to be installed and that have firewalls separating the various internal elements of the LAN. For example, a company may have a LAN/WAN system with elements in which certain sites are less trusted than other sites. Frequently, there is a firewall between a branch site and the central site. In such cases, it is very important to fully understand which ports need to be opened. This useful blog goes into some depth on this subject:

`http://ucmadeeasy.wordpress.com/2011/04/26/deploying-a-lync-sba-watch-out-for-port-444/`

One final element worth noting is that although it is not a firewall as such, the use of IP Security (IPsec) on a network affects Lync traffic—particularly the media components of Lync, which carry real-time communications. IPsec creates a delay as security is negotiated. Therefore, you should turn off IPsec for all media traffic as outlined in Table 3.4.

Table 3.4: The Media Traffic for which IPsec Needs to Be Disabled

Rule Name	Source IP	Destination IP	Protocol	Source Port	Destination Port	Filter Action
A/V Edge Server Internal Inbound	Any	A/V Edge Server Internal	UDP and TCP	Any	Any	Permit
A/V Edge Server External Inbound	Any	A/V Edge Server External	UDP and TCP	Any	Any	Permit
A/V Edge Server Internal Outbound	A/V Edge Server Internal	Any	UDP & TCP	Any	Any	Permit
A/V Edge Server External Outbound	A/V Edge Server External	Any	UDP and TCP	Any	Any	Permit

TABLE 3.4: *(CONTINUED)*

Rule name	Source IP	Destination IP	Protocol	Source Port	Destination Port	Filter Action
Mediation Server Inbound	Any	Mediation Server(s)	UDP and TCP	Any	Any	Permit
Mediation Server Outbound	Mediation Server(s)	Any	UDP and TCP	Any	Any	Permit
Conferencing Attendant Inbound	Any	Any	UDP and TCP	Any	Any	Permit
Conferencing Attendant Outbound	Any	Any	UDP and TCP	Any	Any	Permit
A/V Conferencing Inbound	Any	A/V Conferencing Servers	UDP and TCP	Any	Any	Permit
A/V Conferencing Server Outbound	A/V Conferencing Servers	Any	UDP and TCP	Any	Any	Permit
Exchange Inbound	Any	Exchange Unified Messaging	UDP and TCP	Any	Any	Permit
Application Sharing Servers Inbound	Any	Application Sharing Servers	TCP	Any	Any	Permit
Application Sharing Server Outbound	Application Sharing Servers	Any	TCP	Any	Any	Permit
Exchange Outbound	Exchange Unified Messaging	Any	UDP and TCP	Any	Any	Permit
Clients	Any	Any	UDP	Specified media port range	Any	Permit

Understanding Core Security

By its very nature, Lync was designed to fulfill Microsoft security standards. That is, it is secure by default both in the way it is designed and in the way a deployment using default settings will work. When designing any feature in a product, Microsoft product groups conduct threat assessments to determine how the feature could be subverted to create problems. With this in mind, we will look at some of the key elements that make Lync secure, starting with media security and moving on to authentication and certificates.

Media and Signaling Security

Because it is a wide-ranging communication platform, Lync 2010 is subject to a lot of threats. Many of them involve someone trying to hijack traffic and manipulate it to gain access to the system. For example, common threats include *spoofing* (where someone pretends to be someone they are not), *eavesdropping* (where an attacker tries to look at traffic to ascertain its contents), and *replay* (where an attacker takes the traffic and changes it to gain access or alter content). All of these threats can be mitigated through the use of Mutual Transport Layer Security (MTLS) between trusted servers and Transport Layer Security (TLS) between client and server.

TLS and MTLS allow both encryption of traffic and authentication of endpoints. Lync clients must validate a certificate on the server, which identifies that the server is indeed who it says it is and is issued by a CA that the client trusts. When MTLS is used between servers, both servers exchange certificates from a trusted CA so they can verify (trust) each other's identity. This security is in place between internal servers, and it is used when talking to gateway devices and Edge servers.

So far we have described *signaling traffic*—that is, SIP between servers or clients. There are other types of traffic, including AV media, traffic from gateways to a Mediation server, traffic from the reverse proxy to Lync servers, clients downloading content from meetings, and traffic between Lync and the Monitoring and Archiving servers. All of this traffic is also encrypted. The reverse proxy traffic is encrypted using SSL or TLS as normal, secure web traffic. The traffic from the Mediation server to the gateway can be encrypted, assuming the gateway is capable of supporting a certificate to use for MTLS. The client content download uses standard HTTPS.

A couple of these cases warrant a little further discussion. First, note that the media traffic uses a different protocol, known as Secure Real-Time Transport Protocol (SRPT), a specialized media transfer protocol that supports encryption and traffic authentication. Second, the traffic from the Lync front-end server pool to the Monitoring and Archiving server roles is carried (as you will learn in Chapter 11, "Monitoring and Archiving") using Microsoft Message Queue (MSMQ) technology. By default, this is not encrypted, but it does allow itself to be configured in a secure way using certificates managed by AD. For more information, see "Appendix D: Message Queuing and Internet Communication in Windows Server 2008" at http://go.microsoft.com/fwlink/?LinkId=145238 or "Appendix I: Message Queuing and Internet Communication in Windows Server 2008 R2" at http://go.microsoft.com/fwlink/?LinkId=211883 for Windows Server 2008 R2.

FIPS SUPPORT

Readers in the United States may be pleased to know that Lync supports the Federal Information Processing Standard (FIPS) 140-2 algorithms. Each Lync server would need to be configured to use the correct FIPS algorithms, a process which is described in the following KB article:

```
http://go.microsoft.com/fwlink/?linkid=3052&kbid=811833
```

In summary, all Lync media and traffic is encrypted. This has enabled companies that were concerned with the use of traditional Voice over IP (VoIP) systems, which didn't encrypt traffic, to use Lync in secure environments, such as trading floors. Table 3.5 details the security methods for the different types of Lync traffic.

TABLE 3.5: The Protection Methods Used to Secure Lync Traffic

Lync Communication Type	Security Method
Server-to-server	MTLS
Client-to-server	TLS
Instant messaging and presence	TLS (if configured for TLS)
Audio and video and desktop sharing of media	SRTP
Desktop sharing (signaling)	TLS
Web conferencing	TLS
Meeting content download, address book download, distribution group expansion	HTTPS

Authentication

One of the most fundamental aspects of security is authenticating those who try to access a system. In Lync, there are many ways in which a user can attempt to access the system, including:

- Through an internal Lync client
- Through an external Lync client
- Via a web application
- Anonymously (conferencing or via a web application)
- Through an IP phone device

The most obvious is through the standard desktop Lync client, which operates based on authentication against credentials stored in Active Directory whether the client is internal or external to the network. Earlier in the chapter, we laid out the external authentication path via the Director, so let's look at how the authentication itself occurs. If the client is on the internal LAN, Kerberos V5 is used. For details of Kerberos and the way it operates, see the following URL:

```
http://msdn.microsoft.com/en-us/library/aa378747(VS.85).aspx
```

If the client is outside the network, NTLM (NT LAN Manager) is used, because Kerberos requires direct access to the AD. NTLM is not as secure as Kerberos for many reasons. It doesn't allow mutual authentication; also, with Kerberos, passwords are never sent across the wire, thereby protecting them from man-in-the-middle attacks. Another benefit of Kerberos is that it is an open standard, whereas NTLM is not. Finally, in most recent operating systems including Vista and Windows Server 2008 and later, Kerberos supports AES encryption but NTLM doesn't. For more information about NTLM, see this URL:

`http://msdn.microsoft.com/en-us/library/aa378749(VS.85).aspx`

Because NTLM is less secure, some companies no longer allow it to be used as a method of authentication. This restriction may mean you need to prevent remote access to Lync or you may need to use an alternative, such as Direct Access, to provide connectivity to AD.

That covers the authentication of the main Lync client both inside and outside the network. However, other types of clients with their own types of authentication are used in Lync.

The Lync Web App provides remote access to conferences. It allows you to authenticate using your corporate credentials using either NTLM or Kerberos, depending on where your client is located. Anonymous authentication can also be made available. This works using the Digest Authentication protocol and requires the client/user to have a meeting ID, which can be passed as part of the authentication process. For more information about Digest Authentication, go to:

`http://technet.microsoft.com/en-us/library/cc778868(WS.10).aspx`

For anonymous authentication to be allowed, you must enable it in a couple of places, first on the default Access Edge configuration as follows:

```
Set-CsAccessEdgeConfiguration -AllowAnonymousUsers $True
```

This allows anonymous connections to the Access Edge. However, you must also enable it on one or more of your conferencing policies, as follows:

```
Set-CsConferencingPolicy Identity Global -AllowAnonymousParticipantsInMeetings
$True
```

This would allow anonymous participants in meetings governed by the Global conferencing policy. Both of these steps can also be carried out through the LSCP under the External Access and Conferencing sections, respectively.

The final type of authentication available is Certificate Authentication. This is part of what allows users to authenticate using just a PIN (instead of a full username and password) on IP phone handsets and when signing into conferences. For this to work, each user must have a certificate and the corresponding private key to be able to correctly answer a cryptographic challenge. The certificate needs to identify the user in either the subject or subject alternative name, and it must be issued by a root CA that is trusted by the servers running Lync Server 2010. Also, the certificate must not have been revoked and must be currently valid.

How do these certificates get to the phone devices, and how are they associated with the user? The devices are configured to look at AD for an object with the category of `certificationAuthority`. If one is found, the `caCertificate` attribute is checked and the root CA certificate is installed on the device.

To load the relevant certificate into the `caCertificate attribute`, you must use the following command from an administrative CMD prompt:

```
certutil -f -dspublish "c:\lyncbookCA.cer" cn=gaots-DC01-CA, cn=Certificate
Authorities, cn=Public Key Services, CN=Services, cn=Configuration, dc=gaots,
dc=local
```

This command will insert the `lyncbookCA.cer` certificate, which is the `gaots-DC01-CA` root certificate, into the directory.

As long as the device is able to locate and install the relevant root CA certificate, authentication progresses as follows:

1. Obtain the root CA.
2. Verify the web services Cert using the root CA trust.
3. Store the certificate chain.
4. Take the credentials from the user, consisting of conferencing PIN and phone number.
5. Check the credentials.
6. Request a certificate for the user.
7. Receive the certificate on the device and publish it in the user store.
8. Use the certificate for all further authentication for the user.

Because the certificate needs to be obtained, this procedure must be performed on the LAN the first time a user sets up the phone device. After it is set up, the certificate and PIN combination can be used remotely.

Two-Factor Authentication

In some environments, *two-factor authentication* is a must for any externally accessible system. Two-factor authentication is a system whereby the user has to authenticate with both something they have and something they know (for example, a PIN provided through a token device, as well as a username and password). Of course, Lync is often available externally; however; providing two-factor authentication is not all that simple. In cases where extreme security is a must, various steps can be taken. You could remove external anonymous access so that all conferences require users to know both the conference ID and PIN. Secondly, you could ensure that only business-owned laptops are used to connect to the system externally. This could be done by using an internally signed certificate on the Edge server, which would require you to install the root CA as a trusted certificate on any remote machines. This would sacrifice the availability of PIC federation, but it would provide security. Finally, you could provide two-factor authentication on the remote laptops by using BitLocker and requiring a smart card to boot the machines.

Certificates

We have examined certificates in various contexts in this chapter already, but there are still a couple of areas that need to be addressed to ensure that Lync can use certificates.

First, public certificates should be obtained from a suitable CA. Table 3.6 lists a few of the more familiar CAs that have been validated by Microsoft as properly supporting Lync and Exchange.

TABLE 3.6: Familiar CAs Supported by Lync

CERTIFICATION AUTHORITY	URL
Entrust	`www.entrust.net/microsoft/`
Comodo	`www.comodo.com/msexchange`
DigiCert	`www.digicert.com/unified-communications-ssl-tls.htm`
GlobalSign	`www.globalsign.com/ssl/buy-ssl-certificates/unified-communications-ssl/`

Second, it is important that you set up the required certificate revocation list (CRL) distribution points for internal CAs. A CRL distribution point allows systems to validate whether a certificate has been revoked and, therefore, is no longer valid. More information about this process can be found here:

`http://technet.microsoft.com/en-us/library/cc753296.aspx`

Third, it is important to configure the relevant Enhanced Key Usage (EKU) settings for certificates. All Lync certificates must support the Server Authentication EKU, which is essential for MTLS to function. Also, while previous versions of Microsoft OCS required the Client Authentication EKU, now it is required only on Edge servers that connect to the AOL cloud.

Finally, as discussed in the authentication section, it is possible to allow certificate-based authentication for use on Lync IP Phone devices. This can be enabled or disabled externally using the PowerShell cmdlet:

```
Set-CsProxyConfiguration -UseCertificateForClientToProxyAuth
```

It can be enabled or disabled entirely using:

```
Set-CsWebServiceConfiguration -UseCertificateAuth
```

See Chapter 8, "PowerShell and LMS," for more information about working with PowerShell.

Providing Security Administratively

No matter how secure a system is "out of the box," without correct administration, holes can easily be created through which attackers can penetrate. In this section, you will see how policies can be used to prevent attacks, how the company can meet regulatory requirements through the use of disclaimers, how users can protect their presence information, and how to use antivirus software with Lync.

Client-Version Filtering

To create a secure environment, narrowing down the variables in that environment can be useful. One way of doing this in Lync is to restrict access to a known set of clients. Lync allows you to do this by using the `CsClientVersionPolicy`. This policy is composed of a collection of rules that specify which particular clients, based on their identity in SIP headers, are allowed to connect. By default, a global policy is in place. You can also set policies in a more granular way—for example, at the site or registrar level. This would allow you to have a group of users who must continue to use a legacy OCS client, perhaps because of desktop OS compatibility issues, while most of your other users are mandated to use the latest Lync client. For more information about how policies work, see Chapter 10, "User Administration." For more information about PowerShell, see Chapter 8.

To investigate the global policy, you must first `Get` it using the PowerShell:

```
Get-CsClientVersionPolicy -Identity global
```

This will return the policy, and you will see a blob of text showing the rules. To see each rule individually, you must use the following command:

```
Get-CsClientVersionPolicy -Identity global | Select-Object -ExpandProperty Rules
```

This first gets the policy and then pipes the output to `Select-Object`, which then extracts all the information from the `Rules` attribute and lists them separately. Following is an example of one of the rules:

```
RuleId            : 4730866f-8594-431b-ad57-6f1c798ce0d8
Description       :
Action            : Allow
ActionUrl         :
MajorVersion      : 2
MinorVersion      : 9999
BuildNumber       : 9999
QfeNumber         : 9999
UserAgent         : OC
UserAgentFullName :
Enabled           : True
CompareOp         : LEQ
```

From this output, you can see the elements that go into a rule.

To create a new policy, enter the following command:

```
New-CsClientVersionPolicy -Identity site:EMEA
```

This simple command creates a new policy with the default settings and links it to the EMEA site. However, if you wanted to amend the default rules while creating the policy, you could. To do so, you may use either the `CsClientVersionPolicyRule` cmdlet or the LSCP, as shown in Figure 3.5.

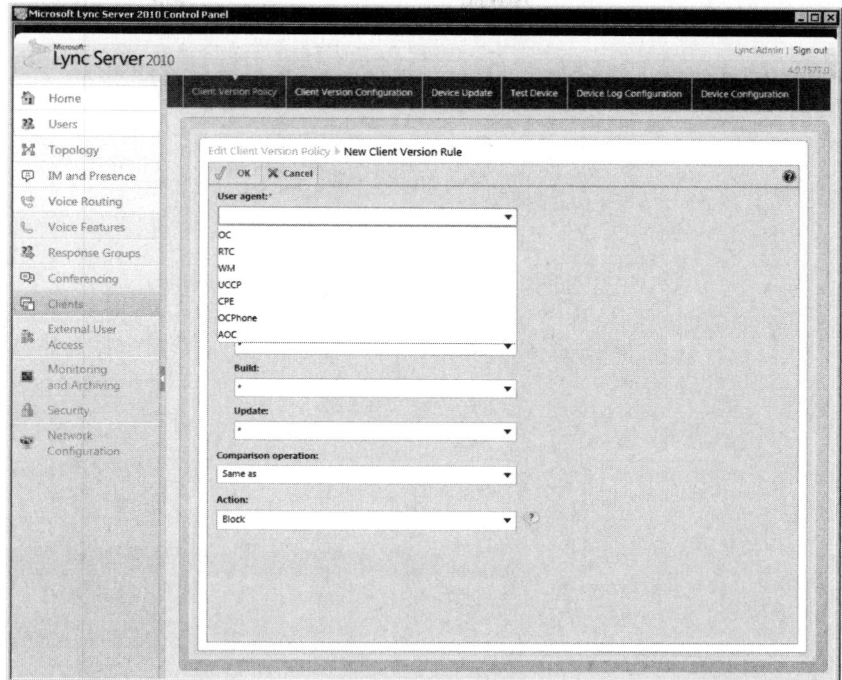

FIGURE 3.5
The client types available in Rules

Whether you use the cmdlet or the GUI, the requirements are relatively complex, so it is important to understand them. First, each rule must have a *unique identifier.* This means it must have a reference to where it will be attached—that is, the scope of the policy to which it will be applied. It must also have a globally unique identifier (GUID). Next, you must specify the client type from those shown in Figure 3.5 and Table 3.7, along with the version that will be referenced in the policy, and whether the client will be allowed, blocked, or one of the other actions. For example, you could allow the client to be blocked and the user shown a URL where they can get more information about why the client has been blocked or even download a newer version. Equally, you could have the client blocked and then automatically upgraded based on software available through Windows Update or Windows Software Update Services. Other elements that can be configured on the rule are, whether it is enabled or not, how the rule is matched; that is, versions equal to that specified, or less than or equal to, and so on. For the full list, see Figure 3.6. Finally it is important to note that the rules in a policy are listed in order or precedence. This is why you have the option to specify the priority of the rule. If you specify a priority which is already in use, the new rule will take the priority number given and all the other rules will move down one.

TABLE 3.7: Client Codes and Associated Clients

CLIENT CODE	CLIENT DETAIL
OC	Office Communicator or Lync client
RTC	LCS clients
WM	Live Messenger
UCCP	Applications such as response groups
CPE	IP Phone
OCPhone	IP Phone
AOC	Attendee only client

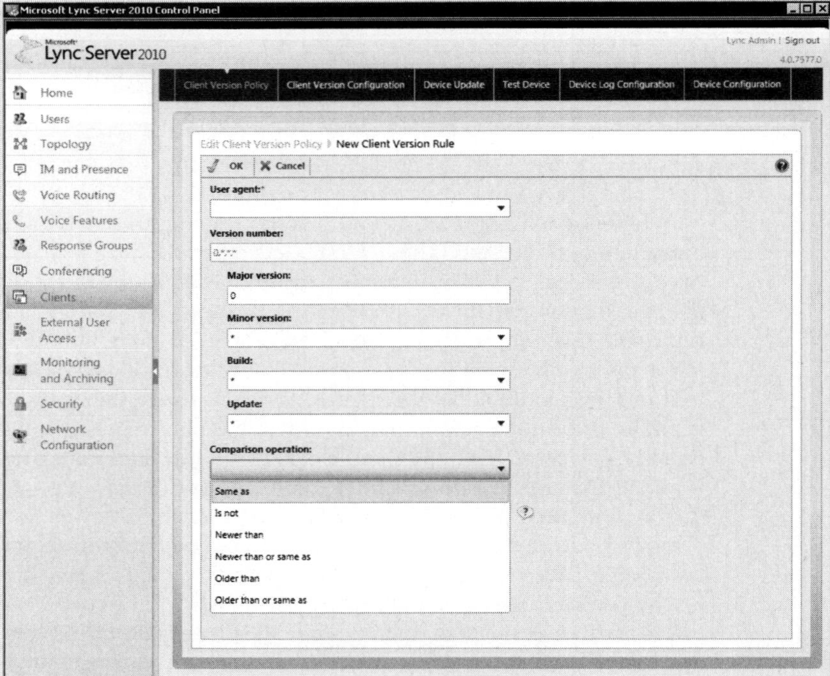

FIGURE 3.6
The match types available in Rules

Now that you've seen the possibilities, let's create a couple of rules for different scenarios. We will do the first one in the LSCP.

1. Log onto the Control Panel with an account that is a member of the `CsAdministrator` RBAC group (for more information, see Chapter 9, "RBAC").
2. Locate the Clients tab and then double-click the Global Policy in the right pane. This will open it for editing.
3. Click New. On the page that opens, specify the client type in the User Agent drop-down shown in Figure 3.7. Select OC, which is the client type for Lync and Office Communicator clients. This becomes the identifier of the rule.
4. Enter the relevant version information to match the client—for example, Lync client version 4.0.7577.275. Newer versions are released each quarter.
5. Set the action, which in this case is to allow and launch a URL. Enter the URL as shown in Figure 3.7 and then click OK.

FIGURE 3.7
The finished rule

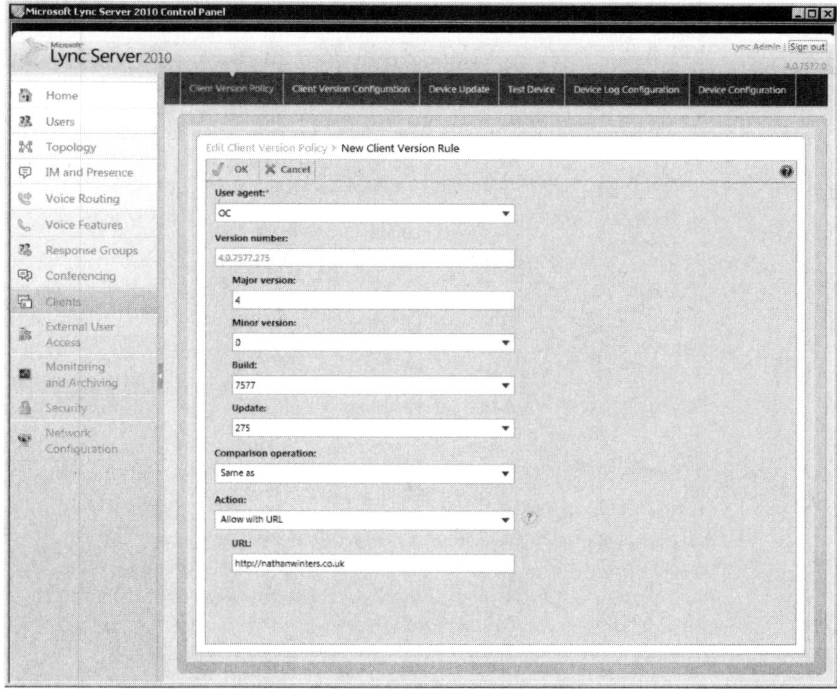

6. On the main policy page, locate the rule, which by default will be at the bottom of the list of rules in the policy. Use the green up and down arrows to position it where needed. Once you are satisfied, click Commit.

Now when users log in using the specified Lync client version, they will be presented with a pop-up in the task bar, which suggests that a new version of the client is available. If they click the pop-up, they will be taken to the appropriate website.

In order to create a similar rule from the LSMS, do the following. First, create a GUID for the rule:

```
$g = [guid]::NewGuid()
```

This generates a GUID and stores it in the `$g` variable. Next, create the rule using the following command:

```
New-CsClientVersionPolicyRule -Parent "Global" -RuleId $g -MajorVersion
4 -MinorVersion 0 -BuildNumber 7577 -QfeNumber 275 -UserAgent OC -Action
AllowWithUrl -ActionUrl "http://nathanwinters.co.uk" -CompareOp EQL -Priority 0
```

This will create the same rule as the one created through the GUI. Do *not* do this if you've already created the rule in the GUI; you will get an error if you do. You will need to change the version details to prevent a duplicate entry to get it to run.

Now you can create new rules and add them to existing policies. You need to understand that the way all Client Version policies are applied is governed by the cmdlet `CsClientVersionConfiguration`. Among other things, `CsClientVersionConfiguration` allows you to modify the default action for clients not specifically mentioned in the active policy, to enable or disable Client Version checks entirely, and to specify the default URL to which clients are pointed if the action of a rule is set to point users to a URL but no URL is specified. The following is an example:

```
New-CsClientVersionConfiguration -Identity site:EMEA -Enabled $True
-DefaultAction Block -DefaultURL "http://nathanwinters.co.uk"
```

This command creates a new Client Version Configuration policy for the Europe Middle East and Africa (EMEA) site; it enables version checking, blocks any clients not specifically listed on Client Version policies, and points any users that match rules with an action pointing to a URL but which do not specify the URL to the `http://nathanwinters.co.uk` site.

Note that both the new client-version policy rule and the new client-version configuration can be configured from the Clients tab in the LSCP.

Message Hygiene

The Lync IM functionality has many uses, and it frequently cuts down on email usage by implementing a quick efficient method of communicating. One element of an IM conversation is the ability to send files and links. Of course, this ability has the potential to open users up to malicious or inadvertent threats because files can contain viruses and links can point to unsafe files or sites. Lync, therefore, allows administrators to control what can and can't be sent in an IM conversation.

The `CsImFilterConfiguration` cmdlet allows you to control what happens when a user attempts to send a link through IM. By default, links are allowed in IM messages. To control this, you can enable the `CsImFilterConfiguration` policy. These settings can either be manipulated as shown, through PowerShell or in the LSCP on the IM & Presence section. Once set, all messages sent by those users within the scope of the policy (for more information about scope, see Chapter 10) will be checked for links. Your options are to block the link so that the message will not be sent, allow it but disable the link by inserting an underscore (_) character at the beginning of the link, or warn the user with a specific message but still allow the link to operate. By default, the `CsImFilterConfiguration` settings pick up the following link types:

- `callto:`
- `file:`
- `ftp.`
- `ftp:`
- `gopher:`
- `href`
- `http:`
- `https:`
- `ldap:`
- `mailto:`
- `news:`
- `nntp:`
- `sip:`
- `sips:`
- `tel:`
- `telnet:`
- `www*`

For example, to create a new policy for the EMEA site, use this command:

```
New-CsImFilterConfiguration -Identity site:EMEA -Action Warn -WarnMessage "This
link could be dangerous, make sure you know where it is taking you!" -Prefixes
http:
```

This will create a new policy for the EMEA site. When it sees a link starting with the `http:` prefix, it will warn users with the text shown next to the `WarnMessage` parameter. Note that if you wanted to have all the prefixes listed as defaults here, you would not specify the `Prefixes` parameter.

To remove the newly created policy, use the following command:

```
Remove-CsImFilterConfiguration -Identity site:EMEA
```

This command removes the `CsImFilterConfiguration` policy assigned to the EMEA site. Basic enabling and disabling of hyperlinks, which you can do through the `CsClientPolicy` using the `EnableURL` setting, is another way to block URLs in IM.

Now that we've looked at how to mitigate one threat, let's look at the threat file transfer via IM. Just as with email attachments, normal antivirus scanning on client machines will provide a lot of protection. However, you can also control whether all or no attachments are allowed and whether specific file types are allowed. This is done using the `CsFileTransferFilterConfiguration` cmdlets.

The `New-CsFileTransferFilterConfiguration` cmdlet is relatively simple. It enables you to create a policy that affects a certain scope of users, defined using the `Identity` parameter as discussed in Chapter 10. The key parameters that make up the policy settings are `Action`, `Enabled`, and `Extensions`. The `Extensions` parameter is simply a list of the allowed (or disallowed) file types. By default, the following file types are part of a policy:

```
.ade, .adp, .app, .asp, .bas, .bat, .cer, .chm, .cmd, .com, .cpl, .crt, .csh, .exe,
.fxp, .grp, .hlp, .hta, .inf, .ins, .isp, .its, .js, .jse, .ksh, .lnk, .mad, .maf,
.mag, .mam, .maq, .mar., mas., .mat, .mau, .mav, .maw, .mda, .mdb, .mde, .mdt, .mdw,
.mdz, .msc, .msi, .msp, .mst, .ocx, .ops, .pcd, .pif, .pl, .pnp, .prf, .prg, .pst,
.reg, .scf, .scr, .sct, .shb, .shs, .tmp, .url, .vb, .vbe, .vbs, .vsd, .vsmacros,
.vss, .vst, .vsw, .ws, .wsc, .wsf, .wsh
```

The `Enabled` parameter lets you turn filtering on or off entirely. By default, file transfers of the types just listed are blocked. The `Action` parameter controls what happens when a file type listed in the `Extensions` parameter is detected. It has two possible settings, `BlockAll` and `Block`. The default is `Block`, which blocks file types listed in the `Extensions` parameter; by contrast, `BlockAll` simply prevents any file transfers.

To create a new file transfer configuration policy for the EMEA site, use the following command:

```
New-CsFileTransferFilterConfiguration -Identity site:EMEA
```

This command creates a new policy for the EMEA site with default extension values. Alternatively, you could specify different file types as shown here:

```
New-CsFileTransferFilterConfiguration -Identity site:EMEA -Extensions .moo, .too
```

If you only want to add to the default types, enter the following:

```
New-CsFileTransferFilterConfiguration -Identity site:EMEA -Extensions @{Add=".
moo",".too"}
```

Finally, you can also add to an existing `CsFileTransferFilterConfiguration` policy, using this command:

```
Set-CsFileTransferFilterConfiguration -Identity site:EMEA -Extensions @{Add=".
doo",".foo"}
```

Configuring Antivirus Scanning

As with other Microsoft server–based systems, having an antivirus product in place on both the servers and the clients is sensible. On the client, antivirus scanning will be most relevant to Lync when using the file transfer and content download features, because these elements will be scanned and protected by the antivirus software. On the server side, there are no such features; however, as a best practice, AV software should still be deployed. It is important to configure that software correctly so that scanning does not compromise Lync performance. To do so, you must configure the following exclusions:

Lync Server 2010 processes:

- ASMCUSvc.exe
- AVMCUSvc.exe
- DataMCUSvc.exe
- DataProxy.exe
- FileTransferAgent.exe
- IMMCUSvc.exe
- MasterReplicatorAgent.exe
- MediaRelaySvc.exe
- MediationServerSvc.exe
- MeetingMCUSvc.exe
- MRASSvc.exe
- OcsAppServerHost.exe
- QmsSvc.exe
- ReplicaReplicatorAgent.exe
- RTCArch.exe
- RtcCdr.exe
- RTCSrv.exe

IIS processes:

- %systemroot%\system32\inetsrv\w3wp.exe
- %systemroot%\SysWOW64\inetsrv\w3wp.exe

SQL Server processes:

- %ProgramFiles%\Microsoft SQL Server\MSSQL10.MSSQLSERVER\MSSQL\Binn\SQLServr.exe
- %ProgramFiles%\Microsoft SQL Server\MSRS10.MSSQLSERVER\Reporting Services\ReportServer\Bin\ReportingServicesService.exe
- %ProgramFiles%\Microsoft SQL Server\MSAS10.MSSQLSERVER\OLAP\Bin\MSMDSrv.exe

Directories:

- %systemroot%\System32\LogFiles
- %systemroot%\SysWow64\LogFiles

Disclaimers

In many countries, regulations specify how a company should identify itself in business communications. IM is just another form of business communication, which, like email, can be used to communicate with other companies. Therefore, applying disclaimers or footnotes to messages is often required. In the United Kingdom this footnote should, for example, contain the company's registration details.

Lync has a couple of places where you can add disclaimers. One is applicable to those who join conferences and is configured using the `Set-CsConferenceDisclaimer`. You could, for example, use the following command to set up a disclaimer that will be shown to anyone joining the conference using a web link, such as the Join URL.

```
Set-CsConferenceDisclaimer -Header "Gaots.co.uk Conference Service" -Body "Please
Note: Conferences can be recorded. You will be notified if a conference is
recorded in the client and can choose to leave."
```

This displays the text in the `Body` parameter to users joining conferences.

The more common disclaimer used in Lync is the one added to IM messages. To apply disclaimers to IMs, you need to use the `CsClientPolicy` cmdlets. In particular, the `IMWarning` parameter must be set as follows:

```
Set-CsClientPolicy -Identity Global -IMWarning "IM message from Company Gaots.
co.uk"
```

This command simply applies the warning text to all users. However, it is possible to target different `IMWarning` text at different users using the standard method of creating new policies with specific User scopes, as described in Chapter 10.

PIN Policy

As discussed in the "Authentication" section, you can log onto Lync using a PIN number in conjunction with your extension or phone number. This is used when connecting to conferences via a phone line rather than using the Lync client and also when using a Lync IP Phone device. As with any other authentication method, controlling the form of credentials that can be used is important. PIN policies allow you to define the minimum length for a PIN and also to configure whether or not to allow common patterns, such as consecutive digits (for example, a PIN like 123456 or 111111). You can also define the length of validity for a specific PIN and the number of PINs the system remembers, so a user can't continually use the same one.

To create a new PIN policy, use the `New-CsPinPolicy` cmdlet. The next command shows how to create one for the EMEA site:

```
New-CsPinPolicy -Identity "site:EMEA" -MinPasswordLength 7 -PINHistoryCount 5
-PINLifetime 60
```

This command will create a new PIN Policy and assign it to the EMEA site. The minimum length will be seven digits, five previous PINs will be remembered, and the PIN will expire in 60 days. As described in Chapter 10, these policies could be assigned to either the site or the per-user scope. This feature can also be configured in the LSCP under the Security section.

Federation and How to Control It

We'll end this section with a discussion of *federation*. This feature enables you to communicate using Lync not only internally but also externally with those who also have Lync and even those on public IM services such as Windows Live Messenger or Yahoo!. Being able to talk not only within your company but with others over voice, video, and of course IM is a great benefit; however, some companies have concerns about the level of flexibility this brings. For example, while it is usually possible to email companies outside your own, your organization may have detailed controls in place to monitor such traffic. These restrictions may not be in place for Lync; therefore, your company may want to restrict your ability to federate entirely or limit it to specific external parties.

By default, federation is disabled. You can enable it during the setup of the Edge server, or afterwards using this command:

```
Set-CsAccessEdgeConfiguration -AllowFederatedUsers:$True
```

This command configures the Access Edge role to allow federation. There is one more step to enable federation. You need to ensure that the users you want to be able to communicate with federated contacts are covered by a `CsExternalAccessPolicy` that enables federation for those users.

To edit the default Global policy, use a command like this:

```
Set-CsExternalAccessPolicy -Identity Global -EnableFederationAccess:$True
-EnablePublicCloudAccess:$True
```

This command enables both standard external federation with other companies and also access to public clouds such as MSN, assuming they have been allowed globally using the `Enable-CsPublicProvider` cmdlet as shown here:

```
Enable-CsPublicProvider -Identity "MSN"
```

This would enable global access to MSN; other options would be `Yahoo!` or `AOL`.

Of course, you may not want to simply enable all federation. This can be controlled using the `Set-CsAccessEdgeConfiguration` cmdlet. For example:

```
Set-CsAccessEdgeConfiguration - EnablePartnerDiscovery:$True
```

This command enables essentially open federation where companies looking to federate will locate each other through DNS SRV records and connect automatically, while setting `EnablePartnerDiscovery` to `$False` would restrict federation to those domains specified manually. This leaves us with how to manipulate the list of allowed or blocked federation domains, which is done using the `CsAllowedDomain` and `CsBlockedDomain` cmdlets. For example:

```
New-CsAllowedDomain -Identity "gaotspartner.com" -ProxyFqdn "edgeserver.
gaotspartner.com" -MarkForMonitoring $True -Comment "Contact: Nathan Winters
(nwinters@gaotspartner.com)"
```

Here we created a new entry to allow the domain `gaotspartner.com` to participate in a federated relationship. We also specified the URL for the Edge server in the federated domain and that we want to monitor the traffic. Finally, we added a comment labeling the domain with a contact person.

The method of blocking domains is similar.

```
New-CsBlockedDomain -Identity "othergaots.com" -Comment "Blocked by Nathan
Winters."
```

This simple command blocks the `othergaots.com` domain from federating with our system and lists Nathan Winters as the person who carried out the configuration. Again, note that although PowerShell is used in this section to perform the configuration, these settings could have been set from the LSCP in the External Access section.

The Bottom Line

Secure External Access Lync utilizes the Edge server and supporting components to provide external access to communications modalities. The Edge server sits in the DMZ and is a proxy between internal and external users. Many layers of security are in place to ensure that communicating externally won't cause security breaches.

Master It Describe the role the Director plays in external access. Why would you use one?

Understand Core Security Lync is designed to be secure by default. It does this in many ways, not least of which is by encrypting all traffic and using certificates as part of mutual authentication of connections.

Master It In different circumstances, Lync can use four different authentication mechanisms. What are they and where are they used?

Provide Security Administratively No matter how secure a product is by design, an administrator can easily open up holes in its defenses. Lync provides many ways in which administrators can participate in tightening or relaxing security. Numerous policies are available to control users, including the clients they are allowed to use and the length and complexity of PINs. Equally, you can configure Lync to block links in IMs and prevent the transfer of files. Finally, Lync can be set up to add disclaimers to messages so that regulatory issues can be managed.

Master It You have been asked to ensure that users in the EMEA site can send only files of type `.txt` in IM messages and that any links in the messages will be prefixed with an underscore character so they must be copied into a browser manually. How would you do this?

Chapter 4

Clients

Client applications tend to be one of the most important aspects of a Lync deployment, and they usually cause the most pain. Lync introduces some new clients and updates others.

Understanding the features the various clients have to offer and how they are configured ensures that the correct clients are deployed to the correct people and that when used, those client applications work.

In this chapter, you will learn to:

- Understand the usage scenarios for each client
- Create client configuration policies
- Configure prerequisites for IP phones

Lync User Clients

In Lync Server 2010, four clients are designed for use by end users: Lync 2010, Lync 2010 Attendant Console, Lync for Mac, and Lync 2010 Phone Edition. They can be grouped into two categories: those designed to run on a user's desktop and those that are standalone IP phones.

Desktop Clients

The three desktop clients are Lync 2010, Lync 2010 Attendant Console, and Lync for Mac; these clients are designed for use by two distinct user sets. The Lync 2010 client is designed for the majority of users and provides access to all features within Lync. The Attendant client is designed for users who need to handle and triage a large number of voice calls and has limited features. Finally, the Lync for Mac client is designed to provide the majority of Lync functionality to Mac users.

Lync 2010

The Lync 2010 client allows users to access all of the features within Lync, and it is the primary client for the majority of users. The client at a high level provides the following features:

- Contacts
- Presence
- Instant messaging

- Voice
- Video
- Application and desktop sharing
- File transfers

These features are similar to those of OCS 2007 R2, but with significant improvements for end users. These improvements include:

- Contact photos
- Simplified selection of audio devices
- File transfers between remote and federated users
- Improved application and desktop sharing, as illustrated in Figure 4.1.
- Visual voice mail
- Activity feeds

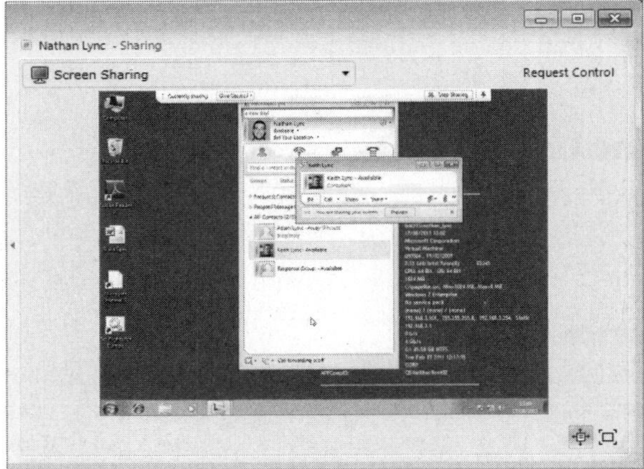

FIGURE 4.1
Desktop sharing in Lync 2010

LYNC 2010 ATTENDANT CONSOLE

Unlike the Lync 2010 client, the Lync 2010 Attendant Console (shown in Figure 4.2) does not require a license to use, but it does require the appropriate Client Access Licenses (CALs). It is designed for users who need to handle large volumes of incoming calls and triage them in a controlled manner. Notes can be assigned to calls before they are placed on hold, for example, allowing the user to easily recall information about the call. As shown in Figure 4.2, the client had lots of extra space; this allows multiple concurrent calls to be handled easily.

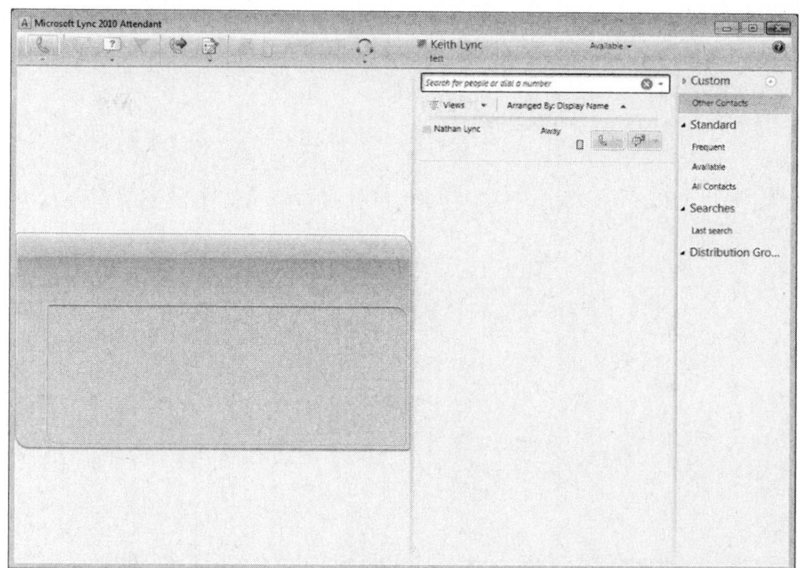

FIGURE 4.2
Lync 2010 Attendant Console

The user can also see the calls build up, and then pick and choose the calls they answer, prioritizing the more urgent calls. Users also have access to voice features such as *consultative transfer*, which allows the user to consult with the person the call is destined for prior to completing the transfer. (Consultative transfer is not available in the Lync client).

In OCS 2007 R2, the Attendant Console was used to handle delegated calls; this functionality is now available in the Lync 2010 client, allowing users who handle delegated call access to functionality such as video calls and application sharing. The functionality remains within the Attendant Console as well. The Attendant Console is limited to the following functionality:

- Instant messages
- Presence
- Contact list
- Voice calls

LYNC FOR MAC

Lync for Mac, illustrated in Figure 4.3, provides a dedicated client for Lync, allowing users to participate in a more immersive experience when using Lync. Although the client does not offer all the functionality of the Windows version, it does provide the features used by the majority of users.

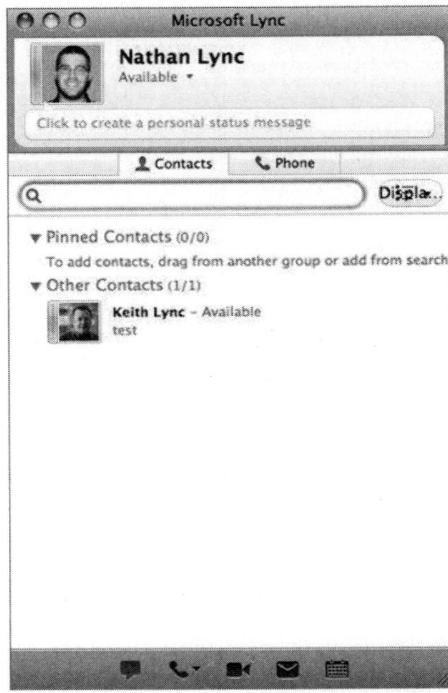

FIGURE 4.3 Lync for Mac

A comparison between Lync for Mac and its predecessor, Communicator for Mac, can be seen in Table 4.1; comparisons to the other Lync clients can be found here:

`http://technet.microsoft.com/en-us/library/gg425836.aspx`

TABLE 4.1: Comparison of Mac Clients

FEATURE	LYNC FOR MAC	COMMUNICATOR FOR MAC
Support for photos	Yes	No
Conference roster	Yes	No
Communicate from within Office applications	Yes	Yes
IM and Presence	Yes	Yes
Display contact card	Yes	Yes
Manual and automatic Presence	Yes	Yes
Call from Contact Card	Yes	Yes
Receive Call Notification	Yes	Yes

TABLE 4.1: Comparison of Mac Clients *(CONTINUED)*

FEATURE	LYNC FOR MAC	COMMUNICATOR FOR MAC
Configure call forwarding	Yes	No
Dial Pad	Yes	Yes
Add phone numbers to contacts	Yes	No
Audio and video calls	Yes	Yes
Audio and video with Windows Live	Yes	No
Schedule conferences (using Outlook)	Yes	No
Ad-hoc conferencing	Yes	No
Join scheduled conferences	Yes	Yes
Share desktop	Yes	Yes
Join and control PowerPoint presentation	Yes	No
Upload files to conference	Yes	No
Initiate PowerPoint presentation	No	No
Use whiteboards or polling	No	No

CLIENT CONFIGURATION

In Lync 2010, the majority of client configuration options have been removed from Group Policy and moved into Lync Server 2010 in-band provisioning. This gives Lync administrators greater control over the settings they need to configure and more granularity in the configuration, because they no longer need Active Directory administrators to perform changes and potentially redesign Group Policy.

Remaining in Group Policy are the items that need to be configured before in-band provisioning is available, such as connection information. This information is usually generic and as such can be set at a higher level within the Organization Unit Structure (OUS) in Active Directory.

Group Policy Configuration

The Group Policy template for Lync is provided only on certain client media; it can be downloaded from this URL:

`www.microsoft.com/download/en/details.aspx?id=27217`

Details of the configuration options can be found in the Lync help file and also in Chapter 10, "User Administration." The following items need to be explained in a little more depth.

Disable HTTP Connect This prevents the client from falling back to using HTTP, which may be required if clients connect via a Proxy server. Disabling HTTP restricts the connections to TCP and TLS only.

Enable BITS for GAL Download Instead of using a standard HTTP download, Background Intelligent Transfer Service (BITS) will be used. This can be useful when the GAL is large, or clients often receive corrupt files. BITS is an efficient transfer mechanism that will adjust the transfer rate of files based on how busy the network is.

Prevent Run This prevents the user from running the Lync client, which is useful when the Lync client has been deployed to client machines but you do not want users to use it. This may occur if the client has been added to a standard computer build image for a machine, but Lync is not ready to be used.

In-Band Configuration

In-band settings are configured through the Client policies; they can be created, modified, removed, and assigned using PowerShell. Policies can be created at the global, site, or user level. Administrators can easily control what features users can and cannot use.

To create a new Client policy, use the `New-CsClientPolicy` PowerShell cmdlet; there are associated `Get`, `Set`, and `Remove` cmdlets, along with a `Grant` cmdlet to assign policies to users. More details on PowerShell can be found in Chapter 8, "Introduction to PowerShell and the Lync Management Shell."

For details of the configuration options in the Lync help file along with an explanation of each, select Lync Server Management Shell ➢ Lync Server 2010 Cmdlets by Category ➢ Client Management Cmdlets ➢ New-CsClientPolicy.

To create a new user policy that would enable Music on Hold, issue the following PowerShell command:

```
New-CsClientPolicy -Identity MoHPolicy -EnableClientMusicOnHold $true
```

Once you've created the policy, you can assign it to users, using `Grant-CsClientPolicy`. Although the cmdlet will only allow you to assign a policy to one user at a time, you can pipe users into the cmdlet; see Chapter 8 for details on redirecting output from one cmdlet to another. Sources could be a CSV file, an LDAP search, or any number of options available within Lync.

To assign the policy you just created to all users in the sales organizational unit, use the following command:

```
Get-CsUser -OU " ou=Sales,dc=gaots,dc=local" | Grant-CsClientPolicy -PolicyName
MoHPolicy
```

Manual Client Configuration

Users can also manually configure the Lync client; this is usually only necessary for testing, as requiring individual users to configure their clients can cause issues. Wherever possible, DNS or Group Policy should be used for connectivity settings and in-band provisioning (discussed in Chapter 10) for client settings.

If you need to configure the Lync server details manually, go into the Settings menu and select Advanced on the General tab, next to where the sign-in name is specified. You'll see the

Advanced Connection Settings window shown in Figure 4.4. You can enter the FQDNs of the internal and external servers there; make sure the external URL ends in `:443`. If this is not specified, port 5061 will be used for external connections.

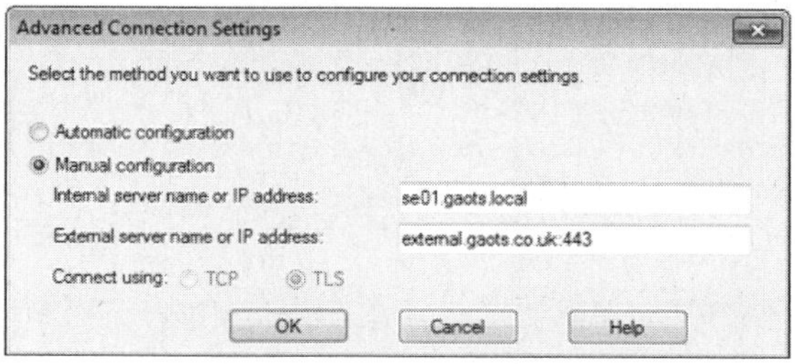

FIGURE 4.4
Specifying server URLs on the client

CLIENT CONNECTION PROCESS

When the Lync client connects to the Lync servers, it goes through a number of steps; this process has changed since OCS 2007 R2 with the addition of user certificates.

Authentication for first-time logins is performed using the user's NTLM (or Kerberos) details. These are passed to the Lync web service, which checks to see if they are valid. If they are, a certificate is returned to the client where it is stored in their personal Certificates Store; the certificate is also published into the Data Store on the user's home pool.

If there is already a user certificate, it is used to perform the authentication. The certificate is used for future logins until it expires (the default expiry period is 180 days and is configurable by an administrator) or is revoked, at which time the authentication process is reset.

Once authentication is complete, the client registers with the Lync pool to which the user is allocated. To locate the correct pool for connection, the Lync client uses DNS to locate the initial connection pool. It will try in the following order:

1. Internal DNS SRV using TLS (`_sipinternaltls.tcp.gaots.co.uk`)
2. Internal DNS SRV using TCP (`_sipinternal.tcp.gaots.co.uk`)
3. External DNS using TLS (`_sip._tls.gaots.co.uk`)

Once it has connected to the initial pool, the client will proceed, assuming it is a single-pool deployment or the user is allocated to this pool. If this initial pool is a Director, or the client is hosted on a different pool, the client will be redirected to the correct home pool.

Once the client has connected to the home pool, it will connect to the registrar. For Standard Edition deployments or single-server Enterprise deployments, there is only one registrar, so it will be used. Where there are multiple registrars in a pool (each front-end server contains a registrar), the client will be redirected to the registrar to which the user has been allocated. This allocation process is defined when the user is created or moved to the pool. It cannot be changed by an administrator. At this stage, the client is registered to Lync, and the registrar address is cached to be used for future connections. Should the registrar become unavailable, the process is started again.

While this may seem like a complicated process, it is not seen by end users and is only exposed to administrators when troubleshooting. The process was changed so that items such as certificates were used in order to support new functionality in Lync, like the Survivable Branch Appliance.

For external clients the process is similar; the only differences are the use of DNS discovery for the server FQDNs and the fact that all communication is relayed via the Edge servers. The DNS records used are the DNS SRVs using TLS and TCP, and the SIP *A* record from DNS, such as `sip.contoso.com`. In addition, the home registrar is cached by the client (in the `EndPointCacheConfiguration.CACHE` file, located in the user profile folder) for future logins. The discovery process occurs only when this file does not exist (on first login) or when the user *home* pool (or server) is unavailable.

SINGLE DNS ZONE? A SOLUTION FOR INTERNAL USERS

Lync relies on DNS to connect to the Lync infrastructure either through autoconfiguration or by resolving preconfigured FQDNs to IP addresses.

Some of the FQDNs used within Lync are explicit internal and external URLs; others need to resolve differently if they are being used internally or externally. Just to make it more complex, some functionality will work even if an internal client connects externally, but this is not an ideal solution.

Therefore, ensuring that clients locate the correct DNS records and resolve them to the correct *A* records is essential.

For organizations that utilize separate internal and external DNS for the SIP domain, an approach commonly known as Split Brain DNS configuration is relatively straightforward, because you can ensure that the clients find the correct records no matter where they are. Problems occur when a single DNS zone is used for the SIP domain.

For example, the SRV record `_sipinternaltls._tcp.gaots.co.uk` is used for internal clients and will resolve to the Lync pool virtual IP or Standard Edition server IP address. This is the first DNS record that Lync looks for during autoconfiguration; if connecting internally, the client will be able to connect. If the client is external with a single DNS zone, the client will retrieve this record and attempt to connect to an internal IP address. After a period of time the client will time out, try the TCP internal address, and again wait to timeout. As that point, the external DNS records will be attempted.

While the client will be able to connect eventually, this method is far from ideal because it creates a bad experience for the end user. To work around this, you can use pinpoint zones. This method creates a DNS zone, which resolves to the exact record that is being searched for rather than an entire domain. This allows the internal records to be excluded from the DNS zone that is being used for DNS lookups internally and externally and allows very specific records to be created in internal DNS.

The DNS records are created using the `dnscmd` command on the internal DNS servers, assuming Windows DNS servers are used.

```
dnscmd . /zoneadd _sipinternaltls._tcp.gaots.co.uk. /dsprimary
dnscmd . /recordadd _sipinternaltls._tcp.gaots.co.uk. @ SRV 0 0 5061 lyncpool.
gaots.co.uk.
```

```
dnscmd . /zoneadd lyncpool.gaots.co.uk. /dsprimary
dnscmd . /recordadd lyncpool.gaots.co.uk. @ A WWW.XXX.YYY.ZZZ
```

These commands create the internal records for the SRV and *A* records for autoconfiguration using a TLS-based connection. The first and third commands create the two zones, and the second and fourth create the SRV and *A* record, respectively. The important thing to note here is that when the SRV and *A* records are created, the @ sign is used for the record name; this is because the zone name is explicit rather than for an entire domain. For example, if you used the following:

```
dnscmd . /zoneadd lyncpool.gaots.co.uk. /dsprimary
dnscmd . /recordadd lyncpool.gaots.co.uk. lyncpool.gaots.co.uk A WWW.XXX.YYY.ZZZ
```

it would not resolve if the DNS request was `lyncpool.gaots.co.uk`. Instead, it would resolve only if `lyncpool.gaots.co.uk.lyncpool.gaots.co.uk` was requested. The @ sign symbolizes that the record is returned when the zone name is looked up; because the zone name is the FQDN that is required, there is no need to specify anything further.

Because pinpoint zones were used, if a DNS lookup were performed for `www.gaots.co.uk`, the internal DNS server would not claim responsibility for this domain but would instead forward it like any other external DNS request.

In summary, while split-brain DNS is preferred, using pinpoint zones provides a solution that does not require re-architecting an organization's DNS setup while still providing users with a seamless login to Lync.

CLIENT UPDATES

In OCS 2007 R2 it was possible to update the OCS client to the latest version; when a new version was made available, the client would download it from the server and then install it. But most organizations could not use this update method because it required administrative privilege and users do not usually have the permissions to install updates. The update method has been improved in Lync. Administrators still use the Client Version filter to specify whether to Allow With Upgrade or Block With Upgrade for a client version, but that is where the similarities end. Lync now uses Windows Update to perform the upgrade; this removes a number of the issues found in 2007 R2.

Windows Update allows updates to be downloaded in a manner specified by the specific organization; this could be through private WSUS (Windows Server Update Service) servers or direct from the public WSUS servers on the Internet. It also provides a mechanism for updates to be installed without the user needing administrative rights. For organizations that perform centralized updating of applications, this method will not need to be used; however, for organizations that want to use it, the pain points from 2007 R2 no longer exist.

Lync 2010 Phone Edition

In Lync 2010, IP phones are provided by a number of vendors, including Polycom, Aastra, and HP. A complete list of certified devices can be downloaded from here:

`http://technet.microsoft.com/en-us/lync/gg278172`

Each of these phones has its own look and feel, but they run the same software, which is Lync 2010 Phone Edition. This software is provided by Microsoft and has the same user interface and functionality regardless of who makes the device.

The IP phones are split into three categories: common area phones, information worker phones, and conference phones. Table 4.2 shows the relevant model numbers for Aastra, Polycom, and HP.

TABLE 4.2: Lync 2010 IP Phone Models

PHONE TYPE	AASTRA	POLYCOM	HP
Common Area Phone	6720ip	CX500	4110
Information Worker Phone	6725ip	CX600	4120
Conference Phone	N\A	CX3000	N\A

In addition to these phone models, the Polycom CX700 and LG-Nortel 8540 are supported and will be updated to Lync 2010 Phone Edition, but they operate with a reduced feature set.

In addition to phones running Lync 2010 Phone Edition, which are referred to as "Optimized for" devices, there are phones that are designed to work with Lync but that do not run Lync 2010 Phone Edition. One vendor of these phones is Snom. These devices are tested to work with Lync but may not offer the same features as the "Optimized for" devices, and they are configured differently. This section only covers Lync 2010 Phone Edition.

COMMON AREA PHONES

Common area phones are designed to be deployed in areas where there is no single user, such as reception areas, warehouses, and so on. Compared to the information worker phones, these phones have a reduced feature set, which is referred to as *basic mode*, and also a reduced hardware configuration. Basic mode offers the following functionality:

- Contacts
- Photos
- Message waiting indicator
- Local call logs
- Remote usage (after intranet provisioning)
- Conference call control

Although referred to as common area phones, they can be used by standard users—for example, in a hot-desking configuration where they are configured as common area phones and also enabled to allow users to log into them. The phones can also be used without common area configuration by a single user.

Information Worker and Conference Phones

From a Lync Phone Edition standpoint, the information worker and conference phone types provide the same functionality, which builds on that of the common area phone and implements what is commonly referred to as *Enhanced mode*.

This Enhanced mode is made possible by connecting the phone to a PC using a USB cable, a technique referred to as *USB tethering*, which is offered on these phones. If a user decides to log in using their extension and PIN instead, they will be restricted to Basic mode. Enhanced mode adds the following functionality: Exchange Calendar including Join Conference, Exchange integrated call logs, and visual voice mail. When a user decides to use USB tethering, they will be prompted to reenter their password when they connect their PC and phone together, as shown in Figure 4.5.

Figure 4.5
Login for USB tethering

These devices, unlike the common area phones, can also be set up from remote locations without needing to be on the corporate network. This allows organizations to drop-ship these devices without needing to preconfigure anything. Users will be required to log in using USB tethering rather than log in with their extension and PIN.

CX700 and 8540 Phones

The CX700 and 8540 phones are upgradable to Lync 2010 Phone Edition but operate with a reduced feature set. The features that are supported are in line with those offered in OCS 2007 R2. The features that are not supported are operating as a common area phone, PIN authentication, and contact photos. For users, the most noticeable change is that they can view their calendar and join Lync Online meetings from the phone.

Configuring IP Phone Prerequisites

A number of elements need to be configured to allow Lync IP phones to operate within your organization so people can use them. The requirements vary depending on how the phone is going to be initially configured. Phones can be configured either through USB tethering or directly on the phone using PIN authentication. USB tethering doesn't depend on the network as much as the method, because the required certificates, SIP URI, and authentication information are synced through the USB cable. The main thing you need is Network Time Protocol; however, depending on your requirements, you may also need Link Layer Discovery and Power over Ethernet. For PIN authentication, the phone needs to locate information about the Lync setup; it needs information in DHCP to provide this.

Irrespective of the method used for the initial configuration, DHCP is needed to provide basic information to the phone, IP address, subnet, and default gateway, along with the DNS domain name and server.

Dynamic Host Configuration Protocol (DHCP)

DHCP is used to provide the information you need for Phone Edition to connect to the Lync server; this information cannot be manually entered into the phone, making the DHCP configuration a requirement for deployment. DHCP provides the following information as part of the in-band provision process:

- Lync registrar address, which could be a Director pool or a Lync pool
- URL of the web services
- Relative URL of the certificate provider on the Lync server
- Protocol for the certificate provider (HTTPS by default)
- Port for the certificate provider (443 by default)

The Lync registrar address is provided in Option 120; the other settings are provided under Option 43, using a vendor-specific MS-UC-Client setting. Both of them are provided as hexadecimal strings.

Two methods are available to provide the required DHCP settings. The first is to use the DHCP server that is provided as part of the Lync registrar. This DHCP server is very limited in functionality and is used to provide the required information. It will only respond to a DHCP request that contains a Vendor Class ID of MS-UC-Client and asks for Option 120 or 43. A fully functional DHCP server is still required to provide an IP address, subnet, and default gateway, along with the DNS domain name and server for the phone. This DHCP server can be useful for labs or for small installations, but once a network becomes segregated by VLANs or WAN connections are used, this method is not usually feasible. To enable the DHCP server, use the following PowerShell command:

```
Set-CsRegistrarConfiguration -EnableDHCPServer $true
```

The second method is to use existing DHCP servers to provide the required configuration settings. This way, you do not have to configure the network to route DHCP requests to the Lync registrar, and you can also use it to deliver additional configuration information to the device.

To help you configure DHCP servers, Microsoft provides a configuration tool that will generate the required DHCP entries. While this tool is mainly aimed at Windows DHCP, the information it generates can be used to configure third-party DHCP servers. The utility, called DHCPUtil, is provided as part of the Lync installation and is located in the `C:\Program Files\Common Files\Microsoft Lync Server 2010` directory, assuming the default installation path. This tool works in conjunction with a batch file called `DHCPConfigScript.bat`, which configures the DHCP server. The DHCPUtil application generates the DHCP configuration, emulates the client to check the DHCP configuration, and finally removes the DHCP configuration.

In order to create the DHCP configuration, at a minimum the batch file needs to be run on the DHCP server with the required settings passed into it as command-line arguments. These settings are generated by the DHCPUtil application and are created from three parameters:

`-SipServer`, which is the FQDN of the Director or Lync pool

`-WebServer`, which is the FQDN of the web services

`-CertProvUrl`, which is the URL of the certificate provider

For a Standard Edition installation, only the FQDN of the SIP server needs to be specified, since it is the same as the web server FQDN. This is also the case for an Enterprise Edition installation in which the SIP server and the web server share the same FQDN, and is usually the case when a hardware load balancer is used. It is usually not necessary to specify the certificate provider URL.

For example, to configure DHCP for a Standard Edition installation with an FQDN of `so.gaots.com`, use the following syntax:

```
DHCPUtil.exe -SipServer se.gaots.com
```

This will produce an output detailing the configuration, along with the syntax required for the `DHCPConfigScript` batch file and will look like this:

```
DHCPConfigScript.bat Configure MS-UC-Client ➥
000273650567616F747303636F6D00 4D532D55432D436C69656E74 ➥
6874747073 73652E67616F74732E636F6D 343433 ➥
2F4365727450726F762F4365727450726F766973696F6E696E6753657276696365652E737663
```

Copy the `DHCPConfigScript` file to the DHCP server and run the previous command to create the DHCP configuration. These configurations are created as server options, and they will be applied to every DHCP scope on the DHCP server. If scope-specific options are required rather than server options, you will need to write your own configuration script. You can use the batch file as a basis for this. If you need to remove the DHCP configuration, run the following command from the DHCP server:

```
DHCPConfigScript.bat -Cleanup
```

The `DHCPUtil` command can be used to test the DHCP configuration; it sends a DHCP INFORM packet, displaying its contents, and also displays the contents of the DHCP ACK packet it receives along with the decoded settings. If the ACK is not received or the decoded settings appear to be wrong, this indicates a configuration issue. You can run the test using the following command:

```
DHCPUtil.exe -EmulateClient
```

The final DHCP-related item you need to look at is how to get the IP phone to switch to a specific VLAN. This is often required in scenarios where a PC is connected via a phone and the two devices need to be on separate VLANs. Using DHCP to do this should always be seen as a fallback option; the preferred method is to use LLDP.

The VLAN configuration is provided through Option 43 in a similar way to the configuration of the actual phone, but it is provided under a different vendor-specific class, CPE-OCPHONE. During the boot stage, the phone will try to retrieve a VLAN ID from LLDP; if this fails, it will perform a DHCP request, looking for a VLAN ID. If it receives one, it will release the IP address it was issued and perform another DHCP request; this is tagged with the VLAN ID it just received. If a VLAN ID is not retrieved, the second DHCP request is still performed to retrieve the server details, because two different vendor class IDs are being used.

Although you could populate DHCP with the server details, there is no utility to populate the VLAN information, so it must be manually created or scripted. The following method is an example of how it can be scripted.

```
netsh dhcp server add class CPEOCPHONE "Lync Phone Edition VLAN Tagging" "CPE-
OCPHONE" 1
netsh dhcp server add optiondef 10 VLANID Word 0 vendor=CPEOCPhone comment="Lync
Phone VLAN"
netsh dhcp server set optionvalue 10 Word vendor=CPEOCPhone "250"
```

This script creates the vendor class, assigns it the VLAN suboption 10 under Option 43, and adds it as a DHCP server option, applicable to all scopes. To use these commands, replace 250 with the voice VLAN you need.

Once DHCP has been updated, the phones will discover the VLAN the next time they are restarted and begin using it. If you ever need to change the VLAN once the phones have been configured, each phone will need to be hard-reset, as the VLAN is cached.

Caching the VLANs does potentially create an issue for one scenario: if an organization requires IP phones to be used remotely via the Edge servers, a cached VLAN can potentially cause problems. If the IP phone is attached to a switch that honors and routes based on the VLAN tag applied by the phone, there is the possibility that the packets will be placed into a VLAN that may not have a DHCP Server configured or internet access, or they may be dropped by the switch completely if the VLAN does not exist. Therefore, if phones need to be configured onsite before being used offsite, scope-specific options should be used for the VLAN configuration rather than server-wide options, and the phone should be connected to switch ports on the correct voice VLAN.

The final item to consider is the actual switch configuration. Because two VLANs are used on a single port, the primary VLAN needs to be set to the VLAN that the computer will use, while the voice VLAN should be set to a supported VLAN for the port.

Link Layer Discovery Protocol (LLDP)

LLDP allows Phone Edition to discover which VLAN it should use. This is the preferred VLAN Discovery method, but it requires network switches that support LLDP-MED, the protocol's Media Endpoint Discovery extension. The configuration varies depending on the switch make and model. The following is a sample Cisco configuration:

```
!-- Enter configuration mode
configure terminal
!-- Enable LLDP
lldp run
!-- Configure Ethernet port 1
interface FastEthernet 1/1
!-- Set Data VLAN to 100
```

```
switchport access vlan 100
!-- Set Voice VLAN to 101
switchport voice vlan 101
!-- Configure as Access Port
switchport mode access
```

This configuration instructs Phone Edition to use VLAN 101, and all network traffic will be tagged with this VLAN, ensuring that the correct DHCP scope is used and the traffic is prioritized correctly.

Power over Ethernet (PoE)

Power over Ethernet allows a Lync phone to be powered by the network switch, rather than requiring a local power supply for the phone. This often simplifies the deployment, because it does not require power sockets local to the phone or additional cables.

The available phones support both 802.3AF and 802.3AT standards for Power over Ethernet; it is important to check that any existing switches support these IEEE standards. If you are upgrading from an existing IP telephony system, the current switches may not support these standards. For example, older Cisco switches use a proprietary PoE implementation that is not compatible with these phones.

Network Time Protocol (NTP)

Because Phone Edition does not allow any configuration on the device, NTP is used to retrieve the current date and time. This lets you check items, such as the certificates, for validity. Phone Edition discovers the NTP server using DNS; the following two DNS records will be tried in order:

- The SRV record, `_ntp._udp.`*`<SIP domain>`* (port 123)
- `time.windows.com`

If there is no SRV record, Phone Edition will fall back to `time.windows.com`. If this is used, the phone will need to be able to access the Internet using UDP on port 123.

If you do not have an internal NTP server and do not want to use `time.windows.com`, then the Windows Time Service, which runs on every Windows server, can be configured to act as an NTP server. You can enable this through a Group Policy change. The Group Policy can be applied to any existing server, and a new policy can be used or an existing one can be changed. The settings that need to be changed can be found at Computer Configuration ➤ Policies ➤ Administrative Templates ➤ System ➤ Windows Time Service ➤ Time Providers.

To enable the Time server on the server to which the Group Policy applies, set Enable Windows NTP Server to Enabled in the Group Policy Management Editor, as shown in Figure 4.6. This will allow the server to respond to NTP requests.

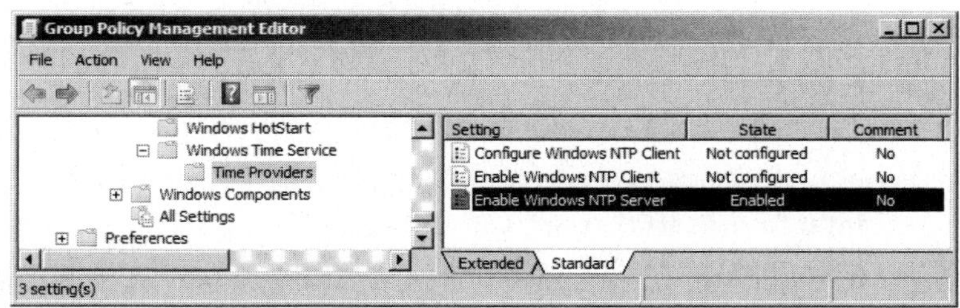

FIGURE 4.6
NTP Group Policy change

Once this has been enabled, the SRV record should be created in the DNS Manager with the server FQDN specified as the Host Offering This Server, as shown in Figure 4.7.

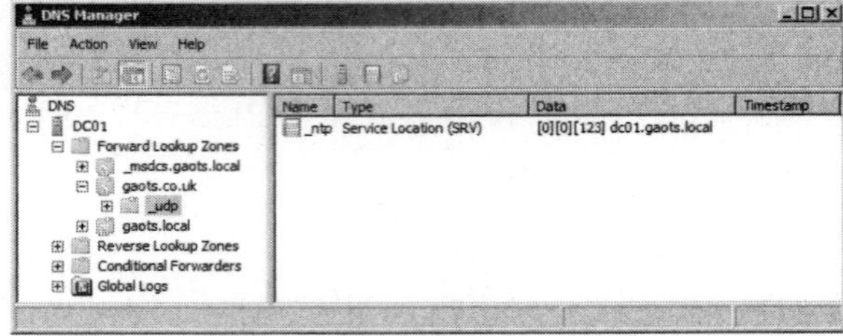

FIGURE 4.7
A Time server SRV record

DEVICE CONFIGURATION

Device configuration is performed in two parts; the first part is performed through in-band configuration and is configured through the Lync Control Panel (Clients ➤ Device Configuration) and PowerShell using the `CsUCPhoneConfiguration` cmdlets (`New`, `Set`, `Get`, and `Remove`).

These settings are available on either a global or a site basis. The following settings are available:

- `Identity`, which is set to global for the global configuration or the Lync site name prefixed with `Site:`
- `SIPSecurityMode`, which is the SIP Signaling Security level for devices
- `LoggingLevel`, which indicates the depth of logging on the device
- `VoiceDiffServTag`, which is the DSCP value for marking voice packets
- `EnforcePhoneLock`, which locks the phone when the timeout occurs
- `PhoneLockTimeout`, which is the length of time until the phone is locked
- `MinPhonePinLength`, which is the minimum length of the device PIN
- `CalendarPollInterval`, which is the interval at which EWS will be polled for changes
- `Voice8021p`, which is the 802.1p value for marking voice packets

The last two settings are exposed only via PowerShell.

Of these settings, the ones most commonly modified are DSCP and Device Lock. The other settings can be left at the factory defaults for most deployments, unless you need to troubleshoot, which requires logging be turned on. If, for example, you needed to modify the global policy to change the device timeout to 5 minutes, the following PowerShell command would be used:

```
Set-CsUCPhoneConfiguration -Identity global -PhoneLockTimeout "00:05:00"
```

The second part of device configuration is done on the devices themselves; it is performed as part of the user sign-in process and allows the following information to be configured:

- Time zone
- Date and time format
- Ringtone
- Phone lock code

Unfortunately, there is no method to configure these settings centrally, and configuring them on a per-user basis in large deployments can be a time-consuming process.

Client Connection Process

Lync Phone Edition connects to the Lync servers in a different way than a Lync client. Phone Edition at a high level goes through the following steps for Internal clients:

1. Tries to locate a VLAN to use.
2. Issues a DHCP request looking for an IP address.
3. Checks for device updates.
4. Downloads certificate chains
5. Authenticates.
6. Receives and publishes the client certificate.
7. Registers with Lync.

The first three steps are covered earlier in this chapter, so we'll focus on the remaining four steps.

In order for Lync Server 2010 Phone Edition to trust the certificates used for web services, the root certificate needs to be downloaded and verified. This process happens only if a root certificate has not already been downloaded. The certificate is downloaded using a standard HTTP query, containing the web services details retrieved from DHCP. Once it is downloaded, an HTTPS request to the web services is performed; this check ensures that the root certificate is valid.

Authentication for first-time logins is performed using either the user's extension and PIN or NTLM details to the Lync web service, which checks to see if they are valid. If the details are valid, a certificate is returned to the client; the certificate is also published into the Data Store in the user's home pool. If the phone already has a user certificate, it is used to perform the authentication, and the client can then automatically log in after a restart.

Once the authentication is complete, the phone needs to register with the Lync pool to which the client is allocated. To locate the correct pool to connect to, the Lync 2010 Phone Edition client uses DNS and DHCP to locate the initial connection pool. It will try to locate the Lync pool address, using the following order:

- DHCP address using Option 120 (Option 43 is used for certificate services discovery)
- Internal DNS SRV using TLS (`_sipinternaltls.tcp.gaots.co.uk`)
- Internal DNS SRV using TCP (`_sipinternal.tcp.gaots.co.uk`)
- External DNS using TLS (`_sip._tls.gaots.co.uk`)

Once it has connected to the initial pool, for single pool deployment or where the user is allocated to this pool, the client will proceed. If this initial pool is a Director or the client is hosted on a different pool, the client will be redirected to the correct home pool.

Once the client has connected to the home pool, it will connect to the registrar. For Standard Edition deployments or single-server Enterprise deployments, there is only one registrar, so it will be used. Where there are multiple registrars in a pool (each front-end server contains a registrar), the client will be redirected to the registrar to which the user has been allocated. This allocation process is defined when the user is created or moved to the pool. It cannot be changed by an administrator.

At this stage, the client is registered to Lync, and the registrar address is cached to be used for future connections. Should the registrar become unavailable, the process is started again.

While this may seem like a complicated process, it is not seen by end users and is exposed to administrators only when they're troubleshooting. The change to using items such as certificates was necessary to support new functionality in Lync, such as the Survivable Branch Appliance.

For external clients, the process is different. The phones must first be logged in internally; once this has occurred and they are taken external, the following process occurs on the phone:

1. Request an IP address from DHCP.
2. Check for device updates.
3. Authenticate.
4. Register with Lync.

These steps are similar to that of an internal client, but at this stage the user certificate already exists. Instead of connecting directly to a Lync pool, all requests are relayed through an Edge server. In addition, only DNS is used to locate the address to connect to:

- DNS SRV using TLS
- DNS SRV using TCP
- SIP *A* Record from DNS—i.e., `sip.gaots.co.uk`

Deploying Phone Edition Updates

As with OCS, updates for Lync 2010 Phone Edition are managed and distributed by Lync Server 2010. This allows updates to be rolled out in a managed way, with the ability to configure test devices and to roll back to a previous version if necessary.

For the most part, you can manage any updates through either PowerShell or the Lync Control Panel. The only thing you must do through PowerShell is upload the update files.

Update files are published on the Microsoft download site and are released periodically. One update file is released for each different hardware vendor, and an update file is released for the Polycom CX700 and LG-Nortel 8540 devices.

Organizations do not usually need to download all of them because they commonly standardize on a single vendor; however, for an upgrade from a previous version, you may need to also download the update for CX700 and 8540 devices.

Each of these update packs have the same filename UCUpdates.exe, therefore if you are downloading files for multiple vendors you need to be careful not to overwrite another update file. These downloads are executable files and will extract to the same location, which is the

`%userprofile%` path. Likewise, they all extract as the same filename, which is `ucupdates.cab`, so make sure that you do not overwrite an existing update file.

Once downloaded and extracted, the update files need to be uploaded to the Lync web services. The following PowerShell command can be used to perform this task; it will upload the file to each Web Services server. This assumes that the `ucupdates.cab` file is located on the root of the C: drive.

```
Get-CsService -WebServer | ForEach-Object {Import-CsDeviceUpdate -Identity
$_.Identity -FileName c:\UCUpdates.cab}
```

Once the updates have been uploaded, they will appear as *pending versions*. When updates are pending, they will be deployed only to test devices. They will not be deployed to other devices until they have been approved.

Device testing, update approval, and version restoration can be managed through either PowerShell or the Lync Control Panel. Test devices are identified using either their MAC address or serial number; both of these should be globally unique, so using either should not cause a problem. In addition, the test devices can be created on either a site or global basis.

To create a test device, use the `New-CsTestDevice` cmdlet, which requires four parameters:

`-Name`, which is the name of the test device

`-Parent`, which is defined as global or `site:`*`sitename`*

`-Identifier`, which is the MAC address or serial number of the device

`-IdentifierType`, which is set to either MACAddress or SerialNumber

To create a test device at the EMEA site using an `Identifier` of AB37_679e, for example, use the following PowerShell command:

```
New-CsTestDevice -Name "Redmond Test Phone 1" -Parent Site:EMEA -Identifier
"AB37_679e" -IdentifierType SerialNumber
```

Once this command has been run, any future uploaded updates will be deployed to this device for testing. You can use the following cmdlets to manage test devices:

`Get-CsTestDevice`

`Set-CsTestDevice`

`Remove-CsTestDevice`

When planning your test devices, choose at least one of each device to test. These devices should not be mission-critical or high-profile users such as C-level executives; they should be users who use the most of their device's functionality.

Once the updates have been tested, they can be approved to be deployed to all the remaining devices. Updates can be approved using either the Control Panel or the `Approve-CsDeviceUpdateRule` cmdlet. This cmdlet takes a single input, which is the unique identity of the update, and it could look like this:

```
Approve-CsDeviceUpdateRule -Identity service:WebServer:se.gaots.local/d5ce3c10-
2588-420a-82ac-dc2d9b1222ff9
```

To retrieve the identities of updates, use the `Get-CsDeviceUpdateRule` cmdlet, which retrieves all available updates and can be filtered as needed. If you want to approve all pending updates after you've tested the update, use the following command:

```
Get-CsDeviceUpdateRule | Approve-CsDeviceUpdateRule
```

If you need to restore to a previous version of Lync 2010 Phone Edition, use the `Restore-CsDeviceUpdateRule` cmdlet. If you want to remove a pending update completely, you can use `Reset-CsDeviceUpdateRule`. Both of these cmdlets use the same syntax as `Approve-CsDeviceUpdateRule`.

Now that you've seen how updates are managed, you need to see how the device updates itself. Updates are handled differently, depending on both the state and the location of the phone. Therefore, we'll look at three different update processes: nonprovisioned devices, internal devices, and external devices.

Nonprovisioned devices are ones that do not have a user signed into them. These devices can be updated only if they are on the corporate network, because access to the updates website is blocked for anonymous users. The update process is as follows:

1. Send a DNS request for `ucupdates-r2.`*<DHCPIssuedDomainName>*.
2. Send an HTTPS request asking if an update is available.
3. If `NumOFFiles = 0` is returned, no update is available.
4. If an update is available, the download path will be provided.
5. The phone downloads the updates, installs them, and after 5 minutes of inactivity reboots the device.

The main issue with this process is that because an HTTPS request is used, the phone needs to trust the certificate that is returned. At this stage, the phone will not trust internal certificates because the root certificate isn't installed; therefore, it will reject it. To work around this, you can use an externally issued certificate or have a user sign in, as this process will download the root certificate.

The update process for internal and external devices is similar with one difference—for external access, the anonymous request is rejected and the phone retries using credentials. The process is as follows:

1. On startup, user login, or every 24 hours, a check for updates using the in-band provisioned URL is performed.
2. If `NumOFFiles = 0` is returned, no update is available.
3. If an update is available, the download path will be provided.
4. The phone downloads the update, installs it, and after 5 minutes of inactivity reboots the device.

When the updates have been applied and the device rebooted, the phone will automatically be logged in as the same user.

Phone Edition Logs

In order to troubleshoot Lync Phone Edition, the log level needs to be specified, and the logs need to be uploaded from the phone to the server and converted. Once at this stage, you can begin analyzing the logs to troubleshoot the issue. This many sound like a cumbersome process, but it is relatively straightforward. The logging level is set through the phone in-band provisioning process, either through the Control Panel or through PowerShell.

To enable logging on a global basis, you can use the following PowerShell command:

```
Set-CsUCPhoneConfiguratoin -Identity Global -LoggingLevel High
```

To disable logging, change `High` to `Off`. The phone will start logging once the settings have been updated. This will be done through the in-band provisioning periodically, but the quickest way is by rebooting the phone.

Since the phone has logging enabled, you can re-create the issue that you are experiencing, and once this is completed the log files need to be sent to the server. To do this, if the phone is logged in, use the phone's Settings menu and select Set Log Settings ➤ Send Logs. If the phone is not logged in or locked, use System Information.

Once the log files have been uploaded, they can be found in `DeviceUpdateLogs\Client\CELog` on the File Store for the pool. At a minimum, there will be a file with a `.clg` extension. There could also be a *Dr. Watson* log file if one has been created; this file is created in case of a crash and is automatically uploaded. It is the `.clg` file you want. It needs to be converted to a readable format using Readlog; the following syntax can be used:

```
readlog.exe -v logfile.clg logfile.txt
```

Now that you have a log file in plain text, you can begin the analysis.

How to Get Your Hands on Readlog

Readlog is part of the Windows CE Platform Builder; it is not freely available but you can use it for a 180-day-trial period. Once you have installed the trial, you can find Readlog here: `C:\WINCE600\PUBLIC\COMMON\OAK\BIN\I386`

Readlog does not depend on any other files, and the executable can be copied to the machine on which you want to convert the files. To install the trial, you will need a trial license key. You can request one at the following URL:

```
www.microsoft.com/windowsembedded/en-us/downloads/download-windows-embedded-ce-6-trial.aspx
```

You will need to log in with your Windows Live ID and complete the registration process. The 180-Day Trial can be downloaded from:

```
www.microsoft.com/downloads/en/details.aspx?FamilyID=7e286847-6e06-4a0c-8cac-ca7d4c09cb56
```

Common Area Phones

In order to use common area phones, you need to create accounts for each phone. These accounts exist only within Lync, but they are represented as contacts within Active Directory and allow users to search for them in the Lync Address Book and call them.

You can create a common area phone through PowerShell using the `New-CsCommonAreaPhone` cmdlet, and you can manage it using the equivalent `Set`, `Get`, and `Remove` cmdlets. There is also a `Move` cmdlet, allowing you to move the phone from one pool to another.

Once you've created the common area phone, you can assign Client, Voice, Conferencing, and PIN policies to it in the same way you assign them to a user. You should create specific policies for these phones, so they can be locked down more than a standard user would be. For example, if you want to create a common area phone for the Headquarters reception, you can use the following PowerShell command:

```
New-CsCommonAreaPhone -LineUri "tel:+14255553827" -RegistrarPool "se.gaots.local"
-DisplayName "HQ Main Reception Phone" -SipAddress "sip:hqmainreception@gaots
.co.uk"
```

This will create the common area phone with a phone number of +14255553827, on the `se.gaots.local` pool with a display name of HQ Main Reception Phone. You can also set a SIP address; this is an optional setting, but if you set it to an address that is easy to remember, it will make it easier to grant policies. If it is not set, a SIP address based on the default domain name and GUID is used.

Once the phone has been created the necessary policies can be assigned to it; this is performed in the same way as a normal user using the `Grant` cmdlets.

The Voice and Conferencing policies should be configured as follows; these settings will suffice for the majority of requirements. The following Voice policy is recommended:

- Call forwarding disabled
- Team call disabled
- Delegation disabled
- Call transfer disabled

The following Conferencing policy is recommended:

- Audio conference disabled
- File transfer disabled

This following is not a Conference setting but is set within the Conference policy:

- Peer-to-peer file transfer disabled

Once the policies have been granted, a PIN needs to be set for the common area phone. Without this, it is not possible to log in to the phone. The PIN is set using the

`Set-CsClientPin` cmdlet. To set it on the common area phone you just created, use the following PowerShell command:

```
Set-CsClientPin -Identity "HQ Main Reception" -Pin 165643
```

Note that the PIN specified must comply with the PIN policy that covers the common area phone. This could be a specific policy or a site or global one. Once the PIN has been set, you can log in to the common area phone using the phone number and PIN.

Enabling Hot-Desking

Hot-desking allows a user to sign into a common area phone, and the phone will become theirs until they sign out or their login times out. This is often useful in conference rooms and offices that have hot-desking or touch-down areas. Users sign into the phone using their phone number and PIN or through USB tethering if the phone supports it.

Hot-desking is enabled through the Client policy using the `EnableHotdesking` and `HotdeskingTimeout` options. The `EnableHotdesking` option is either set to True or False, and the `HotdeskingTimeout` is set in an `HH:MM:SS` format, such as 00:05:00 for 5 minutes. The timeout can be set to a minimum of 30 seconds, with a default of 5 minutes. For most organizations this is too low, as it is common for a user not to use a phone for a period of time but still be using the hot-desk; a setting of at least 60 minutes is usually required.

If you want to enable hot-desking for an existing Client policy and set a timeout of 90 minutes, use the following PowerShell command.

```
Set-CsClientPolicy -Identity SalesHotDeskPhone -EnableHotdesking $true
-HotdeskingTimeout 01:30:00
```

This change will become active once the settings on the phone have been refreshed, either through rebooting the phone or through the regular configuration updates.

Lync Conferencing Clients

Lync 2010 has two dedicated conferencing clients, which are used to allow external participants to participate in Lync online meetings. The first of these is the Attendee client, which is an installable application, and the second is a Silverlight application known as the Lync Web App; each of these clients are covered in further detail in this section.

In addition to the conferencing clients, users can access online meetings using the Lync 2010 client; it can be used by users within an organization or by external parties who are using Lync 2010. Alternatively, a participant can call into a conference allowing them to participate with Voice only; this ability can be useful if they are away from their PCs.

Lync 2010 Attendee

The Lync 2010 Attendee client allows users to participate in all aspects of an online meeting; its functionality is the same as that offered by the Lync client and it has the same look and feel, as shown in Figure 4.8.

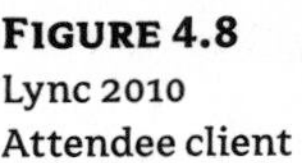

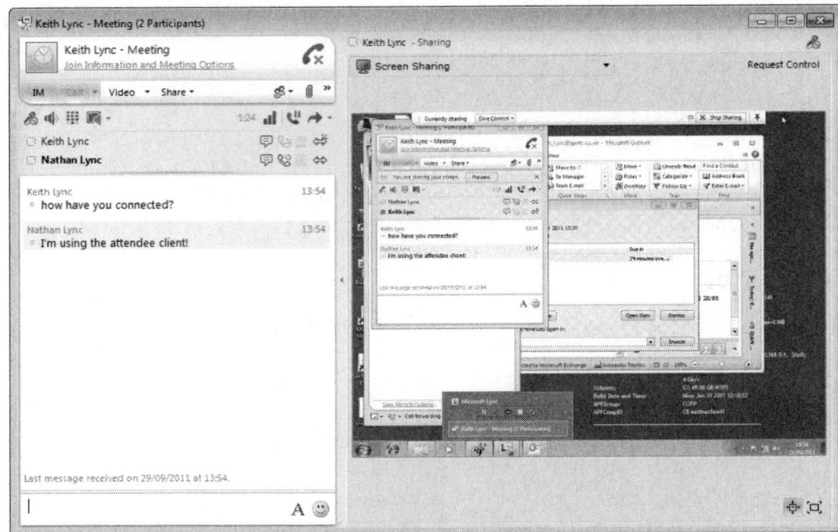

FIGURE 4.8
Lync 2010 Attendee client

This client replaces the LiveMeeting client, which was required for previous versions. Like the LiveMeeting client, the Attendee client is free to use and can be downloaded from the Microsoft website or offered to the user as part of the simplified meeting-join process. Unlike the LiveMeeting client, it cannot be installed on a machine that already has the Lync client installed; however, this shouldn't be an issue, because the Lync client provides the same functionality as the Attendee client.

Two client installers are available. The first, Admin Level Install, is designed for administrators to install on client machines. This installer can be installed using tools such as System Center Configuration Manager; once installed, it is available to all users of the machine. Both of these installers are restricted to the Windows operating system and are supported on 32- or 64-bit platforms.

As part of installing the application, an exception is added to the Windows Firewall. This is an inbound rule, labeled as Microsoft Lync 2010 Attendee, with the following settings:

- Profiles: Domain, Private and Public
- Restrictions: None
- Program: `C:\Program Files (x86)\Microsoft Lync Attendee\AttendeeCommunicator.exe`
- Action: Allow

If you are using a different client firewall, these restrictions will need to be manually created, and they can cause functions to fail if the firewalls block traffic.

The second installer is called the User Level Install. It is designed for nonprivileged users and allows them to install the application for their own use and, in turn, participate in Lync Online Meetings with access to all meeting features.

You don't need administrative rights to install the application, and it is installed only for the user who initiates the installation. The only other difference in the installation is that the firewall exceptions are not created when the client is installed. When the application is first run, the user is prompted with an access request to create the firewall rules (see Figure 4.9). If they decline this or do not have permissions to create the rules, they may not be able to use all features of the online meeting.

FIGURE 4.9 The user prompt for firewall exceptions

By default, the Simplified Join Process will only start the Attendee client if it is already installed on the client machine. You can change this behavior and provide users with the option to either download and install the User Install version or use the Web App. You can do this through the Control Panel (Security ➢ Web Service) or through PowerShell using the following command:

```
Set-CsWebServiceConfiguration -ShowDownloadCommunicatorAttendeeLink $true
```

Once this is enabled, the user has the option to download and install the client from the Meeting Join page, along with the option to use the Web App.

The final item you need to look at is the ability to use Microsoft Communicator 2007 or 2007 R2 to participate in Lync Conference; this is useful for migration scenarios where users are still using the older client or just for allowing external participants to use this. There are some limitations in terms of what is supported:

- Instant messaging
- Voice and video
- Share, View, and Control Desktop or Application (Communicator 2007 R2 only)

This can be configured through the Control Panel (Security ➢ Web Service) or by using PowerShell:

```
Set-CsWebServiceConfiguration -ShowJoinUsingLegacyClientLink $true
```

In addition, using the conferencing lobby is not supported when you are using this client. For people within the organization, this is performed by default; but for external participants, the meeting settings need to be changed on a meeting by meeting basis. Using the Meeting Options, select "Customize access and presenters for this meeting" and set Access to "Everyone including people outside my company."

Lync 2010 Web App

The Lync 2010 Web App allows users who do not have the Lync Attendee client or the Lync client installed to join Online Meetings. The Web App has less functionality than the other available clients but it is sufficient for the majority of scenarios. The Web App is a Silverlight application and can be used on Windows and also with Apple Mac OS X. The only prerequisite is that Silverlight 4 is installed on the client machine.

The Web App allows users to participate in instant message conversations and download files, and it provides access to shared items and polls. Users with Windows can also share their desktop; this requires the installation of an Active X control in a similar way to CWA R2. There is no built-in voice or video, but users can participate in the voice aspect by either using the Dial-In Conferencing functionality or by entering their phone number into the Web App and having Lync call them.

As you can see in Figure 4.10, the Web App has a similar look and feel to the other Lync clients and to Office 2010 applications, providing users with a familiar environment to use. Unlike OCS 2007 R2, Lync Server 2010 does need to have a dedicated role installed on a dedicated server; Web App is provided as part of the Lync 2010 web services, which is installed on the front-end servers. Including this as part of the web services simplifies the deployment and reduces the costs of deployment.

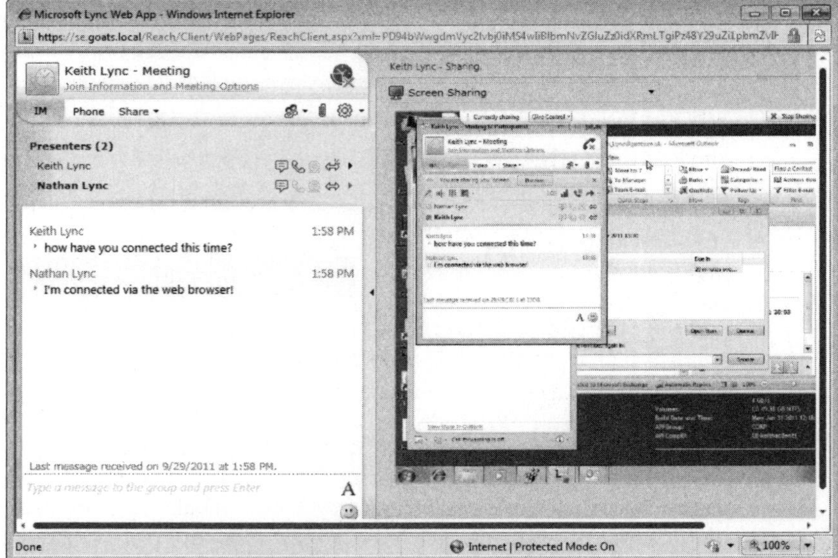

FIGURE 4.10 Lync 2010 Web App

Client Firewalls and Desktop Sharing

For the most part, client firewalls do not cause problems with the Lync Web App because it uses standard web technologies. However, nonstandard ports are used when a participant using the Web App wants to share their desktop. Desktop sharing requires an Active X control to be installed. When this plug-in is first used, the user will be prompted to create firewall exceptions and will have a choice of profiles on which to create the exceptions; they can be domain, private, or public.

For each profile that is selected, two rules will be created. They are identical apart from the protocol; one is for TCP and the other is UDP. A sample rule would consist of the following:

- Name: `communicatorwebappplugin.exe`
- Action: Allow
- Program: `C:\users\`*`Username`*`\appdata\local\microsoft\lyncwebapp\communicatorwebappplugin.exe`

If the user who installed the ActiveX does not have permission to modify the Windows Firewall rules, or if a different client firewall is used, desktop sharing will fail. To overcome this, the firewall entry will need to be created manually.

Legacy Clients

Microsoft Lync Server 2010 supports the use of three legacy clients:

- Office Communicator 2007
- Office Communicator 2007 R2
- Communicator for Mac 2011

Communicator 2007 and 2007 R2

Communicator 2007 and 2007 R2 support is provided to allow a managed migration to Lync 2010. This allows users to be migrated to Lync without requiring the client to be upgraded at the same time.

Although the clients can be used on Lync 2010, users cannot take full advantage of Lync 2010 features until their clients have been upgraded to Lync 2010. Users of the OCS 2007 R2 client will be able to utilize instant messaging, presence, voice, and video. Users of the OCS 2007 client will be able to use the same functionality, as well as the voice features added to OCS 2007 R2 or Lync. These include Call Park, Team Call, and some Response Groups functionality.

The OCS 2007 client can't use features such as desktop sharing, because this functionality was not supported in Office Communications Server 2007. In order for these clients to be used, the latest hotfixes need to be applied. They add the necessary functionality to allow the clients to work within a Lync 2010 environment.

These clients also cannot participate in DNS load balancing, because they do not understand the multiple options returned from the *A* record lookup, which is performed on the pool FQDN. Therefore, they will always use the first option returned; if this server is offline, they will not be able to log in.

Communicator for Mac 2011

Communicator for Mac 2011, illustrated in Figure 4.11, was introduced as a fully featured client for the Apple Mac platform for OCS 2007 R2; this replaces the MSN Messenger client used previously. This client continues to work with Lync 2010 but with the same limitations as Communicator 2007 R2.

FIGURE 4.11 Communicator for Mac 2011

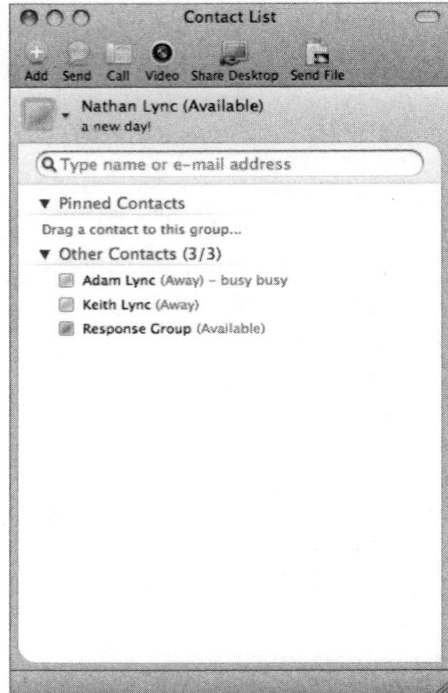

The Bottom Line

Understand the usage scenarios for each client. Each of the Lync clients is designed to be used for specific usage scenarios; for example, the Lync Attendee client allows external users to fully interact with an online meeting.

Master It You have been engaged by a marketing company to design and deploy Microsoft Lync; the company has 500 employees of which 100 use an Apple Mac computer. All users need to be able to use Lync, and no users can be left out.

Manage client configuration policies. In order to prevent users from using certain features, enable more niche features, and change a feature's behavior, client policies can be created. These policies can be configured globally, on a per-site basis, or on a per-user basis.

Master It Users often select Help in Lync and go to the Microsoft-hosted help pages. Your boss has asked you if they can be redirected to custom, internal help pages, so that they can provide more detailed and, in some instances, simplified information.

Configure prerequisites for IP phones. Lync IP phones are designed to be as simple as possible to deploy and receive all of their configuration settings automatically. In order for this to occur, a number of items need to be configured, such as network configuration and DHCP.

Master It You have deployed Lync IP phones, but you are unable to log in to the phones when using extension and PIN authentication; however, logging in using USB tethering works as expected.

Part 2

Getting Lync Up and Running

Chapter 5

Planning Your Deployment

You're probably eager to start implementing Lync Server 2010 in your network and you want to dive in right away.

Stop! Take a step back, breathe deeply, and think about what you want to achieve. Is this a throwaway lab deployment (perhaps virtualized?) utilized just to see what the management interface is like and what changes have been made since Office Communications Server (OCS) 2007 R2? Is this a pilot deployment in a production environment that will be removed once the decision to go ahead with full deployment is made? (Of course, everyone knows the pilot is never thrown away; it's just built on, right?)

The easiest (and best) way to deploy a solid system is to take the time to plan properly. By all means, jump right into a throwaway system deployment; but for any type of test or production system, proper planning will almost always save time in the long run. Even though many of us want to be "doing stuff" such as installing, troubleshooting, and so on, the best deployments are the ones where the appropriate amount of time was spent in the planning phase.

Also remember, having a separate test environment will justify its cost in the long term and it will allow you to catch patches or changes that could inadvertently bring down the system.

In this chapter, you will learn to:

- Use the planning tools available
- Determine when virtualization is appropriate
- Understand the prerequisites

Capturing the Requirements

You would never build a house by starting at the builder's yard, buying some bricks and mortar, and taking them back to a field. The same is true for a deployment. To ensure that you are not repeating work, it is extremely important to plan ahead. For example, if you configure and deploy Lync Server 2010 and later decide to change or add SIP domains, you will have to revisit every pool server and every request certificate again (a significant waste of time, especially if you have a manual certificate requisition process).

In the same sense, there are two ways to approach any project:

- Define the end goal and then determine how to get there.
- Define the current state and then determine what you want.

Understanding What Is Wanted

The preferred approach is to know the end goal first; then you can work out the best route to get there (considering time, cost, or function), rather than building on what is already in place and trying to "morph" something into something else.

Typically, the result ends up being some sort of migration or coexistence state. The longer that coexistence is in place, the longer (and more complicated) a project will be. By planning toward the end goal, you can reduce the time of coexistence and therefore reduce the risk.

Broadly, high-level needs can be divided into four areas:

- Core (instant messaging and presence, peer-to-peer audio/video, internal conferencing)
- Remote access (and/or federation)
- Telephony integration
- High availability

Once you've established (or confirmed) these four key areas, you can begin to get an idea of the infrastructure required. For example:

- It's obvious, but it still needs to be stated: you need at least one pool.
- Remote access means you'll need at least one Edge server.
- Telephony integration means you'll need Mediation servers (possibly colocated) and possibly gateways, or Direct SIP support.
- High availability requires Enterprise pool(s) and hardware load balancers.

Now the infrastructure design is taking shape. As you go further into the discovery process, you'll consider things such as the number of users to determine how many servers (and potentially pools) are needed, and the location of users to determine how many pools and where they will be located.

Once you have determined the functional requirements, you can build the detailed design. For example, if you have a peak requiring 600 concurrent telephony calls through the public switched telephone network (PSTN), this will translate into a requirement of two Mediation servers (plus another for high availability). However, to get to this level of detail requires a lot of investigation and discovery, and it means the organization must already be capturing that type of information from the current telephony system via Call Data Records (CDRs) and it must be able to report the information. Bear in mind that many PBX systems are incompatible with others, resulting in a lot of work to consolidate data across different PBX vendors. Some companies provide consolidation software for reporting purposes on CDRs; however, the software is expensive so it probably won't be used for a migration unless it is already in place.

Understanding What Is Currently in Place

Once the endgame is established, it's important to take a step back and establish what you have already. In some cases, you may be further along than you expect. For customers who have already deployed OCS 2007 R2, you may not need to run the "domain prep" stage, which can save a lot of time when there is a long lead time for change requests to the production environment.

When deploying Lync Server 2010, you will typically be coming from one of the following scenarios:

- Greenfield (a deployment to a company that has never had an instant messaging product in use)
- OCS 2007/OCS 2007 R2
- LCS 2005 (or an earlier Microsoft instant messaging product)
- Other non-Microsoft instant messaging product

The *greenfield* scenario is the easiest and most straightforward of the options because you start with a clean slate and don't need to plan for migration or coexistence.

Migrating from OCS 2007 or OCS 2007 R2 to Lync Server 2010 is the only migration path supported by Microsoft. For details, see Chapter 7, "Upgrades and Migrations."

Migrating from non-OCS and non-Microsoft instant messaging products are similar processes. Because no (current) toolsets are available to simplify the process, dealing with these migrations requires extremely detailed planning to handle the user-experience aspects (for example, are buddy lists migrated or are users expected to re-create them?).

A nonsupported migration approach can be successful, but more likely it will involve problems that result in a nonoperative system or a system that appears to work initially but is hiding a more serious problem. Serious problems may not be obvious at first and may take some time to manifest. When those problems finally do arise, Microsoft may refuse to provide support to resolve them because an unsupported approach was used.

INTEROPERABILITY

Products, such as the XMPP gateway, are available that provide interoperability between Lync Server 2010 and other non-Microsoft instant message solutions. However, these products work in a *federation* scenario, whereby the two applications are federated and each is responsible for a separate SIP namespace; that is, a single domain cannot be shared between the applications.

Now that you have established where you want to go (the features required), as well as where you are (the current state), you can begin planning the more detailed aspects of the design and deployment.

Using the Capacity Planning Toolset

With the launch of OCS 2007, Microsoft provided a Planning Tool application, which guides the administrator to a suggested topology based on a number of questions. Typically, they are feature-driven, such as "Do you wish to use Enterprise Voice?"

From the resulting answers, the Planning Tool draws a recommended topology for each identified site, suggesting the types and quantities of hardware needed. In addition, it provides links to the specific planning and deployment tasks required to implement the suggested topology.

With the release of OCS 2007 R2, the Planning Tool was updated to take into account the new architecture and features provided in this updated version. In addition, a separate Edge

Planning Tool was released, specifically focusing on the Edge role and the complications involving the certificates and DNS and firewall entries required.

As expected, the Planning Tool has been updated again with the release of Lync Server 2010. In addition to supporting the updated topology of Lync, it now incorporates the Edge Planning Tool, so there is only a single tool to use.

DOWNLOADING THE PLANNING TOOL

You can find the Lync Server 2010 Planning Tool at `http://www.microsoft.com/downloads/`, along with versions of the tool for OCS 2007, OCS 2007 R2, and OCS 2007 R2 Edge. Each version of the Planning Tool is specific to the version of the product. As you have chosen a Mastering Lync book, you probably will not need to download previous versions of the tool; however if you are migrating from Live Communications Server 2003 or 2005, you will need to first migrate to a version of OCS.

In addition to the Planning Tool, Microsoft has provided the following additional tools to help you plan:

- Edge Server Reference Architecture Diagrams
- Stress and Performance Tool
- Capacity Calculator
- Bandwidth Calculator

With the exception of the Edge Server Reference Architecture Diagrams (simply a package of Visio diagrams), we will cover all of these tools in this chapter.

The Planning Tool will install and run on the following operating system versions:

- Windows 7, 32-bit edition
- Windows 7, 64-bit edition using WOW
- Windows Server 2008, 64-bit edition using WOW
- Windows Vista, 32-bit edition
- Windows Vista, 64-bit edition using WOW
- Windows XP SP3, 32-bit edition
- Windows XP SP2, 64-bit edition using WOW

Defining a Topology with the Planning Tool

Once downloaded and installed, the Planning Tool will be located in the Lync Server 2010 folder in the Programs menu. Starting the application will take you to the Welcome screen, where you will have two options: Get Started and Design Sites.

As you'll see, Design Sites is more efficient when you know what features you need to implement, but Get Started provides you a little more guidance so it is more helpful. If you follow the Get Started path, you will be prompted with the following questions:

- Would you like to host audio and video conferencing within your enterprise?
- Would you like to deploy dial-in conferencing within your enterprise?
- Do you want to locally host Web conferencing?
- Do you want to deploy Enterprise Voice?
- Do you want to deploy Exchange Unified Messaging?
- Would you like to deploy Call Admission Control?
- Do you want to deploy the Monitoring Server?
- Do you want to deploy the Archiving Server?
- Do you want to enable federation with other organizations or with public IM service providers?
  - Yes, I want to enable federation with other organizations.
  - Yes, I want to enable federation with Office Communications Server 2007 or Office Communications Server 2007 R2 users.
  - Yes, I want to enable federation public IM service providers.
- Is high availability of communications critical to you? If so, do you want to deploy standby servers for failover support?

Once you have answered these questions, you will be taken to the Central Sites page, as shown in Figure 5.1. If you choose the Design Sites button on the Welcome page, this is where you will be taken directly.

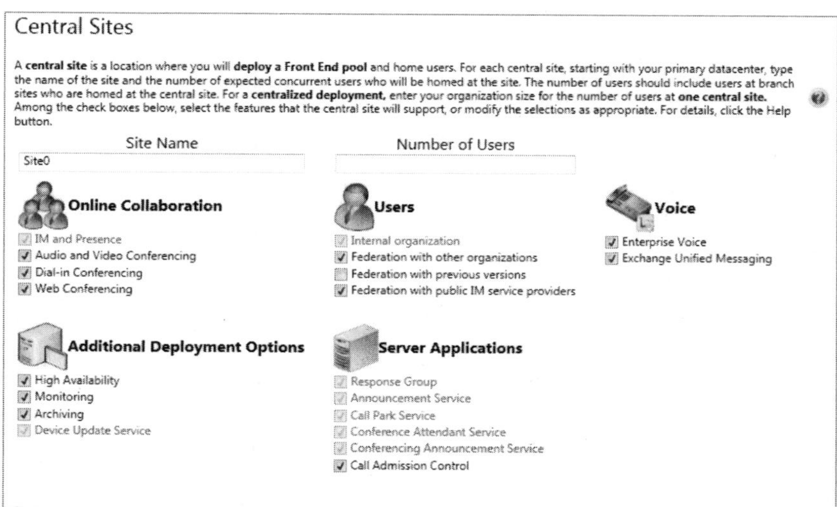

FIGURE 5.1
The Central Sites page

On this page, you can provide the Site Name along with the Number of Users located at this site. In addition, you can modify the answers to any of the previous questions, simply by checking (or unchecking) the boxes next to each option. If you use the Design Sites button, a default of Yes will be assumed for all questions except "federation with previous versions"; using this quick-start approach will save at least 10 clicks of the mouse to get to the same point.

If you follow the wizard and answer the prompted questions, the output will provide a great starting point for a design topology. Because the output file from the Planning Tool can be directly imported into the Topology Builder application, you will need to provide additional information by working through the prompts in the following sections.

A lot of the questions are simply "enable/disable this feature" questions; however, some values will already have default suggestions based on the planning profile used to capture the statistics for recommended hardware. Details of these values can be found in the help file provided with the Lync Server 2010 installation media.

Here are some of the questions you'll be asked in each category:

SIP Domain You'll need to provide a listing of all the SIP domains supported by the deployment. Entering an SIP domain will help generate more accurate output in later sections (such as with the DNS or certificate requirements).

Virtualization You'll be asked whether you want to use virtualized machines in the deployment; the default setting is No.

Conference Settings This section will provide the following prompts with their defaults:

Meeting Concurrency: **5%**.

Meeting Audio Distribution

What percentage of conferences are dial-in? **15%**

What percentage of conferences have no audio (IM-only)? **10%**

Media Mix for Web Conferences

What percentage of conferences are web conferences with audio plus some other collaboration modalities? **75%**

Video is enabled. **Selected**

Application Sharing is enabled. **Selected**

Data Collaboration is enabled. **Selected**

Voice Settings You'll be provided the following prompts:

Enabled users

What percentage of users at this site will be enabled for Enterprise Voice? **50%**

Enable All Users **Not Selected** (This item will force all Enterprise Voice user selection entries to 100%.)

External Phone Traffic

On average, how many calls to the public telephone network do you think that each user at this site will make during the busy hour? **4 calls per hour**

Media Bypass

What percentage of all phone calls will use media bypass? **65%**

Enable All Calls **Not Selected** (If all the locations will have local gateways, this should be selected.)

Types of Calls

What percentage of calls will be UC-PSTN calls? **60%**

Enable All Calls **Not Selected**

Response Groups

What percentage of users use Response Group? **0.15%**

Call Park Service

What percentage of calls will be parked? **0.05%**

Voice Infrastructure You'll be provided the following prompts:

Infrastructure

I plan to deploy gateway using a direct PSTN connection. **Default**

I plan to use SIP trunking.

I have an existing voice infrastructure with a PBX deployed.

PBX (The default is unavailable unless the previous option includes PBX.)

I have an Ip-PBX that is qualified with Microsoft Lync Server (Direct SIP).

I plan to deploy an IP-PBX that requires gateways.

I have already deployed a TDM-PBX.

Infrastructure Supportability (The default is unavailable unless the previous option includes PBX.)

My IP-PBX supports DNS local balancing.

My IP-PBX supports media bypass.

Network Line

Are you using a T1 line or an E1 line? **T1**

Type of Gateway

What type of gateway will you deploy? **4 ports**

Exchange Unified Messaging Settings You'll be provided the following prompts:

Enabled users

What percentage of users at this site will be enabled for Exchange Unified Messaging? **50%**

Enable All Users **Not Selected**

Exchange Unified Messaging Voicemail Traffic

On average, how many times per day do you think users will check their voicemail? **4 times per day**

External User Access You'll be provided the following prompts:

Do you want to enable external user access?

Yes, and I want to deploy Edge Servers in my perimeter network. **Default**

Yes, but I want to use Edge Servers deployed at another site.

No.

What percentage of users are external? **30%**

Enable high availability for my external users. **Selected**

Which type of load balancer do you want to use?

DNS load balancer using NAT. **Default**

Hardware load balancer using public IP addresses.

I want to deploy a Director at this site. **Selected**

Colocation Options You'll be asked how you want to deploy your Mediation servers: colocate them on your Front-End servers or deploy them as standalone Mediation servers. The default value is for Mediation servers to be co-located.

Branch Sites You'll be asked to define your branch sites, including the number of users, whether there is a resilient WAN connection, and whether Media Bypass is available.

Add Another Central Site? Finally, you'll be asked whether to add another central site. Selecting Yes at this point will repeat the entire question set for the next site; the default is No.

Global Topology

Once the site definition is completed, the Planning Tool will present the Global Topology page, as shown in Figure 5.2.

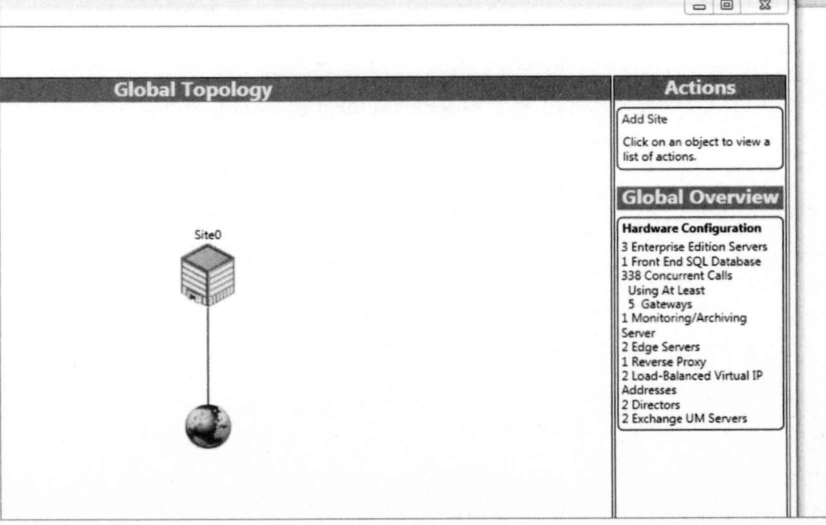

FIGURE 5.2 The Global Topology page

From this page, the Global Topology view provides the total hardware recommendations for all sites defined, based on your answers to the questions on the Central Sites page. The hardware includes not only servers, but also the number of hardware load-balanced IP addresses required, as well as the concurrent call expectation and required gateways. If a single site is selected, the actions list changes to show:

- Add Site
- Add Branch Site
- View Site
- Edit Site

If more than one site is added, the actions list adds a Delete Site item.

Only additional sites may be deleted; the first site created can never be deleted. If it was designed incorrectly, you will need to start fresh or go back and modify the answers.

- Add Site will take you back through the Planning Wizard questions and provide an additional site configuration once completed. You can define a maximum of eight sites.
- Add Branch Site will provide the opportunity to define additional branch sites associated with this site.
- Edit Site will take you back through the questions you already answered for this site and allow you to make changes.
- Selecting a site and then choosing View Site from the actions list, or simply double-clicking a site, will open the Site Topology page, as shown in Figure 5.3.

FIGURE 5.3 The Site Topology page

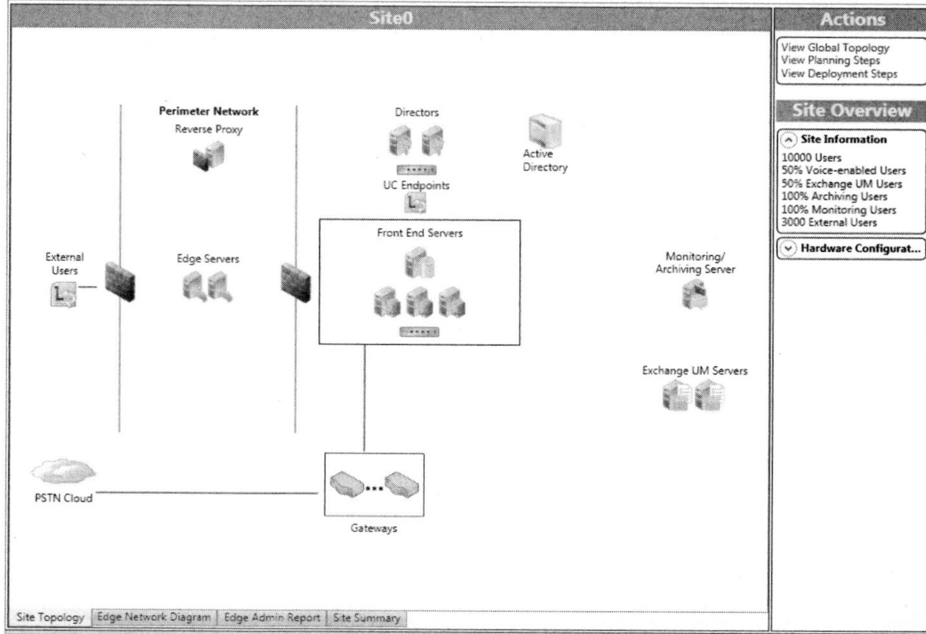

Site Topology

The Site Topology page displays the servers and devices required to support the site as defined in the Question and Answer Wizard. It also provides a breakdown of the specific configuration required (for non-Lync servers, this will be the generic rules).

On the Site Topology page, the actions list includes:

- View Global Topology
- View Planning Steps
- View Deployment Steps

When you select a specific server on the page, a View Server Information item will be added to the actions list. Clicking this action item (or double-clicking the server) will provide a response similar to Figure 5.4. The specific details provided will vary based on the actual server role selected. As you can see, the recommended hardware is displayed in addition to configuration information.

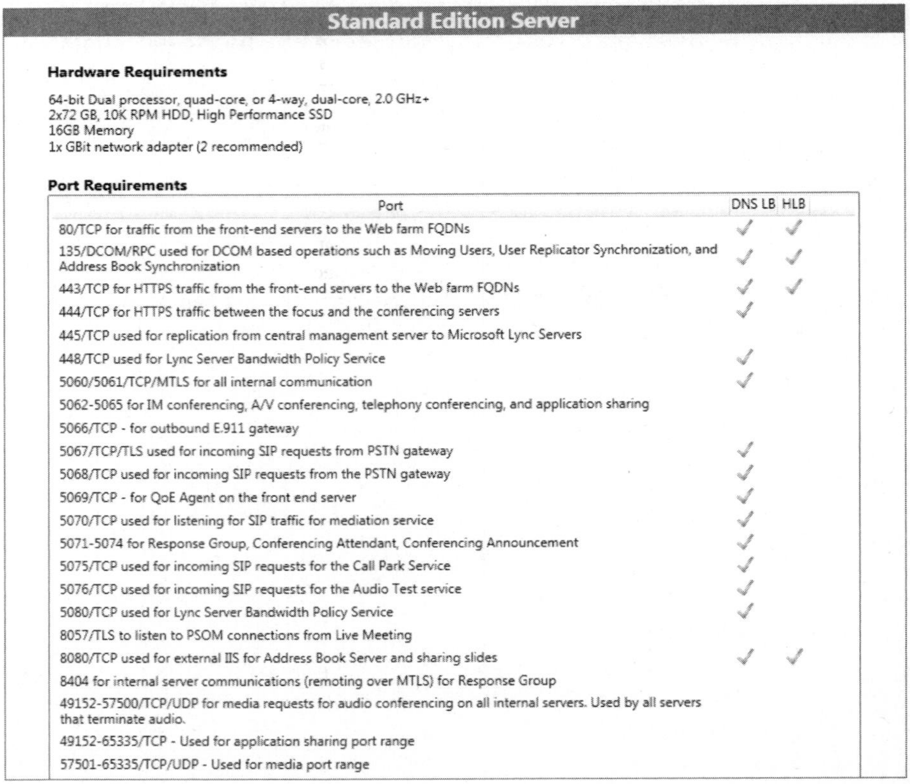

FIGURE 5.4
The Server Information page

Standard Edition Server

Hardware Requirements

64-bit Dual processor, quad-core, or 4-way, dual-core, 2.0 GHz+
2x72 GB, 10K RPM HDD, High Performance SSD
16GB Memory
1x GBit network adapter (2 recommended)

Port Requirements

Port	DNS LB	HLB
80/TCP for traffic from the front-end servers to the Web farm FQDNs	✓	✓
135/DCOM/RPC used for DCOM based operations such as Moving Users, User Replicator Synchronization, and Address Book Synchronization	✓	✓
443/TCP for HTTPS traffic from the front-end servers to the Web farm FQDNs	✓	✓
444/TCP for HTTPS traffic between the focus and the conferencing servers	✓	
445/TCP used for replication from central management server to Microsoft Lync Servers		
448/TCP used for Lync Server Bandwidth Policy Service	✓	
5060/5061/TCP/MTLS for all internal communication	✓	
5062-5065 for IM conferencing, A/V conferencing, telephony conferencing, and application sharing		
5066/TCP - for outbound E.911 gateway		
5067/TCP/TLS used for incoming SIP requests from PSTN gateway	✓	
5068/TCP used for incoming SIP requests from the PSTN gateway	✓	
5069/TCP - for QoE Agent on the front end server	✓	
5070/TCP used for listening for SIP traffic for mediation service	✓	
5071-5074 for Response Group, Conferencing Attendant, Conferencing Announcement	✓	
5075/TCP used for incoming SIP requests for the Call Park Service	✓	
5076/TCP used for incoming SIP requests for the Audio Test service	✓	
5080/TCP used for Lync Server Bandwidth Policy Service	✓	
8057/TLS to listen to PSOM connections from Live Meeting		
8080/TCP used for external IIS for Address Book Server and sharing slides	✓	✓
8404 for internal server communications (remoting over MTLS) for Response Group		
49152-57500/TCP/UDP for media requests for audio conferencing on all internal servers. Used by all servers that terminate audio.		
49152-65335/TCP - Used for application sharing port range		
57501-65335/TCP/UDP - Used for media port range		

To add a View Firewall Diagram item to the list, select a firewall on the Site Topology page. To display the new firewall rule, as shown in Figure 5.5, select it from the action list.

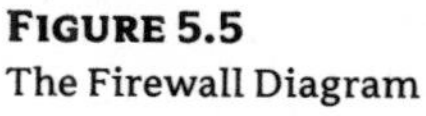

FIGURE 5.5
The Firewall Diagram

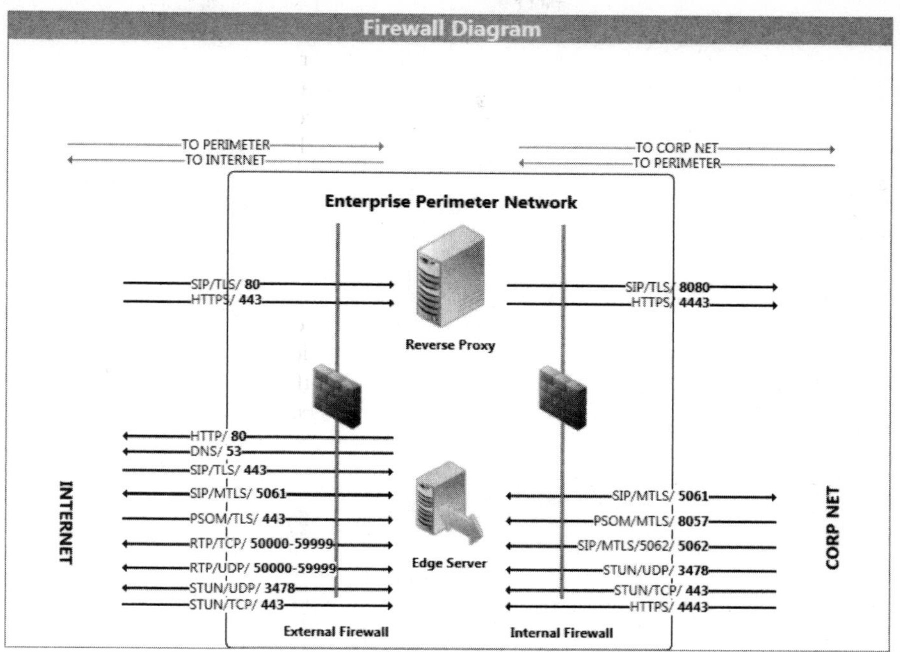

Like the Global Topology page, Site Topology displays the hardware requirements, but only for the site. A site information section describing some of the definition criteria is also included:

- Number of users
- Percentage of voice-enabled users
- Percentage of exchange UM users
- Percentage of archiving users
- Percentage of monitoring users
- Number of external users

EDGE NETWORK DIAGRAM

Selecting the Edge Network Diagram tab on the bottom will display the network diagram view of the edge infrastructure. This will include IP addresses as well as server names, as shown in Figure 5.6.

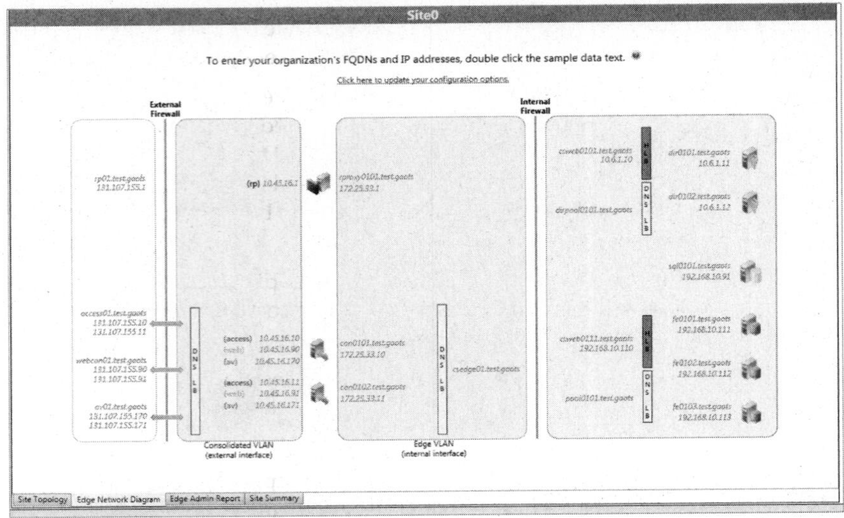

FIGURE 5.6
Viewing the Edge network diagram

At this point, you can populate the detail behind the topology. Double-clicking any of the server icons or the data (server names or IP addresses) will provide a pop-up (also shown in Figure 5.6) through which the server names and IP address information can be added.

Providing this information now allows the topology from the Planning Tool to be exported to a file and directly imported into the Topology Builder, which will save deployment time.

EDGE ADMIN REPORT

The Edge admin report has four sections providing information about the Edge infrastructure; Figure 5.7 shows the beginning of a Summary report.

FIGURE 5.7
The Summary tab of the Edge admin report

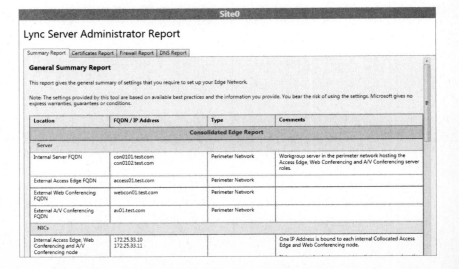

Site0

Lync Server Administrator Report

Summary Report | Certificates Report | Firewall Report | DNS Report

General Summary Report

This report gives the general summary of settings that you require to set up your Edge Network.

Note: The settings provided by this tool are based on available best practices and the information you provide. You bear the risk of using the settings. Microsoft gives no express warranties, guarantees or conditions.

Location	FQDN / IP Address	Type	Comments
Consolidated Edge Report			
Server			
Internal Server FQDN	con0101.test.com con0102.test.com	Perimeter Network	Workgroup server in the perimeter network hosting the Access Edge, Web Conferencing and A/V Conferencing server roles.
External Access Edge FQDN	access01.test.com	Perimeter Network	
External Web Conferencing FQDN	webcon01.test.com	Perimeter Network	
External A/V Conferencing FQDN	av01.test.com	Perimeter Network	
NICs			
Internal Access Edge, Web Conferencing and A/V Conferencing node	172.25.33.10 172.25.33.11		One IP Address is bound to each internal Collocated Access Edge and Web Conferencing node.

Summary Report This report provides the information such as server role, FQDN, IP address, and specific guidance where required (such as static route requirements).

Certificates Report The Certificates report provides the detailed certificate requirements for each of the roles involved with the edge infrastructure (Edge, Reverse Proxy, as well as the Next Hop Pool). This one is very useful for the Reverse Proxy certificate, because the Installation Wizard will generate the Edge and Next Hop certificates. Also included on this report is whether the certificates are required to be internal or public and which specific Enhanced Key Usages are required.

Firewall Report The Firewall report provides all the information required to generate the rules allowing the external configuration. This information is broken down by internal, external, and reverse proxy interfaces.

DNS Report The DNS report provides all the records required, both A and SRV, along with the actual FQDNs to be assigned and the resulting IP address mappings.

In large organizations, the Lync Server 2010 administrator typically is not also the DNS or firewall administrator, so each of these reports can be extremely useful when configuration information needs to be provided to another team.

Site Summary

This page, illustrated in Figure 5.8, provides the list of enabled features as well as the capacity details. A section on topology considerations, detailing how the Planning Tool deals with large numbers of users and splits these across multiple pools, is also provided. In some cases, it may make more sense to adjust the number of servers based on the information here.

FIGURE 5.8
A site summary

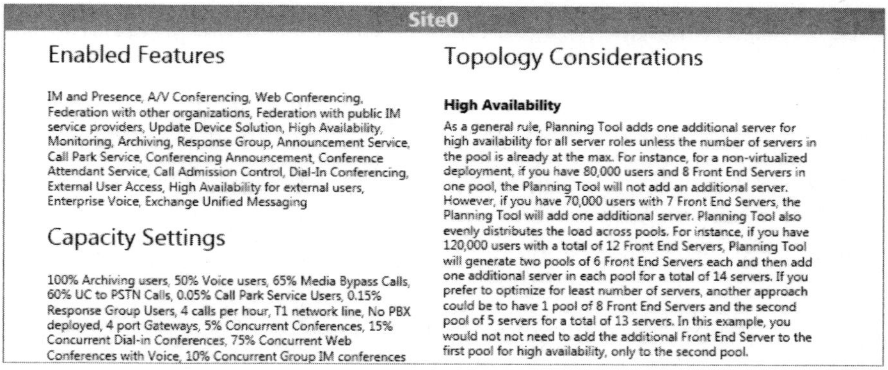

Exporting the Topology

Once the topology has been identified in the Planning Tool, you have several methods to extract that information:

- Export to Visio
- Export to Excel
- Export to Topology Builder

Exporting to Visio

Selecting the Export to Visio option (via the icon or the File menu) provides a prompt for saving the file as a Visio drawing.

The Visio file opens to show the following worksheets as a minimum:

- Global Topology
- Site0
- Site0 Edge Network Diagram

Each additional site (and if defined, associated Edge network diagram) will also be represented on individual worksheets.

These aids are great for inclusion in any design documentation being organized and gathered.

Exporting to Excel

Selecting the Export to Excel option (via the icon or the File menu) provides a prompt for saving the file as an XML 2003 spreadsheet.

By default, opening an XML file will launch Internet Explorer to display the content; however, if you launch Excel and then load the file, Excel opens to show the following worksheets as a minimum:

Summary This worksheet provides a summary of sites and servers hardware required, as well as a per-site breakdown of the features and capacity provided.

Hardware Profile This worksheet provides a summary hardware count and specifications, as well as a detailed breakdown per site and role.

Port Requirements This worksheet summarizes the port requirements per role and provides a list of which ports require hardware load balancing and which can use DNS load balancing.

Virtual Machine Profile If the Use Virtual Machines question was answered positively, this worksheet provides a breakdown of them. It provides the count per site required of each role.

As with the Export to Visio option, this information is ideal for inclusion in any design documentation.

Exporting to Topology Builder

Selecting Export to Topology Builder (again via the icon or the File menu) provides a prompt for saving the file as a Topology Builder document (TBXML). A warning will pop up to notify you if the Planning Tool has not been updated with server names, FQDNs, and IP addresses. The benefits of exporting to a Topology Builder file are negated completely if the data is incomplete.

You'll see more details on the Topology Builder later in this chapter.

Real World Scenario

USING THE PLANNING TOOL OUTPUT IN YOUR DESIGN

As you've seen up to this point, the Planning Tool provides an extremely quick way to determine your design requirements. However, there's no such thing as a free lunch. The output should *not* be used as the definitive design. It should instead be used as a starting point. Because the scenarios are rule-based, they do not (and cannot) deal with small variations in the requirements.

For example, using all the default settings, a single Front-End server (without high availability enabled) will support 8,542 users. If you change the number of users to 8,543, the Planning Tool will indicate that two Front-End servers are required. A third Front-End server is not required until you reach 19,704 users.

According to the help file, a single Front-End server can support up to 10,000 users, and two Front-Ends can support up to 20,000 users.

For most of the customers we work with, we round the number of users to the nearest thousand. We typically start with the Planning Tool output and adjust as needed using the information from the help file and planning documentation.

The Planning Tool does have some inconsistencies within it. For example, it is possible to disable high availability for the pool but enable it for the Edge environment. However, doing so would cause the internal environment to become a single point of failure, and it would affect the external environment too.

Note that the help file and planning documentation are updated more frequently than the Planning Tool; therefore, this documentation is more likely to incorporate user feedback than the Planning Tool.

The Stress and Performance Tool

Of course, the only true way to confirm whether your design meets the defined performance requirements is to stress-test it using the Stress and Performance Tool, which can be downloaded from:

```
http://www.microsoft.com/downloads/en/details.aspx?FamilyID=94b5f191-6d80-4dec-94c2-fca57995f8b7
```

The Stress and Performance Tool can be used to simulate load for the following modalities:

- Instant messaging and presence
- Audio conferencing
- Desktop sharing
- Peer to peer audio (including PSTN)
- Web client conferencing
- Response groups
- Address book download and address book query
- Distribution group expansion
- Emergency calling and location profiles.

The Stress and Performance Tool can support multiple pools and federation. It does not support web Lync 2010 Group Chat or video (either peer to peer or conferencing).

When you deviate from the recommended hardware specifications or usage model, you should carry out performance testing to ensure that the planned design is capable of handling the expected load. This is the only way to validate a deployment prior to deploying in production with live users.

The toolset contains a number of applications to carry out the testing, including:

`Stressconfig.exe` Used to generate user accounts and contacts information used during the testing; these will be created within Active Directory.

`Userprofilegenerator.exe` Provides the wizard to build the input criteria for the tests.

`Lyncperftool.exe` The Client Simulation Tool, which will consume the data created by the other two tools and carry out the testing.

There are also a number of associated files:

`Default.tmx`

`Maxuserports.reg`

Example scripts

Stress and Performance Tool Prerequisites

The `lyncperftool.exe` tool is capable of simulating the load of 2,500 users for every machine matching the following hardware:

- 8GB RAM
- Two dual-core CPUs

In addition, `lyncperftool.exe` requires Windows Server 2008 (64-bit) or Windows Server 2003 R2 (64-bit) with the following software installed:

- Microsoft .NET Framework 3.5 SP1
- Desktop Experience (Windows Server 2008 only)
- Windows Media Format 9.5 SDK (Windows Server 2003 R2 only)
- Microsoft Visual C++ 2008 redistributable package (x64)

The following criteria must also be met:

- The admin running it must be logged on using an account that is a member of the Domain Admins group.
- The "Password must meet complexity requirements" option must be disabled for Domain Policy. (The passwords created must match the user account name for the test accounts).
- `Lyncperftool.exe` cannot be run on a server with Lync Server installed.
- PowerShell V2 must be installed on the server running `stressconfig.exe`.
- `stressconfig.exe` must be run on the Front-End server where the user accounts will reside (Standard Edition or Enterprise Edition).

- Each test account must have a unique phone number.
- The server page file must be system-managed or at least 1.5 times the size of RAM.
- Windows Server 2008 must have Active Directory tools installed.
- Windows Server 2003 R2 must have the `maxuserport.reg` file imported into the Registry to enable more than 5,000 TCP connections to be created.
- The `CapacityPlanningTool.msi` file must be executed on each server being used to simulate clients.
- The Lync server environment must be enabled for the scenarios being tested.

RUNNING THE LYNC STRESS AND PERFORMANCE TOOL

The Lync Stress and Performance Tool is not supported when run in a production Active Directory environment.

Because of the tool's requirements, and the tool's high-risk security requirements needed to access the accounts in Active Directory, this tool should be run only in test environments.

As a general best practice, any sort of performance testing should be carried out in a separate environment on hardware identical to that which will be used in production.

CREATING USERS

Because you'll be running the stress test in a test environment, you'll need to configure some users before you begin testing. To do that, you'll use the `stressconfig.exe` tool. When you run it, the first thing you'll see is the screen shown in Figure 5.9. The information you'll need to provide on each tab is outlined here. Upon first load, the fields will be grayed out and you'll need to load a configuration file, either the sample or a newly created one.

FIGURE 5.9
`StressConfig.exe`

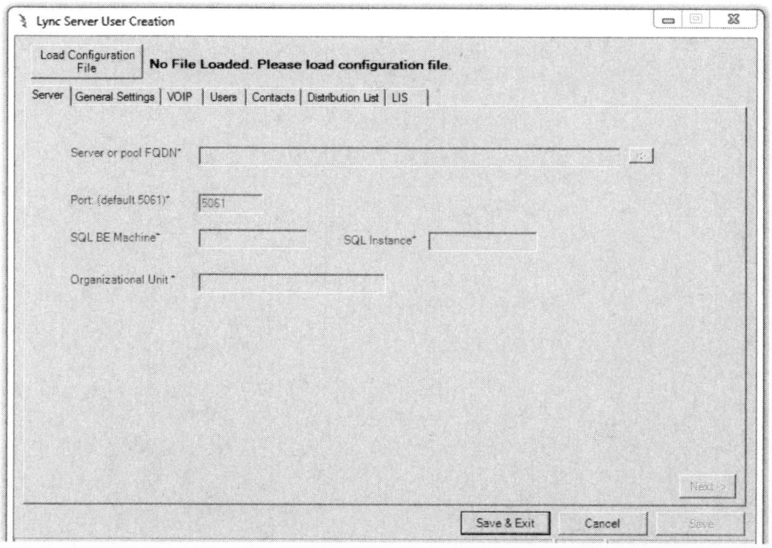

Server Here you'll provide the details of the pool to be stress tested entering the following information:

- Server or pool FQDN
- Port (default 5061): The port number for SIP traffic
- SQL BE Machine: The SQL Server FQDN
- SQL Instance: The SQL instance name
- Organizational Unit: The OU to store users

General Settings Here you'll provide the following information to generate the users:

- Prefix for Username: All usernames will begin with this prefix.
- Start Number for Username: Used to uniquely identify users
- Number of Users
- SIP Domain for Users' URI
- User account domain
- Average number of contacts per user
- Percent of contacts in the same pool
- Average number of groups per user
- Max number of contacts per user
- Percent of contact out of enterprise (federated)
- Max number of groups per user

VOIP Here you'll enter the area code; all numbers are generated using the U.S. numbering format.

Users Once you've entered all the user information, click the Create Users button to run the tool and create all the users as defined.

Contacts Here you'll populate the user's contacts lists by providing the following information (this default information is generated from the previous screens' inputs):

- EntID (This must be unique.)
- FQDN (This is the pool FQDN.)
- Userprefix
- SipDomain
- Startindex
- EndIndex
- CurrentPool (This will be checked for the pool where the contacts will be created/deleted.)

Then click either Create Contacts to create the contacts or Delete Contacts button to delete the contacts.

Distribution List Here you'll provide the following information to allow distribution list creation:

- Distribution List Number
- Distribution List Prefix
- Distribution List OU
- Distribution List Root Tenant

Then click either the Create Distribution Lists button to create the distribution lists or Delete Distribution Lists to delete them.

LIS Here you'll provide the following information to populate the Location Information Services (LIS) database (used to provide location information for emergency dialing):

- Street name
- Street name suffix
- Post directional
- City
- State
- ZIP code
- Country
- Company name
- Number of addresses
- Number of offices per address
- WAP count
- Subnet count
- Switch count
- Ports per switch

It will take some time to populate the users and contacts. In most cases, it is best to allow some time for replication between creating the users and creating the contacts. If replication is not yet completed, an error like the following will appear:

```
Enterprise '{0}' users in pool '{1}' not all accounted for. Users {2} - {3} only
contain {4} actual users.
```

where all the values in brackets ({}) will be replaced with the defined pool names and other values. If you get this error, simply rerun the user-creation stage after you've allowed more time for replication to complete.

Correctly defining the Location Information Services (LIS) content can be quite complicated (especially for locations outside of North America where different address definitions are used), so it's best to simply use the sample data given in the documentation and vary the following data based on the specific number of addresses and access points you want to define:

- Number of addresses
- Number of offices per address
- WAP count
- Subnet count
- Switch count
- Ports per switch

CONFIGURING PROFILES

After you've created the users, you can configure their user profiles. To do that, you'll run `userprofilegenerator.exe`, which displays the screen shown in Figure 5.10. (You'll need to display the profile generator on your own screen to see the details.) The information you'll provide on each tab is outlined next.

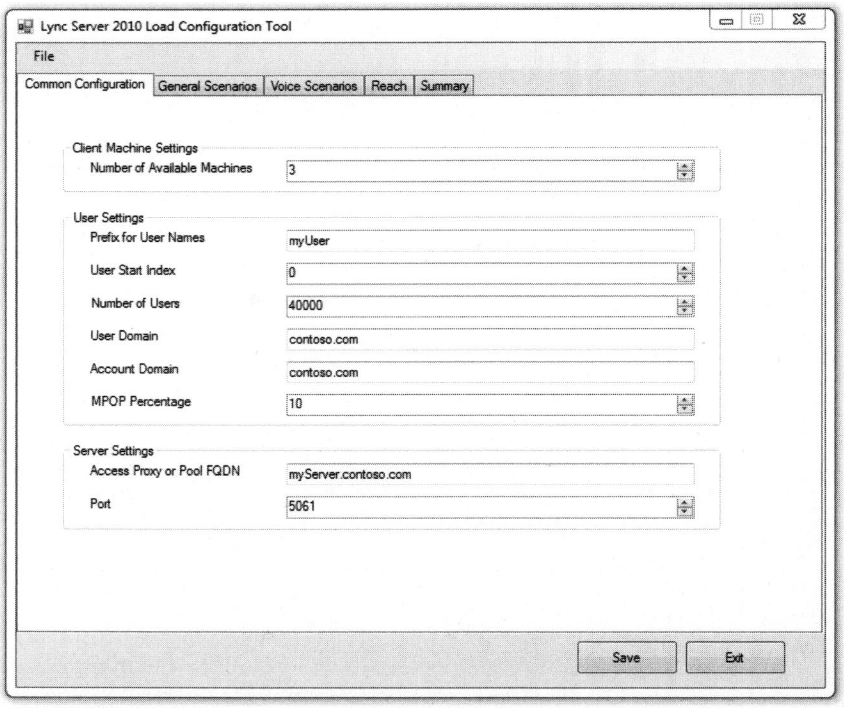

FIGURE 5.10
The screen displayed by `UserProfileGenerator.exe`

Common Configuration Here you'll provide the following information to enable the stress testing to be performed. (At startup, all the information is defaulted to `contoso.com`, so you will have to reenter it).

- Number of machines available (for running the stress testing)
- Prefix for usernames
- User Start Index
- Number of users
- User domain
- Account domain
- MPOP percentage (Multiple Points of Presence support—i.e., how many users will log in via multiple clients)
- Access proxy or pool FQDN
- Port

General Scenarios Here you'll provide the following information to determine the level of testing performed:

- IM load level
- Audio Conferencing load level
- Application Sharing load level
- Data Collaboration load level
- Distribution List Expansion load level
- Address Book Web Query load level
- Response Group Service load level
- Location Information Services load level

Each modality can be configured as followed:

- Disabled
- Low
- Medium
- High
- Custom

The Advanced button allows you to specifically configure each modality as required (detailed information on the default user profile is available in the Lync Server 2010 help file).

Voice Scenarios Here you'll provide the following information specifically detailing the voice modalities:

- VoIP load level
- UC/PSTN Gateway load level
- Conferencing Attendant load level
- Call Parking Service load level
- Mediation server and PSTN

As with the General Scenarios, these options can be configured as follows:

- Disabled
- Low
- Medium
- High
- Custom

The Advanced button allows you to specifically configure each modality, such as length of call, which location profile to use, etc.

Reach Here you'll provide the following information for remote and federated users:

- General Reach settings
- Application Sharing load level
- Data Collaboration load level
- IM load level

Again, as with the General Scenarios, these options can be configured as follows:

- Disabled
- Low
- Medium
- High
- Custom

The Advanced button allows you to specifically configure each modality, such as URLs and the like.

Summary This tab provides an overall summary of the data and allows you to generate custom user ranges.

By default, the system will allocate user ranges for each of the load tests to be performed (see Table 5.1). To allow the User Range column to be manually edited, check the Enable Custom User Range Generation checkbox.

TABLE 5.1: User Range Generation

NAME	LOAD LEVEL	USER RANGE
Distribution List Expansion	Low	0–9
Audio Conferencing	Medium	10–46
Application Sharing Sharer	Low	47–50
Application Sharing Viewer	Low	1–64
Data Collaboration	Medium	65–71
Instant Messaging	High	72–999

When you're ready, press the Generate Files button and indicate where the files should be placed. The test case files will be generated and stored in the specified folder. This folder needs to be copied to each of the client systems that will be executing the stress tests (this folder must be copied to the same folder in which the Stress Tools are installed).

Now that you've created the users and the profiles and have generated the client test cases, you can execute the `runclientx.bat` (where ***X*** is replaced by the client ID—for example, `runclient0.bat` for the first client) file on each of the client computers to begin the execution tests.

Be sure to enable performance counter capturing (using Performance Monitor or `perfmon.exe`) before starting the stress testing.

A number of command prompts will report the testing status (one prompt for each test), as shown in Figure 5.11.

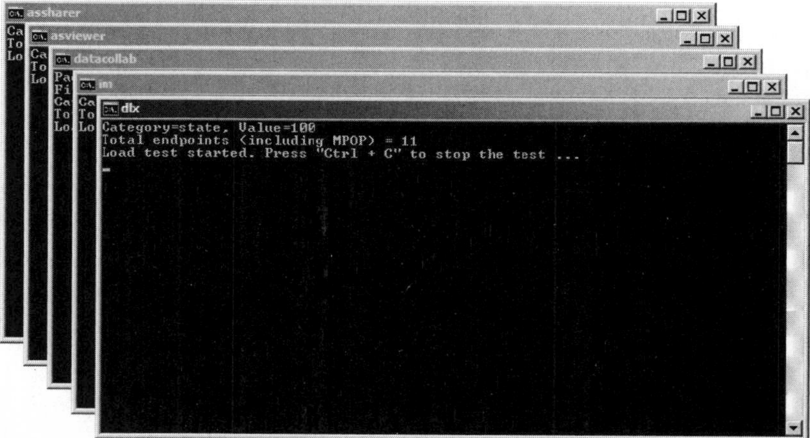

FIGURE 5.11
Client view of stress test execution

Interpreting the Results

Now that you've run the performance tests and the servers haven't turned into smoldering lumps of metal and plastic, what's next?

You'll need to analyze the performance during the testing. It's not enough to say the servers didn't crash, therefore, it must be fine. You need to determine if there was any impact, such as dropped connections or busy responses.

Experience indicates that success counters don't really add value in this scenario; the failure rates are where we can establish when the servers start to come under pressure.

The following counters provide the most information to determine if the pool(s) can cope with the load expected:

- Failed Logons
- 5*xx* Responses for SetPresence
- 6*xx* Responses for SetPresence
- 5*xx* Responses for GetPresence
- 6*xx* Responses for GetPresence
- ABS Full/Delta File Downloads Failed
- ABS WS Calls Failed
- Calls Failed
- Calls Declined
- Calls Received 5*xx* (separate counters for IM, VOIP, App Sharing)
- Calls Received 6*xx* (separate counters for IM, VOIP, App Sharing)
- Conference Schedule Failure
- Join Conference Failure

If these failure numbers are significant, then the load is probably beyond the bounds of the environment's capacity and further investigation is needed. Typically, the causes will be due to poor or inadequate disk or memory performance on the SQL server.

On the other hand, if the numbers are minimal, it is a good indication the servers are reaching their peak capacity, and any further load would put them over the top.

There are no specific guidelines for what values constitute "significant" or "minimal" numbers; they will vary dramatically based on the number of users and the types of customers. For example, a call center will require better consistency from GetPresence-type responses than from Join Conference Failure because the call-center capability, Response Groups, relies on the presence states of users to direct calls. Equally, a failure of one call in a 100-user company will have a larger impact than one failure in a 50,000-user company.

In an ideal world, you would run tests to confirm that the servers are capable of supporting the load expected and then go further to establish the maximum the design can support. By doing that, you will determine the design's capability for future expansion.

Capacity Calculator

The Capacity Calculator Tool provides a way to establish the specific requirements for a server based on a scenario, rather than based on the standard user profile as defined by Microsoft. This calculator can be downloaded from:

```
http://www.microsoft.com/downloads/en/details.aspx?FamilyID=6e8342a7-3238-4f37-
9f95-7b056525dc1a
```

This particular tool is aimed at people who have detailed knowledge of their environment. The answers they supply (things like average calls per user per hour, call duration, and so on) should be factual (or very close approximations) rather than simple guesses.

The calculator is capable of adjusting the server count based on the actual CPU clock speed and processor cycles. The sample server used is a dual-processor, quad-core 2.33 GHz system, resulting in 2,333 megacycles per core, and 18,664 megacycles per second total. If your server specifications differ from this, enter and calculate the appropriate values to provide a true reflection of your server's capability.

From Figure 5.12, you can see some of the configuration options as well as the output recommendations for a physical deployment. The output recommendations for a virtualized deployment are not shown here but are displayed beside the physical outputs in the tool.

FIGURE 5.12 The Capacity Planning Calculator

	Modality/Workload	Workload	Number of users	Front End CPU*	Virtual Machine CPU**
IM/P	Users enabled for Instant messaging and presence	100.0%	80000	80%	160%
	Average number of contacts in Contact list	80	NA		
Enterprise Voice	Users enabled for Enterprise Voice	50.0%	40000		
	Average number of UC-PSTN calls per user	4	NA		
	Percentage of calls that use media bypass	65.0%	NA		
	Percentage of voice users enabled for UC-PSTN calls	60.0%	24000	188%	376%
	Percentage of voice users enabled for UC-UC calls	40.0%	16000	22%	45%
Conferencing	Percentage of users in concurrent conferences	5.0%	4000		
	Percentage of conferences with group IM only (no voice)	10.0%	2200	4%	8%
	Percentage of users using dial-in conferencing	15.0%	600	75%	150%
	Percentage of conferences using voice	90.0%	3600	223%	446%
	Including video	☑	600	46%	92%
	Including application sharing	☑	1500	109%	218%
	Including web conferencing	☑	600	8%	15%
Voice Apps	Response Group Service	0.15%	120	9.78%	19.57%
	Call Park	0.02%	12	0.48%	0.96%
	Address Book Web Query	☑	80000	34%	68%

Recommendations	Physical			
	Servers*	Average CPU Load	Network in Mbps	Memory in GB
Total Front End Servers Required	8	73%	193	11
Edge Servers (based on 30% external)	2	40%	40	8
Directors	2	70%	10	4
Archiving/Call Detail Recording/Quality of Experience services	1	NA	NA	NA
Audio/Video Conferencing Servers required	4	67%	189	8
Back End Database Server Required (Pools Required)	1	NA	NA	NA

Items in orange are the configuration items and profile definitions to be changed based on your own expectations. They are listed here:

- Number of users
- Average number of contacts in Contact list
- Users enabled for Enterprise Voice
- Average number of UC-PSTN calls per user
- Percentage of calls that use media bypass
- Percentage of voice users enabled for UC-PSTN calls
- Percentage of voice users enabled for UC-UC calls
- Percentage of users in concurrent conferences
- Percentage of conferences with group IM only (no voice)
- Percentage of users using dial-in conferencing
- Percentage of conferences using voice (web conferences)
- Response Group Service
- Call Park
- Address Book web query

The values shown in the tool in yellow are the specific resource requirement breakdowns per modality. They are as follows:

- Workload
- Number of users
- Front-End CPU
- Virtual Machine CPU
- Network in Mbps
- Memory in GB
- Megacycles per server

Using megacycles per server rather than a specific CPU type and speed allows different server CPU specifications to be taken into account.

What is extremely useful about the Capacity Planning Calculator is its ability to break down per modality to view the impact on CPU and RAM simply by changing the usage profile.

As with any planning guide and calculator, you should perform a load test before deploying into production.

Bandwidth Calculator

A major piece of feedback that the Lync development team received from OCS deployments was that with the earlier version, admins were unable to determine the bandwidth requirements prior to installation, at which point it was typically too late to do anything. This inability posed a major problem because when there isn't enough bandwidth, users are impacted and other lines of business applications can be too. Call Admission Control (the subject of Chapter 14) helps provide a level of control on this; however, again it provides it after the fact.

The Bandwidth Calculator estimates the bandwidth prior to deploying and configuring Lync Server 2010, thereby allowing additional bandwidth to be purchased before rollout if necessary.

In order to calculate those estimates, the Bandwidth Calculator requires the following information:

- Number of sites
- Number of users per site
- Persona of the users (The persona can be thought of as the user profile. A separate worksheet allows the personas to be customized to indicate low/medium/high usage rates for each modality.)
- Usage model
- WAN connectivity and any restrictions placed on traffic
- Thresholds

Figure 5.13 shows a sample of some of the output generated by the Bandwidth Calculator.

FIGURE 5.13
Output from the Bandwidth Calculator

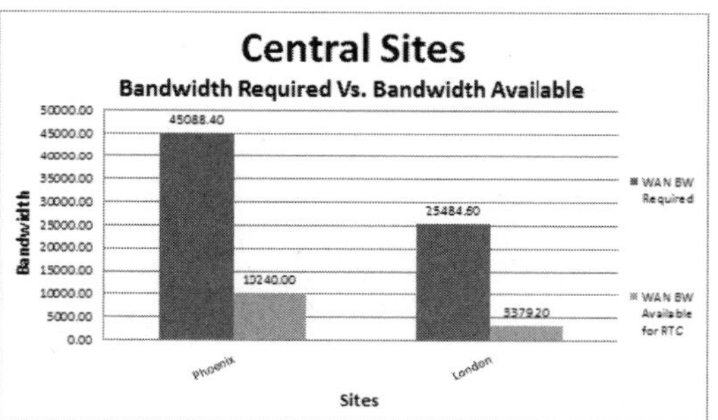

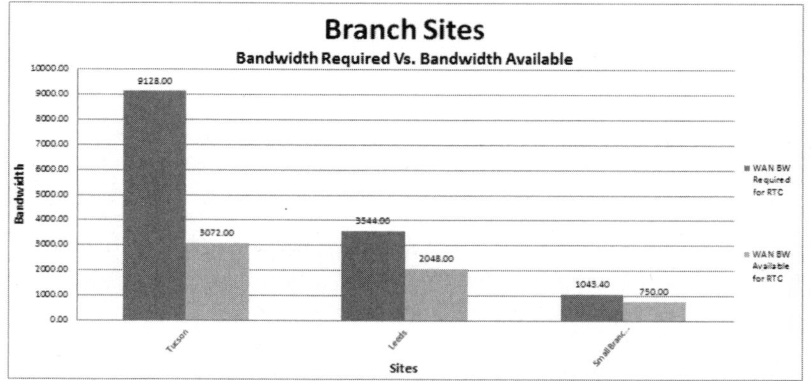

At least for the first few times you use it, you should follow the steps in the flowchart guide (located on the *Start Here* worksheet) to set up the input values (shown reduced to fit the page in Figure 5.14).

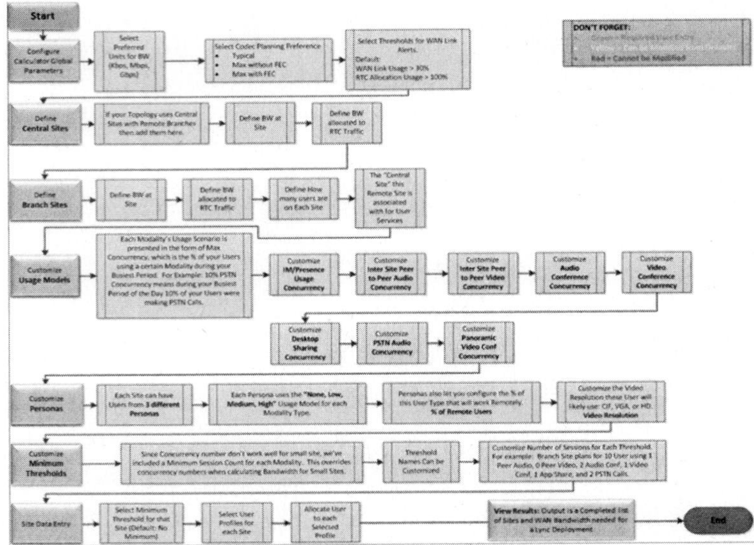

FIGURE 5.14
Bandwidth Calculator flowchart

Using Topology Builder

So far in this chapter, we've been working purely with planning tools. The Topology Builder is the first deployment tool from the Lync 2010 installation media that you will probably use. When you get to this stage, the planning is complete (unless, of course, this is a test or development environment). This stage is where you define the architecture for your deployment; it is also where the first set of automated checks are performed.

The Chicken or the Egg?

Once you have planned your topology, you need to run the Topology Builder, and once you've input the topology you need to publish it into the Central Management Store (CMS), a SQL database. However, the CMS must be in place prior to publishing, and you can't create the CMS until you have defined a SQL database in the topology.

Fortunately, there is a way get around this chicken-or-egg scenario. Run `SETUP.EXE` to go to the Deployment Wizard screen shown in Figure 5.15. On it you will find an item labeled Prepare First Standard Edition Server, which if selected will install the CMS portion into a SQL Express instance on the server it is run.

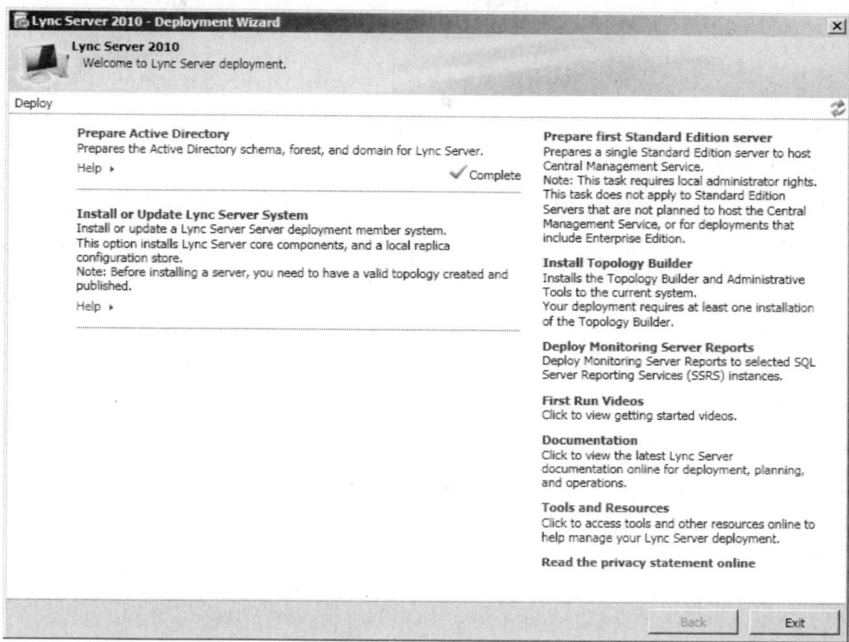

FIGURE 5.15
The Deployment Wizard includes the option Prepare First Standard Edition Server.

What about high availability in an Enterprise Edition deployment? Here you have two options. If the plan is to start with a pilot where you are deploying a Standard Edition server first, you could choose Prepare First Standard Edition Server. When it's time to move to production, define and publish the SQL Server and then move the CMS to it. As an alternative, you could use PowerShell to install and create the database, as the following cmdlet shows:

```
Install-CsDatabase -CentralManagementDatabase -SqlServerFqdn <FQDN of SQL Server>
-SqlInstanceName <named instance> -DatabasePaths <logfile path>,<database file
path> -Report <path to report file>
```

Then, when you want to define the topology, the location is already defined and the database has already been created.

Using Topology Builder

It might make more sense to include this information on the Topology Builder in the planning chapter; however, the Topology Builder is included here because its additional functionality makes it an appropriate tool for planning.

Specifically, although Topology Builder is used to configure, the largest part of its job is to define, *check*, and publish the topology. This ability to check the topology offers a significant advantage over what was available in previous versions.

By verifying that the configuration and dependencies are in place *prior* to making any changes, you can achieve an additional, higher level of verification of your changes. For example, Topology Builder will not let you delete a database or share a file that is still being used. (Of course, it can't stop someone from going to the server itself and deleting the database or share. However, even if someone did that, there would still be a record of what it should be.)

In addition to the checks carried out, after publishing, Topology Builder will provide a To Do list of actions to be carried out and on which servers they need to performed.

PUBLISHING MULTIPLE CHANGES WITH TOPOLOGY BUILDER

The To Do list is an extremely useful feature because it provides the next set of steps (rerun setup, request new certificates, etc.) required to complete any configuration changes.

One thing to note is that no records of the completed actions are kept. For example, if you make a change to the SIP addresses supported in the organization, there will be a reminder to request new certificates for each Front-End server (and possibly Directors and Edge servers, if they are in the environment). If you remove (or add) the Mediation Server role to a specific Front-End server before updating the certificates, the To Do list will report only the last change (the specific Front-End server) and the need to request new certificates may be lost.

Therefore, we recommend that you make all your changes in a single topology publishing step.

The Topology Builder comprises a number of wizards, one for each role. The following list shows the information captured by each wizard. In addition, where a wizard is dependent upon another role (for example, Enterprise pool requires SQL and a File Share), it is possible to launch the new role's wizard from within the running wizard; there is no need to predefine all the dependencies prior to running a wizard.

New Topology Here you'll provide the following information:

- Primary SIP domain
- Additional SIP domain(s)
- First site name
- First site description
- First site address — city
- First site address — state/province
- First site address — country/region code

Enterprise Pool Here you'll provide the following information:

- FQDN of pool
- FQDN of computer(s)
- Features — conferencing
- Features — dial-in
- Features — Conferencing Enterprise Voice

- Features — Call Admission Control
- Colocation — A/V conferencing
- Colocation — Mediation
- Associations — Archiving
- Associations — Monitoring
- Associations — Edge
- SQL
- File share
- Web services URL — override internal FQDN
- External base URL

Standard Pool Here you'll provide the following information:

- FQDN of pool/server
- Features — conferencing
- Features — dial-in
- Features — Conferencing Enterprise Voice
- Features — Call Admission Control
- Colocation — A/V conferencing
- Colocation — Mediation
- Associations — Archiving
- Associations — Monitoring
- Associations — Edge
- File share
- External base URL

File Share Here you'll provide the following information:

- File server FQDN
- File share

SQL Store Here you'll provide the following information:

- SQL Server FQDN
- Named instance (Name) or default instance

Archiving Here you'll provide the following information:

- ◆ FQDN
- ◆ SQL Server
- ◆ File share
- ◆ Associate pools
- ◆ Monitoring
- ◆ FQDN
- ◆ SQL Server
- ◆ Associate pools

Branch On this tab, you'll provide a name and description for the branch site, along with its address comprising city, state/province, and country/region code.

Director Here you'll provide the following information:

- ◆ Pool FQDN
- ◆ Multiple or single computer pool
- ◆ FQDN of computer(s)
- ◆ File share
- ◆ Web services URL — override internal FQDN
- ◆ External base URL

Edge Here you'll provide the following information:

- ◆ Pool FQDN
- ◆ Single FQDN & IP address
- ◆ Enable federation
- ◆ External IP address uses NAT
- ◆ External FQDNs & Ports — SIP Access
- ◆ External FQDNs & Ports — Web Conferencing
- ◆ External FQDNs & Ports — Audio/Video
- ◆ Multiple or single computer pool
- ◆ Internal — IP
- ◆ Internal — FQDN
- ◆ External IP — SIP access

- External IP — web conferencing
- External IP — A/V conferencing
- Next Hop pool

Mediation Here you'll provide the following information:

- Pool FQDN
- Multiple or single computer pool
- FQDN of computer(s)
- Next Hop pool
- Edge server
- PSTN gateways

AV Conference Pool Here you'll provide the following information:

- Pool FQDN
- Multiple or single computer pool

Associate Pools Here you'll provide the following information:

- Gateway
- FQDN or IP address
- Listening port
- TCP or TLS

Trusted Application Servers Here you'll provide the following information:

- Pool FQDN
- Multiple or single computer pool
- FQDN of computer(s)
- Next Hop pool

Survivable Branch Appliance Here you'll provide the following information:

- FQDN
- Front-End pool
- Edge pool
- Gateway FQDN or IP Address
- Listening port
- TCP or TLS

Topology Builder also includes the capability to import the OCS 2007 or OCS 2007 R2 environments via another wizard. Publication of this information is required to ensure that all the Lync Server 2010 servers are aware of and can communicate with any legacy servers.

Most of the data can be captured automatically; however, the Merge Legacy Wizard requires information regarding the legacy Edge servers, because in OCS environments the Edge configuration information is stored only on each Edge server. (Lync Server 2010 instead stores all the information for all the roles in the CMS and requires the CMS to be replicated to all servers.)

Once imported, Topology Builder defines the legacy environment as BackCompatSite; it may be viewed for information about server names and roles, but detailed information is not available in Topology Builder and it must still be managed using the legacy management toolset.

Installation Prerequisites

Once you have completed the planning stage, you are nearly ready to install Lync Server. Before you do, though, you'll need to take care of a few prerequisites for both the infrastructure and the operating system.

Recommended Hardware

The term *recommended hardware* is always a little confusing. Does it mean this is the minimum hardware needed or something else? In the past, it has tended to be a relatively high specification. If you are working for a small company, does this mean Lync Server 2010 is unsuitable for your needs? Can you use lower-spec hardware? Should you virtualize?

The recommended hardware values are based on the tested profiles used by Microsoft (available from the Lync Server 2010 help file) and feedback from the Beta release programs.

By using these capacity tools, it is possible to downsize the scalability of Lync Server 2010 for companies that do not meet the minimum size of 5,000 users and do not want to pay extra to meet the recommended hardware guidelines (especially when based on a usage profile that does not match their own).

Physical Hardware

The best way to determine your hardware needs is to consider the performance characteristics and profiles provided. The recommended hardware is the hardware that has provided the values used in the Microsoft-provided planning tools and guidance, based on the default user profile (which can be found in the Lync Server 2010 help file). If you deviate significantly from the defaults, you should consider more detailed planning.

Table 5.2 shows the recommended hardware for each role.

TABLE 5.2: Recommended Hardware

ROLE	CPU	MEMORY	DISK	NETWORK
Back-End database	64-bit dual processor, quad core 2.0Ghz or quad processor, dual core 2.0Ghz	32GB 16GB for archiving and Monitoring	72GB free disk space10,000 RPM (additional disks for databases)	2 NICs, 1Gbps
Director	64-bit quad core, 2.0Ghz or dual processor, dual core, 2.0Ghz	4GB	72GB free disk space, 10,000 RPM	2 NICs, 1Gbps
All other roles	64-bit dual processor, quad core 2.0Ghz or quad processor, dual core 2.0Ghz	16GB	72GB free disk space, 10,000 RPM	2 NICs, 1Gbps

A single pool will support up to 80,000 users with a maximum of 10 servers (using all modalities). However, this number includes some server capacity for high availability; a pool is capable of supporting all 80,000 users with a minimum of eight Front-End servers.

VIRTUALIZATION

Based on feedback (from the Lync Server 2010 Beta program, previous versions of OCS, and general computing trends), Lync Server 2010 supports virtualization of the server roles; however, support is limited to four CPUs in a virtual environment.

The following virtualization machine managers (also known as *hypervisors*) are supported at the time of writing:

- Windows Server 2008 R2 Hyper-V
- VMware ESX 4.0

See `http://go.microsoft.com/fwlink/?linkid=200511` for updated details of other hypervisors that may be supported.

A mix of virtual and physical servers in the same pool is not supported. For this purpose, Microsoft defines a pool as "two or more servers of the following roles—Front End, Director, Mediation, A/V Conferencing, and Edge."

You can, however, mix virtual and physical pools in the same enterprise deployment (for example, servers in one region could be virtual while servers in another region could be physical). Within the topology, they would be configured in separate pools (and most likely separate central sites).

The other exception to this rule is that having virtual Front-End servers with a physical SQL Server Back-End server is also a supported combination.

There is no requirement to host all types of server roles on the same physical server, such as all virtual Mediation servers on one physical node and all virtual Front-End servers on another. However, you should mix the types of roles deployed on physical nodes to reduce the single points of failure introduced by having all of one role on one physical node.

Quick/live migration is not supported and can introduce additional complexity to the client connectivity.

As a rough rule of thumb, the virtualization of a server role will reduce the capacity of the server by 50 percent. Table 5.3 summarizes the difference between physical and virtual capacity for each role.

TABLE 5.3: Virtual versus Physical Capacity

Server Role	Physical CPU	Physical Memory	Physical User Load	Virtual CPU	Virtual Memory	Virtual User Load
Enterprise Edition Front End (IM & P only)	8 core	12GB	20,000	4 core	10GB	12,500
Enterprise Edition Front End	8 core	12GB	10,000	4 core	11GB	5,000
Standard Edition (IM & P only)	8 core	16GB	25,000	4 core	10GB	12,500
Standard Edition Front End	8 core	12GB	5,000	4 core	16GB	2,500
Director	4 core	4GB	20,000	4 core	4GB	10,000
Monitoring/ Archiving	8 core	16GB	230,000	4 core	8GB	110,000
A/V Conferencing	8 core	16GB	20,000	4 core	11GB	10,000
Mediation	8 core	16GB	800 concurrent calls	4 core	10 GB	400 concurrent calls
Edge	8 core	16GB	15,000	4 core	8GB	7,500
SQL Server	8 core	32GB	80,000	4 core	16GB	40,000

At first glance, some of this table doesn't appear to be correct. For example, consider the load of a physical Front-End server:

Enterprise Edition Front End (IM&P) with 20,000 users

compared to a physical:

Standard Edition (IM&P) with 25,000 users

However, the difference is in the RAM. Regarding the physical versus virtual capacities of the Director role, the CPU and RAM are the same, but the user load is halved. This data is taken from the virtualization white paper available at this link:

```
http://www.microsoft.com/downloads/en/details.aspx?FamilyID=2905fd33-e29c-4709-
a012-e55ea8db63e4
```

In addition, when Front-End servers are virtualized, the maximum number of users in a single conference is halved from 250 (using physical servers) to 125 (using virtual). Using standalone A/V conferencing servers is recommended when you have at least 10,000 users in a physical environment, but the threshold is only 5,000 in a virtual.

There are many reasons to virtualize (green computing, costs reduction, etc.); however, there are also reasons not to virtualize. Don't assume that virtualization is the correct answer to every environment. The white paper is required reading for anyone planning to deploy a virtual environment—and anyone even considering it.

Software Prerequisites

In addition to the hardware requirements just discussed, a number of software prerequisites must be met before you can begin installation. Some of them are at the operating system or application level; others are at the component level.

Active Directory

Of course, before you can install Lync Server 2010, you need to update the Active Directory to support Lync.

The following Active Directory topologies are supported:

- Single forest with single domain
- Single forest with a single tree and multiple domains
- Single forest with multiple trees and disjoint namespaces
- Multiple forests in a central forest topology
- Multiple forests in a resource forest topology

The Active Directory forest version must be Windows Server 2003 Native Mode or higher, and all the domains in which Lync Server 2010 will be deployed must also be Windows Server 2003 Native Mode or higher.

The domain controllers must be Windows Server 2003 (32-bit or 64-bit) or higher, and the Schema, Forest, and Domain prep actions must be performed from a 64-bit machine. There are no tools capable of running the Active Directory updates from a 32-bit machine.

Supported Operating System and SQL Server Versions

Lync Server 2010 is supported on the following Windows Server versions:

- Windows Server 2008 Standard (with SP2)
- Windows Server 2008 Enterprise (with SP2)
- Windows Server 2008 Datacenter (with SP2)
- Windows Server 2008 R2 Standard
- Windows Server 2008 R2 Enterprise
- Windows Server 2008 R2 Datacenter

Only the 64-bit version of the OS is supported, and if virtualization is being used, only Windows Server 2008 R2 versions are supported for the Guest OS.

A question commonly asked is whether service pack updates are supported or not. Service packs are supported upon release, but full version updates are not supported until explicitly tested and confirmed. For example, if SP3 for Windows is released, Lync Server 2010 will automatically be supported with this service pack applied to the operating system, However, if instead of SP3, Windows 2008 R3 is released, Lync Server 2010 will *not* be supported until testing has been confirmed on this new operating system.

In addition to the OS, this rule of thumb also applies to the SQL Server version, of which the following are supported (only 64-bit versions are supported):

- SQL Server 2005 Standard (with SP3)
- SQL Server 2005 Enterprise (with SP3)
- SQL Server 2008 Standard (with SP1)
- SQL Server 2008 Enterprise (with SP1)
- SQL Server 2008 R2 Standard
- SQL Server 2008 R2 Enterprise
- SQL Server Express (for Lync Server 2010 Standard Edition and the local server databases).

Lync Server 2010 supports the use of SQL Server failover clustering in Active-Passive mode (at least one passive node in the cluster).

The administrative tools may also be installed on the following client OSs (they must also be 64-bit):

- Windows 7
- Windows Vista (with SP2)

Remote PowerShell administration does not require installation of the administrative toolset. As discussed in the introduction to PowerShell (Chapter 8, "PowerShell and LMS"), you can instead remotely connect to a Lync Server 2010 Front-End server and access the Lync Server 2010 PowerShell cmdlets as if you were remotely logged into the server and running the cmdlets directly.

Required Operating System Components and Downloads

In addition to the base operating system version, a number of additional components are required:

- Windows PowerShell 2.0
- .NET Framework 3.5 with SP1
- Windows Installer Version 4.5

In addition to the base .NET Framework 5.3 with SP1 installation being required, two additional updates are needed:

- Microsoft Knowledge Base article 981575, "A memory leak occurs in a .NET Framework 2.0-based application that uses the AesCryptoServiceProvider class"
- Microsoft Knowledge Base article 975954, "FIX: When you run a .NET Framework 2.0-based applications, a System.AccessViolationException exception occurs, or a dead-lock occurs on two threads in an application domain"

To learn more about them and download the updates, refer to the following articles:

- http://support.microsoft.com/kb/981575
- http://support.microsoft.com/kb/975954

Depending on your OS, some of these items might be installed already. Pay special attention to the .NET Framework. Version 4.0 may be installed in parallel, but it does not overwrite or replace Version 3.5 (SP1), and Version 3.5 (SP1) is the required version for Lync Server 2010.

Individual roles have different additional component requirements based on their configuration:

Front-End Servers and Directors These require IIS and the following modules installed:

- Static content
- Default document
- HTTP errors
- ASP.NET
- .NET extensibility
- Internet Server API (ISAPI) extensions
- ISAPI filters
- HTTP logging
- Logging tools
- Tracing
- Windows authentication
- Request filtering

- Static content compression
- IIS management console
- IIS management scripts and tools
- Anonymous authentication
- Client certificate mapping authentication

If you attempt an installation without any of these, the response shown in Figure 5.16 will be displayed.

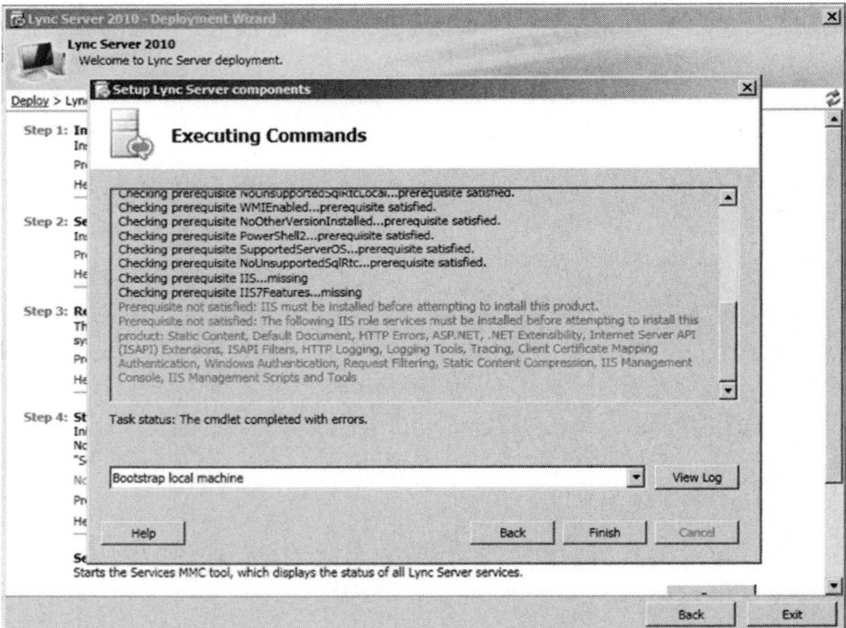

FIGURE 5.16
When IIS modules are not installed, an error message appears.

Unfortunately, this is one of the few generic error messages within Lync Server 2010. The error itself states the problem, but it does not mention which modules are not installed. It simply states that all are needed.

The following PowerShell commands will install all the required Windows features:

```
Import-Module ServerManager
Add-WindowsFeature Web-Static-Content, Web-Default-Doc, Web-Http-Errors,
Web-Asp-Net, Web-Net-Ext, Web-ISAPI-Ext, Web-ISAPI-Filter, Web-Http-Logging,
Web-Log-Libraries, Web-Http-Tracing, Web-Windows-Auth, Web-Filtering,
Web-Stat-Compression, Web-Mgmt-Console, Web-Scripting-Tools, Web-Basic-Auth,
Web-Client-Auth -Restart
```

Servers Running Conferencing Components If conferencing is configured on a server—either as a Front-End server or as a dedicated A/V conferencing server—the Windows Media Format Runtime component must be installed, and this requires a reboot.

For Windows Server 2008, use this command: `%systemroot%\system32\dism.exe /online /add-package /packagepath:%windir%\servicing\Packages\Microsoft-Windows-Media-Format-Package~31bf3856ad364e35~amd64~~6.1.7600.16385.mum /ignorecheck`

For Windows Server 2008 R2, use this command: `%systemroot%\system32\pkgmgr.exe /quiet /IP /m:%windir%\servicing\Packages\Microsoft-Windows-Media-Format-Package~31bf3856ad364e35~amd64~~6.0.6001.18000.mum`

Archiving and Monitoring Components If Archiving and/or Monitoring servers are being deployed, the Microsoft Message Queueing component must also be installed on the Front-End servers as well as on the Archiving and Monitoring servers. The following PowerShell commands will achieve this.

```
Import-Module ServerManager
Add-WindowsFeature MSMQ-Server, MSMQ-Directory -Restart
```

Other Components or Server Roles Lync Server 2010 will also install the following software if it is not already installed:

- Microsoft Visual C++ 2008 Redistributable
- Microsoft Visual J# version 2.0 Redistributable
- URL Rewrite Module version 2.0 Redistributable
- SQL Server 2008 Express SP1
- SQL Server 2008 Native Client

The Bottom Line

Use the Planning Tools available. Lync Server 2010 is an extremely complex application, even when only some of the modalities are being used. Being able to plan for capacity, not just the number of servers, but also bandwidth is extremely critical.

> **Master It** Which of the planning toolsets would you use to determine the required bandwidth on the network?

Determine when virtualization is appropriate. Unlike previous versions, Lync Server 2010 supports server virtualization across all modalities. In certain cases, this enables administrators to reduce the server footprint, giving a better "green computing" deployment.

> **Master It** What is the typical capacity reduction expected when comparing a physical server against a virtual server?

Understand the prerequisites. Like most applications, Lync Server 2010 has a number of prerequisites that must be met prior to installation. These range from Active Directory requirements to individual server role requirements, both at the OS level and the component level.

> **Master It** Which operating systems are supported for deployment of Lync Server 2010?

Chapter 6

Installation

Now you're ready to get up and running with a Lync deployment. If you've deployed OCS, you'll see that Lync deployment is dramatically different but simpler. In Chapter 5, "Planning Your Deployment," you learned that the key difference is in the planning of the topology and how this information is used in deployment. Lync now utilizes a Central Management Store (CMS), which holds information about all the roles and settings in the deployment. This replaces the various data stores that were used in OCS. The benefit of this Central Management Store is that once the topology is defined and published, every installation simply pulls from the defined configuration. This minimizes administrator input and allows automated deployment. Other improvements include the process by which certificates are requested and deployed and the fact that the Edge server role can now be centrally managed; the administrator no longer has to connect remotely to that server to manage it locally.

Like many Microsoft server applications, Lync has a Standard and an Enterprise Edition. The Standard Edition is fully functional but runs on a single server, using a SQL Express back-end database. It is still supported by other roles, such as the Edge, Monitoring, and Archiving roles, which would still run on other physical server hardware. The supporting roles don't have a definition of Standard or Enterprise; they simply support the deployed front-end servers. The Enterprise Edition allows for higher availability and more scalability of the roles to support organizations with hundreds of thousands of users. Both versions of the software can be installed only on a Windows Server 2008 or 2008 R2 64-bit operating system (OS) and must be installed on the full GUI version of those operating systems rather than the Server Core version.

In this chapter, you will learn to:

- Configure Windows Server for a Lync installation
- Prepare Active Directory for a Lync installation
- Install your first Standard Edition server
- Get your first users up and running
- Implement external access through the Director, Edge server, and Reverse Proxy server
- Understand the differences in an Enterprise Edition installation

Getting Up and Running with Standard Edition

In the previous chapters, we explored what Lync is, so you're familiar with its components and the underlying protocols that enable it to function. We also discussed clients and security. Now it's time to get things up and running so you can start to experience Lync hands on!

Lync Standard Edition is designed to support up to 5,000 users on its single server, so it is more than capable of supporting an enterprise. However, it doesn't scale beyond those 5,000, nor does it provide full high availability (HA). That said, it is perfect for smaller enterprises or branch deployments with significant numbers of users to support. For now, though, Standard Edition provides the best environment to learn the key deployment concepts without needing tons of hardware to support it. This is true in home learning or training class scenarios, although in the later scenarios you may have more hardware that will enable the progression to more complex Enterprise-class deployments.

Configuring Windows Server 2008 R2 SP1

The first step to installing Lync is to prepare the supporting server OS with the prerequisites to support Lync. In Chapter 5, we touched on the major elements required from a planning point of view, such as OS version support and capacity planning. Here we will discuss the specifics required on each server before Lync can be installed.

> **OS SUPPORT**
>
> Lync is supported on Windows Server 2008 SP2, Windows Server 2008 R2, and Windows Server 2008 R2 SP1, all 64-bit operating systems. For the bulk of this chapter, we will concentrate on Lync running on Server 2008 R2 SP1, which is the latest version of Windows supported at the time of writing. If you are installing Lync on another OS, see "Preparing for Lync Server on Other Operating Systems" later in the chapter for the differences.

The software prerequisites differ for the various Lync roles. The prerequisites for the Standard Edition server are very similar to those for the Director and Front-End Server roles used in Enterprise deployments. We will discuss the specific requirements of each role as we install it in this and later chapters.

The prerequisites fall into a few different areas. The first requirement is the .NET Framework v3.5 SP1; it is required because Lync is written as *managed code*, a program that will run only under Common Language Runtime. For more information, see the wiki page:

```
http://en.wikipedia.org/wiki/Managed_code
```

The next area of software to install is IIS 7 (on Server 2008) or 7.5 on Server 2008 R2. Lync has many elements that use IIS, including providing access to the Address Book, client updates, meeting content that is stored in the file store and exposed to user via a virtual directory in IIS on the Lync front-end servers, and of course the Meet, Dial-in, and Admin URLs, which provide access to conferences, the dial-in conferencing settings, and the Lync Control Panel.

Table 6.1 lists the IIS modules required by Lync Server Standard Edition.

Table 6.1: IIS Modules Required by Lync Server Standard Edition

Module	Description
`[Web-Static-Content]`	Static Content
`[Web-Default-Doc]`	Default Document
`[Web-Http-Errors]`	HTTP Errors
`[Web-Asp-Net]`	ASP.NET
`[Web-Net-Ext]`	.NET Extensibility
`[Web-ISAPI-Ext]`	Internet Server API (ISAPI) Extensions
`[Web-ISAPI-Filter]`	ISAPI Filters
`[Web-Http-Logging]`	HTTP Logging
`[Web-Log-Libraries]`	Logging Tools
`[Web-Http-Tracing]`	Tracing
`[Web-Windows-Auth]`	Windows Authentication
`[Web-Filtering]`	Request Filtering
`[Web-Stat-Compression]`	Static Content Compression
`[Web-Mgmt-Console]`	IIS Management Console
`[Web-Scripting-Tools]`	IIS Management Scripts and Tools
`[Web-Client-Auth]`	Client Certificate Mapping Authentication
`Anonymous Authentication`	Installed by default when IIS is installed

Finally, some elements are required in specific cases. If your Lync front-end (FE) or Standard Edition server is going to run conferences and you intend to provide music on hold, you will also need the Windows Media Format Runtime. Likewise, if you are installing your first Lync server, from which you intend to prepare your domain, or if you want to be able to manage Active Directory (AD) through the Active Directory Users and Computers (ADUC) snap-in or for that matter PowerShell, you need to install RSAT-ADDS (Remote Server Administration Tools–Active Directory Domain Services). We will include both of them in the Standard Edition configuration in this chapter.

A Lab to Follow

Chapter 5 covered the system requirements and prerequisites to deploy Lync Server 2010 in your network; however, if you want to follow along with this chapter but don't think you will be able to because the specs are so high, don't worry!

Here is what will work (and what we used to write this book): We have a single, desktop-class tower machine, with an Intel Core i7 Quad Core CPU and 16GB of RAM, running Windows Server 2008 R2 with Hyper-V.

This formed the platform for deployment and testing. We ran a domain controller (DC), Exchange, Lync, and SQL boxes on this system. The Standard Edition Lync Server that we are about to install had two CPUs allocated and 2.5GB of RAM. Supporting roles had two CPUs and 1.5GB of RAM, and the DC had a single CPU and 1GB of RAM. SQL had 2GB of RAM and two CPUs.

No, that isn't the supported minimum, and it won't let you run many users, but it works very nicely for learning, whether in a training class or at home. To prepare the server on which you plan to install Lync Standard Edition, you will need to log onto the server as at least a local administrator. Later you will need top-level domain and forest permissions like Schema and Enterprise Administrator. For this exercise, you will perform the steps as the built-in domain administrator account. We will discuss more complex systems where different accounts have different rights later.

The server should already be running Windows Server 2008 R2 SP1, and it should be joined to your test domain and have all the latest Microsoft Update patches installed. This can include .NET Framework v4.0 if that is part of your build.

Be Safe, Segregate!

Please, please, please don't install Lync for the first time in your production network! This has a great chance of becoming an RGE (a résumé-generating event). Lync installation will make significant changes to your Active Directory schema that can't be undone. It also creates a bunch of groups and ACLs/ACEs on many objects in your forest, so you should create a safe environment in which to learn by spinning up a test lab.

As you have just seen, preparing the server for the installation of Lync requires various pieces of software. Lync setup will actually install some of them automatically if they are not in place; however, many must be manually configured. The first you will install is the .NET Framework 3.5 SP1. If you try to run Lync setup before it is installed, you will be prompted to install it, as shown in Figure 6.1.

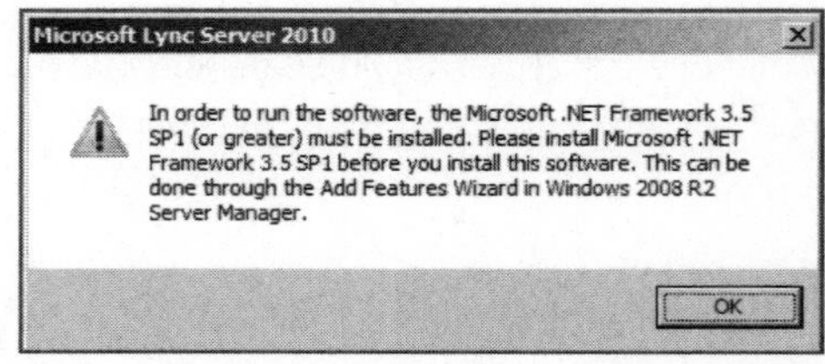

Figure 6.1
Warning to install .NET 3.5 SP1 on your server before installing Lync

NOTE We like to use PowerShell to do these installations because they can be done with a couple of simple commands and they allow installation of all Lync prerequisites in a simple script.

There are a few ways to install .NET Framework 3.5 SP1, including through the GUI's Server Manager Features section or through PowerShell. To perform the installation using PowerShell, you must open up Windows PowerShell as an administrator. Assuming you are logged on as an administrator, type **PowerShell** in the Start menu search area and click on the result, the Windows PowerShell command shell. (You may want to skip to Chapter 8, "PowerShell and LMS," if you need an introduction. You'll use PowerShell for numerous installation tasks in this chapter.)

1. Once in PowerShell, run the command:

```
Import-Module ServerManager
```

   This command will import the module ServerManager. You will learn much more about modules in Chapter 8; however, for now, all you need to know is that it is a way to extend PowerShell with additional functionality. In this case, you are adding the ability to install Roles and Features on the server.

2. Run the command:

```
Add-WindowsFeature NET-Framework-Core
```

   This installs the core .NET Framework code needed to run Lync.

.NET Patches for Installation on Windows Server 2008 SP2 or 2008 R2 RTM

On Windows Server 2008 SP2 or 2008 R2, once you have installed .NET 3.5.1, you need to install two patches to get .NET Framework ready to run Lync. The first is detailed in the Knowledge Base (KB) article KB981575. This patch fixes a memory leak that occurs when a .NET application uses the AesCryptoServiceProvider class. For more detailed information, see the following URL:

```
http://support.microsoft.com/kb/981575
```

To download the patch, use the next URL or see the link from the support page:

```
http://archive.msdn.microsoft.com/KB981575/Release/ProjectReleases.
aspx?ReleaseId=4935
```

Make sure you download the version for x64 and either the NDP35SP1 link for Windows 2008 or the Windows 6.1 version for Windows 2008 R2.

Once you've downloaded the patch, install it.

The second patch you need is detailed in KB 975954. It fixes an issue whereby data in memory can be corrupted and an application can stop responding. For more detailed information, see the following URL:

```
http://support.microsoft.com/kb/975954
```

To download the patch, use the next URL or see the link from the KB page. Again, make sure you use the right version. Windows 6.0 is for Windows Server 2008, and Windows 6.1 is for Windows Server 2008 R2:

```
http://archive.msdn.microsoft.com/KB975954/Release/ProjectReleases.
aspx?ReleaseId=3839
```

When reading about these patches, you will see that they are hotfixes designed to fix a specific issue. Don't be put off by this; they are fully supported and required for use in your Lync installation. To the non-.NET programmer, the descriptions of what these patches actually fix are somewhat cryptic, but suffice it to say that you need them to ensure good performance.

Now that .NET is installed, you should install the other features required by Lync. Start with the web components listed earlier. You can install them in a single PowerShell command, once the ServerManager module has been imported; you did that before you installed the .NET Framework.

3. To install all the required web elements, use the following command:

```
Add-WindowsFeature Web-Static-Content,Web-Default-Doc,Web-Http-Errors,Web-
Asp-Net,Web-Net-Ext,Web-ISAPI-Ext,Web-ISAPI-Filter,Web-Http-Logging,Web-
Log-Libraries,Web-Http-Tracing,Web-Windows-Auth,Web-Filtering,Web-Stat-
Compression,Web-Mgmt-Console,Web-Scripting-Tools,Web-Client-Auth
```

Having run the precious command, you should check the output, which should be as shown here:

```
Success Restart Needed Exit Code Feature Result
------- -------------- --------- --------------
True    No             Success   {IIS Management Scripts and Tools, IIS Man...
```

4. At this point, all the required IIS components should be installed on your Lync server. This just leaves RSAT-ADDS, which can be installed with the following command:

```
Add-WindowsFeature RSAT-ADDS
```

Running this command will get a slightly more detailed output than the web component installation, as you are warned that a reboot is needed:

```
WARNING: [Installation] Succeeded: [Remote Server Administration Tools] AD DS
Snap-Ins and Command-Line Tools. You must restart this server to finish the
installation process.
WARNING: [Installation] Succeeded: [Remote Server Administration Tools] Server
for NIS Tools. You must restart this server to finish the installation process.
WARNING: [Installation] Succeeded: [Remote Server Administration Tools] Active
Directory module for Windows PowerShell. You must restart this server to finish
the installation process.
```

```
WARNING: [Installation] Succeeded: [Remote Server Administration Tools] Active
Directory Administrative Center. You must restart this server to finish the
installation process.

Success Restart Needed Exit Code Feature Result
------- -------------- --------- --------------
True    Yes            Succes... {AD DS Snap-Ins and Command-Line Tools, Se...
```

AUTOMATING THE REBOOT

You have seen that a reboot is needed. If you don't want to wait and manually reboot, you can add the `-restart` parameter to the command to make the system reboot immediately after completing the RSAT-ADDS install.

5. Now that you have installed .NET, ADDS tools, and the web components, reboot the server.

The last piece of preparation needed is to install the Windows Media Format Runtime. This is done in a slightly different manner. The installation command should be run from the `CMD.exe` shell as an administrator.

1. To run the CMD prompt, type **CMD** into the Start menu search box, right-click the result, and select Run As Administrator. Having done so, run the following command:

```
%systemroot%\system32\dism.exe /online /add-package /packagepath:%windir%\
servicing\Packages\Microsoft-Windows-Media-Format-Package~31bf3856ad364e35~a
md64~~6.1.7601.17514.mum /ignorecheck
```

2. This command will install the runtime and then exit as shown in Figure 6.2. As shown, you will need to restart, so type **Y** to do so.

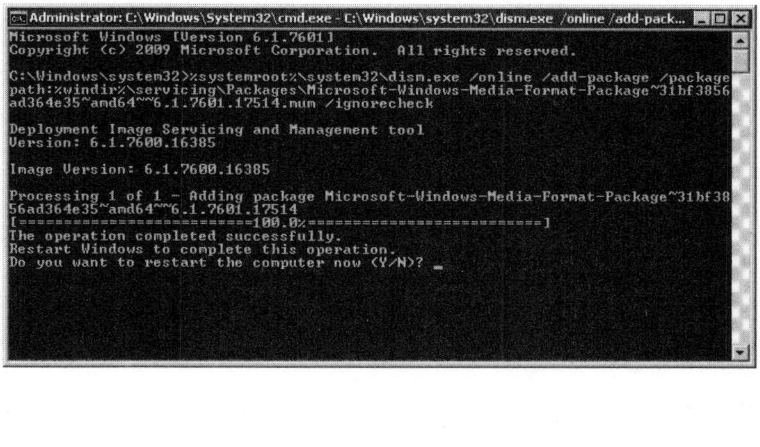

FIGURE 6.2
Installing the Windows Media Runtime Format from the **CMD.exe** shell

```
Administrator: C:\Windows\System32\cmd.exe - C:\Windows\system32\dism.exe /online /add-pack...
Microsoft Windows [Version 6.1.7601]
Copyright (c) 2009 Microsoft Corporation.  All rights reserved.

C:\Windows\system32>%systemroot%\system32\dism.exe /online /add-package /package
path:%windir%\servicing\Packages\Microsoft-Windows-Media-Format-Package~31bf3856
ad364e35~amd64~~6.1.7601.17514.mum /ignorecheck

Deployment Image Servicing and Management tool
Version: 6.1.7600.16385

Image Version: 6.1.7600.16385

Processing 1 of 1 - Adding package Microsoft-Windows-Media-Format-Package~31bf38
56ad364e35~amd64~~6.1.7601.17514
[==========================100.0%==========================]
The operation completed successfully.
Restart Windows to complete this operation.
Do you want to restart the computer now (Y/N)? _
```

PREPARING FOR LYNC SERVER ON OTHER OPERATING SYSTEMS

If you are installing Lync Server on an OS other than Windows Server 2008 R2 SP1, note the following differences:

INSTALLING THE WMFR ON OTHER WINDOWS OPERATING SYSTEMS

To install the Windows Media Format Runtime on servers running Windows Server 2008 R2 RTM, use the following command:

```
%systemroot%\system32\dism.exe /online /add-package /packagepath:%windir%\
servicing\Packages\Microsoft-Windows-Media-Format-Package~31bf3856ad364e35~a
md64~~6.1.7600.16385.mum /ignorecheck
```

To install the Windows Media Format Runtime on servers running Windows Server 2008, use the following command:

```
%systemroot%\system32\pkgmgr.exe /quiet /ip /m:%windir%\servicing\Packages\
Microsoft-Windows-Media-Format-Package~31bf3856ad364e35~amd64~~6.0.6001.18000.mum
```

PREREQUISITES FOR OTHER SUPPORTED OPERATING SYSTEMS

In general, we refer to Windows Server 2008 R2, and specifically SP1, as the platform on which Lync is installed. That is because it is the most recent Microsoft operating system that is supported. However, in the real world, you may not be able to install Lync on the latest and greatest OS or at the latest service pack level. This can occur for a number of reasons, including licensing; your company simply may not have purchased the client access licenses (CALs) for Server 2008 R2. Not having the proper CAL could make deploying Lync cost-prohibitive. Another compelling reason could be that your company has a restricted set of customized OS builds and has yet to prepare one for Server 2008 R2, or it could have one for 2008 R2 but not for the SP1 release. If such were the case, you may have been told to install Lync on Windows Server 2008 or RTM 2008 R2.

To do so, you must realize that there are differences in the prerequisites required and how they are installed.

There are very few differences between Server 2008 R2 and Server 2008 R2 SP1. The differences we have found are mentioned in the sections ".NET Patches for Installation on Server 2008 R2 RTM" and "Installing the WMFR on Other Operating Systems." This section focuses on the differences with Server 2008 SP2.

The key difference is that some elements installed by default on Server 2008 R2 are not in Server 2008. They are the following:

- PowerShell V2
- Windows Installer 4.5
- .NET Framework 3.5 SP1 manual download

To install Windows PowerShell 2.0 on a server running Windows Server 2008 SP2, see the Microsoft Knowledge Base article 968929, "Windows Management Framework (Windows PowerShell 2.0, WinRM 2.0, and BITS 4.0)," which can be found at this link:

```
http://go.microsoft.com/fwlink/?linkid=197390
```

The Windows installer can be downloaded from the Microsoft Download Center using this link:

```
http://go.microsoft.com/fwlink/?linkid=197395.
```

To install .NET Framework manually, download the Microsoft .Net 3.5 Service Pack 1 (Full Package) from the Microsoft Download Center at this link:

```
http://go.microsoft.com/fwlink/?linkid=197398
```

Patches are also required for .NET, as detailed in the section ".NET Patches for Installation on Windows Server 2008 SP2 or 2008 R2 RTM," and a different version of the Media Format Runtime is required as detailed previously.

One final element is that instead of using the PowerShell command prompt to install the OS roles and required features, you use `ServerManagerCmd.exe`. For example, to install the web components, run the following command from an administrative `cmd.exe` prompt:

```
ServerManagerCmd.exe -i Web-Static-Content Web-Default-Doc Web-Dir-Browsing
Web-Http-Errors Web-Http-Redirect Web-Asp-Net Web-Http-Logging Web-Log-Libraries
Web-Request-Monitor Web-Http-Tracing Web-Windows-Auth Web-Client-Auth Web-
Filtering Web-Stat-Compression Web-Mgmt-Console Web-Scripting-Tools
```

To install the ADDS RSAT tools to prepare for Active Directory and for user management, use the following command:

```
ServerManagerCmd.exe -i rsat-adds
```

That is nearly all the prep work that needs to be done manually. All you must do now is run Windows Update again to check for any updates and ensure that the system is fully patched.

You are now ready to start the Lync setup process. Throughout setup, additional pieces of supporting software will be installed. On your first run of setup, you will install the Microsoft Visual C++ 2008 Redistributable. If, for example, you've run setup to install Topology Builder, this will already be installed. As part of the rest of Lync installation, these other elements will be installed:

- Microsoft Visual J# version 2.0 Redistributable
- URL Rewrite Module version 2.0 Redistributable
- SQL Server 2008 Express SP1
- SQL Server 2008 Native Client

Most of them are not likely to cause any problems with your server team; Visual C++ and J# are simply programming interfaces that allow Lync to operate, and the URL Rewrite module is used by the simple URLs (discussed further in Chapter 4, "Clients Access," and Chapter 15, "E.911 and LIS"). However, you may notice that SQL Server Express and its client pieces are installed, which may cause your SQL team some concern. SQL Express is installed on each Lync server and is part of the replication and data storage mechanism used to ensure that each server has a local copy of the CMS. For more information about the CMS and its replication, see Chapter 5. You may need to discuss SQL and Lync Server requirements with your database administrators (DBAs).

Having set up the prerequisites, the next thing you need to do is prepare Active Directory.

Preparing Active Directory

Active Directory (AD) is absolutely critical to your network. It is the central authentication point, so any changes to it should be carried out with appropriate care and attention. As with other Microsoft server applications, Lync makes significant changes to AD as part of setup. There are three key elements to these changes. First, the schema is extended with classes and attributes in which to store information about Lync and its users. Second, the forest is prepared; it creates global settings and universal groups that are used in the management of Lync. Finally, each domain where Lync users or servers will be deployed must be prepared. Let's look at each stage in more depth.

THE SCHEMA

Schema preparation is run against the holder of the schema master FSMO (Flexible Single Master Operation). That doesn't actually mean you must be running at the console of the box, but you do need to be a member of the Schema Administrators group and the Enterprise Administrators group in the root domain.

In this simple installation of Standard Edition, we will be running in a single-forest, single-domain model and the installation will be carried out as the default administrator, so no worries there. Later in the chapter, we will discuss what happens in more complex AD environments, where permissions are heavily locked down, or where different teams manage AD and Lync.

As you learned in Chapter 5, most of the Lync configuration information is now stored in the CMS; however; there is still some info in AD. The schema extension adds attributes to user objects to store information such as the SIP URI of a user (the Lync equivalent of an email address); it also creates classes and attributes for backward-compatibility with OCS 2007 and OCS 2007 R2.

There are two ways to extend the schema during installation. One is through the Lync setup program; the other is through the command line. The cmdlets that handle this are installed as part of the administrative tools package during the Topology Builder installation.

At this point let's prepare the schema. We will use the Setup Wizard for this and come back to the cmdlets later in the chapter when we talk about automating setup.

1. Run `setup.exe` from within the install media *X*`:\Setup\amd64` directory. If you followed the instructions in Chapter 5 to install the Topology Builder, you will not face any prompts and will land at the home page of the Setup Wizard application, shown in Figure 6.3.

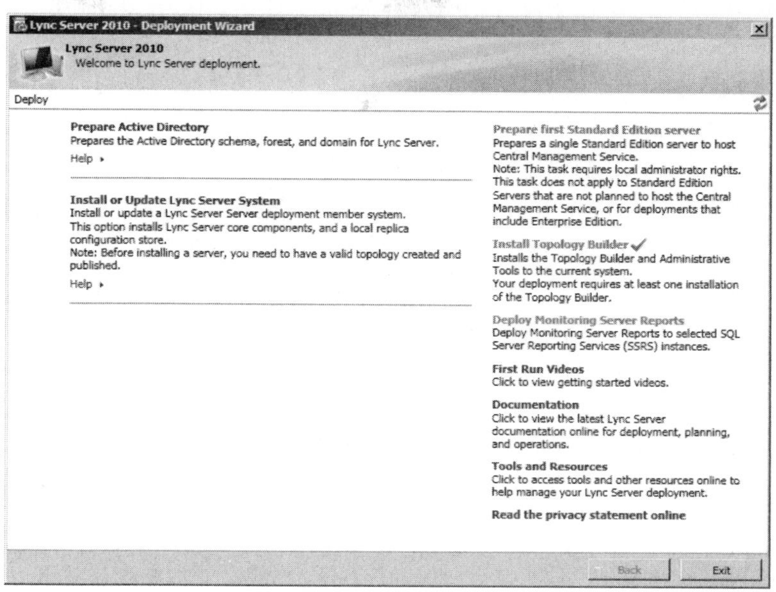

FIGURE 6.3
The Setup Wizard home page, from which all setup activities are run

2. On the home page, click Prepare Active Directory, which will take you to the area where all the AD preparation tasks are chosen. In the Prepare Schema section, click Run to kick off Schema Prep.

3. Follow through the wizard, clicking Next to kick off the process. This will take only a minute at most in this exercise.

   On completion, you will see a summary screen of the cmdlet that ran in the background, allowing you to view the log of the process. As long as there were no warnings shown on the summary screen, there is no need to check the log unless you want to know a little more about what happened during the process.

   If you do want to check the log, click the View Log button next to the drop-down, which will allow you to select a log based on the activity you want to investigate. The log will open in the web browser. If you are using Internet Explorer 9, you will need to click Allow Blocked Content to explore the log. Click Expand All Actions in the top-right of the page to see details of the log.

IT'S ALL POWERSHELL

As mentioned, a PowerShell cmdlet ran in the background during the schema-extension process. As you will see in Chapter 8, Lync is entirely controlled through PowerShell. The GUI simply calls the relevant cmdlets.

4. If you click the Log button, the log will open in Internet Explorer (IE). You must allow IE to run the blocked content, at which point you will be able click Expand All Actions in

the top-right of the window, to show the entire file. Once satisfied, close the browser and click Finish in the wizard to complete schema preparation and return to the AD preparation wizard page.

CHECK SCHEMA REPLICATION

In our small lab with one DC, checking replication is irrelevant because there are no other DCs with which to talk. However, in a larger AD, it is critical to ensure that replication of the schema changes has occurred on all DCs before moving on to the forest preparation.

To do this, log onto a server as a member of the Enterprise Admins group and then load `asdiedit.msc`. Note that ADSI Edit is not installed by default and comes either with the Windows Server 2003 resource kit tools or as part of the RSAT ADDS tools on Windows Server 2008 or 2008 R2 systems.

On the Action menu, click Connect To. In the Connection Settings dialog box under Select a Well Known Naming Context, select Schema, and then click OK.

Under the schema container, search for **CN=ms-RTC-SIP-SchemaVersion**. If this object exists, and the value of the rangeUpper attribute is 1100 and the value of the rangeLower attribute is 14, then the schema was successfully updated and replicated. If not, wait a little longer for replication to occur.

THE FOREST

Now that the schema has been extended, it is time to prepare the forest in which Lync is to be installed. The AD *forest* is a collection of trees (which contain domains) that share a common global catalog and directory schema. The forest represents the security boundary within which users, computers, groups, and other objects reside. The process of forest preparation is what creates the permission structure by which Lync is managed. It creates a bunch of universal groups, which all start with the characters RTC and CS. These groups are combined to provide administrative rights over Lync objects. This is covered in much more depth in Chapter 9, "RBAC." The forest prep also creates various objects in the configuration partition of AD, which is replicated to all domain controllers in the forest.

THE CONFIG PARTITION

The config partition is used as a store of information, which is readily available to all DCs as it is part of the information set of which all DCs hold a replica. In OCS 2007, this configuration information was by default stored in the System container in the root domain of the forest; however, this often caused issues in large distributed ADs where access to the root forest was slow. Therefore, in OCS 2007 R2 the default was changed to the configuration store, and this is maintained in Lync.

Because you ran the schema preparation from the setup GUI, you will run the forest preparation in the same way. Again, you need to be a member of the Enterprise Admins group, but this time not Schema Admins. You will continue running as the default administrator.

1. Either start setup again, if you closed it after schema prep, or carry on from where you left off. This time click Run on the Prepare Current Forest section of the wizard to start the process. Once the wizard starts, follow through with the defaults. Notice that there

is an option to specify a different domain to create the universal groups in; however, for now there will be only the single domain. We will cover this further in the "Enterprise Deployment" section.

2. Once the wizard completes, you must recheck replication. This time there is a Lync cmdlet to do this. Open the Lync Management Shell by navigating through Start, All Programs, Microsoft Lync Server 2010, Lync Server Management Shell. Run the following cmdlet:

```
Get-CsAdForest
```

This will check that your Active Directory forest has been correctly configured to allow installation of Microsoft Lync Server 2010. As long as the output is as shown here, you are fine to proceed:

```
LC_FORESTSETTINGS_STATE_READY
```

3. If you want more detail about what the Get-CsAdForest cmdlet has checked, run the following command to output results to the log file specified:

```
Get-CsAdForest -Report C:\ForestPrep.html
```

This outputs a log file in HTML format that you can open in your browser, and it looks something like Figure 6.4.

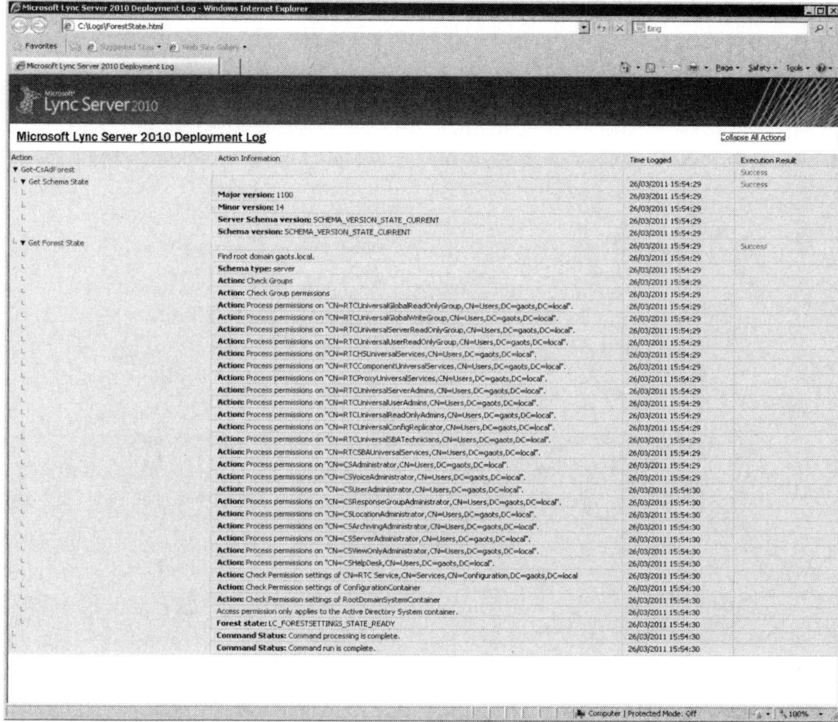

FIGURE 6.4
The deployment log file shows the steps to verify forest prep

For detailed info about PowerShell and Lync, see Chapter 8.

The Domain

The final step in AD preparation is the domain preparation. This step must be carried out in every domain with Lync users and/or servers. To run domain prep, you must be either an enterprise admin or a domain admin in the domain being prepared.

The Access Control Entries (ACEs) that allow members of the RTC groups to manage Lync objects and manipulate user objects in the domain are actually created during domain preparation. The permissions are set on the default containers, users, domain controllers, and at the root of the domain.

Again, this step can be run either through the Shell or through the setup GUI.

1. Continuing from the completion of forest prep, you should be back in the AD Prep home page section of the setup application. To start domain prep, click Run in the Prepare Current Domain section of the page. Run through the wizard, selecting the defaults, and clicking Next to progress and Finish to end.

2. At this point, you once again need to check that things have completed correctly. Run the following command:

```
Get-CsAdDomain -Report "C:\DomainPrepReport.html"
```

   This will check the domain prep steps and output a report with the Get-CsAdForest cmdlet. The expected output is

```
LC_DOMAINSETTINGS_STATE_READY
```

   Assuming this all checks out, you are ready to move on. If things didn't quite work, your next step will be to leave more time for replication; if that doesn't work, then try rerunning the preparatory steps. If this still isn't successful, then use the logs to localize the area of failure. To identify more ways of fixing common problems, see Chapter 12, "Troubleshooting."

Installing the Standard Edition Server

As you learned in Chapter 5, the Lync installation is driven by the topology you define using Topology Builder and publish to the CMS. In Chapter 5, you defined a simple topology for a Standard Edition deployment, so let's retrieve that topology, create the CMS, and publish the topology. Once that is done you can begin the actual installation.

Permissions

In these exercises, we are running all the steps as the default domain administrator account. It has Schema, Enterprise, and Domain admin rights, which give full access to allow setup to be performed. Later in the process, we will create a Lync Admin account, which we will use to administer Lync. At the end of the chapter, "Enterprise Deployments" covers environments where permissions are locked down more tightly.

Retrieving the Topology and Creating the CMS

To retrieve the topology, take the following steps:

1. On the Lync server, open the Topology Builder (this should have been installed in Chapter 5).
2. When you open Topology Builder, you are prompted to load a topology, either by downloading from a CMS, by opening from a saved file, or by creating a new topology. For this example, select Open From File and find the file saved in Chapter 5.

   Once it is opened, all the settings defined in the topology will be visible and you can make any final tweaks. At this point, you need to publish the topology to the CMS, but you haven't actually created the CMS yet.
3. To create the CMS, you need to prepare a SQL database. SQL is installed on each Lync server, but can't install Lync without having published the topology. This sounds like a Catch-22.

   To get around this with the Enterprise Edition (more later), you could have already created the SQL instance. On Standard Edition, where SQL Express is installed on the same box, you must use the Prepare First Standard Edition option in the setup application. This installs SQL Express on the Standard Edition server, which gives you access to a database engine that Topology Builder can use to create the CMS to which you then publish the Topology.
4. To prepare the first Standard Edition (and yes, it is only the first, because once the CMS is created you are no longer in the Catch-22 situation mentioned earlier), you must once again run `setup.exe`. On the home page in the top-right corner, you should click Prepare First Standard Edition Server. This will launch a wizard. The first time you click Next, the wizard will start to install SQL Express. Once the installation completes, click Finish to exit the wizard and return to the home page of setup.

   Once this is done, you don't need to run the Setup Wizard again on any other servers. If you do, all it will do is leave you with an empty SQL Express installation.

Preparing the First Standard Edition Server Might Take a While

You may well find that the preparatory steps take a while, even as long as 10 to 15 minutes on slower systems while nothing much seems to be happening on the console. Don't worry at this point! If you are really concerned, fire up Task Manager and take a look at the following processes:

```
TrustedInstaller.exe
Setup100.exe
SQLsvr.exe
```

You will find that these processes require a fluctuating amount of CPU resources and that the memory consumed by the `Setup100.exe` and `SQLsrv.exe` processes grows.

As long as you see these fluctuations, all is well and you should just keep waiting.

The preparation process not only installs SQL, it ensures that remote computers have access to it; that access is provided by creating relevant firewall rules using the following NetSH commands:

```
> Creating firewall exception for SQL instance
netsh advfirewall firewall add rule name="OCS SQL RTC Access" dir=in action=allow
program="c:\Program Files\Microsoft SQL Server\MSSQL10.RTC\MSSQL\Binn\sqlservr.
exe" enable=yes profile=any
> Creating firewall exception for SQL Browser
netsh advfirewall firewall add rule name="SQL Browser" dir=in action=allow
protocol=UDP localport=1434
```

At this point, you have one final task to perform before returning to the Topology Builder to publish the topology. You must set up the file share, which Lync will use, depending on configuration, to store some or all of the following elements:

- Application Server files
- Archiving Server
- CMS File Store
- Web Services (including elements like the Address Book files, meeting content, and device updates)

1. To create the file share on the server where you are about to install Lync Standard Edition, first run `cmd.exe` to open a command prompt and then enter the following commands:

```
Mkdir c:\lyncshare
```

This will create a folder named `lyncshare` on the `C:` drive, which you will share using the command:

```
NET SHARE lyncshare=c:\lyncshare /GRANT:Administrators,FULL
```

This will share the `c:\lyncshare` folder with Full permissions for the Administrators group, which is all that is needed to allow you to publish the topology. Now you're ready to publish the topology and install Lync.

2. Move back to the Topology Builder and check through the topology opened earlier in the chapter. Verify the following elements:

- Check all simple URLs.
- Confirm that the file share is available and has the proper permissions defined.
- Ensure that you've defined the server roles you need at this time.
- Confirm that any servers defined are online and joined to AD.

Given that you are installing a very simple topology on a single server at this point, and have literally just created the file share, there should be no problems here. If you are uncertain, revisit Chapter 5 for more information.

3. The final thing to check is that the topology references the correct CMS. To do this, right-click at the root of the topology where it says Lync Server 2010 and select Edit Properties, and then on the page that opens, select from the left pane Central Management Server. In the drop-down, select the Standard Edition server as the CMS.

DNS Entries

Before publishing the topology, you must make sure all servers are available. One aspect of this is setting up the relevant DNS entries. These entries are detailed in Chapter 4 and Chapter 5; however, the basics are that you need an A record for the FQDN of the Standard Edition server and SRV records to enable automatic sign in for each SIP domain.

A = `se01.gaots.local` = IP of the Standard Edition server

SRV = `_sipinternaltls._tcp.gaots.co.uk` over port 5061 that maps to the FQDN of the Standard Edition server (`se01.gaots.local`)

You also need to create the Meet, Dial-in, and Admin records:

A = `meet.gaots.co.uk` = IP of the Standard Edition server

A = `dialin.gaots.co.uk` = IP of the Standard Edition server

A = `admin.gaots.co.uk` = IP of the Standard Edition server

Later in this chapter, we will change the DNS A records for the simple URLs (`meet` and `dialin`) to point to the IP address of the Director.

Publishing the Topology

Once you are satisfied with the topology, it is time to publish it.

1. In Topology Builder, click Publish Topology on the right pane.
2. This will kick off a wizard that first gives you a list of requirements to follow before you can publish the topology. You have met all of them, but take a quick read to verify and then click Next to continue.
3. You will be presented with a screen that asks you to select the front-end server on which to create the CMS. It should be prepopulated with the server on which you are installing. If it isn't, select the correct server in the drop-down. You may notice the Advanced button, which is used to be more specific about the directories used when creating SQL databases. It will be covered in more depth later in the chapter. Click Next to begin publishing.

Once publishing completes, Lync gives you the option to check the logs; it also links to a text file telling you which actions need to be performed on other servers. This is something you will see repeated throughout the setup stages and is very useful. In this case, you are reminded that you need to create the relevant DNS records for the Meet and Dial-in URLs, as shown in Figure 6.5.

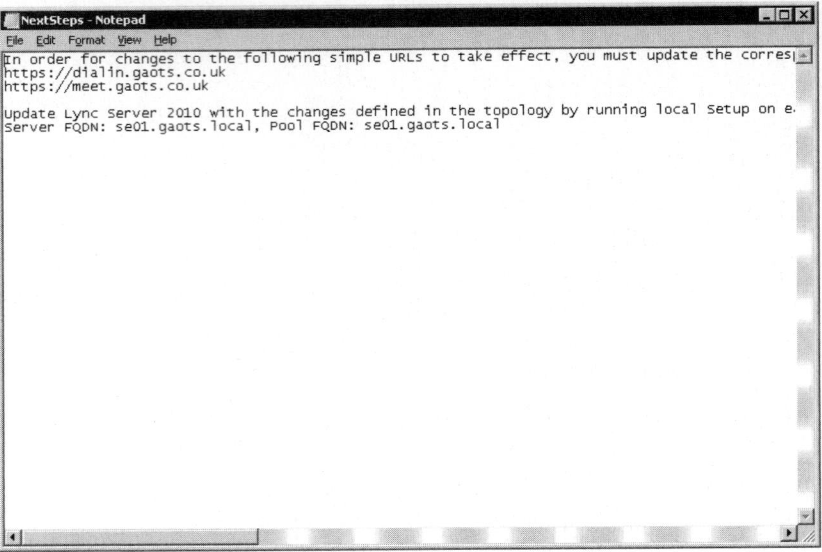

FIGURE 6.5
The actions required after the topology is completely published

The topology is now published, which means that the relevant configuration has been entered into the CMS. This means that when you install Lync, the configuration can be pulled to the Local Configuration Store and used to configure the local server.

FURTHER PREPARATION

The remaining setup steps are relatively straightforward. First, you need to install the Local Configuration Store. This will create a new SQL instance on the server which holds a read-only replica of the CMS.

1. To install the Local Configuration Store, start `setup.exe` from the `\setup\amd64\` folder of the media, and on the setup home page, click Install or Update Lync Server System.
2. This takes you to a setup page which runs through all the tasks to get the server up and running. Click Run in the Install Local Configuration Store section.
3. This kicks off a wizard where you will first be asked from where you want to pull the config. In this instance, you will pull it from the CMS. The other option would be to pull from a file which you will see later when you configure the Edge server. Click Next to begin creating the Local Configuration Store.

   This process will take a few minutes, after which you will get the familiar completion page that allows you to view the steps taken and to launch the log in a browser to delve further into any details. One nice touch to note is that if multiple logs were created for different steps of the process, all of them are available from a drop-down menu.
4. To end the wizard, click Finish.

How the Local Configuration Store Is Populated

We've discussed that the Local Configuration Store is pulled from the CMS. However, you might be wondering how this is actually done.

What happens is that an `Export-CsConfiguration` command is run against the CMS, which creates a ZIP file. Because this is our first Standard Edition server, this file is stored locally; however, if we were building a server remote from the CMS, this would be sent by SMB over port 445 to the remote server. Once it is received, an `Import-CsConfiguration` is carried out with the `-LocalStore` parameter, which imports the configuration into the local configuration database. At this point, the HTTPS SQL replication process kicks in to maintain consistency between the databases.

Installation

Let's return to the Install or Update Lync Server Settings setup page. The next element to complete is the Setup or Remove Lync Server Components section. This is what actually installs the Lync binaries onto the server.

1. To begin the process, click Run in the Setup or Remove Lync Server Components section. This kicks off the Setup Lync Server Components Wizard.

   In the background, setup will look in AD to find a Service Connection Point (SCP), which will tell it where the CMS is held. Setup will review the data in the CMS and then install any required components by checking against the name of the server listed in the topology.

2. On the first page of the wizard, click Next to kick off setup. On completion, click Finish.

The next element to configure is Certificates. This has been simplified somewhat compared to the OCS installation process.

3. Back at the Install or Update Lync Server Settings setup page in the Certificates section, click Run to start the Certificate Wizard. This will open the page shown in Figure 6.6.

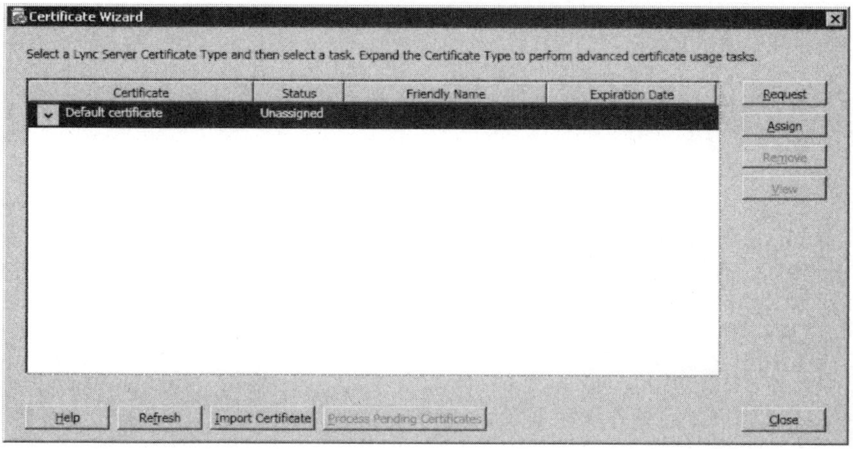

Figure 6.6
The Certificate Wizard

You can see that by default the Lync server requires a single certificate. However, if you click the drop-down by the default certificate, you will see that it is possible to install a certificate for each component, including the Server Default, Web Services Internal, and Web Services External. This flexibility is particularly useful when providing external access through a reverse proxy that cannot trust an internal Certificate Authority (CA), which would cause you to need a trusted public certificate on the External Web Services component. In this case, keep the simple, standard installation because you will be using Forefront Threat Management Gateway as the proxy, as you will see later in the chapter.

4. To create the required certificate, minimize the drop-down and highlight the default certificate. Click Request and then follow the wizard that opens. Click Next to progress to the selection of an online or an offline CA.

   Here, you can choose whether to use a CA that is likely to be internal to your organization and is online to issue certificates automatically, or save the request to a file and submit it to a CA manually. This could be the case either if you use trusted public certificates or if your CA can't provide certificates automatically.

5. In this case, keep it simple and go for the internal CA, which is running as an Enterprise Root CA on Windows Server 2008 R2. Because this is the only CA in the environment, it is the only one in the drop-down, so click Next to continue.

6. On the next page, you can opt to select different credentials to use to access the CA. This can be useful if you are using an account with only enough rights to install Lync so it cannot access the CA. In this case, leave the defaults in place and use the account you are using to run Lync setup (the built-in domain administrator account) which has plenty of rights. Click Next to continue to the next page.

7. Here you can select a custom certificate template instead of using the default Web Server template on the CA. This could be useful if, for example, later you need to be able to export the private key, and your default certificate template doesn't allow that. Leave this blank and thus use the default template and click Next to continue.

8. You are prompted to give the certificate a "friendly name," as shown in Figure 6.7. Make it something meaningful. It is not obviously presented to users, but will show up if they view the certificate that is used by the internal web components.

FIGURE 6.7
Setting the certificate friendly name

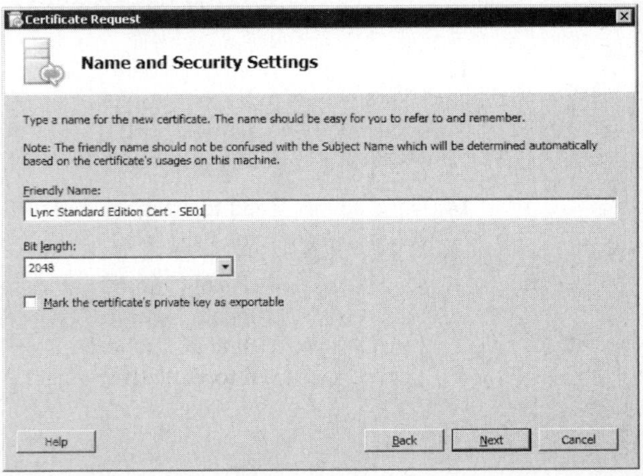

9. Click Next to progress and then follow the next couple of pages entering information about your organization and location, which will be stamped on the certificate.

   Once the information has been entered and you have clicked Next a couple of times, you will get to a summary page that displays the Subject Alternative Names (SANs), which will be used to create the certificate. In Figure 6.8, you can see how this contains the URLs for the simple URLs for conferencing and administration alongside the server FQDN and also the external web services FQDN, which will be used later in the chapter when you provide external access to Lync.

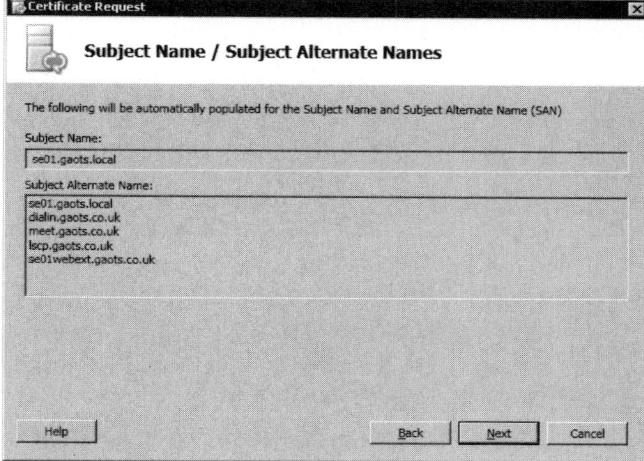

FIGURE 6.8
The summary page shows all the URLs entered on the certificate

10. To complete the request, click Next to move on to choose whether or not to set up any further subject alternative names on the certificate.
11. Ensure that you put the checkbox in the box next to your SIP domain. As noted on the dialog, this would be required because of the way devices connect to Lync and was described in depth in Chapter 4. Again click Next to proceed.
12. On the next screen, you will not need any more SANs so click Next again to reach the summary page.
13. Take a look through and note how the settings you have entered throughout the wizard are represented. Once you are happy, click Next to create the certificate. On completion, you will be presented with the familiar page showing the commands that ran, and you will be given the option to look at the log file that was generated.
14. Finally, you need to assign the certificate. Click Next and then on the next page click Finish to start the Certificate Assignment Wizard.

    The Certificate Assignment Wizard opens and gives you a chance to view the certificate. The View Certificate Details button displays the default info about the certificate such as the expiration date and where it was issued. On the Details tab, shown in Figure 6.9, you can scroll down to view the Subject Alternative Names.

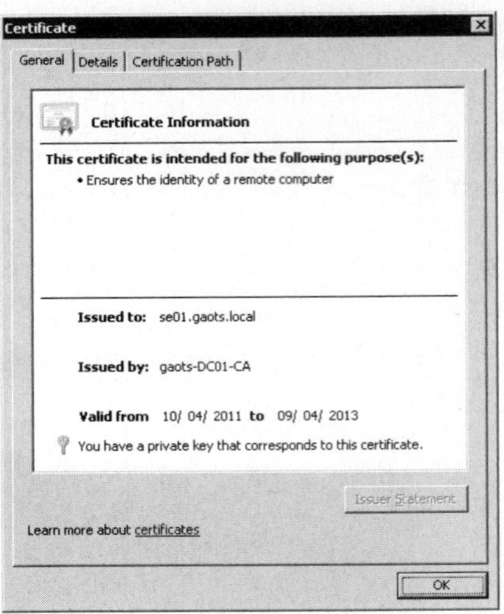

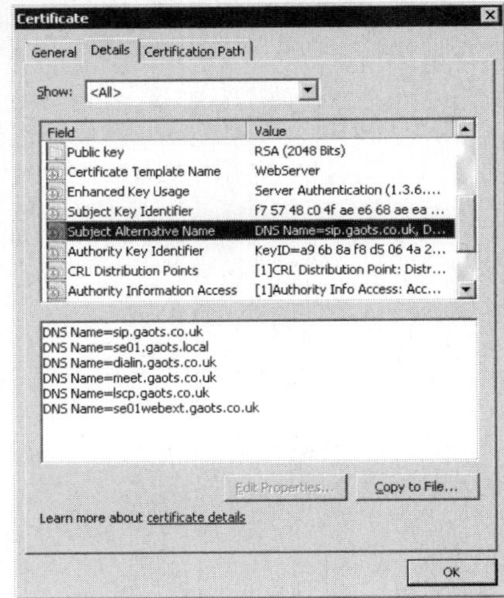

FIGURE 6.9
The certificate shows both the issuing CA (left) and the details of the SANs (right)

15. In the wizard, click Next to get to the summary page and then Next to assign the certificate. Finally, click Finish to exit the Certificate Assignment Wizard.

    Now you return to the first Certificate Wizard, where you can see that you have assigned the certificate you just created. Clicking Close takes you back to the Lync Server Deployment Wizard, where you will see that you are now ready to start the services.

16. Click Run in the Start Services section to start the Services Wizard. Click Next to start the services, after which you can review the log or simply click Finish to exit.

When Lync is being installed, a service may occasionally fail to start, as shown in Figure 6.10. If that happens, check the log and find which service hasn't started. In this case, it simply timed out, so it can be manually started using `Services.msc`.

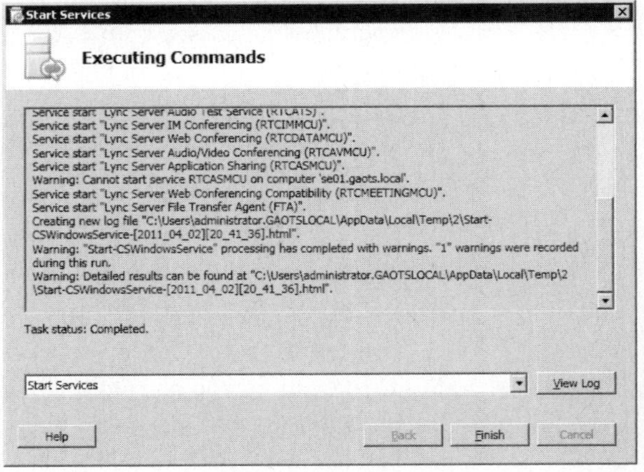

FIGURE 6.10
The summary page of Start Services, showing a warning about the RTCASMCU service

At this point, you are done installing the main Lync components for your first Standard Edition server. You can exit from the Deployment Wizard and run one final check to see if there are any Windows Updates. Install anything you find and then reboot the server. Although the process was lengthy to describe, once you have done it a couple of times you can whip through setup easily, especially if you have taken a suitable amount of time in the planning phase using Topology Builder. Now you're ready to move onto what to do after setup.

Post-Deployment Tasks

Now that you've completed setup of the Standard Edition server, there are several steps you need to perform before you can get users up and running. You need to create an account with basic administrative permissions before you can do anything else. Then you need to test the installation, install any needed updates, and finally configure Kerberos authentication. The following sections discuss each of those steps.

Basic Administrative Permissions

Once you've finished setup, your first task is to give an account full administrative rights to the server. Up to this point, you've been using the administrator account to perform the setup, but now you'll create a Lync administrator account and use it to manage the system in the future.

First, you need to create a new user in Active Directory.

1. Open Windows PowerShell by typing **PowerShell** into the Start menu search area and running the top result.
2. Import the Active Directory module. This can be done with the following command:

```
Import-Module ActiveDirectory
```

3. This imports all the cmdlets needed to manage AD. Now that you have the cmdlets to manage AD objects, run the following command to create the new administrative user.

```
New-ADUser -SamAccountName "lyncadmin" -UserPrincipalName "lyncadmin@gaots.local"
-GivenName "Lync" -Surname "Admin" -DisplayName "Lync Admin" -Name "Lync Admin"
-Enabled $true -path "CN=Users,DC=gaots,DC=local" -AccountPassword (Read-Host
-AsSecureString "AccountPassword")
```

   This will create a new user Lync Admin in the default Users container, and it will prompt you to enter a password. On completion, the account will be enabled. Having done this, you need to add the account to two groups, which will give you all the rights you need to perform basic administration on Lync 2010.

4. The following command adds the Lync Admin account to the required groups:

```
Add-ADGroupMember RTCUniversalServerAdmins lyncadmin ; Add-ADGroupMember
CsAdministrator lyncadmin
```

   This command will first make Lync Admin a member of the RTCUniversalServerAdmins group and then, when it is run again, make Lync Admin a member of the CsAdministrator group.

5. The last thing you need to do to ensure that Lync Admin can make any necessary changes to the local server is to add Lync Admin to the local administrators group. You can do this by copying the next six lines of code into the Windows PowerShell on the Standard Edition Server and running them.

```
$computerName = $env:COMPUTERNAME
$Group = "Administrators"
```

```
$LocalGroup = [adsi]"WinNT://$computerName/$Group,group"
$Domain = "gaotslocal"
$UserName = "lyncadmin"
$LocalGroup.Add("WinNT://$Domain/$userName")
```

Once these commands are run, the Lync Admin domain user will be a member of the local administrators group.

> **POWERSHELL AND PERMISSIONS FOR MANAGEMENT**
>
> At this stage, don't worry if the PowerShell commands you've just seen are unfamiliar. Not only is all of Chapter 8 about PowerShell, Chapter 9 focuses on setup and delegation of management.

Testing the Installation

Now that you've created the Lync Admin user, you are ready to log onto the Standard Edition server as that user and begin testing the installation. The aim is to validate that all server components are installed and communicating correctly and that all services are started before you move onto any complex system configuration.

1. Log onto the Standard Edition server as Lync Admin.
2. Once you're logged in, type **l s c p** (yes, with the spaces) in the Start menu search bar and press Enter.

   This will run the Lync Server Control Panel (LSCP), which allows you not only to administer the majority of Lync settings, but also to validate that setup has completed properly. In this case, start with validation.
3. If prompted, log into the Control Panel with the Lync Admin user credentials and click the Topology tab. This will bring up a view of all the deployed services, as shown in Figure 6.11.

FIGURE 6.11
A warning appears on the Topology tab in Lync Server's Control Panel

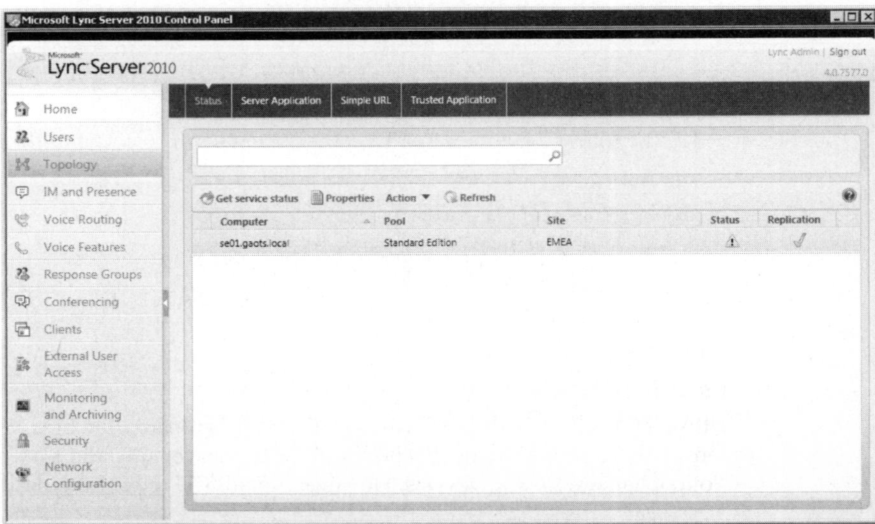

You can see information about the status of the server you installed. Hopefully, everything will have a green tick/icon. However, in the figure, you can see a warning denoted by the yellow triangle in the services column.

4. Double-click the row to drill into the services to find out what is wrong. You can see in Figure 6.12 that the Conferencing server is stopped.
5. To rectify this, select the service row and then click the Actions drop-down and select Start Service. The service will start.
6. Once it is complete, click Close to move back to the first page and you will see all green icons, meaning that the service is healthy.

FIGURE 6.12
Drill into the components to determine the error

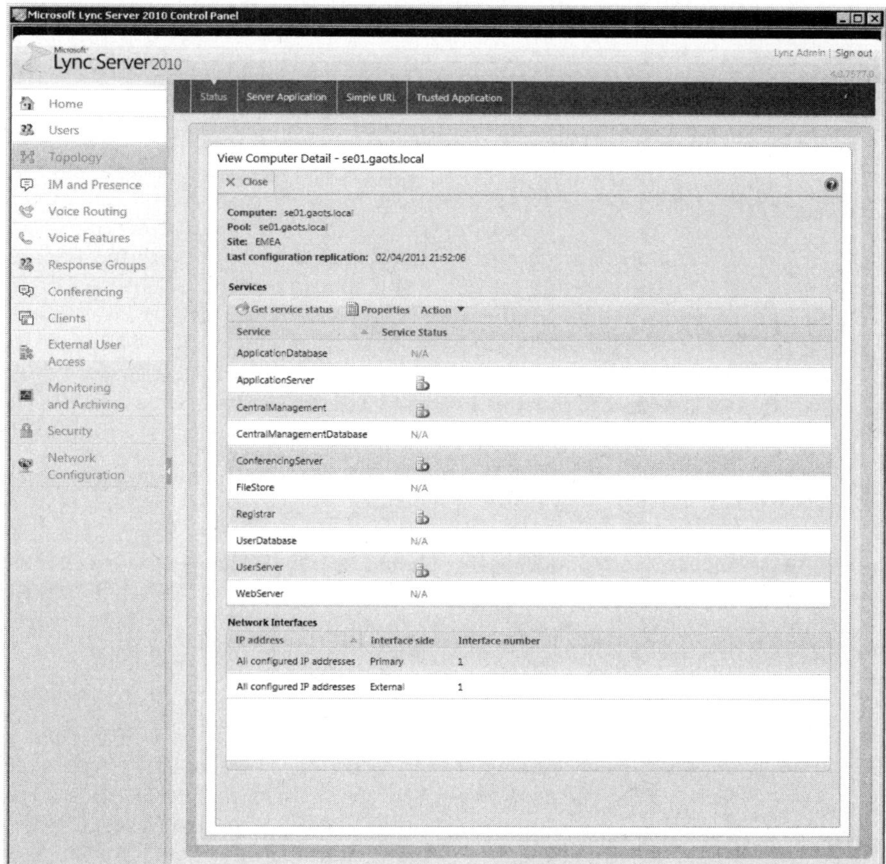

Installing Updates

Within a CU release, there are various files to download, each of which patches a different element of Lync. There can be patches both for the server side and the various clients, including Group Chat and Phone Devices. However, not all CU releases will have patches for all Lync components. One nice thing is that there is no need to install the patches from each subsequent CU. Simply download the latest patches and install them, and that will get you all the patches from previous updates. One very important thing to look out for is that some CU releases will include a database update (CU3 is one that does). These are not installed automatically! People frequently overlook this element of the update and then can't figure out why things aren't working properly. The most important thing you can do in this regard is make sure you carefully read the release notes and KB articles associated with the patch before installation, and ideally test this in a lab environment.

For CU3 the patches are described in the following Knowledge Base (KB) articles:

- Updates for Lync Server 2010: `http://support.microsoft.com/?kbid=2493736`
- Description of the update for Lync Server 2010 Group Chat: July 2011 - `http://support.microsoft.com/?kbid=2571550`
- Description of the cumulative update package for Lync 2010: July 2011 - `http://support.microsoft.com/?kbid=2571543`

In terms of installing the patches, each of these pages has a link to the relevant download site. For the main Lync Server update, you can download patches for each component separately or rather more sensibly, download the `LyncServerUpdateInstaller.exe` file, which will provide all the server-side updates in one file and install them for you in the correct way. As mentioned, `LyncServerUpdateInstaller.exe` will not patch the database, so you will need to do this manually using the `Install-CsDatabase` cmdlet as described in the KB article.

Before you install the patches, make sure that you log on as the user you installed Lync with, in our case the default domain Administrator account, and ensure that all Lync apps like the Control Panel and Topology Builder are shut. Even having done this, you may find that while installing some updates you will be prompted that setup needs to stop and restart one of the services. As with all patches, test them in your lab environment before rolling them out in production.

Kerberos Authentication Configuration

The last piece of post-setup work to be done on this Standard Edition installation is to set up Kerberos authentication. Lync can use either NTLM (NT LAN Manager) or Kerberos for Web Services authentication; however, everyone knows that Kerberos is more secure than NTLM because it uses mutual authentication, so it is important to perform this setup.

This difference in the Lync configuration process compared to that of OCS is because Lync now runs under the Network Service account. OCS ran using service accounts like RTCService. Kerberos relies on the correct Service Principal Names (SPNs) (which are used for mutual authentication) being assigned to accounts; however, it is not possible to link SPNs to the Network Service account under which Lync runs. To work around this, Lync creates a dummy computer account on which to place the SPNs needed by IIS. This is used instead of a user account to get around the default password policy, which might require irritating regular changes of password.

It is only necessary to have a single Kerberos computer account, but it is possible to create multiple accounts to provide one for each site. This might be needed if you have a large distributed topology with many sites, as the process whereby a password change is communicated to each site happens via Distributed Component Object Model (DCOM), which is a set of Microsoft standards allowing distributed software components to talk to each other. If you have a large network, this password reset may take quite sometime to complete; therefore, having local Kerberos accounts may be more sensible.

Just so you get an idea of what SPNs look like, let's check to see what SPNs exist currently for the SE01 computer before you start. Do this by running the following command from an administrative command prompt (`CMD.exe`):

```
SetSPN -L SE01
```

When this is run, you should see output similar to the following, which is a listing of Kerberos SPNs linked to the Standard Edition computer object:

```
Registered ServicePrincipalNames for CN=SE01,CN=Computers,DC=gaots,DC=local:
        MSSQLSvc/SE01.gaots.local:50169
        MSSQLSvc/SE01.gaots.local:RTCLOCAL
        MSSQLSvc/SE01.gaots.local:49806
        MSSQLSvc/SE01.gaots.local:RTC
        http/se01.gaots.local
        sip/se01.gaots.local
        WSMAN/SE01
        WSMAN/SE01.gaots.local
        TERMSRV/SE01
        TERMSRV/SE01.gaots.local
        RestrictedKrbHost/SE01
        HOST/SE01
        RestrictedKrbHost/SE01.gaots.local
        HOST/SE01.gaots.local
```

Next, create the Kerberos account.

1. To create the account, log onto the Lync server as a domain administrator and open Lync Management Shell. Run the following command to create your first Kerberos account.

```
New-CsKerberosAccount -UserAccount "gaotslocal\LondonLyncKerb" -ContainerDN
"CN=Users,DC=Gaots,DC=local"
```

   This command creates an account in the gaotslocal domain, called LondonLyncKerb, within the default Users container. Obviously, you would use your domain name and create an account name that is meaningful to you. You can also put the account in a different container or OU if you want to keep it separated from the main Users container.

2. Next, you need to assign the account to the site, which you do with the following command:

```
New-CsKerberosAccountAssignment -UserAccount "gaotslocal\LondonLyncKerb"
-Identity "site:EMEA"
```

   This will assign the LondonLyncKerb account to the EMEA site, which is the only one you have at the moment.

3. At this point, you need to update the topology, so use the following cmdlet:

```
Enable-CsTopology
```

This registers all the relevant SPNs against the newly created Kerberos account based on the sites you have assigned to it. The penultimate step is to ensure that all machines in the site have registered the password assigned to the account. The account is assigned a random password on creation, but each machine running IIS needs to know it! This is done using the following command:

```
Set-CsKerberosAccountPassword -UserAccount "gaotslocal\LondonLyncKerb"
```

Once you've run this command, all the IIS instances in the site on front-end servers, Directors, or Standard Edition servers will get the password.

4. Finally, run `SetSPN -L` again, but this time with the computer account you just created as the target.

```
SetSPN -L LondonLyncKerb
```

Now, you will see output similar to this:

```
Registered ServicePrincipalNames for CN=londonlynckerb,CN=Users,DC=gaots,DC=local:
        http/se01.gaots.local
```

This is the SPN, which will allow the LondonLyncKerb account to be used for Kerberos authentication for web services rather than using the local Network Service account.

5. Having created the account, assigned, and enabled it, you can run the following command, which will test whether it is operating properly:

```
Test-CsKerberosAccountAssignment -Identity "site:EMEA" -Report "c:\logs\
LondonKerberosReport.htm" -Verbose
```

This runs through a number of tests and outputs to the familiar HTML format log file in the directory you specify.

Before we move on, there are various considerations worth mentioning about Kerberos accounts. One recommended methodology is that before you configure Kerberos, you complete your deployment, or at least all the elements that are going to use Web Services, namely Standard Edition, Director, and front-end servers. Realistically, this may not be possible, which means that when you add a server, like a Director, after setting up Kerberos Authentication you need to configure IIS and set the password on the server. This is described later in the chapter, as part of the process of setting up a Director server, but briefly, you use the `Set-CsKerberosAccountPassword` cmdlet to do this. Similarly, each time you create a new site, you need to decide whether to create a new Kerberos account and link it to the site or reuse an existing one. As mentioned, this depends on the size and scale of your topology. If you choose to use a new Kerberos account, then go ahead and create it and link it as described earlier.

Enabling Your First Pair of Users

Lync is installed and ready to use, but there are aren't any users enabled to test it. You can create a couple of test users either manually through Active Directory Users and Computers, or using PowerShell much as you did when creating the administrative user. For this example, we will use PowerShell, so do the following.

1. Open Windows PowerShell and ensure that you are running it as a domain administrator. Next, import the Active Directory module. This can be done with the following command:

```
Import-Module ActiveDirectory
```

   This imports all the cmdlets needed to manage AD.

2. Now that you have the cmdlets to manage AD objects, run the following command to create the new administrative user:

```
New-ADUser -SamAccountName "testuser1" -GivenName "Test" -Surname "User1"
-DisplayName "Test User1" -Name "Test User1" -EmailAddress "testuser1@gaots.
co.uk" -Enabled $true -path "CN=Users,DC=gaots,DC=local" -AccountPassword
(Read-Host -AsSecureString "AccountPassword"); New-ADUser -SamAccountName
"testuser2" -GivenName "Test" -Surname "User2" -DisplayName "Test User2"
-Name "Test User2" -EmailAddress "testuser2@gaots.co.uk" -Enabled $true -path
"CN=Users,DC=gaots,DC=local" -AccountPassword (Read-Host -AsSecureString
"AccountPassword")
```

   This will prompt you for two passwords, one for each account, and will then create two new, enabled, test user accounts in the default Users container. Importantly, these accounts will have email addresses, which will then be used when enabling for Lync as the SIP address.

3. To enable users, log into the LSCP as the Lync Admin account created earlier. Select the Users tab and click Enable Users. This opens the page shown in Figure 6.13.

FIGURE 6.13
The Add New Link Server User dialog

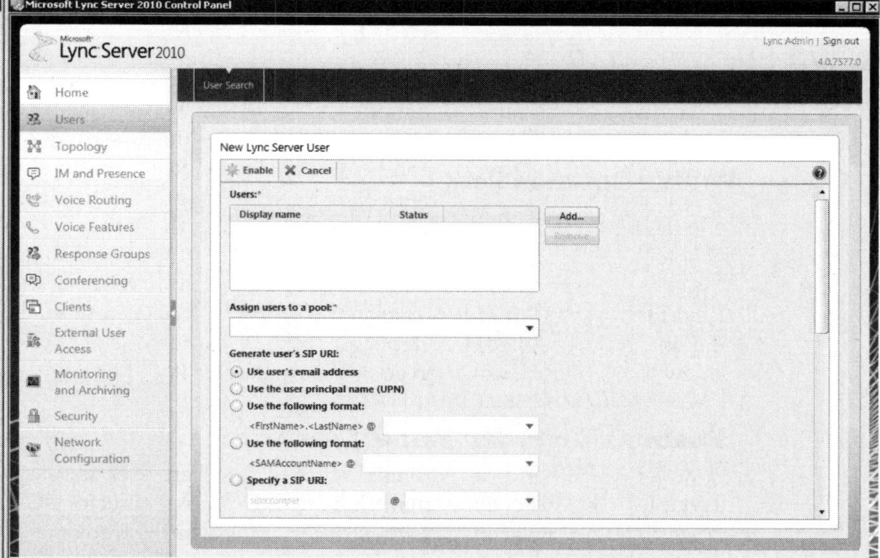

4. Click the Add button and then search for **test** to find Test User 1 and 2.
5. While holding down the Shift key, select both the users so they are highlighted in yellow, and click OK. Back on the first page, assign the users to the `SE01.gaots.local` pool and leave the default setting of Using The Email Address to generate the SIP URI. There are many other settings, but we will cover them in Chapter 10, "User Administration." For now, click Enable to accept all the defaults and enable the two test users for Lync. On completion, you will see the new users as shown in Figure 6.14.

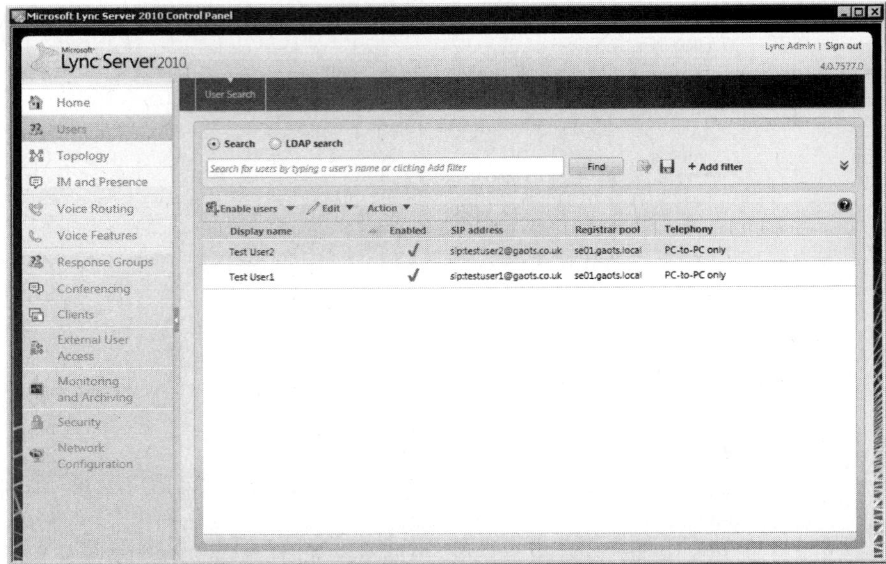

FIGURE 6.14
The newly enabled users

Rolling Out the Client

Finally, you are just about ready to test with actual users. Before you can do that, however, you need to roll out the Lync client. Most likely at this stage, you will simply perform a manual install of the Lync client on a couple of test machines, but you also need to consider how you will install the Lync client on hundreds of machines in your organization. First, we'll run through the manual setup and then discuss options for a wider deployment.

A Manual Lync Client Installation

Installing Lync manually is a simple process. You must first prepare a client machine with the relevant prerequisites. Lync Client supports Windows desktop OS of XP SP3 (with Windows Installer 3.1 pre-installed) Windows Vista and Windows 7, and there is also a Mac version. It also installs fine on the following server versions: Server 2003, 2008, and 2008 R2. Silverlight 4.0 is included as part of the install. For full integration with Exchange and Office, you will need Office 2003, 2007, or 2010 installed and Outlook configured with an Exchange user profile. The Office install is not mandatory, and for now we will simply install on a blank Windows 7 install.

CLIENT VERSIONS

The Lync client has both 32-bit and 64-bit versions. Choose the relevant version for your OS. Lync Server can accept connections from various client versions including OCS 2007, OCS 2007 R2, and Lync itself with different updates applied. It is possible to set up Lync to allow only certain versions of the Lync client to connect, as discussed in the "Client-Version Filtering" section of Chapter 3.

1. Copy the Lync client setup program to the `C:\` drive of the machine on which you intend to install and double-click it.
2. Check the install location, and if you want, check the box to allow information about your usage of Lync to be passed back to Microsoft to help drive improvements in the future. Click Install.
3. You will see that the Visual C++ 2008 redistributable is installed and then Lync. Once setup completes, leave the Start Lync checkbox enabled and click Close. At this point, the Lync client will start, and you will need to enter the details of the user to log on.
4. Repeat this process on another client machine and log in as a second user. Test that Address Book lookup works by using the search bar to search for a user enabled for Lync. Double-click the user found and send them an IM. This should show up on your other client test machine. At this point you can be satisfied because you have a working Lync installation.

WIDER DEPLOYMENT OF LYNC CLIENTS

Clearly, it would be possible in a small deployment to go around to each PC and manually install Lync, but in an organization with hundreds or even thousands of PCs all around the world, this approach isn't practical. Thankfully, there are several ways to deploy the Lync client in large or managed IT environments. First, you can use tools such as Microsoft System Center Configuration Manager 2007 R3 to package and deploy the client. This gives the benefits of scheduling, reporting, and specific features to mitigate the bandwidth challenges associated with pushing packages over a WAN. Other options are the use of the traditional login policy or using the deployment options available in Group Policy.

To dive deeply into the methods available for mass deployment of software would be outside the scope of this book. In many ways, deploying the Lync client is no different from deploying any other piece of Microsoft software. So at this point, we will simply lay out a few of the options and considerations specific to deploying the Lync client through the methods just outlined.

First, you may have noticed that the Lync client setup program is an `.exe` file rather than an `.MSI` package. The key benefits of this are that the `.exe` installer performs a series of prerequisite steps required to ensure a successful installation of the Lync client. For example, the installer will let the user know if any apps need to be closed, and it will install relevant versions of Visual C++ components and also Silverlight. The installer will also remove previous versions of Lync or OCS clients and it will notify the user that Windows Media Player 11 is needed for certain functions to work properly. This simplifies the deployment, as it doesn't require you to automate these steps yourself.

To deploy Lync from a command line, you could try running the following command:

```
en_lync_2010_x64_598497.exe /install
```

This will kick off the full Graphical User Interface (GUI) version of the installer and allow the user to customize settings, which you probably don't want. Instead, you are likely to be better off running this version of the command:

```
en_lync_2010_x64_598497.exe /install /silent
```

This will carry out the install but use all the default setup options and run predominantly in the background without user interaction. Table 6.2 lists other setup options.

TABLE 6.2: Lync Client Deployment Options

COMMAND-LINE ARGUMENT	DESCRIPTION
`/Silent`	Suppresses the installation user interface, and uses default values for other installation options (for example, installation directory). This argument can be used along with the `/Install`, `/Uninstall`, and `/Repair` arguments.
`/Install`	(Default) Installs the client.
`/Uninstall`	Removes previous versions of Office Communicator and add-ins.
`/Repair`	Reinstalls the client to repair any installation issues.
`/InstallDir`	Specifies the installation directory.
`/Help`	Displays the Help text in a dialog box.
`/reg [FileName]`	Registers the settings in the specified file during installation. This Registry file is then used during runtime.
`/uninstalladdin`	Removes the Conferencing add-in for Microsoft Office Outlook, which is the previous version of the add-in (used for scheduling Microsoft Office Live Meeting server- and service-based meetings).
`/fulluisuppression`	Enables Lync 2010 to run in user interface suppression mode.

Two of these options warrant further mention because they both help provide the ability to extend and customize the Lync client. The `/fulluisuppression` mode is used when you need the functionality of Lync, such as presence, to be available on your system but you have perhaps created your own custom app or client through which users interact with real-time communications utilizing the UCMA development APIs. The `/reg` option is used by developers who create applications that integrate with the Lync client and who need to install contextual application settings to the Lync Registry files. These settings enable users to launch applications directly from a link in a conversation window, which enables seamless collaboration through Lync in third-party applications.

INSTALLING FOR MULTIPLE USERS ON ONE PC

The Lync client, once installed, is accessible by everyone who uses the PC; it cannot be restricted to a single profile/user on that PC.

The final method of installing Lync is using an MSI through Group Policy. The first challenge here is where to obtain the MSI file. You will find the MSI by installing from the `.exe` file and then looking in `%Program Files%\OCSetup\Lync.msi` or `%Program Files(x86)%\OCSetup\Lync.msi`, depending on your OS version (32 bit or 64 bit).

Once you have the MSI, you will encounter another problem—Microsoft has prevented installation of the MSI unless a specific Registry key was set. This was done mainly to prevent the issues that the .exe install overcomes from being a problem inadvertently, the thinking being that if you set the Registry key you had likely done the necessary research. What is needed is to create a new DWORD value Registry key called UseMSIForLyncInstallation and set it the value of 1.

The following steps are from the KB article 2477965, which describes the procedure in more depth:

1. Click Start, click Run, type **`regedit`**, and then click OK.
2. Locate and then click the following Registry subkey:
   `HKEY_LOCAL_MACHINE\Software\Policies\Microsoft\Communicator`
3. On the Edit menu, point to New, and then click DWORD Value.
4. Type **`UseMSIForLyncInstallation`**, and then press Enter to name the Registry entry.
5. Right-click UseMSIForLyncInstallation, and then click Modify.
6. In the Value data box, type **1** if that value is not already displayed, and then click OK.
7. Exit the Registry Editor.
8. Restart the computer.

There are other workarounds on the Internet, which involve editing the MSI file to remove the check; however, at this time the method just described is the only supported one. Once you have solved this problem, you are ready to install from the MSI. Just remember that you need to carry out all the prerequisite steps that the .exe would do. So long as you take that into consideration, the deployment will be like any other your packaging team will have carried out, and we will not dive into further detail here.

LOCKING DOWN THE LYNC CLIENT

There are many ways in which you can configure and lock down the Lync client. It is important to understand key policies and settings and how these settings are applied, a user administration topic that is covered in Chapter 10.

Configuring External Access

If you've been following along, you now have a full-fledged Lync installation that is perfectly capable of letting people within your organization communicate and collaborate in a wide variety of ways. However, these capabilities are currently limited by the confines of your firewall. It would be so much better if you could access these tools from anywhere and communicate and collaborate in exactly the same way whether you were in your office or in a coffee shop with Wi-Fi half way around the world. That is exactly what this next section is about: configuring the Lync Edge server and supporting components to allow external access.

Three main components are involved in providing external access to Lync: the Edge role, which does the majority of the work; the Director, which is an optional stop-gap between the front end and the Edge server; and the reverse proxy, which allows you to publish externally the various web components of Lync, such as the Address Book and the software update service.

The process for deploying external access consists of the following major steps:

1. Define the topology.
2. Prepare for deployment.
   a. Meet the software prerequisites.
   b. Set up networking, DNS, and firewalls.
   c. Set up/prepare certificates.
   d. Provision Public IM Connectivity.
3. Set up the reverse proxy.
4. Set up a Director (optional).
5. Set up the Edge server.
6. Configure users for external access.
7. Test.

The first of these steps is already done, as you defined the topology in Chapter 5. The specific prerequisites for each server are outlined in the following sections.

PROVISIONING PUBLIC IM CONNECTIVITY (PIC)

PIC requires specific licensing from Microsoft and is, therefore, not something that is often able to be tested in a lab. There is an online provisioning process, which is covered in depth in the following Technet article:

`http://technet.microsoft.com/en-us/library/ff945947.aspx`

Installing the Director

The Director role is frequently dismissed in designs as just another server, and so it is left out. However, it does have an important role to play. Essentially, a Director is a barrier between the Edge and the front-end server. In this role, it is the Director that performs authentication of users coming in across the Edge server and thus, it not only takes a load off the front-end server but also helps to isolate the front-end server from any malicious traffic generated as a denial of service attack. If, for example, an attacker were to send large amounts of malformed authentication traffic toward the Edge server, it would be passed on to the Director, which would potentially be overloaded. However, the front-end server would be unaffected, so internal users would be able to continue working with limited disruption. There are a couple of other roles where the Director server plays a part. One is as part of a large enterprise deployment, as discussed later in the chapter. The other is by way of a method of distributing information to clients about a backup registrar that was covered in Chapter 4 but is worth reviewing briefly now. Essentially, when a Lync client registers with the server it finds through autodiscover, or is pointed to through manual configuration, if that server is not its home server, the Lync client is sent a redirect given the details of the primary and backup registrar. If the client was configured to connect first to its home server instead of the Director, then if the home server was down, it would never get the redirect request telling it about the backup registrar and thus failover wouldn't work.

Directors, like other components, can be deployed either as a single server or in a pool. If they are deployed in a pool, load balancing must be configured. In this Standard Edition deployment, you will simply deploy a single Director. To do so, you will need a server that is running a supported OS as described in Chapter 5. In this network, you will use another Windows Server 2008 R2 SP1 machine that is fully patched and joined to the domain.

In Lync, the Director is finally a role in its own right. It used to be in OCS that it was a front-end server with various services turned off. The cool thing about this is that now you no longer have to worry about users getting accidentally homed on the Director server, as it simply isn't an available option like it was when it was a cut down front end in OCS. Although a separate role, the Director has very similar prerequisites to the front end (or Standard Edition server). In fact, there are only a couple of differences. The first is that the Windows Media runtime is not required. Similarly, neither are the Active Directory tools (RSAT-ADDS).

Installing on Different OSs

As with the other roles, there are differences if installing on an OS other than Windows Server 2008 R2 SP1. One such difference for the Director and Edge roles is the need to install one additional component. This is a patch, described in KB article 2028827, which prevents problems with network traffic when "on a computer that is running Windows Server 2008 R2 or Windows 7, any application that uses the Transport Driver Interface (TDI) driver for network traffic may stop responding." One thing to note about this hotfix is that you have to request it to be emailed to you. This is a straightforward process, which is initiated by clicking the View And Request Hotfix Downloads link at the top of the page linked here:

```
http://support.microsoft.com/kb/2028827
```

Because we spent quite some time detailing the installation of prerequisites on the Standard Edition server, at this point, we will simply list the commands that should be run from a PowerShell command prompt with administrator credentials on the local server:

```
Import-Module ServerManager

Add-WindowsFeature NET-Framework-Core

Add-WindowsFeature Web-Static-Content,Web-Default-Doc,Web-Http-Errors,Web-
Asp-Net,Web-Net-Ext,Web-ISAPI-Ext,Web-ISAPI-Filter,Web-Http-Logging,Web-
Log-Libraries,Web-Http-Tracing,Web-Windows-Auth,Web-Filtering,Web-Stat-
Compression,Web-Mgmt-Console,Web-Scripting-Tools,Web-Client-Auth
```

Running these commands will first import the cmdlets needed to install software and then install the .NET Framework and the web components. If asked, reboot the server and then perform one final check for patches from Windows Update, and install any that are found.

At this stage, you are ready to deploy the Director role.

1. When you insert the media, Setup will auto-run, and as with the Standard Edition server you will be prompted about installing Visual C++ 2008. Click Yes and then click Install to agree to the location for install files. Obviously, you can change from the default if you choose to place the installation on another drive. Accept the license agreement by placing a check in the checkbox and then click OK to progress with setup.
2. Once installation bootstrapping is complete, you will be at the setup home page. Click Install or Update Lync Server system, which takes you to the steps for deploying the new role.
3. Then, as with all other roles, click Install Local Configuration Store to begin the wizard that installs the SQL Express database to hold the local replica of the CMS.
4. On the first page of the wizard, opt to Retrieve Directly from the Central Management Store and click Next to start the installation.
5. On completion, you can view the log as in previous installs or click Finish to return to the deployment steps page and continue.
6. Next, you will install the Lync files by clicking Setup or Remove Lync Server Components.
7. This takes you to another wizard, where you click Next to kick off a process of installing all the specific services needed for the Director role. On completion, click Finish to return to the setup steps page.

Next, you provision certificates, a procedure very similar to that of the Standard Edition install.

1. Once again there is the option to be very specific about certificates. However, for this example you will request a single certificate with multiple SANs by clicking the Request button.
2. When the wizard opens, click Next and then opt to Send Your Request Immediately To An Online Certification Authority and click Next.
3. Select the same CA as for the Standard Edition install and click Next.

4. Assuming you are logged on as the default domain administrator account, there is no need to specify different credentials, so click Next and then Next again to use the default certificate template.
5. On the next page give the certificate a friendly name such as **Lync Director Cert** and click Next.
6. On the next couple of pages, enter your organizational information and click Next until you reach the Subject Name and Subject Alternative Names page. Here you will notice the simple URLs, the FQDN of the Director pool, and the external name for the Director of web services all in the SAN. The Subject is the Director pool FQDN. Click Next.
7. Select the checkbox next to the SIP domains, to ensure that the `SIP.gaots.co.uk` entry gets populated on the certificate for use later by phone devices, and click Next.
8. There are no other SANs to add, so click Next and then review the summary page and click Next to make the request. Once it is completed, click Finish to run the Certificate Assignment Wizard, which after you click Next twice and then click Finish will have assigned the certificate to the relevant services within Lync.
9. At this point, click Close on the certificate page and then again back on the Install Steps page, and finally click Run in the Start Services section to start the Director services.
10. You can check that all services have started by launching `Services.msc` using the Run button in the Service Status (Optional) section. This is worth doing especially in a situation where limited RAM may make things start rather slowly. Assuming everything has started OK, you should have a running Director.

As mentioned in the earlier Kerberos section, anyone who has configured Kerberos authentication needs to configure it for use on the new Director. Do this from the LMS on a server that has Kerberos already set up (in this case, the Standard Edition SE01), using the following command:

```
Set-CsKerberosAccountPassword -FromComputer SE01.gaots.local -ToComputer
director01.gaots.local
```

This command will synchronize the password and account information from the SE01 server to the new Director.

Perform a final check for Windows Update and install the same level of Lync Cumulative Update as described in the Standard Edition install, and then you'll be nearly ready to move to the next stage, setting up the reverse proxy.

Before you move on, you should check the topology again as you did after installing the Standard Edition server. Open Lync Control panel as the Lync Admin user created earlier and on the Topology tab check that replication has a tick next to both the Standard Edition server and the Director and that the Status is green.

New Prompt When Opening LSCP

After installing the Director, note that there is now a prompt for the URL to use when you open LSCP from the Start menu. This is because both Director and Standard Edition servers have a set of web URLs to offer to users. You can run the LSCP from either URL successfully.

Configuring the Reverse Proxy

Deploying and configuring a Reverse Proxy server or farm is outside the scope of this book and in fact warrants a book of its own. We will, therefore, focus only on setting up the rules needed to publish Lync to the Internet. This installation chapter will assume that you have a Forefront Threat Management Gateway (TMG) 2010 server up and running and configured to allow publishing of websites from the internal network. There are, of course, many other supported reverse proxies, but for now we will stick with TMG.

To begin the process of publishing Lync, it is important to understand what you need to publish via a reverse proxy. As discussed at the beginning of the chapter, Lync makes heavy use of web services to provide access to meeting content, to expand distribution lists, to publish the Address Book, and many more uses. These services are all provided to external users by publishing virtual directories through TMG for external access. You also need to publish the simple URLs, which provide access to meetings and dial-in conferencing settings.

In general, because of the number of virtual directories involved, it is recommended to publish all virtual directories on a given front end (or front-end pool), Standard Edition, or Director (or Director pool) through a single rule. For example, we will be publishing `https://director-webext.gaots.co.uk/*`.

In the simplest deployments (a single Standard Edition server internally and an Edge and reverse proxy in the perimeter network), where a Director is not deployed, you would simply publish all the required URLs from the Standard Edition server. However, given that you followed best practice and deployed the Director, you should use it. Therefore, you need to publish two URLs, one for the Standard Edition and one for the Director. Because the role of the Director is to route traffic to the appropriate front end or Standard Edition server, you will publish the simple URLs from the Director, which will then pass the traffic on to the appropriate internal resource. The Director will also be where the Web Ticket authentication occurs (as discussed in Chapter 3 and Chapter 4), before the connection is passed to the front end or Standard Edition server where the user is homed. This server will then give out its distinct URL for the web services elements mentioned earlier. This is why both the Director and Standard Edition/front-end servers need to be published.

Before you can publish the internal servers, it is important that the reverse proxy resolve the servers to be published. This can be done either through DNS or by editing the HOSTS file on the reverse proxy. Because the TMG server is a member of the internal AD, DNS is pointing to an internal server, which can resolve the Director and Standard Edition servers. For an example of how to edit the HOSTS file, see the installation of the Edge server later in this chapter.

Another thing you need to do to prepare the Reverse Proxy server is to make sure it has an external IP address assigned to its external NIC for each of the servers or pools you intend to publish. In this case, you will be publishing the Standard Edition server SE01 and the Director Director01. Therefore, you need two external IP addresses for the TMG box.

The final step before actually creating the publishing rules is to ensure that you have the correct certificates on the TMG server. You may remember the flexibility Lync allowed in the certificates you installed on the Standard Edition and Director boxes. There was the option either to install a single certificate or to break out the certificates for each component. The reason for this flexibility is that for TMG to successfully publish the virtual directories on the Standard Edition and Director servers, TMG needs to trust the certificates used to authenticate and identify those servers. A single certificate can be used on the internal servers, which can be requested from the internal CA on the domain controller. This works fine when using TMG connected to the domain, because it therefore trusts the AD Enterprise CA. However, if you were using another reverse proxy, which couldn't be made to trust the internal CA, then it might be a problem. You would need to use public certificates instead, which the reverse proxy could trust on the external web services portion of the internal servers. But because the TMG server does trust the internal CA, you have only one final piece to configure, which is the certificates to be used by TMG to identify itself to external users. You need a certificate on the TMG server that corresponds to each URL you publish. In this case, this will be as follows; note the use of SAN certificate for the simple URLs published on the Director:

Standard Edition (SE01)

Subject: `se01webext.gaots.co.uk`

Director (Director01)

Subject: `directorwebext.gaots.co.uk`

SAN: `directorwebext.gaots.co.uk`

SAN: `meet.gaots.co.uk`

SAN: `dialin.gaots.co.uk`

These externally trusted certificates are needed so that TMG can terminate the connection from the external user, view the traffic to check it for threats, and then open a new encrypted connection from TMG to the internal server, this time using the internal certificate.

To get the certificate on the TMG server, you have various options. However, the cleanest one to use is the command line's `certreq.exe` utility. A lot of detailed information on the subject of using `certreq.exe` is available at the following links:

`http://technet.microsoft.com/en-us/library/ff625722(WS.10).aspx`

`http://technet.microsoft.com/en-us/library/cc725793(WS.10).aspx`

Essentially, the process is to create a request template file for each certificate needed and then to use the `certreq.exe` utility, which is installed by default on Windows Server 2008 R2, to create a certificate request file. The template file for the Standard Edition URL is shown in Listing 6.1. You can see that it requests only the one URL. In Listing 6.2, you can see the request template for the Director URLs certificate. Here you can see that the Extensions section is added to create the needed SANs.

LISTING 6.1: *.inf* **File Text Used to Create Standard Edition Certificate**

```
[Version]
Signature="$Windows NT$"

[NewRequest]
Subject = "CN=se01webext.gaots.co.uk,OU=ICT,O=Gaots,L=Croydon,S=Surrey,C=GB"
Exportable = FALSE
KeyLength = 2048
KeySpec = 1
```

```
KeyUsage = 0xA0
MachineKeySet = True
ProviderName = "Microsoft RSA SChannel Cryptographic Provider"
RequestType = PKCS10
FriendlyName = "Standard Edition Ext Web Services"

[EnhancedKeyUsageExtension]
OID=1.3.6.1.5.5.7.3.1 ; Server Authentication
```

LISTING 6.2: `.inf` File Text Used to Create Director

```
[Version]
Signature="$Windows NT$"

[NewRequest]
Subject = "CN=directorwebext.gaots.co.uk,OU=ICT,O=Gaots,L=Croydon,S=Surrey,C=GB"
Exportable = FALSE
KeyLength = 2048
KeySpec = 1
KeyUsage = 0xA0
MachineKeySet = True
ProviderName = "Microsoft RSA SChannel Cryptographic Provider"
RequestType = PKCS10
FriendlyName = "Director Ext Web Services"

[EnhancedKeyUsageExtension]
OID=1.3.6.1.5.5.7.3.1 ; Server Authentication

[Extensions]
2.5.29.17 = "{text}"
_continue_ = "dns=directorwebext.gaots.co.uk&dns=meet.gaots.co.uk&dns=dialin.
gaots.co.uk"
```

Take the following steps to create the certificates:

1. From an Administrator `CMD.exe` prompt, change to the folder where the request template `.inf` file is stored and run the following command:

```
certreq -new se01csr.inf se01.req
```

   This will pull settings from the `se01.csr.inf` file and output to the `se01.req` file in the same directory.

2. Then carry out the same step for the director certificate:

```
certreq -new directorcsr.inf director.req
```

Having run these commands, you have created the certificate request for each required certificate on the TMG. You will need to copy the contents of the `.req` file and send it to your third-party CA, such as Digicert or VeriSign. There are too many third-party CAs to describe all the processes in detail.

3. Once the CA has created the certificate for you, follow its procedure to install it on the TMG machine, making sure that the certificate is in the Computer Account Personal Certificate store and that you have imported any required intermediary root CAs so that you trust the Certificate path.

Once the certificates are installed, you can create the required rules to publish Lync. First, you will publish the Standard Edition server.

1. To do so, open up the TMG management tool and in the left-hand pane, expand the server Forefront TMG (TMG), right-click Firewall Policy, point to New, and then click Web Site Publishing Rule.
2. On the Welcome to the New Web Publishing Rule page, type a display name for the publishing rule, such as SE01 Lync External, and click Next. On the Select Rule Action page, select Allow and click Next.
3. On the Publishing Type page, select Publish a Single Web Site or Load Balancer and click Next.
4. On the Server Connection Security page, select Use SSL to connect to the published Web server or server farm and click Next.
5. On the Internal Publishing Details page, you will enter the Standard Edition server FQDN, which in this case is **`SE01.gaots.local`**, in the Internal Site name box and click Next. See the accompanying discussion for what to use in more complex scenarios.

DETERMINING THE INTERNAL SITE NAME URL

The internal site name URL will vary depending on whether your internal server is a Standard Edition server or an Enterprise Edition front-end pool. If it is a Standard Edition server, the FQDN is the Standard Edition server FQDN. If your internal server is an Enterprise Edition front-end pool, this FQDN is a hardware load-balancer virtual IP (VIP) that load-balances the internal web farm servers.

It is critical that the TMG server be able to resolve the FQDN to the IP address of the internal web server. There are various ways to achieve this; you can use DNS in the perimeter network or point the TMG server to an internal DNS server with the relevant records. Other methods are using the HOSTS file on the TMG server or selecting Use A Computer Name Or IP Address To Connect To The Published Server, and then, in the Computer Name Or IP Address box, type the IP address of the internal web server.

6. On the Internal Publishing Details page, in the Path (Optional) box, type **/*** as the path of the folder to be published and then click Next.

   It is worth noting that you are publishing only one URL (path) in this section of the wizard. That's fine in this case for the Standard Edition server because it is the Director that will host the simple URLs, which require addition paths to be published. These additional paths will be added for the Director by modifying the publishing rule once it is created; the steps are described at the end of this section.

7. On the Public Name Details page, confirm that This Domain Name (Type Below) is selected next to Accept Requests For and then type the external Web Services FQDN (in the example, **`se01webext.gaots.co.uk`**) in the Public Name box and then click Next.
8. On the Select Web Listener page, click New to open the New Web Listener Definition Wizard, and on the Welcome to the New Web Listener Wizard page, type a name for the web listener in the Web Listener name box (in the example, **LyncPublishingListener**).
9. Click Next to open the Client Connection Security page, and then select Require SSL Secured Connections with Clients and click Next.
10. On the Web Listener IP Address page, select External, and then click Select IP Addresses.
11. On the External Network Listener IP Selection page, select Specified IP Address on the Forefront TMG computer in the selected network. Because you will use the same listener to publish the Director server shortly, select two of the available public IP addresses and click Add. Click OK to move back to the Web Listener IP Address page and click Next.
12. On the Listener SSL Certificates page, select Assign a Certificate for Each IP Address, select the IP address that is associated with the Standard Edition external web FQDN (`SE01webext.gaots.co.uk`), and then click Select Certificate.
13. On the Select Certificate page, select the certificate that matches the SE01 FQDN and click Select.
14. Repeat steps 1 to 13 for the other IP address, except this time select the certificate that has the names published on the Director server and then once done, click Next.
15. On the Authentication Setting page, select No Authentication and then click Next.
16. On the Single Sign On Setting page, click Next.
17. On the Completing the Web Listener Wizard page, verify that the Web Listener settings are correct, and then click Finish.
18. Back on the Select Web Listener page, click Next.
19. On the Authentication Delegation page, select No Delegation, But Client May Authenticate Directly and click Next.
20. On the User Set page, click Next.
21. On the Completing the New Web Publishing Rule Wizard page, verify that the web publishing rule settings are correct, and then click Finish.
22. Click Apply in the details pane and then enter any required notes in the Configuration Change Description page and click Apply again to save the changes and update the configuration.

Now that you've created the basic rule and listener to publish the Standard Edition web services externally, you must edit the rule to tweak a couple of the settings, which will complete the configuration.

1. To edit the properties of the web publishing rule, locate the rule in the Firewall Policy section of the TMG management tool, right-click it, and select Properties.
2. On the Properties page, on the From tab in the This Rule Applies To Traffic From These Sources list, click Anywhere and then click Remove. Click Add.
3. In Add Network Entities, expand Networks, click External, click Add, and then click Close.
4. On the To tab, ensure that the Forward The Original Host Header Instead Of The Actual One checkbox is selected.
5. On the Bridging tab, select the Redirect Request to SSL Port checkbox, and then specify port 4443.

   Changing this port number is required because in Lync the internal servers (front-end, Standard Edition, or Director) all have two websites, one listening on the standard SSL port 443 for internal users and the other on port 4443 for external users published via the reverse proxy.
6. Click Apply to save changes, and then click OK.
7. Click Apply in the details pane and then enter any required notes in the Configuration Change Description page and click Apply again to save the changes and update the configuration.

Now you need to repeat the procedure just outlined, but this time to publish the Director. There are a few slight differences when publishing the Director.

- Obviously, you need to give the rule a new name, which in this case you can call the Director Lync External.
- On the Web Listener page, instead of creating a new listener, select the existing one and click Next.
- Finally, when editing the newly created rule at the end, make sure that on the Public Name tab you click Add and enter the first simple URL, in this case `meet.gaots.co.uk`. Click OK and then repeat the process to add the second simple URL, `dialin.gaots.co.uk`.

One other consideration is that if you have phone devices externally, then for device updates and for logging purposes you will need to publish on port 80 as well as 443. This means you will need to configure your existing listener to listen on port 80 and bridge to port 8080 on the internal servers. To do this, on the Firewall Policy section of the TMG management console, in the right pane select the Toolbox tab and drill into Network Objects and through to the Web Listeners folder. Right-click the LyncPublishingListener created earlier and select Properties. On the Connections tab, check the box next to Enable HTTP Connections on Port: and click OK.

Apply these changes in the normal way. Next, open the properties of the Lync publishing rules you created. On the Bridging tab, check the checkbox next to Redirect Requests to HTTP

Port: and enter **8080** in the port box. Click OK and then perform this on each Lync server publishing rule you have created. Then apply the changes in the normal way. At this point Lync phone devices will be able to be updated and carry out logging, externally.

> **DNS ENTRIES**
>
> Of course for all this publishing to work, you will need to create *A* records in DNS for the external URLs and point them to the IP external public addresses through which TMG publishes the URLs.

Having completed the configuration needed, there are various tests you can carry out to prove that everything is working properly. You can test the connection to the Address Book, the Conferencing URL, the Distribution Group expansion URL, and the dial-in conferencing URL. To do so, follow these steps:

1. Open Internet Explorer from a machine on the Internet outside your local network. To test the Address Book service enter:

   `https://se01webext.gaots.co.uk/abs`

   You should receive an HTTP authentication challenge, because directory security on the Address Book Server folder is configured to Windows authentication by default.

2. To test conferencing, use the following URL:

   `https://se01webext.gaots.co.uk/meet`

   This URL will display the page used when joining conferences.

3. For distribution group expansion, use the URL:

   `https://se01webext.gaots.co.uk /GroupExpansion/service.svc`

   As with the Address Book, you should receive an HTTP authentication challenge.

4. In these examples, we haven't configured dial-in conferencing yet, so this URL won't currently work; however, for future reference, you can test external access to the dial-in conferencing site by typing the simple URL for dial-in conferencing shown here, after which the user should be directed to the dial-in page:

   `https://dialin.gaots.co.uk`

   If you have published both Director(s) and front-end or Standard Edition server(s), you should run these tests on each of the published servers.

Installing the Edge Server

The Edge server role is slightly different from the other Lync roles in that it is the only one not connected to your Active Directory domain, and it is installed in the perimeter network.

EDGE BEST PRACTICES

The Edge server should not be connected to your internal Active Directory. Microsoft supports connecting it to an Active Directory forest specifically for use in the perimeter network. In general, it is recommended that the server is a member of a workgroup.

This difference raises various challenges about how best to manage the installation. Lync does a vastly better job than OCS in this regard, as you will see. Now that Lync has the CMS, once the first replication of the configuration is complete (done manually as part of setup), secure push replication is carried out so that all management can be performed from the Topology Builder and Lync management tools.

The first step to deploying an Edge server is to set up a server meeting the prerequisites described in Chapter 5. In this case, you will use another Windows Server 2008 R2 SP1 server, which you will not join to the domain. The server will be called Edge01. Once the server is built and fully patched it then needs the relevant prerequisites installed.

First, it is important to configure the primary DNS suffix to match the internal domain suffix of the Lync server pool; in this case it will be `gaots.local`.

1. To do this, open up Properties of the Computer and click Change Settings in the Computer Name, Domain and Workgroup Settings section.
2. On the Computer Name tab, click Change and then on the Computer Name/Domain Changes tab, click More.
3. Enter the required suffix, and click OK until prompted to reboot, which you should do.

Next, you need to configure the NICs. As we discussed in Chapter 5, the Edge server must have two NICs, each on a different subnet. One is public-facing and the other closer to the internal LAN. In this exercise, you will use public IP addresses on the external interface instead of using NAT, as discussed in Chapter 3 and Chapter 5. Ensure that the external NIC has the default gateway defined pointing to the external firewall or router and that this NIC is at the top of the NIC binding order. To do this, take the following steps:

1. Type **Network and Sharing** into the Start menu search bar and open the Network and Sharing Center.
2. Click Change Adaptor Settings. When the window opens, press the Alt key. This will bring up menu options, from which you should select Advanced and then Advanced Settings.
3. This will open up the Adapters and Bindings window, where you should ensure that the Internet/External NIC is at the top of the bindings, as shown in Figure 6.15.

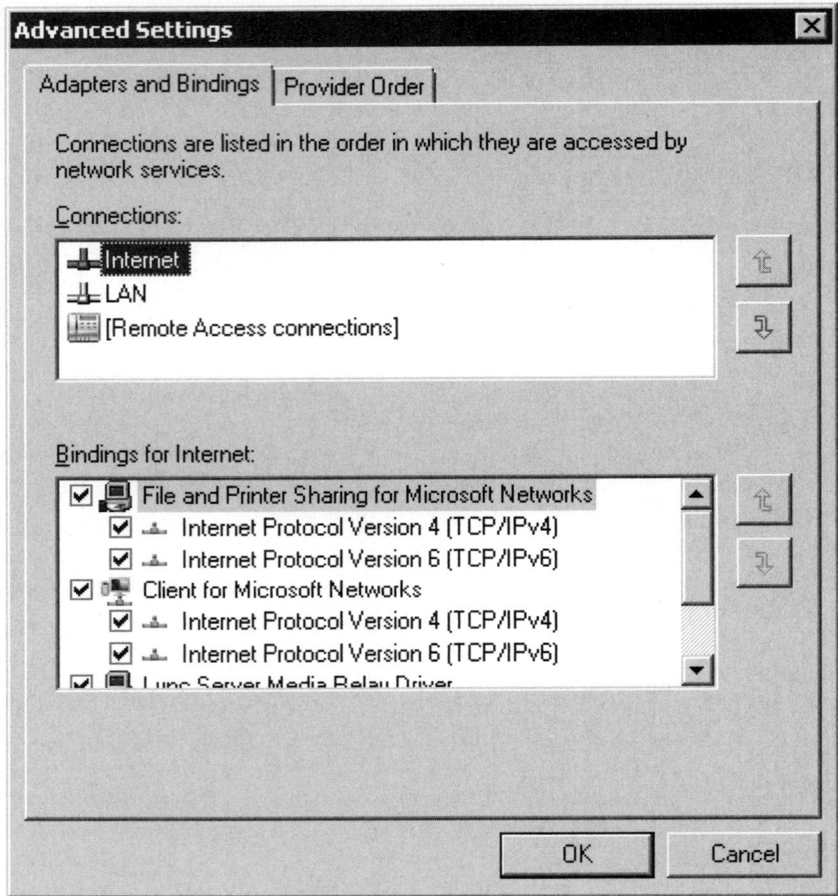

FIGURE 6.15
The NIC bindings on the Edge server

The next step is to ensure that the Edge server can resolve the internal servers by name. There are a couple of options here: using DNS servers you control in the perimeter network or using external DNS servers.

If you have DNS servers in the perimeter network, they must contain *A* records for the internal servers the Edge server needs to talk with—the next-hop server, which will be either the Front-End, Standard Edition, or Director server. If there is a pool of servers, each should have a record under the same name to provide for DNS load balancing.

If you are using external DNS servers, these should be defined purely on the external NIC and should point to public DNS servers. This option will not provide name resolution for the internal server, so you will need to provide entries in the HOSTS file. Figure 6.16 shows how to open the Hosts file, which should be done from Notepad running as Administrator. Figure 6.17 shows the entries in the HOSTS file in our environment.

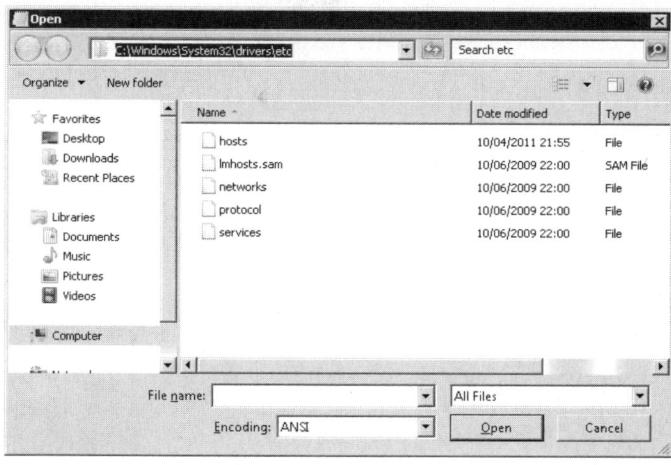

FIGURE 6.16
Opening the HOSTS file using the All Files option

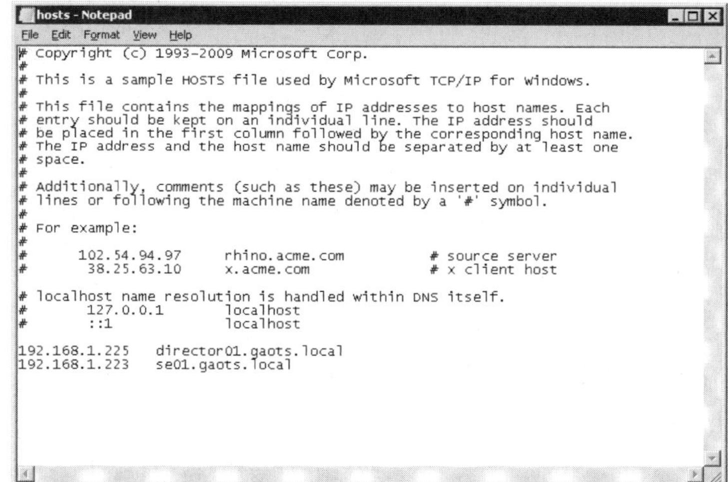

FIGURE 6.17
The HOSTS file entries

At this stage, the basic preparatory steps are done. Now you need to install the prerequisite software, which for the Edge is simply the .NET Framework 3.5 SP1. Install this in the normal way from an administrative PowerShell prompt.

1. Import the `servermanager` module and then install PowerShell:

```
Import-Module ServerManager
Add-WindowsFeature NET-Framework-Core
```

2. Having installed the .NET Framework, start the Lync setup program and allow setup to install Visual C++. As with the previous roles, setup follows the same format, first installing the Local Configuration Store. The difference in the Edge installation is that instead

of pulling the first config synchronization from the CMS, you have to pull it from a file. This means that you need to create the file, which is done on one of the internal servers with the admin tools installed. In this case, go to the Standard Edition server and open the Lync Management Shell. Use the following command to export the topology to a file:

```
Export-CsConfiguration -FileName c:\toplogyexport.zip
```

3. Locate the file and copy it over to the Edge server. Next run local setup and when prompted, select Import From A File and specify the location of the ZIP file copied from the Standard Edition server, as shown in Figure 6.18.

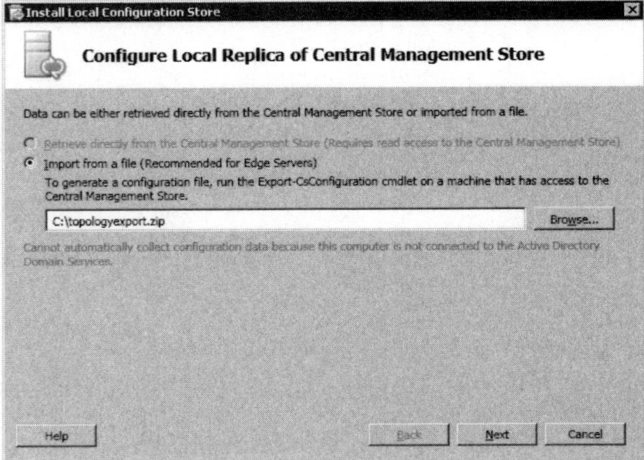

FIGURE 6.18
Importing the topology from a file into the Edge server

Again, as with other roles, you need to install certificates. The specific requirements were discussed in Chapter 5, so for now we will simply list what you need to install on the demo Edge server.

CERT REQUEST FOR EXTERNAL NIC:

Subject: `Accessedge.gaots.co.uk`

SAN: `Accessedge.gaots.co.uk`

SAN: `Webconf.gaots.co.uk`

SAN: `Sip.gaots.co.uk`

Note that the first SAN entry must be the same as the subject name of the certificate because TLS encryption is in use and it simply looks at the SANs of the certificate rather than the subject name.

CERT REQUEST FOR INTERNAL EDGE NIC:

Subject: Edge01.gaots.local

Another difference in the process of requesting the certificates for the internal servers is that this time, you will not be able to submit the requests to an online CA. The external NIC certificate request should be submitted as an offline request to a public trusted CA such as Digicert or VeriSign, and although the internal certificate can and should be issued from the internal CA used for the internal servers, that will also need to be done offline, as it is unlikely that relevant ports will be open from the DMZ to the internal network for online enrollment.

To create the manual requests, take the following steps:

1. Start with the Edge Internal certificate highlighted and click Request. Elect to Prepare The Request Now and click Next.
2. Enter a name and path for where to save the request file and click Next.
3. Click Next on the Specify Alternative Certificate Template window, and then on the Name and Security Settings page enter a Friendly name for the certificate. Use something in the name that will help you identify the server and interface.
4. Click Next to proceed. On the next couple of pages, enter organizational information. Accept the default subject name on the Subject Name / Subject Alternative Names page and then click Next.
5. Don't enter additional SANs, and click Next.
6. Finally, check the summary and click Next to create the certificate request. As long as the request is created without error, click Next and then on the Certificate Request File page, click View to look at the certificate request data. This is the text data that must be sent to the CA.
7. Click Finish to return to the first Certificate Wizard page.
8. Once you have received the certificate and installed it into the Personal store of the Local Computer Account, return to the first Certificate screen and, with the Edge Internal certificate still highlighted, click Assign.
9. On the first page of the Certificate Assignment Wizard, click Next and then on the Certificate Store page, locate the relevant certificate by friendly name to assign, as shown in Figure 6.19.

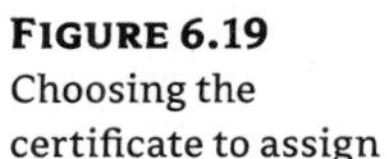

FIGURE 6.19
Choosing the certificate to assign

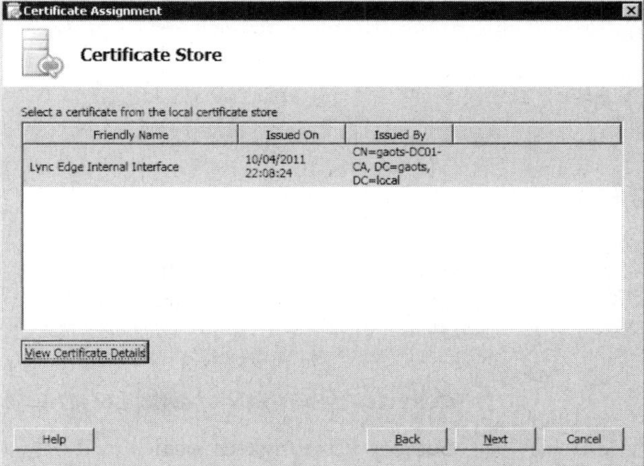

10. Click Next twice to assign the certificate. On the Executing Commands page, check for any errors and view the log if required, and then click Finish to exit.

> **CA Trust for Internal Certificates**
>
> One step to carry out before requesting the certificates is to ensure that the Edge server trusts the internal CA that issues certificates to the internal servers.

When creating the external certificate, follow the same process. As before, when prompted, select the checkbox to create the `sip.gaots.co.uk` SAN entry for later use by phone devices. This certificate request will be sent to an external CA, which will generate and return the certificate. As with the installation of externally trusted certificates on the TMG box, you must follow the installation instructions carefully. Once the certificate is in the personal store of the local computer, go back to the Certificate Wizard and with the external interface certificate highlighted, click Assign and follow the wizard to assign the externally trusted certificate.

Now that you've completed the certificate setup, all that remains is to start the services, install any remaining Windows patches, and update Lync to the same version (currently CU3) as the other servers in the organization.

Enterprise Deployments

In this chapter, we installed Lync Standard Edition and enabled external access with a single Edge server. In essence, this has been a simple, small-business installation. That is not to say that this system can't support a large number of users; it can. Standard Edition will, when run on the right hardware, support up to 5,000 users; however, there are companies with many more users than that. Another aspect of the installation that was simpler than many deployments is the domain and network. We set up a single site and single forest/domain Active Directory. Even some small businesses with far fewer than 5,000 users have many sites that need support. In these more complex environments, there are additional considerations that may change the way deployment is carried out. In the remainder of this chapter, we will look at these issues, starting with installing into a large Active Directory, which potentially has restricted rights for different administrators. Other topics will include specifying how you want install to work with SQL, working in environments with multiple sites (including both small branch offices and those with tens of thousands of users), and finally a discussion of setup automation.

Working in Large Active Directories

As discussed in the "Preparing Active Directory" section, Lync uses Active Directory less than its predecessor OCS did. That said, there is still a need for schema changes and the creation of a significant number of new objects which, therefore, require careful collaboration between all those working with the directory.

So what exactly constitutes a large/complex directory? Anything larger than a single forest, single domain, and single site warrants some discussion. Traditionally, there are various types of structures that form large directories:

- Single forest with a single tree and multiple domains
- Single forest with multiple trees and disjoint namespaces

- Multiple forests in a central forest topology
- Multiple forests in a resource forest topology

The requirements for these directories were discussed in Chapter 5, so this section covers what is needed from an installation perspective. The key rule is to remember the following:

Schema prep needs to be run once in each forest where Lync servers will be deployed.

Coming back to the structure of the forest mentioned earlier, you do not need to run this directly on the schema master (which is likely to reside in the root domain in the forest), so long as the account you run schema prep under has rights to the schema master. This is good news because it means that you don't need to gain access to a machine in the root domain which is likely to be heavily locked down. In a resource forest model, schema prep is run in the resource forest where the Lync servers are, not in the user forest.

The forest prep procedure, which creates the universal group, is run once in a forest that will host Lync servers. It is forest prep that creates the universal groups used to assign permissions to the various Lync components. In a large directory environment you may want to take advantage of the opportunity to create these groups in a domain other than the forest root. You might particularly want to do this if you operate an empty forest root domain and, therefore, want to keep access as limited as possible to the forest root domain. In a resource forest model, forest prep is run in the resource forest where the Lync servers are, not in the user forest.

Domain prep should be run in each domain where Lync users will be enabled. In a resource forest model, domain prep is run in the resource forest where the Lync servers are not in the user forest. This is because although there will be users in the user forest accessing Lync, they will be linked via the disabled user objects in the resource forest, which are what will hold the Lync properties.

SINGLE-LABEL DOMAINS

It should be noted that unlike Exchange 2010, Lync cannot be installed in a *single label domain*. That is, for example, a domain called `.gaots` rather than `.gaots.local`.

When working in an environment that has a complex AD, it is likely is that AD will be managed by a dedicated team of directory experts. In order to make changes to the directory, you will need to describe all the required changes. One of the biggest and most permanent is the schema update. A great deal of detail can be found in the Lync help file; however, in summary what happens is that schema prep imports information from four `.ldf` files in the order shown below:

`ExternalSchema.ldf` This file creates the classes and attributes which allow integration of Lync with Exchange for UM and OWA IM.

`ServerSchema.ldf` This is the primary Lync schema file and contains the majority of classes and attributes associated with Lync.

`BackCompatSchema.ldf` This file provides for interoperability with components from prior releases.

`VersionSchema.ldf` The changes in this file set the version of the schema by which it is possible to check which version of Lync schema is installed.

If you want to take a closer look at these files, you can find them in the `\Support\schema` folder on the installation media. It is even possible to import these files manually in AD with the LDIFDE utility. You would no longer need to provide the directory teams with the ability or training needed to run the Lync setup program, and you'd have a workaround in cases where the only option available is to run the process from a machine that is not 64-bit, which is what Lync setup needs.

Another difference with a large directory is that once you have run the schema and forest preparation, more care is needed to ensure that the changes have replicated around all domain controllers in the forest. It is also worth noting that making these changes will create replication traffic, so it is worth carrying out these changes over a period of low usage to ensure a smooth replication process.

Delegating Setup Permissions

Closely related to the topic of Active Directory is that of administrative permissions needed to carry out setup in an enterprise deployment.

Delegation of setup permissions is much simpler than in OCS 2007 R2. Running local setup now requires only Local Administrator permissions on the Lync server and the ability to read domain-based information and CMS information. These are granted by the Domain Users and RTCUniversalReadOnlyAdmins groups, respectively. This simplification is possible because so much work has already been carried out in the Topology Builder. Of course, a greater level of permissions is needed to publish and enable the changes in a new topology, as discussed in Chapter 5.

The other permissions issue you may come up against when running setup is that of a locked-down AD. This might occur, for example, if your directory team has turned off inheritance on certain sections of the directory to enable delegated security. When Lync setup is run, both the domain prep and server activation steps set permissions on objects within the domain. Not having the relevant security entries can prevent Lync from properly understanding the topology of the system and will prevent user administration. Therefore, if inheritance is blocked on a particular OU, you can use the following command to manually set the required security entries for Lync after domain prep is run.

```
Grant-CsOuPermission -ObjectType "User" -OU "ou=testusers,dc=gaots,dc=local"
-Domain "gaots.local"
```

This will set the required permissions on the user objects within the `testusers` OU in the `gaots.local` domain.

If instead this were a `Computer` OU, which held Lync computer accounts, you could run the following command:

```
Grant-CsOuPermission -ObjectType "Computer" -OU "ou=Servers,dc=gaots,dc=local"
-Domain "gaots.local"
```

This would set the permissions on `Computer` objects in the `servers` OU in the `Gaots.local` domain.

Standalone SQL

One major area that is different in an Enterprise Edition installation is SQL. As you know, SQL is used to store various databases, the most important being the CMS. In Standard Edition, the

CMS and other databases are installed on the Standard Edition server and run on SQL Express. However, when using Enterprise Edition, SQL must be run on a separate server which is often a SQL cluster to provide suitable resilience.

In Lync setup there are two main ways to install the required databases; they offer different levels of control. The Setup Wizard provides some capacity for specifying database file location, but for full control you need to revert to the command line.

The `Install-CsDatabase` cmdlet lets you create databases from the command line. It is a cmdlet with many parameters and a lot of intelligence. For example, you can use it to determine automatically the best available deployment path for the database on the SQL server. However, this only works on a standalone SQL server and not on SQL clusters. Therefore, it makes sense to learn how to use the cmdlet to deploy databases in a syntax that specifies the path for the data and log files.

Before attempting to run any of the commands listed next, make sure that the server you are attempting this from has the following components installed and that Lync AD Preparation has completed successfully.

Component Name	**File Location on Media**
Lync Server 2010 `OCSCore.msi`	`\Setup\AMD64\Setup`
SQL Server 2005 BC (`SQLServer2005_BC.msi`)	`\Setup\amd64`
SQL Server Native Client (`sqlncli.msi`)	`\Setup\amd64`

To prepare the Lync CMS database, open LMS and first run this command:

```
Set-ExecutionPolicy -RemoteSigned
```

This allows local PowerShell scripts to run unhindered while also ensuring that those not created locally need signing to prove their authenticity.

Next, run a command similar to the following:

```
Install-CsDatabase -CentralManagementDatabase -SqlServerFqdn sql01.gaots.local
-SqlInstanceName rtc -DatabasePaths "E:\LyncDB-Logs","D:\LyncDB-CMS" -Report "C:\
Logs\InstallDatabases.html"
```

This will install the CMS database on the SQL server SQL01. The database named `rtc` will be placed in `D:\LyncDB-CMS` while the logs will on `E:\` in the `LyncDB-Logs` folder. Finally, a log file will be written to the `C:\Logs` folder.

Referring to SQL Servers by Name

When you are using the SQL server name in commands, it is important to use the FQDN and not the short (NetBIOS) name. For example, use `SQL01.gaots.local` rather than SQL01.

Having created the CMS database just shown, you can continue through the processes discussed in Chapter 5 to create and publish the topology. Once Lync deployment progresses to the point of installing the server, you should use the following command to create the databases defined in the topology:

```
Install-CsDatabase -ConfiguredDatabases -SqlServerFqdn sql01.gaots.local
-Report "C:\Logs\InstallDatabases.html"
```

This command will install all the databases defined in the topology for the SQL server `SQL01.gaots.local`.

Configuring an AV Conferencing Breakout Server

Another aspect of a large deployment is *scale*. One of the most resource-intensive elements of Lync is AV conferencing. It is for this reason that in an Enterprise Edition deployment of Lync it is possible to break out the conferencing role to provide additional scale and remove load from the front-end server. In an Enterprise deployment, once you have between 4,000 and 6,000 users actively participating in a front-end server pool, you should consider splitting out the Conferencing role. This was discussed in more depth in Chapter 5, so for now let's look at what this means from an installation point of view.

To install an AV Conferencing breakout server, you need to prepare the usual Windows Server 2008 R2 SP1 server (or other supported OS) and have patched it with all the latest patches from Windows Update. You need to install very few prerequisites; in fact the only one that is needed is the Windows Media Format Runtime, which you installed for the Standard Edition role. To install the runtime, you should run the installation command from the `CMD.exe` shell as an administrator. To run the CMD prompt, type **CMD** into the Start menu search box, then right-click the result and select Run as Administrator. Having done so, run the following command:

```
%systemroot%\system32\dism.exe /online /add-package /packagepath:%windir%\
servicing\Packages\Microsoft-Windows-Media-Format-Package~31bf3856ad364e35~a
md64~~6.1.7601.17514.mum /ignorecheck
```

This command will install the runtime and then you will need to restart, so press Y to do so.

Assuming you have published the AV Conferencing Breakout pool in the topology, at this stage you can begin setup. As with all the other roles, setup follows the same steps:

1. Install the Local Configuration Store and have it pull the configuration from the CMS.
2. Run Setup or Remove Lync Server Components.
3. Install Certificates, which are simple single-name certificates matching the AV Conferencing pool FQDN.
4. Start the services.

Once you've carried out these steps, you'll have additional resources to dedicate to serving conferencing requests.

Considerations for Branches

As discussed in Chapter 5, there are various aspects to consider when deploying Lync in branch offices, including the bandwidth available and the reliability of that bandwidth back to the central site, the number of users in the remote site, and the availability of local IT staff. Planning might determine that a local server capable of supporting all workloads is needed at the branch office. This would, therefore, not be a Survivable Branch Appliance, but would instead be a Standard Edition server.

Deploying a Standard Edition server in a branch site is very similar to deploying one in a central site. The main difference is that instead of running the "Prepare first Standard Edition server" step, you can progress straight to installing the Local Configuration Store. That is because you will already have a CMS in one of your other central sites, which you would define the new topology required for the deployment of Standard Edition in the branch office.

TYPE OF SITE FOR STANDARD EDITION DEPLOYMENT IN A BRANCH

Contrary to common sense, to deploy a Standard Edition server in a branch office, you don't create a branch site—which would be the case for a SBA deployment. Instead, you create another central site.

Automating Installation Using PowerShell

Throughout this chapter, if you looked carefully at the summary pages at the end of the various installation steps, you have seen the PowerShell commands that ran. As stated before, Lync is entirely underpinned by PowerShell, which means that it is entirely feasible to carry out the installation directly from the command line without using the GUI setup at all. Although it may not be the most user-friendly option, it is great for documentation and repetition. So if you are rolling out Lync globally, we highly recommend taking a look at this option and working to build a deployment script that will enable you to deploy Lync servers in a known manner without any administrative errors. Given that we have yet to dive into PowerShell in depth, we will leave the details of this script until we introduce PowerShell in Chapter 8. If you are keen, then feel free to skip ahead now.

The Bottom Line

Configure Windows Server for a Lync installation. Installing Lync is relatively simple, but many steps are involved. One of the most important is the preparatory work needed. If you get this wrong, it will slow down your installation and you may find that certain features will not work later down the line.

Master It Lync can be installed on several subtly different operating systems. You have been asked to lay out which OS requires the least amount of preparatory work and what the main preparatory stages are before Lync can be deployed.

Prepare Active Directory for Lync installation. Like many Microsoft server applications, Lync has tight ties with AD. Lync is the first version of Microsoft's real-time communications product to start moving away from the reliance on AD, but nevertheless there are still hard requirements and preparatory steps that must be carried out, which include schema, forest, and domain prep.

Master It You are working in a large corporation with a single forest and multiple domains. You have been instructed to work with your directories team to help them understand the changes that need to be made to the schema as part of setup.

Install your first Standard Edition server. Lync Standard Edition server is a complex environment requiring careful deployment. It has numerous prerequisites that need to be installed. Once you have completed the installation of prerequisites, setup is relatively straightforward following a standard process.

Master It You have been tasked with installing the first Standard Edition Lync server in your network. What is one of the unique preparatory steps required for this Standard Edition, and why? Following that, what are the standard steps that setup takes?

Get your first users up and running. Getting the first users on Lync is slightly more involved than it first sounds. Of course, you need a couple of users with which to test. Enabling them for Lync is straightforward, especially if they already have an email address defined that matches the SIP uniform resource identifier (URI) you want the user to have. The more interesting challenge is getting the client deployed. Of course, this can be done manually, but once things scale out that won't be feasible. This leaves options to install from the command line as part of a logon script or perhaps to use the MSI installer to install via a management tool such as System Center Configuration Manager.

Master It You are rolling out the Lync client to thousands of users. How would you do this, and what are some of the considerations you need to make?

Implement external access through the Director, Edge, and Reverse Proxy servers. There are many elements that come together to provide external access. The Edge server and Reverse Proxy sit in the perimeter network and provide access to media and web components, respectively. The Director sits on the LAN and acts as a routing and security buffer between the external users and the front-end pools. The deployment of the Director follows very similar lines to the Standard Edition or front-end servers and requires similar prerequisites.

Master It You are deploying an Edge server as part of providing remote access to your network. What is different about the install compared to the Standard Edition and Director installs?

Understand the differences in an Enterprise Edition installation. There are many differences when working on an Enterprise deployment of Lync compared to a Standard Edition install. For example, there is the potential for a complex directory to be present, which requires close cooperation with a directories team. Another change is that SQL is installed separately from Lync and does not co-exist with the Lync server as it does with Standard Edition. Finally there is the challenge of scalability and branch offices to overcome.

Master It You have been asked to work with the database team to ensure that everything is in place for the Lync installation. What do you need to explain and how would you instruct the database team to create the databases?

Chapter 7

Migration and Upgrades

If you've followed along in the book so far, you should have a good understanding of much of Lync, including how to deploy it. However, if you already have a Microsoft real-time communication platform in your environment, things are slightly more complex than if you don't. You will need to consider how to upgrade or migrate from one system to the next and negotiate a period of coexistence. There are constraints on exactly which versions are supported during coexistence, and there are some differences between moving from OCS 2007 and OCS 2007 R2. Of course, throughout this period you'll need to work with your users to make sure the transition period is as painless as possible for them as they move from clients they know to the new Lync client.

In this chapter, you will learn to:

- Understand migration considerations
- Consider client pain points
- Migrate to Lync

Understanding Migration

Migration to Lync can take a variety of forms. Possibly the simplest would be to install a new Lync system, not have it talk to the old OCS system, and ask users to re-create all their contacts and meetings. Clearly, this isn't possibly very often! The disruption would simply be too great.

Therefore, a move to Lync from one of the previous Microsoft real-time communication platforms needs to include a period of coexistence. At the time of writing, this period of coexistence can include only two versions of the product at any one time; Lync is one, and the other is either OCS 2007 R2 or OCS 2007. Migration from Live Communications Server (LCS) 2005 directly to Lync 2010 is not supported, tested, or documented, and neither is having both OCS 2007 and OCS 2007 R2 deployed in the same organization and adding Lync to that. If you have a complex environment with a mix of OCS 2007 and OCS 2007 R2, or even an old LCS system, you have to perform some intermediary steps before you can get to Lync.

In order to get to a state where Lync can be integrated and coexist with your existing environment, you need to make sure that any LCS deployments are upgraded to at least OCS 2007 and that LCS is completely decommissioned. Equally, if you have a mixed OCS 2007 and OCS 2007 R2 deployment, then you need to either back out of the OCS 2007 R2 deployment and move back to OCS 2007 or push on, and remove all of the OCS 2007 pools so that you have only OCS 2007 R2 left. Once you've done that, you are ready to move to Lync.

Coexistence

This chapter is called "Migrations and Upgrades," because people use both words interchangeably to describe moving to Lync. You are *upgrading* in the sense that you are moving from one Microsoft real-time communication product to the next version; however, you are *migrating* in the method that you carry out the move. We describe it this way because there is no way to simply put the install media into the existing servers and click Upgrade. The only way to move to Lync is through a side-by-side migration, in which you install Lync on new servers in your existing Active Directory (AD) and then configure it to coexist with your current product, be it OCS 2007 or OCS 2007 R2.

NOTE Although we mentioned that Lync would be installed on new hardware into the existing AD, you must still install a new Lync pool. Lync servers cannot be installed in OCS pools.

One key piece of coexistence is the ability for Lync to talk to OCS. Because there has been a significant architecture change from OCS to Lync, particularly in the move to the Central Management Store, some configuration is needed to make this possible. Once you are happy that you have Lync installed and running satisfactorily on your pilot pool, you must then merge the OCS configuration data from Windows Management Instrumentation (WMI) and Active Directory (AD) into the Lync topology. Then, once everything is configured correctly so that communication can flow, you start the process of moving services and then users over to the new Lync system, and then finally decommission the old OCS setup.

Another key element of coexistence is the way the Edge and Director roles are handled. The first principle is that the Lync Edge and Lync Director roles should always be deployed together. You should not have an OCS Edge talking to a Lync Director, for example. Another similar requirement is not to mix the Lync and OCS versions of the Edge and Mediation roles. For example, a Lync Mediation server should have a route out of a Lync Edge, not an OCS one.

At this point the process for moving from OCS 2007 to Lync is different from moving from OCS 2007 R2 to Lync, particularly at the stage where the Lync Edge and Director roles are deployed. With OCS 2007, an entire Lync pool with Edge and Director should be set up in parallel, whereas with OCS 2007 R2 the Lync front end can talk to the outside world via the OCS 2007 R2 Edge and Director for the first part of coexistence. This chapter will focus on the migration from OCS 2007 R2 to Lync, with a separate discussion covering the differences in migration from OCS 2007 in more depth.

In addition to the major issue of version support, you need to be aware of a couple of more detailed points about coexistence. First, when moving to Lync, there are a variety of options involving the SQL database. You can either create and use an entirely new SQL infrastructure or reuse an existing SQL server. Obviously, you must size the SQL infrastructure correctly in either case so that it can perform adequately for Lync. One thing that is highly discouraged is using an existing SQL instance that is supporting another application. Although it is possible to make this work theoretically, you would not be able to control the way CPU and memory resources were assigned even though you could control where the database resided on the disk. Also, if the existing instance is supporting OCS, you would have a clash of default database names, which is definitely something to avoid! For more information about SQL sizing for Lync, see the following:

To configure SQL Server for Lync Server 2010, refer to:

`http://technet.microsoft.com/en-us/library/gg425848.aspx`

Server hardware platforms:

http://technet.microsoft.com/en-us/library/gg398835.aspx

THE OCS ENHANCED PRESENCE BIT

OCS 2007 introduced the concept of *enhanced presence*, which allowed users to set different levels of access to their presence information, including blocking access altogether. When you're migrating, you need to make sure that Enhanced Presence is turned on for each OCS user when you are configuring. This must be done before you migrate users to Lync. If this is the first time you have turned Enhanced Presence on in OCS, you need to make sure that users have logged on at least once to the OCS client, because this is what completes the Enhanced Presence setup in the OCS database. If they haven't logged on, the migration will produce an error and they will lose their blocked contacts list.

Another aspect of migration to be aware of is that Lync brings some new roles that didn't exist in OCS. For example, when you're using Enterprise Edition, you can split out the AV Conferencing role to scale the capacity for conferences. Both Standard and Enterprise versions of Lync can utilize the new Survivable Branch Appliance, which provides resilience to branch offices. It is recommended to complete the deployment of Lync and the removal of OCS before deploying these new roles.

A final piece to consider about coexistence involves applications that have been written in United Communications Managed API (UCMA). Apps that use v2.0 and are running on OCS 2007 R2 servers can be called into by users migrated to Lync servers; however, if you still have UCMA v1 apps that are running on OCS 2007, they will not work. Either way, for apps to run on Lync server, they need to be written using UCMA v3.0, so as part of your migration, you will need to consider how best to get this done and have the new apps deployed on the Lync servers. This custom development work is outside the scope of this book, so you should contact whoever created the application for you and discuss specific requirements and process for migration with them.

Considering Client Pain Points

When a move to Lync is being planned, one of the most important considerations is how the migration will affect users. After all, it would be a shame to create a negative feeling about such a great new platform. In order to ensure that things go smoothly you need to be aware of common issues and problems that inevitably occur as new functionality is introduced that works differently than its predecessor. This topic is discussed more broadly in Appendix B.

The first consideration is the client. The old client can connect to the new server, but not the other way around; therefore, the client is the last thing to be upgraded. This helps to simplify how things work, but it also means that in a large deployment, if you stick rigidly to the old client, users who have been migrated could miss out on the new features of Lync, such as the new conferencing features of document and program sharing, for a long time until everyone is moved. To avoid that, you might decide to move people and then upgrade their clients, which would mean that will have two different versions in place and that people will have access to different functionality. It is critical to communicate to users exactly what is happening and when and how it will affect their ability to do what they always have done. It also means that you as an administrator will have two different clients to support and manage using the policies available.

Policies

In OCS, there are many policies available to control the client. In Lync, there is a fairly significant change in how policies are applied, which is covered in depth in Chapter 10, "User Administration." However, in the context of a migration, you need to understand a few things. In particular, you need to know how a certain group of settings, which provide client configuration and lockdown for OCS, should be translated into the new Lync policy mechanisms.

In Lync, the majority of policy settings are now set through in-band provisioning. However, there is also a group still provided via Group Policy, which enables settings to be configured before the client logs on. Fortunately for these bootstrapping policies, the same group policy used for an OCS client will work for Lync clients. For example, you might have been using Group Policy to configure an OCS client to connect to a specific server, to use TCP rather than TLS, and not to display the client first run splash screen; this policy will still work with Lync.

Of course, there are differences based on the new policy engine. There are also many new policies to cover new Lync features. Before you complete your rollout of Lync, be sure to read Chapter 10, which covers the policy engine in depth. Also take a look at the "Migrating User Settings to Lync Server 2010" topic in the help file, which can be found here:

```
http://technet.microsoft.com/en-us/library/gg398814.aspx
```

This discussion provides a useful reference point for policies that have the same name, a name change, or are new altogether.

Meetings

The biggest change in client functionality in Lync is that LiveMeeting is replaced in Lync. As part of this move, the old meeting URLs are replaced. In OCS, conference URLs start with `conf://` and LiveMeeting URLs start with `meet://`. In Lync, all meeting URLs start with the `HTTPS://` format, which means that participants can access a meeting via the Meeting Join website. They will be given the option to join via the Lync Web App or to download the Lync Attendee and use it instead. If they already have a suitable client installed (either Lync, Lync Attendee, or Lync Attendant), they will be taken directly into the meeting. The Lync Attendant provides access only to the audio part of the meeting.

CONFIGURING THE MEETING JOIN PAGE

Configure the Meeting Join page in the Lync Server Control panel under the Security ➢ Web Service settings. You can configure the same settings by using the `New-CsWebServiceConfiguration` or `Set-CsWebServiceConfiguration` PowerShell cmdlets with the `ShowDownloadCommunicatorAttendeeLink` and `ShowJoinUsingLegacyClientLink` parameters.

As part of the migration, there is also a change from creating a LiveMeeting for sharing to creating a new Lync Online Meeting. When creating these new Lync Online Meetings, it is important to realize that there are differences in the default settings for meetings. Specifically, with OCS scheduled meetings, anonymous participants could enter straight into the meeting (subject to conferencing policy); in Lync, this is not the case. The new Lobby feature is enabled to capture people who enter a meeting and are not part of your company; this information is ascertained by checking the supported SIP URIs of your organization. In comparison, Lync ad-hoc meetings that are set up using Meet Now from the Lync client by default allow anyone directly into the meeting without waiting in the lobby. You need to be aware of these changes so that you can communicate the new system to your users, or change the defaults to better meet your needs.

PINs and IDs

As with other elements of migration, some things change and others don't. One thing that won't change is a user's PIN to get into conferences from a phone device; one thing that will change is your conference ID. It is changed when you start using the new Lync client Online Meeting add-in to Outlook to schedule meetings. The ID is covered in more depth in Chapter 16, "Extended Voice Functionality"; however, the key thing to note is that although your old ID will continue to work for meetings already scheduled, all new ones will use your new ID.

Of course, not all meetings will be new. It is important to address what happens to recurring meetings or those that are already set up for the future. For meetings that were created on OCS, when a user is migrated to Lync, the meetings are carried over but remain either `conf://` (Conferencing) or `meet://` (LiveMeeting). For `conf://` URLs, a migrated user will use the Lync client. For `meet://` URLs, the LiveMeeting client will still be used. This means you can't simply remove the LiveMeeting client from PCs until all meetings have been moved across to the new Lync format.

Also note that users migrated to the new Lync client cannot create new Live Meetings hosted on OCS. For those conferences or Live Meetings that have been migrated to Lync, there are limits to which settings can continue to be modified. Most meeting settings remain editable as usual; however, if a user modifies the end date, subject, or attendee list of a meeting created on OCS, that meeting will be migrated to the new Lync Online Meeting format. Given that you can create only new Lync Online Meetings once you have been migrated and are using the new client, it may well make sense to move those who are heavy conference users to Lync early in the process so they can begin using the benefits.

Meeting Content

Content in existing meetings that are migrated is not brought across. For example, if your sales people have already set up regular meetings with uploaded PowerPoint slides and polls, even though the meetings will be migrated, the decks and polls will not. You will need to set up this information again.

You also need to understand that although a user migrated to Lync can easily join a meeting set up on OCS, the new features available in Lync meetings will not be available.

So far we have focused on moving to Lync when the new Lync client is in place. The other aspect of migration is when you have been moved to Lync but the new clients have not rolled out. In this instance, a user would continue to use the LiveMeeting conferencing add-in to schedule meetings but would not have access to new features such as lobby management in the meeting or to new Lync collaboration features as provided by the Lync client. Equally, before a user is moved to Lync, they have access to conferences created on Lync, but will not get access to the new conferencing functionality unless they use the Attendee or Lync Web App clients. This is similar to when users still on OCS are invited to meetings hosted on the Lync server. They will find that there are various methods of joining. They can use the browser-based Lync Web App, or download and install the Lync Attendee, or they can be dialed in using the legacy OCS client. However, they will end up with reduced functionality. If coexistence is going to be in place for any length of time, the Lync Attendee client should be rolled out to all users and then replaced with the Lync client as users are migrated.

You may also need to provide access to the new Lync meetings to those outside your company. Instead of using the LiveMeeting client, you need to make sure people use the Lync Attendee or the Lync Web App to join your meetings. These clients are covered in Chapter 4 "Client Access." When access is provided to a federated party, if the meeting organizer uses the Lync feature to lock a meeting so participants come into the lobby, the meeting can't be accessed by federated users using the LCS 2005 or OCS 2007 clients. Participants need to use the Attendee or Web App to enter.

Interoperability

As touched on previously, one of the bigger challenges of your move to Lync is making sure that things work as expected for users. A big part of this challenge is determining how those users still on the old client can work with those on the new client.

Multiple Points of Presence

By default, OCS and now Lync offer the potential for a user to sign in from many different places. For example, a user could be signed in on a phone device, a Mac laptop, and a Windows desktop. Once a user is moved to Lync, there are few limits to which clients they can be signed in from simultaneously. They can use all forms of the Lync client and be signed in with both the current Lync and older OCS 2007 and OCS 2007 R2 client at the same time, subject to your client version policy. There is, however, one important exception. A Lync Attendant user can be signed in simultaneously only with phones running the Lync 2010 Phone Edition. Simultaneous sign-in with other Lync Server 2010 clients is not supported.

Delegating

In OCS 2007 R2, a new feature called *call delegation* enabled managers to delegate phone call handling to one or more administrative assistants or other delegates. When a delegate answered a call, the manager was notified that the call had been answered, along with the name of the delegate who answered. In Lync, delegation has been improved significantly. In OCS 2007 R2, the administrative assistants needed to use the attendant console; in Lync, all of this is now integrated into a single Lync client as part of the push toward a real-time communications client. Of course, for this new functionality to work, both the manager and delegate must be using Lync

2010, so it is very important that you move managers and delegates to Lync at the same time; otherwise, you will disable the delegates' ability to manage their bosses' calls.

FUNCTIONALITY

A few functional areas need to be addressed, especially if you are moving from OCS 2007 but occasionally if you are moving from OCS 2007 R2 as well. These areas particularly affect some of the Enterprise Voice functionality, which is understandable given the rate of development from OCS 2007 to Lync.

As a starting point, let's look at basic communication between different client versions. First, it is important to note that Lync users can only talk to those on the LCS 2005 client if they are federated users—that is, not in the same organization/AD forest. Lync is fully supported to communicate with OCS 2007 or OCS 2007 R2 clients in the same organization and it provides the ability to communicate via IM, voice, and video. The limitations involve specific voice features. For example, it is not possible to retrieve a call parked on Lync (see Chapter 16 for more information) from a non-Lync client. Equally, it is not possible to use response group or team call features when using OCS 2007 clients. With these caveats aside, most communications scenarios will work just fine during your period of coexistence.

On a different but related note, it is important to acknowledge that although Lync provides a feature called Lync Web App (LWA) installed on each front-end server, LWA no longer provides the full IM functionality that Communicator Web Access (CWA) in OCS did. LWA is supported only to gain access to conferences in Lync. Therefore, if you still require the functionality of CWA, you must either deploy CWA and connect it to Lync, which is still supported, or go without this functionality until Microsoft provides a replacement.

Migrating to Lync

Now that you're familiar with a broad outline of the migration process and understand how a migration affects users, it's time to dive in and actually migrate a system. The rest of this chapter will discuss moving from a system on OCS 2007 R2 to Lync 2010.

NOTE **Although the migration-related aspects of the process will be discussed in depth, this chapter assumes that you have read and understand other areas of the book. Given that a migration touches many elements of Lync, if we covered every piece of the process in depth, this chapter would be huge!**

The elements involved in the migration consist of the following machines:

- DC01: The domain controller, which hosts the DNS and certificate services: domain name `gaots.local`
- OCS-SE01: Our OCS 2007 R2 Standard Edition server running Cumulative Update 9
- OCS-Mediation: Providing Enterprise voice functionality via a SIP Trunk to UK provider Gradwell
- OCS-CWA: The Communicator Web Access server providing web based access to IM, Presence, and Conferencing dial-in

- OCS-Edge: Providing full external access and federation for user domain names:
  - `OCS-Edge.gaots.local`
  - `OCSAccess.gaots.co.uk`
  - `OCSConf.gaots.co.uk`
  - `OCSAV.gaots.co.uk`
- Exch: The Exchange 2010 SP1 server, which runs Unified Messaging and also has presence integrated with OWA

The Director role hasn't been deployed, but otherwise this is a great representation of a standard OCS deployment. As part of the migration you will add two more servers:

- Lync-SE01 will be your Standard Edition Lync server: domain name `Lync-se.gaots.local`
- Lync-Edge will provide remote access to Lync users. Domain names:
  - `Lync-edge.gaots.local`
  - `LyncAccess.gaots.co.uk`
  - `LyncConf.gaots.co.uk`
  - `LyncAV.gaots.co.uk`

MONITORING AND ARCHIVING DURING MIGRATION

Although a Monitoring or Archiving server isn't defined in the migration scenario in this chapter, it is something you may need to take into account. This is especially the case when your company relies on archiving for compliance reasons or perhaps monitoring for billing purposes. The main principle is that each version of OCS or Lync only works with the Monitoring and Archiving server from the same version. Therefore, if you are migrating and maintaining these capabilities is critical, you must implement the Monitoring and Archiving roles in your Lync pool before you move any users to Lync. For more information on the Monitoring and Archiving roles, see Chapter 11, "Monitoring/Archiving."

As the migration progresses, when you merge the topology to allow Lync and OCS to communicate, you will find that the existing Archiving and Monitoring policies come across into Lync. Similarly, when users are migrated, if they were archived in OCS they will also be in Lync.

Finally, you should note that the new Lync Archiving and Monitoring servers don't use the same databases as the OCS roles, so if you need to maintain the legacy data, you should back up the databases and keep them available for reporting.

Before you get going with the migration, there are a few things you must pay close attention to throughout the process. First, test at all stages; don't simply plough on after each step without validating that the changes you have made were actually applied correctly.

It is also very important to use the correct tools to manage both systems during coexistence. As you might expect, you should manage the Lync elements using the Lync Server Control

Panel (Control Panel) or Lync Server Management Shell (PowerShell) and OCS using the OCS Management tools. Migrations should all be carried out from the Lync Management tools.

Preparing

When all your planning is complete, the final stage before starting the actual migration steps is to prepare your OCS environment. This takes several forms; some of it is technical and some of it relates to documentation.

The most important step is to ensure that your OCS installation has the latest patches installed. Realistically, this should have been part of normal operations, so most likely it is already complete. However, if it is not, you must at the very least ensure that you have installed OCS 2007 R2 CU5; if you are coming from OCS 2007, then the latest patches are needed. These patches should be installed across all servers and clients, including phone devices.

Once you've completed the updates, it is worth downloading the OCS Best Practice Analyzer (BPA) from the following link:

```
www.microsoft.com/downloads/en/details.aspx?FamilyId=1B90993C-072A-4C84-B385-
B76D23B2F27C&displaylang=en
```

The BPA tool is a way of scanning your environment to check that it is configured correctly and will highlight any issues that you need to either address or acknowledge. Figure 7.1 shows the interface as you kick off the scan.

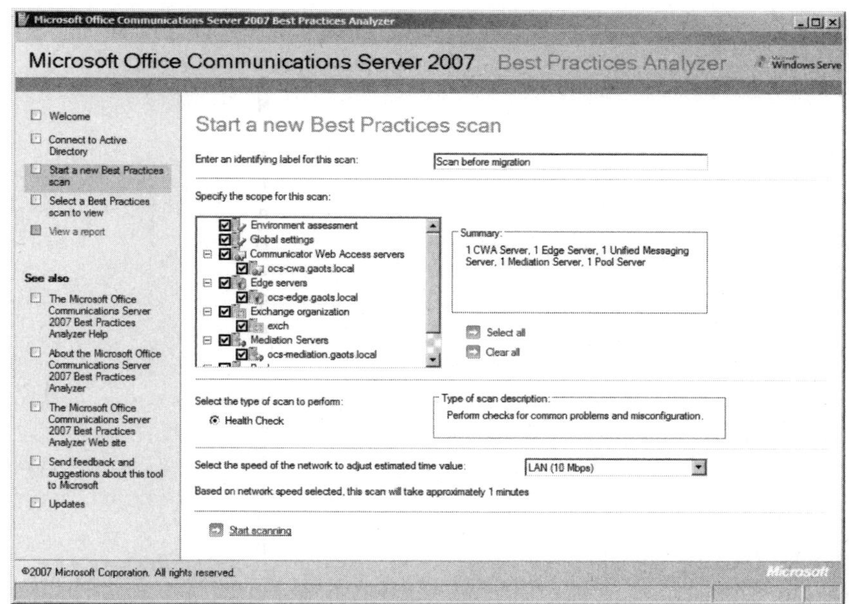

FIGURE 7.1
Beginning a BPA scan

Once you are satisfied that you have resolved any issues the BPA reveals, you should perform your usual backup to ensure that in the event of any unforeseen problem, you have the ability to roll back to a known working state. This should, of course, include an Active Directory system state backup and any OCS databases. At this point, it is also well worth making sure you have up-to-date documentation of the OCS system, showing IP addresses, DNS FQDN and certificate details, pool locations, policies, and any custom configuration.

The final element is to choose which clients should be able to connect to OCS during the coexistence and migration phase. It is highly recommended to make sure that only the clients with the latest updates can connect. Equally important is to ensure that no Lync clients can connect to OCS. This is done using client version filtering on OCS as follows:

1. On the OCS Standard Edition (or front end in an enterprise deployment) in the OCS management console, drill down to the pool name, right-click, hover over Filtering Tools, and then select Client Version Filter.
2. Once in the tool, your first objective is to block Lync clients from connecting to OCS. This is done by adding the following elements as Blocked:

Client	User agent header	Version
Lync 2010	OC	4.*.*.*
Lync Web App	CWA	4.*.*.*
Lync 2010 Phone Edition	OCPhone	4.*.*.*

3. Your second objective is to ensure that only the latest versions of the OCS clients can connect to the OCS pool. This is done by entering the following elements and setting them so that if the client is less than (<) the version it will be blocked. Note that this is current as of the May 2011 LiveMeeting and September 2011 (CU10) Office Communicator R2 updates.

Client	User agent header	Version
Office Communicator	OC	3.5.6907.236
LiveMeeting	LM	8.0.6362.202

4. Once you have entered this information and removed conflicting elements, your client version policy should look something like Figure 7.2. Once you are finished, click OK to apply the policy.

That completes the edit of the client version policy. If you want more details about some of the available options, see the following TechNet articles.

For a discussion of OCS 2007 R2, see the following:

`http://technet.microsoft.com/en-us/library/dd572488(office.13).aspx`

For a discussion of OCS 2007 and details about the User Agent Header see:

`http://technet.microsoft.com/en-us/library/bb936607(office.12).aspx`

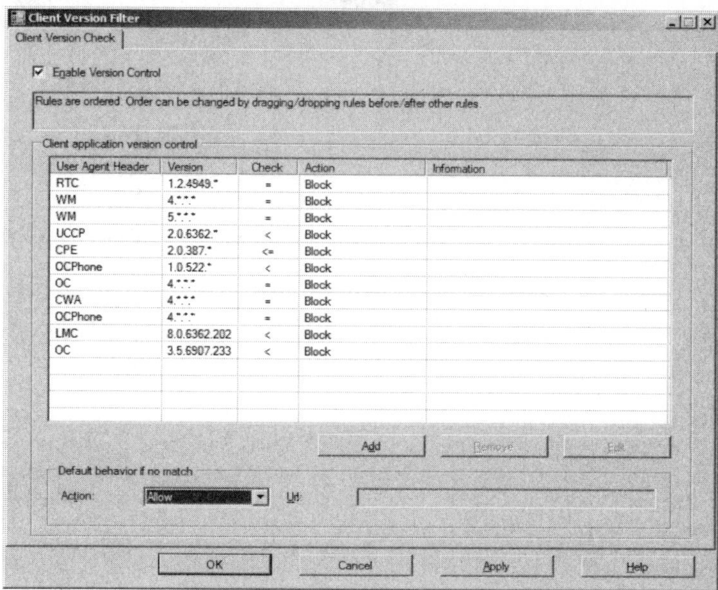

FIGURE 7.2
The newly updated Client Version policy on OCS

Deploying the First Lync Pool

Now that all the checks have been performed and the rollback plans are in place, it's time to install Lync. The procedure follows the same steps described in Chapter 6, "Installation." You'll begin by installing the Lync Standard Edition server, which will also host a colocated Mediation server in time. You'll also be adding a Lync Edge server later in this process. The new servers will be as follows:

- `Lync-SE01.gaots.local`. This hosts the Lync Web App and includes the colocated Mediation server.
- `Lync-Edge.gaots.local`

The key thing about deploying the first pool is that you should install the elements that match what you have in OCS. In other words, you should not add the newer Lync roles (for example, the expanded AV server, or the SBA) until you have removed OCS. This first pool can be used to pilot Lync and thoroughly test integration. It is generally built with minimal hardware, as shown earlier. Once functionality testing is complete, you build out the pool to support the required number of users and provide resilience through load balancing. At that point, the pool will be taken into production.

LARGE-SCALE DEPLOYMENTS

In large-scale deployments, you'll need to choose which pool you want to move to Lync first. If you are moving from OCS 2007 R2, you should start with a pool that does not hold the Edge servers that perform federation. This is different from OCS 2007, where you do start with the Federation pool.

NOTE The first Lync pool is performed as a new deployment; therefore, you can follow the steps outlined in Chapter 5 and Chapter 6. For the Voice elements, you can follow the steps explained in Chapter 13 and Chapter 16. Given that those chapters cover deployment of Lync in depth, this chapter will focus on what is needed for a successful migration and will provide step-by-step guides only when doing so will not cause extensive duplication.

During the process of creating your topology, you will maintain the same primary and secondary SIP domains. When you create the Lync pool, you must give it a unique pool name. Do not attempt to reuse the OCS pool name. In this case, it is called `Lync-Se01.gaots.local`.

Given that Enterprise Voice and Dial-in Conferencing are enabled in OCS 2007 R2, you will enable them here. The Lync documentation talks about using a colocated Mediation server during migration, even if you will eventually move to a dedicated Mediation server. Experience indicates that that this is not essential. You should do whatever you feel is suitable, based on best-practice Mediation-server design principles. In this case, use an SIP trunk from Gradwell .net (a UK ISP and SIP provider). Best practice states that when using SIP trunks to an ITSP (Internet Telephony Service Provider), you should configure the SIP trunk to terminate on a dedicated Mediation server in Lync, because you can frequently end up having to pay for a trunk per front-end member of a load-balanced pool. Given that this migration is in a test environment, not in a real environment, for the sake of minimizing resource requirements and because there is only one front-end server, you will maintain the colocation. You will come back to the EV migration shortly.

Although you'll deploy a Lync Edge server later, at this point you're deploying only the Standard Edition box, so don't use the "Enable an Edge pool to be used by the media component of this Front End pool" option.

Because you opted for a colocated Mediation server, the Topology Builder will prompt you to specify PSTN gateways. At this stage, you will enter none. This is something you will create at the relevant point of the migration. The SIP trunk (like many others) is configured to allow sending and receiving from a specific public IP address and to have certain DDI numbers assigned to that trunk. This trunk is currently assigned to the OCS 2007 R2 Mediation server. Therefore, moving it to Lync at this point is not an option. You must first move all the users to Lync. At that point, you'll need to move the specific external IP address onto the Lync Mediation server and then set up the relevant routes. This, of course, will require an element of downtime, which can be scheduled well in advance. If this is not an option, an alternative would be to set up a second trunk homed on the Lync Mediation server and then gradually reassign the DDI numbers to the second trunk as users are moved. Clearly, this is more administratively complex and requires a second trunk; however, it would ensure that the service remains available throughout the migration.

Having configured the topology, complete the deployment of the Lync pool as covered in Chapter 6. To take care of permissions, remember to add the user installing Lync to the RTCUniversalServerAdministrators group and also add a Lync admin user to the CsAdministrator group.

Creating the Central Management Store (CMS)

Even though you already have an OCS Standard Edition server, you still need to run the Prepare First Standard Edition Server Wizard to prep the SQL database on Lync-SE01 for the Central Management Store (CMS).

Once you have finished, make sure that everything on OCS is still working and that you can add a pair of new users to the Lync pool and have them communicate between themselves. They will, of course, not be able to communicate externally or to users on the OCS system, because you haven't enabled coexistence yet.

Merging the OCS and Lync Topology

At this point, you are ready to introduce the OCS and Lync systems to each other. As previously discussed, OCS and Lync use different structures to store configuration information, so to enable coexistence, you must enable these structures to interoperate. To do this, you must first install the Windows Management Instrumentation (WMI) Backward Compatibility Package on the Lync server. OCS stores configuration information in WMI, and this package enables Lync to understand that information and merge it into the Central Management Store (CMS).

For this exercise, you will install the required component on the machine where the topology merge will be performed. In this case, you have only one, so it will be on the Lync-SE01 machine.

The component is located on the install media in the directory `SETUP\AMD64\SETUP\OCSWMIBC.MSI` Running the MSI is a very quick process.

1. Once the package is installed, open up Topology Builder and have it pull down the configuration from the Central Management Store in the normal way. On the right pane, click Topology to open the drop-down and then click Merge 2007 Or 2007 R2 Topology.
2. When the Merge 2007 Or 2007 R2 Topology Wizard opens, click Next.
3. The Specify Edge Setup window opens. This wizard allows you to specify the configuration of the Edge servers on OCS, where you should add all OCS Edge servers in the environment. To begin, click Add.
4. The next page gives you the option to specify the version of Edge that you are adding, in this case OCS 2007 R2. After you do that, click Next.
5. You are presented with a screen giving a choice of Edge configuration: Consolidated, Load Balanced, or Expanded. The Expanded Edge configuration was a potential OCS 2007 design where the different Edge roles (Access, Conferencing, and AV) were placed on separate servers. This design could have been carried over to OCS 2007 R2 as part of a migration. Lync does not support interoperating with this type of Edge setup, so if you have this setup, you will need to convert it back to either a load balanced or single consolidated Edge setup. In this case, select the Single Edge Server and then click Next.
6. On the next page, specify the ports and Fully Qualified Domain Name (FQDN) at which you want to talk to the Edge. The default ports are populated automatically. For the FQDN, specify `OCS-Edge.gaots.local`, as shown in Figure 7.3, and then click Next.

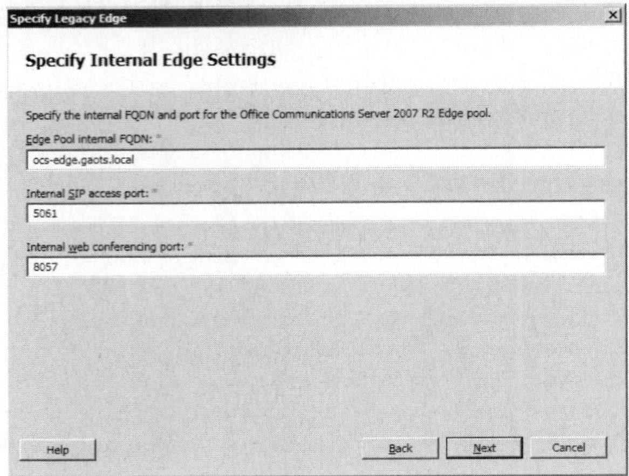

FIGURE 7.3
Specifying the Edge server FQDN and ports

7. On the next screen, enter the FQDN of your external conferencing Edge NIC and the associated port, which again is populated with the default of 443. Assuming the Edge server to which you are connecting is your federation and Public IM connectivity host, check the box as shown in Figure 7.4.

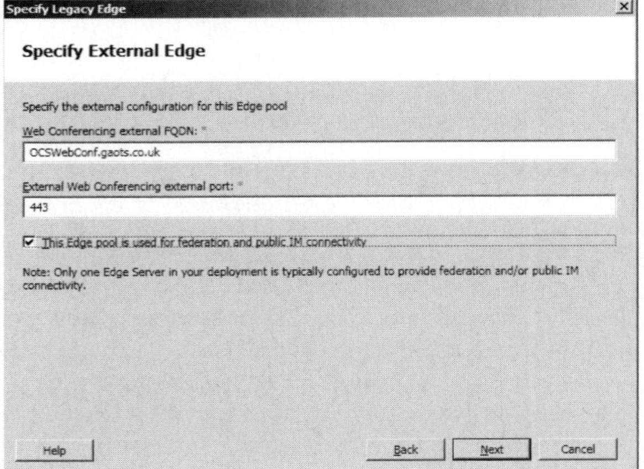

FIGURE 7.4
Selecting the Edge server/pool for federation

8. Click Next and then enter the details of the next hop. Often this will be a system or pool of machines running as Directors, but in this small network you will connect directly to the OCS front end on `OCS-SE01.gaots.local`, as shown in Figure 7.5. To complete the configuration, click Finish.

9. You will return to the Specify Edge Setup page, where you should click Next to continue or repeat the process if you have other OCS Edge systems.

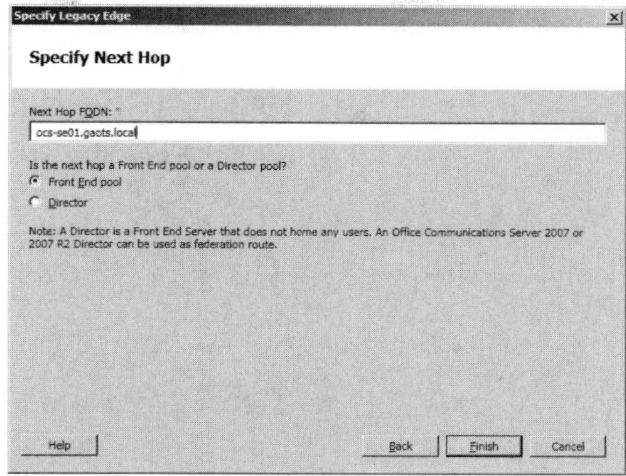

FIGURE 7.5
Configuring the next hop to the internal servers

10. The final step is to specify the internal SIP port on which Lync will communicate with OCS. Assuming you haven't changed this, stick with the default of 5061. If you have changed the ports for any of your internal pools, make sure they are all available and allow remote WMI access, and opt for the Automatic Discovery option.
11. To move to the Summary page, click Next and click Next again to begin merging the topologies.
12. Once it is complete, click Next to review the process. You are given the option to view the XML config file, shown in Figure 7.6. Finally, click Finish to exit the Merge Wizard.

FIGURE 7.6
The XML representation of the configuration imported to Lync


```
<?xml version="1.0"?>
- <TopologyInput xmlns="urn:schema:Microsoft.Rtc.Management.Deploy.LegacyUserInput.2008">
  - <EdgeClusters>
    - <EdgeCluster FederationEnabled="true" Version="OCS2007R2" DP="true" MR="true" AP="true">
        <LoadBalancer ExternalDPFqdn="OCSWebConf.gaots.co.uk" InternalFqdn="ocs-edge.gaots.local"/>
      - <Machines>
          <Machine InternalFqdn="ocs-edge.gaots.local"/>
        </Machines>
        <DirectorOrEdgeNextHop IsDirector="false" Fqdn="ocs-se01.gaots.local"/>
        <Ports InternalDPPort="8057" ExternalDPPort="443" InternalAPPort="5061"/>
      </EdgeCluster>
    </EdgeClusters>
    <RegistrarClusterPort Port="5061" EnableAutoDiscoveryOfPorts="false"/>
  </TopologyInput>
```


Having completed the Merge Wizard, you will now see in Topology Builder a new element on the left pane, called BackCompatSite. This is the representation of the OCS environment in Lync Topology format. You should check that it lists all the OCS pools in your environment and that it contains the Edge servers you defined in the wizard. Now that it is in the topology, you must publish the topology (a process described in Chapter 5, "Planning Your Deployment"), which will write it to the CMS and allow it to replicate among the Lync servers.

The Merge Wizard has given Lync the knowledge of the basic shape of the OCS deployment; for example, it now knows about OCS pools and Edge servers. However, what hasn't yet been brought across are the policies and configuration information, which is set on OCS. For example, version policies, dial plans, dial-in conferencing numbers, and voice routes are all configured in OCS but Lync knows nothing about them yet. To bring these settings across to Lync, you have to move into the PowerShell and run the `Import-CsLegacyConfiguration` cmdlet. (For more about PowerShell see Chapter 8, "PowerShell and LMS"). Note when you run the command that if you have any policies in OCS that contain illegal characters such as the colon (:), you will see the warning shown in Figure 7.7. This is nothing to worry about and is simply for information.

FIGURE 7.7
Warning on import about illegal characters in OCS policy names

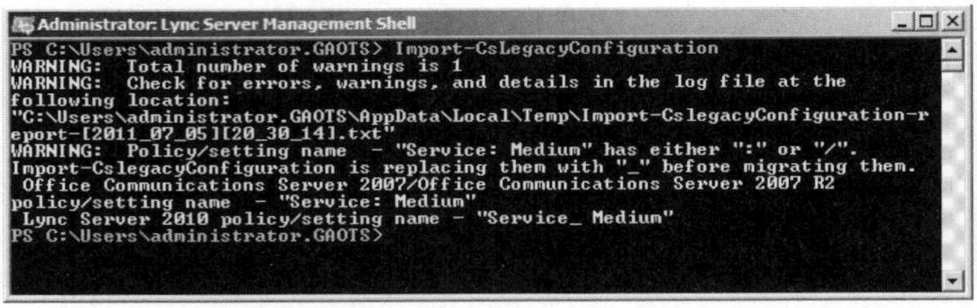

```
Administrator: Lync Server Management Shell
PS C:\Users\administrator.GAOTS> Import-CsLegacyConfiguration
WARNING:  Total number of warnings is 1
WARNING:  Check for errors, warnings, and details in the log file at the
following location:
"C:\Users\administrator.GAOTS\AppData\Local\Temp\Import-CslegacyConfiguration-r
eport-[2011_07_05][20_30_14].txt"
WARNING:  Policy/setting name  - "Service: Medium" has either ":" or "/".
Import-CslegacyConfiguration is replacing them with "_" before migrating them.
 Office Communications Server 2007/Office Communications Server 2007 R2
policy/setting name  - "Service: Medium"
 Lync Server 2010 policy/setting name - "Service_ Medium"
PS C:\Users\administrator.GAOTS>
```

Once the command is run, when you're looking through the relevant areas of the Lync Server Control Panel (Control Panel) such as Voice Routing, Conferencing, and External User Access, you will see that the various objects mentioned now have configuration data from OCS. You will also see the OCS element show up on the Topology – Status section of the Control Panel. Of course, policies in Lync are more granular than those in OCS (as discussed in Chapter 10), so generally the Global Policy in Lync will be what has been updated. Elements to pay careful attention to are the dial-in conferencing numbers. They are also brought across to Lync; however, at this point, they are still homed on the OCS system and should only be modified there. Most importantly, with the dial-in conferencing numbers and other policy settings on OCS, any time you change the configuration on OCS, you should again run the `Import-CsLegacyConfiguration` cmdlet.

If you want to see more details about your newly merged pool, run the following command:

```
Get-CsPool -Identity Lync-SE01.gaots.local
```

This will provide you with similar information to that shown in the LSCP Topology–Status section, and it will add information about services running on the pool.

Finally, check that the conferencing directories merged properly, by running this command:

```
Get-CsConferenceDirectory
```

This will show all conferencing directories where content is stored both on Lync and OCS. Sample output from the exercise environment is shown in Figure 7.8.

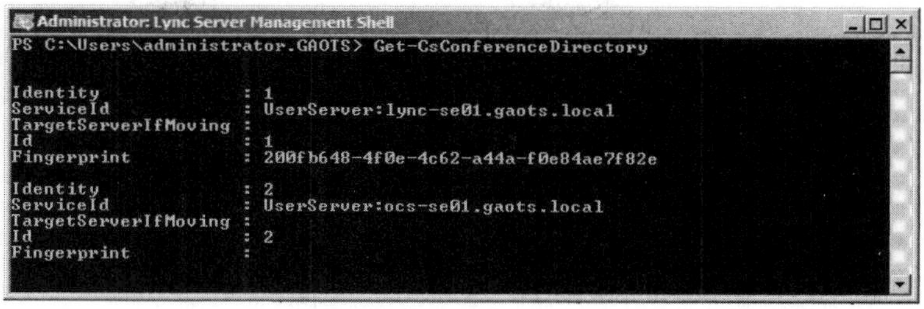

FIGURE 7.8
Displaying both OCS and Lync conferencing directories

```
PS C:\Users\administrator.GAOTS> Get-CsConferenceDirectory

Identity              : 1
ServiceId             : UserServer:lync-se01.gaots.local
TargetServerIfMoving  :
Id                    : 1
Fingerprint           : 200fb648-4f0e-4c62-a44a-f0e84ae7f82e

Identity              : 2
ServiceId             : UserServer:ocs-se01.gaots.local
TargetServerIfMoving  :
Id                    : 2
Fingerprint           :
```

Configuring the First Lync Pool

Now that the Lync pool knows about OCS, you need to configure Lync to properly utilize the OCS components, most importantly the Edge and Mediation servers. As with other major configuration changes, you do this in the Topology Builder with a user account that is a Domain Administrator and member of the RTCUniversalServerAdmins group.

To enable the Lync pool to use the OCS Edge server, two elements need to be configured. The first gives Lync a route for Federation traffic, and the second enables media traffic to pass through the OCS Edge.

1. To proceed, open the Topology Builder and download the configuration from the CMS. Next, right-click the site (in this case, EMEA) and select Edit Properties.
2. On the window that opens, in the left pane click Federation Route. In the Site Federation Route Assignment section at the bottom of the right pane, click Enable, and in the drop-down select the OCS 2007 R2 Edge server you entered during the Merge Wizard previously, in this case `ocs-edge.gaots.local BackCompatSite Edge` (see Figure 7.9). Click OK to save the settings.

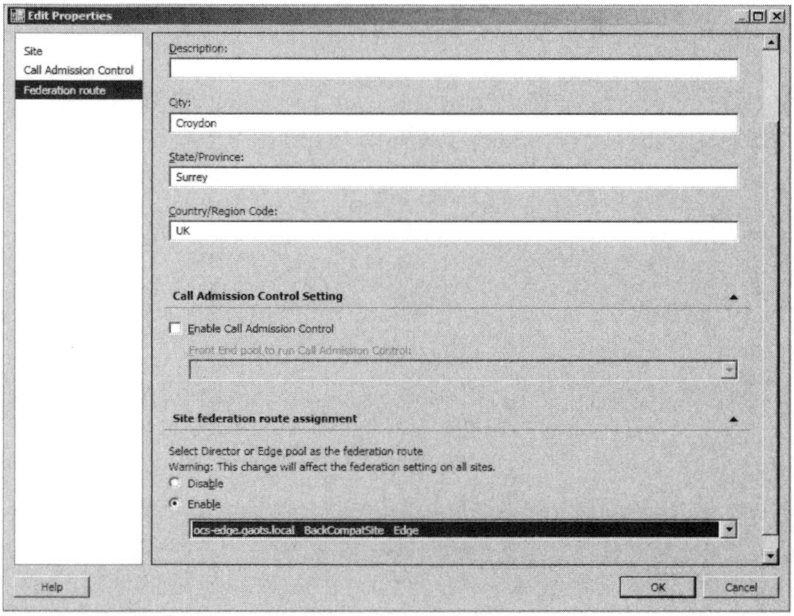

FIGURE 7.9
Configuring the federation route for the new Lync pool

3. Now that you've configured the Federation route, you need to allow media traffic to flow through the OCS Edge. This is done in the Properties section of the front-end pool, or in this case the Standard Edition server. Right-click the server and select Edit Properties. In the right pane, scroll down until you locate the Associations section. Select the checkbox for Associate Edge Pool (For Media Components) and then in the drop-down select the same server as defined in the federation route, in this case `ocs-edge.gaots.local BackCompatSite` (see Figure 7.10). Click OK again to accept the changes.

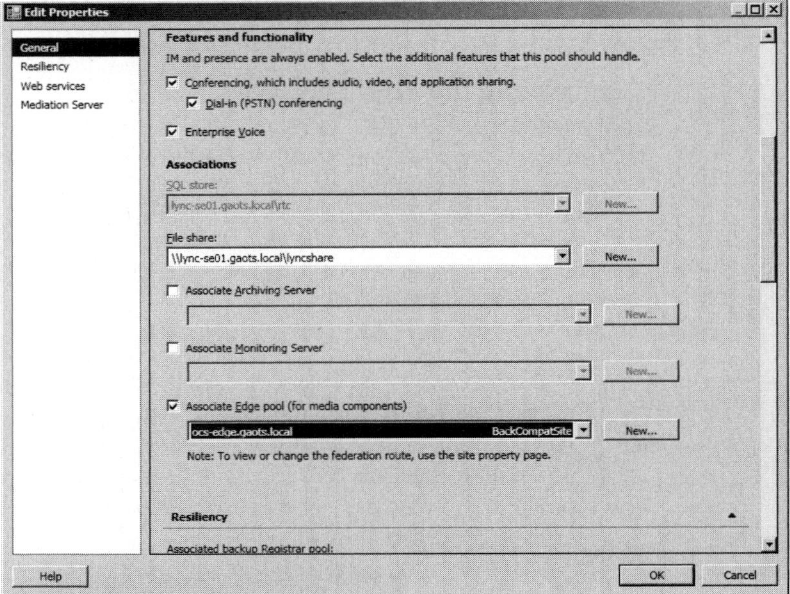

FIGURE 7.10
Configuring the Edge server media route

4. At this point you must again publish the topology, as described in Chapter 5, to lock the changes into the CMS.

5. Once the topology is published, check the Notepad file for the next actions to see if you need to run local setup on any of your Lync servers. (You might need to run local setup on the Standard Edition server.)

Having done so, you must now move to the OCS side of things and ensure that the OCS servers actually trust the Lync front-end pool or Standard Edition server to communicate with it.

To do this, on your OCS Edge server run `Compmgmt.msc` to open the administrative console where you access the OCS Management tools under the Services and Applications node. Right-click the Office Communications Server 2007 R2 node and select Properties. Navigate to the Internal tab and then at the bottom of the window in the Internal Servers Authorized To Connect To This Edge Server section, click Add Server. Add the FQDN of the internal Lync Standard Edition server (or front-end pool) as shown in Figure 7.11 and click OK. If you have more than one Lync server pool that will use this Edge server, you will also enter those server

FQDNs at this time. Likewise, if you are using Directors in your Lync pool, the FQDN of the Director (or Director pool) will need to be added here. Once you have added all the necessary server FQDNs, click OK to complete the process. At this point, the new Lync pool is configured to use the OCS Edge server. Of course, you will also need to make sure the OCS Edge server can resolve the new Lync servers. If you are using an internal DNS server on your OCS Edge, that shouldn't be a problem. However, if you are using a HOSTS file, be sure to add entries for the new Lync servers. Finally, make sure communication is not blocked by firewalls, as discussed in Chapter 3, "Security."

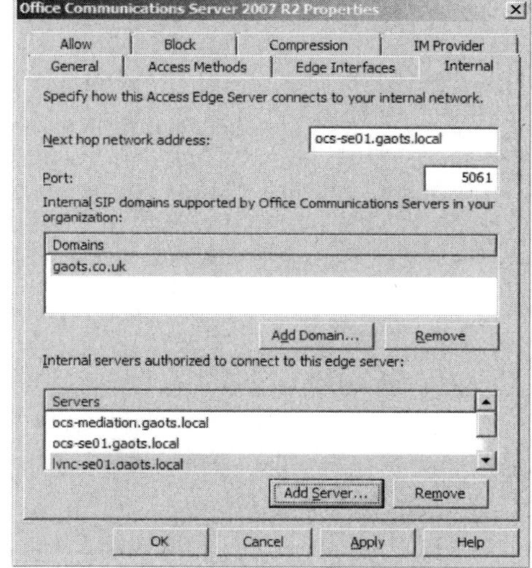

FIGURE 7.11
Authorizing the new Lync server on the OCS Edge

At this point, you can address the other element of configuration, ensuring that the Lync servers can access the OCS Mediation server. Of course, if you are not using Enterprise Voice in your environment, you can skip this step.

Because you already have functional voice routes on OCS 2007 R2, they will have been brought across to Lync by merging the topology and configuration. You can check that this was the case by opening the Control Panel and selecting the Voice Routing tab. You should see your location profiles on the Dial Plan tab and the route to your gateway or SIP trunk on the Route tab.

The final step before you move on to user migration is Unified Messaging integration with Exchange. Given that you have UM-enabled users in this environment, it is important that this functionality continues to work once users are migrated to Lync. To ensure that this is possible, on your Exchange UM server you must rerun the `ExchUCUtil.ps1` script, which you ran as part of UM setup. This script and its function are described in Chapter 17, "Exchange, SharePoint, and Group Chat Integration." For now, though, you will see that it creates a new IP gateway representing the new Lync front-end server and maps it to the existing dial plan. Now that you have carried out this configuration, voicemail will continue to work once you migrate users.

Testing and Migrating Pilot Users

Now you're ready to see if the coexistence really works and begin migrating a handful of users over to the new Lync pool.

The first thing you need to verify is that simple communication is possible between the Lync users you created earlier in the chapter. Test the basic Lync installation and the OCS users. You should test all normal communication methods such as IM, voice, and video. Equally, you should test with combinations of users internal to the network and external to the network for both Lync and OCS users.

Obviously, testing will be different for different organizations because you will use a variety of features and functions. As a starting point, refer to the test plans at the following URL:

```
http://technet.microsoft.com/en-us/library/gg425729.aspx
```

Once you are sure that basic communication is possible, it is time to migrate your first user from OCS to Lync. This can be done either through PowerShell or in the Control Panel. Note that users are essentially pulled across to Lync using the Lync tools, rather than being pushed across using the OCS tools.

To move a user in the Control Panel, you must open and log on to Control Panel as a member of either the RTCUniversalServerAdmins group or the CsAdministrator or CsUserAdministrator RBAC roles. Once in Control Panel, navigate to the Users tab. On the right pane, don't enter any search text and click Add Filter. Make sure the query drop-downs read Legacy User, Equal To, and True. Click Find. This will return a list of all users on Lync, as shown in Figure 7.12.

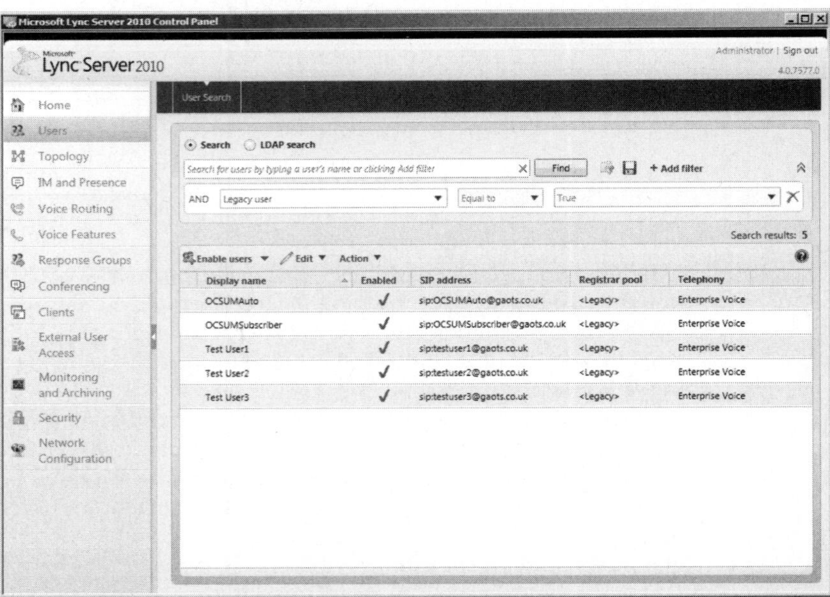

FIGURE 7.12 Using Control Panel to search for legacy users

At this point you should choose a suitable user or group of users to migrate to Lync. Once you have selected the user or users that you want to move, click the Action drop-down and select Move Selected Users To Pool. This opens a dialog in which you select the pool to move to from the drop-down and then click OK.

MOVING BACK TO OCS

You can, of course, also move users back to Lync by locating the user in the Control Panel and then instead of selecting the Lync pool when prompted, moving the user to the OCS pool.

If instead you want to perform the migration from PowerShell, you can use the following commands. First, get a list of all OCS users, using this command:

```
Get-CsUser -OnOfficeCommunicationServer | Select-Object SamAccountName,
SipAddress
```

This will output a list of accounts and display only the `SamAccountName` parameter and the important `SipAddress`, as shown here:

```
SamAccountName                  SipAddress
--------------                  ----------
testuser1                       sip:testuser1@gaots.co.uk
testuser2                       sip:testuser2@gaots.co.uk
                                sip:OCSUMSubscriber@gaots.co.uk
                                sip:OCSUMAuto@gaots.co.uk
testuser3                       sip:testuser3@gaots.co.uk
```

Next, choose the user you want to migrate. In this example, you'll migrate `testuser1`. To move the user, run the following command:

```
Move-CsLegacyUser -Identity "sip:testuser1@gaots.co.uk" -Target "lync-se01.gaots
.local"
```

If the user is logged on at this time, she will be logged off and then Office Communicator will automatically log her back on. When she does get logged back on, the user will still use DNS entries which point users to the OCS server to log on. DNS will redirect them to the Lync server so the user can log on. Later in the process, you will change these DNS records to point users to the Lync server.

To validate that the move occurred correctly, run this command:

```
Get-CsUser testuser1
```

In the output shown below, you can see that the `RegistrarPool` is now our Lync server.

```
Identity                : CN=Test User1,OU=TestUsersOU,DC=gaots,DC=local
VoicePolicy             :
ConferencingPolicy      :
PresencePolicy          :
DialPlan                : HomeLocProf
LocationPolicy          :
ClientPolicy            :
ClientVersionPolicy     :
```

```
ArchivingPolicy          :
PinPolicy                :
ExternalAccessPolicy     : Allow Federation+Outside Access
HostedVoiceMail          :
HostedVoicemailPolicy    :
HostingProvider          : SRV:
RegistrarPool            : lync-se01.gaots.local
Enabled                  : True
SipAddress               : sip:testuser1@gaots.co.uk
LineURI                  : tel:+442031375047
EnterpriseVoiceEnabled   : True
HomeServer               : CN=Lc Services,CN=Microsoft,CN=1:1,CN=Pools,CN=RTC Ser
                           vice,CN=Services,CN=Configuration,DC=gaots,DC=local
DisplayName              : Test User1
SamAccountName           : testuser1
```

Finally, if you want to move multiple users or even all OCS users using LSMS, the following two commands should be used. First, to move a selection of users:

```
Get-CsUser -Filter {DisplayName -eq "TestUser1" -or DisplayName - eq "TestUser2"}
| Move-CsLegacyUser -Target "lync-se01.gaots.local"
```

That command would move both `TestUser1` and `TestUser2` to the `Lync-se01.gaots.local` pool. Alternatively, if you want to move all OCS users to Lync, then the following command would be needed:

```
Get-CsUser -OnOfficeCommunicationServer | Move-CsLegacyUser -Target "lync-se01
.gaots.local"
```

This command gets all the OCS users and pipes them to the `Move-CsLegacyUser` cmdlet, which moves them to Lync.

User Replication Error Prevents Migration

If a migration fails with an error including the text "...the user is not provisioned," you may find that user replication from AD to Lync hasn't finished. This is particularly likely if you have a large number of users in AD and you haven't waited very long since getting Lync up and running before starting the migration. To verify that replication has completed, use the following steps:

1. Log on to the computer where Topology Builder is installed as a member of the Domain Admins group and the RTCUniversalServerAdmins group.
2. Click the Start menu, and then click Run.
3. Type **eventvwr.exe** and then click OK.
4. In Event Viewer, click Applications and Services Logs to expand it, and then select Lync Server.
5. In the Actions pane click Filter Current Log.
6. From the Event sources list, click LS User Replicator.
7. In <All Event IDs>, enter **30024** and then click OK.
8. In the filtered events list, on the General tab, look for an entry stating that user replication has completed successfully.

As you may recall, once the user has been migrated they won't have access to a bunch of the new functionality until the clients are updated. Another thing to remember is that policies and configuration from OCS are brought across to Lync during the configuration import and topology merge. While you are testing, you should make sure that policies that were brought across are working as expected for both Lync and OCS users and that any archiving and monitoring servers (see Chapter 11) are performing adequately.

JOINING CONFERENCES CREATED BY A LYNC USER

As soon as you have users who are migrated to Lync and are using the new Lync client, you should change the default Web Service settings to make joining Lync meetings easier for those still on OCS. You can do this from the LSMS or through the Control Panel. The simplest way is through LSMS by running the following command:

```
Set-CsWebServiceConfiguration -Identity global
-ShowDownloadCommunicatorAttendeeLink $True -ShowJoinUsingLegacyClientLink $True
```

By default when a user with only the OCS client joins a meeting, they will be brought in via the Lync Web App. This doesn't provide audio and video functionality. To deal with this you have a couple of choices. Either roll out the Lync Attendee client (which IT can do via centrally managed tools, or the users can be allowed to download and install it once you have enabled the link to do so via the previous command) or you can allow users to connect using their legacy OCS client, which is also enabled by the previous command. If you choose to allow users to use their legacy OCS client, they will not have all the functionality available in a Lync meeting.

This command is shown to demonstrate the options. Generally, it would be more sensible to roll out the Attendee client as part of coexistence and not allow the user to dial in using the OCS client.

Another conferencing issue is the ability of federated users to attend Lync meetings. You must verify that the conferencing policy assigned to the Lync user has the Allow Participants to Invite Anonymous Users checkbox selected.

Adding Lync Edge and Director Roles

At this point, you can happily leave the system running. Users are now working on Lync and can communicate with users on OCS both internally and externally, and with federated users. Equally, if you have rolled out the Lync client to the newly migrated Lync users, those who have been migrated to Lync can now use the new Lync functionality—for example, the enhanced conferencing and sharing capabilities. However, you are now essentially supporting two systems, OCS and Lync, so you need to begin the process of making sure Lync can start to take up all workloads. The first step to that end is to configure the components that will allow native Lync External Access. Most of the configuration steps were discussed in depth in Chapter 6, we'll highlight the important steps of the migration process here.

The first step will be to configure the Reverse Proxy server to publish the Lync web services externally. Key elements to consider are that you will need a second public IP address on the reverse proxy to publish the Lync components and that you must have the required certificates.

In this case, you are not using the Director role, so you will simply put the Meet and Dial-in URLs on the main Lync Standard Edition certificate and publish them on the main Lync Web publishing rule as you did for the Director in Chapter 6.

Next, you must configure the Lync Edge server. The first part of this is to define a Lync Edge server in the Lync topology using Topology Builder, as described in Chapter 5. While defining this topology, it's important that you do not configure this Edge pool to be the route for federation; leave the option unchecked as shown in Figure 7.13.

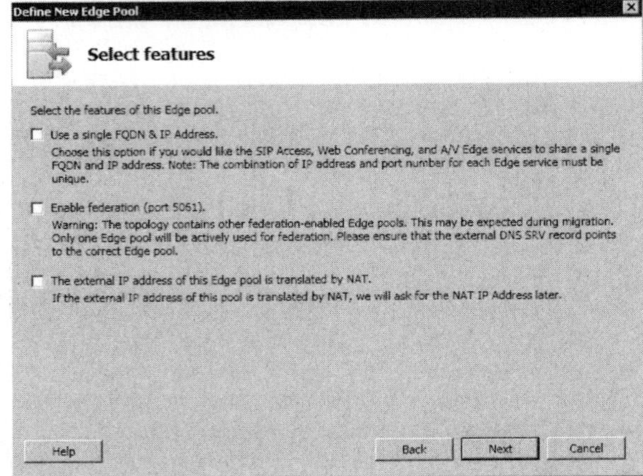

FIGURE 7.13
When configuring the Edge topology, don't enable federation.

To continue, progress through the Topology Builder Wizard (described in Chapter 5), entering the URLs and IP addresses. When prompted, select the Lync Standard Edition (or front-end pool) as the next hop. When prompted on the Associate Front End Pools page, do not associate the Edge server with the Lync front end. You'll do this later, so leave the settings as shown in Figure 7.14.

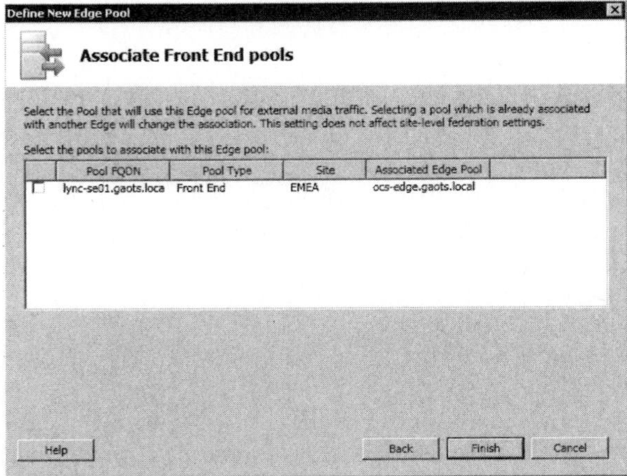

FIGURE 7.14
Make sure you don't associate the Edge with the Lync front-end pool.

Once the Edge installation is complete, make sure as always that the servers are patched and that the latest Lync CU is installed on all Lync boxes including the Edge.

WHAT ABOUT MIGRATION FROM OCS 2007?

This chapter covers migrating to Lync from OCS 2007 R2. However, it is also possible to migrate from OCS 2007. If you are doing that, there are a few differences to the process and some real-world tips that can help you avoid trouble.

The main difference between migrating from OCS 2007 and OCS 2007 R2 is in the order of the migration. The key issue is that the new Lync pool cannot pass media through the OCS 2007 Edge. Therefore, you must deploy a Lync Edge and optionally a Director pool at the same time you deploy your Lync pool rather than later in the process, as with a migration from OCS 2007 R2. You will still use the legacy Edge for federation, but media will pass through the Lync Edge. You must, of course, use different URLs and certificates on the new Lync Edge than the ones on the legacy OCS 2007 Edge.

Two other differences are that there are no Response Groups or dial in conferencing settings to migrate, as these didn't exist in OCS 2007. CWA servers did exist in OCS 2007, but they won't talk to Lync, so anyone using them to provide access to Blackberry users will need to upgrade to the latest Blackberry Enterprise Server 5 SP3 release and will then need to deploy OCS 2007 R2 CWA servers after Lync is deployed and OCS 2007 is removed.

Another change is that although Lync can communicate with UCMA 2.0-based apps hosted on OCS 2007 R2 servers, it cannot communicate with UCMA 1.0 on an OCS 2007 server. This means you will need to deal with these apps earlier in the migration process than you would in a migration for OCS 2007 R2; otherwise, users on Lync won't be able to access the applications.

One tip which might spare you some trouble is that OCS can support 1,024-bit certificates, whereas Lync needs 2,048-bit or longer certificates. If you were planning on reusing any certs, make sure they are the right length for Lync.

For a more detailed view of the migration from OCS 2007 to Lync 2010, see the following TechNet article:

`http://technet.microsoft.com/en-us/library/gg412976.aspx`

Moving the First Lync Pool from Pilot to Production

Now you are at the stage where the majority of the Lync components are installed and configured and you are ready to start moving the bulk of services and the remaining users across to Lync. The first thing you'll need to do is enable the Lync Edge server as the route out for federation and media traffic. Make sure you schedule a little downtime for external access and federation. As noted earlier, the FQDNs for all services on the OCS Edge differ from those on the Lync Edge. Although this means that you need an additional certificate, it does keep things clean and allows you to have everything set up and ready to move, without having to juggle service names and DNS entries.

1. To begin the process, log on to the Lync front end (or Standard Edition) box as a member of the RTCUniversalServerAdmins and Domain Admins groups.
2. Open Topology Builder and download the topology from the CMS. Right-click the site with your first Lync pool in it (in this case, the EMEA site) and select Edit Properties.
3. In the window that opens, in the left pane click Federation Route. Then in the right pane under Site Federation Route Assignment, click Disable, as shown in Figure 7.15. Then click OK, and publish the topology. This has disabled the route for the Lync pool to federate out through the OCS Edge server.

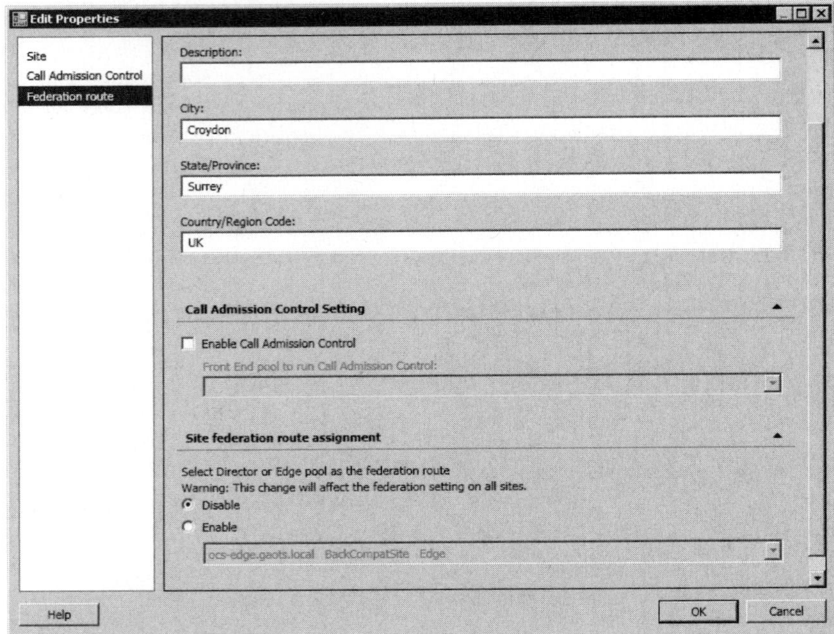

FIGURE 7.15 Disabling the federation route for the Lync pool

Next, you need to rerun the Merge 2007 or 2007 R2 Topology Wizard so you can reconfigure the legacy Edge defined within it.

1. To do this, while still in Topology Builder in the Actions pane, click Merge 2007 or 2007 R2 Topology.
2. On the first page, click Next; this takes you to the Specify Edge Setup page. Select the Edge server defined (in this case `OCS-Edge.gaots.local`) and click Change.
3. Then click through the wizard until you get to the Specify External Edge page. Clear the checkbox by This Edge Pool Is Used For Federation And Public IM Connectivity, as shown in Figure 7.16, and then click Next through to the end of the wizard, keeping the default settings.

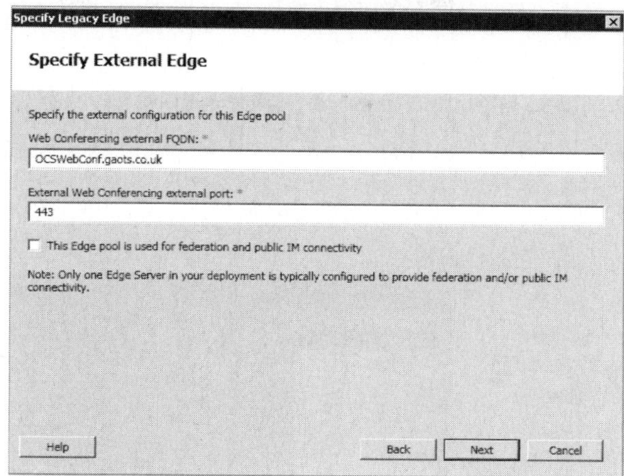

FIGURE 7.16
Ensuring that the OCS Edge isn't used for federation

Once the merge completes, you will likely see the warning:

```
No Office Communications Server 2007 / Office Communications Server 2007 R2 Edge
Has Been Enabled For Federation.
```

This is expected. Again, you need to publish the topology.

Now you are ready to move across to the OCS system and configure it to use the Lync Edge for federation.

1. Log onto the OCS front-end server (`OCS-se01.gaots.local`) as a member of the RTCUniversalServerAdmins group.
2. Open the OCS Admin tool and in the left pane, right-click the forest and select Global Properties. In the window that opens, navigate to the Federation tab and enter the internal URL of the Lync Edge server, in our case `Lync-edge.gaots.local`, as shown in Figure 7.17. To complete the process, click OK.

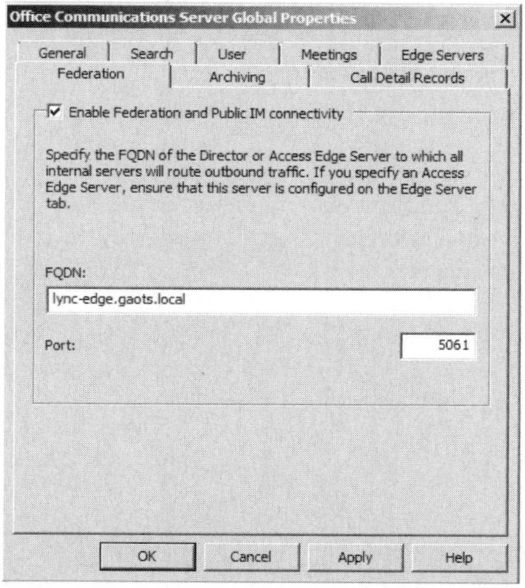

FIGURE 7.17
Reconfiguring OCS to federate through the Lync edge

You're almost done; what remains is to make the Lync Edge server live. You do this back in Topology Builder.

1. Right-click the Standard Edition server and click Edit Properties.
2. In the window that opens, scroll down to the Associations section and on the drop-down in the Associate Edge Pool (For Media Components) section, ensure that the Lync Edge is selected as shown in Figure 7.18.

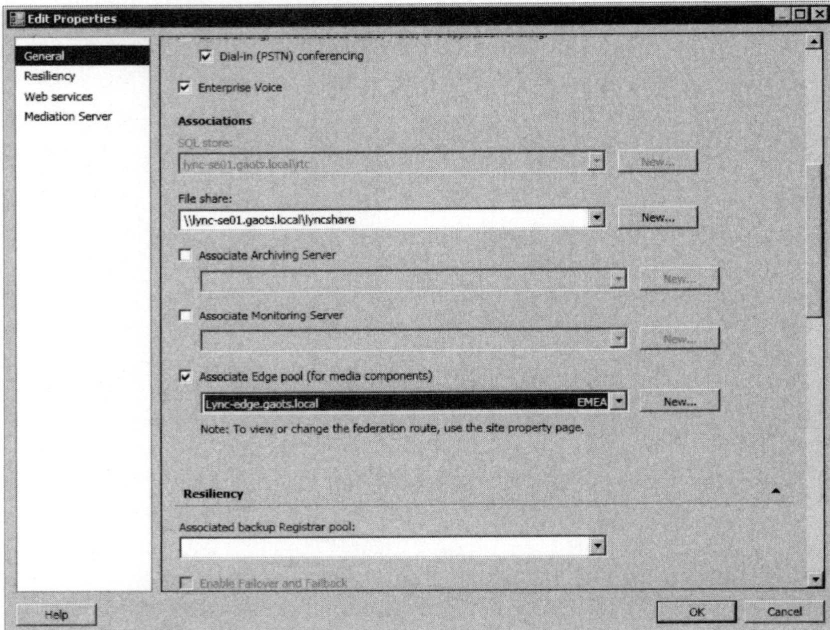

FIGURE 7.18
Routing Lync pool media traffic out of the Lync Edge

3. Click OK and then back in the Topology Builder left pane, right-click the Lync Edge pool and select Edit Properties.
4. In the General section, check the box next to Enable Federation For This Edge Pool (Port 5061), as shown in Figure 7.19. Then click OK and republish the topology.
5. On the Publishing Wizard Complete page, check whether any further steps are needed and carry them out. For example, you might be requested to run local setup on the Lync Edge server.

FIGURE 7.19
Enabling federation on the Lync Edge pool

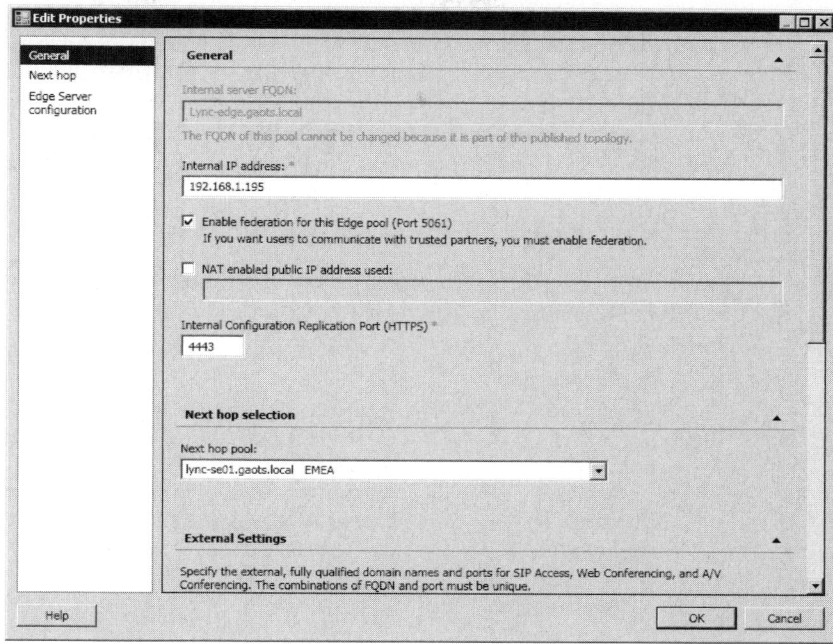

Now it is time to ensure that your firewalls and DNS entries are configured correctly for the Lync Edge server as described in Chapter 3. Then you'll need to reconfigure the DNS SRV records so that all external traffic for federation and remote access will be pointed at the Lync Edge server. This will involve updating the `_sip._tls.gaots.co.uk` SRV record and the `_sipfederationtls._tcp.gaots.co.uk` SRV records so they will be served by the `Lyncaccess.gaots.co.uk` host.

All that remains is to log onto the OCS Edge server where you can stop and disable all the Office Communications Server services. You can also remove the entries allowing access for the OCS Edge from your firewalls and the external DNS entries for the box.

POLICIES TO ENABLE EXTERNAL ACCESS AND FEDERATION

We've already said it a number of times, but just to be absolutely clear, once you move the federation and media over to travel through the Lync Edge server, the Lync policies governing external access and federation come into play. In the Control Panel on the External Access policy, make sure you enable external access and federation on both the External Access policy and the Access Edge configuration.

Now that you've configured the Edge so that federation and media traffic flows through the Lync Edge, you are ready to move the Exchange UM contact objects to Lync. This is a two-step process. First, you move the Subscriber and Auto Attendant contact objects over to the Lync server and then update the Exchange UM server so it knows about the new Lync pool. To move the contact objects, log onto the Lync front end (or Standard Edition) server as a member of at least the RTCUniversalUserAdmins group or CsUserAdministrator RBAC role and open up PowerShell.

Get the contacts that exist, using the cmdlet `Get-CsExUmContact`. This will bring back all Exchange UM contact objects in the forest, so to narrow it down, use the following command to specify objects for migration by display name:

```
Get-CsExUmContact | where {$_.DisplayName -eq "OCSUMAuto" -or "OCSUMSubscriber"}
```

This will get only the object named `OCSUMAuto and OCSUMSubscriber`, as shown in the following output:

```
Identity              : CN=OCSUMSubscriber,OU=UMContacts,DC=gaots,DC=local
RegistrarPool         :
HomeServer            : CN=LC Services,CN=Microsoft,CN=OCS-SE01,CN=Pools,CN=RTC
                         Service,CN=Services,CN=Configuration,DC=gaots,DC=local
Enabled               : True
SipAddress            : sip:OCSUMSubscriber@gaots.co.uk
LineURI               : tel:+442031370989
OtherIpPhone          : {sip:OCSUMSubscriber@gaots.co.uk;opaque=app:exum:OCSUM.
                        gaots.local}
AutoAttendant         : True
IsSubscriberAccess    : False
Description           : Exchange UM Subscriber Access
DisplayName           : OCSUMSubscriber
DisplayNumber         : +442031370989
HostedVoicemailPolicy :

Identity              : CN=OCSUMAuto,OU=UMContacts,DC=gaots,DC=local
RegistrarPool         :
HomeServer            : CN=LC Services,CN=Microsoft,CN=OCS-SE01,CN=Pools,CN=RTC
                         Service,CN=Services,CN=Configuration,DC=gaots,DC=local
Enabled               : True
SipAddress            : sip:OCSUMAuto@gaots.co.uk
LineURI               : tel:+442031370988
OtherIpPhone          : {sip:OCSUMAuto@gaots.co.uk;opaque=app:exum:OCSUM.gaots.
                        local:OCSAuto}
AutoAttendant         : True
IsSubscriberAccess    : False
Description           : Exchange UM Auto-Attendant
DisplayName           : OCSUMAuto
DisplayNumber         : +442031370988
HostedVoicemailPolicy :
```

At this point, you have confirmed that you have the correct objects and you will pipe the output of the previous command into the `Move-CsExUmContact` cmdlet as follows:

```
Get-CsExUmContact | where {$_.DisplayName -eq "OCSUMAuto" -or "OCSUMSubscriber"}
| Move-CsExUmContact -Target lync-se01.gaots.local
```

This will move the previously mentioned contact objects to the `Lync-se01.gaots.local` pool. Now that the contact objects have been moved, you need to run the `ExchUCUtil.ps1` script on the Exchange UM server again to ensure all entries are updated as described in Chapter 17. Having run the script, restart the Lync front-end service on all the Lync front-end or Standard Edition servers so they'll pick up the changes.

The next components that need to be moved across to Lync are your response groups. Response groups are covered in depth in Chapter 16, so we'll simply cover the migration steps here. First, download and install the SQL Server 2005 native client on the Lync server where you will perform the migration, in this case the Standard Edition server. This is required because the database where the configuration is held on the OCS 2007 R2 server is running on SQL 2005. If another version were being used, you would need to use the appropriate client. The required version of the SQL 2005 native client is part of the feature pack for Microsoft SQL Server 2005 - December 2008. Specifically, it is the `SQLNCLI.MSI` package, and it can be downloaded from the Microsoft Download Center here:

```
http://go.microsoft.com/fwlink/?LinkId=204105
```

Because your Lync server is running Windows 2008 Server R2, which is a 64bit OS, you should download the 64-bit version. The installation process consists of simply accepting the defaults and clicking through the installation.

Once that process is complete, make sure you are logged on as a member of the RTCUniversalServerAdmins group and then open PowerShell. Then run the following command to migrate the configuration across to the new Lync pool.

```
Move-CsRgsConfiguration -Source ocs-se01.gaots.local -Destination lync-se01.
gaots.local
```

This command will read the Response Group service configuration from the database on the OCS pool and bring it across to the Lync pool. You should note that the command will bring all the information from the OCS source pool over to the Lync destination pool. There is no way to be more granular. If you need to move any more components around, perhaps to split up pools, do it after you have moved everything across to Lync. Once you have run the command, in typical PowerShell fashion there will be no output if it is successful. To verify that the configuration has moved correctly, you can run the following commands. First, run:

```
Get-CsRgsAgentGroup
```

This brings back the agent groups you set up, and its output will be as follows:

```
Identity                   : service:ApplicationServer:lync-se01.gaots.local/58db
                             633d-179c-4681-ac29-5478deb0f134
Name                       : Agent Group 1
Description                :
ParticipationPolicy        : Informal
AgentAlertTime             : 20
RoutingMethod              : RoundRobin
DistributionGroupAddress   :
AgentsByUri                : {sip:testuser1@gaots.co.uk, sip:testuser2@gaots.co.uk}
```

The next verification cmdlet is:

```
Get-CsRgsQueue
```

This will bring back a list of the queues that you had set up, which in this case is RG Queue 1, as shown in the following output:

```
Identity           : service:ApplicationServer:lync-se01.gaots.local/0584762b-b2
                     f7-4562-87a7-09159f686944
TimeoutAction      : Action=Terminate
OverflowAction     : Action=Terminate
Name               : RG Queue 1
Description        :
TimeoutThreshold   :
OverflowThreshold  :
OverflowCandidate  : NewestCall
AgentGroupIDList   : {service:ApplicationServer:lync-se01.gaots.local/58db633d-1
                     79c-4681-ac29-5478deb0f134}
```

Finally, check on the workflows:

```
Get-CsRgsWorkflow
```

This command brings back a list of the workflows you have set up, which includes the IT Helpdesk workflow set up in the example.

```
Identity                : service:ApplicationServer:lync-se01.gaots.local/2682ac
                          21-7df7-454a-a272-52089640f92d
NonBusinessHoursAction  : Action=Terminate
HolidayAction           : Action=Terminate
DefaultAction           : Prompt=Hi, Welcome to the IT Helpdesk.
                          Action=TransferToQueue
                          QueueId=0584762b-b2f7-4562-87a7-09159f686944
CustomMusicOnHoldFile   :
Name                    : Helpdesk
Description             : IT Helpdesk
PrimaryUri              : sip:helpdesk@gaots.co.uk
Active                  : True
Language                : en-US
TimeZone                : GMT Standard Time
BusinessHoursID         : Service:1-ApplicationServer-1/2242b88a-168e-4ba4-a218-
                          2cc7ac2421d1
Anonymous               : False
DisplayNumber           : +442031375044
EnabledForFederation    : False
LineUri                 : tel:+442031375044
HolidaySetIDList        : {}
```

Of course, if you want, you can see all this from the Control Panel, as shown in Figure 7.20.

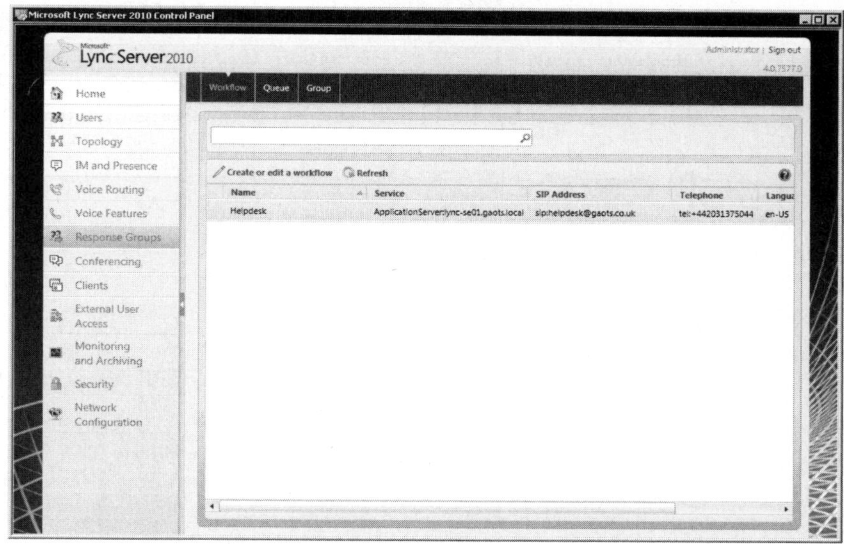

FIGURE 7.20
Verify that the Response Group settings have migrated into the Control Panel.

The last test is performed by making a call into the IT Helpdesk workflow to see if it still works for both internal and external OCS and Lync users, where both Lync and OCS users are agents and calling parties.

MORE COMPLEX RESPONSE GROUPS WITH AGENT SIGN ON

The Response Group system in OCS and now Lync is a very flexible application, and we've only scratched the surface. One thing worth mentioning, and which is covered in depth in Chapter 16, is that agents can be required to log into an Agent Group via a tab added to the OCS client—in which case, users will still be using the OCS 2007 R2 client after they move to Lync. As part of the migration, you will need to make sure that users log into the new URL by updating the customer tab definition file with the new URL, which in a standard edition deployment will be similar to this:

```
https://lync-se01.gaots.local/RgsClients/Tab.aspx
```

(If you are using Enterprise Edition, use the Web URL for the pool.)

Once users move to the Lync client, that client will pick up the URL automatically and prompt the users to sign in.

Now that you have moved all the main pieces across to Lync, there will be limited disruption from here on. You are ready to migrate the remaining OCS users across to Lync; do that following the procedure covered in the "Testing and Migrating Users" section.

Post-Migration Steps

Congratulations! Having moved all your users and main services across to Lync, you are now in production. Of course, a few areas still need to be tidied up a bit. The most disruptive of these is the migration of the Mediation server to Lync, alongside moving the dial-in access numbers.

TELEPHONY

Because telephony is usually a critical subsystem, it is important to schedule a period of down-time for this piece of the migration. The outage should be very short, but give yourself peace of mind and do it on a weekend or late evening. Start by moving the dial-in conferencing access numbers over from the OCS 2007 R2 pool.

1. The first step is to log on to your OCS front-end or Standard Edition server as a member of the RTCUniversalServerAdmins group and open up the OCS administrator console.
2. In the left pane, right-click the forest and select Conferencing Attendant Properties. On the window that opens, on the Access Phone Numbers tab, sort the entries by clicking on the Service By Pool column heading. Double-click any entries serviced by the legacy OCS pool to open the Edit Conferencing Attendant Number window.
3. In the new window, copy the SIP URI, shown in Figure 7.21, which you will need to use in the PowerShell command used to migrate the conferencing attendant number to Lync. Once you have copied all the SIP URIs, close the Properties page.

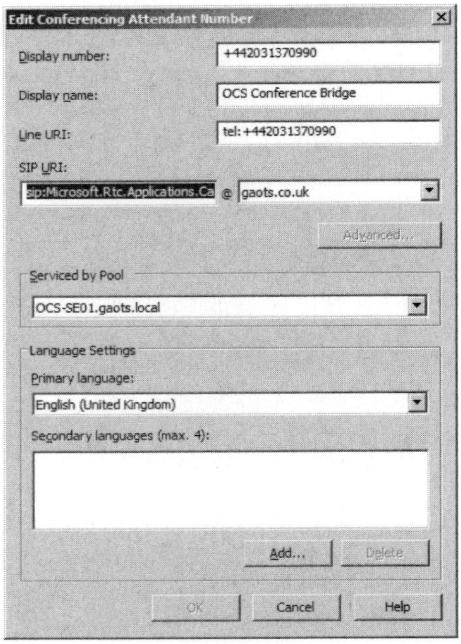

FIGURE 7.21 Making a note of the SIP URI of the conferencing attendant number

4. Now that you have the SIP URI for all conferencing attendant numbers, move over to the Lync front-end server and open PowerShell. Run the following command, making sure to use your SIP URI rather than the example shown here:

```
Move-CsApplicationEndpoint -Identity sip:Microsoft.Rtc.Applications.Caa-14113DE0-
1DCD-4E64-83CB-D193AD62EE9C@gaots.co.uk -TargetApplicationPool lync-se01.gaots
.local
```

5. Repeat this process for each of the conference attendant numbers. When you're done, move back to the OCS server and reopen the Conferencing Attendant Properties to check that none of the conferencing attendant numbers are serviced by the legacy OCS pool.

This should complete the move of the conferencing attendant numbers. Now you still need to move the conferencing directories hosted on OCS over to Lync. This step is important because it enables all migrated meetings to continue working. If you miss it, users will have to set up all their meetings again.

1. Verify that you can correctly access the relevant directories. To do so, run the following command:

```
Get-CsConferenceDirectory | Where-Object {$_.ServiceID -match "ocs-se01.gaots
.local"}
```

   This gets the conference directories that are hosted on the OCS pool as shown here:

```
Identity             : 2
ServiceId            : UserServer:ocs-se01.gaots.local
TargetServerIfMoving :
Id                   : 2
Fingerprint          :
```

2. Make a note of the Identity (a numeric value) because you will need it to migrate the directory. To migrate the conference directories, use the following command:

```
Move-CsConferenceDirectory -Identity 2 -TargetPool lync-se01.gaots.local
```

   This command moves the conference directory over to the Lync pool. That completes the conferencing number and directory migration, so you are ready to migrate the Mediation server across to Lync.

3. You already have the Mediation server enabled on the Lync front-end server, so you need to configure it. Open the Topology Builder, making sure you are logged on as a member of the RTCUniversalServerAdmins and Domain Admins groups, and download the configuration from the CMS. In the left pane, locate the front-end server, right-click it, and select Edit Properties. In the left pane of the new window, click Mediation Server. Depending on your PSTN connection, you will need to configure this section appropriately. (See Chapter 13, "Getting Started with Voice," and Chapter 18, "Third-Party Integration," for more information.) You are connecting to a SIP trunk and need to listen on port 5060, so first check the box to Enable TCP Port and enter **5060** in the data entry box, as shown in Figure 7.22. Next, click New to create a new PSTN gateway.

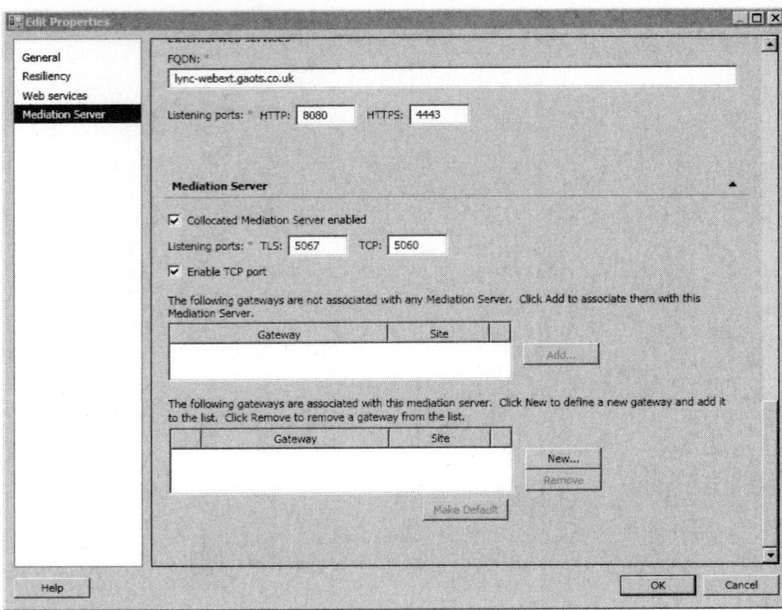

FIGURE 7.22 Configuring the Mediation server

4. In the dialog that opens, configure the IP or URL for the gateway (in this case, the SIP trunk provider's session border controller) and enter the relevant port and protocol information (for this example, that is TCP port 5060, as shown in Figure 7.23).
5. Click OK twice to accept the changes and then publish the topology. If prompted at the end of publishing, rerun local setup on the Lync front-end server.

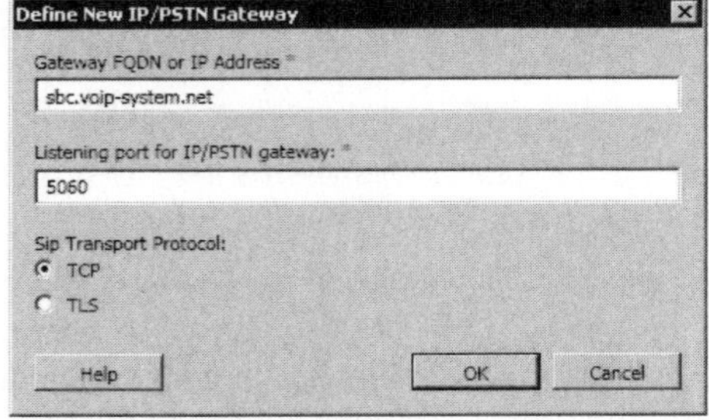

FIGURE 7.23 Setting up a new PSTN Gateway

You are now ready to swap the external IP address, which is the end point for the SIP trunk from the OCS Mediation server over to the Lync front-end server. Your downtime will begin now. Once you have configured the networking on the Lync front-end server appropriately, as it was on the OCS Mediation server, go back into the Topology Builder and download the configuration from the CMS. Then, in the left pane, right-click the front-end server and click Edit Properties.

In the General section, click Limit Service Usage to Selected IP Addresses. In the Primary IP address box, enter the LAN address of the server; and in the PSTN IP address box, enter the newly moved SIP Trunk public IP address, as shown in Figure 7.24. Click OK and then publish the topology.

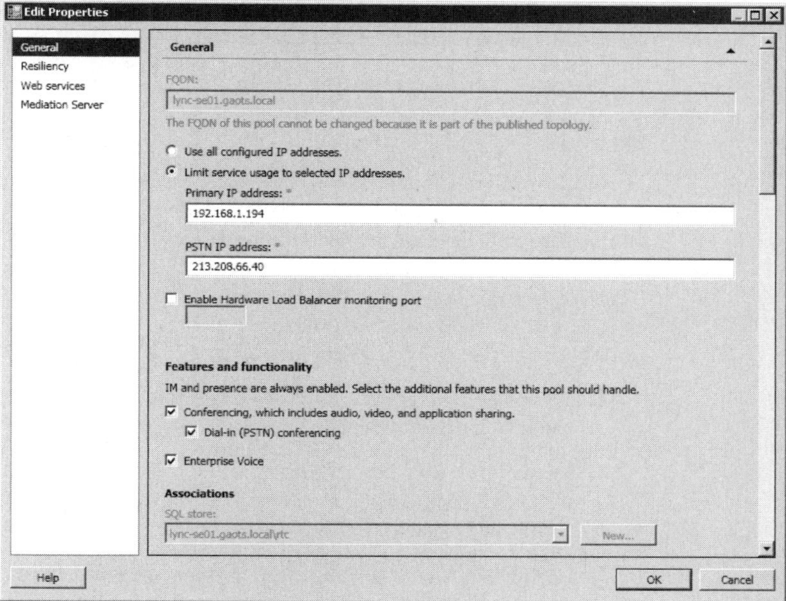

FIGURE 7.24
Configuring the Lync server service IP addresses

Now you have a functioning Mediation server that is set up to communicate with your PSTN gateway using the external NIC. The final step is to set up a new Voice Route so that traffic knows to use the new gateway. This is done in Control Panel, and you need to be logged on as a user who has at least the CsVoiceAdministrator role.

1. In the Control Panel on the left pane, click the Voice Routing tab and then navigate to the Route tab on the right pane. Click New to start creating a new route. Give the policy a name and then scroll down to the Associated Gateways section and click Add.
2. In the window that opens, select the new PSTN gateway you just created and click OK. Next, scroll down to the Associated PSTN Usages section and click Select.
3. On the Select PSTN Usage Record page, select Default Usage or another appropriate usage and then click OK. For more information about Usages and when and where they should be used, see Chapter 13.
4. Back on the New Voice Route page, click OK to create the Voice Route. Select the newly created route and click Move Up until the newly created route is at the top of the list.
5. Finally, click Commit and then select Commit All. On the Summary page, click Commit to apply the changes and then click Close.

> **OCS GATEWAYS AND LYNC**
>
> If you are using media gateways to connect your OCS server to the PSTN, you will need to upgrade them either with new hardware or new software when you move to Lync, because OCS gateways don't support the necessary encryption features that Lync requires. For more on gateways, see Chapter 18.

WEB

Having completed the telephony-related aspects of the migration, you can finish the web aspects. Specifically, you will reconfigure the CWA server to work with the Lync pool and enable the Lync pool for integration with Exchange 2010 SP1 Outlook Web App (OWA) to provide IM and presence access in OWA. You'll begin by redirecting Communicator Web Access (CWA). As you know, Lync doesn't provide a native fully functional IM and presence web application as of CU3, so you must maintain the use of the OCS 2007 R2 CWA server until this functionality is added to Lync natively.

1. To do so, log onto your CWA server as a member of the local Administrators group and the RTCUniversalServerAdmins group, and open the CWA MMC snap-in.
2. In the left pane, expand the name of the computer that hosts the virtual server for which you want to specify a next-hop server (in this case, `OCS-CWA.gaots.local`) and then right-click the name of the virtual server and select Properties.
3. In the window that opens, navigate to the Next Hop tab. From the Next Hop Pool drop-down, select the Lync pool (`Lync-se01.gaots.local`). Unless you have changed it, you can leave the listening port at the default of 5061.
4. Click OK. You have now repointed CWA to the Lync pool. To verify functionality, you should log onto CWA to test.

To complete the web elements of the migration, you need to enable Lync integration with Exchange 2010 SP1 OWA. See Chapter 17 for an in-depth description of the process.

THIRD-PARTY APPLICATIONS

The last server-based piece of the migration concerns third-party applications. There are a variety of types; some, such as video conferencing units, are defined in Lync as trusted application pools. They need to be configured so that they point to the Lync pool as the next hop. This is performed in Topology Builder and is covered in Chapter 18. The other type of application is the type built on a version of UCMA earlier than v3.0. These applications cannot be run on Lync Server and so must be rewritten and then deployed on Lync. That topic is beyond the scope of this book, and you should speak with the vendor who built the application to migrate them.

Now that everything is migrated, you can move the internal SRV records that currently direct clients to the OCS Pool so that they point to the Lync pool.

CLIENT ROLLOUT

The final piece of the migration is to complete the rollout of the Lync client along with the same level of cumulative update as is deployed on your Lync servers. Some considerations for the rollout of the Lync client are as follows:

- Use client version filtering rules on the Lync Front End to ensure that only clients with the correct updates installed are able to sign in, as described in Chapter 3.
- As discussed earlier in this chapter, you may need to configure the Group Policy settings that are required for client bootstrapping.
- Ensure that you have all the required policies in place on Lync and that they are correctly targeted at the necessary Lync users.

Decommissioning Legacy Systems

Now that you've migrated everything to the Lync pool, you are ready to remove the legacy OCS pool. We won't cover the required steps in detail here, but the following documentation will help:

- Decommissioning OCS 2007 Standard Edition:

`http://go.microsoft.com/fwlink/?LinkId=205889`

- Removing OCS 2007 servers and server roles:

`http://go.microsoft.com/fwlink/?LinkId=205887`

- Removing an OCS 2007 Enterprise pool:

`http://go.microsoft.com/fwlink/?LinkId=205888`

Once you have completely removed the OCS servers from your network (except of course for the OCS CWA server you pointed at Lync earlier), you should rerun the Merge 2007 or 2007 R2 Topology Wizard. Running through the wizard will remove all the aspects of the OCS topology except for the CWA server under the Trusted Application Servers node. Of course, if you are not using CWA, then running the merge will also remove the BackCompatSite.

Finally, once you've removed all the OCS servers, rerun the `ExchUCUtil.ps1` script on the Exchange UM server to remove the OCS IP Gateway entries.

The Bottom Line

Understand migration considerations. The process of migrating to Lync involves many aspects of an organization, not least of which are the end users who will have new functionality to exploit and skills to learn. It is very important to thoroughly evaluate all the phases of a migration and communicate clearly and efficiently to the staff. This is particularly true for any phase of coexistence where some users will be on Lync and others on OCS, potentially with different versions of the client in place.

Master It You have been asked to prepare a short presentation covering the key elements of the migration. List areas you would cover.

Consider client pain points. During Lync migration your primary concern should be for your users. Throughout the migration users will face a changing environment. How you deal with this and control the changes both through careful process and configuration of policy will have a large impact on the successful completion of the migration.

Master It You have been asked to prepare a short presentation covering the key difficulties faced by users during migration. List the areas you would cover.

Migrate to Lync Migrating to Lync is a complex set of processes that will move you from a stable OCS environment to a stable Lync environment with minimal downtime.

Master It You have been asked to lay out the steps to migrate to Lync. What are they?

Part 3

Administration

Chapter 8

Introduction to PowerShell and the Lync Management Shell

PowerShell was introduced by Microsoft in 2006 as the long-term plan to unify various scripting languages. It is a framework built on and integrated with the .NET framework and consists of a command-line shell and scripting environment. The first product to take advantage of PowerShell natively was Exchange 2007, and the scope has grown dramatically since then to include almost all of the Microsoft collection of server and system administration products: Windows Server 2008, SQL Server 2008, System Center Operations Manager 2007, System Center Virtual Machine Manager 2007, System Center Data Protection Manager 2007, Windows Compute Cluster Server 2007, SharePoint 2010, and now Lync Server 2010. As PowerShell was initially released in 2006, the hope was that OCS 2007 R2 would natively integrate with PowerShell; instead, a number of PowerShell scripts were provided as part of the Resource Kit toolset, and these PowerShell scripts simply call VBScript or Windows Management Instrumentation (WMI) to perform their tasks. Outside of the Microsoft products, a significant number of third-party vendors, including IBM, Quest, VMware, and NetApp to name a few, provide modules to allow PowerShell integration.

In this chapter, you will learn to:

- Use PowerShell command syntax
- Employ tips and tricks to get more out of PowerShell
- Get help using PowerShell
- Understand PowerShell remoting and scripting

Why Use PowerShell?

If you're wondering why you should use PowerShell, the answer is simple: scripting.

In today's large-scale enterprise environments, it is extremely common to perform the same task on a number of servers or on a number of users. With its proliferation and integration across the Microsoft suite of products (as well as the third-party integration), PowerShell is extremely easy to connect to any of these products using the common shell interface.

Looking to the future and "cloud computing," Microsoft is providing PowerShell management capabilities for the cloud interface, again meaning that a single interface is now capable of providing management both on-premises and in the cloud.

Coming back to the current world and the now-legacy versions of Lync (that is, OCS), there are multiple integration points such as WMI and COM. Developing scripts to simplify administration quite often results in extremely large, complex and difficult-to-maintain VBscript. Tasks that previously required tens (or even hundreds) of lines of code can now be performed with a single command, and in addition, PowerShell allows the results of one command to be piped into another, providing an even more resourceful environment.

The final reason is that there are some cases where the only way to achieve a task is via the shell, so even in single-server, 20-user environments, there are scenarios where the shell *must* be used.

PowerShell is very modular; in Windows Server 2008 R2, the base PowerShell V2 installation has over 200 individual cmdlets. Lync Server 2010 extends this by almost 500 more cmdlets specific to Lync.

Understanding Command Syntax

Unfortunately, every scripting language is different—and typically, as they get more powerful, they become more complicated and, in some cases, more cryptic.

One of Microsoft's goals for PowerShell is to make this language more intuitive, and as a result each PowerShell command typically consists of a verb and noun combination; the verb provides the action and the noun provides the object—for example, `Get-CsUser`. This combination of verb and noun is referred to as a *cmdlet*. The verb will always come first and the noun will follow, separated by a hyphen. The noun begins with a prefix indicating which tool the PowerShell cmdlet belongs to; for Lync, every cmdlet includes `Cs` to indicate it is part of the Lync PowerShell command set. Why `Cs`? It is a reference back to Communication Server. During the Beta program the codename for Lync was "Communications Server 14"—abbreviated to CS. The cmdlets were not changed upon release (and rename) of Lync Server 2010.

Table 8.1 shows some of the common verbs and nouns in Lync.

TABLE 8.1: Common Lync Management Shell Verbs and Nouns

CMDLET PORTION	VERB/NOUN	DESCRIPTION
`Get`	Verb	Probably the most commonly used verb. It will return information as specified by the object.
`Set`	Verb	Next in line of the verbs comes `Set`. It is used to update an object.
`Enable`	Verb	`Enable` is used to turn on functionality.
`Disable`	Verb	`Disable` used to turn off functionality.
`New`	Verb	Used to create new objects, typically policies.
`Move`	Verb	Typically used to manipulate the home server (or pool) attribute for an object.

Remove	Verb	Used in the deletion of objects.
CsUser	Noun	The user object when homed on a Lync pool.
CsLegacyUser	Noun	The user object when homed on an OCS pool.
CsAdUser	Noun	Additional AD attributes of a user.
CsConferencingPolicy	Noun	The object dealing with conference policy.
CsCertificate	Noun	The object properties of a certificate.

The following code:

```
Get-CsUCPhoneConfiguration
```

returns the following information about all Lync 2010 `UCPhoneConfiguration` objects (to return only a single object, specify the `UCPhoneConfiguration` ID as the only parameter):

```
Identity              : Global
CalendarPollInterval  : 00:03:00
EnforcePhoneLock      : True
PhoneLockTimeout      : 00:10:00
MinPhonePinLength     : 6
SIPSecurityMode       : High
VoiceDiffServTag      : 40
Voice8021p            : 0
LoggingLevel          : Off
```

To update a `UCPhoneConfiguration` object, use the following cmdlet:

```
Set-CsUCPhoneConfiguration
```

To create a new `UCPhoneConfiguration` object, use the following cmdlet:

```
New-CsUCPhoneConfiguration
```

The list goes on. You can see that in most cases the cmdlets are self-explanatory; however, there are some scenarios where you'll need to do some trial-and-error to find the right combination. Alternatively, you can use the help file, which is described next.

Finding Help

Figure 8.1 shows the help file index of cmdlets (shown on the left). It also includes a listing by category (on the right), which most people find easier to navigate, at least initially. (You know what you want to achieve, and category-based grouping makes it easier to find these types of cmdlets.) As time goes by, and you become more familiar with cmdlets, you'll probably find that searching directly for the cmdlet is the easiest way to get to the information you want.

(a)

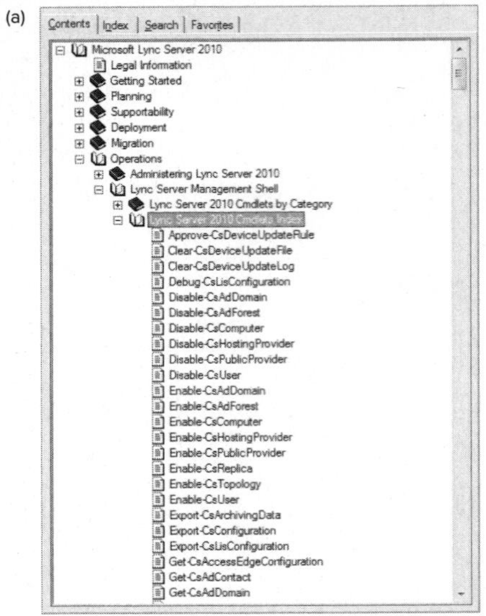

(b)

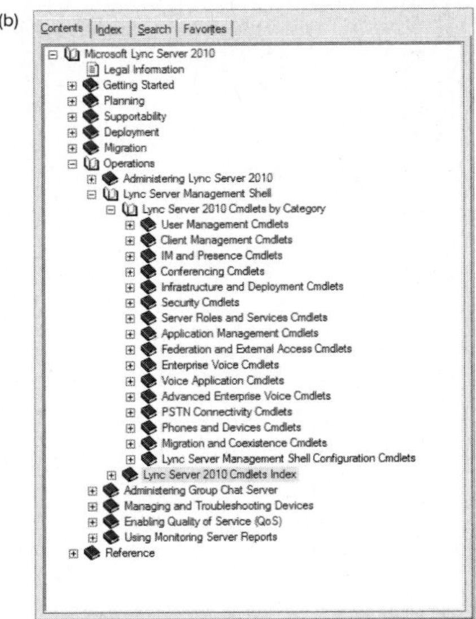

FIGURE 8.1 Use the help file to find cmdlets by name (a) and by category (b)

Selecting a specific cmdlet within the help file will display more detailed information regarding the cmdlet itself, as well as some examples of its usage. Figure 8.2 shows a snippet of the display for the `Move-CsUser` cmdlet.

FIGURE 8.2 View the **Move-CsUser** cmdlet in the help file

Move-CsUser

Send Feedback

See Also Example

Collapse All Language Filter: All

Lync Server Management Shell > Lync Server 2010 Cmdlets by Category > User Management Cmdlets >

Topic Last Modified: *2010-10-01*

Moves one or more user accounts enabled for Microsoft Lync Server 2010 to a new Registrar pool.

Syntax

```
Move-CsUser -Identity <UserIdParameter> -Target <Fqdn> [-Confirm [<SwitchParameter>]] [-DomainController <Fqdn>] [-Force
<SwitchParameter>] [-PassThru <SwitchParameter>] [-ProxyPool <Fqdn>] [-WhatIf [<SwitchParameter>]]
```

Parameters

Parameter	Required	Type	Description
Identity	Required	UserIdParameter	Indicates the Identity of the user account to be moved. User Identities can be specified using one of four formats: 1) the user's SIP address; 2) the user's user principal name (UPN); 3) the user's domain name and logon name, in the form domain\logon (for example, litwareinc\kenmyer); and, 4) the user's Active Directory display name (for example, Ken Myer). User Identities can also be referenced by using the user's Active Directory distinguished name. You can use the asterisk (*) wildcard character when using the Display Name as the user Identity. For example, the Identity "* Smith" returns all the users with who have a display name that ends with the string value " Smith".
Target	Required	FQDN	The FQDN (for example, atl-cs-001.litwareinc.com) of the Registrar pool where the user account should be moved. In addition to a Registrar pool, the Target can also be the FQDN of a legacy Office Communications Server Front End Server or a hosting provider. Any accounts moved to a hosting provider (for example, Microsoft Lync Online 2010) will lose all their associated user data. For example, any conferences the user has scheduled will be deleted and will not be available in Lync Online 2010.
DomainController	Optional	String	Enables you to connect to the specified domain controller in order to retrieve contact information. To connect to a particular domain controller, include the DomainController parameter followed by the computer name (for example, atl-cs-001) or its FQDN (for example, atl-cs-001.litwareinc.com).
ProxyPool	Optional	String	This parameter is used only for Microsoft Lync Online 2010. It should not be used with an on-premises implementation of Lync Server.
Force	Optional	Switch Parameter	If present, moves the user account but deletes any associated user data (such as conferences that the user has scheduled). If not present, both the account and the associated data are moved.
PassThru	Optional	Switch Parameter	Enables you to pass a user object through the pipeline that represents the user account being moved. By default, the **Move-CsUser** cmdlet does not pass objects through the pipeline.

The help file consists of the following sections for all cmdlets:

- Syntax
- Parameters
- Detailed description
- Input types
- Return types
- Example
- See also

It can be quite time-consuming to leave the shell environment to go to the help file and then go back to the shell to continue scripting or running cmdlets (not everyone has two screens!). The solution to this problem is to run a favorite cmdlet: `Get-Help`. There are several other related cmdlets or associated methods of retrieving help, all of them documented in Table 8.2.

TABLE 8.2: Methods of Finding Help

Method	Description
`Get-Help`	Lists the help information for the `Get-Help` cmdlet itself.
`Get-Help` *`Cmdlet`*	Lists the help information for the cmdlet specified.
`Get-Help` *`*Keyword*`*	Lists the help information for the keyword specified. This is typically in Table format, so it is not actually very helpful as the columns are truncated.
`Help`	Same as `Get-Help`.
`Help` *`Cmdlet`*	Same as `Get-Help` *`Cmdlet`*.
`Help` *`*Keyword*`*	Same as `Get-Help` *`*Keyword*`*.
`Get-Command`	Lists all the cmdlets, aliases, and functions in the PowerShell process (including any imported sessions).
`Get-Command` *`*Keyword*`*	Lists all cmdlets, aliases, and functions that contain the keyword. Example: `Get-Command *-Cs*` will return all commands that include `*-Cs*`.
`Cmdlet` `-?`	Lists help specifically for the cmdlet listed.

From within PowerShell, there are different views or output options, providing a method to control the information returned from the `Help` command. They are:

- `Default`
- `Detailed`
- `Example`
- `Full`
- `Parameters`

To use these parameters, enter the `Get-Help` cmdlet in the following format, including the view option:

```
Get-Help Disable-CsUser -Detailed
```

Because you specified `Detailed`, you should get the following output:

```
NAME
     Disable-CsUser

SYNOPSIS
     Modifies the Active Directory account of the specified user or users; this
modification prevents users from using Microsoft Lync Server 2010 clients such
as Microsoft Lync 2010. Disable-CsUser only restricts activity related to Lync
Server 2010; it does not disable or remove a user's Active Directory account.

SYNTAX
     Disable-CsUser -Identity <UserIdParameter> [-Confirm [<SwitchParameter>]]
[-DomainController <Fqdn>] [-PassThru <SwitchParameter>] [-WhatIf
[<SwitchParameter>]] [CommonParameters]

DESCRIPTION
     The Disable-CsUser cmdlet deletes all the attribute information related to
Lync Server from an Active Directory user account; this prevents the user from
logging on to Lync Server. When you run Disable-CsUser all the Lync Server-
related attributes are removed from an account, including the Identities of
any per-user policies that have been assigned to that account. You can later
re-enable the account by using the Enable-CsUser cmdlet. However, all the Lync
Server-related information (such as policy assignments) previously associated
with that account will have to be re-created. If you want to prevent a user
from logging on to Lync Server, but do not want to lose all of their account
information, use Set-CsUser instead. For details, see the Set-CsUser help topic.
<cut for brevity>
```

The output will continue, providing information on each of the following sections:

- Parameters (including details on each parameter)
- Examples
- Remarks (this typically refers to other links for more information)

The `-Examples` option provides only the example information (only one example is included; however, multiple examples will be displayed):

```
NAME
    Disable-CsUser

SYNOPSIS
    Modifies the Active Directory account of the specified user or users; this
modification prevents users from using Microsoft Lync Server 2010 clients such
as Microsoft Lync 2010. Disable-CsUser only restricts activity related to Lync
Server 2010; it does not disable or remove a user's Active Directory account.

------------------------- Example 1 -------------------------
Disable-CsUser -Identity "Ken Myer"
The preceding Example disables the Lync Server account for the user Ken Myer.
In this example, the user's display name is used to indicate his Identity.
```

Knowing about this option is important if, like a lot of technical people, you learn by looking at examples and changing the code to do what you need. This Examples view provides only the NAME, SYNOPSIS, and EXAMPLES sections.

On the other hand, running `Get-Help Disable-CsUser -Full` will display all the sections. From the full output, you can see additional information based on the types of input accepted and output generated. With each parameter, you can also see its associated metadata. Table 8.3 explains each item.

TABLE 8.3: `Get-Help` Cmdlet Metadata

VALUE	DESCRIPTION
`Required?`	`True` or `False` based on whether this parameter is needed.
`Position?`	Specifies the position of the parameter. Most parameters are Named, which means the parameter value must be prefixed by the parameter tag. The `-Identity` parameter is always 1, which means the tag is not required.
`Default`	The value used if none is provided. For most parameters, this is blank.
`Accept pipeline input?`	`True` or `False` based on whether input is accepted from another cmdlet (more on this later in the chapter).
`Accept wildcard characters?`	`True` or `False` and determines whether or not wildcards (such as * or ?) are accepted.

The `-Default` parameter will return the following sections:

```
NAME
SYNOPSIS
SYNTAX
DESCRIPTION
RELATED LINKS
REMARKS
```

Finally, the `-Parameter` option will return only the specific information regarding the parameter specified, including the metadata.

Cmdlet versus Command

Understanding the difference between "cmdlet" and "command" is important. Both terms are used frequently when talking about PowerShell.

- A cmdlet is the verb-noun combination that takes parameters as input, carries out a task, and in most cases provides output.
- A command is the complete string comprising the cmdlet and a specific set of parameters.

For example, `Get-CsUser` is a cmdlet, and `Get-CsUser "sip:keith_lync@gaots.co.uk"` is a command.

When Is a Cmdlet Also a Command?

In some cases (such as the previous one), the cmdlet can stand as a command in its own right. `Get-CsUser` executed on its own will produce the output for every user enabled for Lync. Typically, we refer to a cmdlet when we are only talking about generics, and a command is the full string of cmdlet and parameters.

Shells versus the Prompt

Opening the wrong shell is a common mistake. You can see why because a Lync server can have some or all of the following installed (see Figure 8.3):

- Command prompt (also known as the command shell or DOS prompt)
- Windows PowerShell
- Lync Management Shell
- Windows PowerShell modules

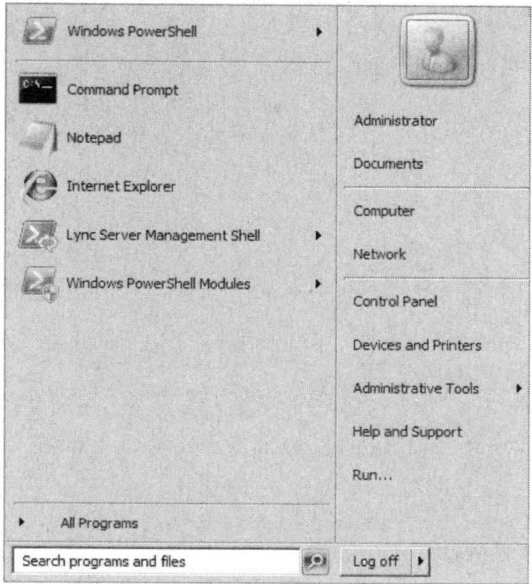

FIGURE 8.3
Common command shells installed on a Lync server

The command prompt has been around since before Microsoft itself was first formed. The version on a Lync 2010 server is the latest incarnation of the old DOS prompt (see Figure 8.4). From a Lync administration perspective, it is almost useless. Yes, there are a few utilities that can be run from the command prompt (mostly from the Resource Kit); however, day-to-day administration requires PowerShell, not a command prompt.

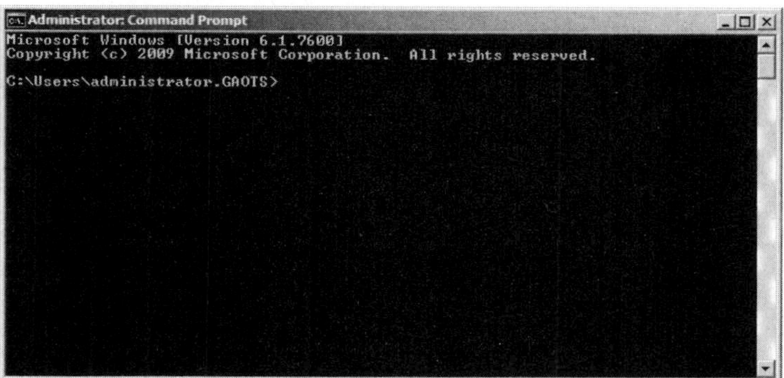

FIGURE 8.4
The command prompt

Next up are the Windows PowerShell and Windows PowerShell modules (see Figure 8.5). Windows PowerShell is the basic shell, with over 200 cmdlets; however, the Windows PowerShell modules add significantly more cmdlets to help administer Windows itself. The ability to incorporate additional modules to extend the capabilities of the shell is an extremely powerful function—and it is exactly what the Lync Management Shell does. Its additional cmdlets are specific to Lync management.

FIGURE 8.5
Windows PowerShell

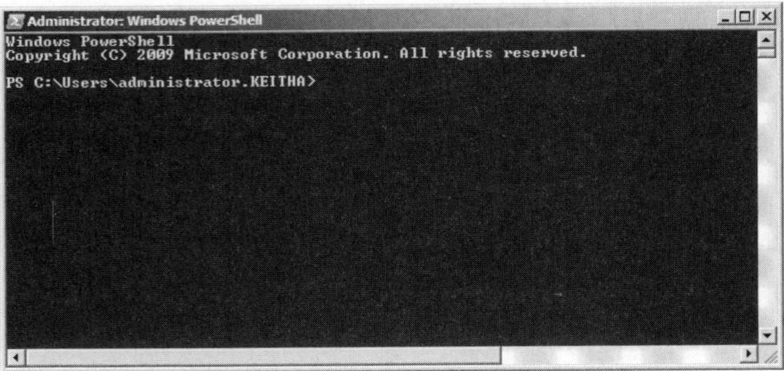

Figure 8.6 shows the Lync Management Shell, and if you open both it and a base Windows PowerShell window, you will notice a difference in the speed at which they start up; the Lync Management Shell is loading the Lync-specific cmdlets in the background.

FIGURE 8.6
The Lync Management Shell

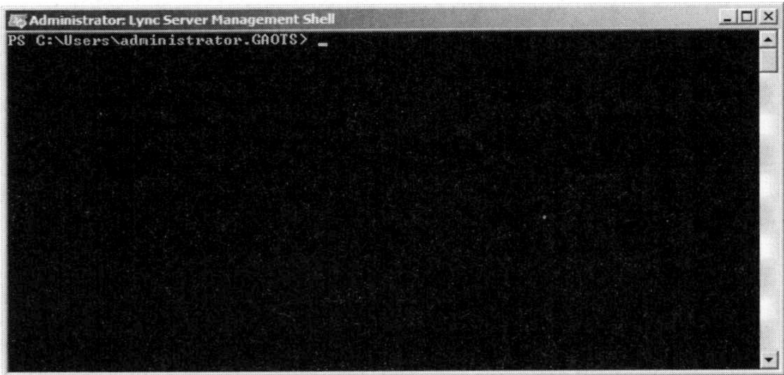

As you can see, the Lync 2010 Management Shell window looks extremely similar to a command prompt, so it's quite easy to use the wrong one; however, very quickly you're going to see errors returned if you try to execute PowerShell commands in a Command Prompt window, or Lync 2010 cmdlets in a basic PowerShell window.

NOTE In the book, we use the term PowerShell to describe the Lync Server Management Shell. Please don't confuse this use of PowerShell with the standard Microsoft PowerShell shell, which is installed on Windows Server 2008 R2 by default. When working with Lync, unless explicitly stated otherwise, you should be using the Lync Server Management Shell. The Lync Server Management Shell can either be launched directly from the Lync Server program group, or by importing the Lync modules into a standard PowerShell session, using the 'Import-Module Lync' command.

Introducing PowerShell Coding

So far, we've looked at individual cmdlets and how to execute them. By linking multiple cmdlets together or working on (or with) the same object, you can develop code (or scripts), which can be saved in a file with a `.PS1` extension and rerun at a later date. By introducing and using variables, along with logic controls based on the values of those variables, the script can adapt to different environments, or indeed different conditions in the same environment. In this section, we'll look at how you can begin to build up from cmdlets into scripts that can query the environment and perform additional tasks based on the results of those queries.

Windows PowerShell has over 200 cmdlets, whereas the Lync Management Shell has almost 500 Lync-specific cmdlets. A brief PowerShell introduction will explain the difference. You've already seen the `Get-Command` cmdlet and how it displays details for a specific command. By providing it with the parameter `*-Cs*`, you can instruct it to return a list of all the cmdlets that include `-Cs` in their name—that is, all the Lync Management Shell cmdlets.

```
Get-Command *-Cs*
```

In the Windows PowerShell prompt, four entries are returned:

```
ConvertFrom-Csv

ConvertTo-Csv

Export-Csv

Import-Csv
```

In the Lync Management Shell, this same command returns too many entries to read. You need to modify the command to the following:

```
$total = Get-Command *-Cs*
```

This is the first piece of PowerShell coding. By specifying **`$total`**, you define a variable and assign the results of the `Get-Command *-Cs*` command to it.

The array, which can be thought of as a list, is **`$total`**. In itself it produces no output; however, you can manipulate it. For example, the variable name alone:

```
$total
```

will produce onscreen the same output as if you simply ran `Get-Command *-Cs*`. Specifying the index, or numeric position within the array, like this:

```
$total[0]
```

will produce the first entry in the list—in this example, `Approve-CsDeviceUpdateRule`.

Finally, adding the `count` parameter:

```
$total.count
```

will return the total number of items in the list—in this example, 556.

TAB COMPLETION

An extremely useful feature of PowerShell is that you can press Tab to complete a cmdlet. This is especially helpful with some of the longer cmdlets. Once you have typed enough to define a unique cmdlet, pressing Tab will complete the cmdlet. If you haven't reached a unique point in the cmdlet, pressing Tab will cycle through the cmdlets that match what you have typed so far.

For example, if you type **A** and then press Tab, the cmdlet will complete to `Approve-CsDeviceUpdateRule`, because only one cmdlet begins with A.

But if you start typing **`Clear-CsDeviceUpdate`** before pressing Tab (or at any point during this cmdlet), you will cycle through both `Clear-CsDeviceUpdateFile` and `Clear-CsDeviceUpdateLog` because you have not reached a unique point.

The tab-completion feature also works with parameters for cmdlets.

Although pressing Tab cycles forward through the cmdlets, if you press Tab too many times and miss the cmdlet you're looking for, you can simply press Shift+Tab to cycle backward to the cmdlet you missed.

PowerShell Variables and Data Types

A variable is a placeholder for a value and can be a string, number, or object. You access the values stored in a variable simply by referencing the variable name. In PowerShell every variable begins with a dollar sign ($) and is an object. Defining the variable as an object means that you can assign any value to it; however, you can force a specific data type if required. This is called *casting*. For example, the following command:

```
$x = [int]5
```

would assign the integer value 5 to the variable `x`, rather than the string "5".

Assigning the output of a cmdlet to a variable creates an *object*, which in turn can be passed to another cmdlet. For example, in this command:

```
$users = Get-CsUser
```

the `$users` variable will contain all of the user objects in the environment. This will result in an array with each entry being an individual user.

In PowerShell, the first item in an array is always numbered 0; therefore, the first user object would be accessed by using:

```
$users[0]
```

PowerShell can define and use any .NET framework data type as a value. There are too many to list here; however, the more commonly used ones are:

- String
- Integer
- Boolean
- DateTime
- XML

Script Control

So that decisions can be made by the script, PowerShell includes a number of standard constructs that check conditions and that control loops.

Conditions are typically checked in this format:

```
If <something> then <do something> else <do something else>
```

Within PowerShell this format becomes:

```
If (condition) {code} else {more code}
```

This can be further extended using `elseif` statements, such as:

```
If (condition1) {code} elseif (condition2) {code2} else {more code}
```

PowerShell also includes the `Switch` construct (known as `Case` in some other languages). It is used in the following format:

```
Switch (variable)
{
Value1 {code}
Value2 {code}
Value3 {code}
Default {code}
}
```

Control loops allow a script to parse through multiple values (such as an array). Combined with condition checking, these loops are the logical flow and execution of the script. PowerShell supports a number of different control loops:

- For looping
- ForEach looping
- While looping
- Do While looping
- Do Until looping

The basic syntax of each of these control loops is as follows, with each of the *code* sections repeated within the loop:

```
For (startvalue;condition;nextvalue) {code}
ForEach (Item in collection) {code}
While (condition) {code}
Do {code} While (condition)
Do {code} Until (condition)
```

It's beyond the scope of this book to go into each of these in detail, but a few of them will be used in the examples later in this chapter.

Input Parameters

You've already been introduced to the concepts of cmdlet parameters and how to query the help (by passing a parameter!) to find out which parameters a cmdlet needs, as well as the metadata definitions of each parameter. Now let's look in more detail.

In Lync 2010, `-Identity` is the most-used parameter and will always be the first parameter in the cmdlet list, so it doesn't need to have the tag included. For example,

```
Get-CsUser -Identity "sip:keith_lync@gaots.co.uk"
```

provides the same result as:

```
Get-CsUser "sip:keith_lync@gaots.co.uk"
```

Other parameters must be tagged with the parameter name as part of the cmdlet. As mentioned previously, the list of parameters for a cmdlet can be queried using the `Get-Help` cmdlet, with the specific parameter `-Parameters`.

The `Get` verb cmdlets are interesting, because the `-Identity` parameter is optional; if it isn't provided, the cmdlet will work on all objects of that type, so `Get-CsUser` will return all enabled users.

The groups of `Set` verbs, on the other hand, require you to provide an `-Identity` tag to determine the object on which to execute changes. What happens if you forget this (or indeed, any) required parameter? Well, PowerShell is intelligent enough to know the parameters that are required, so it will prompt for them; any optional parameters will be left out of the command. Figure 8.7 shows the prompt from running the `Enable-CsUser` cmdlet without a specific `-Identity` parameter.

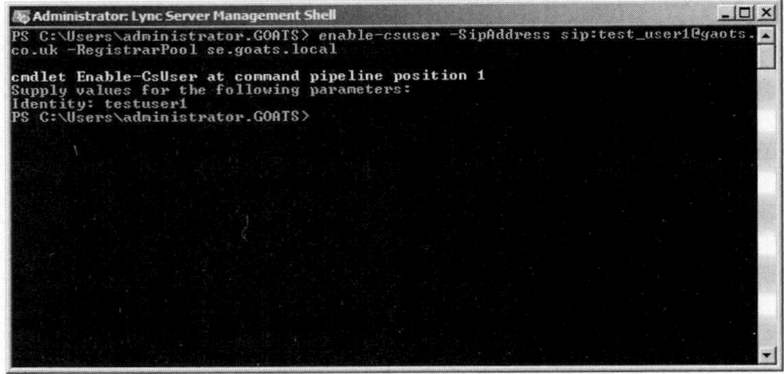

FIGURE 8.7
Prompting for missing parameters

Output Parameters

Because PowerShell is based on the .NET Framework, it uses an object model for data. This means the responses from commands are not text-based (although they will display on screen as text); instead, they are objects. Cmdlets will have a default display (content and format) of the data being returned, but because the data takes the form of objects, you can easily override this default and display the data you want to see. You do that by specifying output parameters. For example, here's the default output of `Get-CsPool` for the example system:

```
Get-CsPool

Identity  : se01.gaots.local
Services  : {UserServer:se01.gaots.local, Registrar:se01.gaots.local,
       UserDatabase:se01.gaots.local, FileStore:se01.gaots.local...}
Computers : {se01.gaots.local}
Fqdn      : se01.gaots.local
Site      : Site:APAC

Identity  : sql01.gaots.local
Services  : {MonitoringDatabase:sql01.gaots.local,
       ArchivingDatabase:sql01.gaots.local,
       UserDatabase:sql01.gaots.local,
       ApplicationDatabase:sql01.gaots.local}
Computers : {sql01.gaots.local}
Fqdn      : sql01.gaots.local
```

```
Site      : Site:APAC

Identity  : dc01.gaots.local
Services  : {FileStore:dc01.gaots.local}
Computers : {dc01.gaots.local}
Fqdn      : dc01.gaots.local
Site      : Site:APAC

Identity  : monitor01.gaots.local
Services  : {MonitoringServer:monitor01.gaots.local}
Computers : {monitor01.gaots.local}
Fqdn      : monitor01.gaots.local
Site      : Site:APAC

Identity  : archive01.gaots.local
Services  : {FileStore:archive01.gaots.local,
       ArchivingServer:archive01.gaots.local}
Computers : {archive01.gaots.local}
Fqdn      : archive01.gaots.local
Site      : Site:APAC

Identity  : lyncpool.gaots.local
Services  : {UserServer:lyncpool.gaots.local,
       Registrar:lyncpool.gaots.local,
       WebServer:lyncpool.gaots.local,
       ConferencingServer:lyncpool.gaots.local...}
Computers : {fe01.gaots.local, fe02.gaots.local}
Fqdn      : lyncpool.gaots.local
Site      : Site:APAC

Identity  : ocsse02.gaots.local
Services  : {Registrar:ocsse02.gaots.local,
       UserServer:ocsse02.gaots.local,
       ApplicationServer:ocsse02.gaots.local}
Computers : {ocsse02.gaots.local}
Fqdn      : ocsse02.gaots.local
Site      : Site:BackCompatSite
```

You can manipulate this output by changing the format. The default format for many cmdlets is `Format-Table`, which typically results in a minimal set of parameters being displayed in the output.

```
Get-CsPool | Format-Table

Identity              Services
--------              --------
se01.gaots.local      {UserServer:se01.gaots.local, Registrar:se01.g...
sql01.gaots.local     {MonitoringDatabase:sql01.gaots.local, Archivi...
dc01.gaots.local      {FileStore:dc01.gaots.local}
monitor01.gaots.local {MonitoringServer:monitor01.gaots.local}
archive01.gaots.local {FileStore:archive01.gaots.local, ArchivingSer...
lyncpool.gaots.local  {UserServer:lyncpool.gaots.local, Registrar:ly...
ocsse02.gaots.local   {Registrar:ocsse02.gaots.local, UserServer:ocs...
```

As you can see, the content of the field may be truncated with `Format-Table`. Depending on the size of your window, you may get more columns than shown here, and if you export the output to a file (using `Output-File`), you will get the full column content; however, the individual columns may still be truncated.

`Format-List` will provide all the properties of the returned object:

```
Get-CsPool | Format-List
```

`Format-List` is the default output of many `*-Cs*` commands, so in this case the output is the same as shown for `Get-CsPool` alone, as if you did not include the `Format-List` cmdlet.

In addition, you can specify only the parameters you are looking for, reducing the amount of screen clutter.

```
Get-CsPool | Ft Site, Fqdn

Site                          Fqdn
----                          ----
Site:APAC                     se01.gaots.local
Site:APAC                     sql01.gaots.local
Site:APAC                     dc01.gaots.local
Site:APAC                     monitor01.gaots.local
Site:APAC                     archive01.gaots.local
Site:APAC                     lyncpool.gaots.local
Site:BackCompatSite           ocsse02.gaots.local
```

ALIASES

In the previous example, the `Format-Table` has been replaced by `Ft`. This is known as an *alias*. Aliases are shortcut references to longer cmdlets. In the native PowerShell installation, almost 150 aliases are predefined.

You can create your own aliases for frequently used commands by using the `Set-Alias` cmdlet.

WHEN OUTPUT EQUALS INPUT

Often it is useful to run one command to retrieve information and directly use that information as the input for another command. You have already seen this in the previous couple of examples, where one command's output is directed to a second command using the pipe (|) symbol:

```
Get-CsPool | Format-Table
```

Here you are sending the output of the first cmdlet into the `Format-Table` cmdlet, as well as providing additional information in the form of parameters to filter the results.

Not all cmdlets will support piping between them; however, where the noun portions of the cmdlets match, it will always work. For example:

```
Get-csuser <something> |set-csuser <something>
```

Using the `Get-Help` cmdlet with the `-Full` parameter will provide the details to describe each parameter and whether it will accept pipeline input or not.

When interacting between cmdlets that do not support piping, the `ForEach` cmdlet can usually be used to process the data in a loop:

```
ForEach  ($user in $users)
{
            Write-Host $user.Name
}
```

This code snippet would cycle through each `$user` object in the `$users` collection and output the `Name` parameter.

Filtering the Output

Rather than limiting the properties returned, you may be interested only in a subset of the objects. For example, you may want to select only the users on a particular Lync pool and apply a change to them. This is where filtering comes in. You are running the command on the full environment; however, you then provide a filter across this complete data showing a view of only the data in which you are interested. Here's an example:

```
Get-CsUser | Where-Object {$_.poolname -like 'SE01'}
```

Breaking down this command, run the `Get-CsUser` command (in this form it is a command rather than cmdlet) to return all the users. This output is piped to the `Where-Object` cmdlet, and using the filter parameters enclosed in `{}`, you will retain only the objects that match the criteria. In this case, the `$_.poolname` property must match the `'SE01'` value provided. Here, you have introduced another new concept, because `$_` refers to the current object and is used when you want to iterate through a complete list of objects, in this case comparing each one to the filter criteria.

Table 8.4 shows a list of common operators that can be used with filtering.

Table 8.4: Shell Values and Operator Descriptions

Shell Value	Operator	Description
`-eq`	Equal	The property must match exactly the value.
`-ne`	Not Equal	The property must not match the value.
`-gt`	Greater Than	Integers only. The property must be greater than the value.
`-ge`	Greater Than or Equal to	Integers only. The property must be greater than or equal to the value.
`-lt`	Less Than	Integers only. The property must be less than the value.
`-le`	Less Than or Equal to	Integers only. The property must be less than or equal to the value.
`-Like`	Contains	Text. The string can match exactly or wildcards can be used to indicate the string being a substring.
`-Notlike`	Does Not Contain	Text. The string must not match exactly or wildcards can be used to indicate the string must not be a substring.

PowerShell V2

Until now we've been discussing functionality that is contained within both versions 1 and 2 of PowerShell. Windows 7 and Windows Server 2008 R2 introduced PowerShell Version 2, bringing some fantastic new features, such as remoting and the Integrated Scripting Environment.
For older operating systems, PowerShell Version 2 is available as a download from this link (separate downloads are available for each operating system):

`www.microsoft.com/download/en/search.aspx?q=powershell+2.0`

In this section, we'll look specifically at some of these new features.

Remoting

Remoting is the term given to managing an environment from a remote shell. You launch a local PowerShell prompt and initiate a remote PowerShell session against the machine (or environment) you want to manage, and then you import that session to your current session:

```
$session = New-PsSession -ConnectionUri https://se01.gaots.local/ocspowershell
-Authentication NegotiateWithImplicitCredential
Import-PsSession $session
```

At this point, the remote PowerShell modules become available in the local session.

This is an extremely useful function, because it means that you don't need to install local administration tools and you can provide separate administration credentials (ensuring a separation of user and admin roles) through the connection session.

Managing Multiple Environments from a Single PowerShell Session

By taking advantage of PowerShell's remoting capabilities, you can connect a single PowerShell session to multiple environments, which will allow you to modify users for Lync and Exchange at the same time. This concept will work with services located both on the premises and in the Cloud; PowerShell doesn't care where the services are located, only that it can reach the administration point.

Take the following script:

```
$ExchangeSession = New-PsSession -ConfigurationName Microsoft.Exchange
-ConnectionUri http://ex01.gaots.local/PowerShell -Authentication Kerberos

Import-PsSession $ExchangeSession

$CsSession = $CsSession = New-PsSession -ConnectionUri https://se01.gaots.local/
ocspowershell -Authentication NegotiateWithImplicitCredential

Import-PsSession $CsSession

Enable-Mailbox gaots\PS_DemoUser

Enable-CSuser -identity gaots\PS_DemoUser -SipAddress sip:ps_demouser@gaots.
co.uk -RegistrarPool se01.gaots.local

Enable-UMMailbox gaots\PS_DemoUser -UMMailboxPolicy "UK Default Policy" -
SipResourceIdentifier PS_DemoUser@gaots.co.uk -Extensions "1234"
```

By running this script in a Windows PowerShell session, you first connect to and import an Exchange session (`$ExchangeSession` and `Import-PsSession`) and then connect to and import a Lync session (`$CsSession` and `Import-PsSession`). Then you have a single PowerShell session connected to both Exchange and Lync, and you can enable a user with a mailbox and Lync account, and finally you enable Exchange Unified Messaging—all from within the remaining three lines of code.

The Integrated Scripting Environment

PowerShell V2 also provides a graphical user interface called the Integrated Scripting Environment (ISE), which includes a handy debugging tool. On Windows Server 2008 R2, the ISE must be installed by adding the Windows PowerShell Integrated Scripting Environment feature from Server Manager. The ISE can be launched by typing **ISE** in a PowerShell window. Figure 8.8 shows the ISE when started.

FIGURE 8.8 The Integrated Script Environment

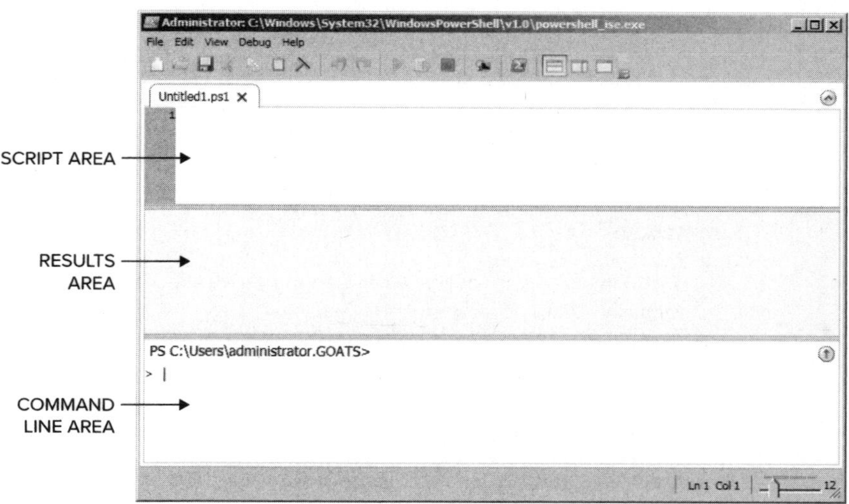

Commands are entered in the bottom pane, with the results displayed in the middle pane. The top pane is used for scripting. Figure 8.9 shows the working environment where the `Get-Service` cmdlet was entered in the command line, and the results appeared (the screen has been scrolled back to show the start of the output).

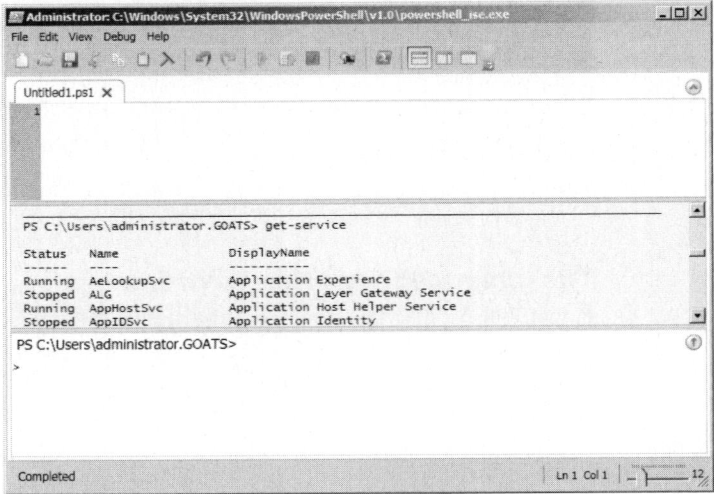

FIGURE 8.9
The ISE is working

ISE does not include any PowerShell extensions (such as Lync 2010 or Exchange) and is required to use the remoting feature to connect to and import a Lync 2010 (or Exchange) session.

Figure 8.10 shows the script introduced in the example (to open select File ➢ Open). Each script is opened in a separate tab, which allows multiple scripts to be opened at the same time.

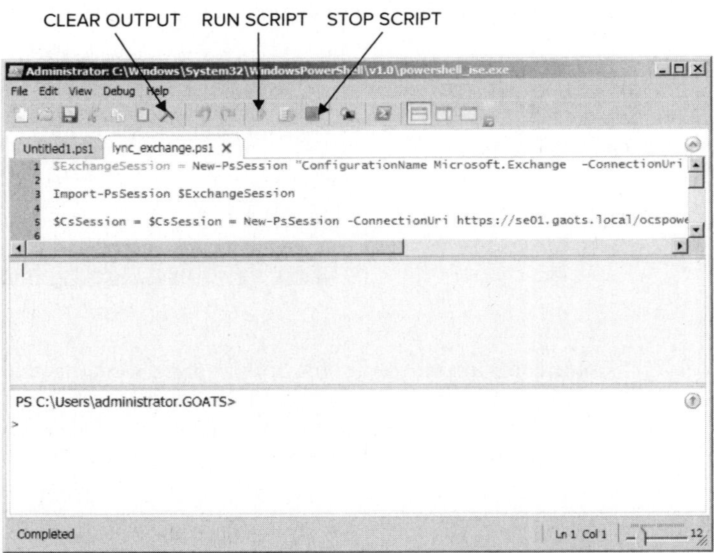

FIGURE 8.10
Scripting via ISE

Although you can't see it in the figure, the scripting section uses color highlighting to make it easier to write scripts and view variables, functions, and cmdlets. The color highlighting allows you to easily spot where the script blocks start and end. When code is written, quote marks (") are frequently placed in the wrong location (or forgotten), starting or ending a string in the wrong place. The highlighting makes it obvious that this has occurred.

Each line in the script area is numbered, as are any errors from PowerShell are numbered. This allows you to easily locate an error (use Ctrl+G to jump to a specific line in the script).

Once the script has been saved (File ➤ Save), debugging is enabled. This allows breakpoints to be set in the script by placing the cursor on a line of code and pressing F9 (or selecting Debug-Toggle Breakpoint). A *breakpoint* is a point in the code where execution will pause, allowing detailed interrogation of the script to determine specific values of the variable at that stage. This technique is used to help resolve errors in the code that may otherwise be difficult to find. Breakpoints are highlighted in dark red. Once a breakpoint has been configured and the script executed, assuming the line of code is reached, the script will pause.

At this point, you can interrogate any variable simply by entering the variable name in the command window; you can also execute PowerShell cmdlets in it. Additional commands become available once the script is paused:

- **Step Over (F10):** Allows line-by-line execution of the script, and if the line is a function, will not step into the function, but will execute it.
- **Step Into (F11):** Allows line-by-line execution of the script, and if the line is a function, will continue debugging the function line-by-line.
- **Step Out (Shift+F11):** Continues execution of a function, and pauses once the function is completed.
- **Continue (F5):** Continues executing the script until the next breakpoint.
- **Stop (Shift+F5):** Stops the execution of the script.

Figure 8.11 shows the ISE running a basic script, which will count from 0 to 10, outputting the value each time, and when the value is equal to five will write the text "the value is five" rather than the number. At the point of capture of the screenshot, the *breakpoint* has been reached. The [DBG] indicates that the output screen and the command window are in Debug mode.

FIGURE 8.11
ISE in Debug mode

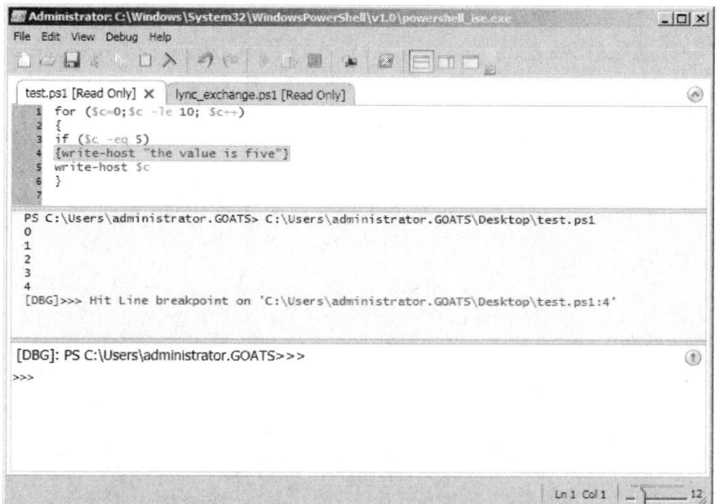

Managing Output

Although PowerShell is the interface used to configure and administer Lync, more often than not it will be used to provide data in a form either for human consumption or for input to other applications. As a result, it is often necessary to massage the results of the command output.

Lists and Tables

You've already seen how to display the output as a list (`Format-List`) or a table (`Format-Table`), and you've seen how to limit the properties displayed by using the `Format` cmdlet.

The next thing you may need to do is sort or group the output. Sorting is provided by the `Sort-Object` cmdlet, which can take a number of parameters. Here it is receiving the output of `Get-CsUser`:

```
Get-CsUser | Sort-Object
```

The output will be sorted in ascending alphabetical order, by the default sort property, and return the following:

```
Identity    : CN=Keith Lync,CN=Users,DC=gaots,DC=local
SipAddress  : sip:keith_lync@gaots.co.uk
DisplayName : Keith Lync

Identity    : CN=Keith OCS,CN=Users,DC=gaots,DC=local
SipAddress  : sip:keith_ocs@gaots.co.uk
DisplayName : Keith OCS

Identity    : CN=Nathan Lync,CN=Users,DC=gaots,DC=local
SipAddress  : sip:nathan_lync@gaots.co.uk
DisplayName : Nathan Lync

Identity    : CN=Nathan OCS,CN=Users,DC=gaots,DC=local
SipAddress  : sip:nathan_ocs@gaots.co.uk
DisplayName : Nathan OCS
```

LIMITING OUTPUT

Actually, we cheated a little in the sorted output and throughout this chapter. To ensure brevity, we appended:

```
| fl identity, sipaddress, displayname
```

at the end of the command to display only those fields—otherwise, this chapter would contain lots of not very useful content! In fact, the command we entered was this (remember that `fl` is a default alias created for the `Format-List` cmdlet):

```
Get-CsUser | Sort-Object | Fl Identity, SipAddress, DisplayName
```

To sort in ascending alphabetical order, by the named property (this would show the same output as the previous command), you would enter the following:

```
Get-CsUser | Sort-Object -Property <property name>
```

To sort in descending alphabetical order, by the named property:

```
Get-CsUser | Sort-Object -Property IdentityDescending=$True
```

This gives the following output:

```
Identity    : CN=Nathan OCS,CN=Users,DC=gaots,DC=local
SipAddress  : sip:nathan_ocs@gaots.co.uk
DisplayName : Nathan OCS

Identity    : CN=Nathan Lync,CN=Users,DC=gaots,DC=local
SipAddress  : sip:nathan_lync@gaots.co.uk
DisplayName : Nathan Lync

Identity    : CN=Keith OCS,CN=Users,DC=gaots,DC=local
SipAddress  : sip:keith_ocs@gaots.co.uk
DisplayName : Keith OCS

Identity    : CN=Keith Lync,CN=Users,DC=gaots,DC=local
SipAddress  : sip:keith_lync@gaots.co.uk
DisplayName : Keith Lync
```

`Sort-Object` also has the capability to return only the unique values in a list:

```
Get-CsUser | Sort-Object -Unique
```

You can sort by multiple fields (and in differing directions if required) with an extension to the `Sort-Object` cmdlet. This is typically used to provide a specific format to output. To sort first by `Enabled` in descending order and then by `DisplayName` in ascending order, the command would be as follows:

```
Get-CsUser | Sort-Object -Property @{Expression="Enabled";Descending=$True},@{Exp
ression="DisplayName";Descending=$False}
```

This command will display the full user object for each order, sorted with the `Enabled` users first and each of them sorted based on the `DisplayName`. The output isn't included because it would stretch to several pages!

This last example is a method of grouping. You can also use the `Group-Object` cmdlet to give a slightly different output.

```
Get-CsUser | Sort-Object -Property SipAddress| Group-Object -Property Enabled

Count Name   Group
----- ----   -----
    4 True   {CN=Keith Lync,CN=Users,DC=gaots,DC=local,
              CN=Keith OCS,CN=Users,DC=gaots,DC=local,
              CN=Nathan Lync,CN=Users,DC=gaots,DC=local,
              CN=Nathan OCS,CN=Users,DC=gaots,DC=local}
```

As you can see, the Sort-Object and Group-Object cmdlets provide extremely powerful output manipulation features in PowerShell.

Output to File

So far you've seen the command output on the screen in table or list formats. In many cases, it is useful to store data in files. PowerShell provides a number of cmdlets to let you do just that. In this section, we'll look at the Out-File, Export-Csv, and Export-CliXml cmdlets.

Out-File

Out-File captures the command output and stores it directly in a file:

```
Get-CsUser -Identity "keith lync" | Out-File c:\get-csuser.txt
```

Opening the file c:\get-csuser.txt shows this:

```
Identity                : CN=Keith Lync,CN=Users,DC=gaots,DC=local
VoicePolicy             :
ConferencingPolicy      :
PresencePolicy          :
DialPlan                :
LocationPolicy          :
ClientPolicy            :
ClientVersionPolicy     :
ArchivingPolicy         :
PinPolicy               :
ExternalAccessPolicy    : Allow No Access
HostedVoiceMail         :
HostedVoicemailPolicy   :
HostingProvider         : SRV:
RegistrarPool           : se01.gaots.local
Enabled                 : True
SipAddress              : sip:keith_lync@gaots.co.uk
LineURI                 :
EnterpriseVoiceEnabled  : False
HomeServer              : CN=Lc Services,CN=Microsoft,CN=1:1,CN=Pools,CN=RTC Servi
ce,CN=Services,CN=Configuration,DC=gaots,DC=local
DisplayName             : Keith Lync
SamAccountName          : keith_lync
```

Export-Csv

Export-Csv exports the data into CSV format:

```
Get-CsUser -Identity "keith lync" | Export-Csv c:\get-csuser.csv
```

Opening the file c:\get-csuser.csv shows:

```
#TYPE Microsoft.Rtc.Management.ADConnect.Schema.OCSADUser
```

```
"SamAccountName","UserPrincipalName","FirstName" <other fields cut for brevity>

"keith_lync","keith_lync@gaots.local","Keith"," <other fields cut for brevity>
```

EXPORT-CLIXML

`Export-CliXml` exports the data into XML format.

```
Get-CsUser -Identity "keith lync" | Export-CliXml c:\get-csuser.xml
```

Opening the file `c:\get-csuser.txt` shows this:

```
<Objs Version="1.1.0.1" xmlns="http://schemas.microsoft.com/powershell/2004/04">
  <Obj RefId="0">
    <TN RefId="0">
      <T>Microsoft.Rtc.Management.ADConnect.Schema.OCSADUser</T>
      <T>Microsoft.Rtc.Management.ADConnect.Schema.OCSADUserBase</T>
      <T>Microsoft.Rtc.Management.ADConnect.Schema.OCSEndPoint</T>
      <T>Microsoft.Rtc.Management.ADConnect.ADObject.ADObjectBase</T>
      <T>Microsoft.Rtc.Management.ADConnect.ADObject.ADRawEntry</T>
      <T>Microsoft.Rtc.Management.ADConnect.Core.ConfigurableObject</T>
      <T>System.Object</T>
    </TN>
    <ToString>CN=Keith Lync,CN=Users,DC=gaots,DC=local</ToString>
    <Props>
      <S N="SamAccountName">keith_lync</S>
      <S N="UserPrincipalName">keith_lync@gaots.local</S>
      <S N="FirstName">Keith</S>
      <S N="LastName">Lync</S>
      <S N="WindowsEmailAddress">keith_lync@gaots.co.uk</S>
<remainder cut for brevity>
```

Graphical Display and Filtering with *Out-GridView*

Keeping with the output types, `Out-GridView` is a new cmdlet introduced with PowerShell V2. With this cmdlet, the output appears (as shown in Figure 8.12) in a graphical display that provides its own filtering interaction. This reduces the need to use other cmdlets to sort and filter data, such as the `Where-Object` and `Sort-Object` cmdlets mentioned previously.

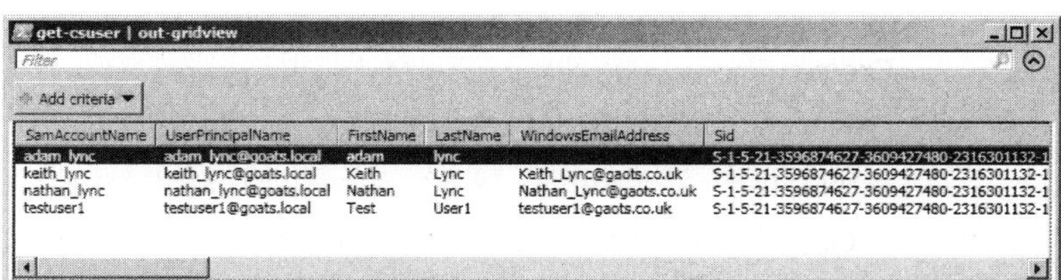

FIGURE 8.12
Out-GridView

Running Scripts

So far we've been looking at individual cmdlets or in some cases piping the output from one command to another. As you become more proficient with PowerShell, the commands will get more complex, and you won't want to keep working out complex commands every time you need to repeat the same task. This is where scripting comes in.

POWERSHELL SCRIPT FILES

PowerShell script files have the `.ps1` extension and must always be prefaced with the directory path. If you want to run a script in the local directory, preface it with `.\`, as shown here:

```
.\listusersscript.ps1
```

Running Scheduled Scripts

The advantages of scripting really come into play when you consider scheduling. If, for example, you want to move a user from one pool to another, use the command:

```
Move-CsUser -Identity "keith lync" -Target "lyncpool.gaots.local"
```

However, you probably don't want to risk interrupting users during the working day (of course, as an admin you don't want to work overnight). You can save the move command in a file with a `.ps1` extension (let's call it `move_user.ps1`) and leverage the Windows Task Scheduler to schedule the command to run after working hours.

You can find the Windows Task Scheduler by choosing Start ➢ Administrative Tools ➢ Task Scheduler; the Microsoft Management Console (MMC) shown in Figure 8.13 will appear.

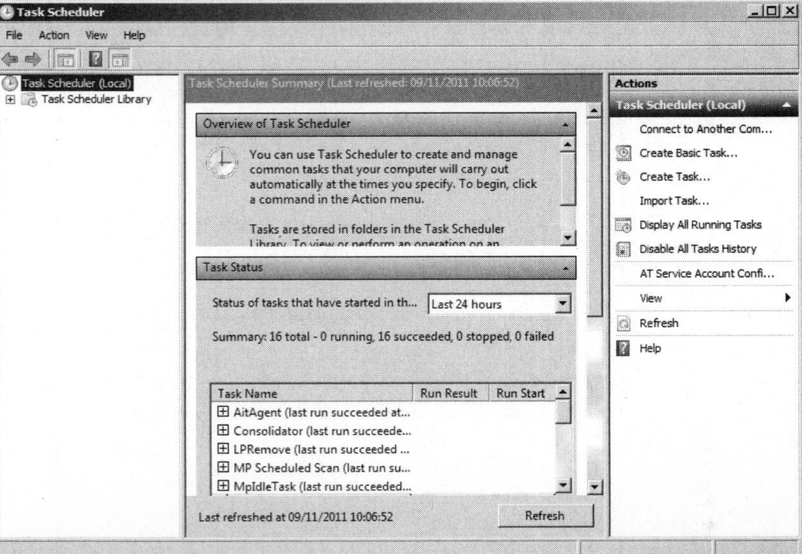

FIGURE 8.13
The Windows Task Scheduler

Click Create Task in the right Actions panel to open the Task Wizard (shown in Figure 8.14).

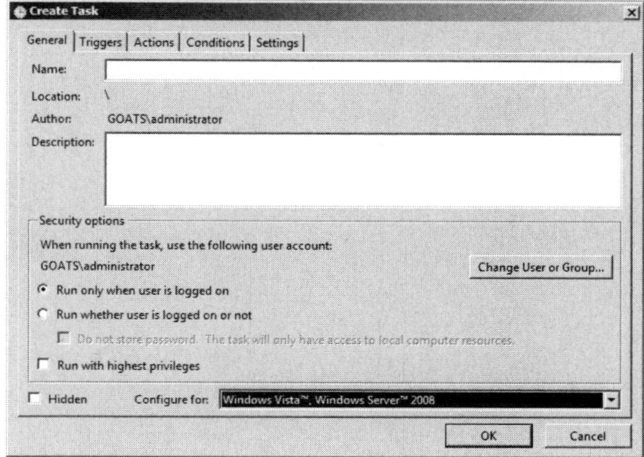

FIGURE 8.14
Create a new task

Using this wizard, you can define the task and the triggers that initiate it. You can also put conditions in place–for example, to ensure the task does not run too long. Each of the sections is explained here:

General Define the name of the task, along with the security controls associated with it, including which user account to use and whether the user must be logged on or not.

Triggers This is where you define how the task will be started; the options include On A Schedule, At Log On, At Startup, and so on. You can further modify this to include repetition options and expiry dates.

Actions This is where you define the actual task to be executed; the options include Start a Program, Send an Email, and Display a Message.

Conditions The Conditions section allows you to check to ensure the system is in a capable state; for example, you could decide to start the task only if the computer is running on AC power or only if a particular network connection is available.

Settings Miscellaneous settings that do not fit anywhere else, such as Allow Run on Demand, Restart If the Task Fails, and what to do if the task is already running.

The Task Scheduler does not allow PowerShell scripts to be run directly, so you must create a *batch* file (a list of executable commands for the command prompt, whose name ends with a *.bat* extension) and have the PowerShell script called from the batch file. You would create a new file and call it `move_user.bat`; this batch file would contain the following code.

```
PowerShell -command "& 'move_user.ps1'"
```

Now within the Task Scheduler, you call the task `Move User` and define the trigger to be scheduled for 8:00 PM, with the Action to be executed `Move_user.bat.` Figure 8.15 shows the results of creating the task (with the Action tab highlighted).

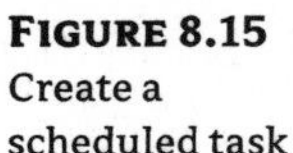

FIGURE 8.15
Create a scheduled task

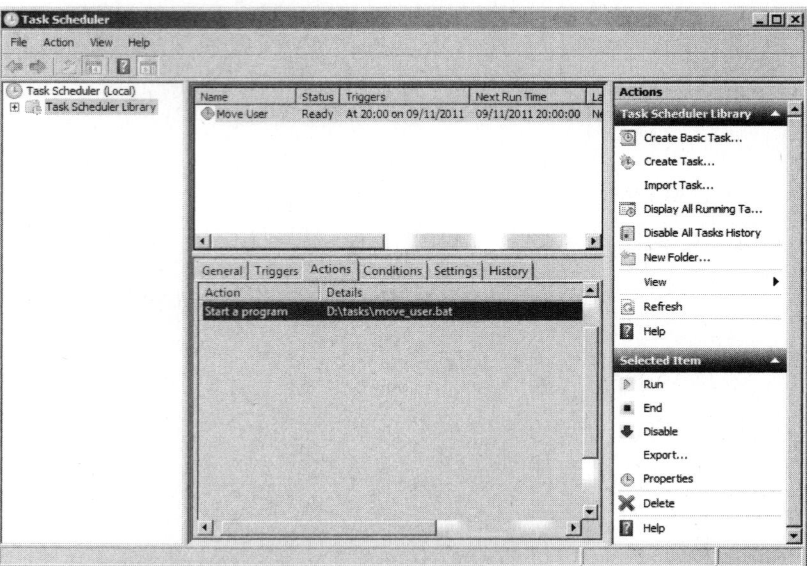

Now you can leave for the night and come back in the morning to view the report showing the user move information. Of course, scheduling a single user move is not a very useful scheduled script; more likely you would move multiple users in the following way, perhaps as shown to move all users to a new pool:

```
Get-CsUser | Move-CsUser -Target "lyncpool.gaots.local
```

CHANGING POLICY BASED ON TIME

A customer recently needed to limit the number of calls permitted on their network during the day; for the evenings, this limit was lifted. The Call Admission Control (see Chapter 14) functionality within Lync does not provide any time-based policy controls.

However, by using the PowerShell scripting functionality, combined with Windows scheduling, and having two scripts—one to enable the restrictions and one to remove them—we were able to meet this requirement quite easily.

The restriction script runs at 08:00 every day, and the unrestricted script runs at 18:00.

Learning from the GUI

Unlike Exchange 2007 and Exchange 2010, the Lync Server Control Panel does not provide a user-friendly view of the PowerShell script being executed. With Exchange this allows you to cut and paste from the Exchange Console into your own scripts, making script creation simpler.

However, that said, the naming system used on the Control Panel screens in most cases is easily understood and translated into the PowerShell cmdlet parameters. For example, Figure 8.16 shows a sample screen from the Control Panel, and Table 8.5 shows the corresponding parameters.

TABLE 8.5: PowerShell versus Control Panel Namin

CONTROL PANEL	POWERSHELL PARAMETER
Scope	No direct parameter—it is included in the Identity parameter
Name	`Identity`
Description	`Description`
Enable communications with federated users	`EnableFederationAccess`
Enable communications with remote users	`EnableOutsideAccess`
Enable communications with public users	`EnablePublicCloudAccess`
N/A	`EnablePublicCloudAudioVideoAccess`

The final entry in the PowerShell column highlights again the fact that the shell is more powerful than the GUI; more functionality is exposed using PowerShell than through the GUI (approximately 80 percent of the PowerShell capability is presented within the GUI). For example, in Figure 8.16 you are looking at the External User Access configuration and the `New-CsExternalAccessPolicy` (or in the case of changing an existing policy, `Set-CsExternalAccessPolicy`).

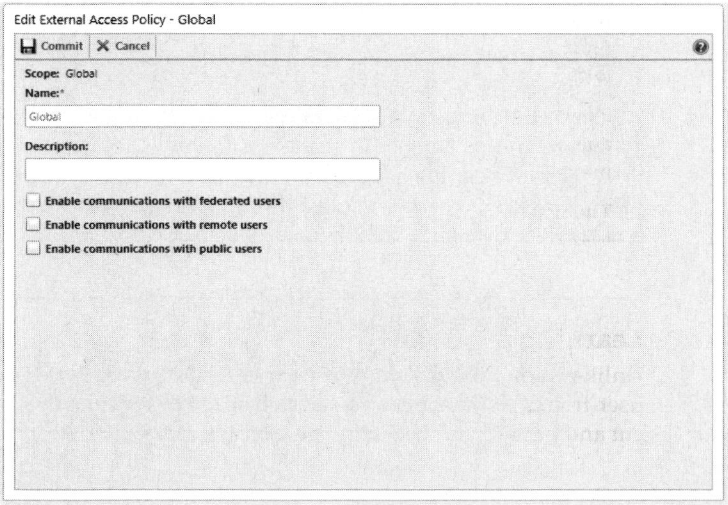

FIGURE 8.16
A sample Control Panel screen

To determine the cmdlet parameter names from within PowerShell, use the following command:

```
Get-Help New-CsExternalAccessPolicy
```

As described previously, the help information is returned for the particular cmdlet selected (in this case `New-CsExternalAccessPolicy`). You're only interested in the Syntax section, so the rest has been omitted for clarity.

```
SYNTAX
    New-CsExternalAccessPolicy -Identity <XdsIdentity> [-Confirm
[<SwitchParameter>]] [-Description <String>] [-EnableFederationAccess <$true |
$false>] [-EnableOutsideAccess <$true | $false>] [-EnablePublicCloudAccess <$true
| $false>] [-EnablePubl
    icCloudAudioVideoAccess <$true | $false>] [-Force <SwitchParameter>]
[-InMemory <SwitchParameter>] [-WhatIf [<SwitchParameter>]] [<CommonParameters>]
```

Here you can see the full list of parameters that can be provided, and if you want to see further detail about a specific parameter, you can use the following command:

```
Get-Help New-CsExternalAccessPolicy -Full
```

As previously shown, this has been shortened for clarity, to show only the information from a single parameter.

```
-EnablePublicCloudAccess <$true | $false>
Indicates whether the user is allowed to communicate with people how have SIP
accounts with a public Internet connectivity provider such as MSN. The feault
value is False.

Required?                    False
Position?                    Named
Default value
Accept pipeline input?       False
Accept wildcard characters?  false
```

So what have you learned here? From the GUI, you can see the option Enable Communications with Public Users, and from the cmdlet help you can see that the equivalent parameter is `EnablePublicCloudAccess`. This example was chosen to illustrate that although not all parameters are an exact match (without spaces), enough information should be provided in the GUI to infer a match with a parameter.

How can this help you? While Exchange administrators may be used to cutting and pasting their PowerShell into scripts from the GUI, Lync 2010 administrators can still learn from the GUI. However, creating a script from the actions taken is a manual process—but it is achievable with a little thought and effort!

The 80 Percent Rule

One of the aims of the Lync Server development team was to provide 80 percent functionality via the Control Panel interface. As a result, some functionality is available only by using PowerShell.

Example Script Development

In this section, you're going to look at some real-world examples of scripts and how to develop them from scratch, putting into practice some of what you learned in this chapter. The scripts shown here are available to download from this link:

```
www.sybex.com/go/masteringlyncserver
```

UPDATING USER INFORMATION

A reasonably common task is to update users' information details; this may be due to a change in name of the department, a building move, or similar occurrences.

In this example, you'll look at updating the Lync 2010 user phone information (we won't consider updating any Active Directory information in this script). This may happen when users move between buildings or when a telephone provider changes the area code (because they need a larger numbering scheme). So, the principle here is to change each user from area code 555 to area code 556.

This high-level approach is as follows:

1. Get a user.
2. Check the user's phone number.
3. If the number includes area code 555, change it to 556.
4. Get the next user.

Let's start with `Get-CsUser`. It allows you to retrieve user information (remember that `Get-CsUser` will return all the users, unless you supply a specific `-Identity` parameter). Because you want to check the user phone number details, you'll want to store the returned information in a variable (`$users`). The script so far looks like this:

```
$users = Get-CsUser
```

Next, you want to take each individual user in turn; to achieve this, you'll use the `ForEach` control-loop capability:

```
ForEach ($user in $users) {code}
```

Now, you want to look at the phone number field for a user; this is called `LineUri` and can be accessed by using `$user.LineUri` (the `$user` variable is used only within the `ForEach` loop and refers to the current user object).

Next, you want to check that this will include the area code in the number and ensure that you are dealing only with the users from a specific country (you don't want to change users with the same area code, but a different country). You need to define the area code as `+44555`. Indeed, the `LineUri` parameter contains `Tel:` at the beginning, so you'll be looking for an entry that begins with `Tel:+44555`. The script line looks like:

```
If ($user.LineUri.Startswith("Tel:+44555")) {code}
```

Once you have identified a user that needs to be updated, you'll need to generate the new number for that user, and you can use the `Replace` function in PowerShell to do that. You also need to store this new number in a variable (`$newnumber`):

```
$newnumber = $user.LineUri.Replace("Tel:+44555","Tel:+44556")
```

then update the user object with the new value, using this command:

```
Set-CsUser -Identity $user.SipAddress -LineUri $newnumber
```

Bringing this all together, the script will look like this:

```
$users = Get-CsUser
ForEach ($user in $users) {
        If ($user.LineUri.Startswith("Tel:+44555")) {
  $newnumber = $user.LineUri.Replace("Tel:+44555","Tel:+44556")
  Set-CsUser -Identity $user.SipAddress -LineUri $newnumber
        }
}
```

Indentation is normally used to make the script more readable—each indentation refers to a control loop or a condition check. The closing brackets line up with the starting command.

Of course, this script updates only the `LineUri` field. What about users who have private lines? Now that you've worked through this section, you can update the script for those users on your own for extra practice. (Look for the `PrivateLine` field.)

Installing Prerequisites

The first script you examined dealt with updating user information, something that probably happens rarely in batches. This script will look at something significantly more useful, especially if you regularly build a lot of Lync 2010 servers for demos or test labs.

Here, you're going to look at configuring the prerequisites for a Lync 2010 front-end server installation, either a Standard Edition or Enterprise Edition. It's worth noting that this procedure can also be used to install other server roles; however, the other roles will have fewer prerequisites, so they should be used only in a lab environment; you don't want to install unused services if you don't need them.

The server is assumed to have only Windows Server 2008 R2 installed and be part of the domain, which matches the SIP domain. The goal is to finish with a deployed and functional Lync 2010 front end.

In addition, there is no way to manage the topology using PowerShell, so the topology is assumed to be already configured and published, with the file share definitions available.

From Chapter 5, "Planning Your Deployment," you know you should make a list of server features you'll need to install Lync Server 2010. First, you need to import the `servermanager` module to modify the feature list.

```
Import-Module servermanager
```

Next, you need to install the required features using `Add-WindowsFeature`. The actual names of the features can be found by running `Get-WindowsFeature` if you want to learn more.

```
Add-WindowsFeature Web-Static-Content, Web-Default-Doc, Web-Http-Errors, Web-
Asp-Net, Web-Net-Ext, Web-ISAPI-Ext, Web-ISAPI-Filter, Web-Http-Logging,
Web-Log-Libraries, Web-Http-Tracing, Web-Windows-Auth, Web-Filtering, Web-
```

```
Stat-Compression, Web-Mgmt-Console, Web-Scripting-Tools, Web-Basic-Auth, Web-
Client-Auth -Restart
Add-WindowsFeature MSMQ-Server, MSMQ-Directory -Restart
Add-WindowsFeature Net-FrameWork
Add-windowsfeature RSAT-ADDS-Tools, RSAT-AD-AdminCenter
Add-windowsfeature IH-Ink-Support, Desktop-Experience
```

The final line adds support for media playing, which is necessary for any server running the A/V conference MCU (assuming the deployment will have it enabled). Unfortunately, this will typically need a reboot, and further installation will fail if a reboot is pending, so you need to check for a reboot.

In addition to listing all the available features, the `Get-WindowsFeature` cmdlet will also tell you if a reboot is pending, so you can use the following commands to query the state and issue the `Restart-Computer` cmdlet to reboot if there is a pending reboot.

```
$features = Get-WindowsFeature
if ($features.restarttneeded -eq "yes"){Restart-Computer}
```

Once the computer has rebooted, you can rerun the script, and it will execute to this stage with no ill effects. Even though you are starting to add features, if they are already added, nothing will happen, and the check for reboot this time will return `FALSE`, so it will not issue the reboot.

Next, you'll register the DNS records, but first you need to query and capture the domain name. In this example, you'll use a system call to get the domain information. If you establish that the server is not domain joined, you'll exit the script (using `exit`); however, do expect to be domain joined, so you'll store the domain name in the variable `$dn_name`.

```
$domain = [system.directoryservices.activedirectory.domain]::GetComputerDomain()
if ($domain -eq $null){
    $domain_joined = $false
    exit
}
else{
    $dn_name = ([ADSI]"").distinguishedname
}
```

Capture your own server name from the WMI object `Win32_ComputerSystem`, using the following query, with the hostname stored in the Name field of the variable.

```
$computer = Get-WmiObject -Class Win32_ComputerSystem
$hostname = $computer.name
$seserverfqdn = "$hostname.$dn_name"
```

As you can see from the hostname (`$computer.Name`) and the domain name queried earlier (`$dn_name`), you build the server FQDN (`$seserverfqdn`).

You can't manipulate a DNS record directly within PowerShell; you need to use the `DNSCMD.EXE` executable. Of course, you first need to find out your own IP address so that you can register it. To do that, query a WMI object, `Win32_NetworkAdapterConfiguration`. You're interested only in enabled network interfaces, assuming the first enabled interface is the one you want to use (remember, the first item in an array is numbered 0).

```
$ip = (get-wmiobject win32_NetworkAdapterConfiguration -filter
"IpEnabled='True'")
$seserveripaddress = $ip.IPAddress[0]
```

You're going to need the address of the DNS server and, fortunately, the same WMI object holds that data.

```
$dnsserver = $ip.dnsserversearchorder[0]
```

For the actual DNS entries, you want to create the SRV record along with the `meet`, `admin`, and `dialin` entries too.

```
Dnscmd $dnsserver /recordadd $dn_name _sipinternaltls._tcp srv 5 0 5061
$seserverfqdn
Dnscmd $dnsserver /recordadd $dn_name meet a $seserveripaddress
Dnscmd $dnsserver /recordadd $dn_name admin a $seserveripaddress
Dnscmd $dnsserver /recordadd $dn_name dialin a $seserveripaddress
```

Now that the script has installed the prerequisites and created the necessary DNS entries, you need to install the appropriate software from the Lync 2010 DVD. For this example, we'll assume you are using drive X: for the DVD. You need to install the following:

- Visual C++ Redistributable
- SQL Native Client
- SQL Backwards Compatibility Toolset
- Unified Communications Managed API (UCMA)
- Lync Core Components
- Lync Admin Tools

To install them, you can use the following commands. Each software package may take some time to complete, and as we rely upon the package being installed later we will want to pause while the installation is under way using the `Start-Sleep` cmdlet (ensuring the package has completed installation by the time we need it):

```
$lync_media_directory = "x:"
#Install Visual C++ Redistrubute
$lync_media_directory\setup\amd64\vcredist_x64.exe /q
start-sleep -s 120

#Install SQL Native Client
$lync_media_directory\setup\amd64\sqlncli.msi -quiet
start-sleep -s 60

#Install SQL backward compat tools
$lync_media_directory\setup\amd64\SQLServer2005_BC.msi -quiet
```

```
start-sleep -s 60

#install ucma
msiexec /qn /i $lync_media_directory\setup\amd64\Setup\ucmaruntime.msi
REBOOT=ReallySuppress /QN EXCLUDETRACING=1 BOOT=1
start-sleep -s 60

#Install Lync core components
msiexec /qn /i $lync_media_directory\setup\amd64\Setup\ocscore.msi
INSTALLDIR=`"C:\Program Files\Microsoft Lync Server 2010\`" ADDLOCAL=Feature_
OcsCore
start-sleep -s 60

#Install Lync admin tools
msiexec /qn /i $lync_media_directory\setup\amd64\Setup\admintools.msi
start-sleep -s 60
```

At this point, you've done all you can do without running the Lync 2010 PowerShell, so you need to import that module:

```
Import-Module -name 'C:\program files\common files\microsoft lync server 2010\
modules\lync'
```

These examples have assumed the topology was published; however, you can check this by using `Get-CsTopology`, and in this case you'll exit the script if it has not. This will allow the script to install all the prerequisites (including Topology Builder) for you and then wait until you define and publish the topology. This is useful if you're deploying only one server. Simply rerun the script after the topology is published and the script will continue:

```
$topology = Get-CsTopology
If ($topology -eq $null){exit}
```

Now you're getting to the actual deployment stages, the first part of which is to install the local SQL Express for the replica of the Central Management Store (CMS). Next, start the Lync Replica Service to allow the data to replicate from the CMS to the new server.

```
"C:\Program Files\Microsoft Lync Server 2010\Deployment\Bootstrapper.exe" /
BootstrapLocalMgmt /SourceDirectory:$lync_media_directory\setup\amd64\
start-sleep -s 120
Enable-CsReplica
Start-CsWindowsService Replica
```

You could wait for replication or use PowerShell to speed it up. Naturally, you'll want to speed it up! Exporting the configuration file from the CMS and importing it locally has the same effect as waiting, but it is quicker! Here, you're temporarily storing the data in the `$config` variable:

```
$config = Export-CsConfiguration -asbytes
Import-CsConfiguration -byteinput $config -LocalStore
```

Now you've reached the stage where the prerequisites (both server-side and Lync 2010 specific) are installed, the DNS entries are created, and the topology is replicated to the local CMS replica. All you need to do is run the installation routine, get certificates, and start the services.

The Lync 2010 installation routine checks the local topology to see which roles are defined for the current server, and it will install only what is needed. Because this process is part of the installation, the script does not need to determine which roles are required to be installed; you can simply run the installer.

```
"C:\Program Files\Microsoft Lync Server 2010\Deployment\Bootstrapper.exe" /
SourceDirectory:$lync_media_directory\setup\amd64\
```

At this point, a reboot may be required to complete the installation; however, you still need to get certificates, and this will succeed whether a reboot is pending or not.

Requesting a certificate is relatively easy using Lync PowerShell; however, the tricky part is to find the Certificate Authority (CA) details, which are held in Active Directory. You have to connect to Active Directory and search specifically for the `pKIEnrollmentService`, and from the response you need to determine the DNS name of the server. There may be multiple entries of this type; however, this script simply takes the final entry as the one to use.

```
$root = [ADSI]"LDAP://CN=Configuration,$dn_name"
$query = new-object system.directoryservices.directorysearcher($root)
$query.filter = "(&(objectClass=pKIEnrollmentService)(cn=*))"
$query.SearchSCope = "subtree"
$result = $query.findall()
```

If the results of the Active Directory search are empty, set the `$ca_found` variable to `$false` (you'll use this later) and if they're not empty, capture the CA name in the correct format (*`dnsname\cnname`*) and set the *`$ca_found`* variable to `$true`.

```
if ($result -eq $null){
$ca_found = $false
}
else{
        foreach ($ca in $result) {
        $o = $ca.getdirectoryentry()
        $dnsname = $o.dNSHostName
        $cn = $o.cn
        $ca_name = "$dnsname\$cn"
        $ca_found = $true
}
}
```

Now that you have the certificate details, you can request and assign the certificate and finish starting the services. If the `$ca_found` variable is set to `$true`, you will automatically request and assign the certificates using the CA; however, if it is `$false`, the process will be manual. Once the certificate is assigned, the services can be started:

```
If ($ca_found){
    $Certificate = Request-CsCertificate -New -Type Default,WebServicesInternal,W
ebServicesExternal -CA $Ca_Name -FriendlyName Default -AllSipDomain
```

```
    Set-CsCertificate -Thumbprint $Certificate.Thumbprint -Type Default,WebServic
esInternal,WebServicesExternal
    Enable-CsComputer
    Start-cswindowsService
}
```

In summary, this script has achieved the following:

- Installed the server prerequisites for Lync Server 2010 Front End
- Installed Lync Server 2010 prerequisites
- Created the DNS records
- Installed SQL Express for the RTCLocal instance
- Replicated the topology
- Installed Lync Server 2010 to the configuration specified in the topology
- Requested an application of a certificate
- Started the Lync Server 2010 Services

At this point, users can be enabled and clients will be able to connect.

The Bottom Line

Use the PowerShell command syntax. PowerShell is an easy-to-use command-line interface that provides more control over the manipulation and configuration of Lync (as well as other Microsoft and third-party products).

PowerShell cmdlets consist of a verb, indicating the process (`New`, `Enable`, `Set`, and so on) and a noun, indicating the object (`CsUser`, `CsPool`, `CsExternalAccessPolicy`, and so on).

Master It You need to enable a new user for Lync Server 2010. Which is the correct cmdlet to use?

- `Enable-CsUser`
- `Set-CsUser`
- `New-CsUser`

Employ tips and tricks to get more out of PowerShell. PowerShell has many built-in capabilities native to PowerShell itself; extensions such as Lync provide the specifics to manage an application environment.

One of its most powerful features is the ability to pipe output from one command to another. This ability lets you easily and quickly perform repetitive tasks.

Master It You want to enable all users for Enterprise Voice. How would you do this?

Get help using PowerShell. The ability to provide detailed help information on any cmdlet, as well as use case examples, without leaving the PowerShell environment is an invaluable timesaver.

Master It You need to manipulate some pool configuration items but you can't remember which cmdlet to use. How can you identify possible cmdlets to use?

Understand PowerShell remoting and scripting. PowerShell provides a wealth of scripting capability, allowing relatively easy automation of everyday tasks which previously could be very complex.

Remoting extends PowerShell even further. Now you don't need to install individual administration toolsets for every application on an administrator's workstation; simply connect remotely to a PowerShell session and you can use the cmdlets.

Master It You want to administer the Lync Server 2010 configuration from your local workstation without installing any local administration tools and without using Remote Desktop. How would you connect to a remote PowerShell?

Chapter 9

Role-Based Access Control

Implemented first in Exchange Server 2010 and now in Lync Server 2010, Role-Based Access Control (RBAC) changes the granularity and ease with which an administrator can be granted permissions required for their job and only their job, allowing specific delegation of functionality to groups of people.

In this chapter, you will learn to:

- Use PowerShell to list the standard RBAC groups
- Understand the permissions available to each role
- Undertake planning for RBAC roles
- Create custom RBAC roles and assign them to administrators
- Carry out general administration, including granting and removing RBAC roles
- Report on the use of RBAC roles

RBAC Overview

In medium to large organizations, the same person does not necessarily administer every system. RBAC was created to address the problems that can arise as a result. In addition, Microsoft and security professionals in general espouse the principle of *least privilege*, whereby each administrator is granted only the minimum permissions needed to carry out his or her job. Until RBAC was built into the product, companies were forced to work within the constraints of the rather lackluster delegation often provided by Microsoft server applications, or they had to look for a third-party delegation product. This led to the development of rather complex and costly products such as Active Roles, from Quest, which enabled more granular delegation based on the need to perform certain tasks, which grouped together formed roles. If you didn't have the time or budget for such products, you were left with native tools and the myriad possibilities of manually hacking Access Control Lists (ACLs) and below them, individual Access Control Entries (ACEs) in Active Directory (AD).

Administration of Microsoft server products has long been intertwined with permissions. Administrators need rights to modify, create, and delete objects. Until recently, this required granting complex levels of permissions on Active Directory and file system objects. OCS 2007 R2 RTCUniversalReadOnlyAdmins made a token gesture toward granting permissions based on job role. However, membership in the AD group aligned to the role didn't give all the permissions necessary to do the job, as other AD group memberships to allow basic account access were required.

Thankfully, in Wave 14 (the 2010 release of Microsoft products) Microsoft answered the call to build in this type of functionality. Starting with Exchange 2010 and now in Lync 2010, there is an implementation of Role Based Access Control (RBAC), which allows for granular delegation of tasks based on role, and targeting of objects where the administrator can carry out tasks without the need to manually set ACLs.

Roles and Scopes

The concept of RBAC is very simple. An administrator is granted the rights to run certain PowerShell cmdlets (a *role*) on a certain group of users or servers (a *scope*).

An RBAC role is built up by defining a set of cmdlets that can be run. Generally, these cmdlets are grouped together to form a set of cmdlets related to a job role. A scope defines the target objects where those cmdlets can be run. For example, a scope could be defined to servers (grouped within a site), a group of users (in an OU), or to the whole organization using a *global scope*.

Each role has a config and a user scope. This means that you can delegate a role both to a set of users and to a site where servers are contained, allowing you great granularity in the way delegation is carried out.

Each role membership is controlled by a linked AD group, which is specified at the creation of the role. The standard role AD groups are created in the Users container of the domain specified during AD forest preparation. As discussed in Chapter 6, "Installation," although this must be run from a machine in the root forest, the domain specified can be anywhere in the forest and doesn't have to be the root. Given that the membership of these groups governs the roles an administrator holds, if your company heavily locks down the root domain of the forest, you may decide to create these groups in a child domain. Figure 9.1 shows the key elements of role, AD group, and scope in diagram form for the standard role AD group CsAdministrator.

FIGURE 9.1
The key elements of RBAC: role, group, and scope

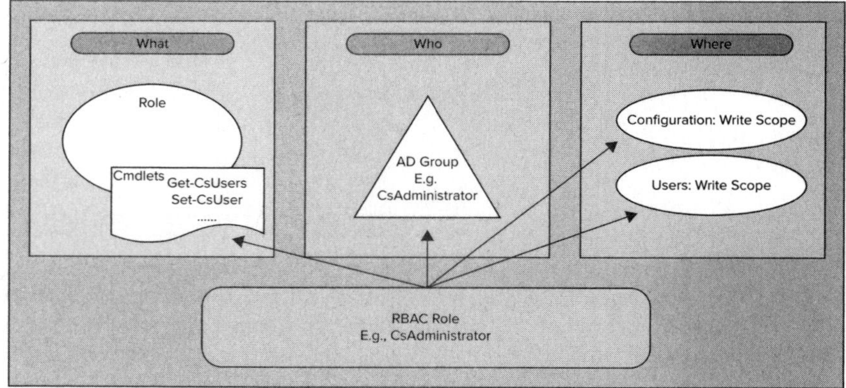

CU2 Updates Bring Cross-Domain Support

One nice improvement that was made in Lync Server 2010 Cumulative Updates 2 (CU2) is the ability to scope to a child domain. When Lync was first released, its inability to use scope caused problems; the common name (CN) of the organizational unit (OU) to be delegated under the control of a scope could only be in the root domain. Thankfully, this is now fixed, so it is possible to let different groups of administrators, from different child domains, control the users in the domains they administrate.

Lync Roles and PowerShell

Chapter 8 covered the PowerShell basics and showed how Lync utilizes its cmdlets. As you learned, all administration can be undertaken through PowerShell in Lync 2010. In fact, even when you are using the Lync Server Control Panel (LSCP), you are actually calling PowerShell commands in the background. This chapter relies primarily on PowerShell, as it provides the only way to manipulate Lync roles.

It is this reliance on PowerShell that enables RBAC to work. When you access PowerShell remotely—as described in Chapter 8—either through the LSCP or through remote PowerShell rather than directly on the Lync server via the Lync Server Management Shell (LSMS), Lync parses the commands to which you have access based on the roles you are assigned. In fact, when accessing Lync through remote PowerShell, when you run `Get-Command` you only see the commands you can run. This is also reflected in the GUI, as shown in Figure 9.2, which shows the LSCP accessed by a full administrator and an Archiving administrator logged on. The difference is clear to see, with far less functionality being made available to the archiving administrator.

FIGURE 9.2
The Control Panel accessed by an administrator holding the CsAdministrator role, with full administrative rights (top); the CsArchivingAdministrator role, with limited admin rights (bottom)

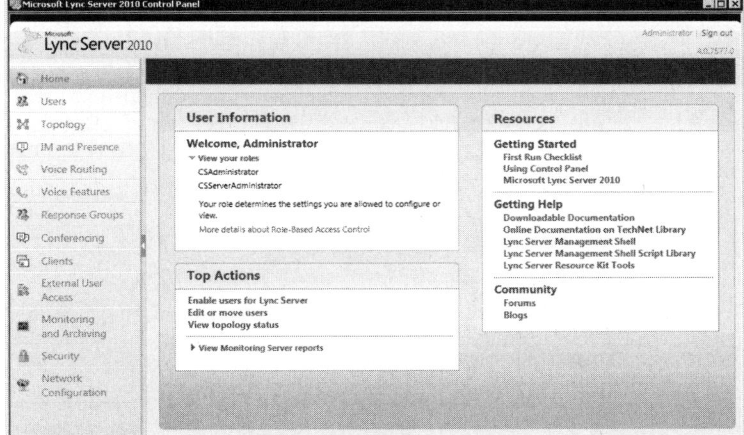

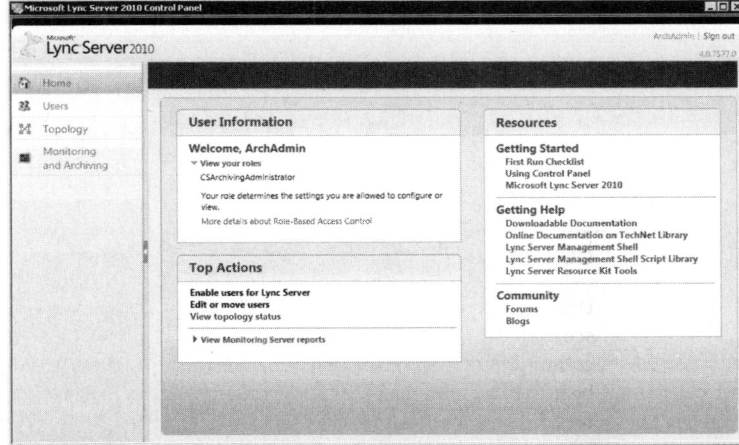

So how does this actually work? When an administrator connects to Lync, either through remote PowerShell or via LSCP, they are authenticated. At this point, the Lync Management Web Service will create a run-space for the user, which contains only the cmdlets the user has access to run as assigned by their role membership. When the administrator then runs a command, authorization is performed to confirm that indeed the administrator does have rights to run that cmdlet and that the cmdlet is targeted at a location (scope) where the administrator has been granted access. At this point, assuming all checks are passed, the CS Management Web Service executes the cmdlet.

Command Filtering in the Lync Server Control Panel

You can actually see this filtering of commands in action in the Lync Server Control Panel. On a slow system, when you log onto LSCP as an administrator with limited permissions, you can see the various elements of the graphical user interface (GUI) to which you don't have access disappear as the role is applied.

How does this work, given that the administrator doesn't need special permissions in AD? Each RBAC role has an associated Universal security group in Active Directory (AD). The groups for the standard roles are shown in Table 9.1.

Table 9.1: Details of the Standard RBAC Role Groups

Group Name	Group Type	Description
CsAdministrator	Security Group - Universal	Members of this group can perform all administrative tasks in Lync Server 2010.
CsArchivingAdministrator	Security Group - Universal	Members of this group can create, configure, and manage archiving-related settings and policies in Lync Server 2010.
CsHelpDesk	Security Group - Universal	Members of this group can view the deployment, including user properties and policies, and can execute specific troubleshooting tasks in Lync Server 2010.
CsLocationAdministrator	Security Group - Universal	Members of this group have the lowest level of rights for E911 management. They can create E911 locations and network identifiers, and associate them with each other in Lync Server 2010.
CsResponseGroupAdministrator	Security Group - Universal	Members of this group can manage the configuration of the Response Group service in Lync Server 2010.

Group Name	Group Type	Description
CsServerAdministrator	Security Group - Universal	Members of this group can manage, monitor, and troubleshoot Lync Server 2010 and services.
CsUserAdministrator	Security Group - Universal	Members of this group can enable and disable users for Lync Server 2010, move users, and assign existing policies to users.
CsViewOnlyAdministrator	Security Group - Universal	Members of this group can view the Lync Server 2010 deployment, including server information, in order to monitor deployment health.
CsVoiceAdministrator	Security Group - Universal	Members of this group can create, configure, and manage voice-related settings and policies in Lync Server 2010.

However, the role group in AD doesn't grant any special permission; it is just a placeholder provided so Lync can manage membership of the role. How are the cmdlets run? They are run under the local machine account of the server to which the administrator has the remote connection. This works because that local machine account is itself a member of various AD groups. These groups will be familiar to anyone who has installed any form of OCS—for example, the Real Time Communications (RTC) groups—and they are still the groups that govern what happens when you don't use remote PowerShell. If you access the console of the front-end server and run the Lync Server Management Shell, for example, you will not be authenticated and managed by RBAC.

RBAC Only Works Using Remote Connections

If you rely on RBAC to delegate administrative access, you must be careful to protect console access, either via RDP or physically at the server. RBAC only works remotely, so anyone who gains physical access will be governed by membership of the RTC groups, not RBAC roles. It is, therefore, also very important to monitor and manage access to the relevant AD group memberships.

When the admin logs on locally and uses LSMS on the console of the Lync server, administration rights are governed by membership of the RTC named groups, which are created by Lync forest prep. This system is almost identical to that which was in place with OCS 2007 R2. There is no simple provision for scoping of access.

So how are these groups and the RBAC role groups intertwined? The RBAC groups are not granted permissions on anything directly. As mentioned earlier, what actually happens when an RBAC user runs a command is that the CS Management Web Service first confirms that the user is entitled to run the cmdlet and then runs it under the local Lync Server machine account. These machine accounts get their rights to run cmdlets from membership in the various RTC groups shown in Table 9.2, such as RTCUniversalServerAdmins and RTCUniversalUserAdmins.

TABLE 9.2: RTC Groups in the Users Container in Active Directory Users and Computers (ADUC)

GROUP NAME	GROUP TYPE	DESCRIPTION
RTCUniveralUserReadOnlyGroup	Security Group - Universal	Members have read access to RTC-related user attributes or property sets.
RTCUniversalUserAdmins	Security Group - Universal	Members can manage RTC users in this forest.
RTCUniversalServerReadOnlyGroup	Security Group - Universal	Members have read access to RTC-related server AD objects in the forest.
RTCUniversalServerAdmins	Security Group - Universal	Members can manage all aspects of RTC server in this forest.
RTCUniversalSBATechnicians	Security Group - Universal	Members have read access to Lync Server 2010 configuration and are placed in the Local Administrators group of survivable branch office appliances during installation.
RTCUniversalReadOnlyAdmins	Security Group - Universal	Members can only read RTC-related server and user properties in this forest.
RTCUniversalGlobalWriteGroup	Security Group - Universal	Members have write access to RTC global settings.
RTCUniversalGlobalReadOnlyGroup	Security Group - Universal	Members have read access to RTC global settings.
RTCUniversalConfigReplicator	Security Group - Universal	Members can participate in configuration replication.
RTCSBAUniversalServices	Security Group - Universal	Members have read access to Lync Server 2010 configuration for survivable branch office installation.
RTCProxyUniversalServices	Security Group - Universal	Members can be used as RTC proxy service logon.
RTCHSUniversalServices	Security Group - Universal	Members can be used as RTC IM service logon.
RTCComponentUniversalServices	Security Group - Universal	Members can be used as RTC MCU and web component services logon.

The RTC groups are then assigned permissions through the setup process on objects in AD. Figure 9.3 shows the Security tab for a user account, which clearly shows the Access Control Entry (ACE) for the RTCUniversalUserAdmins group.

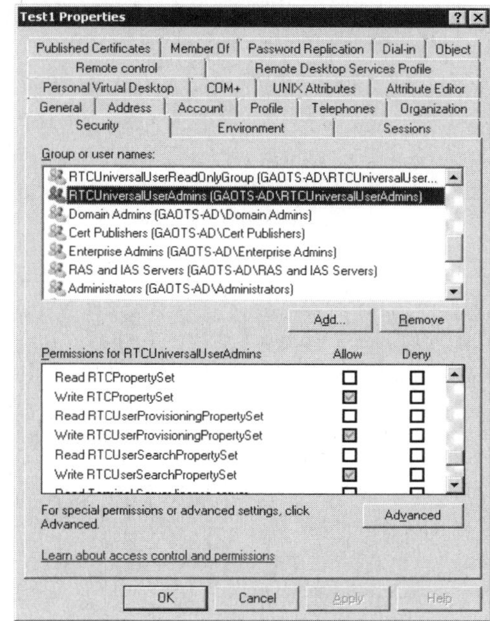

FIGURE 9.3: The Security tab of a standard user showing the ACE for RTCUniversalServerAdmins

Now that we've looked at the building blocks, let's move on and examine the roles available in Lync out of the box.

Understanding Lync's Standard Roles

Out of the box, Lync ships with nine roles, a range that gives you a fair amount of flexibility in grouping your administrators. You may find that you don't want to split things quite as they are out of the box, and this is one area where you might be disappointed. Of course, you can give administrators several roles, or perhaps utilize the ability to create custom roles, as described later in this chapter. However, what you can't do is carve up the cmdlets yourself to make custom roles; you can only make the administrator a member of several roles. The key thing about creating custom roles is that you can be specific about the scope of the role, whereas the standard roles are always locked to a global scope covering all objects. With that said, the provision of the standard roles has been well thought through, so let's dive into some PowerShell and see how to view the roles.

On the Lync Standard Edition server you installed in Chapter 6, make sure you are logged on locally either through RDP to the console or physically at the server console. Ensure that you are logged on as a member of the RTCUniversalServerAdmins group in AD. Open up the Lync

Server Management Shell (LSMS). The simplest command you can use to get Lync to output a list of the roles:

```
Get-CsAdminRole
```

This will bring back any roles, including those you might have created yourself.

You can then be a little more specific and bring back just a single role—for example, the CsAdministrator role as follows:

```
Get-CsAdminRole -Identity CsAdministrator
```

The output, as listed next, shows you the Role Identity, the Security Identifier (SID) of the group it is linked to in AD, that it is a standard role, the beginning of the list of cmdlets that are available to those holding the role, and the scopes of the role. At the bottom of the output you will see the template. For the default roles, this is empty; however, as you will see later, when you create custom roles, this is something that you will have to specify.

```
Identity       : CsAdministrator
SID            : S-1-5-21-4086828924-2878421486-2829562594-1196
IsStandardRole : True
Cmdlets        : {Name=Get-CsAddressBookConfiguration, Name=Set-CsAddressBookCo
                 nfiguration, Name=Remove-CsAddressBookConfiguration, Name=New-
                 CsAddressBookConfiguration...}
ConfigScopes   : {Global}
UserScopes     : {Global}
Template       :
```

To bring back a nicely formatted list of just the standard roles, you need to extend the first PowerShell cmdlets as follows:

```
Get-CsAdminRole | Where-Object {$_.IsStandardRole -eq $True} | fl Identity
```

This pipes the output of the plain `Get-CsAdminRole` cmdlet into `Where-Object`, which checks each role to see if the attribute `IsStandardRole` is set to `True`. It then pipes those role objects into the `Format-List` cmdlet and shows only the `Identity` attribute.

Having done this, you will have successfully listed all nine standard roles and will obtain the following output:

```
Identity : CsAdministrator
Identity : CsVoiceAdministrator
Identity : CsUserAdministrator
Identity : CsResponseGroupAdministrator
Identity : CsLocationAdministrator
Identity : CsArchivingAdministrator
Identity : CsViewOnlyAdministrator
Identity : CsServerAdministrator
Identity : CsHelpDesk
```

As mentioned, a Lync role is a group of cmdlets. As you can see, the list of cmdlets is begun but then tails off in an ellipsis. In order to see all of the cmdlets that make up each role, you need to jump back into PowerShell. For example, to see all the cmdlets assigned to the CsAdministrator role, you would use the following command:

```
Get-CsAdminRole -Identity CsAdministrator | Select-Object -ExpandProperty Cmdlets
| Out-File c:\csadminrolecmdlets.txt
```

This command first gets the CsAdministrator role, pipes its attributes to `Select-Object` and then expands the `Cmdlets` attribute. The results are then piped to the `Out-File` cmdlet, which will write them to a text file. Later in this chapter, you'll see a script created by a member of the Lync product group that lists all the cmdlets available to each role.

Now that you've seen how to list the standard roles, let's take a closer look at each one.

CsAdministrator

Of all the RBAC roles, this is the most powerful. It gives the assigned user the full range of Lync functionality, including the ability to carry out user, server, and device administration and to create and assign RBAC roles and other policies. This is the role to which the setup process asks you to add a user, who will become the first Lync administrator. Essentially, this role would be given only to the most senior administrators who require access to deploy and control all aspects of Lync.

One final thing to note about the CsAdministrator role is that although it gives the most functionality available in a role, it doesn't enable you to run all the commands that exist in the Lync PowerShell module.

PowerShell Modules

For more on the use of PowerShell modules and in particular the Lync module, see Chapter 8. To output all the commands in the module to a text file called AllLyncCmds.txt, you would run this version of `Get-Command`:

```
Get-Command -Module Lync -CommandType All | Out-File c:\AllLyncCmds.txt
```

If you compare the cmdlets available in the Lync module and those available to the CsAdministrator role, you will see that many are not included in the CsAdministrator role. These are generally system-altering cmdlets like those that allow the preparation of the domain, such as `Prep-Domain`. They, therefore, need greater permissions than granted through Lync groups alone—for example, Domain Administrator permissions. They are also required to be run locally on the Lync server through LSMS rather than through remote PowerShell.

Related Exchange Role

Given that Exchange 2010 also implements RBAC, it is useful to understand the similar roles available. If your administrators run both Exchange and Lync, then you will understand how to assign the standard RBAC groups in Lync to match those in Exchange.

A similar role in Exchange to Lync's CsAdministrator role would be the Organization Administrator role.

CsUserAdministrator

The CsUserAdministrator role enables the holder to manage users. Specifically, it can enable users for Lync, although it cannot create new AD users, and it can move users between Lync pools and disable Lync users. It also allows the holder to assign policies to users, but not to create policies. This role also allows the management of devices such as analog and common area phones. Interestingly, the role also allows the creation of the contacts used when integrating Lync with Exchange Unified Messaging (UM) for voicemail provision. For more information about UM, see Chapter 17, "Exchange, SharePoint, and Group Chat Integration."

It is likely that this role would be given to second-level support engineers who were specifically focused on end-user support rather than support of the server infrastructure, which might be left for third-level support and higher.

Related Exchange Role

A similar role in Exchange would be Mail Recipients.

CsServerAdministrator

The CsServerAdministrator role is the most far-ranging role outside of the CsAdministrator role. It allows control of a significant amount of Lync functionality.

In general, the main thing that this policy can't do is grant policy to end users. For that, you need the CsAdministrator role or the CsUserAdministrator role. It can't enable or disable users either. The other key thing it can't do is create new RBAC roles for which the CsAdministrator role is needed.

Other than that, this role does give the ability to manage and monitor the back-end aspects of Lync. It allows the management of services, testing of services, and ability to bring servers up and down through the draining process.

This role is likely to be granted to senior or third-level admins who are focused on maintaining and managing Lync on a day-to-day basis.

Related Exchange Role

A similar role in Exchange would be the Server Management role.

CsViewOnlyAdministrator

The CsViewOnlyAdministrator role grants the holder the ability to monitor the Lync implementation. It is made up almost entirely of `Get-` cmdlets that pull back information about a wide variety of Lync elements, such as policies, server configuration, voice configuration, call admission control, and users. The one exception is the `Debug-CsLisConfiguration` cmdlet, which allows you to pull back detailed configuration information about the Location Information Service.

This role is intended to give reporting powers and would perhaps be granted to architects or compliance officers to enable them to monitor the progress of deployment or see the settings of various policies.

Related Exchange Role

There is a very similar role in Exchange: View-Only Organization Management.

CsArchivingAdministrator

The CsArchivingAdministrator role in Lync gives the holder the ability to run a limited set of cmdlets pertaining only to managing the archive and archive policies in Lync. This is the only role other than CsAdministrator that is able to create, grant, and alter archiving policies.

This role is most likely to be delegated to a security/compliance officer who would be specifically tasked with managing archiving by creating and assigning policies to users.

Related Exchange Role

In Exchange, there is the Discovery role; however, it is more about performing searches than configuring journaling and retention policy. More similar roles would be Retention Management and Legal Hold.

CsHelpDesk

In some ways, the CsHelpDesk role is similar to the CsViewOnlyAdmin role in that it is made up of mostly `Get-` cmdlets giving visibility of configuration. However, the CsHelpDesk role also has many `Test-` cmdlets, which can be run to validate end-to-end functionality and thus troubleshoot user issues and also three PIN-related cmdlets (`Set-CsClientPin`, `Lock-CsClientPin`, and `Unlock-CsClientPin`), which allow control over user access. This role is likely to be given to first-line support to enable them to fix basic issues like resetting the user PIN and then to provide a useful report to the more senior engineers after running the relevant `Test-` cmdlets.

Related Exchange Role

There is a very similar role in Exchange: HelpDesk.

CsVoiceAdministrator

The CsVoiceAdministrator role is a wide-ranging one; it allows configuration and control over the PBX elements of Lync, including Phone devices, response groups, location setup, and call routing. In many organizations where unified communication systems haven't been deployed, the teams who manage the PBX and those who manage servers are different. This role allows that type of split to continue.

Related Exchange Role

There is no equivalent role in Exchange. These teams are often separate. The only possible consideration is whether these administrators might take control over aspects of Unified Messaging on Exchange. If there were still a "hard" division between those working on telephony and those on servers, UM would probably be handled by the Exchange team in collaboration with the Telephony team.

CsResponseGroupAdministrator

The CsResponseGroupAdministrator role is another role related to the telephony side of Lync. It gives holders the ability to manage response groups to manage call flow and agents who are members of each queue. This role might be given to a suitably trained contact-center administrator so he or she can change queues and implement working-hour automation as necessary without troubling the wider support team.

Related Exchange Role

As with the CsVoiceAdministrator role, there is no equivalent role in Exchange.

CsLocationAdministrator

The CsLocationAdministrator is another limited role, much like the archiving role. It allows the holder to manage location information and, as such, might be used by a facilities or networking administrator who would be tasked with managing and maintaining the mapping of locations to subnets, switches, and buildings.

Related Exchange Role

As with the CsVoiceAdministrator role, there is no equivalent role in Exchange.

Differences from Exchange 2010 RBAC

In Exchange 2010, RBAC is somewhat more advanced than in Lync 2010. For example, in Lync, roles are assigned to Administrators only. Exchange 2010 provides more granularity by allowing you to create custom roles that can run only the specific commands defined, whereas Lync restricts custom roles by allowing them to be only a copy of an existing role with a specific scope. In Exchange 2010, roles are granted not only to administrators but to users, which allows users to undertake basic admin tasks such as updating contact information and carrying out message tracking.

Creating New Roles

At this point, we have covered what Lync offers out of the box, and you have a lot to consider. It is critical to plan the use of RBAC carefully. Taking the easy road will end up with administrators having too many permissions, which as everyone knows, can lead to disaster. Therefore, at this stage you really need to think through how you want administration to work in your organization. The following sections will outline various options and then take you through the steps required to create new roles and perform RBAC management tasks.

Planning Combinations

Now that you've seen the standard roles, you can understand that there is a fair amount of flexibility in the way administrative power can be delegated. One thing to consider is that the structure of the administrative teams in many organizations won't necessarily fit the exact way the standard roles are laid out. It is, therefore, possible to use the standard roles as templates for custom roles that will give more flexibility in what each administrator can do.

Also bear in mind that each of the standard roles has a global scope, so one recommendation is to follow the process of applying least privilege and create custom roles based on the standard roles but with more suitably targeted scope. For example, if there were a group of administrators on a help desk who needed to administer only users in one OU, you would configure a new custom role with a user scope for that specific OU and use the CsUserAdministrator role as the template.

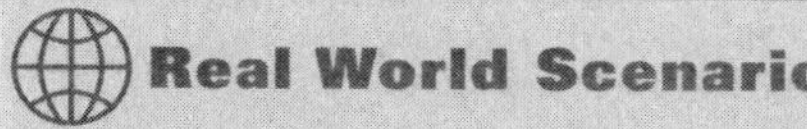

SPLIT ADMINISTRATORS FOR A SINGLE SITE: TRADERS AND RESEARCHERS

Throughout our consulting work, we have seen certain organizations where there were significant regulatory reasons to keep groups of users from communicating and, therefore, have separate IT teams to manage those groups. In these cases, users could be in the same site, but separation of admin rights was needed.

Lync RBAC can deal with these types of situations through the creation of custom roles. Instead of using the global scope, you can create two new roles, one for each set of administrators. Each group's config (site) scope will be the same, but you can apply different user scopes, specifically focused on the specific OU containing the users to be administered. This will enable the administrators to manage the servers in the site as needed, but not to access each other's users.

In addition to the role template and role scope, another consideration is the naming of custom roles, which has two elements. First, it is important to realize that the name of the RBAC group must match the SAMAccountName of the group created to hold the members of the role. Therefore, if you have an AD group-naming policy, you must consider how this will affect the name of the RBAC group. Second, to follow best practices, the name of the RBAC role should enable an administrator to easily understand what the role does, identifying, for example, the role template and scope. You could, for example, call your group `CsAdministrator-EMEA`.

A final consideration is how you might group roles together. To help you decide how you might group roles together, one of the Lync Program Managers, Cezar Ungureanasu, put together the following script. It will run through all the standard roles in Lync and output which cmdlets they contain to a tab-separated values file. This file can be opened in Excel, where it provides an easy reference and comparison method to see which cmdlets are in each role and how they overlap. You can download the script from `www.sybex.com/go/masteringlyncserver`

```
$roles = Get-CsAdminRole  | where-object { $_.IsStandardRole -eq $true} | Sort
Identity
$d = "Cmdlet"
foreach($role in $roles)
    {
        $d = $d + "`t" + $role.Identity
    }
Out-File -FilePath "C:\cmdlettorole.tsv" -InputObject $d
$x = Get-Command -module Lync -commandType cmdlet | Sort Name
foreach($i in $x)
    {
        $a = $i.Name
        $c = $a +"`t"
        foreach($role in $roles)
            {
                if ($role.cmdlets -match $i.Name)
                    {
```

```
                        $c = $c + "yes" + "`t"
                    }
                else
                    {
                        $c = $c + "no" + "`t"
                    }
            }
        Out-File -FilePath C:\cmdlettorole.tsv -InputObject $c -Append
    }
```

In order to run the script, you should enter it into your favorite text editor (Notepad will do) and save it as a PowerShell `.ps1` file. You would then run it from your Lync Front End server. For more details about saving and running PowerShell scripts, see Chapter 8. The output file can be opened in Excel, and an extract from it is shown in Table 9.3. Of course, for space reasons, we have cut this down because it is a large sheet encompassing all the roles and cmdlets available. You can find the entire spreadsheet at `www.sybex.com/go/masteringlyncserver`

TABLE 9.3: An Extract from the Roles Analysis Spreadsheet

CMDLET	CSADMINISTRATOR	CSARCHIVINGADMINISTRATOR	CSHELPDESK
`Approve-CsDeviceUpdateRule`	yes	no	no
`Clear-CsDeviceUpdateFile`	yes	no	no
`Clear-CsDeviceUpdateLog`	yes	no	no
`Debug-CsLisConfiguration`	yes	no	yes
`Disable-CsAdDomain`	no	no	no
`Disable-CsAdForest`	no	no	no
`Disable-CsComputer`	no	no	No

By looking at the spreadsheet in Excel, you can clearly see that certain roles overlap in functionality, which may mean that if you have a fairly small administrative team where there aren't so many tightly focused roles, you can use the more broadly scoped roles. For example, the CsResponseGroupAdministrator is entirely a subset of the CsServerAdministrator, the CsVoiceAdministrator, and, of course, the CsAdministrator. Therefore, this might be one role that you can do without if you have a relatively small administrative team and don't need one person to manage only response groups.

In addition, the CsLocationAdministrator role is a subset of the CsVoiceAdministrator role; so again, where there is not one person or group of people specifically responsible for management of network locations (for example, network engineers), then granting the CsVoiceAdministrator role would cover all functionality.

On a different note, and as mentioned previously, the CsAdministrator and CsArchivingAdministrator are the only roles that can create and grant archiving policy.

Finally, and rather more obviously, the CsViewOnlyAdministrator is a subset of the CsAdministrator role.

This type of analysis, in conjunction with your understanding of how administration works in your organization, should help you decide how you will use RBAC roles in your Lync deployment.

 **Real World Scenario**

DIFFERENT ORGANIZATION TYPES

Through our consulting experience, we have found that organizations come in all shapes and sizes. In general, administration is organized in one of two ways.

Some organizations centralize their administrative efforts. This may be representative of a company in a single site, or simply that they have a central team to deal with all users or systems for a particular application. In such cases, a single group controls the entire Lync organization, and there are likely to be tiers of administrators, starting with first-line help desk personnel who take basic queries and attempt immediate fixes, such as resetting passwords or PINs. More difficult problems are passed up to second-line support, who may visit users at their desks, and this is followed by third- and fourth-level support, who mainly deal with the back-end servers and architecture as a whole. Given this type of organization, a global scope would be assigned to the roles, so the default roles could be used.

The second type of organization is a highly distributed environment. In this case, the company might have grown from various acquisitions or be a global company where different regions operate as somewhat separate entities; however, they have chosen to merge their IT systems. These companies often have multiple child domains underneath an empty root forest. To work in this environment, Lync roles would be targeted at specific sites and specific end-user OUs. There would likely still be the same type of tiered support, but it would be regional.

Finally, another issue we have seen occurs when an organization is simply not structured to manage a unified communications system. Lync is an application that brings together two different worlds: that of Windows servers and that of telephony. In many cases, these are managed by totally separate groups of people, each of whom want to keep control and fear change. In these cases, Lync has the ability to delegate the telephony administration to the telephony group without requiring the telephony administrators to have full domain-admin rights or other extensive infrastructure permissions.

Creating the Role

Once you have completed planning and understand what custom roles, if any, you will need in your organization, you are ready to create your custom roles. You need to collect various pieces of data to create a role. First, you need a name for the role. As mentioned previously, it is worth sticking to a naming convention that helps identify the role. Having decided on the name, you must create a new Universal security group with the same name as the new role. For example, if your new RBAC role is to be called "EMEA-CsAdmin", you can create the group using the following command:

```
New-AdGroup -Name "EMEA CsAdministrator" -GroupScope Universal -SamAccountName
emea-csadmin -GroupCategory Security
```

Notice how this command creates a Universal security group with a display name containing spaces, but the SamAccountName, which is what must match the RBAC role name, is without spaces and is shorter than 20 characters.

With this command, the group will be created in the Users container in the domain to which you are connected. Unlike the standard roles, whose related groups are always in the Users container of whichever domain was specified during forest preparation, the groups created for custom roles can be placed in any OU in any domain in the forest. To do this, specify the common name (CN) of the parent container as follows:

```
New-AdGroup -Name "EMEA CsAdministrator" -GroupScope Universal -SamAccountName
emea-csadmin -GroupCategory Security -Path "ou=EMEA,ou=GroupsOU,dc=gaots,dc=local"
```

That command will create the same group as before, but this time in the GroupOU under the EMEA OU.

Once you have created the relevant group in AD, you can create the new custom RBAC role using this command:

```
New-CsAdminRole –Template CsAdministrator –Identity emea-csadmin
```

This will create a role with all the power of the CsAdministrator role and with a global scope and output as follows:

```
Identity       : emea-csadmin
SID            : S-1-5-21-170417243-3997822658-2177595193-1163
IsStandardRole : False
Cmdlets        : {Name=Get-CsAddressBookConfiguration, Name=Set-
CsAddressBookConfiguration, Name=Remove-CsAddressBookConfiguration, Name=New-
CsAddressBookConfiguration...}
ConfigScopes   : {Global}
UserScopes     : {Global}
Template       : CsAdministrator
```

Of course, the reason for creating custom roles is to be specific about where you want them to apply—in other words, to set the scope. To do this, you need to add one or two more parameters to the command used to create the group. For example, if you want to create a role with a specific site scope so as to control objects only in an EMEA site, run the command as follows:

```
New-CsAdminRole –Template CsAdministrator –Identity emea-csadmin –ConfigScopes
Site:1
```

This will create the same role as before, but this time those granted the role will only be able to carry out administration in the EMEA (SiteID:1) site. Note that the Site is referred to by its numerical site ID, which you can get by running the command Get-CsSite. This will give you output similar to the following for each site you have:

```
Identity        : Site:EMEA
SiteId          : 1
Services        : {UserServer:lync-se01.gaots.local, Registrar:lync-se01.gaots
                  .local, UserDatabase:lync-se01.gaots.local, FileStore:lync-se0
                  1.gaots.local...}
Pools           : {lync-se01.gaots.local}
FederationRoute :
Description     :
DisplayName     : EMEA
SiteType        : CentralSite
ParentSite      :
```

Once you have created the new role, the output is different in the ConfigScopes area, as you can see next:

```
Identity       : emea-csadmin
SID            : S-1-5-21-170417243-3997822658-2177595193-1163
IsStandardRole : False
Cmdlets        : {Name=Get-CsAddressBookConfiguration, Name=Set-
CsAddressBookConfiguration, Name=Remove-CsAddressBookConfiguration, Name=New-
CsAddressBookConfiguration...}
ConfigScopes   : {Site:1}
UserScopes     : {Global}
Template       : CsAdministrator
```

Assuming that you are using a template group that had user-related commands (perhaps CsAdministrator or CsUserAdministrator), you could instead lock down the new role to a specific OU that contains users that would allow those allocated the role to manage only those users in the OU specified. In that case, you would run the following command:

```
New-CsAdminRole -Template CsAdministrator -Identity emea-csadmin -UserScopes "OU:
ou=TestUsersOU,dc=gaots,dc=local"
```

This command would create the same new role, but administration would only be possible on users in TestUsersOU. Note that when specifying the OU, you must preface the distinguished name with the `OU:` keyword.

Again, this produces different output, this time in the UserScopes area:

```
Identity       : emea-csadmin
SID            : S-1-5-21-170417243-3997822658-2177595193-1163
IsStandardRole : False
Cmdlets        : {Name=Get-CsAddressBookConfiguration, Name=Set-
CsAddressBookConfiguration, Name=Remove-CsAddressBookConfiguration, Name=New-
CsAddressBookConfiguration...}
ConfigScopes   : {Global}
UserScopes     : {OU:ou=TestUsersOU,dc=gaots,dc=local}
Template       : CsAdministrator
```

Finally, if you want to scope to multiple sites or user OUs so as to enable one group of administrators to have permissions over a range of objects but not the entire deployment, run a command like the following one:

```
New-CsAdminRole -Template CsAdministrator -Identity emea-csadmin -UserScopes "OU
:ou=TestUsersOU,dc=gaots,dc=local"," OU:ou=AnotherTestUsersOU,dc=gaots,dc=local"
-ConfigScopes "Site:1","Site:2"
```

This more complex-looking command will create the same old role, but this time scoped for user administration on users in the TestUsersOU and AnotherTestUsersOU and for Site 1 and Site 2.

BE CAREFUL WITH SCOPES

One thing that is worth highlighting is that the default scope for a new role is global. Therefore, if you create a new role and scope it for a site using the ConfigScopes parameter but do not specify a user scope for that role, the administrative permissions will apply to all users. Don't expect the users to be scoped to the site just because you apply a config scope!

Now that you have seen how to create new custom RBAC roles, let's move on to learn how to carry out basic day-to-day administration on either the standard or custom RBAC roles.

Manipulating Roles

Now that we've discussed how RBAC works in Lync and how to create custom roles, let's finish this chapter by reviewing the key ways of manipulating roles: assigning users to and removing them from roles, deleting roles, filtering specific roles, and reporting on them.

Assigning and Removing Roles

You assign a role by adding the user who needs to carry out the role's tasks to the relevant AD group. This is a Universal security group, and for the standard roles is named equally to the role and is found in the Users container of whichever domain was specified during forest prep. Table 9.1 shows the groups for the standard RBAC roles.

Because granting a role is as simple as placing the new member's user account in the relevant group, it is important to consider the security of Active Directory, as well as that of other systems, such as Lync itself; otherwise, the roles could easily be overridden.

Helpfully, the users who are assigned roles do not necessarily need to be Lync-enabled. This is good, because it means that the separate administrative accounts, which should be used to follow the principle of separation of powers, do not need to be Lync-enabled and, therefore, will not show up in address books and the like.

In the same way that assigning roles is done through membership of an AD group, the removal of a role is as simple as removing the member from the relevant administrative group.

Deleting Roles

You may find that over time sites get decommissioned or OUs are removed, and this means that RBAC roles that were scoped to those areas are no longer needed. In order to remove the role, use the following command:

```
Remove-CsAdminRole -Identity nameofroletoremove
```

This command will prompt you to verify that you really want to remove the RBAC role; if you enter **Y**, it will remove the role with the name *nameofroletoremove*.

> **DOES REMOVING A ROLE REMOVE THE AD GROUP?**
>
> No! So what can you do? You could remove the group manually, but perhaps you want a command-line method.
>
> If you have the Active Directory module loaded as shown in the CsAdministrator section earlier, you can do something like the following:
>
> ```
> $Name = nameofroletoremove
> Remove-CsAdminRole -Identity $name; Remove-ADGroup $name
> ```
>
> This first sets a variable, denoted by the $ sign, with the name of the role to remove. It then runs two PowerShell commands on one line, through the use of the semicolon delimiter (;), and thereby first removes the RBAC role as shown previously and then uses the Active Directory module cmdlet Remove-ADGroup to remove the AD group.

Filtering Specific Roles

You've already seen a few examples of how to view the roles; once you have built up a significant group of roles with a suitable naming convention, you might want to pull back all the roles for, say, a certain site. As is often the case in PowerShell, there are a few ways in which you can achieve this. One is to use the `-Filter` parameter:

```
Get-CsAdminRole -Filter "*EMEA*"
```

This will bring back all the roles with *EMEA* in the identity as shown here:

```
Identity       : emea-csadmin
SID            : S-1-5-21-170417243-3997822658-2177595193-1164
IsStandardRole : False
Cmdlets        : {Name=Get-CsAddressBookConfiguration, Name=Set-CsAddressBookCo
                 nfiguration, Name=Remove-CsAddressBookConfiguration, Name=New-
                 CsAddressBookConfiguration...}
ConfigScopes   : {Site:1}
UserScopes     : {OU:ou=umcontacts,dc=gaots,dc=local}
Template       : CsAdministrator
```

Note the use of the wildcard (*) within the quotes to allow the return of any roles that contain the word EMEA.

Reporting on Roles

During the day-to-day management of a Lync system, it is very likely that the following questions will arise:

- What roles does a specific user have?
- Which users have a specific role?
- Which roles have access to certain users?
- Which roles have access to certain sites?

Thanks to PowerShell, it is relatively easy to find the answers.

What Roles Does a Specific User Have?

This can be answered with the following command:

```
Get-CsAdminRoleAssignment -Identity "Useralias"
```

This command will return a list of all the roles for the user "Useralias."

Which Users Have a Specific Role?

To answer this question, in the PowerShell console you must first import the Active Directory module:

```
Import-Module ActiveDirectory
```

This command will import all the cmdlets related to AD management, such as group creation, deletion, and manipulation.

Once the AD module has loaded, you can use the following command to list the members of the group linked to a specific role, in this case the CsAdministrator:

```
Get-ADGroupMember -Identity CsAdministrator | Select name
```

This command brings back all the members of the group "CsAdministrator," as shown here:

```
name
----
Administrator
```

To list members of all the roles, try this:

```
Get-CsAdminRole | ForEach-Object {$_.Identity; (Get-ADGroupMember -Identity
$_.Identity) | fl name}
```

This final command gets all the admin roles and then iterates through them by identity. Within the iteration, another command is run within the parentheses to get the AD group membership of each of the corresponding roles in the AD group. Finally, the output is passed to the Format-List format cmdlet, and the name of each member is printed as shown here:

```
CsAdministrator
name : Administrator

CsVoiceAdministrator

CsUserAdministrator
```

```
name : RTCUniversalUserAdmins

CsResponseGroupAdministrator
CsLocationAdministrator
CsArchivingAdministrator
CsViewOnlyAdministrator

CsServerAdministrator
name : RTCUniversalServerAdmins

CsHelpDesk

emea-csadmin
name : Test User1
```

Which Roles Have Access to Certain Users?

To list which roles can access a certain OU, run the following command:

```
Get-CsAdminRole | Where-Object {$_.UserScopes -match "OU:ou=TestUsersOU,dc=Gaots,
dc=local"}
```

This command first gets all the admin roles and then lists each role that has a user scope of the OU common name (CN) entered.

Which Roles Have Access to Certain Sites?

In a similar way, you can also find roles that have access to certain servers, based on the site, as follows:

```
Get-CsAdminRole | Where-Object {$_.ConfigScopes -match "site:1"}
```

This command first gets all the admin roles and then lists where any of the roles has a config scope of the site entered.

> **Limitations of RBAC**
>
> Now that we've reviewed RBAC, it's only fair to point out a few of its limitations. First is granularity; although it is possible to create custom roles, you can't go nearly as deep in that customization as you can with Exchange. There is no way to be specific about exactly which cmdlets a role contains. Secondly, RBAC does nothing to prevent access on the local machine. It is fundamentally something that protects remote PowerShell connections. Therefore, if an administrator gets access to the local server console, they can run any cmdlets that their AD group membership allows. Finally, although it's not a massive problem, Lync requires the Universal security groups used by RBAC roles to be in the Users container in the root forest. For those with very strict requirements about what can and can't go in the root domain, this could be an issue.

The Bottom Line

Use PowerShell to list the standard RBAC groups. RBAC in Lync 2010 is administered through the Lync Server Management Shell (LSMS). There are nine standard roles that ship with Lync; they provide an organization the ability to delegate administration with a reasonable degree of granularity.

> **Master It** You are in the middle of planning your enterprise Lync deployment and have been asked by the senior architect to research the available options for administrative delegation. You have been asked to provide a list of standard RBAC roles.

Understand the permissions available to each role. There are nine RBAC roles in Lync. These roles range from granting high-level administrative access using the CsAdministrator role to read-only access with the CsViewOnlyAdministrator. To use them properly, you need to know what each role does and understand any overlaps where different roles provide the same capability.

> **Master It** As part of an investigation into how to make the best use of RBAC, you have been asked to identify a list of cmdlets each role grants access to so that it can be analyzed to see which RBAC role best fits the way your administrative teams work.

Undertake planning for RBAC roles. Your implementation of RBAC roles should relate to the way your organization is set up for administration. Some organizations are centralized and others are distributed. You must understand your organizational structures and take them into account when planning RBAC roles. It is also important to follow the principle of least privilege, granting only the rights necessary for an administrator to do the job. This may mean utilizing custom roles and targeted scopes either at user OUs or Lync sites.

> **Master It** You are in the middle of planning your enterprise Lync deployment and have been asked by the senior architect to plan the RBAC deployment in your organization. What should you consider?

Create custom RBAC roles and assign them to administrators Lync allows the creation of custom RBAC roles. These are not as flexible as in Exchange, because you cannot grant access to specified single cmdlets. When creating a custom RBAC role, you must specify a template role from one of the nine standard roles and then set an appropriate scope.

> **Master It** Having carried out a planning exercise, you have decided that the standard Lync roles are not adequate for your organization. Because you have a separate site supported by a separate team of junior admins who only need to manage users in one site, you need to be more specific about the areas that certain administrators can manage. How would you create an RBAC role to ensure that the junior admins don't have too many permissions?

Carry out general administration including granting and removing RBAC roles. There are few cmdlets that allow management of RBAC roles in Lync 2010 and most use the `CsAdminRole` verb. All PowerShell roles are assigned through the membership of a linked Active Directory Universal security group.

Master It A colleague who administered Lync has moved to a new role, and his replacement starts on Monday. You have been asked to ensure that the new staff member has the appropriate rights to do his job.

Report on the use of RBAC roles. Given that the purpose of RBAC is to provide people with administrative access to a system, there will always be a need to review and provide reports to management on who has what access. Reporting on RBAC takes various forms but can all be done through LMS.

Master It You have been asked to provide details on which roles have access to the APAC site and list the membership of those roles. How would you proceed?

Chapter 10

User Administration

"The job would be easy if it weren't for the users!" Or so the saying goes. This chapter is all about how Lync handles users. There are simple elements, such as the ability to use Lync Server Control Panel (LSCP) and Lync Server Management Shell (LSMS, commonly known as PowerShell) to find, enable, disable, and generally manipulate users both individually and collectively. Then there are more complex elements, such as understanding how to set the wide variety of policies available in Lync. This aspect has changed dramatically since OCS 2007 R2. The vast majority of policy is now set using in-band provisioning rather than the mix of Group Policy Objects (GPOs), in-band provisioning, and Registry settings required in OCS 2007 R2. This means you now have a single place to configure and assign policy, making things far simpler to manage. In addition to the changes in of the way you apply policy, many more settings are available to give organizations plenty of control over exactly what users can and can't do with Lync.

In this chapter, you will learn to:

- Search for users in the LSCP and PowerShell
- Carry out basic user administration in the LSCP and PowerShell
- Understand Lync policies
- Manipulate Lync policies
- Choose the right policy for the job

User Configuration Basics

The starting point for user configuration in Lync is the Lync Server Control Panel (LSCP). As detailed in Chapter 9, "Role-Based Access Control," to carry out the full range of user administration, you must be logged in with an account that has been delegated the CsAdministrator or CsUserAdministrator RBAC roles through membership of the CsAdministrator or CsUserAdministrator groups.

LYNC USER ADMIN

To make the screenshots of the LSCP in this chapter cleaner, we decided to create a Lync User Administrator (LyncUserAdmin) account the same way we created the Lync Admin account in Chapter 6, "Installation." However, this time, instead of granting the Lync Administrator role (CsAdministrator), we added the user to the CsUserAdministrator group to make him a Lync User Administrator. This is the account we will be using throughout the chapter.

LSCP can be accessed in various ways. You can do so directly on the Lync server using the LSCP icon by clicking Start and choosing All Programs ➢ Administrative Tools ➢ Microsoft Lync Server 2010 ➢ Lync Server 2010 Control Panel.

You can also install the administrative tools on another machine; this approach gets you not only the icon from which to launch the LSCP but also the Topology Builder and PowerShell. If you are planning to install on an administrative workstation, refer to Chapter 5, "Planning Your Deployment," where this was covered in detail. Essentially, the workstation must meet the following prerequisites:

- OS as supported by Lync Server with the addition or Windows Vista SP2 x64 or Windows 7 x64.
- Browser with Silverlight Plug-in version 4.0.50524.0 or later
- .NET Framework 3.5 SP1
- PowerShell v2.0

IE Support

Interestingly, at the time of writing, there is a support message in LSCP which states that when running in Internet Explorer 9, "You are using a web browser or operating system that is not supported for use with Lync Server Control Panel." It then recommends the use of either IE 8 or IE 7. This also occurs when using Firefox 4.0 or Chrome 10, which also have the relevant Silverlight plugin installed. This may be fixed in a future CU (Cumulative Update).

Finally, you can use the admin simple URL defined in Topology Builder. For the examples used in this chapter, that was `https://admin.gaots.co.uk`. To actually access the LSCP from the admin URL, you must append `/cscp`, which is the required virtual directory. Following these steps allows you to log into the LSCP from any computer with a supported browser.

Once you have logged in with our LyncUserAdmin account, you will see the LSCP with only the interface elements related to user administration visible, as shown in Figure 10.1.

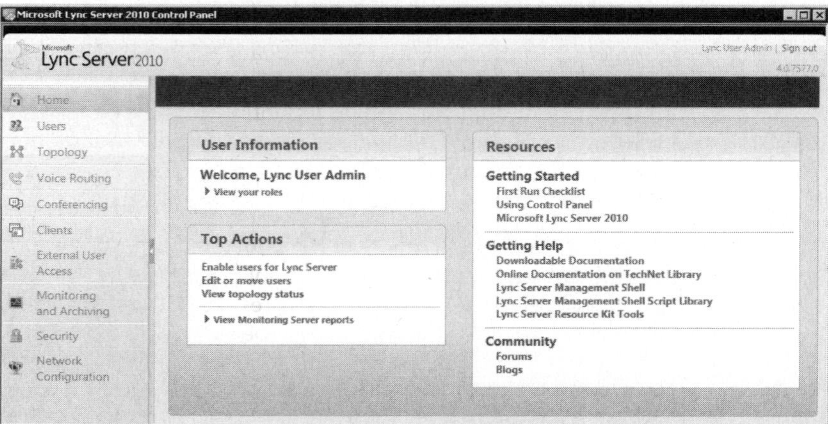

FIGURE 10.1
Logged into the Lync Server Control Panel as Lync User Admin

Now that you've gained access to the LSCP, the first task you need to master is searching; this will allow you to locate users for administration. Each tab of the LSCP has a search interface, and all of them except the one on the Users tab are very basic. The first thing to note about the searches that can be performed is that they only return objects that are Lync-enabled. Don't get caught out by this if you are looking for users to enable! This is done in a similar way but in a different location, which we will discuss shortly.

To carry out a search, first switch to the Users tab. At this point if you click Find, you will simply bring back all Lync-enabled users. Thankfully, the search interface on the Users tab allows you to customize certain search parameters. For example, you can perform a standard or LDAP search. The standard search will search for users by display name, first name, last name, Security Accounts Manager (SAM) account name, SIP address, or line Uniform Resource Identifier (URI). Note that wildcards will not work in this search and that unless you are planning to enter the entire contents of the attribute you are searching on (for example, Nathan), you must enter what it starts with rather than any other part of it (for example, **Nat** rather than **han**). If you want to search on SIP or line URI fields, you must include the **tel:** or **sip:** preface to the attribute data; otherwise, no results will be returned. The LDAP search allows even greater flexibility. You can use any attribute available through an LDAP query to be very granular about which objects are returned. For example, to start with you could use the following filter to bring back only user objects:

```
(objectclass=user)
```

Selecting the radio button next to LDAP Search and entering this filter brings back all Lync-enabled users. That's not very exciting, so how about this:

```
(description=Marketing)
```

This brings back all users with a description of Marketing. This next one brings back users with the letter U in their common name:

```
(cn=*u*)
```

Finally, this last one is much more complex:

```
(&(objectCategory=person)(objectClass=user)
(userAccountControl:1.2.840.113556.1.4.803:=2))
```

This brings back all Lync users who have a disabled AD account—as might be the case if the AD team had disabled a user in preparation for deletion but not told you yet.

As you can see, there is a huge amount of flexibility with which you can experiment. For more information about the syntax of the search query for LDAP filter, look at the resource here:

```
http://msdn2.microsoft.com/en-us/library/aa746475.aspx
```

Another feature of the Lync search capability is its ability to create quite complex searches using only the GUI. Clearly a lot is possible through LDAP searches, but if you just want to put together something without needing to research LDAP, you can use the Search Filter feature. Search filters allow you to add various operators to a basic search and only operate in basic search mode rather than LDAP mode. You cannot use wildcards in the search filters, but you can use the operators that PowerShell allows:

- ◆ Starts with
- ◆ Ends with
- ◆ Equal to
- ◆ Not equal to
- ◆ Contains
- ◆ Not contains

To add a filter, click the Add Filter button on the search bar. You can add up to 15 filters to build significantly complex queries. These queries can be saved and reloaded at a later date if this search is regularly used. Saved searches are stored as `.usf` files. This approach might be useful if, for example, it is needed to regularly check whether a certain group of users have the correct PIN policy. You could set up the relevant saved query, perform the search, and then use the assign policy action to ensure that all the users had the relevant policy.

Figure 10.2 and Figure 10.3 show the filter interface and some of the attributes that can be used in searches built with filters.

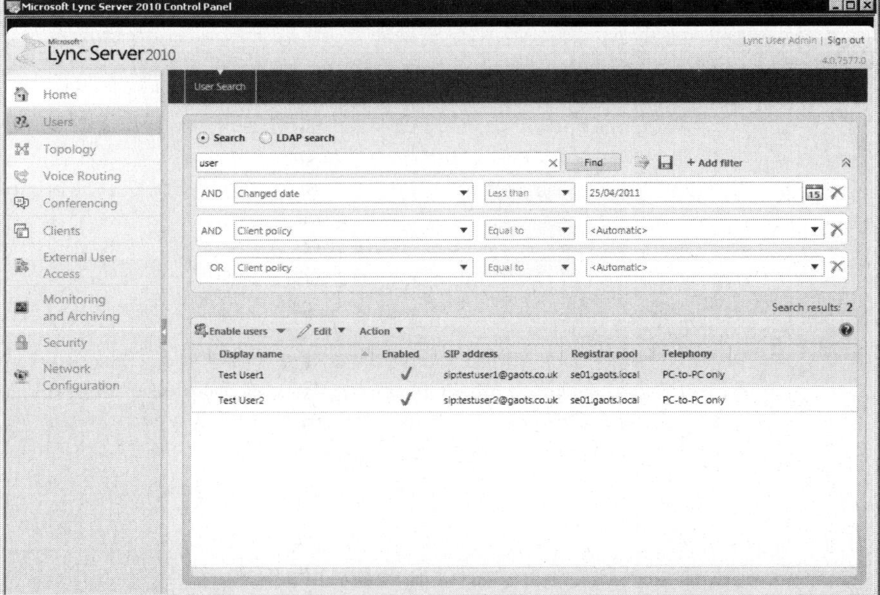

FIGURE 10.2 The Filter interface showing the AND and OR operators, the Add Filter, and the Save and Import query buttons

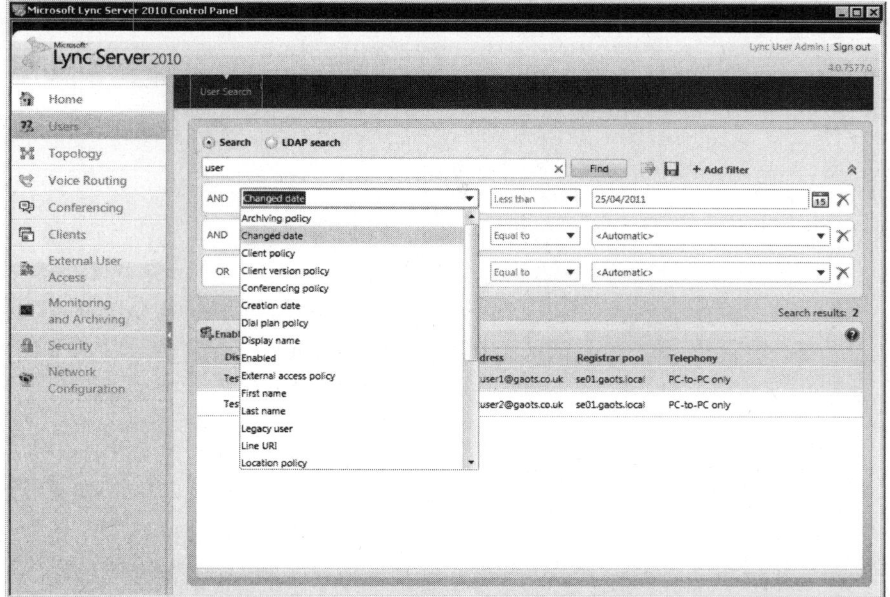

FIGURE 10.3
Some of the attributes that can be added to searches based on filters

Once the results are returned, you can perform actions on the resulting set of users by selecting one or many of them using either Shift+click or Ctrl+click and using the Actions drop-down; you'll learn more about this shortly.

When you are searching in LSCP, you might run into a couple of issues: the search interface can return only 200 users, and you can't customize the way data results are displayed. For example, you couldn't perform a simple LSCP search to find and display all the DDI numbers deployed. You could search and return all users with a DDI; however, to see the DDIs you would have to go into the properties of each user. For this level of data manipulation, you would have to dive into PowerShell.

If you want to search using PowerShell, a couple of useful PowerShell cmdlets are available for finding users to manipulate: `Get-CsUser` and `Get-CsAdUser`. `Get-CsAdUser` retrieves all user accounts in Active Directory Domain Services (AD DS), Lync-enabled or not, whereas `Get-CsUser` retrieves only Lync-enabled users inside AD DS.

In this section, we will discuss `Get-CsUser`, a cmdlet that focuses on Lync-enabled objects and Lync-specific attributes. `Get-CsUser` allows similar searches to those described in the section above. We will cover `Get-CsAdUser` in the next section on enabling user accounts for Lync.

To run these cmdlets, you need to be connected via a remote PowerShell console to the Lync server using our Lync user admin account. You can do this manually as described in Chapter 8, "PowerShell and LMS," or if you've installed the administrative tools, you can use LSMS, which is a little simpler because the connection is made automatically. Once at the prompt, you have even more flexibility than you had in the LSCP. For example, you can search for all Lync-enabled users in a specific OU and return up to two billion results, which should be enough for most people!

CREDENTIALS

Both the `Get-CsUser` and the `Get-CsAdUser` cmdlets have a rather useful parameter that allows you to run them under a user account other than the one with which you are connected to remote PowerShell. To do this, you must first create a PSCredential object using the `Get-Credential` cmdlet, which prompts for credentials and stores them in a variable. Use the following command:

```
$cred = Get-Credential
```

This will bring up a standard credential dialog, which will capture the credentials, including username and password, and store them in the variable `$cred`.

Then, by using the `-Credential` parameter and passing those stored credentials, the `Get-CsUser` or `Get-CsAdUser` cmdlet will run using those credentials. An example would be as follows:

```
Get-CsUser -Credential $cred
```

This would run the command under the credentials stored in the `$cred` variable and return all Lync-enabled users.

To get started, simply run `Get-CsUser`, which will return a list of all Lync-enabled users. Next, you can be more specific about which user or users you will return, by using the `-Identity` parameter as follows:

```
Get-CsUser -Identity "Test User1"
Get-CsUser -Identity "Test User*"
```

The first command brings back only `Test User 1`, and the second brings back any user starting with `Test User`.

WILDCARDS

Interestingly, PowerShell, unlike the LSCP, accepts wildcards. However, it accepts only the asterisk (*) wildcard. You cannot use the whole range of wildcards, such as ? and so on. Another thing to bear in mind is that wildcards work only on the Display Name attribute of a user rather than the department and other names.

You could, for example, use the following command to find all users starting with `test`.

```
Get-CsUser -Identity test*
```

Now, you can be more specific and search within an OU:

```
Get-CsUser -Identity "Test User1" -OU "cn=users,dc=gaots,dc=local"
```

Again, as with the LSCP, you can use filters. They can be of the usual PowerShell filter, as implemented in a ***`Where-Object`*** command, or they can be LDAP filters. You should note that only one of these parameters can be used in any one `Get-CsUser` command. The next command shows the use of a PowerShell filter:

```
Get-CsUser -Filter {RegistrarPool -eq "se01.gaots.local"}
```

This command will bring back all users homed on the "se01.gaots.local" pool. As you have seen, the simple Get-User command outputs all of the properties on which the user can be filtered. The previous filter was simply performed with only one parameter. You can expand the filter to create complex searches. For more specifics about how to format the filter string, see the following link:

```
http://technet.microsoft.com/en-us/library/ee177028.aspx
```

The other type of filter is the LDAP filter. It works in much the same way as through the LSCP but through PowerShell:

```
Get-CsUser -LDAPFilter "(Description="Office Based")"
```

This command will pull back all users where the description contains the Text "Office Based" and the Title is Manager.

Here's another:

```
Get-CsUser -LDAPFilter "!(Department=Marketing)"
```

This will pull back all users who are not in the Marketing department. As you can see, a great deal of flexibility is available to enable you to retrieve only the users you want.

Now that you know how to search and filter users in the LSCP and in PowerShell, let's move on to what you can do to the users you find.

Enabling and Disabling

Enabling users in the LSCP is relatively straightforward.

1. Open the LSCP as a user with CsAdministrator or CsUserAdministrator rights and click the Users tab. In the main pane, click Enable Users, which will open the main page to select and enable users, as shown in Figure 10.4.

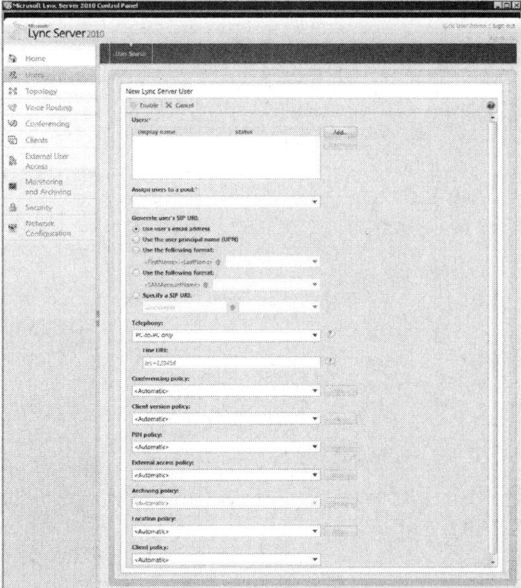

FIGURE 10.4
The main configuration page with options for enabling users

2. Click Add and locate the user or users you want to enable through the searching methods that were described earlier in the chapter. Once you have located and selected the relevant users, click OK.

   Note that multiple users can be selected either in one block using the Shift+click method or individually using the Ctrl+click method, which should be familiar from Windows Explorer.

3. You should be back in the main configuration page shown in Figure 10.4, this time with users listed in the Users section. You must assign the users to a Registrar pool. In Figure 10.4, this will be `se01.gaots.local`, which is the only pool available in the drop-down; however, your organization may have pools in different locations around the world. You must also select a method to generate a SIP URI (uniform resource identifier). We will cover these choices in more depth later when discussing how to enable the user from PowerShell. At this point, you will simply select Use User's Email Address because you know the email address field is populated with an address which fits the naming scheme of the SIP domain, `@gaots.co.uk`.

   At this point, you could simply accept the defaults and click Enable to finish setting up the users; however, you should be aware of a few other settings.

4. The Telephony section allows you to configure the way in which the user can use Lync features to make telephone calls. The default is PC-to-PC Only, which is what you should leave set for the user. This setting allows Lync voice and video calls to be made only within the Lync system between machines with the relevant Lync client installed. Other options are to enable coexistence with a third-party PBX, to configure the user to use Lync as a PBX, or to disable audio and video entirely. These settings will be covered in more detail in Chapter 13, "Getting Started with Voice."

5. The rest of the settings you can configure on this page enable you to assign immediately the various policies Lync provides to enable control of the user environment. For now, leave them at the default settings. We will discuss many of the policies in much more depth later in this chapter; at that point, you can come back and change those policies assigned to users if you like.

6. After you've looked through all the settings available, click Enable to make the users selected live on Lync.

Managing Users Who Are Domain Admins

We've used LSCP throughout this chapter to manage users; however, domain admins can't be managed this way. At this point, we would like to emphasize what a bad idea it is to have domain administrator permissions on users who are enabled for services like Lync and Exchange and who do "regular" work like web browsing. Of course, it does happen in organizations. You may, therefore, come across an LSCP limitation: because of the rights it runs under, LSCP cannot manage domain admins; it can only present information about them in a read-only manner. Therefore, to manage domain admin Lync users, you must use LSMS and be logged on as a domain admin to do so.

Although the LSCP is fine for enabling a single user, and even acceptable for doing them in bulk, some people just love to do things from the shell. For those people, here's how you enable a user from PowerShell. As discussed earlier, you need to locate the relevant user or users. When working in PowerShell that means using the `Get-CsAdUser` cmdlet, unless you know the display name of the user, in which case you can simply start with the `Enable-CsUser` cmdlet. In this case, you know the display name is *`Test User1`*, so you can move right on; but if you didn't know the name, you could use the `Get-CsAdUser` cmdlet to bring back the relevant user or users and pipe the output of `Get-CsAdUser` into the `Enable-CsUser` command, discussed next.

As you saw in the LSCP, certain fields are mandatory. First, of course, you must identify the user or users, using AD Display Name, SIP Address, User Principal Name (UPN), or Domain\SamAccountName. Again, in this case, you can stick with AD Display Name. Next, you need to specify the Registrar pool and the SIP address. In this simple example setup, this is pretty straightforward because there is only one Registrar pool (`se01.gaots.local`). The choice of SIP address is possibly more complex. As a rule of thumb, the SIP address should match the email address of the user if at all possible. However, unless Exchange is installed, the email address field might not be populated. Make sure it is for the user account you will be creating so you can use it later. In this example, Test User1 is set up with the email address: `testuser1@gaots.co.uk`.

To enable the user, use the following command:

```
Enable-CsUser -Identity "Test User1" -RegistrarPool se01.gaots.local
SipAddressType EmailAddress
```

This command will enable the user Test User1 for Lync on the `se01.gaots.local` pool with a SIP address matching the email address `testuser1@gaots.co.uk`. The one parameter here that may not be immediately obvious is the `SipAddressType`. It could have been very specific, used the `SipAddress` parameter, and manually specified the SIP address `testuser1@gaots.co.uk`; however, the `SipAddressType` parameter is potentially more useful because it allows various options to form the SIP address. One thing you will note is that when you use certain of the `SipAddressType` settings, you will need another parameter, `SipDomain`. In this environment, things are simple with only the one `SipDomain`: however, large organizations commonly need to support multiple domains, perhaps to represent different brands or company units.

The options for `SipAddressType` are as follows:

`EmailAddress`: As shown previously, this uses the email address from the user in AD and doesn't require the `SipDomain` parameter.

`SamAccountName`: This uses the SamAccountName from AD and does require the `SipDomain` parameter to specify the suffix of the name after the `@` sign.

`UserPrincipalName`: This uses the UPN of the user in AD and, as the UPN is in the same form as an email address, doesn't require the use of the `SipDomain` parameter.

`FirstLastName`: This takes the first and last name of the user and puts a period between them—for example, `nathan.winters`. It requires the use of the `SipDomain` parameter.

PIPING OUTPUT FROM THE *ENABLE-CSUSER* CMDLET

One thing that you may be used to in PowerShell is the ability to pipe the output from one command into the input of the next. This is one of PowerShell's most useful features. It allows you to do the following:

```
Get-CsAdUser -OU "cn=users,dc=gaots,dc=local" | Enable-CsUser -RegistrarPool
se01.gaots.local SipAddressType EmailAddress
```

This would enable all the users in the Users container in AD using their email addresses as the SIP Address. However, you may not be aware that piping from the output of the `Enable-CsUser` cmdlet doesn't work by default. This is by design, because `Enable-CsAdUser` enables the given User object for Lync and doesn't pass the User object. Thankfully, if you add the `-PassThru` parameter it will enable the output to be piped to other cmdlets so that you can set specific settings for the newly enabled user—for example, enabling them for Enterprise Voice.

You now know how to find and enable users for Lync. As you have seen, the `SipAddress` is key. This forms the unique ID and is what makes users show up in searches carried out for Lync-enabled users. On occasion this can cause unintended results, as you might ask yourself what happens if a user already has a SIP address populated in his `msRTCSIP-PrimaryUserAddress` attribute. This could happen as part of a previous deployment when the user maybe became orphaned. Thankfully, there is a PowerShell command that can help identify these users and get them all set up for Lync:

```
Get-CsUser -UnassignedUser | Select-Object DisplayName
```

When run, this command will identify any users with an SIP address but who are not assigned to a Registrar pool. It will then output their display name. You could, of course, simply pipe the output to the `Enable-CsUser` cmdlet and get them set up directly for Lync.

Making Changes to Lync Users

Now that you've enabled some users for Lync, you no doubt feel suitably pleased. However, it won't be very long before the changes start rolling in. For example, someone might move to a different office or even a different country and be served from of a different Lync pool. Another typical occurrence is when a name changes due to marriage; and of course, people will leave your organization temporarily or permanently and their accounts will need to be disabled and then deleted. As with all the other Lync user administration tasks, the first requirement with these tasks is to make sure you target the relevant user or users; that is where the search skills you've learned early come in handy.

The LSCP is well laid out, so by now you should be pretty familiar with it. On the Users tab, search for the user you need to alter. Once you've selected it, you can explore the available options and find the Edit and Action drop-downs.

The Edit drop-down is very straightforward. It gives you an easy option to select all the users returned by a search, after which you can move to the options on the Action menu, which we'll discuss shortly. Other than that, the only option is Show Details, which takes you to the configuration page for that particular user. This will look familiar from the steps taken to enable the user in LSCP described earlier. The Action drop-down gives many more options, as shown in Figure 10.5.

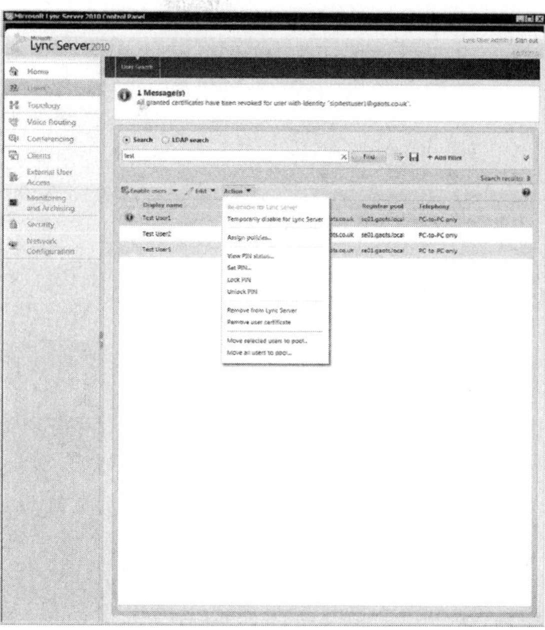

FIGURE 10.5
The options on the Action drop-down

MOVING USERS

As you can see, moving users to another pool is simple. You select the relevant user or users, and then on the Action menu click the Move Selected Users To Pool entry. This opens a dialog box where you can choose the pool in the drop-down shown in Figure 10.6. There is also a checkbox entitled Force which should be used if the standard process for moving fails. The standard process of moving users between pools will take across their conferences and buddy lists. If for some reason the source pool is unavailable, you would have to use the Force checkbox to move the user without this data from the source pool. This is discussed in more detail in Chapter 12, "Troubleshooting."

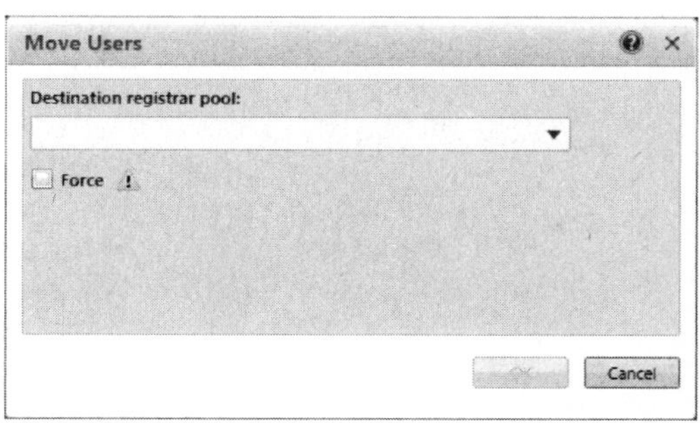

FIGURE 10.6
The Move Users dialog box allows you to move selected users to a pool.

Selecting the Move All Users To Pool option will bring up a dialog that allows you to select both a source and destination pool and enables moving all users from the source to the destination, as shown in Figure 10.7. Again, the Force checkbox allows scenarios where the source pool isn't available.

FIGURE 10.7
The Move Users dialog box allows you to move all users between pools.

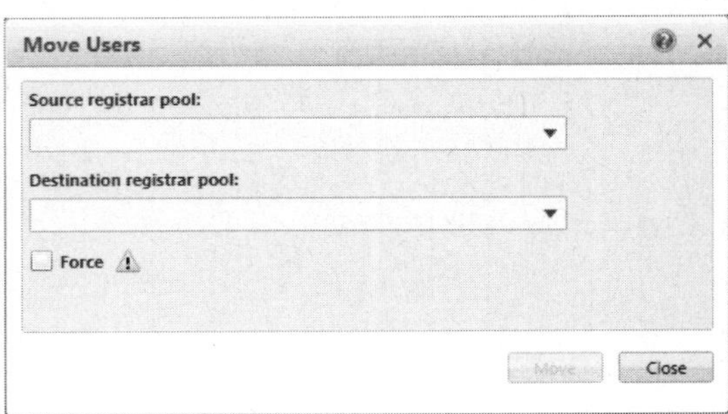

To perform these moves from PowerShell, you would use the `Move-CsUser` cmdlet, a very simple cmdlet. The required parameters are `-Identity` to target a specific user and `-Target` to specify to which pool to move. There is also the `-Force` parameter, which provides the same functionality to move users in failure scenarios without taking user data across to the new pool.

```
Move-CsUser -Identity "Test User1" -Target "newpool.gaots.local"
```

This command moves `Test User1` to the Newpool pool.

Instead of having a separate cmdlet to allow all users to be moved from one pool to another, this time the PowerShell pipe is used for functionality:

```
Get-CsUser -Filter [RegistrarPool -eq "se01.gaots.local"} | Move-CsUser -Target
"newpool.gaots.local"
```

This command first runs the `Get-CsUser` command you are familiar with, and using a filter it selects all users on the `Se01.gaots.local` pool. These are then piped to the `Move-CsUser` cmdlet, which moves them to the `Newpool.gaots.local` pool.

CHANGING USERNAMES

In addition to moving users between pools, another commonly needed task is to change usernames, usually after a marriage. In this case most of the work will be done by other teams, namely the AD guys and the Exchange guys. (Of course that might be you, but that's a topic for a whole other book!) In Lync terms, when the AD guys have made their changes the user will show up in Lync searches with a new display name. However, what won't have changed is the SIP URI, which as we have said should match the primary email address of the user. To ensure that is the case, in LSCP locate the user and on the Edit drop-down click Show Details. In the configuration pane that opens, edit the SIP Address field as required and then click Commit. To do the same process from PowerShell, use the `Set-CsUser` cmdlet as follows:

```
Set-CsUser -Identity "Test User1" -SipAddress testmarried1@gaots.co.uk
```

This command will update the SIP Address of Test User 1 to: `testmarried1@gaots.co.uk`.

Disabling and Removing Users

There are actually a couple of ways of disabling users, which have slightly different effects. On the Edit drop-down, if you click Show Details, one of the options on the user configuration page is a checkbox entitled Enabled for Lync Server. If this checkbox is cleared, a Lync user cannot log onto Lync, but it doesn't remove any of the user's settings from Lync and doesn't remove Lync attributes, like the SIP URI, from the user object. This is a sensible option if the user in question is going to be out of the organization for a period of time but will return. In PowerShell, this is the same as running the following command:

```
Set-CsUser -Identity "Test User1" -Enabled:$False
```

This command will ensure that a user can't log onto Lync but doesn't delete any settings or policy assignments.

To reverse the process, simply run the following command:

```
Set-CsUser -Identity "Test User1" -Enabled:$True
```

This command will bring the user back to life and ensure that they can log onto Lync again as before. These steps can be carried out from the Action drop-down using the Temporarily Disable for Lync Server and the Re-enable for Lync Server options. If instead, you want to be more permanent, then you need to use the Action drop-down in the LSCP or the `Disable-CsUser` cmdlet in PowerShell. With the relevant user or users selected, move to the Action drop-down and select Remove from Lync Server. You will be prompted to click OK if you are sure. This action will remove the user entirely from the Lync Server by removing Lync attributes on the user account and wiping out Lync user data such as buddy lists and policy assignments. It will not remove the Active Directory user object. To carry out the same action in PowerShell, use the following command:

```
Disable-CsUser -Identity "Test User1"
```

This will remove the user from Lync. At this point if you wanted to re-enable the user, you would have to go back and use the `Enable-CsUser` cmdlet or the LSCP process just described.

> **Bulk Changes**
>
> Using the GUI, it is possible to manage more than one user at a time. But unless you really enjoy repetitive tasks, if you need to manage tens or hundreds of Lync users, PowerShell is critical. We've covered some of the basics in this chapter, but take a look at Chapter 8 for more detailed information.

Other User Actions

The other options on the Action menu that we haven't covered are Assign Policies, the various PIN settings, and the Remove User Certificate setting. We will cover the Assign Policies option in the rest of this chapter, and the PIN settings are covered in the Voice chapters of this book, so the final element to cover is the Remove User Certificate option. As explained in Chapter 3, "Security," Lync allows users to be authenticated not only through traditional username and password combinations, but also through the use of a certificate and PIN. This makes authentication from phone devices simpler because users only need to enter the numeric PIN. Of course, as an administrator, you may want a way to prevent a user logging in this way. That is what the Remove User Certificate option does. Although it doesn't remove the certificates from the devices, it does remove them from the server, which prevents the user logging on. Through PowerShell the same thing can be carried out using the `Revoke-CsClientCertificate` cmdlet.

Understanding Lync Policies

The ability to control systems through the use of policies is critical to an enterprise. It is standard to have different groups of people carrying out a certain function and to provide them with only the required tools to do the job. In this way, systems can be sized correctly and security can be maintained. In OCS 2007 and OCS 2007 R2 there were, of course, policies to enable control and management of the user experience. However, these policies could not always be applied in a way that provided the same experience for users no matter where they logged on. The policies were also applied in different ways and did not always allow enough granularity of control without significant effort. Thankfully, Lync Server 2010 uses a completely different methodology for policies. There are numerous policies that can be applied in very granular ways to give a single consistent experience to users and to ensure that Lync administrators can control Lync users without constantly needing the approval of other IT teams (as was the case when Group Policy was used). The remainder of this chapter looks in depth at just what you can do—and how—to keep order in your Lync environment.

In-Band Provisioning

In-band provisioning describes the application of policy to the client through information contained in SIP messages and passed to the client during usage so that settings apply immediately. For a really detailed description of how this works, see this TechNet article:

```
http://blogs.technet.com/b/csps/p/cmgmtprovisioning.aspx
```

Because of the way policy is applied, different types of clients apply the relevant policy settings to the functionality they offer. Whatever the client, the user will have the same experience, because this method of applying policy is as relevant to the browser client as it is to the PC that's not domain-joined and even to the domain-joined PC. Another benefit is that administrators are not constrained to fit Lync policies around another policy engine, such as Group Policy in OCS. Almost all Lync policies can be created and applied either through the LSCP or through PowerShell (see "What about Group Policy" later in the chapter for the exceptions). Not using group policies provides greater flexibility, as policies can be applied at Global, Site, Service, and User levels, and these policies take effect immediately rather than having to wait for a Group Policy refresh cycle.

Understanding Where Policies Apply

One of the principal benefits of moving to the new Lync in-band provisioning model is that Lync policy can closely follow Lync architecture and users, allowing a high degree of granularity.

As discussed in Chapter 5, Lync has added to the architectural concepts of OCS 2007 R2 (the *organization* and the *pool*) and includes the concept of *sites*, which generally map to data centers. It is now possible to apply policy at all these levels. Default policies are applied at the Global level, but administrators can create certain types of policies at other levels, such as the Site, Service, or Tag level. Tag-level policies are what allow policy to be assigned to an individual user or selection of users. (As you will see, the search skills you learned earlier can be used to locate users to apply policy to, thereby giving you the very flexible ability to specifically target users.)

Of course, all these different levels mean that you need to understand their precedence. The following rules apply:

- If a per-user policy is assigned to the user, then the per-user policy is used.
- If no per-user policy is assigned to the user, then the service policy is used.
- If there is no per-user or service policy, then the site policy is used.
- If there is no per-user, service, or site policy, then the global policy is used.

Simply summarized, the policy set closest to the user wins! Understanding this is important because it has a material effect on which settings are applied to users. For example, certain settings in a policy could be left blank, at the user's discretion. For example, you could allow the user to choose whether or not to display a photo by leaving the DisplayPhoto section of the CsClientPolicy blank. But what would happen if you set the DisplayPhoto section of the CsClientPolicy to force the use of the AD stored photo on the global policy but then left that setting blank on a policy closer to the user (that is, site or user tag)? The user would still be able to choose. The whole policy is applied even if settings are blank, not just settings that have an explicit value.

To understand the various levels more closely, you need to understand the difference between policy name and scope, which defines how policies are referenced using the `-Identity` parameter in PowerShell. Following are some examples of how different policies are referenced:

`Identity global` This will pull back the global policy of whichever cmdlet is used.

`Identity site:PolicyName` This reflects a policy that is assigned to a site.

`Identity registrar:server.domain.xxx` This reflects a policy that is assigned to a specific service, in this case a registrar.

`Identity Tag:PolicyName` This reflects a policy that is assigned to users.

You can see clearly the concept of policy name and policy scope. The element in the identity before the colon (:) is the scope; the element after the colon is the policy name. In the case of either site or service scopes, the policy name matches that of the site or service where the policy is to be assigned. In the case of the tag scope, the policy name should describe where the policy will apply. You will see how this works when you create and assign policies later in this chapter.

What About Group Policy?

We've mentioned that all policies could be created through LSCP or PowerShell; however, that is not quite true. When the Lync client starts up, it needs certain bootstrapping settings passed to it. For example, if you are not using auto-configuration through DNS SRV records, the client would need to be provided the Lync server to log onto. Another such configuration is to enable or disable the welcome screen that pops up when the Lync client is launched for the first time. Clearly in-band provisioning won't work in these instances, as the client hasn't logged on nor been able to check settings. Therefore, the use of Group Policy is maintained for these client bootstrapping settings only.

In order to apply these Group Policy settings, you will need to obtain the relevant `.adm` template file. This file is available only on the retail disc images of the Lync 2010 Client (in the support folder). It is not available on the Trial, MSDN, or TechNet versions because they are `.exe` downloads rather than ISO images. Strangely, no separate download is available on the Microsoft website. The file you are looking for is called `communicator.adm`.

On the RTM version of the Lync retail disc, there is an irritating error in the ADM file that produces an *`Error 62`* when you try to load it. To repair the problem, open the `.adm` file using a text editor, such as Notepad.

Locate the `[strings]` section and ensure that the `PolicyGalUseCompactDeltaFile` section reads as follows:

```
POLICY !!PolicyGalUseCompactDeltaFile
EXPLAIN !!ExplainText_GalUseCompactDeltaFile
PART !!PolicyGalUseCompactDeltaFile DROPDOWNLIST NOSORT
VALUENAME "GalUseCompactDeltaFile"
ITEMLIST
NAME !!GalUseCompactDeltaFileVal0 VALUE NUMERIC  0
NAME !!GalUseCompactDeltaFileVal1 VALUE NUMERIC  1 DEFAULT
NAME !!GalUseCompactDeltaFileVal2 VALUE NUMERIC  2
END ITEMLIST
END PART
END POLICY
```

If you have trouble implementing this fix, the file is also available on the Internet, at `http://www.microsoft.com/download/en/details.aspx?id=27217`. This file includes the Microsoft Lync 2010 administrative template file (`Communicator.adm`) and a spreadsheet that lists the Group Policy settings.

Once you have the template file, you will need to load it into a Group Policy Object (GPO), which will then be applied at the level in AD where you want to control settings. This is subject to all the usual constraints, such as delays in policy propagation as mentioned earlier.

1. To load the template into a GPO, on a domain controller (or anywhere else you have the Group Policy Management tools installed) click Start ➢ Administrative Tools ➢ Group Policy Management.

2. On the left pane, drill down into the forest and domain and right-click on Group Policy Objects. Select New, as shown in Figure 10.8.

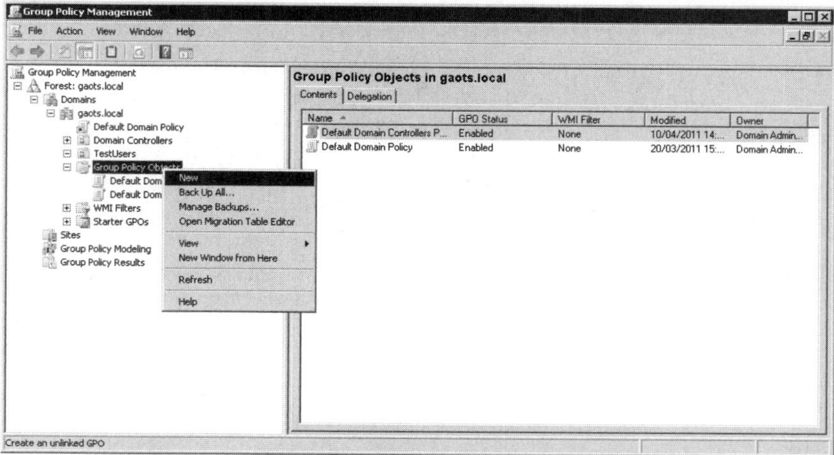

FIGURE 10.8
Creating the new GPO object

3. Give the policy a name, but don't select a starter GPO, and click OK.
4. Right-click the new GPO and click Edit. In the left pane, drill down to User Configuration ➢ Administrative Templates: Policy Definitions (ADMX Files) Retrieved from the Local Machine. (Don't worry that it mentions ADMX files, as the older ADM files work just fine.) Right-click the Administrative Templates folder and click Add/Remove Templates.
5. On the next window, click Add and then locate the ADM file. Click OK and then Close. You will see a new folder called Classic Administrative Templates (ADM), under which if you drill down you will see the Lync Bootstrap policy settings. Each setting is fairly self-explanatory and comes with a useful help article built into the GPO, as shown in Figure 10.9.
6. After you set up the policy as needed, you can apply it to the relevant group of users by using the standard method.

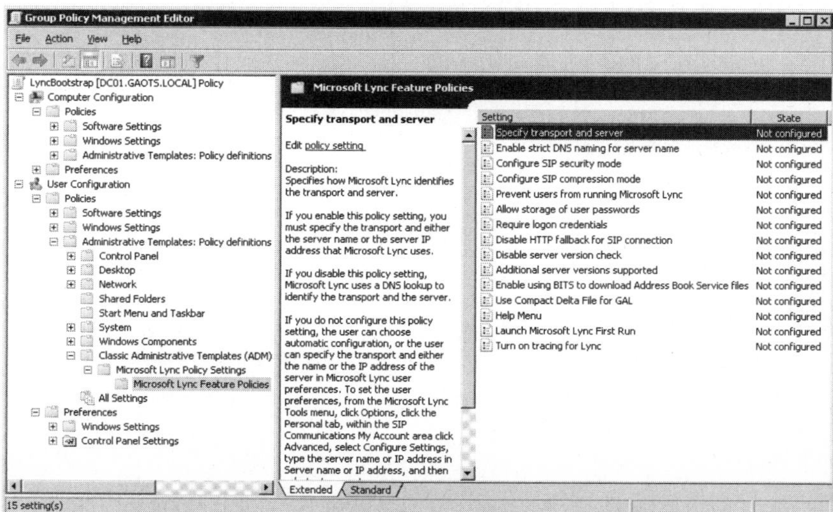

FIGURE 10.9
The newly created GPO with the Lync settings imported

Manipulating Policies

You are getting close to the process of testing policies. As you will soon come to expect, Lync policies can be manipulated in the usual two ways: either though LSCP or PowerShell. In general, though, most manipulation is done through PowerShell, as the policies are very wide-ranging. Because these policies must be manipulated using PowerShell, administrators must take the time to really think through what they were doing as they prepare and research the necessary commands. One final thing to note before you dive right in: although the `LyncUserAdmin` used in this chapter's examples so far can assign policies to users, it can't create them; therefore, to carry out the operations discussed next (except for the assignment of policies), you should be logged on as a member of the CsAdministrator RBAC role.

Viewing Policies

You will undoubtedly want to know what policies already exist before you create new ones. Lync comes with a global policy set up for each policy type available, and the default settings are hard-coded into the software. You will see this in action later in the chapter when we discuss what happens if you try to delete a global policy.

Because we discussed some of the policies earlier in this chapter, you already know several of the policy types. In LSCP, they are spread out in the various tabs to which they apply. For example, to see the available ClientVersionPolicies, you would navigate to the Client tab in LSCP; and in the main pane under Client Version Policy, you would see all available policies. This is shown in Figure 10.10.

FIGURE 10.10
Viewing the Client Version Policy tab in LSCP

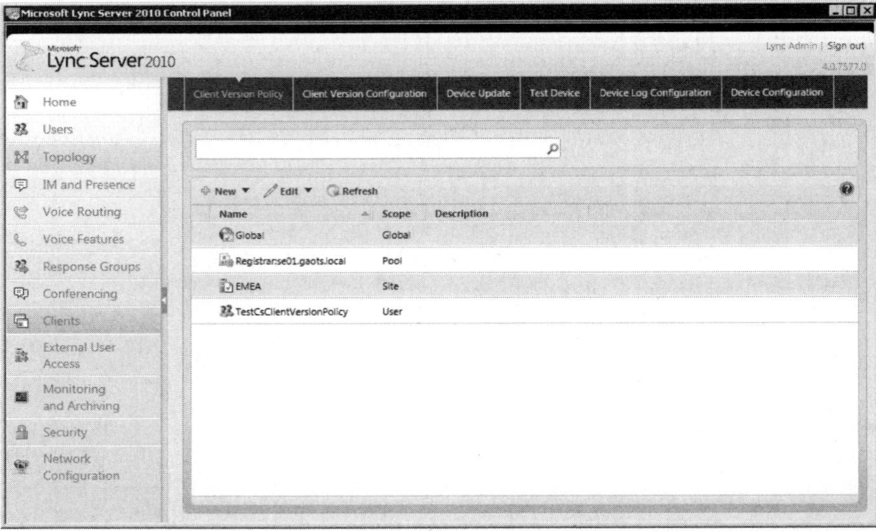

What you can see is not only the default global policy, but also some other more focused policies which you will create shortly. If you view one of the other policy sections, under the

External User Access tab, you can see the External User Access policy. If you double-click the global policy, you will see the settings in Figure 10.11.

FIGURE 10.11
Viewing the settings of the default global External User Access policy

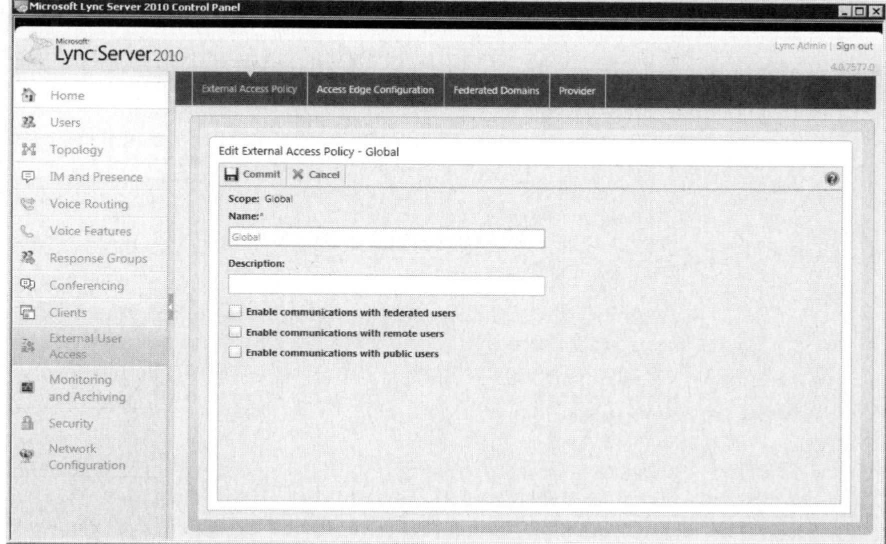

To change any of the settings, simply check the relevant checkbox and then click Commit. You can see how easy it is to retrieve policy information and change settings in the LSCP. If you look carefully enough at all the possible options, you will also notice that some of the more-wide ranging policies like the CsClientPolicy are not visible through the LSCP.

Given that some of the settings are not available through LSCP and in keeping with the rest of the book, let's take a look at how you would use PowerShell to view policies.

As we have already discussed, there are various default global policies. To retrieve one of them, the CsClientPolicy type, you would use a command such as this:

```
Get-CsExternalAccessPolicy -Identity global
```

Because you want to retrieve the default global policy, notice the naming convention. Also notice the output of this command, which shows the current settings that you saw in Figure 10.11:

```
Identity                          : Global
Description                       :
EnableFederationAccess            : False
EnablePublicCloudAccess           : False
EnablePublicCloudAudioVideoAccess : False
EnableOutsideAccess               : False
```

To get the remaining policies, you simply need to identify the relevant cmdlets. Sadly, this is not as simple as it could be, because the developers didn't quite stick to a naming convention. Most of the cmdlets are formatted like the previous one, `Get-CsXxxPolicy`. However, there are a couple that stand out. First, note that although the `Get-CsNetworkIntersitePolicy` follows the relevant naming format, it actually works with Call Admission Control (CAC) and as such is not related directly to users. This is covered in Chapter 14, "Call Admission Control." The other anomaly is the `Get-CsDialPlan` cmdlet, which retrieves dial plans related to Enterprise Voice that are applied to users. Dial plans are covered in Chapter 13, "Getting Started with Voice." With this knowledge, you can run the following command to get a list of all the relevant cmdlets:

```
Get-Command -Module Lync | Where-Object {(
$_.Name -like "Get-Cs*Policy" -and $_.Name -notlike "*Network*") -or $_.Name
-like "Get-Cs*DialPlan"}
```

This command will first get all the commands in the Lync module, and then sort through them listing only those that fit the previous plans and not the CsNetworkIntersitePolicy, which wasn't needed. When it is run, you will see the following output:

```
CommandType    Name                          Definition
-----------    ----                          ----------
Cmdlet         Get-CsArchivingPolicy         Get-CsArchivingPolicy [[-Ide...
Cmdlet         Get-CsClientPolicy            Get-CsClientPolicy [[-Identi...
Cmdlet         Get-CsClientVersionPolicy     Get-CsClientVersionPolicy [[...
Cmdlet         Get-CsConferencingPolicy      Get-CsConferencingPolicy [[-...
Cmdlet         Get-CsDialPlan                Get-CsDialPlan [[-Identity] ...
Cmdlet         Get-CsExternalAccessPolicy    Get-CsExternalAccessPolicy [...
Cmdlet         Get-CsHostedVoicemailPolicy   Get-CsHostedVoicemailPolicy ...
Cmdlet         Get-CsLocationPolicy          Get-CsLocationPolicy [[-Iden...
Cmdlet         Get-CsPinPolicy               Get-CsPinPolicy [[-Identity]...
Cmdlet         Get-CsPresencePolicy          Get-CsPresencePolicy [[-Iden...
Cmdlet         Get-CsVoicePolicy             Get-CsVoicePolicy [[-Identit...
```

Now you have a useful list of all the cmdlets that can be used to retrieve policies. They all (even `Get-CsDialPlan`) take the same command structure as shown earlier to get the Global Policy settings.

It's useful to see the current settings for each of the global policies, but sometimes you'll want to see the default settings. There are a few ways of doing this:

- Check the help file. This method doesn't require any discussion.
- Create a new, empty policy and retrieve it to display its settings. This method has a disadvantage we'll discuss next.
- Create a new policy but use the `-InMemory` parameter. This final way is rather clever.

As mentioned, creating a new policy with no parameters other than a name will create a policy using the default settings. For example:

```
New-CsClientPolicy -Identity TestDefaultSettings
```

This command would create a new client policy called TestDefaultSettings. However, you don't really want to have to create policies every time you want to see the default settings because it would be too easy to forget one and clutter up the system. Fortunately, another option is available. One of the parameters of the `New-CsXxxPolicy` cmdlets is `-InMemory`. When appended to the command just shown, it creates a policy but holds it in memory and never writes it to the configuration store. To see this parameter in action, run the following command:

```
New-CsClientPolicy -Identity TestDefaultSettings -InMemory
```

This will output the default settings of the client policy but not actually create the policy. Of course, this functionality is not provided just to let you see the default settings of a policy. It will also allow you to create a new policy in memory and assign it to a variable. You can then manipulate the policy settings as you need, and then put the policy into action, thereby ensuring that the correct settings are applied immediately. We will cover this in the next section.

We've looked at how to retrieve the global policies and the default settings, but what about easily viewing the other policies of a specific type? The next command will list all policies of a certain type:

```
Get-CsClientVersionPolicy | Select-Object Identity
```

This command will list all the CsClientVersionPolicies, as in the output shown here:

```
Identity
--------
Global
Site:EMEA
Service:Registrar:se01.gaots.local
Tag:TestCsClientVersionPolicy
```

This output nicely demonstrates the naming conventions showing scope and assignment. The `Tag:TestCsClientVersionPolicy` entry is ready to be assigned to users.

Creating and Assigning Policies

So far we've covered the basics of creating a policy using the `New-CsXxxPolicy` cmdlets. We know that simply using the cmdlet followed by an identity will create a new policy with the default settings. We've also discussed the basics of what the different identities for the policy mean to where they apply, but it will be useful to recap that here. This time we will use the `New-CsClientVersionPolicy`, because it can be created against all of the various scopes available as follows:

```
New-CsClientVersionPolicy -Identity global
New-CsClientVersionPolicy -Identity Site:EMEA
New-CsClientVersionPolicy -Identity registrar:se01.gaots.local
New-CsClientVersionPolicy -Identity TestDefaultSettings
```

These commands will create policies with the default settings. Of course, you can also create new policies through the LSCP. One of the benefits of this is that you get guidance in creating the policies of different scope as shown in Figure 10.12.

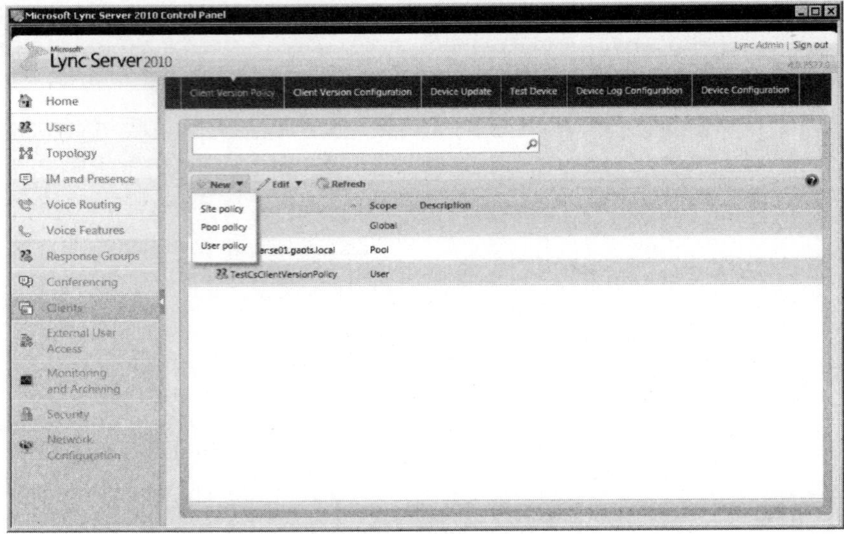

FIGURE 10.12 Creating a new CsClientVersionPolicy through LSCP, showing the different policy scopes available

Once you have selected the scope type, you will be presented with a search box to locate the relevant pool (registrar) or site, or taken straight into the policy settings windows with a text box to name the policy if it is to be a user (`Tag:`) policy.

After policies have been created in LSCP or PowerShell, the next stage is the assignment of these policies. Global policies, site policies, and service policies don't need to be assigned; they just work immediately on creation because their identity specifically references an element of Lync architecture where they are to be active. That's why the name of a policy can be edited only with user policies. Of course, this means that you can't use one site policy on another site; you must create a new one, as the naming format is specific to the site, such as Site:EMEA or Site:ASIA. If you do need to do this, there is no simple method. It would be worth reviewing the article linked here, which details a possible workaround:

`http://blogs.technet.com/b/csps/archive/2011/03/21/copypolicies.aspx`

The user policy (sometimes called Tag level) will need to be assigned. This is where the `Grant-CsXxxPolicy` cmdlets come in. In the case of the policy about to assign the TestDefaultSettings Client Version Policy to Test User 1, you would need to do the following:

```
Grant-CsClientVersionPolicy -Identity "Test User1" -PolicyName
"TestDefaultSettings"
```

This will apply the policy to Test User1. But suppose you want to apply this policy to all members of a department, or to those with a special customer attribute, or specifically to members of an AD group.

Well, this is once again where PowerShell comes in. You can again utilize the searching skills you learned at the start of this chapter. You first locate the relevant group of users you need and then pipe the output to the relevant `Grant-CsXxxPolicy` cmdlet. Here is an example:

```
Get-CsUser -LdapFilter "Department=Marketing" | Grant-CsClientPolicy -PolicyName
"TestCsClientPolicy"
```

This will first use an LDAPFilter to get all the members of the Marketing department who are Lync-enabled and then apply the TestCsClientPolicy to them. If you are using the LSCP to assign policy, things follow much the same format. You would use the search skills covered earlier to locate the relevant Lync-enabled users. Then you would select the users, and on the Action drop-down, click Assign Policies. This will open the window you see in Figure 10.13. You can assign the relevant policies to the users by using the relevant drop-down menus and clicking OK to apply.

FIGURE 10.13
Assigning policies in the LSCP

Applying a policy to members of a specific AD group is unfortunately not quite so simple. Like many things, though, it can be achieved with a line of PowerShell.

You first need to get the members of the group. This can be done as follows:

```
Import-Module ActiveDirectory
Get-AdGroupMember -Identity TestGroup
```

Here, you are first importing the AD module so you can manipulate AD objects and then get the members of the group TestGroup. However, the output looks like this:

```
Get-ADGroupMember -Identity TestGroup
distinguishedName : CN=Test User5,CN=Users,DC=gaots,DC=local
name              : Test User5
objectClass       : user
objectGUID        : 1870d540-28f4-47eb-90fd-b98c339cd6d5
SamAccountName    : testuser5
SID               : S-1-5-21-97327702-4139054532-3539935471-1143
```

If you try to pipe that directly into the `Grant-CsXxxPolicy` cmdlet you will get an error, as the `Grant-CsXxxPolicy` cmdlet doesn't understand the input. So to work around this, you need to understand the type of input that the Grant-CsXxxPolicy cmdlet takes. You can get this from the help file, as shown here:

```
String value or Microsoft.Rtc.Management.ADConnect.Schema.ADUser object. Grant-
CsClientPolicy accepts pipelined input of string values representing the Identity
of a user account. The cmdlet also accepts pipelined input of user objects.
```

This tells you that the cmdlet accepts pipelined user objects, as you proved when passing it output from Get-CsUser, and that it also accepts strings which represent user accounts. Therefore, what you need to pass the Grant-CsXxxPolicy cmdlet is something in the form of "Test User5."

As you can see from the output from the Get-AdGroupMember cmdlet, this particular format is found under the .name attribute. You can, therefore, use the following PowerShell command to grant policy to the membership of a specific AD group:

```
Get-ADGroupMember -Identity testgroup | ForEach-Object {Grant-CsClientPolicy
-PolicyName testcsclientpolicy -identity $_.name}
```

This command first gets the members of the group and then for each member runs the Grant-CsClientPolicy cmdlet using the .name attribute for the identity.

Real World Scenario

THE NEED TO AUTOMATE POLICY ASSIGNMENT

In many recent discussions with customers, a common scenario has arisen. As you have seen, assigning policy is a process that requires a command to be run. It is perhaps a slight disadvantage to the new way of doing things. With Group Policy, assuming a new user account fell under the scope of a GPO, that new user account would automatically get the new policy applied. In Lync this is not the always the case. For example, suppose a new user is created in the Marketing department. Even if you have followed one of the earlier examples to assign a specific policy to all those members of the Marketing department using the LDAPFilter method, this new member of the Marketing department won't get the same policy as the rest of the department. Instead, he or she will get the nearest policy to it, following the normal inheritance method. This could either be a service (depending on which pool they register to), a site (depending on which site they are homed in), or the global policy, if none of the others apply.

What is required is a way to ensure that users get the policies they should get. At this point, there is really no good way that we have come up with for doing this. You could of course have scripts which are scheduled, but it would only be reasonable to run those, for example, at the end of each day. This means a user could be live on the system for a day without the correct policies. If this were an archiving policy, that could leave you open to some serious legal consequences!

All we can suggest in this case is to make the assignment of Lync policy part of your provisioning process. This could mean ensuring that assigning policy is added to the checklist of steps taken when creating a user. Or, you may have an automated method, given that PowerShell makes it so simple to assign policy based on user attributes. If so, you can ensure that when the user object is created by Forefront Identity Manager (FIM), which is a Microsoft meta directory and directory synchronization tool used in many provisioning systems, FIM will validate the relevant attributes based on user type (such as Marketing) and then run the relevant PowerShell commands to apply policy.

Finally, as part of operational management of Lync, you could report on Lync policies each month to double-check that people have the correct policies and no one has slipped through the net.

Realistically, you probably don't want to create all your policies with the default settings. After all, there would be little point in that, as you could simply use the default global policies. So to create new policies with settings other than the default, you need to specify what settings you want in the `New-CsXxxPolicy`. As an example, creating a custom Presence Policy enables you to manage two important aspects of presence subscriptions: prompted subscribers and category subscriptions as shown here:

```
New-CsPresencePolicy -Identity MarketingPresencePolicy -MaxPromptedSubscriber 750
-MaxCategorySubscription 900
```

This would create a new Presence Policy using the settings entered. The `MaxCategorySubscription` parameter lets you control the maximum number of category subscriptions allowed at any one time. A category subscription represents a request for a specific category of information—for example, an application that requests calendar data. The `MaxPromptedSubscriber` parameter enables you to control the maximum number of prompted subscribers a user can have at any one time. By default, any time you are added to another user's contacts list, a notification dialog appears on screen informing you of this fact and giving you the chance to do such things as add the person to your own contacts list or block the person from viewing your presence. Until you take action and dismiss the dialog box, each notification counts as a prompted subscriber.

Creating a Presence Policy in this way is easy. However, what about a policy that has many more options you could set, like a Client Policy? In that case, you need to plow through them and set the ones you want. The settings that you don't explicitly set will take on the default settings for that policy.

As you've seen, it is also possible to create policy using the LSCP. In this case, configuring the relevant settings is simply a case of using the GUI and then clicking Commit.

Editing Existing Policies

We have created several policies, but what about editing the existing ones? Editing policies is also a simple matter in PowerShell or LSCP. With PowerShell, you would use the relevant `Set-CsXxxPolicy` cmdlet and identify the policy using the naming conventions outlined previously (*Scope*:*Name*) and then use the relevant parameter to change the setting. For example:

```
Set-CsPresencePolicy -Identity Tag:MarketingPresencePolicy -MaxPromptedSubscriber
200 -MaxCategorySubscription 400
```

There is at least one policy that works slightly differently than the others. That is the Client Version Policy. This policy is made up of rules to allow or disallow certain versions, and it uses the `CsClientVersionPolicyRule` set of cmdlets to amend and create rules. They are covered in the final section of this chapter.

So having created and assigned all these policies, the last thing we will cover in this section is how to see which user has which policy assigned. After all, it could get rather complex with all those different levels in play!

To see the policies applied to a user, run the following command:

```
Get-CsUser -Identity "Test User5"
```

This will output something similar to the following:

```
Identity                  : CN=Test User5,CN=Users,DC=gaots,DC=local
VoicePolicy               :
ConferencingPolicy        :
PresencePolicy            :
DialPlan                  :
LocationPolicy            :
ClientPolicy              : testcsclientpolicy
ClientVersionPolicy       :
ArchivingPolicy           :
PinPolicy                 :
ExternalAccessPolicy      :
HostedVoiceMail           :
HostedVoicemailPolicy     :
HostingProvider           : SRV:
RegistrarPool             : se01.gaots.local
Enabled                   : True
SipAddress                : sip:testuser5@gaots.co.uk
LineURI                   :
EnterpriseVoiceEnabled : False
HomeServer                : CN=Lc Services,CN=Microsoft,CN=1:1,CN=Pools,CN=RTC Ser
                            vice,CN=Services,CN=Configuration,DC=gaots,DC=local
DisplayName               : Test User5
SamAccountName            : testuser5
```

Note that although some of the policies applied are shown, others are not! This is because the only ones shown here are the ones assigned specifically to the user; namely, the `Tag:` policies.

To see all the policies that apply to the user, you need to dig a little deeper and write a fairly serious PowerShell script. Thankfully, the guys at the Lync Server PowerShell Blog have already done that for us. For more information, including the script, take a look here:

`http://blogs.technet.com/b/csps/archive/2010/06/07/scriptuserpolicyassignments.aspx`

Removing or Resetting Policies

With all the experimenting with policies you've done in this chapter, you have probably ended up with lots of policies you don't want! You also may well have changed the settings of the default global policies and, for that matter, other policies as well. So what can be done about that? Well, removing a policy at any of the levels other than global is simple. Use the relevant `Remove-CsXxxPolicy` cmdlet with the identity of the policy as follows:

```
Remove-CsClientVersionPolicy -Identity Site:EMEA
Remove-CsClientVersionPolicy -Identity registrar:se01.gaots.local
Remove-CsClientVersionPolicy -Identity TestDefaultSettings
```

In LSCP removing policies is just as simple; you simply select the relevant policy and then from the Edit drop-down select Delete.

Interestingly, when you remove a policy, you remove the policy but not the assignment to the user. Of course, removing site and service policies automatically removes their assignment, as the identity and assignment are intrinsically linked. It is different for user or Tag policies, as you will see if you run the following `Get-CsUser` command:

```
Get-CsUser -Identity "Test User5"
```

Assuming you have removed one of the previously assigned user policies, you will see that the user still has a reference to that policy although not by name:

```
Policy with identity X (Numerical value based on anchor) has been removed.
```

This essentially shows that the policy can't be found.

WHAT ARE ANCHORS?

An *anchor* is a unique value assigned to each policy of a certain type; the values increase by one each time a policy is created. If you had five policies, they will be anchored 1 through 5. If you delete number 3, then the next policy created will still take number 6, and number 3 will never be reused.

As discussed in the inheritance section, what will happen now is that the next closest policy to the user will take precedence. Although this looks slightly messy, there is no need to take any further steps to clean up.

USER MOVING TO A NEW LOCATION

If a user moves from one place to another and, therefore, needs different policies, you don't need to first remove the policies from the user; you simply apply the new policies in the same way you did before (as discussed previously). The user—and for that matter, the site, service, and global levels—can have only one policy applied at any one time.

Interestingly, if you try to delete the default global policies, Lync won't let you! Essentially, all that happens is that any changes you have made to the Global Policy revert back to the default settings. To try this for yourself, you would use a command like the one below:

```
Remove-CsClientVersionPolicy -Identity global
```

When you run this, you will reset the global CsClientVersionPolicy to its default settings. By way of warning, you will see the following output:

```
WARNING: Global configuration for "ClientVersionPolicy" cannot be removed.
Instead of removing it, the Global configuration for ClientVersionPolicy" has
been reset to the default value.
```

Choosing the Right Policy for the Job

We have looked at the changes in policy architecture in Lync and have seen how policies operate, how they are targeted, and also where Group Policy is still needed. We have also looked at the basics of manipulating policies in Lync. Finally, we will dive in and look at the individual policies and the settings they control.

The first element of examining individual policies is knowing where to view and change those settings. Clearly, LSCP gives access to many policy elements, including the ability to edit and assign policies as well as create and delete them. However, not all policies can be accessed in this way. Table 10.1 lists the elements of LSCP that deal with policies (for example, assigning them to various scopes) and it shows how the settings in LSCP equate to PowerShell cmdlets; it also indicates which chapter of this book covers the related policies.

TABLE 10.1: A Mapping of LSCP Settings to PowerShell Cmdlets

LSCP Tab	LSCP Setting	PowerShell Cmdlet	Notes	Chapter Covered
IM & Presence	File Filter	`CsFileTransferFilter Configuration`		3
IM & Presence	URL Filter	`CsImFilterConfiguration`	Note that the IM Filter Configuration is different from the basic enabling and disabling of hyperlinks that is possible through the CsClientPolicy through the EnableURL setting.	3
Voice Routing	Dial Plan	`CsDialPlan`		13
Voice Routing	Voice Policy	`CsVoicePolicy`		13

Voice Routing	Trunk Configuration	`CsOutboundTranslationRule`
		`CsTrunkConfiguration`
		`CsVoiceRegex`
				13

Conference	Conferencing Policy	`CsConferencingConfiguration`		16
Conference	Meeting Configuration	`CsMeetingConfiguration`		16
Conference	PIN Policy	`CsPinPolicy`	Note this is the same policy defined in the Security tab and controls both Conferencing and Device access	3, 16

LSCP Tab	LSCP Setting	PowerShell Cmdlet	Notes	Chapter Covered
Clients	Client Version Policy	`CsClientVersionPolicy`		3, 10
Clients	Client Version Configuration	`CsClientVersion Configuration`	Allows you to modify the default action for clients not specifically mentioned in the active policy	3
Clients	Device Log Configuration	`CsUCPhoneConfiguration`		4
Clients	Device Configuration	`CsDeviceUpdateConfiguration`		4
External User Access	External Access Policy	`CsExternalAccessPolicy`		4
External User Access	Access Edge Configuration	`CsAccessEdgeConfiguration`	Note this is a global-only setting	4
Monitoring and Archiving	Call Detail Recording	`CsCdrConfiguration`		11
Monitoring and Archiving	Quality of Experience Data	`CsQoEConfiguration`		11
Monitoring and Archiving	Archiving Policy	`CsArchivingPolicy`		11
Monitoring and Archiving	Archiving Configuration	`CsArchivingConfiguration`		11
Security	Registrar	`CsProxyConfiguration`		3
Security	Web Service	`CsWebServiceConfiguration`		3
Security	PIN Policy	`CsPinPolicy`		3, 16
Network Configuration	Global Policy	`CsNetworkConfiguration`		14
Network Configuration	Location Policy	`CsLocationPolicy`		15

What you may notice in Table 10.1 is that there is no mention of the CsClientPolicy, CsPresencePolicy, PrivacyConfiguration, or UserServicesConfiguration. Some of the most far-reaching policies can be changed only through PowerShell. In the rest of this chapter, we will drill into the settings of these polices and any particular quirks of operation related to individual policies.

OTHER POLICY TYPES

There are, of course, many other policy types that we are not covering in this chapter. There are settings for conferences, voice, archiving, and simple URLs among others. Although these policies can all be applied to users, they are applied in the context of specific areas of Lync functionality that are described in other chapters of this book, so we cover the relevant policies settings there, too.

ClientPolicy

The ClientPolicy is manipulated using the `CsClientPolicy` cmdlets. It is this policy that replaces the vast majority of settings that would previously have been set using group policies in OCS 2007 R2. Client policies can be applied at the site or user scope.

It is the ClientPolicy which allows the configuration of such elements as these: MaximumNumberOfContacts, whether to add a disclaimer message to an IM with the IMWarning setting, whether to force saving of IMs in Outlook with the EnableIMAutoArchiving setting, and whether to display a photo with the DisplayPhoto setting.

Of course, there are many more settings available, which are all described in detail in the Lync help file. However, if the setting is not in the default scope, there is a way to make client policies even more flexible. You can use the `New-CsClientPolicyEntry` cmdlet to add additional areas of control to the Lync ClientPolicy. This functionality has to be used in conjunction with Microsoft, who would potentially add the relevant new element to control in a cumulative update as detailed here: `http://technet.microsoft.com/en-us/library/gg399046.aspx`. In the past, this was used to add a method for providing a link to a feedback URL to capture client requests during the beta of Lync 2010.

ClientVersionPolicy

The client version policy is set to ensure control over which different clients can register to a Lync pool. Client version policies are made up of rules that identify specific clients. These rules are defined using the `ClientVersionPolicyRule` cmdlets. Each SIP client sends identifying information in its SIP headers. This identifying information is then matched against the defined rules.

SPOOFING HEADERS

Because clients report their version in an SIP header, it is possible that given a correctly manipulated client, the header could be changed. This would allow a way around the policy. Therefore, you should not think of this as a top security policy—rather, think of it as something that can provide a good consistent service and as a line of defense against casual attackers.

These policies are used to ensure both a consistent user experience and security, by making sure that old, unpatched clients cannot connect to the service.

Client Version policies can be applied at the global, site, service (registrar) and the user scope.

ClientVersionConfiguration

The `ClientVersionConfiguration` cmdlets allow you to control, at either the Global (default) or Site (new policy) level, what happens when clients attempt to connect to Lync. This is where you turn on or off the facility in Lync to check client version. If this policy is enabled, the ClientVersionPolicies apply. The other side to the ClientVersionConfiguration is what happens when Lync denies access to a client. You can use the settings to set the default action if a client version is not specifically noted in a ClientVersionPolicy. You can also configure whether to prompt the user with a URL to get an updated client, if they have a client that is not compliant with the policy.

PrivacyConfiguration

Presence is a great resource; the ability to see whether someone is available can significantly streamline communication. However, some people are not eager to present this information. Lync 2010 introduces a new way of managing this situation, by applying Privacy Configuration settings. The fundamental aim of these settings is giving users control. It allows users to only show their status to those people on their contacts list.

Given that only allowing contacts to see your status is very restrictive, you can help users prepopulate their contacts list with their manager and direct reports, using the `AutoInitiateContacts` setting. Other settings configure Lync to ensure that the user must specifically opt in to sharing photo and location information with others.

Policies can be configured at the global, site, and service scope. At the service scope, it can only be applied to the User Services service.

PresencePolicy

The PresencePolicy controls two settings, the MaxCategorySubscription and the MaxPromptedSubscriber. Presence as a concept is all about providing information about whether someone or something (a group, for example) is available. However, the simple process of providing that information creates network traffic and database load, as all the people who are tracking an object are communicated with and logged. Lync is a fairly efficient system and scales to hundreds of thousands of users; however, if all those users subscribed to a single object, then when it came online or changed status, that would generate hundreds of thousands of messages to let all those users know.

To mitigate this potential flood of network traffic, you can use the settings in the PresencePolicy. The first setting, MaxCategorySubscription, controls the individual types of information that each user can subscribe to—for example, calendar information.

The MaxCategorySubscription property enables you to limit the number of category subscriptions a user can have.

The second setting is the MaxPromptedSubscriber setting. Each time you are added to another user's contacts list, the default Lync behavior is to prompt you with a pop-up that gives you the chance to reciprocate and add the user to your contacts list. Each of these prompts counts as someone subscribed to the requesting user's presence. It is common practice to limit the number of unacknowledged presence subscriptions; this can be done with the MaxPromptedSubscriber property. If a user were to reach the maximum number, she would not receive new contact notifications until some of the outstanding prompts have been acknowledged.

The `CsPresencePolicy` cmdlets can apply at the global, site, or per-user scope.

UserServicesConfiguration

User Services are the services that control the basic settings for maintaining presence for users and also some base meeting settings. The meeting settings cover the length of time an anonymous user can remain in a meeting without an authenticated user, and the maximum time that any meeting can remain active. On the user side, you can set the maximum number of contacts each user can have and the maximum number of meetings that they can schedule.

The UserServicesConfiguration policies are applied at site or service scope. You can also edit the Global policy.

When the UserServicesConfiguration settings and the ClientPolicy settings are in conflict (for example, when different maximum number of contacts per user has been set), the lower number wins.

The Bottom Line

Search for users in the LSCP and PowerShell. Lync offers huge flexibility in what can be done to configure and control the Lync user experience. However, in order to work efficiently in Lync, being able to identify and retrieve information about different groups of users based on various criteria is critical. It is this skill which enables you to target specific groups with specific policies. As with most administration, you can search for users in both LSCP and PowerShell.

Master It You have been asked to run a report on two groups of users. How would you handle the following requests? Can you use two different types of search?

Locate all users in Marketing.

Locate all users who register to the `se01.gaots.local` pool.

Perform basic user administration in the LSCP and in PowerShell. As would be expected, most basic administration can be performed in LSCP and in PowerShell. New users can be created, deleted, enabled, and disabled in both. You can, of course, also change various Lync properties—in particular, things like the SIP URI of a user and the pool to which they register. User administration is generally carried out by a user who is a member of the CsUserAdministrator RBAC role.

Master It You have been asked to enable all users, except those who are in Marketing, for Lync. How would you do this? In addition, one of your colleagues, who is a domain administrator, has asked you to make some changes to his account. What problems might you face?

Understand Lync policies. Lync has significantly improved the policy architecture since OCS 2007 R2. Although AD Group Policy still can have a role to play in getting the Lync client up and running, Lync enforces the majority of policy through in-band provisioning. It uses SIP messages to push policy out to the client instantly and ensures that there is no requirement for domain membership. Users get a consistent experience no matter where they log on. To apply

Lync policies properly, it is important to understand the new scope model, in which polices can be applied at the Global, Site, Service, and User levels and how inheritance works so that the policy closest to the user wins.

Master It You have been asked to explain to a new Lync administrator the different scopes at which a policy can be applied and how different scopes affect the identity of the policy. What would you tell her?

Manipulate Lync policies. Lync policies are controlled and applied to users either through PowerShell or LSCP. When in the shell, your search skills are critical to ensure you can closely target relevant user groups. It is here that the piping capabilities of PowerShell are so useful. You can, of course, also apply policy through LSCP, which has a helpful Assign Policy page where you can apply applicable policies to one or many users from a single screen.

Master It You have been asked to create a new Client Policy for the APAC site. You first need to check the default settings for the policy and then customize it to limit the number of users a person can have on their contacts list to 300. How would you proceed?

Choose the right policy for the job. There are a vast range of policy settings in Lync. One of the hardest things an administrator must do is understand where to make certain configurations. LSCP makes available many policy settings, but it is not always obvious which PowerShell cmdlet sets which setting, compared to what is presented in the LSCP. Equally, it is not possible to carry out all configuration through the LSCP, with some of the most wide-ranging policies only being configured through PowerShell.

Master It You have been asked to design a set of policies for your Lync organization. Where would you gather more information about specific settings?

Chapter 11

Archiving and Monitoring

Any company facing the world of compliance will probably need to account not only for who is IM'ing with whom and when, but also for the content of those messages. This is where the Lync Server 2010 Archiving role comes into play.

Its partner role is the Monitoring role. Monitoring is often associated with service availability up/down reporting capabilities, but the Lync Server 2010 Monitoring role is responsible for the quality-based call monitoring, as well as the Call Detail Records capability normally associated with PBXs. Server (and service) availability monitoring is the responsibility of System Center Operations Manager, and Lync Server 2010 has a management pack available to provide specific service alerting and reporting into System Center.

In this chapter, you will learn to:

- Understand the architecture of the Archiving and Monitoring roles
- Provide reporting on the data available from the Archiving and Monitoring roles
- Use the capabilities in the System Center Operations Manager management pack to report on the availability of the Lync Server 2010 service

Deploying the Architecture for Archiving and Monitoring

Live Communications Server introduced the archiving and CDR capability; however, the Monitoring server role was not available until OCS 2007.

In both LCS (2003 and 2005) and OCS 2007, the archiving database contained the IM logs as well as the CDR data. The monitoring database introduced with OCS 2007 contained only the Quality of Service (QoE) data; however, with the move to OCS 2007 R2, the CDR data was removed from the archiving database and included with the QoE data. This configuration has been maintained with Lync Server 2010; archiving contains only the IM logs, and monitoring includes both CDR and QoE data.

In this chapter, we'll look at the prerequisites required (not just on the Archiving and Monitoring servers, but also the associated front-end servers), the deployment architecture, and the policies required to enable the archiving and monitoring capability for users.

Prerequisites

The Archiving and Monitoring roles both require Microsoft Message Queuing (MSMQ) to be installed, not only on the Archiving or Monitoring role server itself, but also on any front-end server that will be forwarding the captured information. MSMQ is part of the operating system; however, it is not installed by default. With Windows Server 2008 (and R2), MSMQ can be added through the Add Features Wizard of Server Manager.

Figure 11.1 shows the queues created on a front-end server when both Archiving and Monitoring roles are enabled for collection. The Archiving or Monitoring roles aren't enabled specifically; once they are defined in the Topology Builder and associated with a pool, they will be collecting messages.

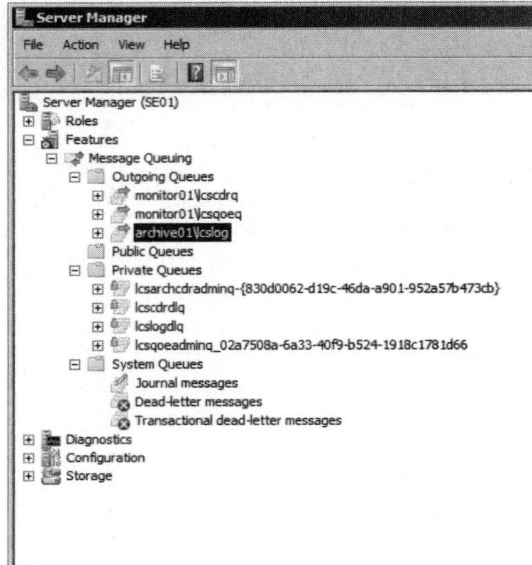

FIGURE 11.1
Message queuing on a front-end server

The queues listed in the Outgoing Queues section of Figure 11.1 correspond to the public queues on the Archiving and Monitoring servers. From this public queue, the archiving (or monitoring) service will take the data and insert it into the relevant SQL database.

Database Support and Architecture

Microsoft recommends you deploy separate instances for each of the archiving and monitoring installations; however, it does support sharing an instance between archiving and monitoring. Typically, separate instances are used when performance of SQL is critical.

The Archiving instance creates a single database called LCSLOG, whereas the Monitoring instance creates two databases, LCSCDR, containing Call Data Record information, and QoEMetrics, containing Quality of Experience information.

Lync Server 2010 also provides more than 40 reports for accessing and reporting on the Quality of Experience data, allowing administrators to help diagnose and troubleshoot call quality problems. You'll see some of these later in this chapter.

Both roles require the 64-bit version of SQL to be used; the monitoring reports pack requires SQL Reporting Services. The following versions of SQL are supported (or later service packs):

- SQL Server 2005 Standard (with SP3)
- SQL Server 2005 Enterprise (with SP3)

- SQL Server 2008 Standard (with SP1)
- SQL Server 2008 Enterprise (with SP1)
- SQL Server 2008 R2 Standard
- SQL Server 2008 R2 Enterprise

Role Colocation and Capacity

Not only does Microsoft support colocating the databases in the same instance, but it also supports colocating both roles on the same server. In addition, these roles can be colocated with the SQL database server (assuming SQL Server is not clustered), or in the case where SQL is deployed on a separate server, both roles may be colocated with a Standard Edition Lync 2010 server.

Table 11.1 shows the capacity figures based on colocation.

TABLE 11.1: Capacity Figures for Archiving and Monitoring Colocation

ROLE	CAPACITY	COLOCATION STATE
Archiving	500,000	SQL server only
Monitoring	250,000	SQL server only
Both	100,000	Both roles and SQL server

Either (or both) roles can support multiple pools and multiple sites.

High Availability

Currently, there is no high availability solution for the Archiving or Monitoring roles; however, if there is a failure in the message delivery chain (shown in Figure 11.2), the MSMQ messages will continue to queue until either the queue becomes available, the local MSMQ storage is exhausted, or the MSMQ message timer expires.

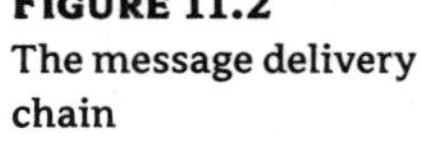

FIGURE 11.2 The message delivery chain

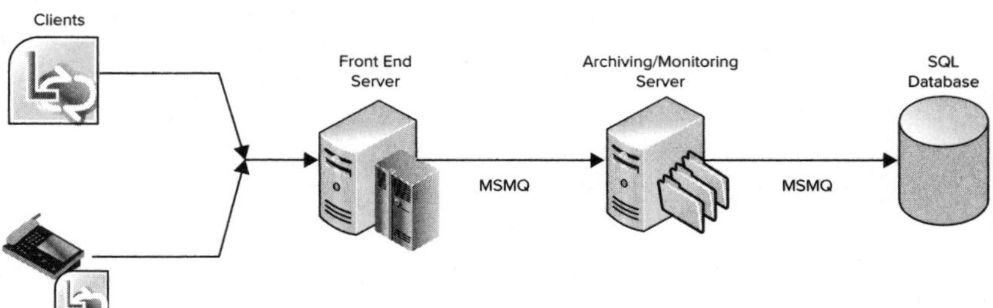

Local MSMQ storage is 1GB by default and can be increased by modifying the properties of the Message Queuing feature within Server Manager (as shown in Figure 11.3).

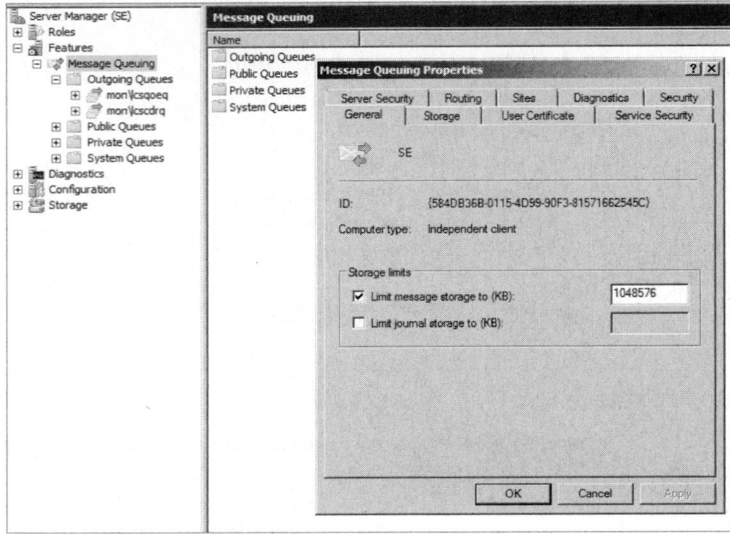

FIGURE 11.3
Modification of the MSMQ storage limit

Policy Configuration

The Archiving and Monitoring configuration is defined in the same location within the Control Panel application, as shown in Figure 11.4.

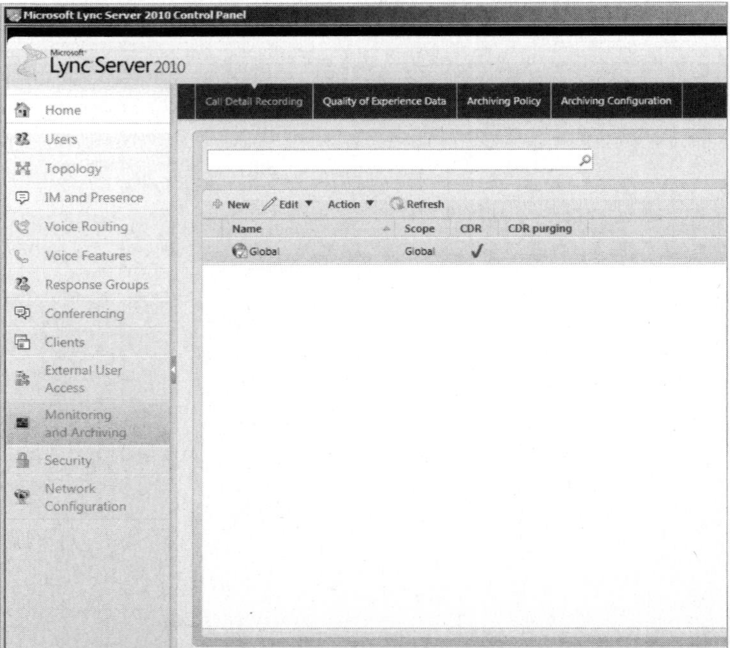

FIGURE 11.4
The Archiving and Monitoring Configuration menu

Both Call Detail Recording and Quality of Experience Data have the same options:

- Scope
- Enabled
- Purging
- Number of days for data to be kept (if purging is enabled)

To define the CDR policy using PowerShell, enter this command:

```
New-CsCdrConfiguration -Identity site:London -EnableCDR $true -EnablePurging
$true -KeepCallDetailForDays 30 -KeepErrorReportForDays 30 -PurgeHourOfDay 3
```

To configure the QoE data, use the `New-CsQoeConfiguration` cmdlet.

The `PurgeHourOfDay` parameter allows you to customize when the old data will be purged. Common sense suggests that you define this outside normal office hours; however, other operations (such as backups) may occur at the default time (02:00 AM), and you may find it useful to change this.

Archiving can be enabled for internal and/or external communications. You can define additional policies to allow this distinction to be made on a per-user or per-site basis if required.

The `New-CsArchivingConfiguation` cmdlet provides the options shown in Table 11.2 to configure the actual policy (using `New-CsArchivingPolicy`).

TABLE 11.2: Archiving Configuration Cmdlet Parameters

PARAMETER	DEFAULT	NOTES
`ArchiveDuplicateMessages`	True	Used when dealing with cross-pool messages. If set to True, the message will be archived once per pool of users involved. If False, it will be archived only once.
`BlockOnArchiveFailure`	False	If set to True, IMs will be refused if there are any issues with the archiving service. False enables message flow to continue in the event of problems.
`CarchPurginInternal`	24	Defines how often the system cache is purged of messages when none of the participants are enabled for archiving.
`EnableArchiving`	None	Specifies what is archived: None ImOnly ImAndWebConf
`EnablePurging`	False	If set to True, messages will be removed from the database if older than the value specified in `KeepArchivingDataForDays`. If False, messages are not removed.

TABLE 11.2: Archiving Configuration Cmdlet Parameters *(CONTINUED)*

PARAMETER	DEFAULT	NOTES
KeepArchivingDataForDays	14	Number of days that messages are kept for (between 1 and 2,562, approximately 7 years)
PurgeExportedArchivesOnly	False	If True, only messages that have been exported will be purged (overrides KeepArchivingDataForDays value).
PurgeHourOfDay	2	Time value (hour only) when the data purging will occur.

A common archiving requirement is for compliance purposes, and typically it requires data to be kept for more than the default 14-day period. To create a new policy configuration with a one-year retention period, use the following command:

```
New-CsArchivingConfiguration -Identity site:EMEA -KeepArchivingDataForDays 365
-EnableArchiving ImAndWebConf
```

If the Archiving role has not yet been deployed, a warning will appear to remind the administrator that enabling archiving requires the Archiving server role to be deployed.

Using `Get-CsArchivingConfiguration` will return the following data for our new policy configuration:

```
Identity                  : Site:EMEA
EnableArchiving           : ImAndWebConf
EnablePurging             : False
PurgeExportedArchivesOnly : False
BlockOnArchiveFailure     : False
KeepArchivingDataForDays  : 365
PurgeHourofDay            : 2
ArchiveDuplicateMessages  : True
CachePurgingInterval      : 24
```

To apply this configuration as a policy, you need to create an associated policy using the `New-CsArchivingPolicy` cmdlet; this will allow you to define whether the configuration applies to internal or external (or both) types of communication.

```
New-CsArchivingPolicy -Identity 1-year-external -ArchiveExternal  $True
```

Here, you have created a user policy with only external archiving enabled.

Using `Get-CsArchivingPolicy` will display the following configuration:

```
Identity        : Tag:1-year-external
Description     :
ArchiveInternal : False
ArchiveExternal : True
```

Given that you created a site-based policy configuration and a user-based policy, when you assign the user-based policy to users (with the `Grant-CsArchivingPolicy` cmdlet) this specific site policy will take effect only when users are part of the EMEA site; for locations outside of EMEA, the global policy is in effect with the default values.

Deploying the Reporting Pack

The Quality of Experience(QoE) data can be complicated, but Microsoft has provided a pack of over 40 built-in reports to help you understand the data captured. They range from simple usage and trending reports to detailed troubleshooting reports.

They are deployed into a SQL Reporting Services instance, using the Deployment Wizard setup application (shown in Figure 11.5).

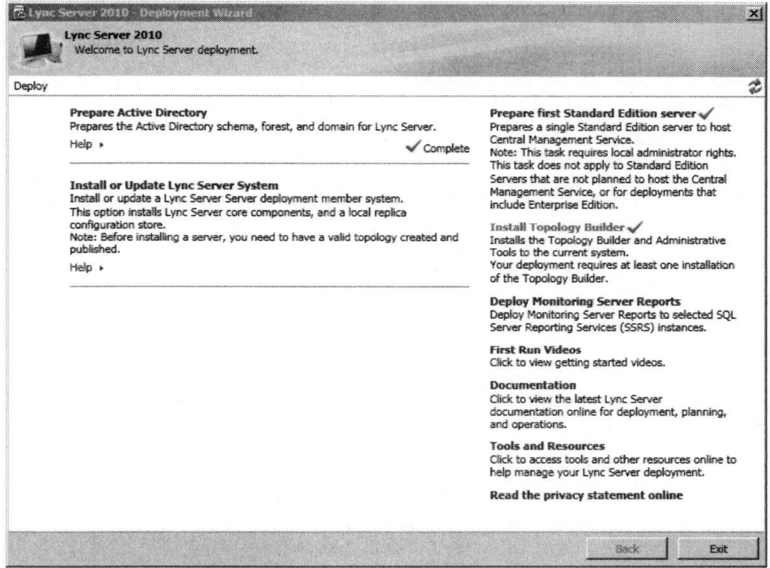

FIGURE 11.5
The Deployment Wizard allows you to deploy Monitoring server reports

Once you select Deploy Monitoring Server Reports, the Deployment Wizard prompts you for the following information:

- Monitoring Server
- SQL Server Reporting Services Instance
- SQL Server Account credentials (for use by the SQL Reporting Services)
- User Group (to provide Read-Only access to the reports)

By default, the wizard will attempt to create a secure web page on which to publish the reports (shown in the link on the home page of the Control Panel); however, you don't have to install a certificate on this website, and you can access it without deploying a certificate if required. In that case, you will manually enter the website address and not link it from the Control Panel home page.

Unfortunately, the Reporting Pack covers only the monitoring server databases (CDR and QOE); from an IM perspective, the best information that can be retrieved from this is the fact that two users had an IM conversation. The contents of that conversation (assuming archiving is enabled) are stored in the Archiving server database (LCSLog), which does not have any associated Reporting Pack.

Access to this data is via a SQL query, which, providing the user has the correct permissions, can be achieved using any product that supports Open Database Connectivity (ODBC) to retrieve and then manipulate the data. The actual IM conversation is held in Rich Text Format (RTF), which may require further manipulation before it is readable.

Archiving for Compliance

The Archiving server role is not compliant with many of the regulatory compliance standards found throughout the globe, such as MoReq, UK Companies Act, Sarbanes-Oxley, HIPAA, FSA, and so on.

A copy of the IM data is stored in the SQL database. However, no further controls are in place to protect that data; any user with the appropriate permissions can get to the data and change it, with no record whatsoever of the access or change made. In addition, file transfers are not stored with the conversation transcript for easy recovery, and content from Group Chat channels is put in a separate repository.

To provide this level of compliance, you are required to use a product such as Vantage from Actiance (`http://actiance.com/products/vantage.aspx`).

Vantage installs an agent on each front-end server and, as in the MSMQ approach from Microsoft, the agent captures the data and sends it to a Vantage server for processing, and then onward to a SQL Server repository. This repository is tamper-proof, ensuring message and conversation integrity.

As well as providing a compliant repository, Vantage has a built-in capability for IM reporting, both from a system administrator perspective (for policy setting) and a reviewer perspective (for eDiscovery and regulatory compliance reviews).

In addition to the compliance aspect of Vantage, it has other useful features, which either augment existing Lync 2010 features or provide new control capabilities such as:

- Central policy-based logging and analytics.
- Global, group, inter-group or user-based controls.
- Authentication and Authorization. For example, ethical boundaries can be configured to stop users within the same organization from communicating with each other, as well as provide granular control over federation.
- Antivirus and Antimalware controls. For example, integration with several popular anti-virus scanning engines.
- Keyword and regular expression triggers to block or alert on content.
- Granular SpIM (spam over IM) and URL blocking controls (including the ability to customize rules).
- Control over legal disclaimer (including the ability to customize disclaimers).
- File transfer capture—that is, it captures complete file data, not just the name.
- Comprehensive analytics engine to show—for example, the volume of Lync usage by users.

The following Transcript Search is an example of the reporting capabilities from Vantage:

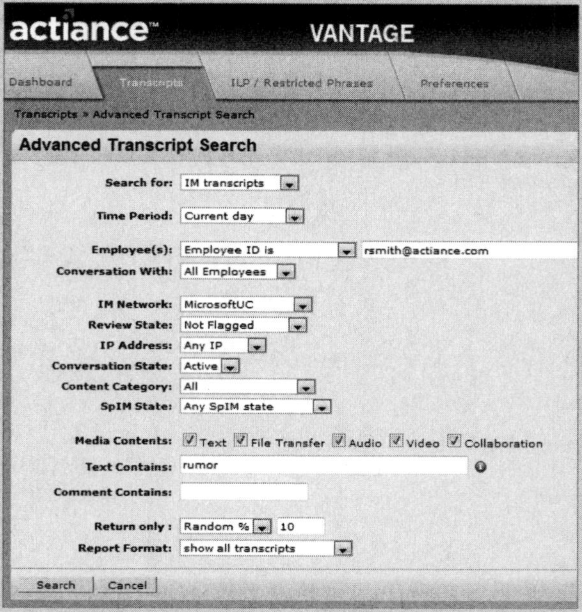

actiance™ VANTAGE

Dashboard | Transcripts | ILP / Restricted Phrases | Preferences

Transcripts » Advanced Transcript Search

Advanced Transcript Search

Search for: IM transcripts
Time Period: Current day
Employee(s): Employee ID is rsmith@actiance.com
Conversation With: All Employees
IM Network: MicrosoftUC
Review State: Not Flagged
IP Address: Any IP
Conversation State: Active
Content Category: All
SpIM State: Any SpIM state
Media Contents: Text File Transfer Audio Video Collaboration
Text Contains: rumor
Comment Contains:
Return only : Random % 10
Report Format: show all transcripts

Search | Cancel

Interpreting the Monitoring Server Reports

Data is useless unless it can be interpreted and understood; the data provided by the Monitoring Reporting Pack is extremely rich and can be used in a number of ways:

- Troubleshooting
- Trend analysis for future capacity planning
- Usage analysis for Return on Investment (ROI) calculations

This section will cover the metrics used and how to interpret them as well as provide details on the reports available.

Understanding Voice Quality

Before delving into the details about the reports and how to interpret them, you really need to understand how voice quality is measured and what steps are taken to ensure that quality is retained throughout the call even when outside events impact that quality.

Some of the key metrics measured per call are listed here:

- Endpoint IP address
- Endpoint subnet

- Internal/External connectivity
- Codec used
- Network connectivity type (wired versus wireless)
- Link speed
- Any bandwidth restrictions applied (due to Call Admission Control)
- Signal level send
- Signal level receive
- Echo
- Device CPU
- Device driver/firmware versions
- Packet loss
- Round trip time
- Latency
- Jitter
- Burst
- Listening MOS
- Sending MOS
- Network MOS
- Audio healer metrics

Individually, these metrics may report values that would be considered "good"; in spite of that, however, the call may still be considered poor quality, because often it is the combination of many of the metrics together that result in a poor call. For example, latency, jitter, roundtrip time, and packet loss may individually be within tolerances; however, the combination of packets being dropped along with packets that do arrive but are late will likely create problems on the call from which the healing metrics are unable to recover.

Mean Opinion Score (MOS)

Traditional telephony provides a subjective assessment of voice quality, based on a scale of 1 to 5, with 5 being perfect and 1 being very poor. A typical PSTN call will rate 2.95 on this scale.

The scoring is carried out by a group of testers listening to an output signal and rating it. This is where the subjective nature of the assessment comes in. It is up to the individual to mark the score, and the average is provided as the final rating.

Because this is a subjective rating, the results can vary from one test to another. Lync Server 2010 uses an objective approach, where the output signal is compared to a model to predict the perceived quality, in a similar way to the Perceptual Evaluation of Speech Quality (PESQ) standard. As previously mentioned, there are four types of MOS value.

LISTENING QUALITY MOS

This value is commonly used in VoIP deployments, but it does not consider bidirectional effects such as delay or echo. The following three metrics are wideband MOS-LQ scores:

- Network MOS
- Listening MOS
- Sending MOS

CONVERSATIONAL QUALITY MOS

This value considers the quality on both ends and includes bidirectional effects such as delay and echo. There is one narrowband MOS-CQ score in Lync Server 2010, Conversational MOS.

NETWORK MOS

The Network MOS value takes into account only network-related factors (packet loss, jitter, and so on) and can be used to identify network conditions that impact audio quality.

LISTENING MOS

The listening MOS value is a prediction of the wideband quality of an audio stream being played to a user; it considers the output aspects of the device, as well as codec, transcoding, speech level, and background noise. Problems encountered with the sound output will be identified within Listening MOS.

SENDING MOS

Sending MOS is the counterpart to Listening MOS, and it is a prediction of the wideband quality of an audio stream being *sent* by a user. It deals with the input levels of the signal, considering the same aspects as Listening MOS. Both Listening and Sending MOS problems typically highlight device issues.

CONVERSATIONAL MOS

In addition to those aspects considered by Listening and Sending MOS, Conversational MOS also takes into account those bidirectional aspects such as echo and delay.

MOS Values by Codec

Being able to understand the different areas of impact in a call will help you narrow down the problem; if one user reports problems hearing a call, but another user reports all is well, it can suggest that you should start investigating the Listening MOS and the values associated there. What about comparing calls with each other?

Well, it's extremely difficult to replicate network conditions at any given time; starting with a comparison between the different expectations by codec is useful (shown in Table 11.3).

TABLE 11.3: MOS Value by Codec

CALL TYPE	CODEC USED	MAX NETWORK MOS
Media Bypass	G711	4.30
UC-UC	RTAudio (wideband)	4.10
UC-PSTN	RTAudio (narrowband)	2.95
UC-PSTN	SIREN	3.72
Conference Call	G722	4.30
Conference Call	SIREN	3.72

COMPARING CALLS BY CODEC

It is not feasible to compare two calls simply by the codec used to determine which was "better." Because both calls are inherently different, based not only on their own attributes but also the state of the network at the time of the calls, it is impossible to re-create the same conditions to allow any sort of comparison.

A much better approach to comparing calls is to evaluate how much each call has degraded, almost like determining the "least worst" call.

By taking this approach, you can determine which call has been impacted most by the network conditions and establish which has been degraded the most.

Viewing the Reports

Lync Server 2010 offers several improvements to Office Communications Server 2007 R2, including an increase in the number of available reports, tooltips, and color highlighting. (Highlighted text is visible when the mouse is hovered over text. It ensures that potential issues are visible to the reader and easily understood.) Some diagnostic reports are generated only when there is enough data to be worthwhile. For example, problematic-server quality reports are available only on the dashboard when more than 30 data points have been captured.

By default the Reporting Pack is installed at the following location (reachable via a web browser):

```
Http:<SQL server name>:80/ReportServer_<SQL instance name>
```

There are two top-level report types:

Dashboard Provides a weekly or monthly snapshot of the state of the environment, allowing an administrator to quickly see trends in both user usage and hotspots for problems. Each report is a hyperlink to the next level of detail. Figure 11.6 shows the weekly dashboard.

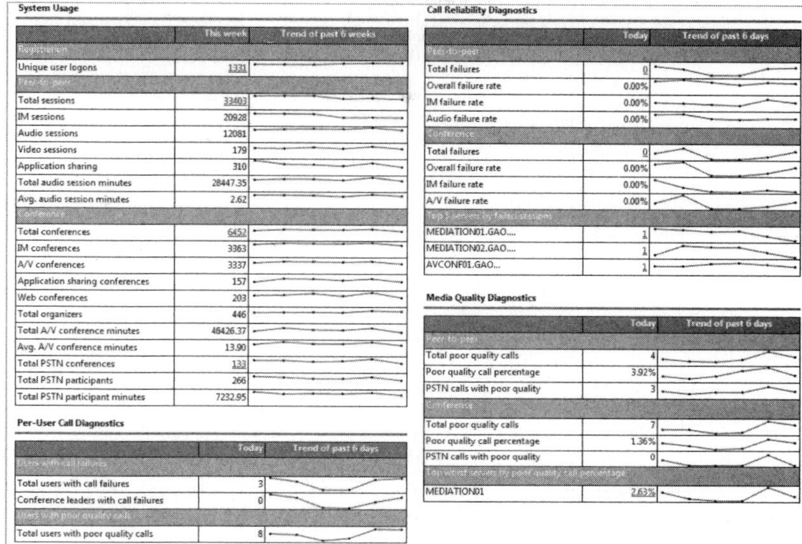

System Usage

	This week	Trend of past 6 weeks
Registration		
Unique user logons	1331	
Peer-to-peer		
Total sessions	33403	
IM sessions	20928	
Audio sessions	12081	
Video sessions	179	
Application sharing	310	
Total audio session minutes	28447.35	
Avg. audio session minutes	2.62	
Conference		
Total conferences	6452	
IM conferences	3363	
A/V conferences	3337	
Application sharing conferences	157	
Web conferences	203	
Total organizers	446	
Total A/V conference minutes	46426.37	
Avg. A/V conference minutes	13.90	
Total PSTN conferences	133	
Total PSTN participants	266	
Total PSTN participant minutes	7232.95	

Per-User Call Diagnostics

	Today	Trend of past 6 days
Users with call failures		
Total users with call failures	3	
Conference leaders with call failures	0	
Users with poor quality calls		
Total users with poor quality calls	8	

Call Reliability Diagnostics

	Today	Trend of past 6 days
Peer-to-peer		
Total failures	0	
Overall failure rate	0.00%	
IM failure rate	0.00%	
Audio failure rate	0.00%	
Conference		
Total failures	0	
Overall failure rate	0.00%	
IM failure rate	0.00%	
A/V failure rate	0.00%	
Top 5 servers by failed sessions		
MEDIATION01.GAO....	1	
MEDIATION02.GAO....	1	
AVCONF01.GAO...	1	

Media Quality Diagnostics

	Today	Trend of past 6 days
Peer-to-peer		
Total poor quality calls	4	
Poor quality call percentage	3.92%	
PSTN calls with poor quality	3	
Conference		
Total poor quality calls	7	
Poor quality call percentage	1.36%	
PSTN calls with poor quality	0	
Top worst servers by poor quality call percentage		
MEDIATION01	2.63%	

FIGURE 11.6
Weekly dashboard report

Reporting Provides the same types of reports; however, they can be customized based on date ranges or targeted to specific pools or locations.

The reports can be loosely grouped into four categories:

- System Usage
- Per-user Call Diagnostics
- Call Reliability Diagnostics
- Media Quality Diagnostics

Each of the reports can be further expanded by clicking on the built-in hyperlinks in the report to drill further into the details behind the numbers. Figure 11.7 shows the Reporting page.

FIGURE 11.7
Reports Home page

Microsoft Lync Server 2010

Monitoring Server Reports

Dashboard | Help
Version : 4.0.7577.0

System Usage Reports

User Registration Report
Peer-to-Peer Activity Summary Report
Conference Summary Report
PSTN Conference Summary Report
Response Group Usage Report
IP Phone Inventory Report
Call Admission Control Report

Call Diagnostic Reports (per-user)

User Activity Report

Call Diagnostic Reports

Call Diagnostic Summary Report
Peer-to-Peer Activity Diagnostic Report
Conference Diagnostic Report
Top Failures Report
Failure Distribution Report

Media Quality Diagnostic Reports

Media Quality Summary Report
Server Performance Report
Location Report
Device Report

System Usage Reports

Within this section, you will find reports used for trend-based analysis, showing the number of connections and typical system usage.

User Registration Report This report will provide an at-a-glance view of user login information broken into the following categories:

- ◆ Total logons
- ◆ Internal logons
- ◆ External logons
- ◆ Unique logon users
- ◆ Unique active users

By default, this returns both tabular and graphical format broken down on a daily total for all pools; however, this breakdown and pool selection can be modified if required.

Peer-to-Peer Activity Summary Report The Activity Summary Report provides the total breakdown of sessions (the default is daily), for the following communications types:

- ◆ Total peer-to-peer sessions
- ◆ Total peer-to-peer IM sessions
- ◆ Total peer-to-peer IM messages
- ◆ Total peer-to-peer audio sessions
- ◆ Total peer-to-peer audio minutes
- ◆ Average peer-to-peer audio session minutes
- ◆ Total peer-to-peer video sessions
- ◆ Total peer-to-peer video minutes
- ◆ Average peer-to-peer video session minutes
- ◆ Total peer-to-peer file transfer sessions
- ◆ Total peer-to-peer application sharing sessions

Figure 11.8 shows a sample section of this report, with a breakdown of peer-to-peer sessions: Total, Audio, and IM only on the top graph; with video, file transfer, and application sharing shown on the bottom graph. At this level, you're simply looking at the trend and, as expected, there is minimal traffic over the weekend; however, the various modalities show different peaks.

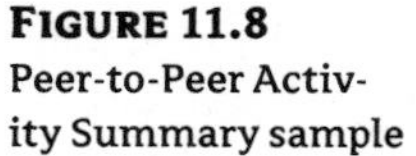

FIGURE 11.8
Peer-to-Peer Activity Summary sample

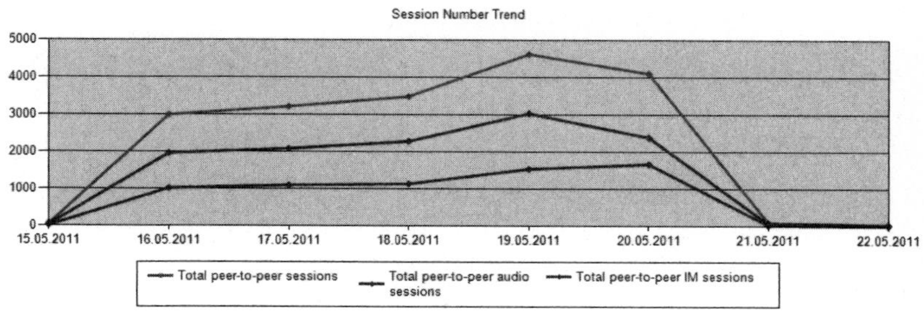

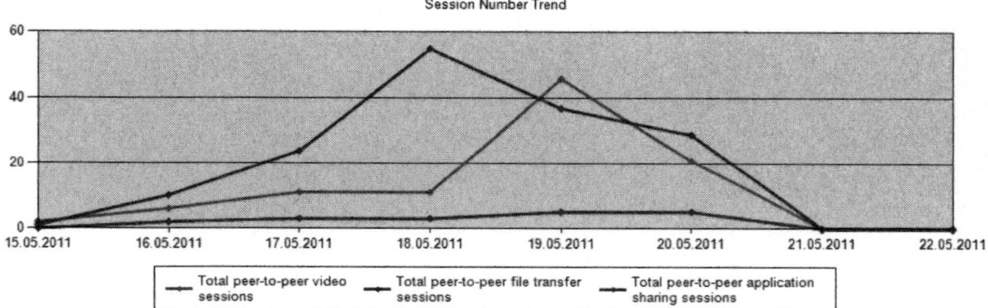

Conference Summary Report Similar to the Peer-to-Peer Activity Report, the Conference Summary Report provides an insight into the conferencing statistics, with the following data reported (default daily):

- Total conferences
- Total participants
- Avg participants per conference
- Total A/V conferences
- Total A/V conference minutes
- Total A/V conference participant minutes
- Avg A/V conference minutes
- Total unique conference organizers
- Total conference messages

Within these reports, drilling into the detail also shows the conference type, either Audio/Video or Application Sharing.

Figure 11.9 shows a snapshot of the more detailed Conference Activity Report, which is reached via the Conference Summary Report, when selecting a specific day to view the conference breakdown. This detailed report goes on to break down the different conference types, connection types, and connection locations.

FIGURE 11.9 Conference Activity Report

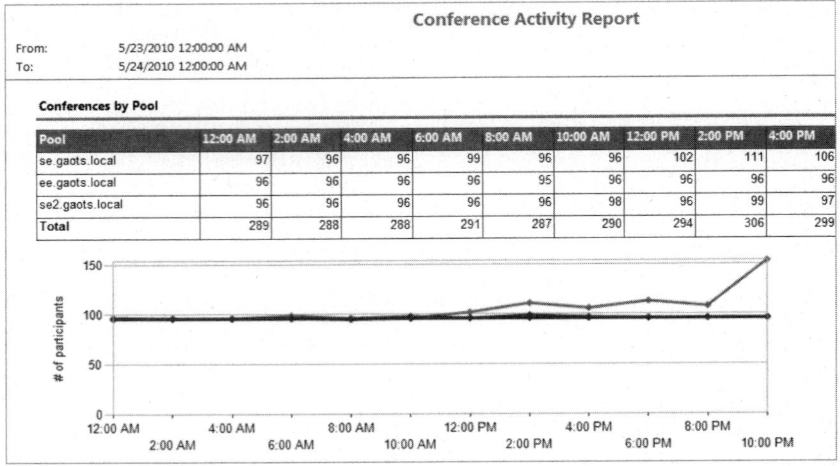

Conference Activity Report

From: 5/23/2010 12:00:00 AM
To: 5/24/2010 12:00:00 AM

Conferences by Pool

Pool	12:00 AM	2:00 AM	4:00 AM	6:00 AM	8:00 AM	10:00 AM	12:00 PM	2:00 PM	4:00 PM
se.gaots.local	97	96	96	99	96	96	102	111	106
ee.gaots.local	96	96	96	96	95	96	96	96	96
se2.gaots.local	96	96	96	96	96	98	96	99	97
Total	289	288	288	291	287	290	294	306	299

PSTN Conference Summary Report The PSTN Conference Report provides a view of the conferences that includes PSTN dial-in participants and shows the following:

- Total PSTN conferences
- Total participants
- Total A/V conference minutes
- Total A/V conference participant minutes
- Total PSTN participants
- Total PSTN participant minutes
- Unique conference organizers

Response Group Usage Report This report provides a view of the number of calls being placed to the response group service, and how they are being answered. The following fields are provided in the initial report:

- Received calls
- Successful calls
- Offered calls
- Answered calls
- Percentage of abandoned calls
- Average call minutes by agent
- Transferred calls

IP Phone Inventory Report This report provides a view of the deployed phone hardware devices in the environment, specifically:

- Manufacturer
- Hardware version
- MAC address
- User URI
- User agent
- Last logon time
- Last logoff time
- Last activity

Call Admission Control Report This report (shown in Figure 11.10) provides a detailed view of how many calls are being rerouted or rejected based on the policy settings, as well as a breakdown of the information per location.

A Diagnostic value of 5 indicates a call has been rerouted via the PSTN.

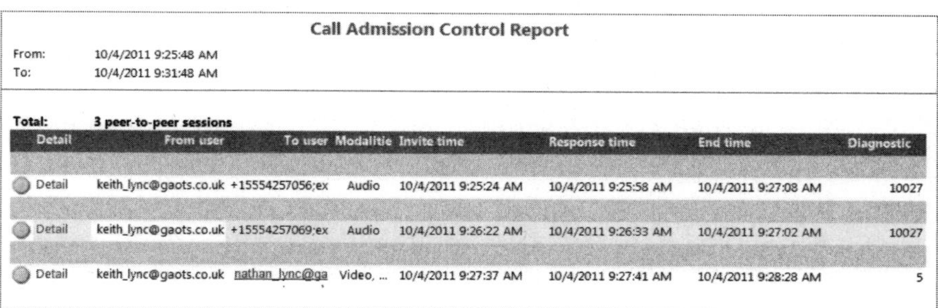

Call Admission Control Report

From: 10/4/2011 9:25:48 AM
To: 10/4/2011 9:31:48 AM

Total: 3 peer-to-peer sessions

Detail	From user	To user	Modalitie	Invite time	Response time	End time	Diagnostic
Detail	keith_lync@gaots.co.uk	+15554257056;ex	Audio	10/4/2011 9:25:24 AM	10/4/2011 9:25:58 AM	10/4/2011 9:27:08 AM	10027
Detail	keith_lync@gaots.co.uk	+15554257069;ex	Audio	10/4/2011 9:26:22 AM	10/4/2011 9:26:33 AM	10/4/2011 9:27:02 AM	10027
Detail	keith_lync@gaots.co.uk	nathan_lync@ga	Video, ...	10/4/2011 9:27:37 AM	10/4/2011 9:27:41 AM	10/4/2011 9:28:28 AM	5

FIGURE 11.10 Call Admission Control Report

CALL ADMISSION CONTROL REPORTING

Over time, understanding the impact of Call Admission Control is important. If the values are set too high, then potentially the network is overspecified and costs may be reduced by decreasing the capacity. On the other hand, it's more likely that Call Admission Control will reject or re-route calls. If a significant number are reported, this may indicate that Call Admission Control is configured too low. In parallel to this, if the network is nearing capacity, it is an indication that the network is under pressure and bandwidth may need to be increased. See Chapter 14, "Call Admission Control," for more information.

CALL DIAGNOSTICS REPORTS (PER-USER)

This report is targeted at help desk staff, and it is used for analysis of activity based on a specific user. The following fields are provided:

- From User
- To User
- Modalities
- Response Time
- End Time
- Diagnostic ID

CALL DIAGNOSTICS REPORTS

The diagnostics reports are most likely to be of interest to network and server administrators; these are the reports that tell you what is going wrong and what needs to be fixed. Within this section, you'll see values such as Expected Failures and Unexpected Failures. Expected Failures are items such as a caller hanging up, or no answer, unless there are a significant number of these events, they can typically be ignored. Unexpected Failures are the ones that typically need to be investigated and corrected.

This is the section of reporting that has had the biggest change compared to Office Communications Server 2007 R2.

Call Diagnostics Summary Report This diagnostics report covers both peer-to-peer sessions and conferences. A breakdown is provided showing the following data:

- Total Sessions
- Failure Rate
- Session Count by Modality (IM, app share, audio, video, file transfer)
- Failure Rate by Modality

Peer-to-Peer Activity Diagnostic Report The Peer-to-Peer Diagnostics Report focuses only on the peer-to-peer aspect, and it provides a daily breakdown of sessions and failures further broken down by modality. The report shows the following data fields (summary and per modality):

- Date
- Success
- Expected Failure
- Unexpected Failure
- Total Sessions

Conference Diagnostic Report Unsurprisingly, the Conference Diagnostic Report provides the same view as the Peer-To-Peer Diagnostic Report, but for conferences.

Top Failures Report This report covers the top failures based on Reported Sessions, also providing the number of users impacted and the weekly trend of a particular failure over the previous eight weeks. Each specific failure item provides the following data in the failure information field:

- Request Type
- Response
- Diagnostic ID
- Category
- Component
- Reason
- Description

This information provides the administrator with a great starting point to begin troubleshooting. Figure 11.11 shows the failure information and trend volume graph for a specific failure item.

Based on this report, the admin would know that the gateway in question is suffering from a relatively steady number of failures before experiencing a sudden peak at the end of the week. This may correlate to a matching increase in call volume, suggesting the actual failure rate is steady; however, the specific error shown in this case (Unexpected - 500 - Server Internal Error) suggests an issue that needs to be resolved by taking some action. Because it refers to a gateway, this may be faulty hardware or firmware. In this case, further investigation is needed on the gateway itself to determine the cause and resolution.

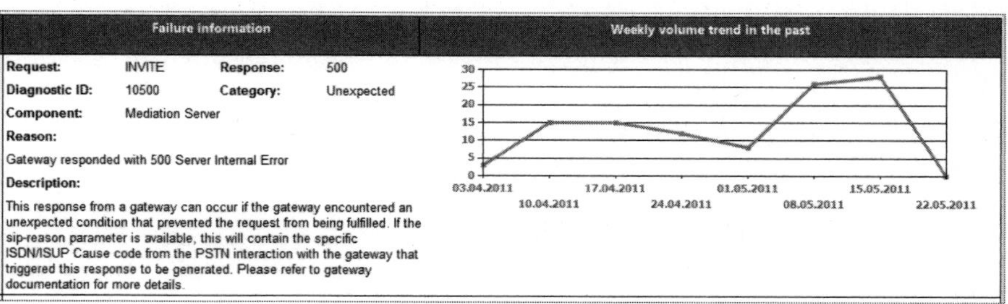

FIGURE 11.11
Top Failures Report

Failure Distribution Report The Failure Distribution Report provides an overview of the top 10 items on each of the following lists:

- Session Distribution by Top Diagnostic Reasons
- Session Distribution by Top Modalities
- Session Distribution by Top Pools
- Session Distribution by Top Sources

- ◆ Session Distribution by Top Components
- ◆ Session Distribution by Top From Users
- ◆ Session Distribution by Top To Users
- ◆ Session Distribution by Top From User Agents

Figure 11.12 shows a sample section from this report. Based on this section, the admin would know that the majority of failures are due to issues with at least one gateway. This is a summary section showing the total of each error type; however, each diagnostic reason is a hyperlink to further break down the issues allowing specific gateways to be identified.

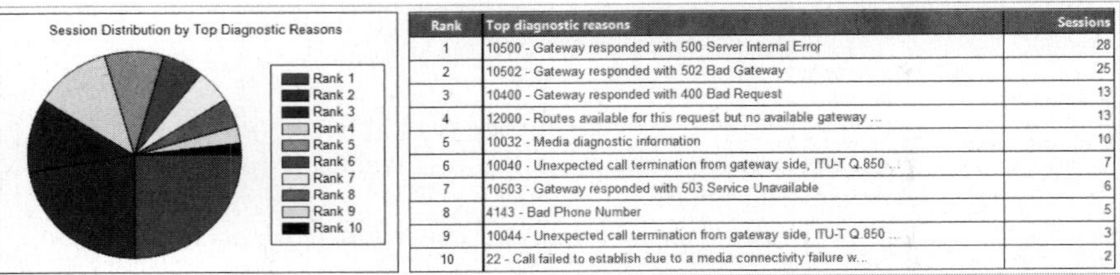

Rank	Top diagnostic reasons	Sessions
1	10500 - Gateway responded with 500 Server Internal Error	28
2	10502 - Gateway responded with 502 Bad Gateway	25
3	10400 - Gateway responded with 400 Bad Request	13
4	12000 - Routes available for this request but no available gateway ...	13
5	10032 - Media diagnostic information	10
6	10040 - Unexpected call termination from gateway side, ITU-T Q.850 ...	7
7	10503 - Gateway responded with 503 Service Unavailable	6
8	4143 - Bad Phone Number	5
9	10044 - Unexpected call termination from gateway side, ITU-T Q.850 ...	3
10	22 - Call failed to establish due to a media connectivity failure w...	2

FIGURE 11.12 Session Distribution by Top Diagnostic Reasons Report

MEDIA QUALITY DIAGNOSTICS REPORTS

The final section on the reports' home page deals with call quality and diagnostics. These reports provide good information on how the individual components are coping in the environment, such as servers, devices, and network locations.

Media Quality Summary Report This report provides the quality view of the different endpoints, broken down by the following categories:

- ◆ UC Peer to Peer
- ◆ UC Conference Sessions
- ◆ PSTN Conference Sessions
- ◆ PSTN calls (non-bypass): UC Leg
- ◆ PSTN calls (non-bypass): Gateway Leg
- ◆ Other Call Types

Each of these categories is further broken down by specific software versions of the client or device.

For each combination entry, the following data is displayed:

- ◆ Endpoint type
- ◆ Call volume
- ◆ Poor call percentage

- Call volume (wireless call)
- Call volume (VPN call)
- Call volume (external call)
- Round trip (ms)
- Degradation (MOS)
- Packet loss
- Jitter (ms)
- Healer concealed ratio
- Healer stretched ratio
- Healer compressed ratio

CODEC HEALING

The implementation of the media codecs in Lync 2010 allows healing aspects within them.

These healing capabilities enable the codec to recover from missed or delayed packets, in effect *healing* the media, so that in most cases the user will be unaware of the missing packets because the call will continue and the problems will be undetectable.

- High values in *healer concealed ratio* will typically result in distorted or lost audio. This is typically due to packet loss or jitter.
- High values in *healer stretched ratio* will typically result in distorted or robotic sounding audio. This is typically caused by jitter.
- High values in *healer concealed ratio* will typically result in distorted or accelerated sounding audio. This is typically caused by jitter.

Server Performance Report The Server Performance Report provides insight into the performance of the individual server roles and gateways. It provides data similar to that of the Media Quality Summary Report:

- Server
- Call volume
- Poor call percentage
- Round trip (ms)
- Degradation (MOS)
- Packet loss
- Jitter (ms)

- Healer concealed ratio
- Healer stretched ratio
- Healer compressed ratio

In addition, an option to view the data trended for the previous week is provided for each server role or gateway.

Location Report Whereas the previous two reports look at the breakdown per endpoint, this report looks at the network viewpoint and shows per subnet (caller and callee).

The following data is provided:

- Caller subnet
- Callee subnet
- Call volume
- Poor call percentage
- Round trip (ms)
- Degradation (MOS)
- Packet loss
- Jitter (ms)
- Healer concealed ratio
- Healer stretched ratio
- Healer compressed ratio

Device Report The Device Report looks at the specific hardware device model or individual drivers used by the operating system to provide a view on the data. This can provide a useful view of which noncertified devices are being used in the environment, or more likely which calls are being made using built-in devices.

The following view is provided of the data:

- Capture device
- Render device
- Call volume
- Poor call percentage
- Unique users
- Ratio of voice switch time
- Ratio of microphone not functioning
- Ratio of speaker not functioning

- Call with voice switch (%)
- Echo in microphone (%)
- Echo send (%)
- Calls with echo (%)

The Call Detail Report

As mentioned, many of these reports link through to other reports, each of which reduces the scope and provides more detailed data resulting in the Call Detail Report, which provides a full breakdown of all the interaction and statistics of the call.

There is no direct method to access this report, as it deals with a single call only and, therefore, the data must be filtered in some method first. The quickest route to get call details is to use the User Activity Report to filter on a specific user and then to select the detail of a specific call.

We will discuss the usefulness of this report in Chapter 12, "Troubleshooting"; however, an example section is shown in Figure 11.13 (note that the "Call Information" section is closed in the screenshot). This report is also known as the Peer-to-Peer Session Detail Report.

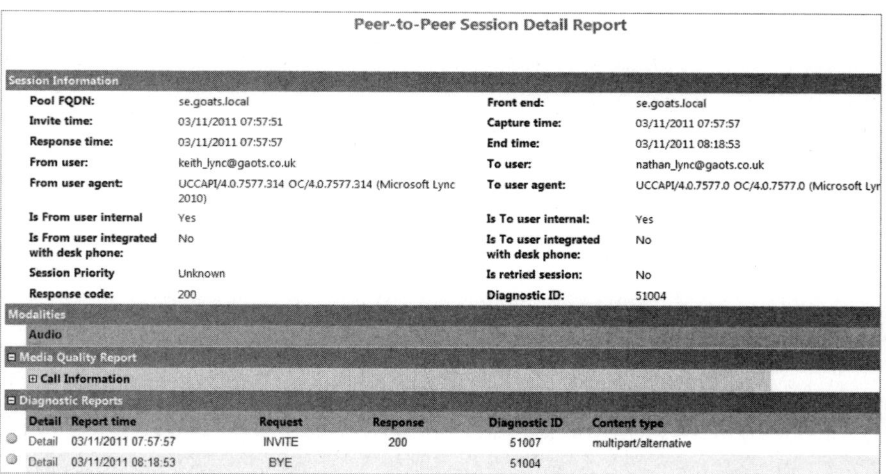

FIGURE 11.13 Peer-to-Peer Session Detail Report

This report contains almost 200 fields of information, broken down into the following sections:

Call Information Here you will see information regarding the users (or PSTN number) involved in the call, start time, and duration, along with client hardware and software version information.

Media Line (Main Audio) - MediaLine Information The MediaLine information section deals with the network identifiers such as network address information, internal/external connectivity, connection speeds, and whether any bandwidth controls are in place due to Call Admission Control.

Media Line (Main Audio) - Caller/Callee Device and Signal Metrics Both caller and callee have separate sections here, providing device identifiers (including device driver versions), signal send and receive information, as well as any hardware (microphone/speaker) issues detected.

Media Line (Main Audio) - Caller/Callee Client Event Again, this is repeated for both caller and callee, and this section provides reporting on the percentage of issues detected around the device hardware and signal.

Media Line (Main Audio) - Audio Stream (Caller ➢ Callee)/(Callee ➢ Caller) This section deals with the specific audio stream in one direction. The following section provides the same data in the other direction. Here you see information regarding the codec used and network impacts (packet loss, jitter, and so on).

Typically, this is the most viewed section because it provides the summary impact due to the underlying network conditions.

Media Line (Main Audio) - Video Stream (Caller ➢ Callee)/(Callee ➢ Caller) The final two sections provide the same information as the preceding except in dealing with the video stream. This is included only for calls that have a video aspect.

A massive amount of information is captured with every call. Some of the fields will be self-explanatory, but you will need more information to understand some of the other fields. In these cases, tooltips are provided, but not all fields have tooltips because they are presumed to be familiar.

Also, to help you understand which values are potentially causing problems, color coding is enabled on the reports. Yellow indicates a warning, and red indicates a high risk of problems.

Customizing Reports

While the number of reports has increased dramatically since the launch of Office Communication Server 2007, they still fall short of the requirements of many customers.

The database schemas for both QoE and CDR databases are detailed in the Lync Server 2010 help file and can also be downloaded from the following link:

```
www.microsoft.com/download/en/details.aspx?id=18099
```

Provided the correct permissions are assigned to a user, it is relatively easy to connect to those databases via ODBC and retrieve the data you'll need to provide customized reports. You can also use SQL Server 2008 Report Builder to generate reports that can be added to the web page, enabling easy generation and a single storage/execution location for reports.

Service Monitoring with the Management Pack

The other aspect of monitoring is server or service monitoring, which is needed so that system administrators can alert their users when aspects of the Lync Server 2010 service fail (or begin to fail). Management packs provide a prepackaged set of rules and alert thresholds you can use to quickly set up and monitor the Lync Server 2010 environment. The Lync Server 2010 Monitoring Management Pack is available to download from the following location:

```
www.microsoft.com/download/en/details.aspx?displaylang=en&id=12375
```

Management Pack Improvements

In the feedback that Microsoft received about the previous management packs for Office Communications Server 2007 (specifically the R2 version), one of the most important findings was that the thresholds were set too low, resulting in a deluge of alerts almost upon installation of the management pack. This typically caused administrators to disable the alerts without coming back to tune and enable them at a reasonable level.

Based on this feedback, the management pack was included as part of the Lync Server 2010 beta code availability so that customers could provide further feedback.

The management pack configuration should be tailored to each individual environment (baselined) to ensure that these thresholds do not produce inappropriate alerts. The last thing any administrator wants is to be paged at 1:00 AM for a problem that could wait until morning!

A good example of this scenario is in an Enterprise Edition pool with four front-end servers; if one server fails, the actual Lync 2010 services (registrar, routing, Address Book, conferencing, and so on) provided by the pool will continue to operate, and hopefully has been scaled to cope with a single server failure, so the impact will be minimal (quite possibly negligible) to the users. The server could wait until morning to be repaired.

Detailed steps on how to configure SCOM are beyond the scope of this book; however, assuming SCOM has been installed and configured with the Lync 2010 management pack deployed to discover the Lync 2010 topology, the next few steps will show how to change thresholds on alerts from the default.

From within the System Center Operations Manager 2007 R2 console, select the Authoring tab, and with Object Discoveries selected, change the Scope (using the button on the toolbar) and select View All Targets. The results are shown in Figure 11.14.

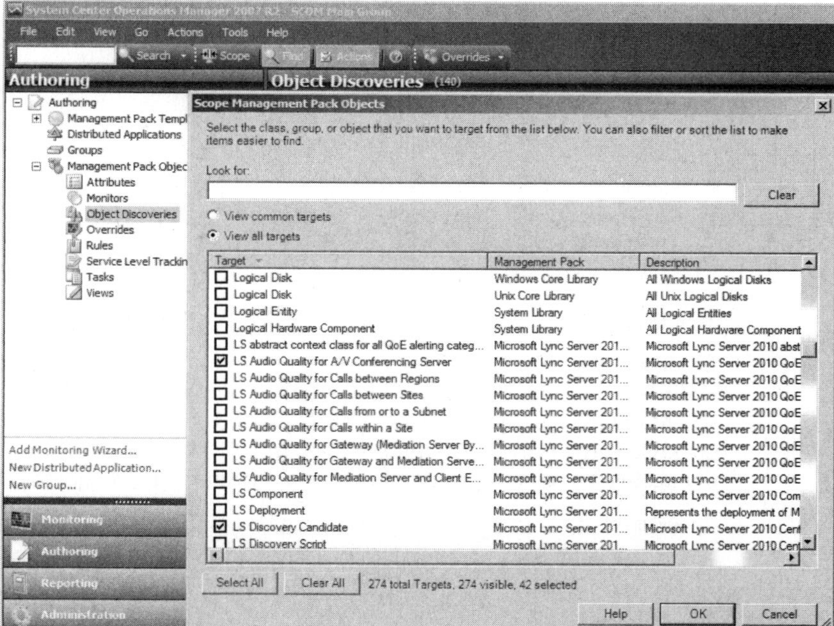

Figure 11.14 Changing the scope within SCOM to show Lync objects

In this example, you will change the audio quality metrics for conferencing, so selecting LS Audio Quality for A/V Conferencing Server and pressing OK will take you back to the Object Discoveries view, this time including the LS QoE Discovery entry under the selected type (LS Audio Quality for A/V Conferencing Server).

Right-click LS QoE Discovery and select Overrides ➢ Override the Object Discovery ➢ For All Objects of Class: LS QoE Monitoring. See Figure 11.15.

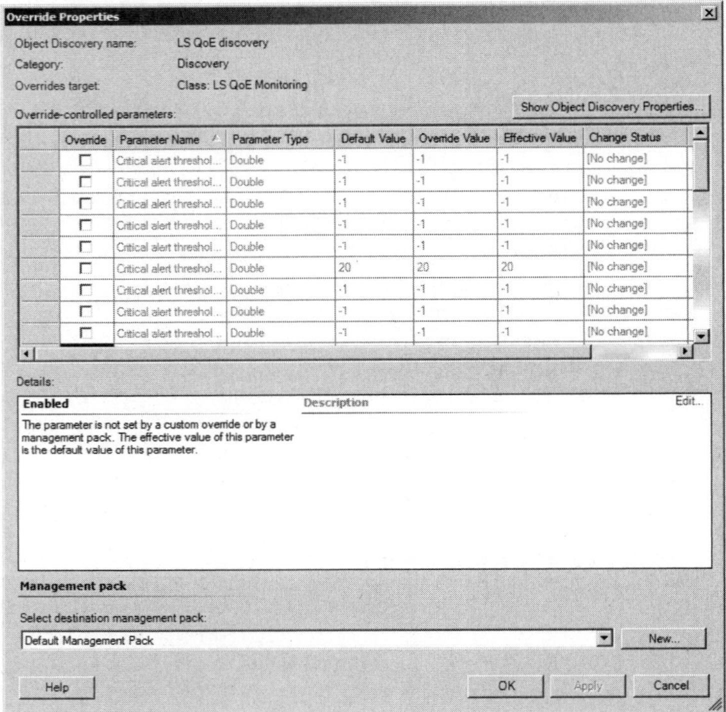

FIGURE 11.15
Enable Overrides on Lync Server 2010 Monitored values in SCOM.

The Parameter Name column indicates the items queried from the database, and the description is provided in the Details window. Selecting an item in the Override column will enable the specific row to be modified at the necessary value, and selecting OK will apply the change.

The management pack raises alerts at different levels, ensuring the correct response based on the impact. The alerts raised provide relevant information to help identify the causes and help troubleshoot, hopefully resulting in a faster recovery time. In some cases, there will be links directly to the CDR or QoE record itself.

The management pack will leverage the information from the Central Management Store to determine the topology, which will help you accurately assign the rules to the server roles with limited administrative interaction.

End-to-end verification is provided through the use of *synthetic transactions*, which can test almost the complete range of functionality required from a client (including simulation of PSTN calling).

These synthetic transactions can be configured to run periodically (it is recommended to have dedicated accounts configured for this), and a failure can be used to generate a high priority alert, which is automatically resolved if the command is successful on the next attempt. Synthetic transactions can be run without integration with SCOM; however, for full automated alerting and reporting, SCOM is required. Table 11.4 shows the full list of all synthetic transactions.

TABLE 11.4: Synthetic Transactions

CMDLET	DESCRIPTION
`Test-CsAddressBookService*`	Tests the functionality of the Address Book service. This can be used to simulate an individual user.
`Test-CsAddressBookWebQuery*`	Similar to the `Test-CsAddressBookService`, except it tests the web query functionality.
`Test-CsAVConference*`	Tests audio video conference functionality using a pair of users.
`Test-CsCertificateConfiguration`	Returns information on the certificates in use.
`Test-CsClientAuth`	Confirms whether a user can log on when using the Lync 2010–provided user certificate.
`Test-CsComputer`	Verifies that services are running, Active Directory groups have been configured correctly, and the firewall ports have been opened.
`Test-CsDialinConferencing*`	Confirms whether a user can utilize Dial-in Conferencing by testing the ability to dial the specified conference numbers.
`Test-CsDialPlan`	Tests a phone number against a dial plan, returning the normalization rule, which will be applied, and the results of that normalization.
`Test-CsFederatedPartner`	Confirms the status of federation with an external domain.
`Test-CsGroupExpansion`	Confirms the functionality of the group expansion capability on the pool.
`Test-CsGroupIM*`	Tests the ability of two users to carry out an IM conference.
`Test-CsIM*`	Tests the ability of two users to carry out a peer-to-peer IM.
`Test-CsKerberosAccountAssignment`	Verifies that the assigned Kerberos account is working correctly.
`Test-CsLisCivicAddress`	Verifies address information against the Master Street Address Guide held by the E911 provider. This is the only test cmdlet that is not a synthetic test. It is capable of updating the LIS database.
`Test-CsLisConfiguration`	Confirms the address configuration when given a specific subnet (or other location identifier).

TABLE 11.4: Synthetic Transactions *(CONTINUED)*

CMDLET	DESCRIPTION
`Test-CsLocationPolicy`	Determines which location policy will be used.
`Test-CsOUPermission`	Verifies the permissions have been applied correctly within the Active Directory OU.
`Test-CsP2PAV*`	Tests audio/video functionality using a pair of users in peer-to-peer mode (rather than conferencing).
`Test-CsPhoneBootstrap`	Verifies that the environment is configured to allow Lync 2010 Phone Edition devices to connect and that a user can log on.
`Test-CsPresence*`	Confirms that a user can log on and publish presence information, as well as receive presence updates from another user.
`Test-CsPstnOutboundCall`	Tests the ability of a user to make a PSTN call. A call will actually be placed and must be answered for this test to succeed.
`Test-CsPstnPeerToPeerCall*`	Similar to Test-CsPstnPeerToPeerCall, except the cmdlet places a call to another user via the gateway, and will answer the call on behalf of the user.
`Test-CsRegistration*`	Confirms whether a user can log on to Lync 2010 or not.
`Test-CsSetupPermission`	Confirms that Active Directory has been configured to allow Lync to be installed.
`Test-CsTopology`	Allows testing of the validity of a server or service.
`Test-CsTrunkConfiguration`	Confirms the operation of the trunk configuration when presented with a phone number.
`Test-CsVoiceNormalizationRule`	Tests a phone number against a specific normalization rule and returns the resulting number after the rule has been applied.
`Test-CsVoicePolicy`	Tests a phone number against a specific voice policy and returns the determined route.
`Test-CsVoiceRoute`	Tests a phone number against a specific route pattern and returns success or fail based on whether the number is accepted by the route.
`Test-CsVoiceTestConfiguration`	Tests a combination of dial plan and policy to confirm that routing works as expected.
`Test-CsVoiceUser`	Confirms the route for a PSTN call from a specific user based on the voice configuration.

** Indicates items that can be used by SCOM for continuous synthetic transaction testing.*

For component monitoring (via SCOM), the alerts are separated into Key Health Indicators and non-Key Health Indicators. A Key Health Indicator is a service impacting issues (which is worth being paged about at 1:00 AM!), and non-Key Health Indicators are those aspects that do not impact service; for example, components which have resiliency. These are automatically resolved if the service returns to health.

Chapter 12 provides more details (and examples) of running synthetic transactions from within PowerShell (without using SCOM integration).

Deploying Synthetic Transactions with SCOM

While running the synthetic transactions from the PowerShell environment is a relatively straightforward task, configuring automatic transaction execution and monitoring within SCOM is a multistep process.

You'll need to define one or more watcher nodes. A *watcher node* is a server responsible for executing synthetic transactions for a pool. If you have deployed multiple pools and want to have automatic synthetic transactions run on each of them, you will need one server per pool.

The server should have the following minimum specifications:

- 4 core processor 2.0 Ghz or higher
- 4 GB RAM
- 10GB free disk space, 7200 RPM drive
- 1 Gbps network adapter
- Windows Server 2008 SP2 or Windows Server 2008 R2

In addition to having a SCOM Agent installed, the Lync Server 2010 core and Lync Server Replica MSI files need to be installed onto the watcher node. The easiest way to do this is via the Lync Server 2010 setup program by selecting both Install Topology Builder and Install Local Configuration Store. Because the watcher node is not directly part of the topology, a trusted application pool must be configured with the watcher node a member server of the application pool. Once the pool is created, a trusted application service is created.

Both of these tasks must be performed using PowerShell because there are no options to configure trusted applications in the Control Panel.

To create a new Trusted Application Pool, first, identify the `SiteId` for the site to which the application pool will be associated. Figure 11.16 shows the output of `Get-CsSite`.

FIGURE 11.16
Get-CsSite

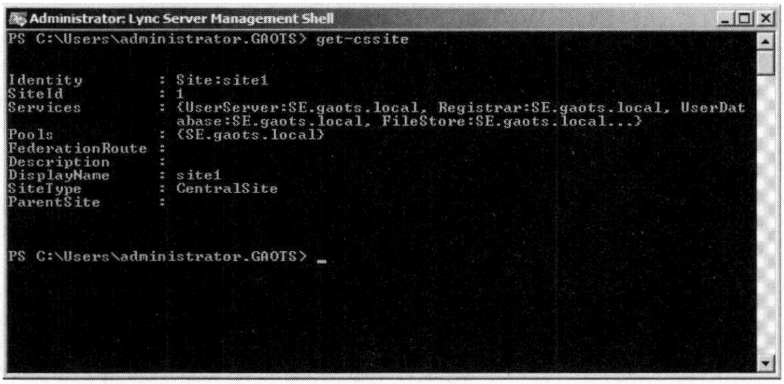

```
Administrator: Lync Server Management Shell
PS C:\Users\administrator.GAOTS> get-cssite

Identity          : Site:site1
SiteId            : 1
Services          : {UserServer:SE.gaots.local, Registrar:SE.gaots.local, UserDat
                    abase:SE.gaots.local, FileStore:SE.gaots.local...}
Pools             : {SE.gaots.local}
FederationRoute   :
Description       :
DisplayName       : site1
SiteType          : CentralSite
ParentSite        :


PS C:\Users\administrator.GAOTS> _
```

With the `SiteId`, run the following command:

```
New-CsTrustedApplicationPool -Identity wn.gaots.local -Site 1 -Registrar
se.gaots.local
```

Where the `Identity` parameter is the FQDN of the watcher node. The response will be similar to this:

```
Identity               : 1-ExternalServer-1
Registrar              : Registrar:se.gaots.local
FileStore              :
ThrottleAsServer       : True
TreatAsAuthenticated   : True
OutboundOnly           : False
RequiresReplication    : True
AudioPortStart         :
AudioPortCount         : 0
AppSharingPortStart    :
AppSharingPortCount    : 0
VideoPortStart         :
VideoPortCount         : 0
Applications           : {}
DependantServiceList   : {}
ServiceId              : 1-ExternalServer-1
SiteId                 : Site:site1
PoolFqdn               : wn.gaots.local
Version                : 5
Role                   : TrustedApplicationPool
```

`Get-CsPool` can also be run to verify that the application pool is configured.

The trusted application service is created using the following command:

```
New-CsTrustedApplication -ApplicationId "STWatcher-Site1"
-TrustedApplicationPoolFqdn wn.gaots.local -Port 5587
```

The `ApplicationId` parameter can be any text entry. You can include the site name or ID so that it is easy to identify which application is dealing with which site. The `Port` parameter can be any unused port.

The result of this command will be similar to that shown in Figure 11.17.

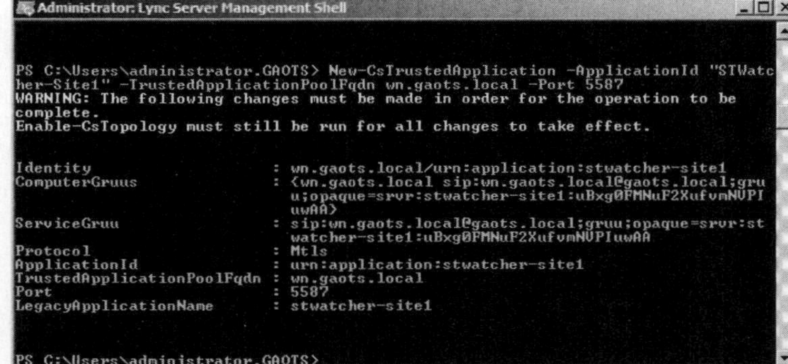

FIGURE 11.17
New-CsTrusted Application

The Enable-CsTopology cmdlet needs to be run in order to apply these topology changes. There is no output from this cmdlet, and once replication is confirmed, the watcher node computer account should be added to the RTCUniversalReadOnlyAdmins group in Active Directory. Then the Enable-CsComputer cmdlet should be run to assign group memberships and permissions. You'll need to create and assign user accounts to the Health Monitoring Configuration entry, using the following command:

```
New-CsHealthMonitoringConfiguration -TargetFqdn se.gaots.local
-FirstTestUserSipUri sip:test1_lync@gaots.co.uk -SecondTestUserSipUri sip:test2_
lync@gaots.co.uk

Identity               : se.gaots.local
FirstTestUserSipUri    : sip:test1_lync@gaots.co.uk
FirstTestSamAccountName :
FirstTestUserSipUri    : sip:test1_lync@gaots.co.uk
FirstTestSamAccountName :
TargetFqdn             : se.gaots.local
```

The *Health Monitoring Configuration* is the stored configuration that is used for the synthetic transactions. Test-Cs* cmdlets that require user accounts will use accounts from this configuration, if available, otherwise they will prompt for the account information. Obviously, for a noninteractive solution within SCOM, you'll need to use this stored configuration.

Additionally, some Registry settings are required for the watcher node; they can be configured using the following PowerShell:

```
New-Item -Path  "HKLM:\Software\Microsoft\Real-Time Communications\Health"
New-ItemProperty -Path "HKLM:\Software\Microsoft\Real-Time Communications\Health"
-Name "IsSTWatcherNode" -Value true
New-ItemProperty -Path "HKLM:\System\CurrentControlSet\Services\HealthService\
Parameters"  -Name "Thread Pool CLR Max Thread Count Min" -propertytype DWord
-value 200
```

Optionally, you can enable logging using the following Registry entry:

```
New-ItemProperty -Path "HKLM:\Software\Microsoft\Real-Time Communications\Health"
-Name "LogOpsMgr" -PropertyType DWord -value 2
```

A certificate (of the default type) needs to be requested and installed using the Request-CsCertificate cmdlet or the setup application.

A restart of the Health Service will enable the automatic synthetic transaction monitoring. Further details (including troubleshooting) can be found in the management pack guide available from the same download link as the main Lync Server 2010 Monitoring Management Pack.

Figure 11.18 shows the synthetic transactions in operation. In this case, the front-end server has been shut down, so you can see the synthetic transaction failure alerts. When the servers come back online, they will automatically clear (when the next synthetic transaction is successful).

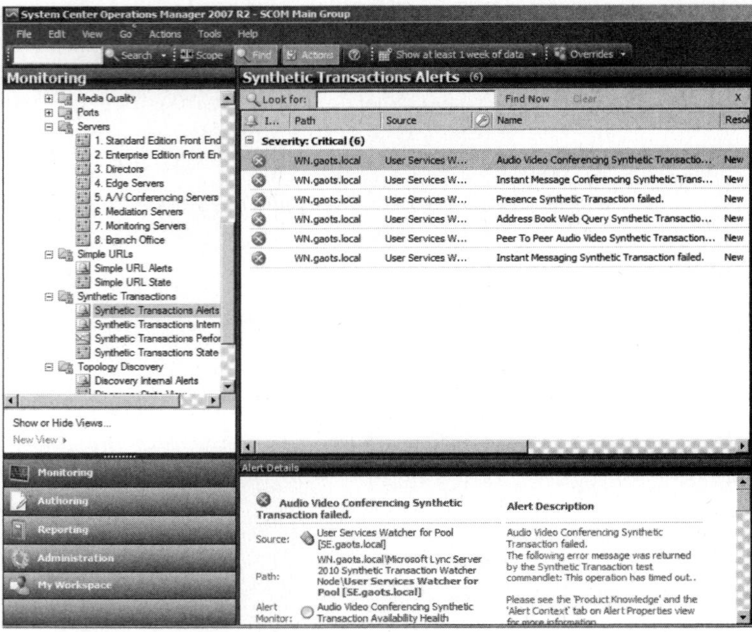

FIGURE 11.18
Synthetic transaction failure alerts

Useful information is contained within the "Alert Details" section, providing initial suggestions on the problem and where to begin troubleshooting.

The Bottom Line

Understand the architecture for the Archiving and Monitoring role. Although related to different aspects of the data, the Archiving and Monitoring server roles are very similar in function, and they have similar back-end requirements. This allows them to be easily colocated and share the same database.

Master it What are the names of the MSMQ queues created by the Archiving and Monitoring server roles?

Provide reporting on the data available from the Archiving and Monitoring roles. Lync Server 2010 provides a monitoring server report pack containing almost 50 reports, which focus on the QoE data. Non-Microsoft vendors provide additional report capability for the other databases and, of course, you can always write your own reports.

Master It What options are available for creating customized reports?

Use the capabilities in the System Center Operations Manager management pack to report on the availability of the Lync 2010 service. With the implementation of the Lync Server 2010 Monitoring Management Pack for System Center Operations Manager 2007, administrators have a consolidated approach and location for collating and monitoring system (and service) uptime.

Master it Which synthetic transactions will confirm the status of the Address Book service?

Chapter 12

Troubleshooting

Sooner or later you'll have to deal with troubleshooting, the topic no one wants to think about but everyone needs to learn. In an ideal world, every system would work perfectly as soon as it was installed and would continue to work until decommissioned. As we all know, this is never the case, and quite often the simple things (typically, the ones assumed to be correct) are what cause us problems.

Lync Server 2010 is no different in this respect. You need to make sure the simple things are correct before you can progress to the complex areas—and with the integration points that Lync provides with third-party hardware (gateways, devices, and so on), as well as its strong integration points with the underlying infrastructure, there are many areas to check when it comes to troubleshooting.

In this chapter, you will learn to:

- Confirm that the basics are in place from the infrastructure side
- Understand how to troubleshoot the client
- Know how to enable troubleshooting on the server
- Understand and use the troubleshooting tools available

Troubleshooting Basics

So, you receive a call from a user saying something is broken (can't log in, can't make calls, or the like). Where do you start?

First, you should ask the usual questions:

- Did it ever work?
- What did the user change?
- What has an administrator changed?

NOTE When we were working in support, we never had anyone admit making a change that broke something; however, as administrators we all knew it happened! When you're troubleshooting, always check to see if an administrative change could've caused the break.

First, you need to establish the scope of the problem. Is it related to a single user, a single location, or is everything down for everybody? The larger-scale impact issues tend to be easiest to troubleshoot, but they also tend to be the ones with the greatest amount of pressure. When 10,000 users are without phone service, the problem can very quickly be escalated to the top!

When it comes to networking investigation, the usual suspects typically include:

- Ping
- Telnet (not installed by default on Windows since Windows Vista was released)
- NSlookup (don't forget to configure to check SRV records)
- The browser (for checking certificates, and so on)

Confirming a Network Connection

Simply put, if a user can't log in, something is wrong with their connection to the server (assuming the account is enabled and not locked).

Using automatic login on an internal network, the Lync 2010 Communicator client will attempt to discover the address of a pool (and therefore registrar) in the following order:

- `_sipinternaltls._tcp.`*`<sip domain>`*
- DHCP Option 120
- `sipinternal.`*`<sip domain>`*
- `sip.`*`<sip domain>`*

The Lync 2010 Phone Edition client will use the following methods:

- DHCP Option 120
- `_sipinternaltls._tcp.`*`<sip domain>`*
- `sipinternal.`*`<sip domain>`*
- `sip.`*`<sip domain>`*

The Lync 2010 Phone Edition device prefers to use Option 120 (in conjunction with Option 43 for certificate services) to allow the phone to be directed to a Lync Server 2010 server rather than a legacy OCS 2007 or OCS 2007 R2 server, which does not provide certificate (or PIN) authentication.

Using the Lync 2010 Communicator client, you can modify the connection type to be manual (see Figure 12.1) and enter the FQDN address of the pool to see if that connection is working. Using this test, you can confirm that the issue is within the DNS resolution of the automatic server discovery or the redirect from another pool.

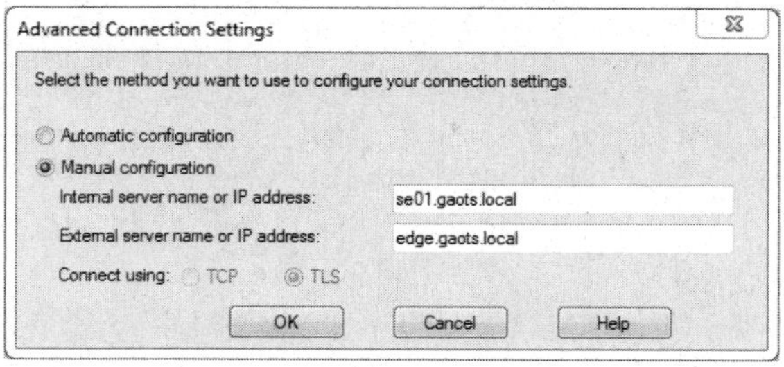

FIGURE 12.1
Configuring a manual server connection

To confirm the connectivity to a server, you can use ping; however, many network administrators will block ping on the firewall, especially when you're trying to communicate with the servers in the DMZ. To confirm communications on a specific port, you must use telnet and provide the server (or pool) name and the port.

For example, to confirm SIP connectivity via a hardware load balancer, use this command:

```
telnet <pool name> 5061
```

The result, rather confusingly, is a blank window. However, this shows that the telnet client has successfully connected to the server. If there is a problem, the client will indicate that it cannot connect, and although the error may not be particularly descriptive, you should be able to determine whether it was a DNS issue (if you used the FQDN) or a network connectivity issue (routing or firewall). The potential DNS issue can be determined simply by repeating the test using the IP address in place of the FQDN.

Using the client logs (enabled as shown in Figure 12.2), you can see the following entries, showing the failed DNS resolution for some of the automatic lookup addresses:

```
06/08/2011|21:43:25.361 2074:1E08 INFO  :: domainName:gaots.com:
serviceName:sipinternaltls: transportName:tcp:
06/08/2011|21:43:25.361 2074:1E08 INFO  :: domainName:gaots.com: serviceName:sip:
transportName:tls:
06/08/2011|21:43:25.372 2074:1E50 INFO  :: QueryDNSSrv - DNS Name[_
sipinternaltls._tcp.gaots.com]
06/08/2011|21:43:25.614 2074:1E50 ERROR :: QueryDNSSrv GetDnsResults query:
_sipinternaltls._tcp.gaots.com failed 8007251d
06/08/2011|21:43:25.614 2074:1E50 ERROR :: DNS_RESOLUTION_
WORKITEM::ProcessWorkItem ResolveHostName failed 8007251d
06/08/2011|21:43:25.614 2074:1E50 INFO  :: QueryDNSSrv - DNS Name[_sip._tls
.gaots.com]
06/08/2011|21:43:25.614 2074:1E08 INFO  :: CUccDnsQuery::UpdateLookup - error
code=80ee0066, index=0
06/08/2011|21:43:25.614 2074:1E08 INFO  :: CUccDnsQuery::CompleteLookup - index=0
06/08/2011|21:43:25.823 2074:1E50 ERROR :: QueryDNSSrv GetDnsResults query:
_sip._tls.gaots.com failed 8007251d
06/08/2011|21:43:25.823 2074:1E50 ERROR :: DNS_RESOLUTION_
WORKITEM::ProcessWorkItem ResolveHostName failed 8007251d
06/08/2011|21:43:25.824 2074:1E08 INFO  :: CUccDnsQuery::UpdateLookup - error
code=80ee0066, index=1
```

```
06/08/2011|21:43:25.824 2074:1E08 INFO  :: CUccDnsQuery::CompleteLookup - index=1
06/08/2011|21:43:25.824 2074:1E08 INFO  :: Function: CUccServerEndpoint::
OnDnsQueryCompleted
06/08/2011|21:43:25.825 2074:1E08 ERROR :: HRESULT API failed: 80ee0066 =
hrStatus. CUccDnsQuery::GetResults
```

FIGURE 12.2
Enabling client logs

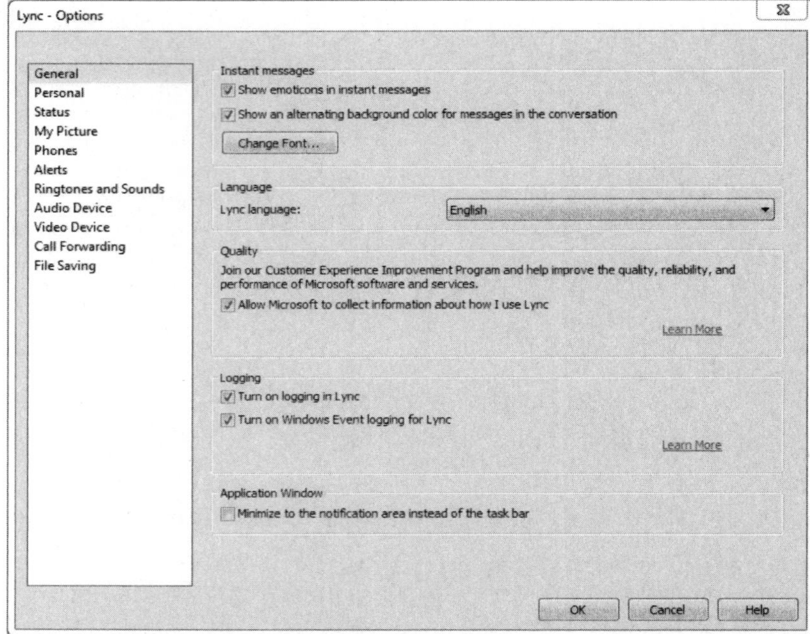

The client logs provide extremely detailed information in terms of what is going on at the client end. You'll see a lot more of them in this chapter.

Confirming Secure Connectivity

Once you have the name resolution, routing, and firewall problems out of the way, the next part of the connectivity path is the certificate on the server. With the improvements made to the Lync Server 2010 Certificate Wizard, the task of configuring the certificates became a lot easier; however, changes can still be made and the certificates still might not be updated, which could lead to connectivity issues.

To test for the correct certificate configuration, you can use the following URL (similar to the successful telnet connection, expect a blank screen, but this time white):

```
https://<poolname>/lmstaticdata/slidefiles/blank.png
```

Figure 12.3 shows the result when the certificate is correctly configured (above) and incorrectly (below).

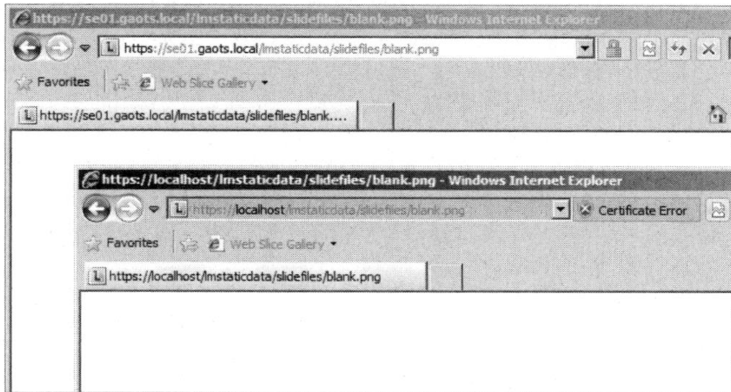

FIGURE 12.3
Confirming the correct certificate

This process can be repeated to confirm each of the expected Subject Alternate Names (SAN) in the certificate, simply by replacing the *<poolname>* entry with each of the SAN entries.

Checking for Audio/Video Peer-to-Peer Connectivity

Now that you've established the basics for client connectivity to the servers, the next step is to confirm connectivity between clients when establishing a call. IM connectivity always flows through the server, whereas the clients must negotiate peer-to-peer connectivity between themselves. Where direct connectivity is not available, clients must connect via NAT or the Edge server. Figure 12.4 shows the connectivity options for a client, depending on the path available between them.

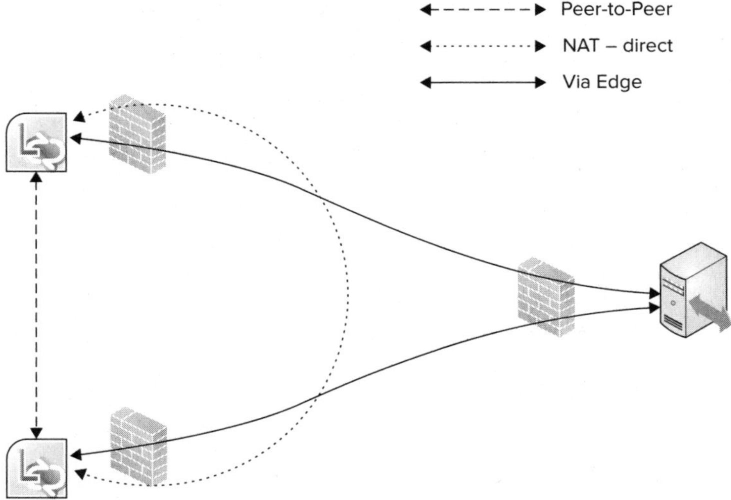

FIGURE 12.4
Client connectivity options

The client logs capture these IP addresses and ports negotiated (known as candidates) during the call initiation (audio, video, or desktop sharing). This Internet Connectivity Exchange (ICE) is shown here:

```
v=0
o=- 0 0 IN IP4 94.245.124.239
s=session
c=IN IP4 94.245.124.239
b=CT:53980
t=0 0
m=audio 56498 RTP/AVP 114 9 112 111 0 8 116 115 4 97 13 118 101
a=candidate:IOj2VRG1VNQG4cWj248JT8iqlOD42gmKoa8xdt4quqo 1 w4WZzoBiHwS3VeihjFFTuw
UDP 0.830 10.154.244.71 50028
a=candidate:IOj2VRG1VNQG4cWj248JT8iqlOD42gmKoa8xdt4quqo 2 w4WZzoBiHwS3VeihjFFTuw
UDP 0.830 10.154.244.71 50029
a=candidate:PZWZ6iscBZZ9TjL4kOKnxvcZDP4wODZKIklqiA/YLek 1 fCq9RqLw2pcibQlONAJULQ
TCP 0.190 94.245.124.238 53882
a=candidate:PZWZ6iscBZZ9TjL4kOKnxvcZDP4wODZKIklqiA/YLek 2 fCq9RqLw2pcibQlONAJULQ
TCP 0.190 94.245.124.238 53882
a=candidate:3aT5M3vcWbnE4FzWub2fX5CjNq6oDM61ZlcRKb0u5rQ 1 N9yLzNb17mpUVbCqNC2lAQ
UDP 0.490 94.245.124.239 56498
a=candidate:3aT5M3vcWbnE4FzWub2fX5CjNq6oDM61ZlcRKb0u5rQ 2 N9yLzNb17mpUVbCqNC2lAQ
UDP 0.490 94.245.124.239 55800
a=candidate:H46GRbUExoCxH7kQHprA5E2uVHxBroGV6aTGb56IowU 1 X1veRGhvsDShUEB8ND7GGQ
TCP 0.250 10.166.24.59 50004
a=candidate:H46GRbUExoCxH7kQHprA5E2uVHxBroGV6aTGb56IowU 2 X1veRGhvsDShUEB8ND7GGQ
TCP 0.250 10.166.24.59 50004
a=candidate:/fsTFKnb2oinetEHwrP5PkreyGP6dHnfhEsmI9V9xS8 1 fRqU3IuSWy2KXVF8MPZ7DA
UDP 0.550 195.226.18.36 50036
a=candidate:/fsTFKnb2oinetEHwrP5PkreyGP6dHnfhEsmI9V9xS8 2 fRqU3IuSWy2KXVF8MPZ7DA
UDP 0.550 195.226.18.36 50037
a=cryptoscale:1 client AES_CM_128_HMAC_SHA1_80 inline:kDgLmPIv2ufDNctJasFOKIkFq5w
/6iXpUDMeWrDW|2^31|1:1
a=crypto:2 AES_CM_128_HMAC_SHA1_80 inline:s40wuCQ33Rw6SysXZs5f7C66IxsF/
GdQRqiqcD3M|2^31|1:1
a=crypto:3 AES_CM_128_HMAC_SHA1_80 inline:SljnKOkFx6RtiWHywiCIVavo1SxLE/
ztysYrFhZb|2^31
a=maxptime:200
a=rtcp:55800
a=rtpmap:114 x-msrta/16000
a=fmtp:114 bitrate=29000
a=rtpmap:9 G722/8000
a=rtpmap:112 G7221/16000
a=fmtp:112 bitrate=24000
a=rtpmap:111 SIREN/16000
a=fmtp:111 bitrate=16000
a=rtpmap:0 PCMU/8000
a=rtpmap:8 PCMA/8000
```

```
a=rtpmap:116 AAL2-G726-32/8000
a=rtpmap:115 x-msrta/8000
a=fmtp:115 bitrate=11800
a=rtpmap:4 G723/8000
a=rtpmap:97 RED/8000
a=rtpmap:13 CN/8000
a=rtpmap:118 CN/16000
a=rtpmap:101 telephone-event/8000
a=fmtp:101 0-16
a=encryption:optional
```

Each line beginning with `a=candidate` is an IP address/Port/Protocol combination on which the client can be reached, and the long, seemingly random text is the username/password combination, ensuring that this connection is secured. (This text string is exchanged via the SIP signaling path, which is already secured.)

Let's look at a sample candidate entry:

```
a=candidate:I0j2VRG1VNQG4cWj248JT8iq1OD42gmKoa8xdt4quqo 1 w4WZzoBiHwS3VeihjFFTuw
UDP 0.830 10.154.244.71 50028
```

Broken down, it consists of the following elements:

`a=candidate:` is the session attribute.

`I0j2VRG1VNQG4cWj248JT8iq1OD42gmKoa8xdt4quqo` is the username.

1 specifies that RTP is to be used (2= RTCP).

`w4WZzoBiHwS3VeihjFFTuw` is the password.

`UDP` is the protocol.

`0.830` is the weighting (a higher number is preferred).

`10.154.244.71` is the IP address.

`50028` is the port number.

This same information is also provided in a previous ICE format, which is shown next (to ensure compatibility with legacy OCS clients):

```
v=0
o=- 0 0 IN IP4 94.245.124.239
s=session
c=IN IP4 94.245.124.239
b=CT:53980
t=0 0
m=audio 53046 RTP/AVP 114 9 112 111 0 8 116 115 4 97 13 118 101
a=ice-ufrag:hGFI
a=ice-pwd:cfwrCdU41RuOe53ZFvWCSpJ4
a=candidate:1 1 UDP 2130706431 10.154.244.71 50020 typ host
a=candidate:1 2 UDP 2130705918 10.154.244.71 50021 typ host
```

```
a=candidate:2 1 TCP-PASS 6556159 94.245.124.238 57358 typ relay raddr 10.166.24.59
rport 50001
a=candidate:2 2 TCP-PASS 6556158 94.245.124.238 57358 typ relay raddr 10.166.24.59
rport 50001
a=candidate:3 1 UDP 16648703 94.245.124.239 53046 typ relay raddr 195.226.18.36
rport 50004
a=candidate:3 2 UDP 16648702 94.245.124.239 50913 typ relay raddr 195.226.18.36
rport 50005
a=candidate:4 1 TCP-ACT 7076863 94.245.124.238 57358 typ relay raddr 10.166.24.59
rport 50001
a=candidate:4 2 TCP-ACT 7076350 94.245.124.238 57358 typ relay raddr 10.166.24.59
rport 50001
a=candidate:5 1 TCP-ACT 1684797951 10.166.24.59 50001 typ srflx raddr
10.154.244.71 rport 50001
a=candidate:5 2 TCP-ACT 1684797438 10.166.24.59 50001 typ srflx raddr
10.154.244.71 rport 50001
a=candidate:6 1 UDP 1694234623 195.226.18.36 50004 typ srflx raddr 10.154.244.71
rport 50004
a=candidate:6 2 UDP 1694234110 195.226.18.36 50005 typ srflx raddr 10.154.244.71
rport 50005
a=cryptoscale:1 client AES_CM_128_HMAC_SHA1_80 inline:kDgLmPIv2ufDNctJasFOKIkFq5w
/6iXpUDMeWrDW|2^31|1:1
a=crypto:2 AES_CM_128_HMAC_SHA1_80 inline:s40wuCQ33Rw6SysXZs5f7C66IxsF/
GdQRqiqcD3M|2^31|1:1
a=crypto:3 AES_CM_128_HMAC_SHA1_80 inline:SljnK0kFx6RtiWHywiCIVavo1SxLE/
ztysYrFhZb|2^31
a=maxptime:200
a=rtcp:50913
a=rtpmap:114 x-msrta/16000
a=fmtp:114 bitrate=29000
a=rtpmap:9 G722/8000
a=rtpmap:112 G7221/16000
a=fmtp:112 bitrate=24000
a=rtpmap:111 SIREN/16000
a=fmtp:111 bitrate=16000
a=rtpmap:0 PCMU/8000
a=rtpmap:8 PCMA/8000
a=rtpmap:116 AAL2-G726-32/8000
a=rtpmap:115 x-msrta/8000
a=fmtp:115 bitrate=11800
a=rtpmap:4 G723/8000
a=rtpmap:97 RED/8000
a=rtpmap:13 CN/8000
a=rtpmap:118 CN/16000
a=rtpmap:101 telephone-event/8000
a=fmtp:101 0-16
a=encryption:optional
```

Broken down, a sample entry in the legacy format:

```
a=candidate:2 1 TCP-PASS 6556159 94.245.124.238 57358 typ relay raddr 10.166.24.59
rport 50001
```

looks like this:

`a=candidate:` is the session attribute.

2 is the candidate ID.

1 specifies that RTP is to be used (2 = RTCP)

`TCP-PASS` is the protocol type (`TCP-PASS` = TCP Passive, `TCP-ACT` = TCP Active, UDP).

`6556159` is the weighting (a higher number is preferred).

`94.245.124.238` is the IP address.

`57358` is the port number.

`typ relay` is the type of relay (`direct` = UDP only; `relay` = TCP-PASS, TCP-ACT or UDP; `srflx` = self-reflective, TCP-ACT or UDP).

`raddr 10.166.24.59` is the remote IP address.

`rport 50001` is the remote port number.

The clients both exchange a candidate (and codec) list and will try each address in preference order. The logs will also show the address list provided by the remote client. Once you have this information, you can ensure manually that the clients can connect.

Once compatibility is confirmed via the IP address, port, and protocol selection, the remaining task is to establish a common codec. The previous listings include this codec map (`a=rtpmap:`); the clients will negotiate this and will continue to negotiate throughout the duration of the call, ensuring that the codecs adapt to any change in the network conditions. Later in this chapter, you'll see an excerpt from the Media Quality Logs which shows the codec selection.

Device Connectivity

Phone devices don't have the same requirements for connectivity as desktop clients, specifically the need for DHCP configuration.

To enable certificate-based authentication (making sure the phone can connect with no Active Directory available), the phone is required to connect to the certificate provisioning website on a Lync Server 2010 pool. This is provided via DHCP Option 43.

In addition, unless DHCP Option 120 is also configured (you need to provide the SIP registrar information), the phone will display an error to the user while it is performing a DNS query on the SRV records (although, once the DNS records are discovered it will connect as normal).

The `DCHPUTIL.EXE` tool (and `DHCPConfigScript.bat` file) provided in the `C:\Program Files\Common Files\Microsoft Lync Server 2010` folder provides instructions for configuring a Microsoft-based DHCP server.

Device Error from the Field

A colleague recently reported a strange user experience from one of his customers—when the customer logged into the Lync 2010 client, everything functioned normally; however, when logged into a Lync 2010 Phone Edition client, the following functionality was missing:

- Voice Mail
- Calendar Integration
- Call Logs

These functions are provided by Exchange Web Services, so we suggested troubleshooting the EWS service and verifying that it was operational. However, as our colleague pointed out, this was all functioning from the Lync 2010 client.

Next on the list was network routing and address resolution from the device (typically, phone devices are allocated to a separate VLAN). In this case, the device was on the same VLAN as the PC.

The end result was that the EWS service had been signed by a different certificate chain than the Lync Server 2010 front-end certificates had been. When the phone device connected to the front-end server to download the certificate chain, it had no way of downloading the chain for the Exchange server and, therefore, did not trust it.

There were two possible ways to resolve this certificate issue with the Exchange server:

1. Ensure that the Exchange server certificates came from the same Certificate Authority as the certificates user on the front-end servers

or

2. Use the `New-CsWebTrustedCACertificate` cmdlet to define the certificates used by the Exchange servers to be loaded onto the front end servers and, therefore, trusted by the Lync Phone Edition client.

As the Lync 2010 Phone Device will download the Front End server certificates (and Root Certificate Authority certificate chain) anyhow, option 1 was the choice used. However, both have the same result, and in some cases it may not be possible to easily replace certificates in use by Exchange.

Sniffing the Network

After you've verified that name resolution, routing, and the firewalls are working and all appears to be fine, the next step is to better understand the actual traffic being sent and received on the network. Two popular tools that are used for network sniffing are:

- Microsoft Network Monitor
- Wireshark

These tools intercept the network traffic and provide a breakdown of the traffic, including the protocol and meaning of the packets being transmitted or received. Figure 12.5 shows Microsoft Network Monitor examining generic network traffic.

FIGURE 12.5
Microsoft Network Monitor in action

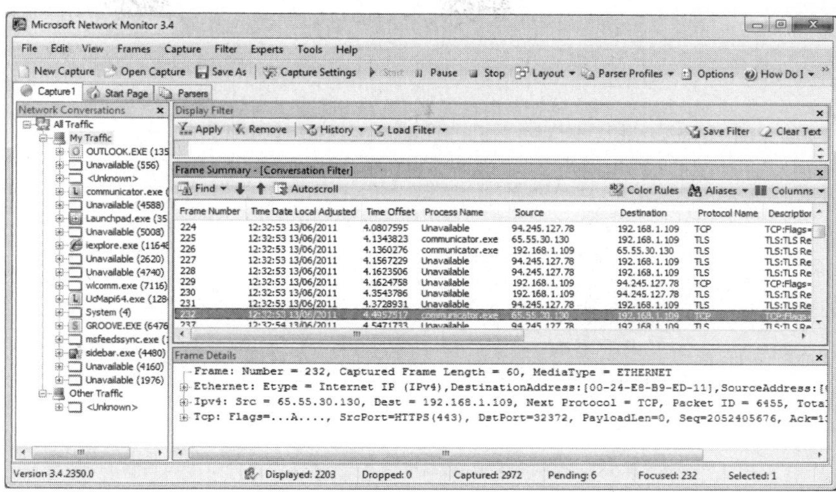

Immediately, from the highlighted section in Figure 12.5, you can see the process (`communicator.exe`) so you know you're looking at the correct network traffic as well as the source and destination IP address information; this means that you are connecting to the server (or device) that you should be. You can also see the specific protocol (in this case TCP) and ports in use.

Although Network Monitor provides protocol parsers for SIP, it is normally much easier to enable logging on the server or client and import the logfile into `SNOOPER.EXE` for analysis. Where Network Monitor comes into its own is in understanding the communications layer. Two important scenarios of it are:

- Understanding and establishing the certificate exchange (handshake)
- Understanding the Hardware Load Balancer interaction

Certificate traffic analysis will indicate the names being provided by the certificate, ensuring that you can match those names with the ones you expect. By contrast, with the Hardware Load Balancers, a common misconfiguration is the timeout values; here, you may capture a `TCP-RESET` packet showing that the timeout is configured incorrectly.

Now that you've looked at the methods of troubleshooting connectivity, and introduced the snippets of the log files, we'll look at tracing.

Introducing Tracing

Both the server and the client provide a method to access what is happening "under the covers" by enabling logging. *Logging* enables the server and client to write detailed information to a text file to provide a means for an administrator or support engineer to understand what is occurring at any given time.

The server provides a means to enable subsets of components to log; on a busy server there is too much information to simply log it all and then parse it. In this section, you'll see how to enable and manage individual server components.

The client doesn't have as much information to log because it is dealing only with a single user's interactions and, therefore, everything is either enabled or disabled.

Figure 12.2, earlier in the chapter, shows where you enable logging on the client; it can also be enabled via policy.

The log files are stored at the location `%USERPROFILE%\Tracing` and are named either `Communicator-uccapi-0.UCCAPILOG` and `Communicator-uccapi-1.UCCAPILOG` (for the Communicator client) or `AttendeeCommunicator-uccapi-0.UCCAPILOG` and `AttendeeCommunicator-uccapi-1.UCCAPILOG` (for the Attendee client). These log files use *circular logging*, so there will always be a minimum of two files (ocassionally there may be more). Once the second is full, the first will be overwritten, and once this is full, the second will be overwritten, and repeat.

As mentioned, these are text-based log files and can be opened and viewed with any text viewer (such as `NOTEPAD.EXE`); however, you'll see later in this chapter how a Resource Kit tool called `SNOOPER.EXE` makes reading and interpreting these log files much easier.

Using *OCSLOGGER.EXE*

On the server, there is a dedicated tool (`OCSLOGGER.EXE`) that provides granular control over components, traces, and levels of logging enabled. Figure 12.6 shows `OCSLOGGER.EXE` in action.

FIGURE 12.6
`OCSLOGGER.EXE`

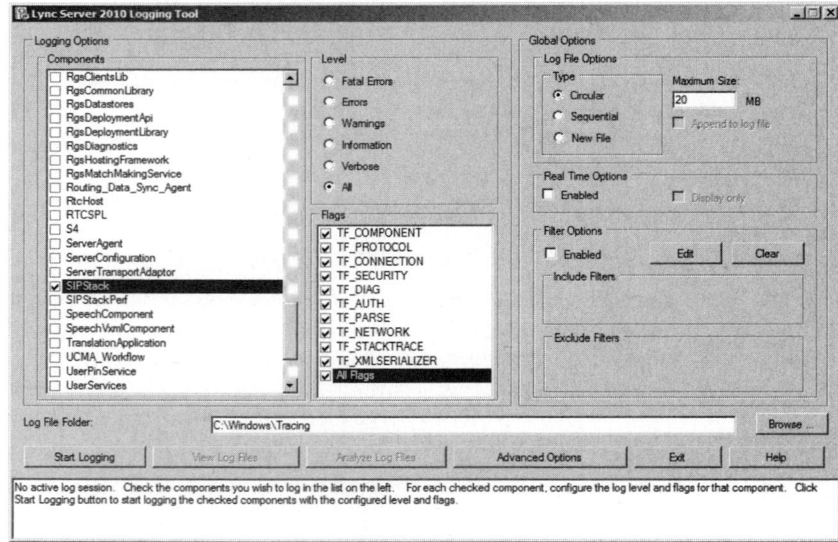

To use this tool, work through its tabs from left to right:

- Components
- Level
- Flags

- Global Options
- Other

Components

The components installed vary, not only with the specific role installed, but the specific components installed on a role. For example, if a pool is enabled for Call Admission Control, the PDP and MRAS components will be installed. Some of these components are self-explanatory based on their naming, others won't be. Some commonly used components are listed in Table 12.1, and the full table can be found at `www.sybex.com/go/masteringlyncserver`.

Table 12.1: `OCSLOGGER.EXE` Components

Component Name	Installed Via	Notes
ABCommon	Front-End Director	Used for troubleshooting the Address Book
ABServer	Front-End Director	Used for troubleshooting the Address Book
ABServerHttpHandler	Front-End Director	Used for troubleshooting the Address Book, specifically web-based access (in conjunction with the IIS logs)
ADConnect	OCS Core Components	Provides logging information on the AD connectivity
AdminUI	Front-End Director	Provides logging information of the Control Panel interactions and calls
PowerShell	OCS Core Components	Allows capture of most of the PowerShell interfaces from the Control Panel
S4	Admin Tools	Signaling information
SipStack	Front-End Director Edge	Signaling information
XDS_File_Transfer_Agent	CMS Installation	Logging of replication data, specially the file transfer aspects
XDS_master_replicator	CMS Installation	Logs creation of replication packages and notifications
XDS_replica_replicator	Local Configuration Store	Logs receipt of replication packages and notifications

Understanding the Underlying PowerShell Scripts Called

Unlike Exchange Server, the Lync Server 2010 Control Panel provides no explanation of what PowerShell cmdlets are being called, making it hard to understand and develop scripts to help manage the environment.

However, by enabling the PowerShell component in OCSLOGGER and then enabling logging and performing an action in Control Panel, you can capture the cmdlets used. By doing this, you can see what is going on behind the covers.

Level

In this tab, you can set the depth to which the logging occurs—that is, whether you are looking for informational messages or error messages. The level selected also includes levels above it. It's easy to capture the log details and filter through them afterward, so you may never find a reason not to select All Levels. The Traces tab within `SNOOPER.EXE` will show the corresponding breakdown of Levels if you do want to limit the amount of logging data.

Flags

The Flags tab allows you to choose the specific areas you want to look at within the component. For example, you might only be interested in the authentication traffic (select `TF_AUTH`) or the network interface traffic (`TF_NETWORK`). These entries are not cumulative, and each Flag item may be enabled individually (unless the All Flags item has been selected). Not all components will offer a detailed breakdown in this type of granularity. As with the Level, you may never find a reason to be selective about the Flags chosen and will always select All Flags. The Traces tab within `SNOOPER.EXE` will show the corresponding breakdown of Flags if you do want to limit the amount of logging data.

Global Options

This section allows you to set up the specific options for the log file as well as any filtering. The log file can be configured to be any size in MB, and it provides the following options for the type of logging:

Circular When the file reaches the defined size, the log entries will begin to overwrite existing entries.

Sequential Old log files are kept, and when the file reaches the defined size, a new file is created.

New A new file is created when logging starts and any existing files are overwritten.

The real-time options can be configured to display in a separate window the log file as it is created—typically too much data is written for the log to be readable, and this would be a good example of when the Level and Flags could be used to limit the amount of data displayed.

You can enable filtering for specific URI or FQDN entries; this is useful if you are trying to capture only a specific user (or two) when you have a server with thousands of users homed and active. Note that not all components include URI information, so this may be of limited use.

Other

The final section of OCSLOGGER, across the bottom of the screen, provides the location of the log files (the default path is `%SYSTEMROOT%\Tracing`) and the ability to change it.

If you were planning to enable logging to capture a lot of information—either with a lot of components or for a long period of time—and you had sequential logging enabled, you should move the logfile folder to a location that won't impact anything if it fills up. You don't want to crash the server by filling the system drive with logs!

The buttons have the following purposes:

Start Logging This button begins logging and changes to a Stop Logging button when logging is in progress.

View Log Files Pressing this button will open another window where the administrator can choose which log files to open and view within `Notepad.exe`. This will include any logfiles stored in the folder, not simply the one recently captured.

Analyze Log Files This button provides the same selection window as the View Log Files button, but instead of opening the files in `Notepad.exe`, it will launch `Snooper.exe` if installed. The next section covers `Snooper.exe` in detail.

Advanced Options Here you can modify the data that is captured (such as inclusion of the component, level, flag name, or the time), as well as sizing the capture buffers.

Exit This button will close the OCSLOGGER tool.

Help This button will open the OCSLOGGER help file.

Oops! Made a Mistake!

In many cases, you may have started the `OCSLOGGER.EXE` tool, clicked Start Logging, and then realized you didn't correctly configure logging.

All of the Components, Levels, and Flags are dynamic and can be enabled or disabled during logging; there is no need to stop and restart the logging process.

Using *Snooper.exe*

In a previous section, you viewed the log file snippets as text. The log file is a text-based file, but it can very quickly grow very large. Snooper is the tool that makes interpreting the logs extremely easy and straightforward. Snooper is shown in Figure 12.7 with a file loaded.

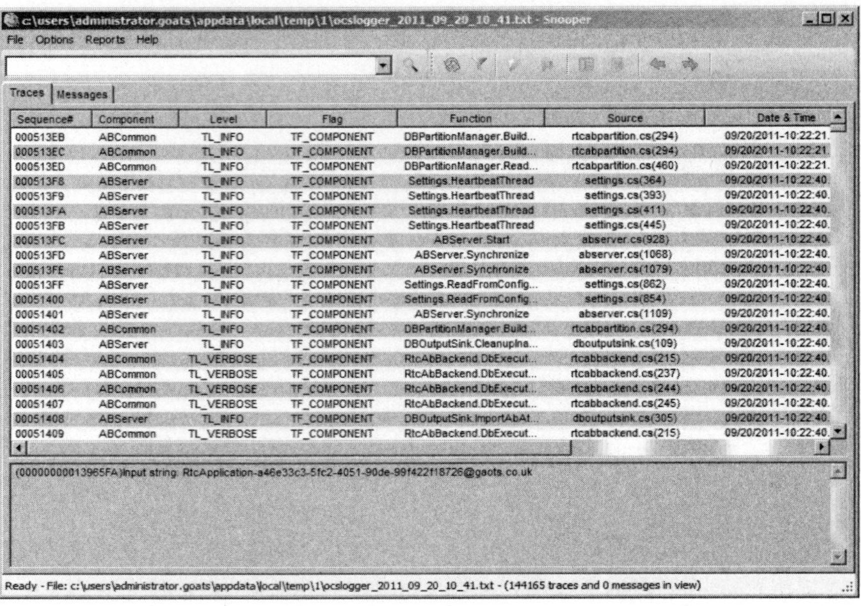

FIGURE 12.7
The Snooper Traces tab

Immediately upon loading a file, Snooper will display the Traces tab (as shown in Figure 12.7) and provide an additional Messages tab (shown in Figure 12.8). If the file is too large (over 25MB), a prompt will appear, asking if you want to load Traces, Messages, or Both.

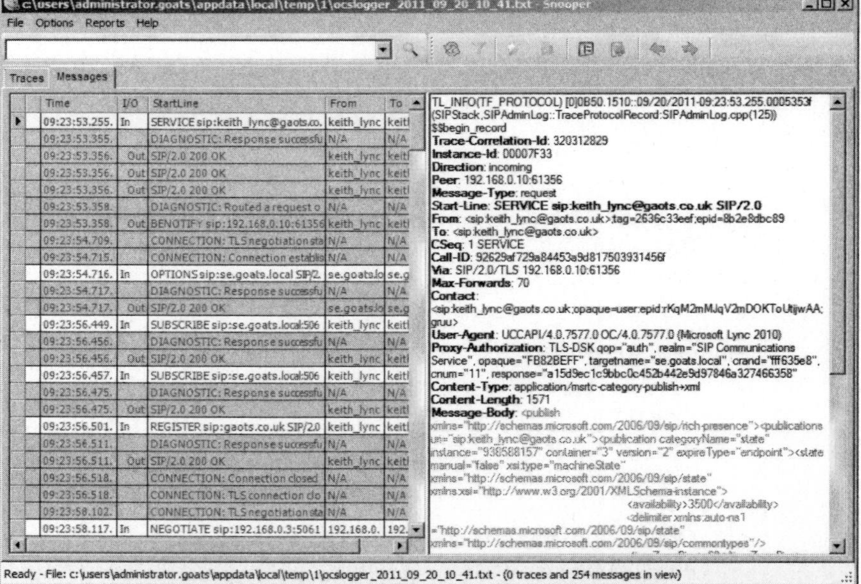

FIGURE 12.8
The Snooper Messages tab

Errors will be highlighted in red, allowing a quick and easy identification process. You may not always be interested in the errors on the Tracing tab because they typically show the result of the problem rather than the cause.

On the client, the component view shows UCCP (Unified Communications Client API); however, server logs provide many different component options (as listed in Table 12.1). Many of these traces are typically of more use to the Microsoft Product Support Services (PSS) than to the administrator.

The Messages tab is more useful to the administrator. Here, you can see the SIP flow of the client. Selecting a single message not only displays the associated content on the right, but also highlights all associated messages. For example, selecting a `SIP INVITE` message will display the content directly associated with that particular message, but it will also highlight the relevant message thread, all the way through to the `BYE` message.

However, where Snooper really comes into its own is the search capabilities, quickly allowing you to find the relevant parts of the log file that you are interested in. You can manually add entries into the search bar if you know the criteria to search for (simply type into the search bar)—typically, this starts with an error message or a username (or number) related to the problem.

The simple Search menu (shown in Figure 12.9) allows you to quickly build a search string from the text within the message to quickly narrow down the content in the log file. This becomes more relevant when you are dealing with server-generated log files, rather than the client.

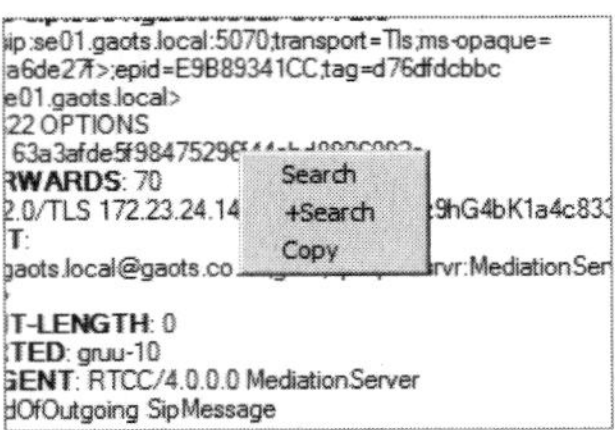

FIGURE 12.9
Searching with Snooper

Selecting Search will simply replace the current search criteria with the selection; however, selecting *+Search* will allow the selection to be added to the current search criteria. Figure 12.10 shows the search bar with a search string (created using +Search).

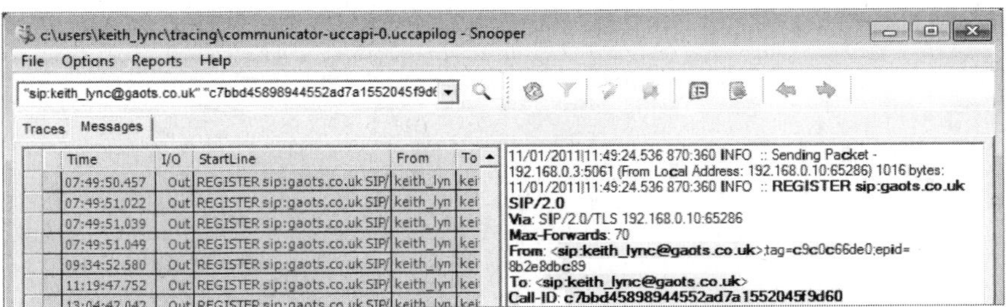

FIGURE 12.10
Building Search strings in Snooper

Obviously, being able to understand the expected process (that is, a SIP call flow) makes the troubleshooting easier because you know roughly what to expect and can interpret deviations from this expected flow to troubleshoot.

An overview of the SIP call flow process is provided in Chapter 2, "Standards and Protocols."

Diagnostic Message Text

One more feature is worth mentioning in the context of tracing. Besides providing Snooper to help you narrow down a problem, Lync Server 2010 has improved significantly on previous versions by including descriptive diagnostic text with all the messages. Some of these messages are shown here:

```
13004; reason="Request was proxied to one or more registered endpoints"
13014; reason="The routing rules did not result in a final response and callee is
not enabled for Unified Messaging"
51004; reason="Action initiated by user"
51007; reason="Callee media connectivity diagnosis info"
```

Other Troubleshooting Options

So far, we've covered only the server and client side logging of the Lync 2010 application itself. In this section, we'll look at some of the other areas where troubleshooting may be required, outside of the OCSLOGGER tool and the client logs.

We'll also touch on the performance counters available to provide a view into how the hardware is actually performing, as well as the synthetic transaction capability to provide automated testing of the Lync 2010 environment. Ideally, this would be integrated with System Center Operations Manager 2007 R2, providing the administrators with monitoring and alerting.

We'll have another look at the CDR report, this time in more detail, and we'll see which parts are of particular interest in troubleshooting.

Finally, we'll show how to capture the client configuration information, which will help confirm that the client is actually connecting to the correct servers!

Investigating Web Components

While most of the web components have specific entries within the OCSLOGGER tool for debugging, they are still web-based, so IIS logs will also need to be investigated.

There are two websites to consider (one for internal client connectivity and one for external client connectivity—we have separate websites as the security configurations are different on each, and indeed some capability—such as administration—is only available internally), each with its own set of log files. These log files will capture every web-based interaction; in a large deployment, they can grow in size very quickly, because every single client will make multiple web queries upon login (for Address Book updates, client updates, and so on).

> **FINDING THE IIS LOGS**
>
> First, you have to determine if the user is connecting to the internal web site or the external and then you need to establish to which server the client is connecting. For a Standard Edition pool this is straightforward, but you could be connecting to any front end in an enterprise pool, and not only that, but different connection types could be going to different servers!
>
> OCSLOGGER is similar and needs to be enabled on each server.

Control Panel

The Control Panel is a Silverlight application, so any issues involving connectivity and loading this page are going to fall under IIS also.

Device Troubleshooting

In the event of problems with devices (assuming the device has connected), there is a Send Logs option within the device menu itself, forcing the device to upload its log file to the web server to the following location:

```
%Lync Pool WebServices Folder%\DeviceUpdateLogs\
```

These logs are in Windows CE logfile format and require the use of the `ReadLog.exe` tool, which is part of Windows Embedded CE. This can be downloaded from the following location:

```
www.microsoft.com/windowsembedded/en-us/develop/windows-embedded-products-for-developers.aspx
```

Performance Counters

Windows servers come with a tool called `PerfMon.exe`, which can display a detailed view of counters within the server and any applications installed. Figure 12.11 shows `PerfMon.exe` in action.

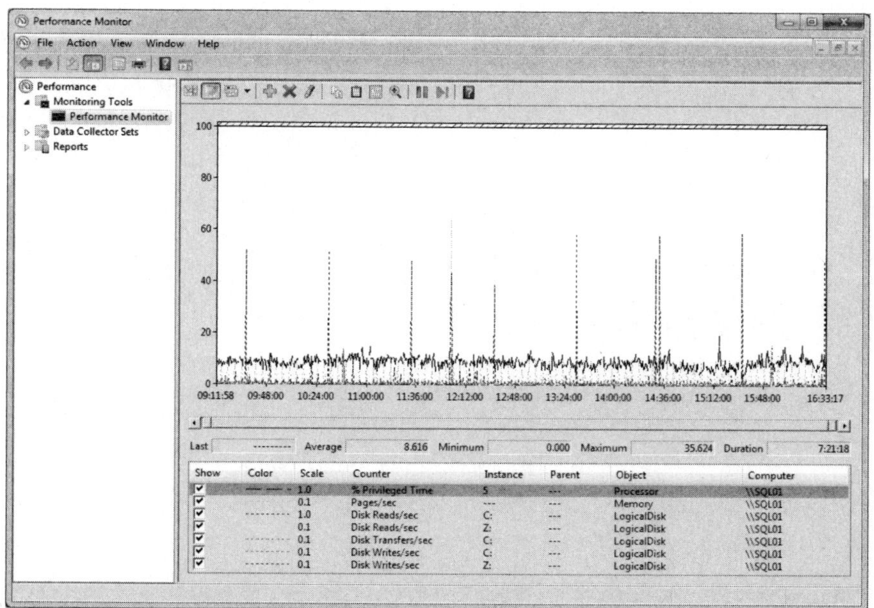

Figure 12.11 PerfMon.exe

Typical counters used to indicate generic server problems include:

- Processor
- Disk (both LogicalDisk and PhysicalDisk)
- Memory
- Network

As can be seen in Figure 12.11, multiple counters can be viewed at the same time, allowing for correlation of conditions. For example, if both network and disk activity increased simultaneously, it could indicate that a file is being copied across the network to (or from) the server.

Most applications will install application-specific counters; Lync Server 2010 is no different and installs over 100. Listed here are some of the more common counter categories, and specific objects within those categories (these were originally detailed in a blog entry regarding server health determination for OCS, at `http://blogs.technet.com/b/nexthop/archive/2007/09/20/how-can-i-tell-if-my-server-is-healthy-in-less-than-10-counters.aspx`; the counters and points in the blog are still relevant to Lync).

- LS:USrv - 01- DBSTORE\002 Queue Latency
- LS:USrv - 01- DBSTORE\004 Sproc Latency
- LS:SIP - 07 - Load Management\SIP - 000 - Average Holding Time for Incoming Messages
- LS:SIP - 01 - Peers\Flow Controlled Connections
- LS:SIP - 04 - Responses\SIP - 053 - Local 504 Responses/sec
- LS:SIP - 01 - Peers\SIP - 017 - Sends Outstanding

The full counter list can be found at `www.sybex.com/go/masteringlyncserver`.

Each of the counter categories (for example LS:SIP - 01 - Peers or LS:SIP - 04 - Responses) has a number of specific counters (for example Flow Controlled Connections) associated with it. In most cases, they will provide rates of message flow—for example, success per second—and can be used to determine the rate of successful connections, or more likely in the case of troubleshooting—the rates (and count) of failures can be interesting.

SQL also installs counters, and because SQL Express is installed on every Lync Server 2010 role, these allow further in-depth visibility of the databases. (SQL-specific counters are beyond the scope of this book).

Synthetic Transactions

Introduced in Chapter 11, "Archiving and Monitoring," the set of PowerShell cmdlets known as synthetic transactions are most useful when integrated with Microsoft System Center Operations Manager; however, they can be used effectively when troubleshooting because they simulate the activities carried out by the client. You can find the full list of cmdlets in Chapter 11. You'll only need a few of them for troubleshooting in this chapter.

Some of the cmdlets really are for one-time testing—for example, to test permissions prior to installation. The ones you are interested in, though, require a user ID as the parameter; this ensures that when a user reports a problem, an administrator can emulate all the correct policies that the user will be receiving, so the test is an accurate reflection of the settings applied to the user.

Before you can use the `Test-Cs` cmdlets that are based on user ID, you need to configure a Health Configuration. This consists of two test user accounts, typically disabled, but enabled for Lync, which the `Test-Cs` cmdlets will use for their accounts to simulate traffic.

```
New-CsHealthMonitoringConfiguration -TargetFqdn se.gaots.local
-FirstTestUserSipUri sip:test1_lync@gaots.co.uk -SecondTestUserSipUri sip:test2_
lync@gaots.co.uk

Identity                 : se.gaots.local
FirstTestUserSipUri      : sip:test1_lync@gaots.co.uk
FirstTestSamAccountName  :
FirstTestUserSipUri      : sip:test1_lync@gaots.co.uk
FirstTestSamAccountName  :
TargetFqdn               : se.gaots.local
```

Once the Health Configurations are configured for the pool, you can use the synthetic transactions to help troubleshoot.

For example, this command:

```
Test-CsIm -TargetFqdn se.gaots.local
```

will return the following if there are no problems:

```
TargetFqdn : se.gaots.local
Result     : Success
Latency    : 00:00:00.0203802
Error      :
Diagnosis  :
```

Some of the `Test-Cs` cmdlets require authentication and will produce a lot of screen data prior to the results. For example, before an Address Book is created (by default 01:30 AM the morning after the pool has been installed), this command:

```
Test-CsAddressBookWebQuery -TargetFqdn se.gaots.local
```

will return:

```
Connecting to web service : https://se.gaots.local/webticket/webticketservce.svc
Using Machine certificate authentication
Successfully created connection proxy and website bindings
Requesting new web ticket
Sending Web-Ticket Request:
```

This is followed by lots of XML, which has been shortened for brevity, and then, finally:

```
Creating WebTicket security token request

TargetUri   : https://se.gaots.local/groupexpansion/service.svc
TargetFqdn  : se.gaots.local
Result      : Failure
Latency     : 00:00:00
Error       : Address Book Web server request has failed with response code
NoEntryFound.
Diagnosis   :
```

On the other hand, if the web server itself is not running, the same command will return the following:

```
TargetUri   : https://se.gaots.local/groupexpansion/service.svc
TargetFqdn  : se.gaots.local
Result      : Failure
Latency     : 00:00:00
Error       : ERROR - No response received for Web-Ticket service.
Diagnosis   :
```

This response still provides the XML data; however, you can see that the error code gives a good indication of where the issue is located. Restarting the web service and allowing the Address Book to be generated (or using `Update-CsAddressBook`) gives the following response to the `Test-CsAddressBookWebQuery` command:

```
TargetUri   : https://se.gaots.local/groupexpansion/service.svc
TargetFqdn  : se.gaots.local
Result      : Success
Latency     : 00:00:20:5385645
Error       :
Diagnosis   :
```

Monitoring Reports

As mentioned in Chapter 11, the Call Detail Report provides an extremely detailed analysis of an individual call with almost 200 individual data points captured.

Some of these data points help to set the scene (network address information and client hardware and software versions, for example). However, the ones of particular interest in identification of a root cause of a problem are in the Media Line (Main Audio)—Device and Signal Metrics, Client Events, and Audio Stream sections. Each of these sections reports in a single direction for the call (such as caller to callee); however, the CDR report includes both directions, so you can compare what is sent and what is received.

Figure 12.12 shows these the three sections from the report (intervening sections have been removed for brevity).

FIGURE 12.12
Using the CDR report

Caller Device and Signal Metrics			
Capture device:	Headset Microphone (GN	Capture device driver:	Microsoft: 6.1.7600.16385
Render device:	Headset Earphone (GN 2000	Render device driver:	Microsoft: 6.1.7600.16385
Microphone glitch rate:	0 per 5 minutes	Speaker glitch rate:	0 per 5 minutes
Microphone timestamp drift:	0.00%	Speaker timestamp drift:	0.00%
Microphone timestamp error:	0.02 ms	Speaker timestamp error:	0.02 ms
Echo event cause:		Voice switch cause:	
Echo percent send:	1.50%	Echo percent microphone in:	14.19%
Send signal level:	-17 dBoV	Receive signal level:	-18 dBoV
Send noise level:	-55 dBoV	Receive noise level:	-56 dBoV
Echo return:		Initial signal level RMS:	4860.392
Caller Client Event			
CPU insufficient time:	0.00%	Microphone not functioning	0.00%
Speaker not functioning time:	0.00%	Clipping time:	0.00%
Echo time:	0.00%	Glitch time:	0.00%
Voice switch time:	0.00%	Low SNR time:	0.00%
Low speech level time:	0.00%	Near end to echo time:	0.00%
Device howling event count:	0	Device multiple endpoints	0
Low network bandwidth time:	0.00%	High network delay time:	35.00%
Poor network receive quality	0.00%	Poor network send quality	26.00%
Audio Stream (Callee -> Caller)			
Codec:	x-msrta	Sample rate:	16000
Audio FEC	False	Bandwdith estimates	431 Kbps
Packet utilization:	15689		
Avg. packet loss rate:	0.26%	Max. packet loss rate:	1.55%
Avg. jitter:	23 ms	Max. jitter:	47 ms
Avg. round trip:	551 ms	Max. round trip:	2157 ms
Burst duration:	0 ms	Burst gap duration:	310580 ms
Burst density:	0.00%	Burst gap density:	100.00%
Avg. concealed samples	3.00%	Avg. stretched samples ratio:	3.00%
Avg. compressed samples	9.00%		
Avg. Network MOS:	3.9	Min. Network MOS:	3.33
Avg .Network MOS	0.2	Max. Network MOS	0.77
NMOS degradation (jitter):	0	NMOS degradation (packet	0
Avg. Sending MOS	2.99	Min. Sending MOS	1.3
Avg. Listening MOS	3.41	Min. Listening MOS	1.42

DEVICE AND SIGNAL METRICS

The Device and Signal Metrics section of the report provides the hardware and software versions of the device in use, but more importantly from a troubleshooting perspective it provides the Send and Receive sound levels.

By comparing the caller *Send* values with the callee *Receive* values (and vice-versa), you can determine how much (if any) signal loss there has been due to the transmission.

Also included here is the amount of echo received by the microphone and the amount actually sent in the signal; this is a representation of how well (or badly) the echo cancellation in the device is working.

Caller Client Event

This section deals with the hardware associated with the device (including the PC if you are using built-in or USB-connected headphone and speakers).

Pay particular attention to the *time* values because they indicate how long the device has been malfunctioning; any value in the fields in this section indicates a problem with the call. Other sections of the report provide informational data, whereas any data in this section indicates a problem. You may need to refer to other sections to determine exactly what the problem is.

Audio Stream

The Audio Stream section covers the network impact to the call and provides information on the specific codec used for the call.

This section will help to determine if the network is causing any of the problems because this is where you can see information related to the packet loss, jitter, and round trip time. Also included here is information on how much healing was carried out on the call. Finally, the MOS values show how much impact the network conditions have had on the call quality.

In the example in Figure 12.12, the Avg. Round Trip value is excessive when compared to the expected values, and has been highlighted in red (which appears black in the printed book!); however, where values are slightly higher than expected, they would be highlighted in yellow.

Client Side

The connected client configuration can be determined by holding down the left Ctrl key and right-clicking the Lync 2010 icon in the system tray to bring up a menu from which you select the Configuration Information item. This will call up the screen shown in Figure 12.13.

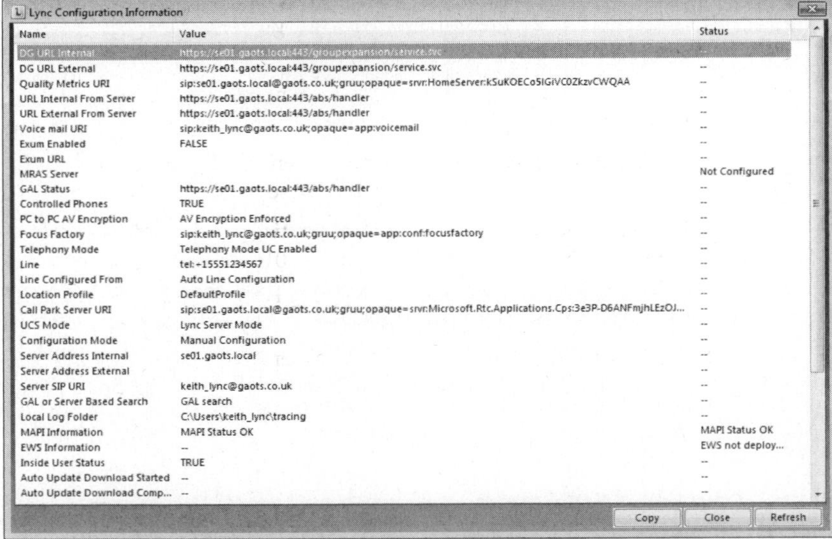

FIGURE 12.13
Configuration information

The Lync 2010 client will cache a significant set of information, ranging from configuration items and search query results to photos and voicemails.

To ensure that the latest configuration information is being provided to the client and remove the possibility of stale cached information, the cache files in the following folder location should be deleted:

```
%USER PROFILE%\AppData\Local\Microsoft\Communicator\sip_<sip address>\
```

For the Lync 2010 Attendee client, replace `Communicator` with `AttendeeCommunicator` in the previous path.

The Bottom Line

Confirm that the basics are in place from the infrastructure side. Lync Server 2010 relies on a range of additional infrastructure to be able to provide its functionality—such as Active Directory, SQL, DNS, Network, and so on. If any of these additional areas suffer interruptions or misconfigurations, it is extremely likely that Lync 2010 will begin to demonstrate issues also.

Master It An internal Lync 2010 client is having difficulty connecting to its home pool when using automatic configuration. Describe the flow of DNS and connection attempts made for a client on the corporate network.

Understand how to troubleshoot the client. The Lync 2010 client provides a lot of information in the configuration section as well as the log files to aid with troubleshooting and should not be overlooked.

Master It Where are the client log files stored?

Know how to enable troubleshooting on the server. The Lync Server 2010 roles each have individual components that require logging and also provide performance counter objects that can be monitored.

By default, logging is not enabled on the servers, and it has a number of different levels to which it can be applied.

Master It Which tool is used to enable logging and configure the specific logging parameters on a Lync Server 2010 server?

Understand and use the troubleshooting tools available. In addition to the built-in logging functionality of Lync Server 2010, additional tools can (and should) be downloaded and installed on each of the servers to provide a better range of data, which is ready to be captured in the event of a problem.

Master It Which tool is recommended to be used for analyzing SIP logs or message traces? And where can it be found?

Part 4

Voice

Chapter 13

Getting Started with Voice

Lync Server 2010, unlike its predecessors, is capable of matching and replacing most (if not all but the very largest) PBXs and providing fully fledged voice capability to the user both via the Lync 2010 Communicator client and the desktop phone device.

Because users' expectations for voice have increased to be on par with PBX, this is important. Can you remember the last time your company had a problem that caused the PBX to fail? In most cases, this is extremely rare! People expect to pick up a phone and have it just work. Lync Server 2010 must match this level of expectation if it is to replace a PBX.

In this chapter, you will learn to:

- Understand the Voice Capabilities
- Understand the Voice Architecture
- Configure Voice Policies and Routing

The Back Story

In the early days of the Microsoft Unified Communications suite (before it was even called Unified Communications), Live Communications Server provided a feature called Remote Call Control, and while this feature is slowly being deprecated with each new version, it was the first way to integrate an instant message product with voice functionality (albeit through a traditional style telephony system). Remote Call Control works by allowing the Communicator client to send signaling information to the PBX, via a dedicated server/interface, allowing control of the desk handset—you clicked (or typed) a number and then picked up the handset to talk.

Office Communications Server 2007 introduced the concept of Enterprise Voice, whereby the Communicator client itself was considered a phone (either hardware or software) and integrated via a media gateway device into a traditional (or IP) PBX or, indeed, directly to the PSTN. Office Communications Server 2007 R2 developed the voice functionality further and moved closer to being a PBX; however, there was still functionality whereby the PBX was required—only in certain cases (typically, small companies or branches) could OCS 2007 R2 be considered capable of replacing a PBX.

As you'll see in the following pages, Lync Server 2010 is designed to overcome that limitation.

Understanding the Voice Capabilities

As mentioned previously, Lync Server 2010 expands the voice capabilities previously developed in versions of Office Communications Server 2007 (and 2007 R2). Table 13.1 shows the feature set and when each feature was first introduced. These are all cumulative; if a feature is listed as OCS 2007, it is also available in OCS 2007 R2 and Lync Server 2010 unless specifically indicated.

TABLE 13.1: Voice Feature Set

FEATURE NAME	FIRST AVAILABLE	SUMMARY
Inbound/outbound PSTN dialing	OCS 2007	Basic call functionality.
Call Forward	OCS 2007	This is the ability to have incoming calls automatically forwarded to another contact or external number.
Simultaneous Ring	OCS 2007	Similar to call forwarding, but instead of redirecting the call, it allows both the UC endpoint and the other endpoint to ring and be answered at either endpoint.
Unified Messaging	OCS 2007	Voice mail capability.
Single Number Reach	OCS 2007 R2 (scheduled for release in a later Lync Cumulative Update)	This is the ability to place a call from a mobile device and have that call routed via the OCS 2007 R2 infrastructure to enable the presentation of the OCS 2007 R2 user caller ID, and the capture of Call Detail Records (CDRs).
Delegation/Team Call	OCS 2007 R2	Allows others to handle calls on your behalf.
SIP trunking	OCS 2007 R2	Allows direct connection to a Mediation server without the use of a media gateway.
Dial-in Audio Conferencing	OCS 2007 R2	Provides audio-only conferencing to PSTN users.
Response Group	OCS 2007 R2	Provides small-scale call center capability.
Call Admission Control	Lync Server 2010	Provides controls for the quality and quantity of calls on the network.
Call Park	Lync Server 2010	Provides the capability to *park* a call from one Lync device and *retrieve* from another.
Unassigned Number Handling	Lync Server 2010	Allows for handling of incoming calls to numbers that have not been assigned to users.
Media bypass	Lync Server 2010	Endpoints can connect directly to another non-Lync endpoint (via G711) without the need to have the media transcoded by a Mediation server.

TABLE 13.1: Voice Feature Set *(CONTINUED)*

FEATURE NAME	FIRST AVAILABLE	SUMMARY
E911	Lync Server 2010	Support for the Enhanced 911 emergency services requirements to provide location information with an emergency call.
Analog Devices	Lync Server 2010	Support for analog device integration, allowing for application of policy and capture of CDR information from non-Lync devices.
Common Area Phone	Lync Server 2010	Provides the ability to designate a device as a common area device (for use in areas such as a lobby), allowing the device to be available for inbound and outbound calls under a generic policy, and the capacity to allow a user to log in and use the device as their own, but be automatically logged out after a time period.
Private Line	Lync Server 2010	Provides a user with a second number allowing the direct receipt of incoming calls
Malicious Call Trace	Lync Server 2010	Allows a call to be flagged as malicious in the CDR database.

A number of these Lync Server 2010 capabilities are covered elsewhere in this book. Table 13.2 provides a cross reference to those chapters.

TABLE 13.2: Lync Server Capability Cross Reference

CAPABILITY	CHAPTER
Call Admission Control	14
Call Park	16
Unassigned Number Handling	16
E911	15
Analog Devices	4
Common Area Phone	4
Private Line, Malicious Call Trace, Media bypass (covered in more detail in this chapter)	1

Private Line

A private line allows a user to have a second Direct Inward Dial (DID) number assigned to them, which will directly notify the user of an incoming call. As indicated by the name, it is intended to be for private calls only; therefore, the call does not follow any team-call or delegation configured rules. It also ignores any presence-based rules such as Do-Not-Disturb, ensuring that it will always get through.

The private line can only be set via PowerShell, using the `Set-CsUser` cmdlet, as in this example:

```
Set-CsUser -identity "sip:keith_lync@gaots.co.uk" -PrivateLine "tel:+15557654321"
```

The number assigned to the private line does not appear anywhere within Active Directory (ensuring it remains private) and indeed is even hidden within Lync Server. To view the number (and other hidden attributes), you must use the `Get-CsUser` cmdlet with the following syntax:

```
Get-CsUser -Identity "sip:keith_lync@gaots.co.uk" | fl *
```

The resulting output looks like this:

```
SamAccountName                      : keith_lync
UserPrincipalName                   : keith_lync@gaots.co.uk
FirstName                           : Keith
LastName                            : Lync
WindowsEmailAddress                 : Keith_lync@gaots.co.uk
Sid                                 : S-1-5-21-51255695-3231353671-2943866482-78963
LineServerURI                       :
OriginatorSid                       :
AudioVideoDisabled                  : False
IPPBXSoftPhoneRoutingEnabled        : False
RemoteCallControlTelephonyEnabled : False
PrivateLine                         : tel+15557654321
AcpInfo                             : {}
HostedVoiceMail                     :
DisplayName                         : Keith Lync
ProxyAddresses                      : {eum:34567;phone-context=test.gaots.local,
EUM:Keith_lync@gaots.co.uk; phone-context=test.gaots.local, sip:keith_lync@gaots.
co.uk, SMTP:keith_lync@gaots.co.uk....}
HomeServer                          : CN=Lc Services,CN=Microsoft,CN=1:1,CN=Pools,C
N=RTC Service,CN=Services,CN=Configuration,DC=gaots,DC=local
TargetServerIfMoving                :
EnabledForFederation                : True
EnabledForInternetAccess            : True
PublicNetworkEnabled                : True
EnterpriseVoiceEnabled              : True
EnabledForRichPresence              : True
LineURI                             : tel:+445551234567
SipAddress                          : sip:Keith_lync@gaots.co.uk
```

```
Enabled                           : True
TenantId                          : 00000000-0000-0000-0000-000000000000
TargetRegistrarPool               :
VoicePolicy                       :
ConferencingPolicy                :
PresencePolicy                    :
RegistrarPool                     : se01.gaots.local
DialPlan                          :
LocationPolicy                    :
ClientPolicy                      :
ClientVersionPolicy               :
ArchivingPolicy                   :
PinPolicy                         :
ExternalAccessPolicy              : Allow No Access
HostedVoicemailPolicy             :
HostingProvider                   : SRV:
Name                              : Keith Lync
DistinguishedName                 : CN=Keith Lync,CN=Users,DC=gaots,DC=local
Identity                          : CN=Keith Lync,CN=Users,DC=gaots,DC=local
Guid                              : a64a9537-de65-4740-9198-9d83314fde96
ObjectCategory                    : CN=Person,CN=Schema,CN=Configuration,DC=gaots
,DC=local
ObjectClass                       : {top, person, organizationalPerson, user}
WhenChanged                       : 16/08/2011 09:01:02
WhenCreated                       : 05/05/2011 15:09:24
OriginatingServer                 : dc01.gaots.local
IsValid                           : True
ObjectState                       : Unchanged
```

Although Private Line can be configured without enabling Enterprise Voice, the user must be Enterprise Voice–enabled for Private Line to work.

The bold entries indicate the attributes that are not shown on-screen by default, but that are returned by the `Get-CsUser` cmdlet. One attribute of significant note is the `TargetServerIfMoving` attribute. It is set to True if the user is in the process of moving pools. No other cmdlets will succeed for a user if this attribute is True.

Malicious Call Trace

Lync Server 2010 provides the ability for a user to flag the previous call as malicious immediately after hanging up the call. The data is flagged within a CDR record and, as such, requires the Monitoring server role to be deployed and configured. When a call is flagged, an entry is logged in the CDR database and allows the administrator to identify the call as well as the associated information: calling number, gateways used, duration of call, and so on.

Figure 13.1 shows the user interface to flag a malicious call.

FIGURE 13.1
Flagging a malicious call

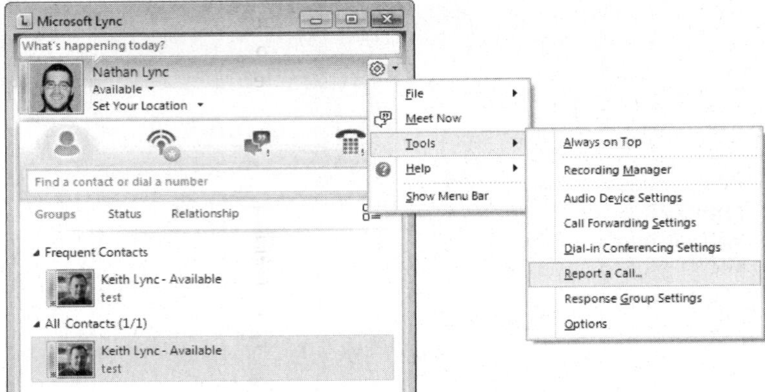

Malicious call tracing is enabled as part of the Voice policy applied to users via the `Set-CsVoicePolicy` cmdlet, or through the Control Panel ➤ Voice Routing ➤Voice Policy page (see Figure 13.2).

FIGURE 13.2
Enabling malicious call tracing via the Control Panel

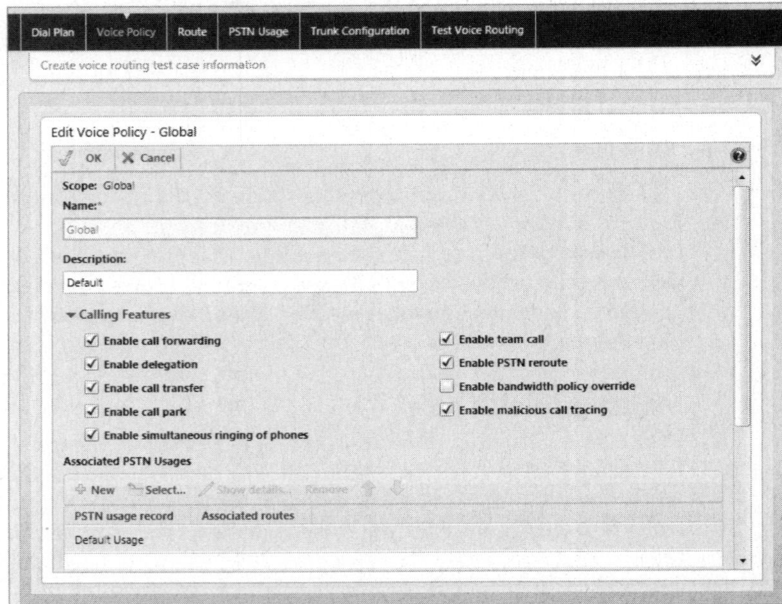

It is important to understand that aside from the entry being logged in the CDR database, there is no automated process to alert an administrator of a malicious call. You must monitor the database via System Center Operations Manager or other similar alerting system to enable some sort of automated alerting.

A manual query can be performed using the Top Failure Report from the Monitoring server report pack. To filter for malicious calls, you must select the following filter items:

Category: Both expected and unexpected failures

Diagnostic ID: 51017

Figure 13.3 shows an example of the filtered report.

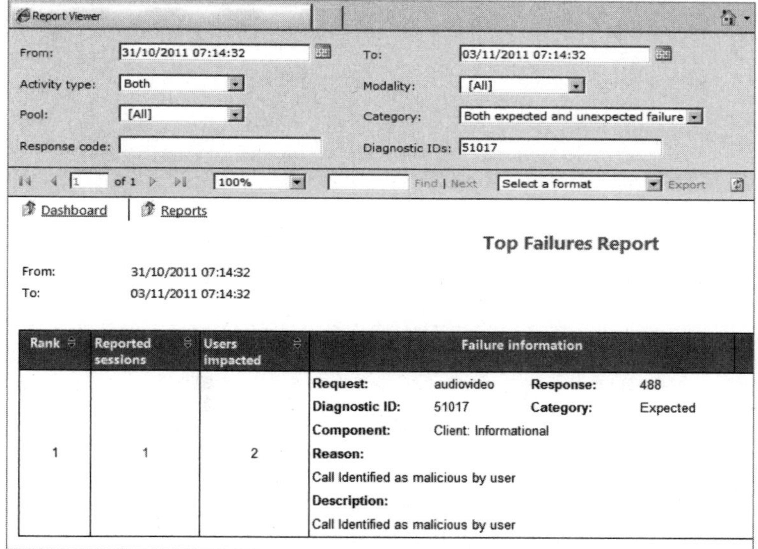

FIGURE 13.3
Malicious call reporting

Media Bypass

Lync Server 2010 introduced an important key feature called media bypass, which allows an organization to reduce the number of servers required (specifically reducing the load on Mediation servers).

So what's the big deal? Well, media bypass allows the Lync 2010 clients to talk directly to non-Lync (or OCS) endpoints without transcoding the media stream by the Mediation server. Reducing the need for transcoding from native OCS codecs (such as RTAudio) to PSTN-style codecs (such as G711) improves the quality of the audio stream by reducing the number of network hops as well as reducing the loss when changing codecs.

OCS 2007 R2 introduced the capability for clients to use a G711 codec natively; however, the media stream still had to pass through the Mediation server (even though no transcoding occurred) when making a PSTN call.

The G711 codec uses more bandwidth but provides a better-quality signal than RTAudio; however, the RTAudio codec copes better on congested networks. Therefore, it is a better choice across WAN connections, and G711 is preferred on a LAN.

Where the media gateway (or compatible IP-PBX) is located on the same LAN, it makes more sense to use the higher-quality codec because it is likely the LAN will be able to cope with the (small) increase in traffic. Enabling media bypass allows this to happen and delivers the media stream directly to the gateway (or IP-PBX).

Signaling traffic (SIP) will continue to pass through the Mediation server. Figure 13.4 shows the path of each type of traffic for a PSTN call.

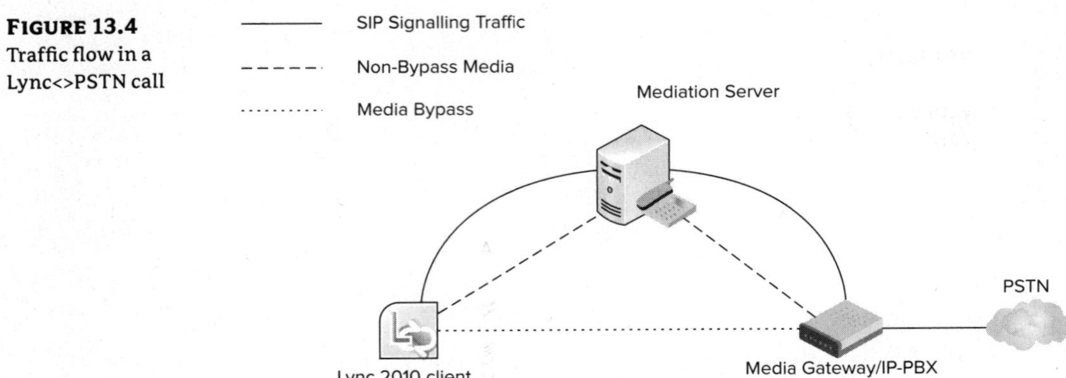

FIGURE 13.4
Traffic flow in a Lync<>PSTN call

Removing the transcoding from a Mediation server dramatically increases the concurrent call capability of the server, and it allows the server role to be colocated with a front-end server, reducing the number of servers required in a voice deployment.

Understanding the Voice Architecture

Media bypass is a good context in which to look at the voice architecture within Lync Server 2010 and understand what is needed to provide Enterprise Voice capability to users.

Obviously, you need a pool (either Standard or Enterprise Edition) on which the users are to be homed. In addition, you need the Mediation server role to be installed and a certified integration device (either: media gateway, IP-PBX, or SIP trunk). These functions no longer have to be physical hardware because virtualization is fully supported. Figure 13.5 shows the minimum requirements for Enterprise Voice.

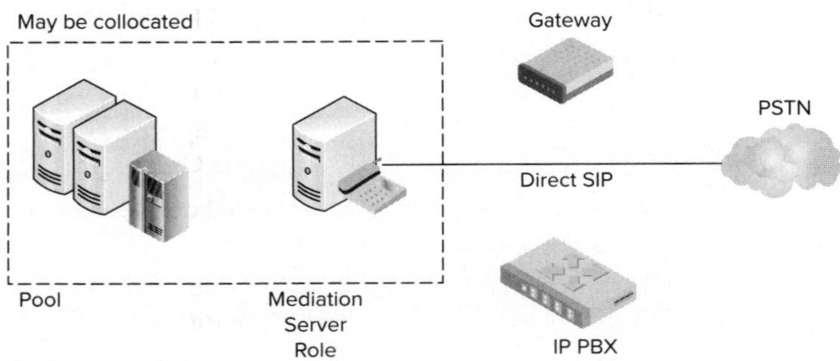

FIGURE 13.5
Minimum requirements for Enterprise Voice

Again, this configuration is the minimum required in order to provide Enterprise Voice. More realistically, we will be looking at additional configuration such as high availability and resiliency options, improved reporting and troubleshooting, expanded client (device) support, and increased configuration items such as E911 or Call Admission Control. This is where you'll start to get into the depths of the voice requirements for a design, not only hardware capability but configuration as well.

The full scope of Enterprise Voice interaction or requirements is shown in Figure 13.6.

FIGURE 13.6
Voice architecture within Lync Server 2010

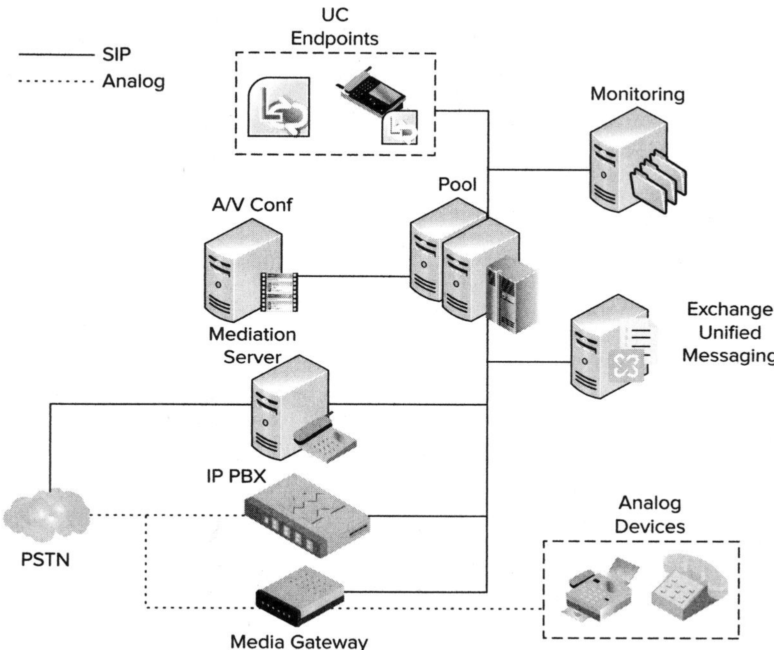

With this view of the building blocks of Enterprise Voice, you can examine the role that each component will play:

UC Endpoints This is the actual user device; it may be the softphone Communicator client or a desktop device running Lync 2010 Phone Edition.

Pool This is the "heart" of the system. Clients register against a pool and receive a policy, which in turn will determine what can be made by each user, as well as the feature set provided to each user. In addition, configuration items such as call routing, Call Admission Control, E911, Call Park, and Response Groups are all configured on the pool.

A/V Conf This role may be colocated on the front-end servers, and is responsible for the audio conferencing capabilities.

Mediation Server This role may be colocated on the front-end servers and is responsible for all PSTN call-signaling information. In addition, it will transcode the media traffic when required.

IP PBX A certified device capable of media bypass. If not certified, it requires connectivity via a certified media gateway; if not capable of media bypass, it requires a Mediation server role to transcode the client media. A non-IP PBX (legacy) may be connect via a certified media gateway.

Media Gateway A certified device capable of media bypass. If not capable of media bypass, it requires a Mediation server role to transcode the client media. Also capable of supporting the connectivity of analog devices (such as a FAX machine) and allowing Lync Server 2010 to control these devices.

Monitoring Captures the CDR and Quality of Experience (QoE) information, allowing the reporting and troubleshooting of calls. This role is not required but is strongly recommended when you're deploying Enterprise Voice.

Exchange Unified Messaging Exchange 2007 SP1 (or higher) provides the voice mail capability for Lync Server 2010.

We've already covered a lot of these integration points in other chapters, so let's focus on the PSTN integration aspect now—Mediation servers.

Understanding Mediation Servers

In both versions of Office Communications Server 2007, the Mediation server had a 1:1 relationship with a media gateway (or IP-PBX). This meant that a large number of Mediation servers were required, and there was no flexibility for the supported hardware. It didn't matter how many calls your Mediation server was handling through the gateway on the other side; the same hardware was required for the server. In addition to this, a failure in either the Mediation server or the gateway would invalidate that route for calls.

With Lync Server 2010, that 1:1 relationship has gone away. Now there is no practical limit to the number of gateways a single Mediation server can service; there is only the maximum number of concurrent calls a single Mediation server can handle, of course! Even this maximum number is now variable based on the specifications of the hardware in use.

Not only that, but Mediation servers can now be pooled in Lync Server 2010, providing an additional level of resiliency to the call flow.

Figure 13.7 compares the Office Communications Server approach and the Lync Server 2010 approach to Mediation servers.

FIGURE 13.7
The OCS 2007 versus Lync Server 2010 Mediation server approaches

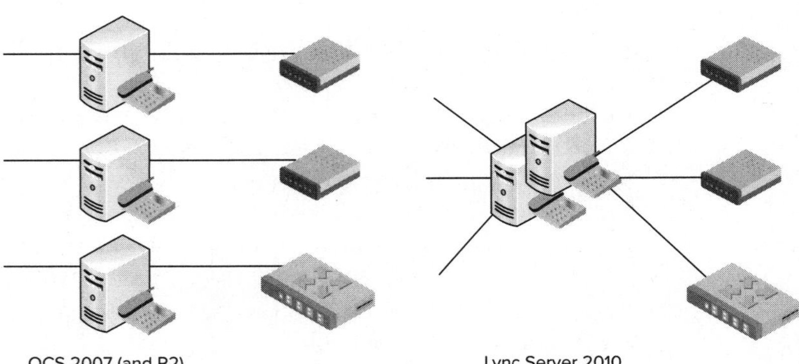

The Office Communications Server approach is still valid with Lync Server 2010 even if media bypass is not enabled. That is, the Mediation server will deal not only with SIP traffic, but also the media transcoding.

In the SIP trunk scenario, a dedicated Mediation server is required to provide a termination point for the Lync 2010 endpoints.

High Availability and Resiliency for Voice

When Lync Server 2010 replaces a PBX, the user's expectations don't change. Telephony has been around for decades, and the expectation of always being able to make a call when you pick up a handset is normal.

Rightly or wrongly, user expectations about the uptime and availability of IT services are still very poor, based mostly on the early "Blue-Screen-of-Death" experiences of Windows NT despite the massive steps forward since then.

Lync Server 2010 has to overcome this preconception, so that when there are challenges with the integrity of the IT infrastructure (whether networking or server related) the telephony service will continue and users will (hopefully) be unaffected. This is not possible in all cases, but Lync Server 2010 does a fantastic job of overcoming the majority of these cases to ensure that service continues.

The different failure scenarios that will be considered here include:

- Individual server failure: Front-end
- Individual server failure: Mediation
- Multiple server failure: Complete pool
- Multiple server failure: Complete datacenter
- Remote site: WAN failure
- Active Directory failure

In general, high availability is achieved by adding more servers of the same role to the configuration, either as standalone (using some sort of round-robin resource allocation) or as pool-based (using DNS or hardware load balancing) resources. If one of the servers fails, the others of the same role will take over the services of that server. In most cases, this is seamless; however, in a few cases, there may be a small impact.

Before you review each case, you need to understand the call flows involved in making an Enterprise Voice (PSTN) call. Although you'll review only a PSTN call in detail here, all of this applies equally to a peer-to-peer call, except for the Mediation server role. Figure 13.8 shows the anatomy of a call; the Mediation server role is broken out separately so you can better understand the call flow.

FIGURE 13.8
Call flow of an Enterprise Voice call

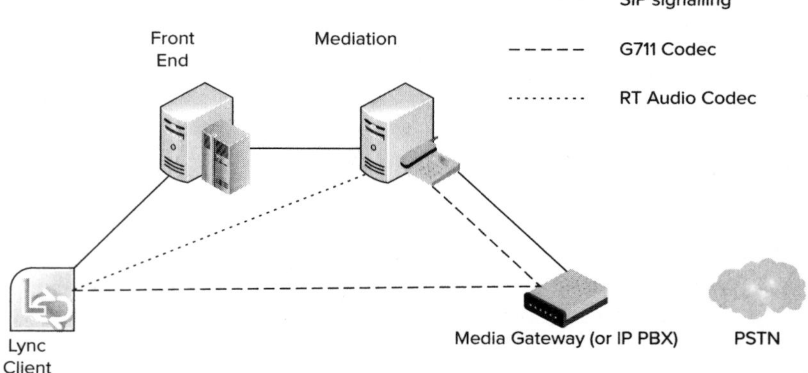

You can see the signaling traffic flows from the Lync 2010 client through the front-end server to the Mediation server and finally to the gateway or IP PBX. Media takes a more direct route, from the client through the Mediation server to the gateway—or, if media bypass is supported and enabled, directly from the client to the gateway itself.

Individual Server Failure: Front-End Server

The failure of an individual front-end server in an enterprise pool does not have a significant impact on users logged in or to calls already in progress. If a user was logged in via the failed server, they will automatically reconnect to another front-end server in the pool (via either hardware or DNS load balancing). If the user is in a call at the time of their server failure, the call will continue unaffected (this functionality was introduced in Office Communications Server 2007 R2); however, signaling will be unavailable until the Lync 2010 client is signed into another front-end server. Figure 13.9 shows the user experience of the call in progress while the client is unable to connect to the front-end server.

Figure 13.9 User experience mid-call with a front-end failure

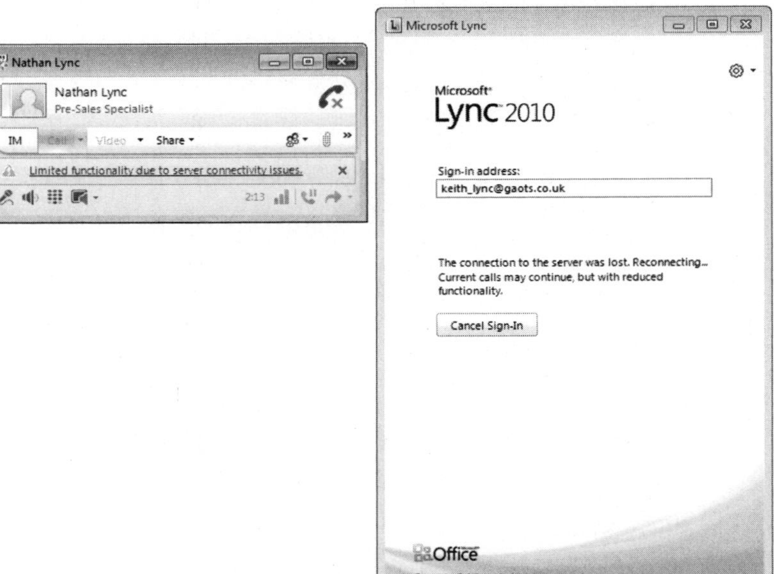

The impact of signaling not being available is that although the media traffic continues, no changes can be made to it, such as call transfer or placing the call on hold. These functions will automatically become available again when the client (automatically) signs in to another front-end server, or when the failed server is returned to service (whichever occurs first).

If a user is dialed into a conference hosted on the failed front-end server, they will be disconnected and will have to redial to rejoin the conference—which will be moved to an available server in the same pool.

INDIVIDUAL SERVER FAILURE: MEDIATION SERVER

The loss of a Mediation server is very similar to the loss of a front-end server unless the Mediation server is performing media transcoding for a call, in which case the call will be dropped.

The call flow is as shown in Figure 13.7, and the user experience is as shown in Figure 13.8, with the exception that the client will remain signed in.

Once the mediation server is in a failed state, the routing processes on the front-end servers are notified of the downed Mediation server and will route any calls being placed to other suitable Mediation servers.

For incoming calls, the gateway will be aware of the failure (because of the failed heartbeat SIP message exchange) and will redirect calls to another Mediation server.

MULTIPLE SERVER FAILURE: COMPLETE POOL

Previously, when a user's complete pool failed, the user would be logged out and unable to carry out any tasks. A call in progress at this point would continue to operate with no signaling functionality available—assuming Office Communications Server 2007 R2 rather than Office Communications Server 2007 (where it would be dropped).

Lync Server 2010 introduces the concept of a *backup* registrar; this is where the client will connect in the event of a failure in its primary registrar. A primary registrar failure comprises all the servers in the pool failing.

There are a few items that must be configured to achieve this. First, the topology of a pool must be configured (and published) to have a backup registrar assigned (shown in Figure 13.10). Associated with this configuration are some timeout values:

- Failover timeout (default 300 seconds)
- Failback timeout (default 600 seconds)

These default values are deliberately set slightly high to ensure that simple "blips" on the network do not cause all the clients to fail over to another pool and back again in quick succession.

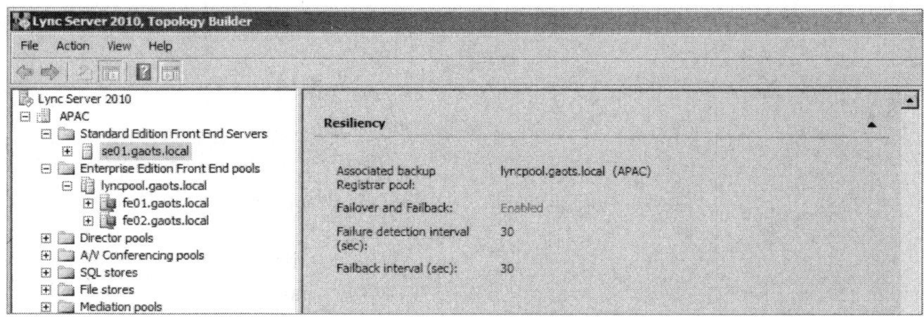

FIGURE 13.10 Configuring a backup registrar

Next, you are required to configure the DNS SRV record for automatic login to have multiple entries, possibly with different priorities (this will depend on the environment). If you are using a Director in the environment, this will have the highest priority for the SRV record, with the primary pool being next. The highest priority record is the one that all clients will attempt to connect to first. This setting is more important in a widely distributed deployment; you may not want European clients attempting to connect to a U.S.-based pool for their first attempt, even though the traffic is quite a small SIP request.

The use of multiple entries for the same SRV record ensures that if the first record directs to a pool that is unavailable, the client will try the next and so on until it finds an available pool to which to connect. Once connected, this pool will redirect to the correct pool (either primary or backup) if online.

The `SIP REGISTER` redirect request for the initial login will include a response like this:

```
01/08/2011|13:19:57.260 4D4:6F8 INFO  :: SIP/2.0 301 Redirect request to Home
Server
Contact: <sip:se01.gaots.co.uk:5061;transport=TLS>;q=0.7
Contact: <sip:lyncpool.gaots.co.uk:5061;transport=TLS>;q=0.3
```

This means that the client will attempt to register with the primary pool first, indicated by the `q=0.7`, and if that is unavailable will fail over to the backup pool, indicated by the `q=0.3`.

When the primary pool has failed, and the client has connected to the backup registrar, not all functionality is available. Some of the built-in functionality is specific to a pool, such as:

- Response Groups
- Call Park
- Conferencing
- Buddy List
- Presence-based Routing (such as Do-Not-Disturb)

The client goes into Survivable mode and displays a warning message to the user (see Figure 13.11). When the primary registrar comes back online, the client will automatically fail back; however, that does not happen immediately, as it's based on the failback timeout value.

FIGURE 13.11
Client Survivable mode

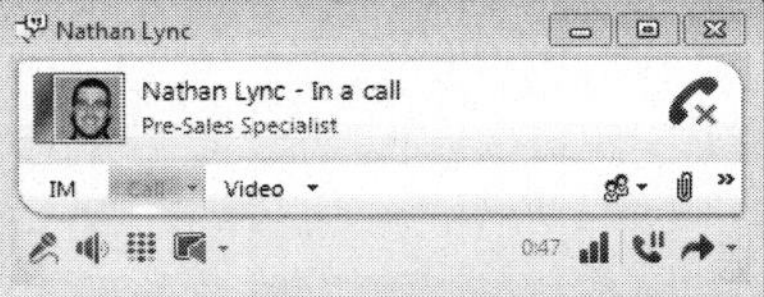

In summary, once the backup registrar is configured, in the event of failure of the primary pool, the client will automatically connect in Survivable mode to the backup pool. In Survivable mode, the client will continue to be able to make and receive PSTN calls but will have limited pool functionality.

Geographical Pool Failure

The primary and backup registrar functionality will work over a global network, but for the PSTN calling feature to be still available, the telephony capability must also be available globally. For example, a U.S.-based pool could have its backup provided by a pool in Europe, but the users would still have a United States phone number. Although Lync Server 2010 fully supports this, the telecom provider must also support rerouting the calls globally in the event of failure.

A pool can be the backup for any other pool, and Enterprise and Standard Edition pools can be used as backups for each other. If this mixed approach is taken, you must be aware of the scaling and consider that if a Standard Edition pool is the backup for an Enterprise Edition pool, the capacity of the Standard Edition pool must not be overloaded in the event of the Enterprise pool failing (bearing in mind that the capacity of a Standard Edition Lync Server 2010 is 5,000).

The Survivable Branch Appliance (SBA) is a combination *primary* registrar (only), Mediation server, and gateway, and it works in conjunction with a pool. If a pool failure occurs in this scenario, even though the client is still connected to a *primary* registrar, it will go into Survivable mode, as its connection to the main pool is lost.

Multiple Server Failure: Complete Datacenter

Now that you've considered the complete pool failure in the previous section, what about the next level up—the significant event of a loss of a datacenter?

Well, in many cases this is simply the same as the loss of a pool; there is a second datacenter with its pool configured as the backup registrar, and additional roles such as the Mediation server and gateways in this datacenter. In fact, this may be an active datacenter with the users split between both datacenters, or it could be a standby ready and waiting for the disaster to happen. In this case, to be supported it must be active but with no users homed on it. Microsoft does not support having this as a "cold standby" pool.

Another option to handle this failure level is the Metropolitan pool approach (introduced in Chapter 1), where a single pool is *stretched* between both datacenters. This is possible when the datacenters are well connected and have a network latency of less than 20ms; this requirement allows the SQL cluster (with synchronous data replication) to support the pool back-end database, which requires a stretched layer-2 VLAN to operate.

The Metropolitan architecture is shown in Figure 13.12. In addition to the pool itself being stretched between the two datacenters, additional infrastructure that the pool relies on must also be stretched, such as the file share.

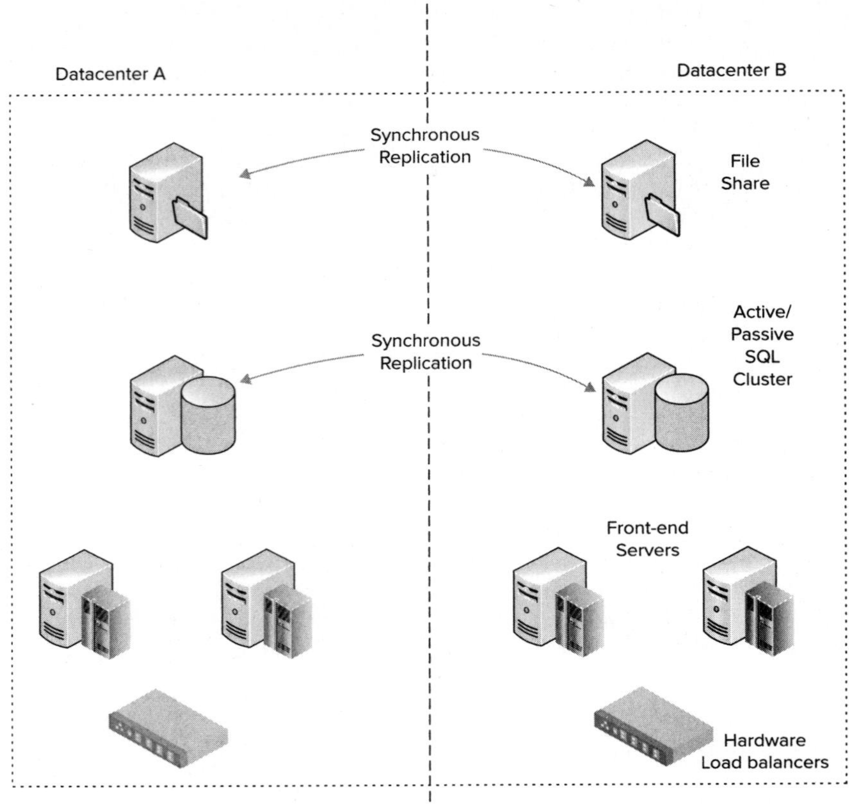

FIGURE 13.12 Metropolitan datacenter architecture

This approach provides a level of resilience above and beyond that offered by the primary/backup registrar; however, the cost comes in the complexity of the networking requirements.

All front-end servers are active and dealing with clients; and in the event of a failure of one datacenter, the SQL cluster will fail over and the remaining server will continue to operate normally. There may be a brief outage to the client during the SQL failover time (the client may go into Survivable mode during this time); however, all the functionality available within a pool is available once SQL is online again.

When sizing this environment, it is important to size for the worst-case scenario—datacenter failure. Therefore, each datacenter should be sized to cope with a 100 percent load, which will significantly increase the number of servers required.

It's worth noting that the Metropolitan datacenter approach could be combined with the backup registrar configuration to allow continued telephony operation in the event of two datacenter failures.

Remote Site: WAN Failure

The last few sections looked primarily at the datacenter and considered failures to individual servers and the complete datacenter. But what happens to those branch offices in the event of a network failure? Is there a solution for them? Well, as you've already seen, the Survivable Branch Appliance (SBA), has been designed to handle this scenario. Specifically, the SBA is designed for offices with between 25 and 1,000 users; different hardware versions of the SBA can handle different sized workloads. The SBA, as its name implies, is an appliance device. The Lync Server 2010 aspects are centrally configured and will replicate to it when installed.

So what is an SBA? It's a hardened version of Windows Server 2008 R2, with only the registrar and mediation services installed from Lync Server 2010. Once joined to a domain and initialized, the Lync Server 2010 installation will replicate the configuration from the Central Management Store. Then the device will become an active part of the topology and will be able to host users. The SBA is configured through Topology Builder as part of the Branch Site settings, as shown in Figure 13.13. Notice that the Resiliency options are configured by default for an SBA.

FIGURE 13.13
Configuring an SBA

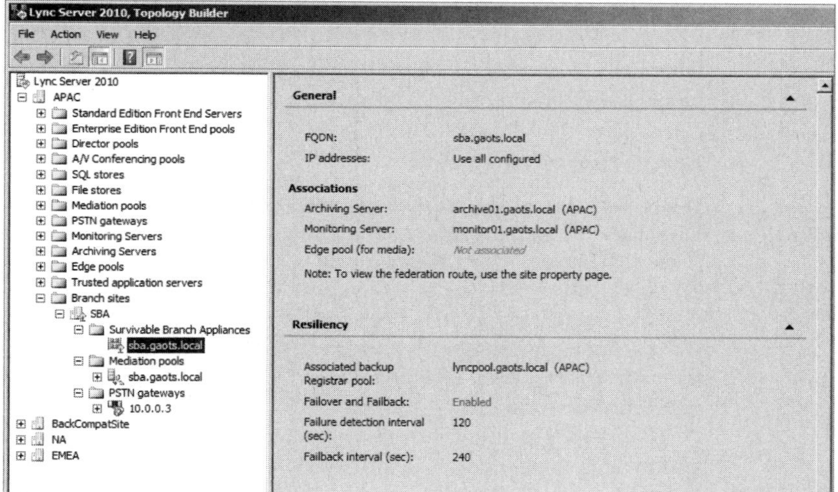

In addition to the Windows Server 2008 R2 and Lync Server 2010 installations, the SBA also includes a media gateway device; this is what will vary in size or type depending on number of users to be supported.

Users register in the same way with an SBA as they would with a pool; however, they are automatically associated with a backup pool as part of the SBA configuration. The SBA does not provide user services (conferencing and buddy list) capability, so the clients associate with the SBA for registration, but continue to use the pool for conferencing and buddy lists.

In the event of an outage to the WAN (or the datacenter), the SBA will be unaffected, because the client will go into Survivable mode and local PSTN calling will continue to operate (via the built-in media gateway).

Some customers will provide DHCP and DNS information from the datacenter, so a WAN outage will also affect these. To accommodate this scenario, the SBA can be configured to provide DHCP information to allow the clients to connect. This is not a full DHCP server; it will not provide IP address information, only DHCP option 43 (pool provisioning URL) and option 120 (SIP registrar), which would enable a client to connect in Survivable mode.

Why would an organization deploy an SBA rather than a Standard Edition server? Well, really this comes down to the number of users at a location and cost. The SBA is expected to be cheaper to purchase and maintain than a full-blown server (even though to provide PSTN integration you would still need a gateway to purchase, configure, and deploy). Conferencing is also a consideration—should each branch host its own conferencing services? Will they all need high availability for this? If so, it may make more sense to centralize and provide that to everyone.

It is also possible to deploy a server-only version of the SBA. This is called the Survivable Branch Server (SBS) and will scale up to 5,000 users (similar to the Standard Edition server), but it only provides the functionality of the SBA (registration and mediation); a standalone media gateway is required to provide PSTN connectivity. This option may be suitable for customers who already have a number of gateways deployed as part of an OCS 2007 deployment (some gateways will need only a firmware update to be certified for Lync Server 2010).

Active Directory Failure

What happens if the previous section's WAN outage also removes your access to Active Directory? Perhaps you centralized the domain controllers, and while users can log on to their client PCs, how do they authenticate with Lync Server 2010? What about Lync Server 2010 Phone Edition? It doesn't have cached credentials, so how will users log in using it?

After being used to an "always on" telephony system for decades, the last thing users want is to lose access simply because they can't log in—especially if they can log into their computers. Well, unsurprisingly, Lync Server 2010 has a solution for this—a certificate-based login.

The first login attempt from a client will use NTLM (default) or Kerberos protocols to log in; and for this to be successful, you need Active Directory to be available. However, as part of this login process, the client will receive a Lync Server 2010 certificate and can present this certificate for any future login, bypassing the need to use Active Directory then.

It is important to understand that this certificate is available only for client-based authentication against the front-end server where the client is homed (not the pool). It cannot be used for any other purpose and is signed only by the front-end server.

This certificate is stored in the local user Certificate Store (see Figure 13.14) and by default is valid for 180 days. The validity period can be changed only by using the following PowerShell command:

```
Set-CsWebServiceConfiguration -DefaultValidityPeriodHours 4320
```

The value 4320 is the number of hours for which the certificate is valid; in this case the default 4320 is equal to 180 days.

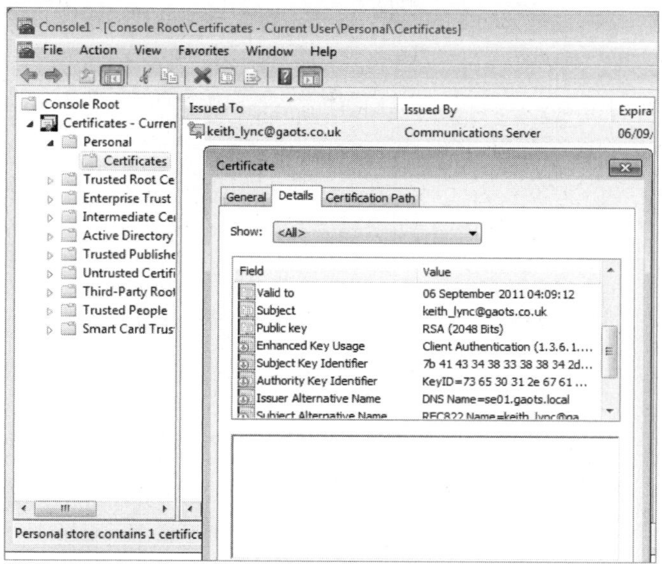

FIGURE 13.14
A certificate used for certificate-based authentication

No additional PKI infrastructure is required for this functionality to operate. Figure 13.15 shows the login process for a client. Note that the Active Directory connections occur only on the first login for a particular client (not user).

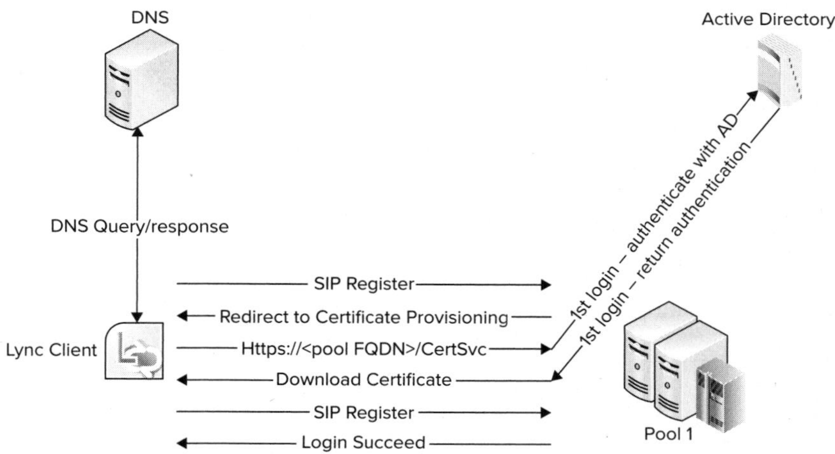

FIGURE 13.15
The client login process

Now that the client is logged in, the next thing to do is enable and configure the Enterprise Voice capability.

Configuring Enterprise Voice

The configuration of Enterprise Voice is best approached in two distinct parts:

Client This includes items such as the Address Book generation, Dial Plan creation, number normalization, and specific feature enablement (such as call forward) in the Voice policy.

Server Here you'll specifically look at the routing aspect of Enterprise Voice and how to configure and control it.

Once these two aspects have been defined, the user must be enabled for Enterprise Voice and should have a phone number assigned to them. If a phone number is not assigned, it is possible for the user to make PSTN calls but not receive them. Once enabled, the user will be assigned to a Dial plan and a Voice policy, and by default this would be the Global Dial plan and the Global Voice policy; however, an administrator would likely apply a specific Dial plan and Voice policy.

Configuring the Client Enterprise Voice Options

The Lync client is the interface between users and the back end of the system. As such, it is needed to translate what the user inputs to what the system expects. Not only that, but it needs to do that seamlessly to the user—without prompting!

The client also needs to adapt to the user's location if some specific configuration is required that may differ from location to location. A good example of this is emergency dialing; a U.S. user who is travelling to Europe may dial 911 to access the emergency services, not knowing that the emergency services number is different in Europe (and indeed from one country to the next).

Configuring Number Normalization

Normalization means adapting the various internal, local, national, or regional phone number formats into a universal standard format. Although Lync Server 2010 can work without normalizing numbers, it is recommended (and much easier) if all numbers are normalized to E.164 format, a global standard that defines the format of telephone numbers, and guarantees uniqueness globally. It is defined as such:

Country code = 1, 2, or 3 digits

Nationally significant number = 15 (country code digits)

The result is a maximum length of 15 digits, which in addition is prefixed with a + character, for example:

+15550123456

The United States country code is one digit (1), followed by the nationally significant area code and local number, with no spaces or other characters. A common misconception is that simply adding the + to the start of a number will make it E.164-compliant; this is not the case.

If all numbers were presented in E.164 format, Lync Server 2010 would have no issue, but this is not the case. Many numbers are stored without country codes, or only the internal extension may be stored, for example. In addition, this storage can be anywhere—Active Directory, local contacts, web pages, and so on.

To make this understandable and routable, Lync Server 2010 allows you to configure a set of rules that will manipulate the number entered and output as an E.164 format number. This number can then be presented to a gateway or PBX for further routing if required.

Number normalization is configured as part of the dial plan: users are assigned to a dial plan when enabled for Enterprise Voice (a user may only be in a single dial plan at any time).

A sample dial plan is shown in Figure 13.16; it has the following configuration items:

- **Name**
- **Simple name:** Used to match against Exchange Unified Messaging dial plans (versions prior to Exchange 2010 SP1 required the dial plans to match by name)
- **Description**
- **Dial-in conferencing region:** Creates an association with dial-in access numbers
- **External access prefix:** Allows numbers to be dialed by users without an external access prefix. Completing this field will automatically add the prefix if listed
- **Associated normalization rules**

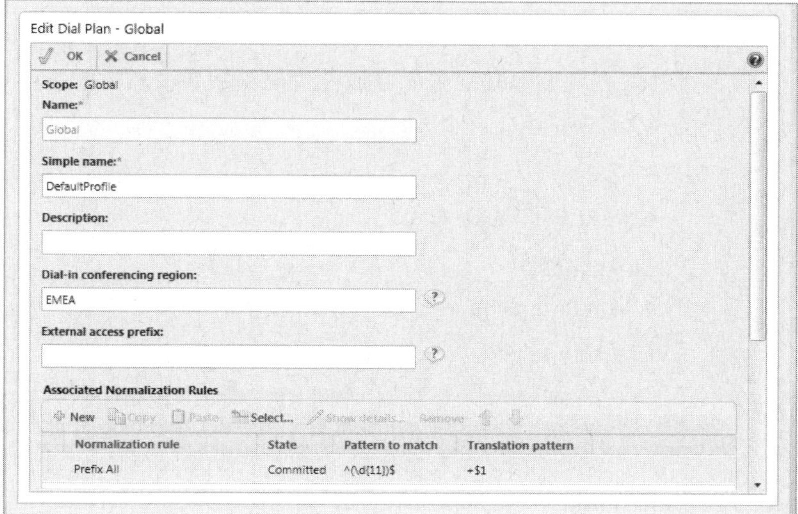

FIGURE 13.16
Configuring a sample dial plan

The command to create a dial plan from PowerShell looks like this:

```
New-Csdialplan -identity "LyncEnterpriseVoice" -description "default dial plan
for all users" -dialinconferencingregion "Birmingham" -ExternalAccessprefix 9
-simplename "LyncEnterpriseVoice"
```

Normalization rules are created using regular expressions (RegEx), and administrators already familiar with using RegEx will find this method quite easy. But if you are new to RegEx, you don't need to worry; Lync Server 2010 has improved significantly over Office

Communication Server 2007 in this, and it provides a basic input system that will build the RegEx for you (see Figure 13.17).

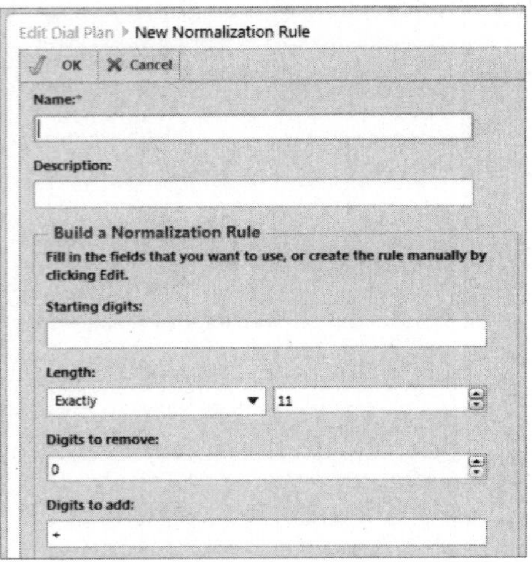

FIGURE 13.17
Configuring a new normalization rule

Here you build out the following information for each rule:

- Name
- Description
- Starting digits
- Length
- Digits to remove
- Digits to add

Here's an example. In the United Kingdom, it is still very common to dial local numbers from a landline, so if someone is located in Birmingham (U.K.), where the national area code is 0121, they can dial the following Birmingham number in several different ways:

Birmingham Central Library: 0121 303 4511

Local dialing (from within the Birmingham area): 303 4511

National dialing (from within the U.K.): 0121 303 4511

International dialing (from outside the U.K.): +44121 303 4511. In this case, the + symbol is introduced; this represents the international dialing access code. In the U.S., this will be 011. In France, it will be 00.

Telephony service that accommodates each of these formats allows users to continue to use their current (known) method to access numbers, and reduces the extent of change they need to adjust to when using Lync 2010 (the less change for users, the more likely they are to accept it).

You can also create normalization rules using the `New-CsVoiceNormalizationRule` cmdlet, for example:

```
New-csvoicenormalizationrule  -identity
"tag:LyncEnterpriseVoice/Prefix Local call without external prefix"
-Description "Local call without external line prefix"
-Pattern "^(\d{8})$" -translation "+44121$1"
```

So, let's take each of these formats and create a normalization rule to get to our target E.164 format.

Local Dialing

Here the input is seven digits and the output is going to include the +44121 prefix.

You will need the following information:

Starting digits: N/A

Length: Exactly 7

Digits to remove: N/A

Digits to add: +44121

Once you have added this information, scroll to the bottom of the tab. The Pattern to Match and Translation Rules will already be created for you (as shown in Figure 13.18).

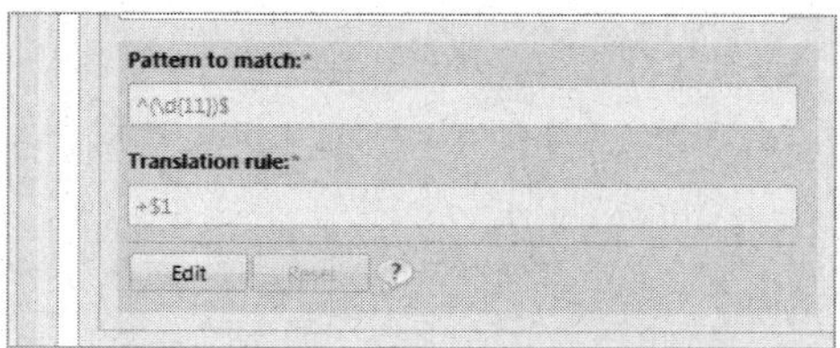

FIGURE 13.18
Automatic RegEx creation

National Dialing

Here your input is 10 digits and the output is going to include the +44 aspect.

So the information you need is the following:

Starting digits: 0

Length: Exactly 10

Digits to remove: 1

Digits to add: +44

With this combination of data, the Pattern to Match and the Translation Rule will be:

Pattern to Match: ^0(\d{9})$

Translation Rule: +44$1

International Dialing

The dial plan is U.K.-focused, so you probably won't be dialing the +44 aspect of a U.K. number; however, you might use the Click-To-Call functionality, which could already have the UK number defined. Here your input is not necessarily a defined length and the output is going to add only the +.

So the information you need is the following:

Starting digits: 001

Length: At Least 11

Digits to remove: 3

Digits to add: +

With this combination of data, the Pattern to Match and the Translation Rule will be:

Pattern to Match: ^001(\d{7}\d+)$

Translation Rule: +$1

Internal Dialing

Of course, all of this is dealing with external number dialing, but what about calling other Lync users or internal PBX users? Well, assuming you have a four-digit extension range, you will need to normalize these numbers to E.164 too. The first thing Lync Server 2010 will do is attempt a reverse number lookup on the phone entered number to try to find a matching user—and because all of the TelUri information is expected to be in E.164 format, that is what you need to resolve to.

For this, you need to enter the following data:

Starting digits: N/A

Length: Exactly 4

Digits to remove: N/A

Digits to add: +44121555

With this combination of data, the Pattern to Match and the Translation Rule will be:

Pattern to Match: ^(\d{4})$

Translation Rule: +44121555$1

ENABLING ADDRESS BOOK GENERATION

Once you have configured all the required normalization rules within the dial plan, you need to configure the Address Book in a similar fashion. The difference is that these rules will be used to map the entries from Active Directory into the E.164 format you need.

In an ideal world, Active Directory would be populated with E.164 format, and you would not have to do this at all; or a common format would already be applied to all the phone number entries, allowing you to keep the number of Address Book rules required to a minimum. Rarely is this the case, which results in a large number of normalization rules also being required for the Address Book generation.

These rules are stored in a file called `Company_PhoneNumber_Normalisation_Rules.txt`, and this must be stored in the following directory:

```
\\<Lync file share>\<Server-id>\ABFiles\
```

Because one Address Book is generated per pool, this file must be duplicated for each pool too; it is important that when multiple Address Book files are in use, and they are kept in sync. This unfortunately is a manual process.

This file is simply a text file and includes each of the normalization and translation rules on a separate line, as shown here:

```
^0(\d{9})$
+44$1

^001(\d{7}\d+)$
+$1

^(\d{4})$
+44121555$1
```

By default, the Address Book is generated daily at 1:30 AM; this can be changed by using the following PowerShell command:

```
Set-CsAddressBookConfiguration -RunTimeOfDay 01:30
```

If the Address Book needs to be updated immediately, the `Update-CsAddressBook` cmdlet is used (no parameters are required). It will take a few minutes to regenerate the Address Book. Clients will only check for a new Address Book file once every 24 hours.

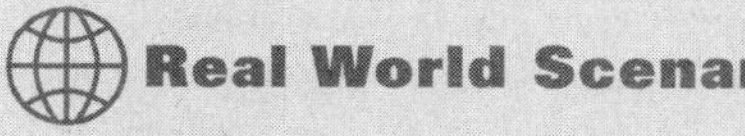

CORRECTING ACTIVE DIRECTORY DATA

When new Address Book data is generated, an output file listing all the incorrectly formatted phone number data can be generated too. This file is only generated if more than one globally unique identifier (GUID) is associated with the deployment. By default, all users and contacts created use the default GUID 00000000-0000-0000-0000-000000000000, and no error file is generated.

Modify the `msRTCSIP-GroupingID` attribute value of a contact using ADSIEDIT (shown here) to any value other than the default. The existence of two separate GUID values for this attribute is what triggers the generation of the error file; the actual value of the second GUID is irrelevant (although it must be a GUID format).

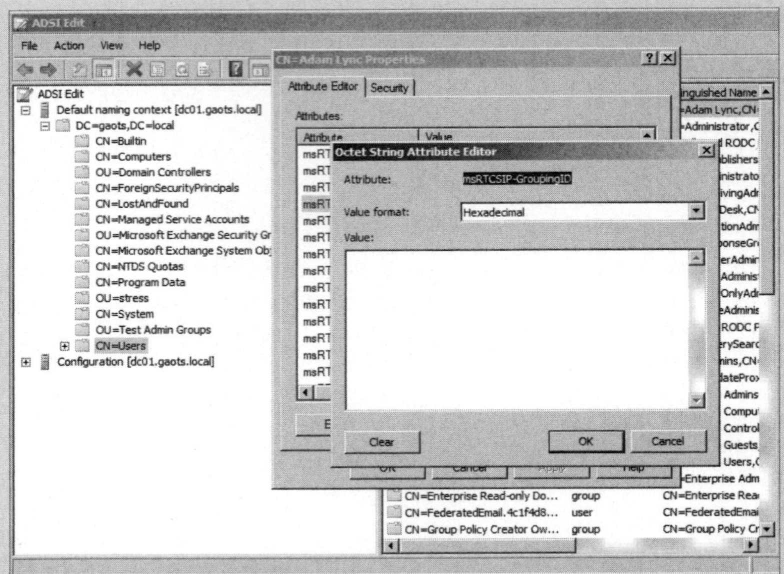

It is important to note that this second GUID generates a second set of Address Book files (associated with this new GUID value), and users associated with one Address Book file cannot search the Address Book for those users associated with the other. For this reason, you should create a dummy value and assign a dummy phone number to the account used in this process.

The error file can be found in the following location:

```
\\<Lync file share>\<server-id>\
ABFiles\00000000-0000-0000-0000-000000000000\00000000-0000-0000-0000-000000000000
```

and is called `Invalid_AD_Phone_Numbers.txt`.

From this error file, you can determine the accounts remaining in Active Directory that do not have a corresponding normalization rule associated and take one of the following appropriate actions:

- Correct the specific user account information in Active Directory.
- Create a new normalization rule to account for the number format.

Voice Policy

Where the Dial plan determines the rules used for each user to provide the number normalization capability, the Voice policy determines the features available to a user:

- Enable call forwarding
- Enable delegation
- Enable call transfer

- Enable call park
- Enable simultaneous ringing of phones
- Enable team call
- Enable PSTN reroute
- Enable bandwidth policy override
- Enable malicious call tracing

The Voice policy is also used to determine the PSTN Usages assigned to a user. This can be considered similar to Class of Service in the legacy telephony world, or equally accurately, the type of call (such as Local, National, or International) that the user is permitted to make.

Figure 13.19 shows the Voice Policy Creation screen.

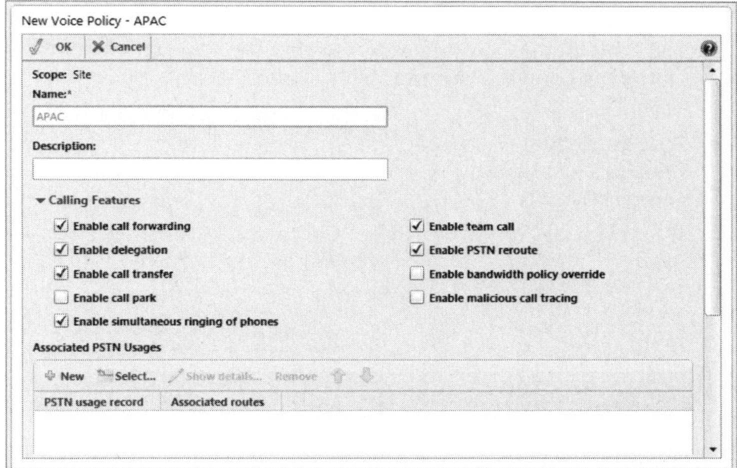

FIGURE 13.19
Creating a new Voice policy

The following sample PowerShell command creates a Voice policy and associates it with some predefined PSTN Usages; you'll see them in the next section:

```
New-Csvoicepolicy -identity "standard" -allowcallforwarding $true
-allowsimulring $true -description "Default policy for all users"
-enablecallpark $false -enablecalltransfer $true
-enabledelegation $false -enablemaliciouscalltracing $true
-enableteamcall $true -name "Standard" -pstnusages
@{add="Internal", "Local", "National", "Mobile", "Emergency"}
```

Configuring the Server Enterprise Voice Options

Now that you have configured the user-side information, you need to configure the server side to route the call to the correct gateway as well as ensure you have the correct permissions (PSTN Usages) to place the call.

ROUTING

Because the server is expecting a normalized (E.164) number, basing the routing on E.164 numbering is the recommended approach to routing the call.

A global enterprise is likely to have at least one gateway in each country where an office is located. This provides the potential savings of Least Cost Routing (LCR), where the call is routed internally across the company WAN to the in-country gateway; by contrast, in a traditional PBX the call would be long distance (or international) rate.

The definition of a route is similar to that of a Dial plan; you need to define it using the RegEx notation shown earlier, although for this example you'll simply use the starting digits.

For instance, to define a route for calls to the United Kingdom (country code 44), you would use the following RegEx: \+44

Notice that you do not define the number of digits, simply the starting digits of the normalized number. The more specific the definition (the more digits provided), the more granular the control over the target gateway you can have. For example, if you have multiple offices in the U.K., with a gateway in each office, you could use the following RegExes to specify regional dialing capability: \+44161 (Manchester), \+44121 (Birmingham), and so on.

Using the Control Panel to define the routing information is shown in Figure 13.20 (you need to scroll down to see the PSTN Usage section).

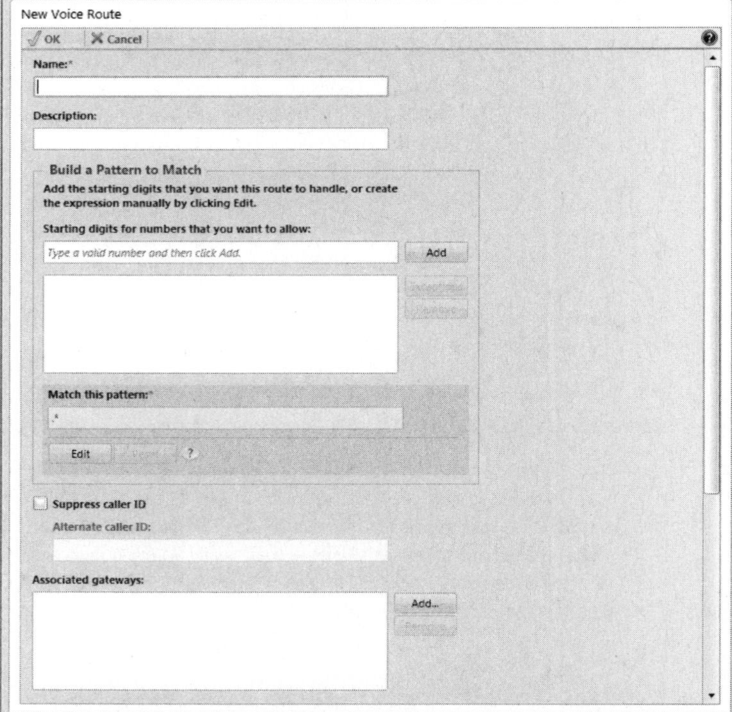

FIGURE 13.20
Creating a route with Control Panel

The equivalent PowerShell is:

```
Set-CsVoiceRoute -identity "LocalRoute"
-description "local number routes"
-numberpattern "^(\+44121{7})$"
-pstnusages @{add="Local"} -pstngatewaylist
@{add="pstngateway:10.0.0.1", "pstngateway:10.0.0.2"}
```

PSTN Usages

By defining the routes and associated PSTN usages, you tie the calling capability of the user to the permissions of the routes. When a user logs in successfully, the Voice policy is applied (containing the user-permitted routes), and when a PSTN call is placed, a check is performed against the matching routes to compare these against the permissions (PSTN usages) allowed.

An easy way to think of this is in the same way as permissions to files are granted:

- Create a group (PSTN Usage).
- Assign the group to the file/folder (Route).
- Add the user to the group (Voice Policy).

Testing Call Patterns

Once the client and server configuration are defined, you need to be sure they work as expected. One option would be to apply the policy to a test account and confirm the operation; however, in a large environment this is impractical. The solution to this is the Test Voice Routing option in the Voice section of the Control Panel.

Here you can provide the number dialed as well as the expected results when you run the test. Once the details are entered, you can save the option to run again in the future. This is where the benefits of scale come into play; once the numbers are saved, you can quickly rerun the tests any time the environment is changed, ensuring that any changes work as expected prior to deploying to users.

Figure 13.21 shows a test case being defined.

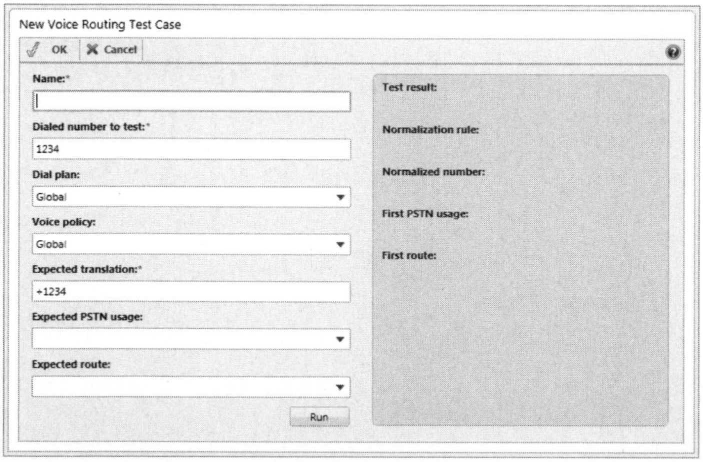

Figure 13.21
Creating a voice test case

The Bottom Line

Understand the voice capabilities. Lync Server 2010 has dramatically expanded the capabilities provided by Microsoft in the Unified Communications space to be almost on par with enterprise PBXs (and certainly equal to, if not better, than departmental PBX offerings).

Master It Describe the benefits of media bypass.

Understand the voice architecture. With the introduction of media bypass and the support for virtualization, the architectural requirements to deploy Voice have been consolidated into a smaller server footprint, and at the same time additional functionality has been included in the product. Significant investment has been made in the high availability and resiliency deployment models.

Master It Describe the user experience when the user's home pool fails and a backup registrar has been configured.

Configure voice policies and routing. Aside from the architectural requirements, to enable Enterprise Voice requires configuration to be applied to users (policies) and back-end configuration to be applied to the servers (routing).

Master It What configuration joins the user configuration to the server configuration and provides the permissions to enable (or block) a call?

Chapter 14

Call Admission Control

In the early days of OCS 2007, Microsoft made a big deal about how the codecs used were dynamic and could adapt to your network. A lot of people misinterpreted this to mean that you could simply install it and it would work. As you know, introducing a new application onto a network also introduces network traffic. If your network is already saturated, introducing more traffic will only make matters worse, resulting in a poor user experience. Lync finally provides an easy way to control the amount (and type) of traffic between users, allowing better understanding of the impact of this new application.

In this chapter, you will learn to:

- Identify Call Admission Control–capable endpoints
- Configure policy-based Quality of Service controls
- Design a Call Admission Control solution
- Configure Call Admission Control

Understanding Call Admission Control

In the legacy telephony world, Call Admission Control was inherent in the infrastructure and not something that overly concerned people. Bandwidth was defined in *trunks* and *lines*. If you tried to make a call and there wasn't enough *bandwidth*, you would receive a *busy* tone, as the system would be unable to route your call to the destination because it had no available capacity. Typically, you tried again sometime later. Advancements in PBX technology introduced a monitoring concept (*ring back*) that allowed the system to call you and connect your call when enough bandwidth was available.

The introduction of Voice over IP (VoIP) systems enabled these typically fixed-capacity trunks to become network links, which were much easier to change in size and therefore capacity. In addition, voice traffic could be routed across traditional network links, providing a potential cost saving to business by combining both voice and data links. In taking this approach, bandwidth control has become problematic. First, how do you ensure that there is enough bandwidth to cope with the calls that you want to allow? Second, how do you ensure that this traffic on a shared link does not impact other data traffic?

The early VoIP systems used a fixed-size codec, thereby ensuring that the required capacity per call was a known value (the number of concurrent calls times the codec size equals the required capacity). Then, however, Office Communication Server 2007 introduced RTAudio (see Chapter 2, "Standards and Protocols," for details), which added the complexity of a codec that changes dynamically (based on the network conditions) and attempts to calculate the bandwidth required.

You still know the number of concurrent calls; however, now you can't determine how much bandwidth is required per call, so can't predict how much bandwidth is required. This can lead to unhappy users if the network is under-provisioned, as the dynamic nature will reduce the quality of the call to ensure that all the calls can be completed.

Assuming the network link shown in the top half of Figure 14.1 is already saturated with calls, the impact of adding an additional call can be seen in the lower half of Figure 14.1.

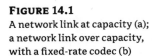

FIGURE 14.1
A network link at capacity (a); a network link over capacity, with a fixed-rate codec (b)

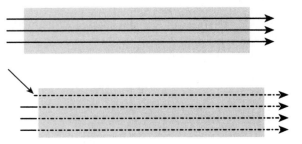

You can see that an additional call from a nondynamic codec will impact all other calls on the link. Because these are fixed-bandwidth calls, the only option is for some packets to be lost or delayed. The result is that all users will suffer a loss of quality.

On the other hand, using a dynamic codec would allow the situation shown in Figure 14.2. The calls in place (as well as the new one) would adapt and potentially use a lower-quality codec, but this means there would be no packet loss and, in many cases, no noticeable impact to users. Figure 14.2 shows all calls being impacted equally, but more likely only a few would be impacted.

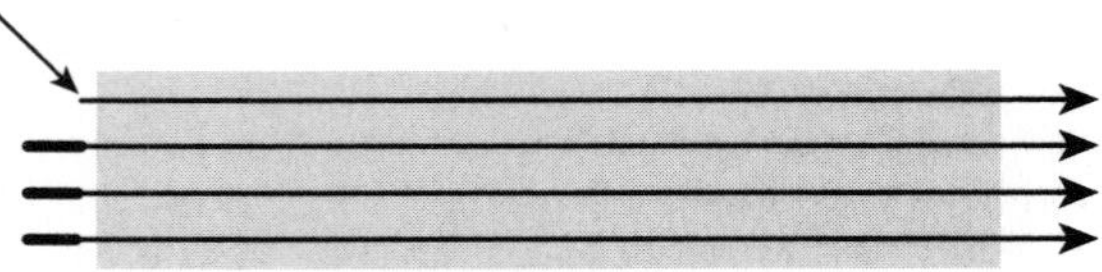

FIGURE 14.2
A network link over capacity with a dynamic-rate codec

Having dynamic codecs does have a downside. Another call introduced would reduce the existing call quality again, as would another and another and another. Eventually, all calls would be operating at such low quality they would be either unintelligible or dropped. A dropped call would allow some "breathing space," but the cycle would continue. It is almost impossible to plan for or control.

With OCS and OCS R2, only three workarounds were available:

MaxAudioVideoBandwidth Registry Key By setting this value, an administrator could determine the maximum bandwidth combined for audio and video; in most cases where this has been set, it results in video being unavailable. Because you don't have the capability to set the minimum value required, you can still continue to add calls to the network; all you are doing is restricting the maximum used by OCS.

Disable Video By disabling the video capability, you reduce the functionality of the product; however, the benefit is that significant bandwidth is not being used for video and is available for use by audio or other applications.

Enable Diffserv By enabling QoS on the network, you can provide a guaranteed bandwidth to OCS, and in return provide a guaranteed bandwidth available to other applications.

None of these workarounds provide the capability to manage at the application (Lync) layer; typically, the results are the same as if the value were not enabled and the codec left to dynamically adjust.

Something had to be done to allow a business to accurately size the network and provision the correct amount of bandwidth for the number (and quality) of calls permitted on the network.

This something is Call Admission Control (CAC), which can be enabled as part of a Lync deployment with no extra hardware requirements (it is part of the front-end services) and requires no specific network hardware, because it interacts at the application layer.

How Call Admission Control Works

The aim of Call Admission Control is to provide a guaranteed quality (user experience) for calls placed on the network. From a user perspective, a rejected call (with explanation), as shown in Figure 14.3, is usually a better experience than a call connected but of extremely low quality. From an admin perspective, CAC introduces a way to allow the network to be accurately architected and protected against unexpected spikes in call volumes.

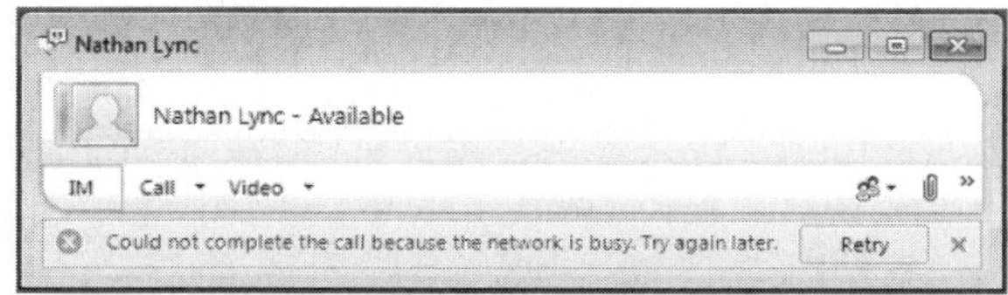

FIGURE 14.3
A rejected call notification due to insufficient bandwidth

Lync configuration includes the definition of the network and details for the number of calls and quality permitted for each leg of the network. We'll implement this configuration later.

Each pool will replicate the number of current calls in place on the network; when a new call is attempted, a query is made to establish if enough bandwidth is available to handle another call and how much bandwidth is permitted for each modality use.

Within this query, the Lync client will provide the Policy Decision Point (PDP) with its IP address, along with the IP address of the calling party client. From these two pieces of information, the PDP can determine the route and establish the current usage on that route.

IS LYNC INTEGRATED WITH THE NETWORK?

Lync's Call Admission Control operates purely at the application layer, so it is not integrated with the network. There are no ties to the underlying network infrastructure to reserve the bandwidth or ensure that it is actually available to handle the call.

The result of the query is one of the following:

Permitted The call may be placed.

Rejected The call may not be placed.

Rerouted The call must take another route, which may be via Edge servers or via the PSTN.

For call rerouting, both modalities are handled together; therefore, it is not possible for the video portion of an audio and video call to be rerouted via the Edge servers and the audio portion to continue across the WAN, or even via the PSTN. If the call cannot be routed via the Edge servers, the video modality will be dropped and, assuming the user is permitted to make a PSTN call, the call will be attempted via a PSTN gateway.

As you can see in Figure 14.4, to enable routing via the Internet, each pool (not shown) must have an associated Edge server or, to connect via the PSTN, a Mediation server (or in the case of media bypass, a supported gateway).

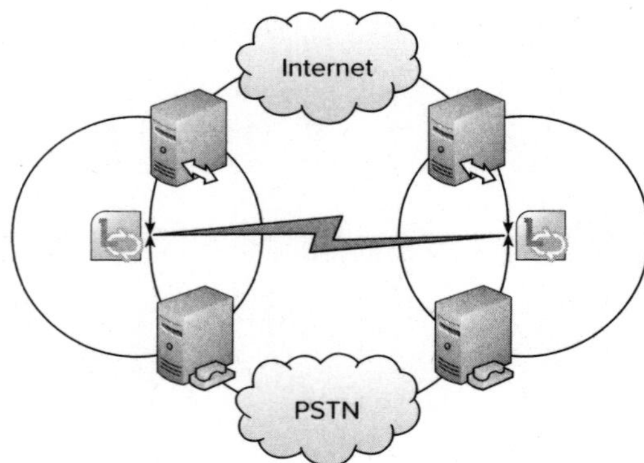

FIGURE 14.4
Call Admission Control rerouting

In Figure 14.5, the calling party will initiate the call. Without the recipient user being aware, the called-party Lync client will receive the request for call signaling and query the Policy Decision Point (PDP) of the site (only a single pool per site runs this process). The PDP will return a response based on the current (real time) capacity of the link as defined within Lync. As noted, this will be permitted, rejected, or rerouted; based on this response, the calling-party Lync client will take appropriate action.

1. User places the call.
2. Receiving endpoint queries PDP.
3. Decision is made and returned to called-party client.
4. The client will take appropriate action based on the response.

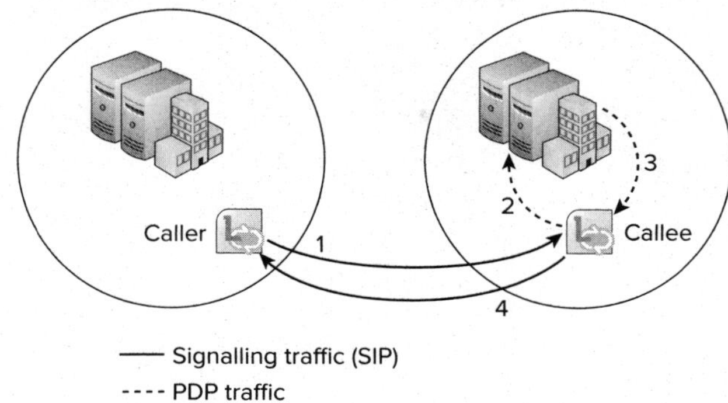

FIGURE 14.5
Signaling call flow for Call Admission Control, where the called party is local to the pool

In the scenario in Figure 14.6, the user is not in a location that has a pool. The subnet will be defined within Lync, and the client will query back to its home-pool (site) PDP, receiving the same responses as before. The scenario is the same for users who roam from site to site.

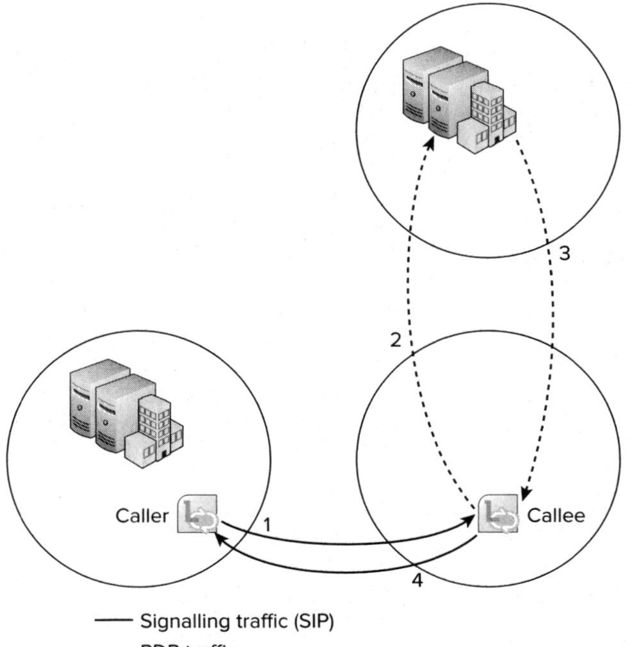

FIGURE 14.6
Signaling call flow for Call Admission Control, where the called party is not local to the pool

EMERGENCY CALL OVERRIDE?

Emergency calls do not override Call Admission Control. CAC is used to guarantee the quality of the calls placed on the network. If there is not enough capacity to accept another call, even if the call is an emergency call, it is not permitted. It would not be a good idea to connect an emergency call if the network is not capable of providing the capacity, because the call quality would most likely be poor. You'll find more details in Chapter 15, "E911 and LIS"

Voice policy can be configured to override Call Admission Control and policies assigned to users or sites. This will allow Call Admission Control to be ignored for users assigned to the policy. Using this option should be an exception rather than the norm, because it defeats the purpose of Call Admission Control.

Where Call Admission Control Works

The endpoint will always query the pool on which it is associated; there is no requirement for a PDP role to be located in the same site as the endpoint. It is important to note that only one pool per central site should be enabled for Call Admission Control; having multiple pools enabled in the same site will prevent Call Admission Control policies from being applied on calls between some users. If the pool to which the endpoint is associated is not enabled for Call Admission Control, the request is simply proxied to the relevant pool.

The receiving endpoint always makes the query to the PDP, and the calling party never makes it (for reasons which will be explained shortly). Multiple Points of Presence (MPOP) are fully supported with each endpoint carrying out a separate query. This may result in a scenario where a user is logged in with multiple endpoints, and some users being able to receive the call and others not. In this scenario, only the endpoints capable of establishing the call will provide a toast/ringtone, and those not capable of call establishment will not.

If a call cannot be established, there is no indication to the intended recipient of a missed call. The user experience could be affected if someone saw a call attempt but was unable to do anything about it (except possibly start an IM conversation). On the other hand, the calling party will see a notification indicating that network issues are preventing the call from being established, or that rerouting may cause a delay in establishing the call.

In Figure 14.7, where the recipient of the call is logged in on multiple devices, it is permissible that some devices will return a positive response, whereas others return negative following the PDP query stage.

FIGURE 14.7
Call Admission Control in a multiple-point-of-presence scenario

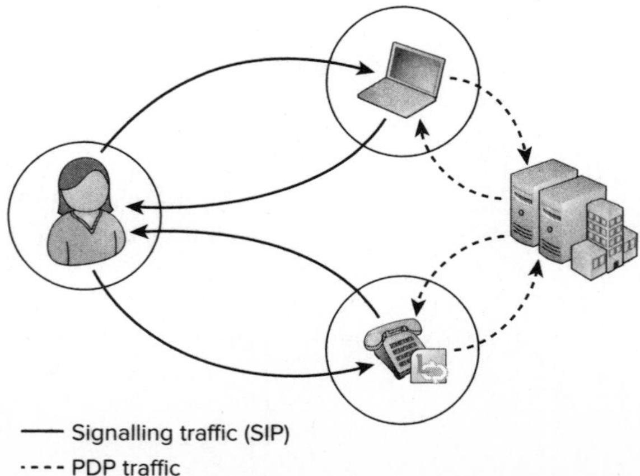

For example, assume the recipient is logged in via both a desk phone and a laptop, which may be connected via wireless. The administrator has configured Lync to be aware of the wireless subnet and has restricted the number of calls available via the wireless LAN to ensure quality. In this case, the desk phone will return a positive response, and the laptop will return a negative one. As a result, only the desk phone device will ring.

Note that there is no indication of a call on the laptop device. This is to prevent the attempted establishment of a call where the network is not capable of delivering a quality call. If the desk phone is not answered, a single missed call notification will be generated and delivered as normal, or the call will be forwarded to Exchange Unified Messaging if configured.

Only a Lync endpoint is capable of querying for Call Admission Control data, so when it is used in a legacy interoperability scenario, calls to legacy clients (OCS 2007 or OCS 2007 R2) will always succeed. A call from a legacy client to a Lync client will create a PDP query, and the result will obey the conditions imposed by the Call Admission Control policy.

In the case shown in the upper half of Figure 14.8, either endpoint will query the PDP for permission, as both are Lync endpoints (and endpoint can be any Lync client or any Lync server role). However, as shown at the bottom of Figure 14.8, the legacy endpoint will not make a query.

FIGURE 14.8
Call Admission Control Query conditions for Lync endpoints (top); for combination or legacy endpoints (bottom)

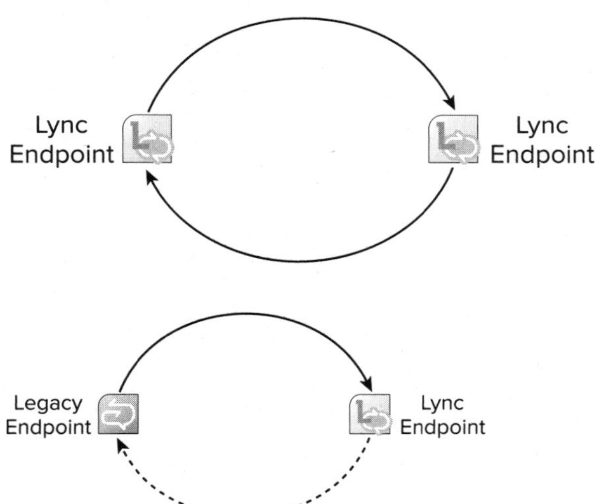

When you're planning a migration, this scenario is extremely important to understand. When receiving a call, any legacy client will permit the call to be placed.

Consider a remote branch office where you want to limit the number of calls being placed across the WAN link to the head office. If you delay the client upgrade at the site, leaving them on a legacy client, then any calls being made *from* the site will be subject to Call Admission Control policy; however, any calls being made *to* the site will not. This could cause potential degradation of calls for all parties using that link.

To ensure that each PDP in each topology site is fully aware of the state of the network—remember, the client will only query its home PDP—each PDP is required to synchronize the data containing its call information. This synchronization occurs via HTTPS.

Underlying Network Requirements

Although Lync Call Admission Control does not *require* Quality of Service (QoS) to be configured on the network, to ensure that the bandwidth is properly reserved for Lync to manage, we *recommend* that you to apply QoS to the network.

Without QoS in place you can define the maximum bandwidth used by Lync for each call modality, as well as the maximum for the total concurrent calls of each modality. However, by not deploying QoS to guarantee the bandwidth when needed, you are in effect allowing other network traffic to eat into the Lync-defined bandwidth. As a result, the Lync codec will adapt dynamically to this lower bandwidth and likely reduce the quality of the call.

By configuring QoS, you ensure that Lync has the guaranteed bandwidth when needed, and any other network traffic will be required to adapt. This ensures that the quality and quantity of calls is as defined in Call Admission Control and enforced on the network by QoS.

Figure 14.9 shows configuration using only Call Admission Control to manage bandwidth. This will ensure that each individual call session will not increase above a given bandwidth value, shown here to be 40 percent, and subsequently codec type, as well as ensure that the total will not increase above a total value. The other network traffic may increase past the 60 percent nominally allocated, as there is no interaction between the network and Lync. If this increase does occur, the Lync traffic will dynamically decrease with a corresponding decrease in quality.

FIGURE 14.9
Impact of configuring only Call Admission Control on the network

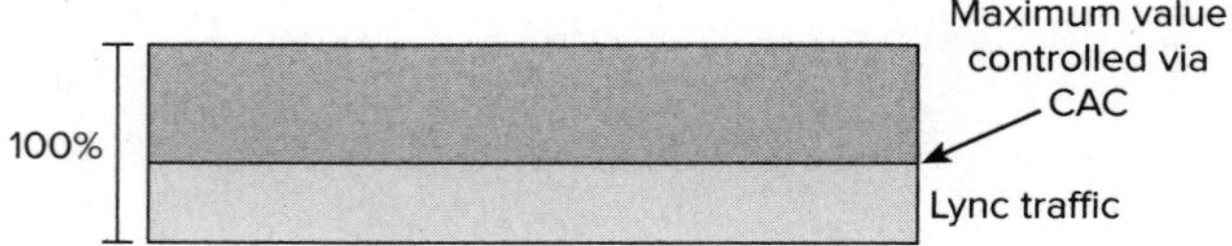

Figure 14.10 shows the same configuration, this time enforced using QoS but with no Call Admission Control in place. In this scenario, you can again ensure that the Lync traffic will not increase beyond the 40 percent value; however, you have no control over the number of Lync calls that can be placed or the codecs in use. This is the same situation you'll have when using OCS or OCS R2.

FIGURE 14.10
Impact of configuring only Quality of Service on the Network

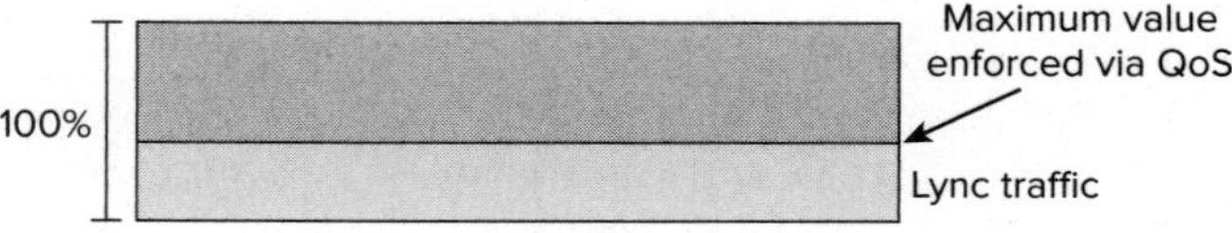

The QoS value can be managed in either direction; assigning 40 percent to Lync will guarantee that 40 percent will be available when Lync needs it, and it will allow increases beyond 40 percent if there is available bandwidth, managing the other data to reduce to below 60 percent when needed.

On the other hand, you can configure the limit to be on the alternative data, ensuring there is a minimum of 60 percent available for it, and forcing Lync to adapt if the other data is deemed more important. To ensure voice quality, the guarantee should be configured on the Lync network traffic.

Figure 14.11 shows the ultimate goal, having both Call Admission Control and QoS complement each other on the network. Call Admission Control provides the application layer control over the network traffic placed on the network, and QoS provides the guarantee that traffic is prioritized when it is on the network.

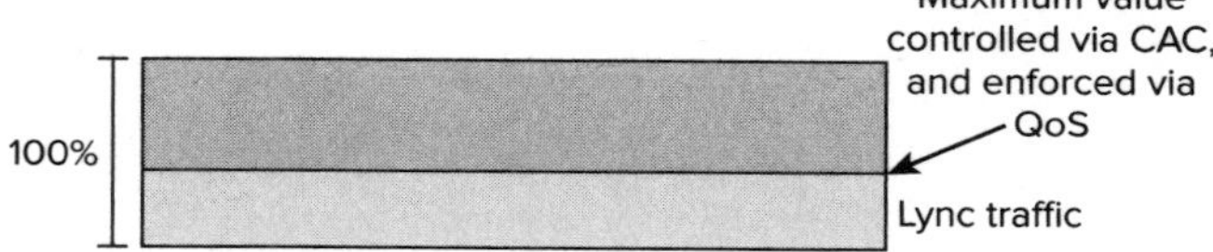

FIGURE 14.11
Impact of configuring both Call Admission Control and Quality of Service on the network

Finally, Figure 14.12 shows a scenario where Call Admission Control has been configured to allow more calls than the network is capable of handling. Because the PDP is not aware of the underlying network capacity, in this situation calls will be permitted to be set up by Lync and the other calls on the network will be affected immediately. The codec bandwidth will be reduced dynamically, thereby reducing the quality of each call. Needless to say, the rest of the network will be impacted as well. This is not much different from not configuring Call Admission Control at all.

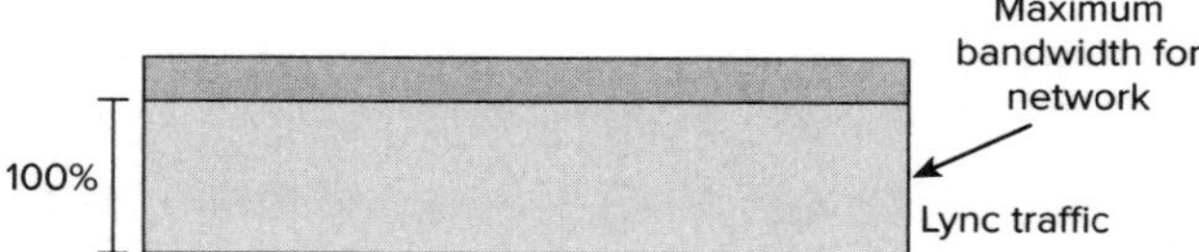

FIGURE 14.12
Impact of over-configuring Call Admission Control on the network

QoS Tagging

By default, Lync will use Differentiated Service Control Point (DSCP) tagging in the headers of the network traffic to allow the underlying network to control and route the traffic based on the configuration required. Table 14.1 shows the default QoS marking for Lync. These values may be changed if required; however, this should only be carried out in conjunction with the network management team of your organization, because straying from the defaults could mean significant reconfiguration required on the network devices (switches, routers, firewalls).

TABLE 14.1: Default DSCP Marking per Modality

MEDIA TYPE	PER HOP BEHAVIOR	QUEUING AND DROPPING	NOTES
Audio	EF	Priority Queue	Low loss, low latency, low jitter, assured bandwidth. Pair with WAN Bandwidth Policies on constrained links.
Video	AF41	BW Queue + DSCP WRED	Class 4. Low drop priority. Pair with WAN Bandwidth Policies on constrained links.
SIP Signaling	CS3	BW Queue	Class 3. Bandwidth allocation should be sufficient to avoid drops.
App Sharing	AF21	BW Queue + DSCP WRED	Class 2. Low drop priority. Pair with end-user policy caps.
File Transfer	AF11	BW Queue + DSCP WRED	Class 1. Low drop priority. Pair with end-user policy caps.

The Per Hop Behavior column indicates the DSCP tag applied to the packet (with a value providing further differentiation where listed):

EF: Expedited Forwarding

AF: Assured Forwarding

CS: Class

COMPARING LYNC CALL QUALITY

Before a full rollout of Lync (or any application for that matter), it is normal to pilot the new technology. When a pilot is running, it is extremely important that the same packet marking is used when comparing with another VoIP deployment.

We have had customers report that Lync is performing badly when compared to their existing deployment, and the reason has quite often been traced to the fact that they prioritize the existing VoIP packets.

In addition, the ports used for each modality can be defined both on the server side and the client, allowing control and prioritization of traffic based on port ranges. If the port range approach is taken, you should define the client range as a subset of the server range of ports; this will reduce the quantity of specific network configuration rules required. For example:

Server port range = 50,001 – 55,000

Client port range = 50,001 – 50,100

Taking this approach, network administrators can configure the network devices to use the range 50,001 – 55,000 for the prioritizing of audio traffic, rather than having to configure two ranges (one for the servers and one for the clients).

Here is a list of the configuration points for the client side:

ClientMediaPortRangeEnabled	True/False
ClientMediaPort	Start port value eg 5,000
ClientMediaPortRange	Number of ports eg 20
ClientAudioPort	Start port value eg 6,000
ClientAudioPortRange	Number of ports eg 20
ClientVideoPort	Start port value eg 7,000
ClientVideoPortRange	Number of ports eg 20
ClientAppSharingPort	Start port value eg 8,000
ClientAppSharingPortRange	Number of ports eg 20
ClientFileTransferPort	Start port value eg 9,000
ClientFileTransferPortRange	Number of ports eg 20
ClientSipDynamicPort	Start port value eg 10,000
ClientSipDynamicPortRange	Number of ports eg 20

How Many Ports Do I Need?

Some customers want to restrict the number of ports a client can open. For most users, we recommend that this be no less than 20 ports per modality. The reason for so many is that during call establishment the ports are negotiated, and there may be several different ways to connect clients (peer to peer, via the edge, and so on), so multiple ports are required during this phase. Once the call is established, two ports per modality are required. This is explained in detail at:

`http://technet.microsoft.com/en-us/library/dd572230(office.13).aspx`

Although this is an OCS R2 document, the content also holds true for Lync.

Users who handle more calls (such as personal assistants) will need a higher number, based on the number of calls expected.

With operating systems before Microsoft Vista, potential rogue applications could leverage this port prioritization; however, Vista (and Windows 7) provides policy-based control, allowing the tagging of packets based on the application itself, which reduces the risk of a rogue application introducing prioritized traffic onto the network.

DEFINING A POLICY-BASED CONTROL

Take the following steps to define a policy-based control:

1. In the Group Policy Management Editor, you'll see that the Policy-Based QoS option is available for both Computer Configuration and User Configuration policies. In this example, you'll use a computer-based policy, so click there and select Create New Policy, as shown in Figure 14.13.

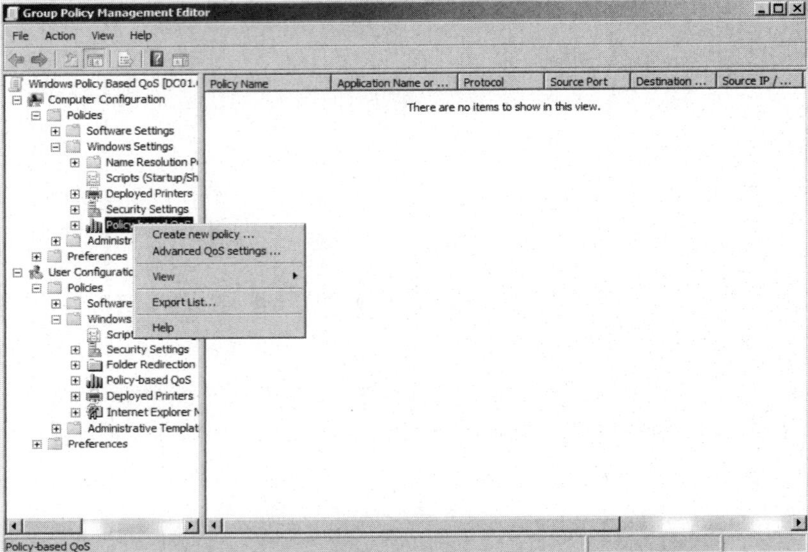

FIGURE 14.13
Choosing to create a new QoS policy in the Group Policy Management Editor

2. Complete the configuration options on the Policy-Based QoS screen, shown in Figure 14.14. In addition to naming the policy and defining the bandwidth rate, notice that the DSCP value is listed as a decimal value; this decodes to the values previously noted, as shown in Table 14.2.

TABLE 14.2: Decoding Default DSCP Values

PER HOP BEHAVIOR	DECIMAL VALUE
EF	46
AF41	34
CS3	24
AF21	18
AF11	10

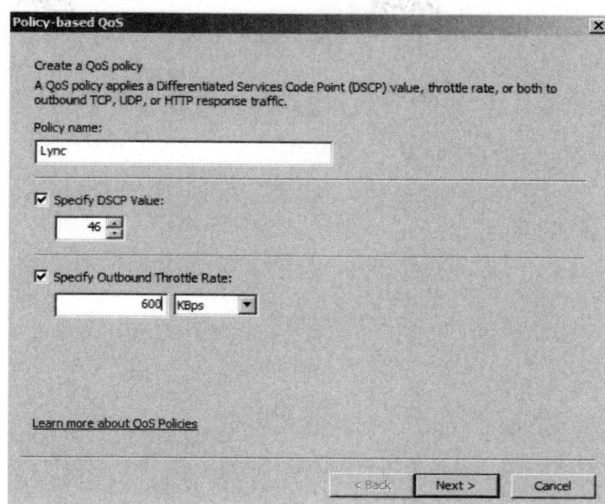

FIGURE 14.14
Entering a QoS policy value and throttle rate

3. The next screen (Figure 14.15) is where you specify the application to which this policy will apply in the Lync case (and OCS); the filename is `communicator.exe`.

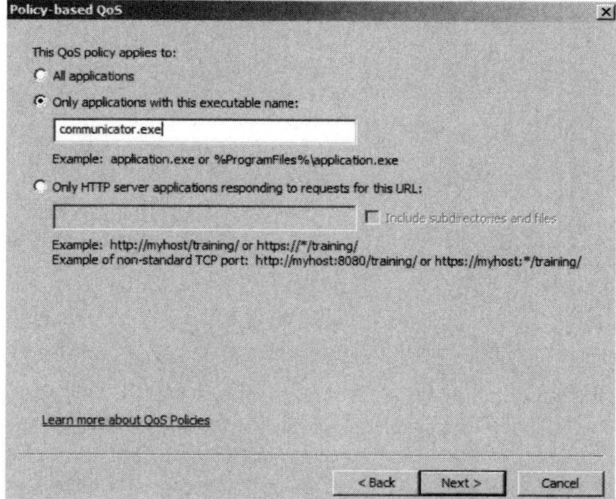

FIGURE 14.15
Specifying application restrictions for the QoS policy

4. The next screen asks for source and destination information. This could be used to mark traffic specific to leaving a site, but in most cases it is likely this would be left as default.

5. Figure 14.16 shows where the port range and protocol can be specified. Choose Finish to complete the policy creation. From there the policy can be applied like any other group policy object.

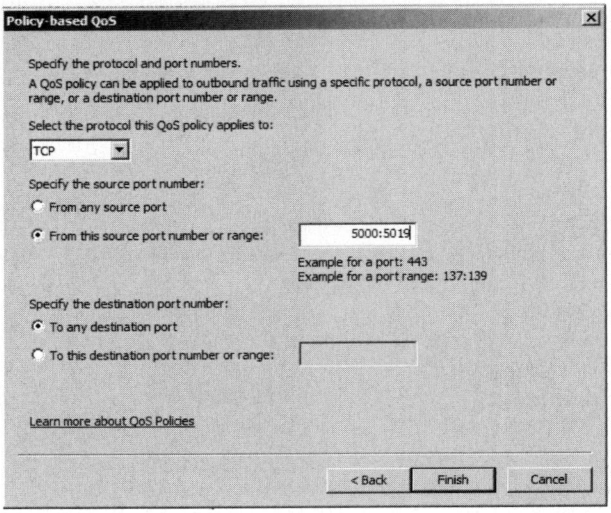

FIGURE 14.16
Specifying a protocol and port range for the QoS policy

Designing for Call Admission Control

The aim of designing the Call Admission Control policies is to ultimately associate IP subnets with locations and, with each location, to define the number of individual calls as well as the total number of calls permitted from (and to) each site. The association of IP subnets is how each client's location is determined for the PDP query.

The following example assumes a company with offices in the following locations, with available network bandwidth shown in brackets. Inter-regional links are from Chicago to London and from London to Sydney:

- North America
  - Chicago (100,000kbps)
  - New York (50,000kbps)
  - Washington, D.C. (50,000kbps)
  - Seattle (5,000kbps)
  - San Francisco (5,000kbps)
- EMEA (Europe, Middle East and Africa)
  - London (10,000kbps)
  - Dublin (5,000kbps)
  - Paris (3,000kbps)

APAC (Asia and Pacific)

Sydney (5,000kbps)

Hong Kong (5,000kbps)

Tokyo (5,000kbps)

To do this, you start by defining the network into regions, or central sites. Any addresses within a region are policy-free—that is, they can establish any number of calls without being blocked or rerouted. You can include multiple physical locations in a single region (or site); in fact, this is recommended when you do not care to control the bandwidth between specific sites.

Next, you'll define the sites and associate each site with a region. Calls within a site are policy-free; however, calls across sites or regions will have policy applied and controls put in place.

From the previous example data, you can see that Chicago, New York, and Washington, D.C. are well enough connected that you don't need to put any controls in place for calls between these locations. Table 14.3 shows the associations.

TABLE 14.3: Region, Site, and Bandwidth Associations

REGION	SITE	AVAILABLE BANDWIDTH (KBPS)
North America	Chicago	100,000
North America	New York	50,000
North America	Washington, D.C.	50,000
North America	Seattle	5,000
North America	San Francisco	5,000
EMEA	London	10,000
EMEA	Dublin	5,000
EMEA	Paris	3,000
APAC	Sydney	5,000
APAC	Hong Kong	5,000
APAC	Tokyo	5,000

For each site, you need to define the bandwidth for the link to the central site or define a *cross-link* tying together two sites. Once you have the total bandwidth defined, you need to establish how much bandwidth will be assigned to total audio and how much bandwidth to total video. (In the example, Paris will be defined not to permit any video calls.)

Table 14.4 shows the required configuration.

TABLE 14.4: Site Total Session Definitions per Modality

REGION	SITE	AVAILABLE BANDWIDTH (KBPS)	TOTAL ASSIGNED TO AUDIO	TOTAL ASSIGNED TO VIDEO
North America	Chicago	100,000	Not controlled	Not controlled
North America	New York	50,000	Not controlled	Not controlled
North America	Washington, D.C.	50,000	Not controlled	Not controlled
North America	Seattle	5,000	2,000	1,200
North America	San Francisco	5,000	2,000	1,200
EMEA	London	10,000	Not controlled	Not controlled
EMEA	Dublin	5,000	2,000	1,200
EMEA	Paris	3,000	1,000	0
APAC	Sydney	5,000	Not controlled	Not controlled
APAC	Hong Kong	5,000	2,000	1,200
APAC	Tokyo	5,000	2,000	1,200

Chicago, New York, and Washington, D.C. will not have policy applied because they are well connected; London and Sydney will be defined as the central site in each region. It is important to note that the central site does not have to tie in with a physical location or indeed a data center. It can be considered a placeholder to which the other locations are connected. In most cases, it makes sense to associate with a location; however, in this example, three locations are being treated as one.

From these definitions, you define the maximum value for each modality that is permitted for a single call, as shown in Table 14.5.

TABLE 14.5: Site Individual Session Definitions per Modality

REGION	SITE	AVAILABLE BANDWIDTH (KBPS)	TOTAL ASSIGNED TO AUDIO	AUDIO SESSION LIMIT	TOTAL ASSIGNED TO VIDEO	VIDEO SESSION LIMIT
North America	Chicago	100,000	Not controlled	Not controlled	Not controlled	Not controlled
North America	New York	50,000	Not controlled	Not controlled	Not controlled	Not controlled
North America	Washington, D.C.	50,000	Not controlled	Not controlled	Not controlled	Not controlled
North America	Seattle	5,000	2,000	100	1,200	600
North America	San Francisco	5,000	2,000	100	1,200	600
EMEA	London	10,000	Not controlled	Not controlled	Not controlled	Not controlled
EMEA	Dublin	5,000	2,000	100	1,200	600
EMEA	Paris	3,000	1,000	60	0	0
APAC	Sydney	5,000	Not controlled	Not controlled	Not controlled	Not controlled
APAC	Hong Kong	5,000	2,000	100	1,200	600
APAC	Tokyo	5,000	2,000	100	1,200	600

Using Seattle as the first example, 2,000kbps was assigned for total audio sessions, and 100kbps was assigned for a maximum per audio session. This will permit a maximum of 20 concurrent calls (total sessions divided by individual session limit) on this connection (into the North America region). On the video configuration, 1,200kbps are assigned for the total sessions and 600kbps are assigned for each individual session, giving a maximum of two concurrent video sessions.

In the case of Dublin, 1,000kbps are assigned for the total audio sessions, and 60kbps are assigned for each individual session, giving a concurrent call rate of 16 calls. For video traffic, none is permitted.

These two examples highlight the capability to control the quality of each individual call. Using Table 14.5, you can determine which codec will be used in the best case; you can also determine the capabilities to dynamically adapt if network issues are encountered during a call.

You can see that Seattle users can hold calls using the G711 codec, ensuring better call quality. However, if the network encounters issues, such as lost packets, and the codec requires the introduction of Forward Error Correction (FEC), then the Lync client cannot introduce FEC on G711 because that would require 156kbps. Instead, it must dynamically drop down to wideband RT-Audio and introduce FEC, using 86kbps.

You can find full details at:

```
http://technet.microsoft.com/en-us/library/gg413004.aspx
```

The bandwidth used by each codec is listed in Table 14.6.

TABLE 14.6: Codec Bandwidth Usage Definitions

AUDIO CODEC	SCENARIOS	TYPICAL VALUE (KBPS)	MAX WITHOUT FEC (KBPS)	MAX WITH FEC (KBPS)
RTAudio Wideband	Peer-to-peer	34.8	57	86
RTAudio Narrowband	Peer-to-peer, PSTN	25.9	39.8	51.6
G.722	Conferencing	42.8	99.6	163.6
G.711	PSTN	59.8	92	156
Siren	Conferencing	22	51.6	67.6
RTVideo	Main Video CIF	250	50	N/A
RTVideo	Main Video VGA	600	350	N/A
RTVideo	Main Video HD	1500	800	N/A
RTVideo	Panoramic Video	350	50	N/A

Where multiple regions have been defined, you also need to establish the links between regions and permitted values of traffic across each, as in Table 14.7.

TABLE 14.7: Inter-Region Link Definitions

NAME	REGION 1	REGION1	TOTAL ASSIGNED TO AUDIO	AUDIO SESSION LIMIT	TOTAL ASSIGNED TO VIDEO	VIDEO SESSION LIMIT
NA_EMEA	North America	EMEA	10,000	60	1,750	350
EMEA_APAC	EMEA	APAC	2,000	60	1,750	350

Finally, you need to associate IP subnets with each site, as shown in Table 14.8. As mentioned earlier, it is from these subnets that a client is able to determine which policy will apply.

TABLE 14.8: Subnet Associations per Site

REGION	SITE	SUBNETS
North America	Chicago	10.0.1.0/24, 10.0.7.0/24, 10.43.23.0/24
North America	New York	10.0.2.0/24, 192.168.3.0/25
North America	Washington, D.C.	10.1.0.0/16
North America	Seattle	10.0.3.0/24, 10.0.54.0/24
North America	San Francisco	10.0.4.0/24
EMEA	London	10.25.1.0/24, 192.168.3.128/25
EMEA	Dublin	10.25.2.0/24
EMEA	Paris	10.25.3.0/24
APAC	Sydney	10.0.9.0/24, 10.37.1.0/24
APAC	Hong Kong	10.37.2.0/24
APAC	Tokyo	10.37.3.0/24

The final Call Admission Control policy looks Figure 14.17.

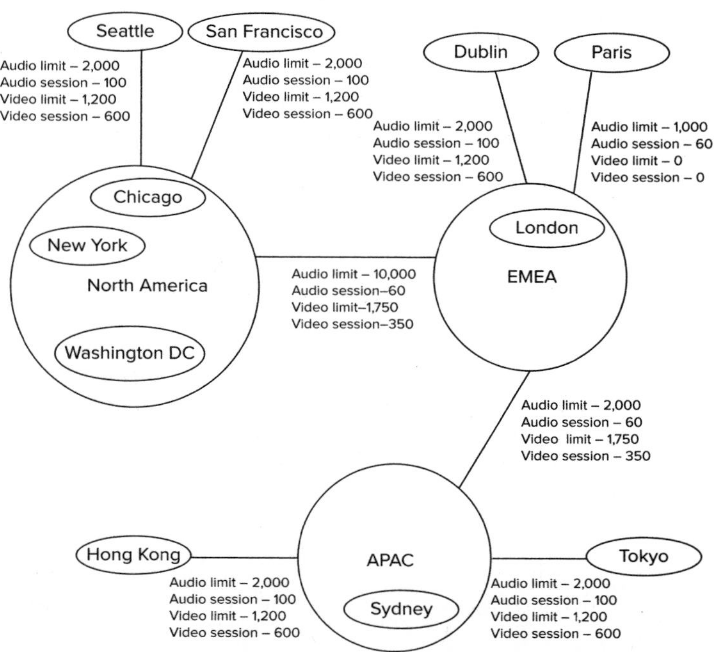

FIGURE 14.17 Diagrammatic representation of Call Admission Control Configuration

When a user in Seattle calls a user in Tokyo, Call Admission Control will assess the following connection links:

Seattle to North America Region

North America Region to EMEA Region

EMEA Region to APAC Region

APAC Region to Tokyo

If any of these links are saturated, the call will not proceed. If the call is established, the call details will be replicated to all PDPs in the topology to ensure that each is fully aware of the current network state.

In this example, we have not considered any rerouting capabilities. We will look at those in the "Configuring Call Admission Control" section later in this chapter.

Real World Scenario

WHAT ABOUT MPLS?

MPLS networks can give the impression that all sites connected to the network are only one hop away from each other. This can cause confusion for anyone attempting to configure CAC in this type of scenario, as you would normally have to configure a site link from each site to every other site—leading to a massive meshed network configuration, which would be extremely difficult to manage properly.

By simply treating the MPLS mesh as a separate site and configuring links from each *actual* site to this imaginary site, you regain control over the network capacity used by Lync. Because you won't assign any network subnets to this imaginary site, no clients will be considered as if they are located within the mesh.

Taking the example from the previous section and replacing the inter-region links with a global MPLS network will give the configuration shown here:

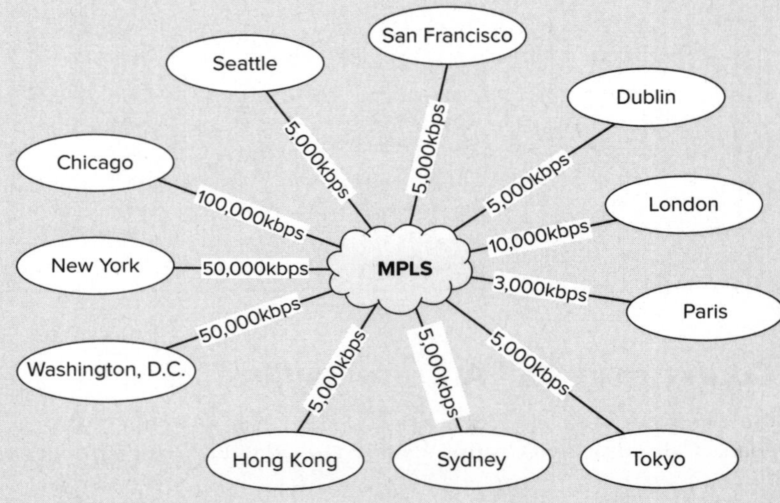

Configuring Call Admission Control to manage this network could prove difficult. Following the logic shown, you would create regions and individual sites again; however, this would lead to misrepresentation on the network. It would be possible but extremely difficult to come up with a configuration where each site theoretically would have multiple links leaving the site but would not be represented as such from the network perspective, where there is only a single MPLS connection. The next illustration indicates how this might look.

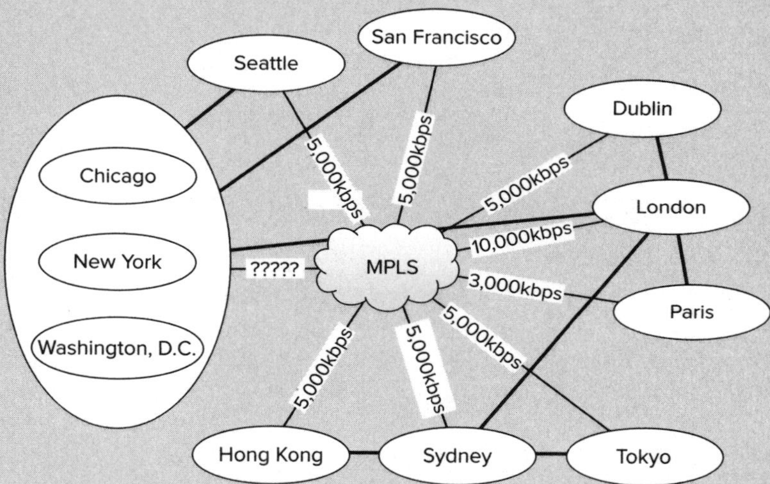

Taking London as the starting point, there are four connections: Dublin, Paris, APAC (Sydney), and North America; all of which Call Admission Control would handle individually, with no understanding of the underlying network where all the calls are actually following the same path. This could result in calls from London to North America being inadvertently impacted when the London–Dublin link is busy.

In addition, how would you manage the North America bandwidth?

A much cleaner approach is to treat the MPLS network *cloud* (MPLS networks are often referred to as *clouds* due to the way in which the actual network connections are abstracted from the user and appear as a single hop) as a Call Admission Control Region in its own right. By taking this approach, you are back to the first diagram in this sidebar, but now you have control over each individual link; because all the links are to the cloud, the PDPs will be aware of the current concurrency rates on every link in the network and can efficiently manage the control of the call flow. This also allows multiple MPLS clouds to be managed easily.

Configuring Call Admission Control

We'll keep using the original example to show how the configuration is built. To configure and enable Call Admission Control, you need to individually configure the following sections (the

Control Panel view is shown in Figure 14.18, with the Global tab open):

- Global
- Location Policy (not related to Call Admission Control)
- Policy Profile
- Region
- Site
- Subnet
- Region Link
- Region Route

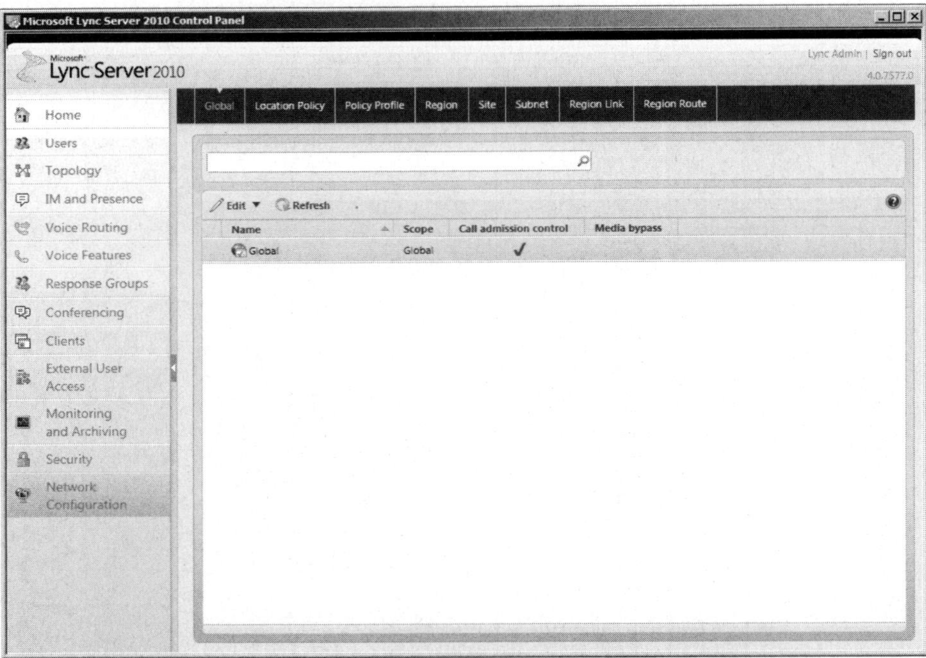

FIGURE 14.18
Using Control Panel to Configure Call Admission Control

Although it is possible to configure all of Call Admission Control via a single `Set-CsNetworkConfiguration` command, that approach is extremely complex and not recommended. It is much easier to configure section by section.

Configuring the Global Setting

Because Call Admission Control is configured at the individual component level, the only setting on the policy in the Global tab is to enable or disable it.

Figure 14.19 shows Call Admission Control enabled in the Control Panel. The equivalent command in the Lync Management Shell would be either:

```
Set-CsNetworkConfiguration -EnableBandwidthPolicyCheck $True
```

or

```
Set-CsNetworkConfiguration -EnableBandwidthPolicyCheck $False
```

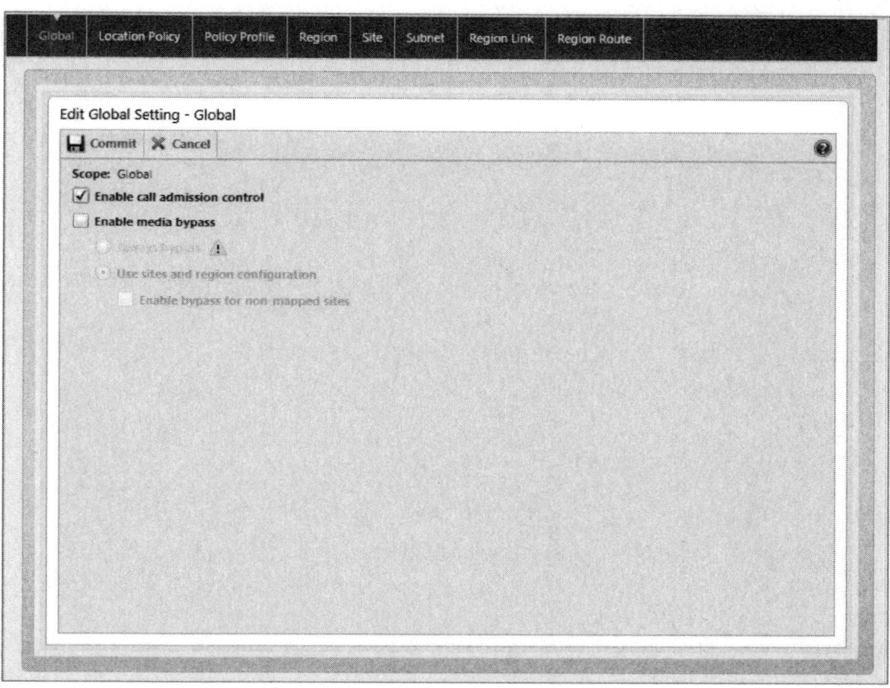

FIGURE 14.19
Enabling Call Admission Control

Additional policies may be created and applied if Call Admission Control is not being controlled globally, or if the network setup does not allow a single global approach. Each policy can be enabled or disabled individually.

Using the `Get-CsNetworkConfiguration` cmdlet allows you to verify the state of each policy:

```
Identity                    : Global
MediaBypassSettings         : Enabled=False;InternalBypassMode=Off;EnternalBypassMode
=Off;AlwaysBypass=False;BypassID=
BWPolicyProfiles            : {}
NetworkRegions              : {}
NetworkREgionLinks          : {}
InterNetworkRegionRoutes    : {}
NetworkSites                : {}
```

```
InterNetworkSitePolicies  : {}
Subnets                   : {}
EnableBandwithPolicyCheck : True
```

Figure 14.18 shows the Control Panel view of this command.

Defining the Policy Profile Settings

The Policy Profile page is where you define both the audio and video limits that will be assigned to the links between each site and region. Later you will link these polices to the relevant network sites. (Note that even though a policy may not allow audio or video across a link by setting the audio or video limit to 0, the individual session limit still requires a value to be added.)

Figure 14.20 shows the Control Panel input page and from the shell; the following command is used to create a bandwidth policy:

```
New-CsNetworkBandwithPolicyProfile -Identity "Global Default Policy"
   -AudioBWLimit 2000 -AudioBWSessionLimit 100
   -VideoBWLimit 1200 -VideoBWSessionLimit 600
   -Description "Global Policy"
```

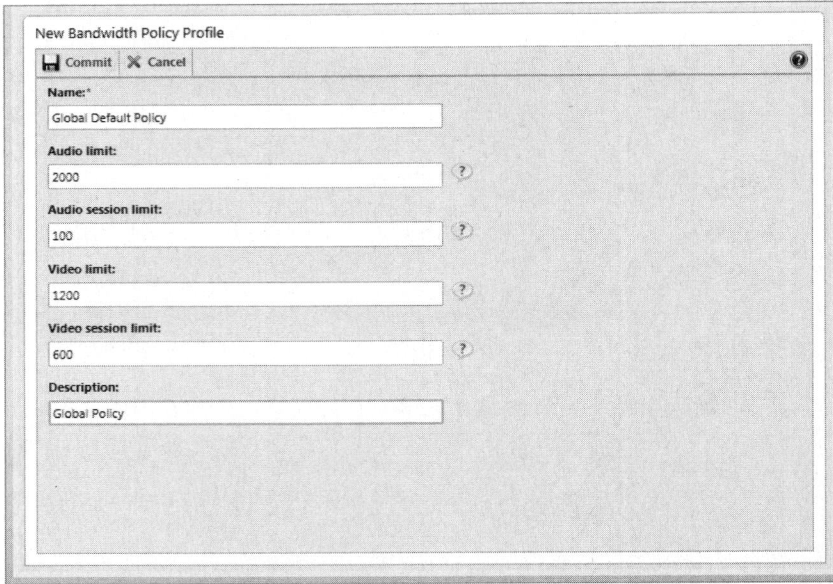

FIGURE 14.20
The New Bandwidth Policy Profile page

An inter-region policy is simply a bandwidth policy applied to a region policy, so is created and configured in exactly the same way.

Once the profile is fully configured, you will see the following output:

```
Get-CsNetworkBandwidthPolicyProfile

Identity            : Paris Bandwidth policy no video
BWPolicy            : {BWLimit=0;BWSessionLimit=60;BWPolicyModality=Audio, BWLimit=0;
BWSessionLimit=100;BWPolicyModality=Video}
BWPolicyProfileID : Paris Bandwidth policy no video
Description         : No video permitted

Identity            : Global Default Policy
BWPolicy            : {BWLimit=2000;BWSessionLimit=100;BWPolicyModality=Audio,
BWLimit=1200;BWSessionLimit=600;BWPolicyModality=Video}
BWPolicyProfileID : Global Default Policy
Description         : Global Policy

Identity            : NA_EMEA Bandwidth Policy
BWPolicy            : {BWLimit=10000;BWSessionLimit=60;BWPolicyModality=Audio,
BWLimit=1750;BWSessionLimit=350;BWPolicyModality=Video}
BWPolicyProfileID : NA_EMEA Bandwidth Policy
Description         : NA-EMEA Bandwith Policy

Identity            : EMEA_APAC Bandwidth Policy
BWPolicy            : {BWLimit=2000;BWSessionLimit=60;BWPolicyModality=Audio,
BWLimit=1750;BWSessionLimit=350;BWPolicyModality=Video}
BWPolicyProfileID : EMEA_APAC Bandwidth Policy
Description         : EMEA-APAC Bandwidth Policy
```

Defining Regions

Regions are the hubs of Call Admission Control, and calls within a region do not have any restrictions placed on them.

Each region is required to be assigned to a central site; this is as defined (and published) via the Topology Builder shown in Figure 14.21. (Topology Builder is a separate installation item, installed via SETUP.EXE; however, it must be installed on at least one server to create and publish the initial topology).

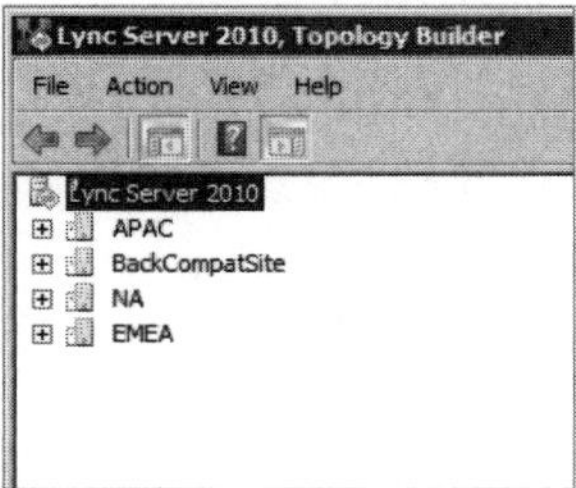

FIGURE 14.21
Central Site representation in Topology Builder

Defining a region using the Control Panel is shown in Figure 14.22, and requires the following information:

- Name
- Central site
- Enable audio alternate path
- Enable video alternate path
- Description
- Associated sites (you'll define the sites in the next section)

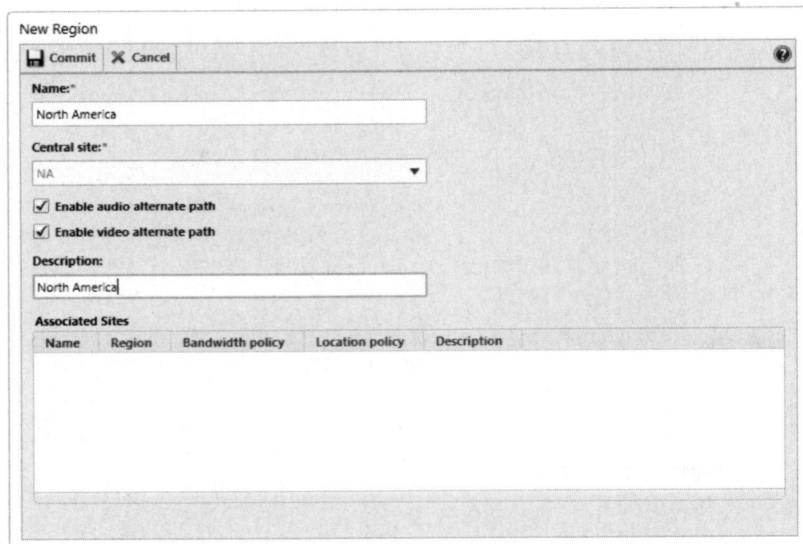

FIGURE 14.22
New region definition

Configuring the information for the remaining regions via the Lync Server Management Shell would look like this:

```
New-CsNetworkRegion -Identity EMEA -CentralSite EMEA -AudioAlternatePath $true
   -VideoAlternatePath $true -Description "EMEA Region"
```

Including `-AudioAlternatePath` and `-VideoAlternatePath` (and setting to `$True`) configures the region to reroute audio and video if Call Admission Control reports that not enough bandwidth is available on the links. This provides us with the capability to provide an alternate path for voice but not video if required.

Get-CsNetworkRegion will return:

```
Identity          : North America
Description       : North America Region
BypassID          : 6d278a1c-c994-4a28-b6de-a4a3773335ec
CentralSite       : Site:NA
BWAlternatePaths  : {BWPolicyModality=Audio;
     AlternatePath=True,
     BWPolicyModality=Video;AlternatePath=True}
NetworkRegionID   : North America

Identity          : EMEA
Description       : EMEA Region
BypassID          : ca72a529-277f-4757-aa8f-e13c681cc462
CentralSite       : Site:EMEA
BWAlternatePaths  : {BWPolicyModality=Audio;
     AlternatePath=True,
     BWPolicyModality=Video;AlternatePath=True}
NetworkRegionID   : EMEA

Identity          : APAC
Description       : APAC Region
BypassID          : d1b4c334-de17-40e8-950d-1ffe6bfd4c06
CentralSite       : Site:APAC
BWAlternatePaths  : {BWPolicyModality=Audio;
     AlternatePath=True,
     BWPolicyModality=Video;AlternatePath=True}
NetworkRegionID   : APAC
```

Defining Sites

Sites are within and connected to regions. Lync clients are associated with sites, based on the actual subnet from which they are connecting. It is possible for a user to be connected with multiple Lync clients, each of which could be in a different site.

Figure 14.23 shows the Control Panel Configuration screen for a new site. This is where you can define the following items:

- Name
- Region (must be previously defined)
- Bandwidth Policy
- Location Policy (not Call Admission Control–related)
- Description
- Associated Subnets (subnets are being defined next)

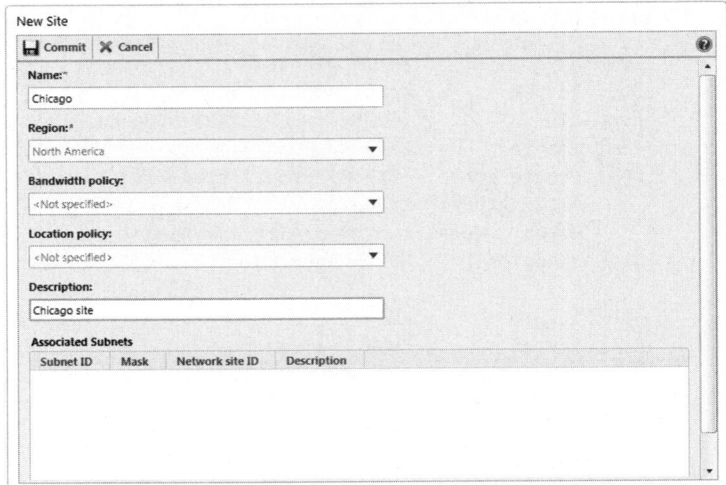

FIGURE 14.23
New site definition

Sites are defined using the `Set-CsNetworkSite` cmdlet:

```
New-CsNetworkSite -Identity "London"
    -NetworkRegionID EMEA
    -Description "London Site"
```

In the North America region, multiple sites are defined even though the example stated there will be no bandwidth controls. It is good practice to define *all* the sites in the environment, because that will make them easier to match up and adjust in the future when—not if—the requirements change.

Not only will troubleshooting be easier when the complete environment is defined, but the fact that a site is defined but has no policy means the client will be correctly assigned within the logs, making them easier to follow when you're trying to understand a problem.

If this were a new site being introduced after Lync had already been deployed, it would make sense to fully populate the policy and location information sources at this point. Because this is the London site and we don't want to place any controls on the bandwidth usage for the example, we won't come back to assign a bandwidth policy; however, the subnets do need to be assigned. Location policy will be discussed in Chapter 15.

The full configuration of the defined sites looks like this:

```
Get-CsNetworkSite

Identity           : Chicago
NetworkSiteID      : Chicago
Description        : Chicago site
NetworkRegionID    : North America
BypassID           : 6d278a1c-c994-4a28-b6de-a4a3773335ec
BWPolicyProfileID  :
LocationPolicy     :

Identity           : New York
NetworkSiteID      : New York
```

```
Description        : New York Site
NetworkRegionID    : North America
BypassID           : 6d278a1c-c994-4a28-b6de-a4a3773335ec
BWPolicyProfileID :
LocationPolicy     :

Identity           : Washington DC
NetworkSiteID      : Washington DC
Description        : Washington DC Site
NetworkRegionID    : North America
BypassID           : 6d278a1c-c994-4a28-b6de-a4a3773335ec
BWPolicyProfileID :
LocationPolicy     :

Identity           : London
NetworkSiteID      : London
Description        : London Site
NetworkRegionID    : EMEA
BypassID           : ca72a529-277f-4757-aa8f-e13c681cc462
BWPolicyProfileID :
LocationPolicy     :

Identity           : San Francisco
NetworkSiteID      : San Francisco
Description        : San Francisco Site
NetworkRegionID    : North America
BypassID           : 86b36862-bd48-49de-a1d6-49561ce50bd9
BWPolicyProfileID :
LocationPolicy     :

Identity           : Seattle
NetworkSiteID      : Seattle
Description        : Seattle Site
NetworkRegionID    : North America
BypassID           : 2049a6b0-02e1-4f71-b76b-db93aa7d130c
BWPolicyProfileID :
LocationPolicy     :

Identity           : Dublin
NetworkSiteID      : Dublin
Description        : Dublin Site
NetworkRegionID    : EMEA
BypassID           : 1f0c441c-aac1-4ba4-b835-43b20fb95686
BWPolicyProfileID :
LocationPolicy     :

Identity           : Paris
NetworkSiteID      : Paris
Description        : Paris Site
```

```
NetworkRegionID   : EMEA
BypassID          : 7c638937-4c0b-4a8f-9918-cebe7a7b7284
BWPolicyProfileID :
LocationPolicy    :

Identity          : Sydney
NetworkSiteID     : Sydney
Description       : Sydney Site
NetworkRegionID   : APAC
BypassID          : d1b4c334-de17-40e8-950d-1ffe6bfd4c06
BWPolicyProfileID :
LocationPolicy    :

Identity          : Hong Kong
NetworkSiteID     : Hong Kong
Description       : Hong Kong Site
NetworkRegionID   : APAC
BypassID          : d6e14fc5-2082-4731-8973-8489cd4e6cde
BWPolicyProfileID :
LocationPolicy    :

Identity          : Tokyo
NetworkSiteID     : Tokyo
Description       : Tokyo Site
NetworkRegionID   : APAC
BypassID          : 4baa4383-c037-414e-b4dd-b780e4c88ee2
BWPolicyProfileID :
LocationPolicy    :
```

Defining Subnets

Each client will determine its site location and, therefore, policy restrictions based on its subnet. To enable this tie-up between site and subnet, you must first define the subnets in the environment and then assign them to the correct sites.

Figure 14.24 shows the Control Panel approach to define a subnet:

- Subnet ID
- Mask
- Network Site ID (must be previously defined)
- Description

The Subnet ID must be the first address in the subnet range (known as the network address or *subnet-zero*). The mask must be in numeric format (e.g., 24), not the more common Classless Inter-Domain Routing (CIDR) format (e.g., /24).

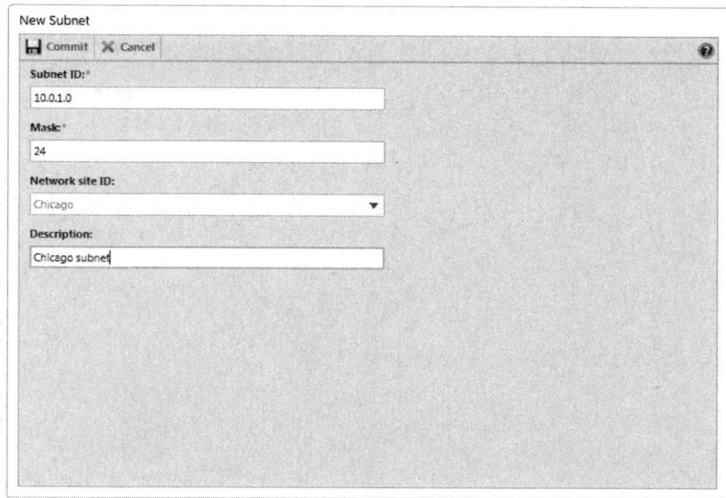

FIGURE 14.24
New subnet definition

The cmdlet to use for this function is `New-CsSubnet`:

```
New-CsNetworkSubnet -Identity 10.0.7.0 -Mask 24
   -NetworkSiteID Chicago
   -Description "Chicago subnet"
```

Once fully populated, the environment looks like this:

```
Get-CsSubnet

Identity      : 10.0.1.0
MaskBits      : 24
Description   : Chicago subnet
NetworkSiteID : Chicago
SubnetID      : 10.0.1.0

Identity      : 10.0.7.0
MaskBits      : 24
Description   : Chicago subnet
NetworkSiteID : Chicago
SubnetID      : 10.0.7.0

Identity      : 10.43.23.0
MaskBits      : 24
Description   : Chicago subnet
NetworkSiteID : Chicago
SubnetID      : 10.43.23.0

Identity      : 10.0.2.0
MaskBits      : 24
Description   : New York subnet
```

```
NetworkSiteID : New York
SubnetID      : 10.0.2.0

Identity      : 10.0.3.0
MaskBits      : 25
Description   : Paris subnet
NetworkSiteID : Paris
SubnetID      : 10.0.3.0
```

The output has been cut for brevity, because the definitions for subnets are the same for each and there really isn't a lot to configure.

Defining Region Linksscruffs

Now that you've defined the regions, sites, and associated subnets, you need to tell Lync Server 2010 how much bandwidth is available between regions. Region links are how you can do this. Region links also represent the logical connections from one region to the next.

Figure 14.25 shows the values required to create the region link between North America and EMEA. To do that, you need to configure the following items:

- Name
- Network Region #1 (must already have been defined)
- Network Region #2 (must already have been defined)
- Bandwidth Policy

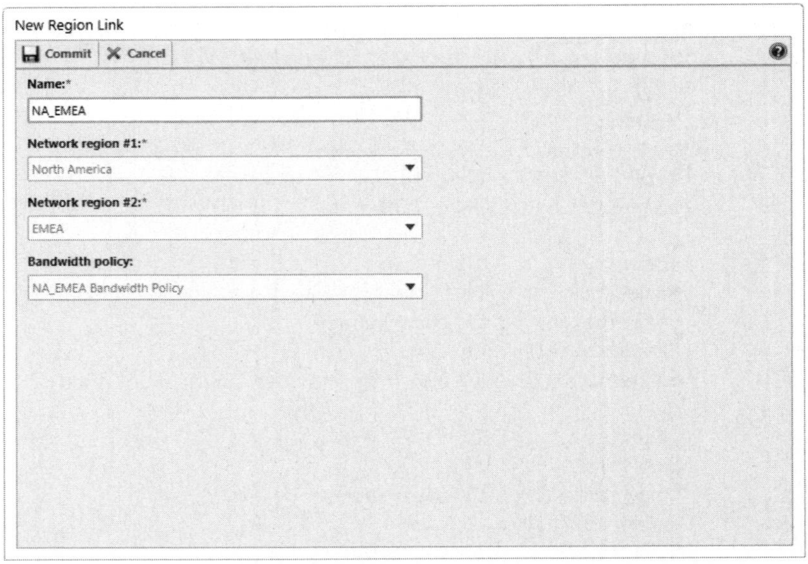

FIGURE 14.25
New region link definition

To define a connection between EMEA and APAC, and assign the relevant bandwidth policy, use this command:

```
New-CsNetworkRegionLink -Identity EMEA_APAC
     -NetworkRegionID1 EMEA
     -NetworkRegionID2 APAC
     -BWPolicyProfileID "EMEA_APAC Bandwidth Policy"
```

Once all region links are defined, the environment will look like this:

```
Get-CsNetworkRegionLink

Identity              : NA_EMEA
BWPolicyProfileID     : NA_EMEA Bandwidth Policy
NetworkRegionLinkID : NA_EMEA
NetworkRegionID1      : North America
NetworkRegionID2      : EMEA

Identity              : EMEA_APAC
BWPolicyProfileID     : EMEA_APAC Bandwidth Policy
NetworkRegionLinkID : EMEA_APAC
NetworkRegionID1      : EMEA
NetworkRegionID2      : APAC
```

Assigning Region Routes

Once all the regions have been defined, Lync needs to understand how they are connected. The connections are defined in the Region Route section in the Control Panel. This is similar to the Region Link configuration, except that rather than defining the policy applied on a link, you are defining the routes to take between regions.

The actual network route taken by the data is not affected by this definition; it is used only internally within Lync Server 2010 to allow an understanding of the network within the Call Admission Control aspect of Lync Server 2010.

Figure 14.26 shows the Control Panel implementation, which requires the following items:

- Name
- Network Region #1 (must have already been defined)
- Network Region #2 (must have already been defined)
- Network Region Links (must have already been defined)

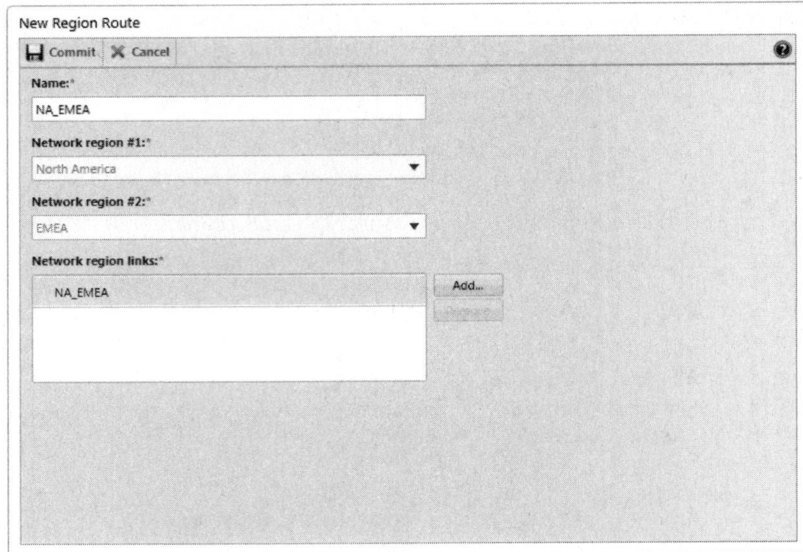

FIGURE 14.26
Region route definition

The equivalent PowerShell cmdlet is `Net-CsNetworkInterRegionRoute`. Here is an example:

```
New-CsNetworkInterRegionRoute -Identity EMEA_APAC
   -NetworkRegionID1 EMEA -NetworkRegionID2 APAC
   -NetworkRegionLinks EMEA_APAC
```

The fully configured environment will be like this:

```
Get-CsNetworkInterRegionRoute

Identity                    : NA_EMEA
NetworkRegionLinks          : {NA_EMEA}
InterNetworkRegionRouteID : NA_EMEA
NetworkRegionID1            : North America
NetworkRegionID2            : EMEA

Identity                    : EMEA_APAC
NetworkRegionLinks          : {EMEA_APAC}
InterNetworkRegionRouteID : EMEA_APAC
NetworkRegionID1            : EMEA
NetworkRegionID2            : APAC
```

Assigning Policies

Now that the environment is fully populated, the final step in configuring it is to apply the policy controls. The previous two sections have shown how to assign policy to the region links; however, you also need to go back and assign the policy to a number of sites.

At this point, all calls within a region are uncontrolled; only the inter-region calls have had policy applied to them. In the example, you want to control calls on a number of site links and leave the remaining as uncontrolled within region NA.

To assign policy to a specific site, use the `Set-CsNetworkSite` cmdlet:

```
Set-CsNetworkSite -Identity "Paris" -BWPolicyProfileID "Paris Bandwidth policy no
video"
```

You can also apply policies using the Control Panel; simply open the specific site (from the Site configuration tab in the Network Configuration section) by double-clicking the site entry. Once the site is opened, you will be taken to the Edit Site page (shown in Figure 14.27). From the defined Bandwidth policy section there, you can choose which policy will be applied on this link.

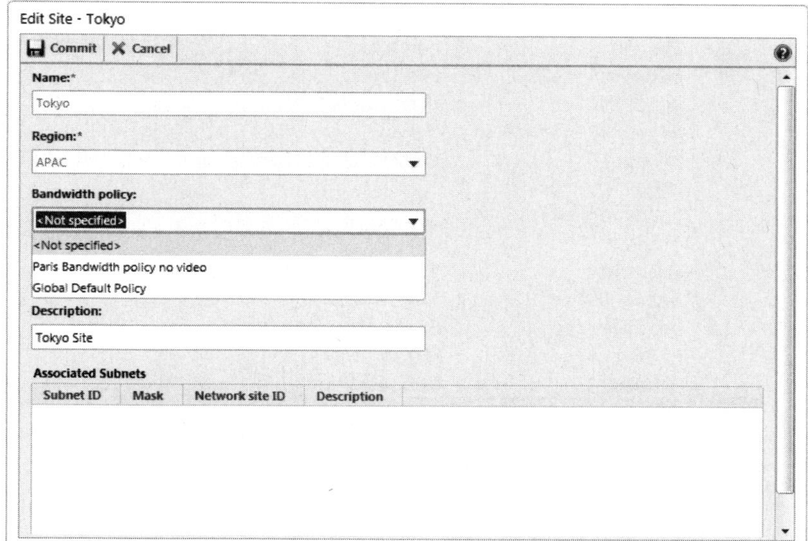

FIGURE 14.27
Assigning a policy to an existing site

Finally, the fully configured site listing looks like this:

```
Get-CsNetworkSite

Identity           : Chicago
NetworkSiteID      : Chicago
Description        : Chicago site
NetworkRegionID    : North America
BypassID           : 6d278a1c-c994-4a28-b6de-a4a3773335ec
BWPolicyProfileID  :
LocationPolicy     :

Identity           : New York
NetworkSiteID      : New York
```

```
Description       : New York Site
NetworkRegionID   : North America
BypassID          : 6d278a1c-c994-4a28-b6de-a4a3773335ec
BWPolicyProfileID :
LocationPolicy    :

Identity          : Washington DC
NetworkSiteID     : Washington DC
Description       : Washington DC Site
NetworkRegionID   : North America
BypassID          : 6d278a1c-c994-4a28-b6de-a4a3773335ec
BWPolicyProfileID :
LocationPolicy    :

Identity          : London
NetworkSiteID     : London
Description       : London Site
NetworkRegionID   : EMEA
BypassID          : ca72a529-277f-4757-aa8f-e13c681cc462
BWPolicyProfileID :
LocationPolicy    :

Identity          : San Francisco
NetworkSiteID     : San Francisco
Description       : San Francisco Site
NetworkRegionID   : North America
BypassID          : 86b36862-bd48-49de-a1d6-49561ce50bd9
BWPolicyProfileID : Global Default Policy
LocationPolicy    :

Identity          : Seattle
NetworkSiteID     : Seattle
Description       : Seattle Site
NetworkRegionID   : North America
BypassID          : 2049a6b0-02e1-4f71-b76b-db93aa7d130c
BWPolicyProfileID : Global Default Policy
LocationPolicy    :

Identity          : Dublin
NetworkSiteID     : Dublin
Description       : Dublin Site
NetworkRegionID   : EMEA
BypassID          : 1f0c441c-aac1-4ba4-b835-43b20fb95686
BWPolicyProfileID : Global Default Policy
LocationPolicy    :

Identity          : Paris
NetworkSiteID     : Paris
```

```
Description        : Paris Site
NetworkRegionID    : EMEA
BypassID           : 7c638937-4c0b-4a8f-9918-cebe7a7b7284
BWPolicyProfileID : Paris Bandwidth policy no video
LocationPolicy     :

Identity           : Sydney
NetworkSiteID      : Sydney
Description        : Sydney Site
NetworkRegionID    : APAC
BypassID           : d1b4c334-de17-40e8-950d-1ffe6bfd4c06
BWPolicyProfileID :
LocationPolicy     :

Identity           : Hong Kong
NetworkSiteID      : Hong Kong
Description        : Hong Kong Site
NetworkRegionID    : APAC
BypassID           : d6e14fc5-2082-4731-8973-8489cd4e6cde
BWPolicyProfileID : Global Default Policy
LocationPolicy     :

Identity           : Tokyo
NetworkSiteID      : Tokyo
Description        : Tokyo Site
NetworkRegionID    : APAC
BypassID           : 4baa4383-c037-414e-b4dd-b780e4c88ee2
BWPolicyProfileID : Global Default Policy
LocationPolicy     :
```

Identifying Calls on a Network

During the early stages of the beta program, customers had a question: "If the system knows what the current state of calls is throughout the network, where can an administrator find that information?"

A subsequent version of the beta (and released) code provided the following management shell command:

```
Set-CsBandwidthPolicyServiceConfiguration -EnableLogging $true
```

This enables CVS file logging to the following location:

```
<ocs share>/1-ApplicationServer-1/AppServerFiles/PDP/
```

Several files are created:

PDP_*<servername><date><time>*_Links This file is updated hourly, or when the Call Admission Control configuration is changed. It will contain one line per site or region and list the current permitted total and the current utilization for both audio and video traffic. It is a CSV format file.

PDP_<*servername*><*date*><*time*>_BwCheckFailure This file is updated with every entry based on the local PDP failures and includes data such as the IP addresses of the clients involved, as well as the minimum and maximum requested bandwidth values. This data does not get replicated to any other PDP in the topology. It is a CSV format file.

PDP_<*servername*><*date*><*time*>_Topology This file is generated once per day at 00:01, as well as when any changes are applied to the Call Admission Control configuration. It is an XML format file.

Reporting on Call Admission Control

Over time, understanding the impact of Call Admission Control is important. If the values are set too high, then potentially the network is over-specified, and costs may be saved by reducing the capacity. On the other hand, it's more likely that Call Admission Control will be rejecting calls, and if a significant number are reported, this may indicate that Call Admission Control is configured too low. In parallel to this, if the network is nearing capacity, it is an indication that the network is under pressure and may need to be increased.

From the reporting pack installed with the monitoring server, you can run the Call Admission Control report, which will provide a detailed view on how many calls are being rerouted or rejected based on the current policy settings. This is covered in Chapter 11, "Monitoring and Archiving."

The Bottom Line

Identify Call Admission Control–capable endpoints. Before designing and configuring Call Admission Control, you need to understand where it can be applied to ensure the proper configuration is identified.

Master It You are in the process of defining a migration from OCS R2 to Lync Server 2010. Users previously reported some issues with call quality due to the capacity on the network, so Call Admission Control is required. Which user endpoints can be restricted by the Call Admission Control policy?

Configure policy-based Quality of Service controls. Call Admission Control provides application-layer management of the call bandwidth; however, to truly provide this guarantee to clients, Quality of Service is required to operate on the network layer. Windows Vista introduced policy-based Quality of Service controls.

Master It You have restricted the port range to be 5000 – 5999, and you will deploy Lync 2010 to your users. An application utilized in the finance department uses the port range 5500 – 5599. How can you ensure that only the Lync 2010 traffic is prioritized on the network?

Design a Call Admission Control solution. Call Admission Control can be complex in large interconnected networks. A properly designed solution will ensure two important requirements of Call Admission Control are met: user call quality is high and the network is not saturated.

Master It What special considerations should be given to an MPLS network?

Configure Call Admission Control. Once designed, Call Admission Control needs to be configured and applied to the Lync 2010 servers. The servers will keep each other constantly updated as to the number of the calls and bandwidth used on the network. By using the built-in logging functionality, it is possible to capture an hourly snapshot of the state, with more detailed reporting available via the monitoring server.

Master It What needs to be defined and applied to configure Call Admission Control?

Chapter 15

E911 and Location Information Services (LIS)

Being able to dial emergency services is probably the most critical requirement for any telephony system. Face it; if someone needs emergency services, something serious is probably happening.

Although Office Communications Server 2007 and R2 were both capable of calling emergency services, Lync Server 2010 is also compliant with the North American requirement to provide location-based data with calls, known as Enhanced 911, or E911.

In this chapter you will learn to:

- Describe the E911 requirements for North America
- Configure Lync Server 2010 to meet E911 requirements
- Understand how Location Information Services can be used by callers outside North America

Understanding E911

In the early days of telephony, each exchange could use a different number for contacting emergency services. Over 70 years ago, the United Kingdom was one of the first locations to introduce three-digit emergency service dialing. This informal standard has since spread worldwide, where almost all countries have three-digit dialing for the main emergency services: police, fire, and medical.

There is no common global number for emergency services; 911 is used in North America, 112 in Europe, and 999 in the United Kingdom, for example. Moreover, in many locations separate phone numbers are used for each of the emergency services, with no central public safety operator.

Where a central public safety operator is used, the safety operator establishes the specific emergency need and may route the call to the specific service or act as an intermediary and collect additional information such as the location, or may provide verbal assistance and guidance until the emergency services arrive.

Figure 15.1 shows a typical interaction in a legacy telephony system.

FIGURE 15.1
Traditional interaction from an emergency operator

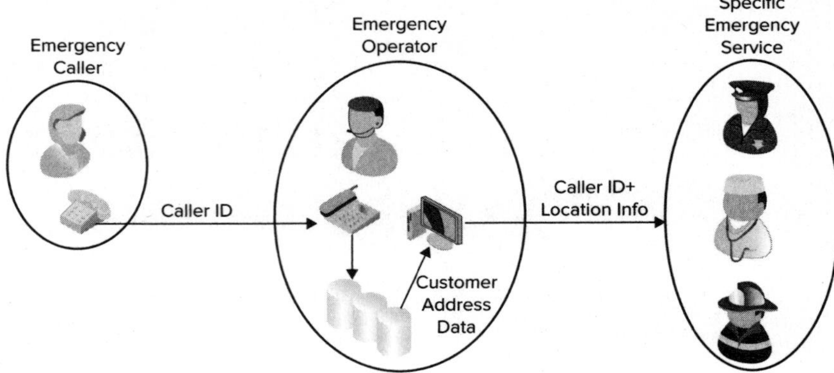

As phone systems developed, and in many cases became nationalized, it was possible to determine the phone's location based on the billing records for an individual line. In large organizations, the information was typically not detailed enough for this to occur; however, at least some of the address information could be discerned.

However, the introduction of cellular-based mobile devices removed this capability—in most cases, the caller was not at the billing address of the handset, rendering billing information useless.

Mobile handsets also introduced the concept of *roaming*, and the complication of enabling users (when travelling out of country) to dial their home country's emergency number and have it translated to the local country number as well as being routed locally. Most devices accept 112, 911, and 999 as preprogrammed emergency service numbers. SIM cards may also have additional data programmed.

Mobile integration with the emergency services differs within each country, but there is normally a provision for the mobile carrier to provide the location information based on the cell tower details through which the handset is provided, as shown in Figure 15.2.

FIGURE 15.2
Cellular provision of location information

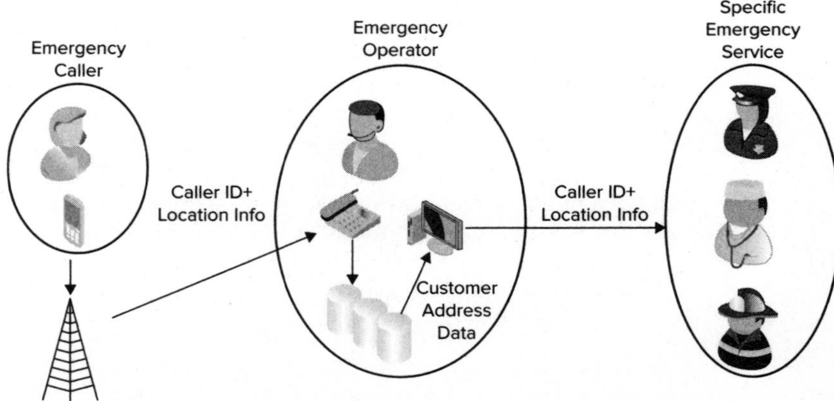

Including location information automatically ensures not only that emergency services are provided the information, saving valuable time, but also that the call is routed to the nearest Public Safety Answering Point (PSAP), guaranteeing that the emergency services in the vicinity of the emergency are notified.

Telephony has moved away from the traditional "fixed line" idea to the data network provision of Voice over IP (VoIP), and the copper lines to desks became network lines to anywhere. Continuing the trend is the concept of soft phone clients such as Lync 2010, and you can see that the need for location-based information continues to become more apparent.

In the early implementations of VoIP systems, emergency calling was specifically excluded, because of the flexibility of the potential location of the caller. Financial penalties imposed by governments over lack of emergency service calling provision soon made this approach unreasonable.

Enhanced 911 (E911) is the provision of the emergency call as well as the location information associated with it. Lync Server 2010 implements E911, as shown in Figure 15.3.

FIGURE 15.3
E911 Implementation within Lync Server 2010

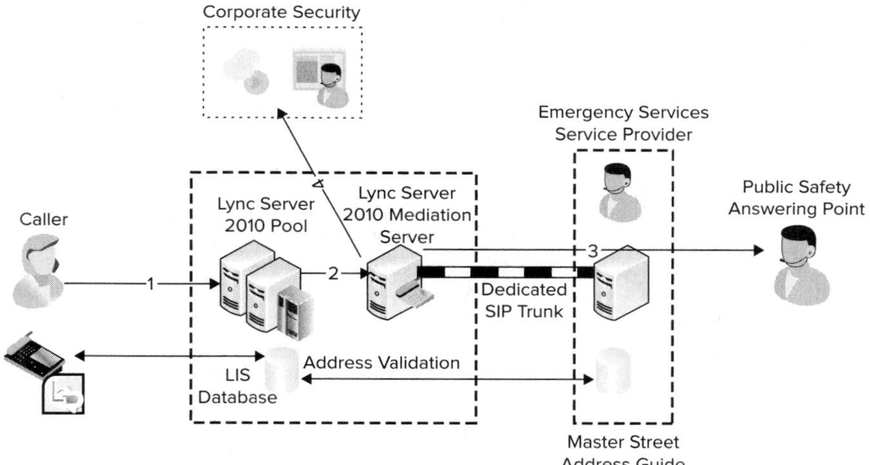

The process is as follows:

1. A call is placed to emergency services.
2. The call is routed to the appropriate Mediation server, with Session Initiation Protocol (SIP) information that includes location details.
3. The call is routed via the Emergency Services Service Provider to the appropriate Public Safety Answering Point (PSAP). If at this stage the location information has not been validated via the Master Street Address Guide database, then an Emergency Services Service Provider Operator will handle the call and verbally confirm location information prior to routing the call to the PSAP.
4. Optionally, the corporate security desk may be informed, via instant message (IM) and/or inclusion in a conference call.

Current Legislation

As of May, 2011, 16 states across North America have legislation requiring businesses, schools, and government agencies to provide E911 capabilities. Other states in North America and other countries throughout the world are considering similar legislation and approaches for provision of location information.

Real World Scenario

The Consequences of Getting It Wrong

Providing location information to emergency services helps improve response times; however, in extreme cases, when this information is out of date or even wrong, it can lead to fatalities simply because the emergency responders are sent to the wrong location.

The first fatality due to failure to deliver the correct location for the caller's address happened in Canada in 2008.

A family moved their home and, realizing the benefits of VoIP, continued to use the same telephony service provider and number at their new location. However, somehow the old street address was retained for the customer. Due to a miscommunication caused by language barriers, the Emergency Services Operator was unable to confirm the address, and the emergency services were dispatched to the old (incorrect address).

This highlights the need to ensure not only that the technology is location-aware, but that the correct street address information reflects the actual location—addresses may still be valid, but associated with an incorrect subnet or switch.

Configuring E911

Now that you understand why you need to configure E911 dialing and location services, how do you go about it?

Well, simply put, E911 calling is a voice route using a dedicated SIP trunk, so you'll need to define the following:

- PSTN usage
- Location policy
- SIP trunk
- Voice route

Configuring PSTN Usage

As described in Chapter 13, "Getting Started with Voice," Public Switched Telephone Network (PSTN) usages are used to provide call authorization to users when attempting to place calls via the Lync 2010 client. A PSTN usage ties a voice policy to a user and also a route to a gateway, giving permissions for a user to use a particular route.

It is recommended that a separate usage be defined for emergency services dialing, and that all users are permitted to use this.

The command to define a PSTN usage is:

```
Set-CsPstnUsage -Identity global -Usage @{add="EmergencyUsage}
```

Configuring Location Policies

The location policy contains the definition of the emergency service dialing implementation. Policies can be assigned to specific subnets or individual users. If neither of these is in place, the global policy takes effect.

Using the `New-CsLocationPolicy` or the `Set-CsLocationPolicy` cmdlets, the additional parameters shown in Table 15.1 provide the PowerShell method of configuration.

TABLE 15.1: `CsLocationPolicy` Parameters

PARAMETER	OPTIONAL?	EXAMPLE
Identity	Yes	Global
EnhancedEmergencyServicesEnabled	No	$True
LocationRequired	Yes	yes
UseLocationForE911Only	Yes	$True
PstnUsage	Yes	EmergencyUsage
EmergencyDialString	Yes	911
EmergencyDialMask	Yes	112
NotificationUri	Yes	Sip:security@gaots.co.uk
ConferenceUri	Yes	Sip:+155512347890@gaots.co.uk
ConferenceMode	Yes	TwoWay
Description	Yes	Global emergency location policy

`Identity` This defines the `CsLocationPolicy` to modify or create. If a policy is being scoped ("Tagged") to a specific site, the entry must be in the form `site:`*<site name>*—for example, `site:UK`.

`EnhancedEmergencyServicesEnabled` The `EnhancedEmergencyServicesEnabled` parameter tells the Lync 2010 client whether or not to retrieve and provide location information with an emergency call.

LocationRequired When the Lync 2010 client is logging, the LocationRequired parameter is used in the event that location information cannot be retrieved from the location configuration database. This parameter can be one of three options:

no The user will not be prompted for any location information, and location information will be unavailable for the emergency services call. The call will be answered by the emergency services provider, asking verbally for the location information before rerouting to the correct emergency services operator.

yes The user is prompted for location information; however, it is not mandatory to be completed and can be dismissed. In this scenario, if the information is provided, the call is first answered by the emergency services provider to verify the location information, before rerouting to the emergency services operator.

disclaimer Similar to yes, except that its prompt may not be dismissed without completing the location information. An emergency call can still be completed, following the no definition, but no other calls can be placed until this information is completed.

UseLocationForE911Only Other applications integrated with Lync 2010 may be able to leverage location information. For example, an application for booking conference rooms could prioritize available rooms closest to your current location; the UseLocationForE911Only parameter controls this capability.

PstnUsage The route associated with this PstnUsage must already exist and should point to a SIP trunk dedicated to emergency calls.

EmergencyDialString This value is the number dialed to reach emergency services. It will differ from country to country; for example, the United States uses 911, while most of Europe uses 112.

EmergencyDialMask The EmergencyDialMask allows multiple numbers to be used to dial emergency services. For example, suppose a user has traveled from Europe to the United States and needs to dial the emergency services, without having to figure out what number to dial; they could continue to dial 112, and have this automatically translated to 911.

You can include multiple entries in this string, by separating each one with a semicolon:

```
EmergencyDialMask "112;999"
```

NotificationURI In addition to providing location information to the emergency services, Lync Server 2010 provides the ability to notify SIP-based contacts through an instant message, which also includes the location information.

Multiple SIP URIs can be included by use of a comma-separated list:

```
-NotifcationURI "sip:security@gaots.co.uk,sip:facilities@gaots.co.uk"
```

ConferenceURI As well as providing the instant message notification via the NotificationUri parameter, the ConferenceURI parameter allows a third party to be conferenced into the voice conversation between the initiator of the emergency call and the emergency service provider/operator. This is used in conjunction with the ConferenceMode parameter.

ConferenceMode When the ConferenceUri is specified, the ConferenceMode parameter determines whether the third party can only listen to the conversation, or can be an active participant. The values permitted are:

oneway Listen only

twoway Actively participate

`Description` As with all the cmdlets, the `Description` parameter allows descriptive text to be entered.

The following command modifies the global policy:

```
Set-CsLocationPolicy -Identity Global -EnhancedEmergencyServicesEnabled $True
-LocationRequired "Yes" -PstnUsage "EmergencyUsage" -EmergencyDialString
"911" -ConferenceMode "twoway" -ConferenceUri "sip:+155512347890>@gaots
.co.uk" -EmergencyDialMask "112" NotificationUri "sip:security@gaots.co.uk"
-UseLocationForE911Only $True
```

`PstnUsage` must be defined prior to running the `CsLocationPolicy` command. If `LocationRequired` is set to `Disclaimer`, the disclaimer test must be set using the following command:

```
Set-CsEnhancedEmergencyServiceDisclaimer -Body "Text to display in the disclaimer
window"
```

The default disclaimer is shown in Figure 15.4.

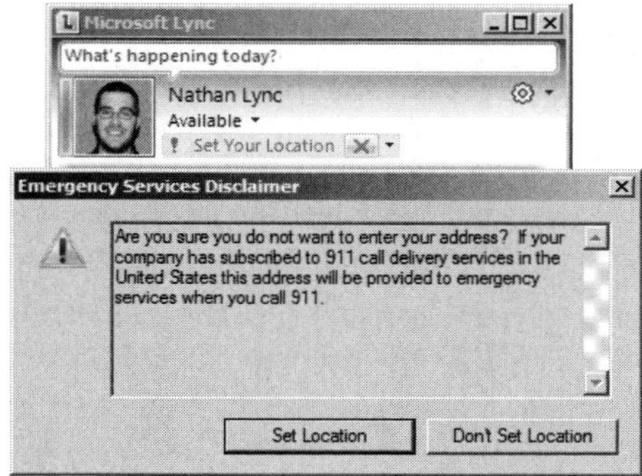

FIGURE 15.4
An emergency services disclaimer

NOTE **When you are configuring `EmergencyDialMask`, make sure you consider Call Park routing—doing so is extremely important. Call Park routing will take precedence, and as such, the numbers used in the `EmergencyDialMask` should be excluded from the Call Park Orbit.**

Creating individual policies allows different policies to be applied directly to specific sites or even individual users. These policies show up with `Tag:` prefixed to their name, and are also known as Tagged policies. This strategy provides more granular control over routing of emergency services, and certainly makes sense in globally distributed companies.

The Location policy information is provided via in-band provisioning and can be assigned by one of three different ways:

- Network Site associated
- User associated
- Global

This allows specific configuration for individual sites, perhaps to enable E911 or not, ensuring that any user, even visitors to a location, will provide the required location information when placing an emergency call.

Defining the SIP Trunk

The SIP trunk will be a dedicated trunk to the emergency services provider, and we need to enable support for the additional payload of the location information. This is provided via a Presence Information Data Format Location Object (PIDFLO) payload type within the SIP message.

To configure this support, use the following command:

```
Set-CsTrunkConfiguration Service:PstnGateway:192.168.3.241 -EnablePIDFLOSupport
$true.
```

By default `EnablePIDFLOSupport` on all trunks is `False`.

Configuring the Voice Route

As introduced in Chapter 13, voice routes define for Lync Server 2010 the path from client to destination for the defined number (in this case the emergency services number).

Once we have the PSTN Usage, Location Policy, and SIP trunk defined, the last remaining step is to define the voice route itself:

```
New-CsVoiceRoute -Name "EmergencyRoute" -NumberPattern "^\+911$" -PstnUsages
"EmergencyUsage" -PstnGatewayList @{add="e911-gateway-1"}
```

This command defines the route to the emergency service provider via the dedicated SIP trunk. In addition to this, you should define at least one secondary route to use if the SIP trunk fails and an emergency services call needs to be placed via a "normal" PSTN connection (which may be via a separate SIP trunk or some other legacy-style connection). The command would look like this:

```
New-CsVoiceRoute -Name "LocalEmergencyRoute" -NumberPattern "^\+911$" -PstnUsages
"EmergencyUsage" -PstnGatewayList @{add="e911-gateway-1"}
```

The parameter `NumberPattern` defined here must use the number defined in the `EmergencyDialString` used in the `CsLocationPolicy` cmdlet. In addition, the + must be included, because Lync Server 2010 automatically adds a + to emergency calls.

Location Information

The previous section covered how to enable Lync Server 2010 to provide the location information; however, it did not show how to configure the location information itself.

Configuring the Location Database

The Lync 2010 client can use a number of methods to establish its location, determined from one of the following:

- Wireless Access Point
- Subnet
- Port
- Switch
- Manual

Upon sign-in, the client requests its location information from the server. In order for the server to determine the location of the client, it must be provided with as much information as possible. The following is an example request where the subnet information is provided:

```
<GetLocationsRequest xmlns:xsi="http://www.w3.org/2001/XMLSchema-instance"
xmlns:xsd="http://www.w3.org/2001/XMLSchema">
<Entity>sip:keith_lync@gaots.co.uk</Entity>
<RSSI>0</RSSI>
<MAC>00-15-5d-19-41-06</MAC>
<SubnetID>192.168.3.0</SubnetID>
<IP>192.168.3.77</IP>
</GetLocationsRequest>
```

The client provides the location identifier to the server, which in turn queries the LIS database to return the specific location information to the client, as can be seen in Figure 15.5.

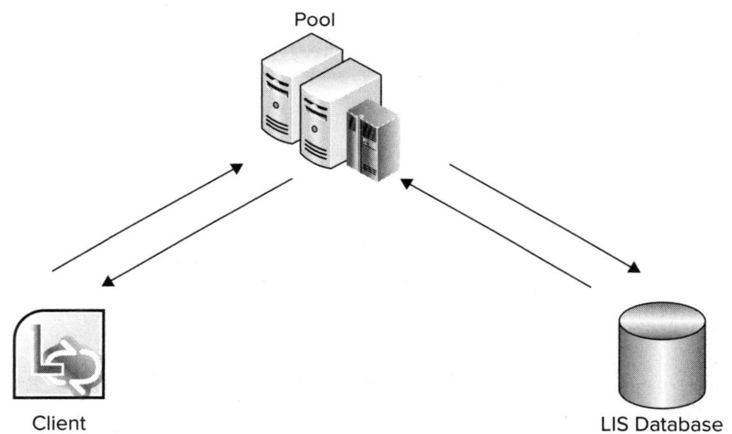

FIGURE 15.5
Client, Pool, and LIS database interaction

The server will return the response containing the address information:

```
<GetLocationsResponse xmlns:xsi="http://www.w3.org/2001/XMLSchema-instance"
xmlns:xsd="http://www.w3.org/2001/XMLSchema">
<ReturnCode>200</ReturnCode>
<presenceList>
<presence entity="sip:keith_lync@gaots.co.uk xmlns="urn:ietf:params:xml:ns:pidf">
<tuple id="_LIS:0">
<status>
<geopriv xmlns="urn:ietf:params:xml:ns:pidf:geopriv10">
<location-info>
<civicAddress xmlns="urn:ietf:params:xml:ns:pidf:geopriv10:civicAddr">
<country>UK</country>
<A1/>
<A3>London</A3>
<PRD />
<RD>Gaots Way</RD>
```

```
<STS />
<POD />
<HNO>1</HNO>
<HNS />
<LOC>London</LOC>
<NAM>Gaots Corporation</NAM>
<PC>NE3 2AB</PC>
</civicAddress>
</location-info>
<usage-rules>
<retransmission-allowed xmlns="urn:ietf:params:xml:ns:pidf:geopriv10:basicPolicy"
>true</retransmission-allowed>
</usage-rules>
</geopriv>
</status>
<timestamp>2011-05-13T11:45:43.9369076Z</timestamp>
</tuple>
</presence>
</presenceList>
</GetLocationsResponse>
```


The client would see the address as:

Gaots Corporation

1 Gaots Way

London, NE3 2AB

UK

To ensure this is a correctly formatted address, the LIS database entries must be verified against a public provider's address records.

Address Verification Outside North America

For the world outside North America, verifying address information via a public provider is not currently possible. In fact, addresses had to be configured manually by users themselves until the release of Cumulative Update 1 (CU1) for Lync Server 2010 in January 2011.

CU1 changed the process so that if the location database returns a single entry for the location information as requested by the client, the client will trust the information.

However, in the event of an emergency call being placed in North America using this location data, the system itself does not trust this information, and the call will be answered by an emergency services provider (rather than operator) to confirm the address information.

Allowing the client to retrieve and use this information means that users can benefit from the location-aware services across the globe.

Once connected and signed in, the Lync 2010 client will display the location field in one of three different modes (depending on the `LocationRequired` parameter as configured in the `CsLocationPolicy` command). The default view can be seen in Figure 15.6.

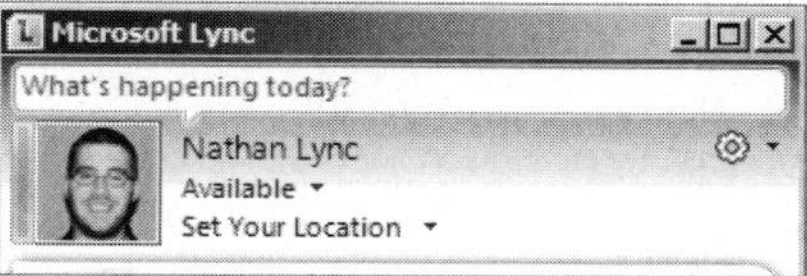

FIGURE 15.6
The Lync 2010 client displays the Location field options

The location information for the E911 location is stored in the LIS database, which is replicated to all servers along with the XDS (Configuration Management server) database in the RTCLOCAL instance. This ensures that there are no delays when location information is requested for emergency calls, and it also ensures that local server (or Survivable Branch Appliance) functionality can still provide this data in the event of a WAN outage to the datacenter.

Unfortunately for the administrator, this location information is separate from the location information provided for the Call Admission Control functionality (see Chapter 14, "Call Admission Control," for more information), and must be defined separately.

Locations can be defined independently using the `Set-CsLisLocation` cmdlets. Table 15.2 shows the parameters accepted by `Set-CsLisLocation` with a description of each.

TABLE 15.2: `Set-CsLisLocation` Parameters

PARAMETER	DESCRIPTION
`Instance`	A location object
`City`	Maximum 64 characters
`CompanyName`	Maximum 60 characters
`Country`	Maximum 2 characters
`HouseNumber`	Maximum 10 characters
`HouseNumberSuffix`	Maximum five characters (additional information, such as "A")
`Location`	Maximum 20 characters (the name for this location, such as "Suite" or "Office")
`PostalCode`	Maximum 10 characters
`PostDirectional`	Maximum two characters (in `1st Avenue NW`, the PostDirectional is NW)
`PreDirectional`	Maximum two characters (in `NW 1st Avenue`, the PreDirectional is NW)
`State`	Maximum two characters
`StreetName`	Maximum 60 characters
`StreetSuffix`	Maximum 10 characters (this is the "Street" or "Avenue" part of the address)

All the parameters are listed as "required"; however, blank entries are acceptable—because the address information is targeted to the United States, not all fields will be required, or indeed make sense, for other countries.

Each of the cmdlets used to input (and manage) the association of the location data has, as would be expected, a different dataset requirement for the determination of the location. Here are the cmdlets and the additional parameters required:

`Set-CsLisPort`

  `ChassisID`

  `PortId`

  `PortIDSubType`

`Set-CsLisSwitch`

  `ChassisID`

`Set-CsLisSubnet`

  `Subnet`

`Set-CsLisWirelessAccessPoint`

  `BSSID`

The associated Get cmdlets will return the information about each type of location provision:

`Get-CsLisPort`

`Get-CsLisSwitch`

`Get-CsLisSubnet`

`Get-CsLisWirelessAccessPoint`

Determining which cmdlet is the correct one to use will be a combination of the specific legal requirements in each location and the level of detail required, as well as the current configuration of the network. For example, to be able to provide the location information down to the level of specific port configuration would require that port configuration to be in place; this can be a significant administrative overhead for the network's team. On the other hand, if the network configuration is a subnet per floor per building, that can be quite easily defined and imported to the database:

```
Set-CsLisSubnet -Subnet 192.168.3.0 -City London -CompanyName "Gaots Corporation"
-Country UK -PostalCode "NE1 2AB" -HouseNumber 1 -StreetName "Gaots Way"
-Location London -Description "London Location"
```

The cmdlet `Get-CsLisCivicAddress` is used to view the address information specifically—that is, it does not return the company or location names, only the following fields:

`HouseNumber`

`HouseNumberSuffix`

`PreDirectional`

`StreetName`

`StreetSuffix`

`PostDirectional`

`City`

`State`

`PostalCode`

`Country`

`MSAGValid`

To return the additional information, the cmdlet `Get-CsLisLocation` is required and includes the additional fields shown:

`Location`

`CompanyName`

Once all the location information is defined don't forget to publish it! Use `Publish-CsLisConfiguration` to achieve this task. (Note that there is no feedback from this cmdlet; even when using the `-Verbose` switch, the detail doesn't report anything useful, only that the cmdlet is being performed!)

If you have forgotten to publish the data, you can simply reopen a Lync PowerShell session and run the `Publish-CsLisConfiguration` cmdlet. It is not specific to location information posted in the PowerShell session; rather, it will publish any waiting location information.

Retrieving the Location Data by a Client

The client can be provided three types of address entry:

Validated These addresses are defined by the administrator and are stored within the LIS database. They have been confirmed against a valid address from the Master Street Address Guide by an E911 service provider. This is achieved using the `Test-CsLisCivicAddress -UpdateValidationStatus $true` command. This in turn will update the `MSAGValid` attribute to `True`, as you can view in the output of the `Get-CsLisCivicAddress` cmdlet.

Suggested These addresses are defined as with the *Validated* addresses; however, the `MSAGValid` attribute is `False`, because they are not confirmed. This is how countries outside North America can leverage location information services.

Custom These addresses are entered manually by the user and up to a maximum of 10 are stored in the `PersonalLISDB.cache` file on the user's computer, in the `%userprofile%\AppDate\Local\Microsoft\Communicator\`*<SIP URI>* folder.

In conjunction with the `LocationRequired` and `EnhancedEmergencyServicesEnabled` parameters, Table 15.3 shows the breakdown of the configuration options and the end result for the user (assuming `EnhancedEmergencyServicesEnabled` is `True`).

TABLE 15.3: User Experience Based on Configuration Options

LOCATION REQUIRED	EXISTING LOCATIONS	USER EXPERIENCE
Yes	Validated location exists.	The location name is displayed automatically and cannot be changed, unless `EnhancedEmergencyServicesEnabled` is False. If this is the case, then a new custom location can be created.
Yes	Single nonvalidated location exists.	The location name is displayed automatically and cannot be changed, unless `EnhancedEmergencyServicesEnabled` is False. If this is the case, then a new custom location can be created.
Yes	Multiple nonvalidated locations exist.	The user is provided with a "Set Your Location" prompt, with a single suggested location entry. Note: Lync Server 2010 cannot provide multiple nonvalidated locations; however, a secondary source may.
Yes	Validated and custom locations exist.	The custom location is given preference.
Yes	Single nonvalidated and custom locations exist.	The suggested location is given preference.
Yes	Multiple nonvalidated and multiple custom locations exist.	The user is provided with a "Set Your Location" prompt in black text and may select other locations in the drop-down menu.
Yes	Custom location only.	The custom location information is automatically displayed.
Yes	None	The user is provided with a "Set Your Location" prompt in red text to highlight the missing data.
No	None	The user is provided with a "Set Your Location" prompt in black text.
Disclaimer	None	The user is provided with a "Set Your Location" prompt in red text to highlight the missing data, along with X. It is not possible to dismiss the prompt, and the emergency services disclaimer is displayed if the user attempts to do so.

Other contact location information can be seen in the contact card shown in Figure 15.7. Keith's Office is defined as in the UK; his Work and Mobile numbers are defined; and his Location is defined as The Office. In addition, time zone information is replicated here, so that you can see the local time for the user, which is extremely useful when you need to communicate globally.

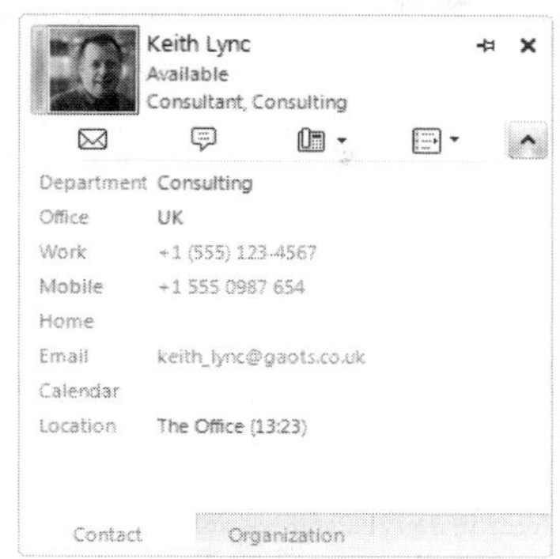

FIGURE 15.7
Contact card location information

Roaming Users

Custom definitions allow users to store manually created entries for which the Lync 2010 client can automatically populate the location information field for frequently visited locations. When returning to a location for a second (or subsequent) time, the Lync 2010 client will not prompt the user; instead, it will read the data already entered into the cache file.

Figure 15.8 shows the blank custom location capture page—the user chooses which information to provide; not all of this information is required, even when the `LocationRequired` parameter is set to `Disclaimer` or `Yes`.

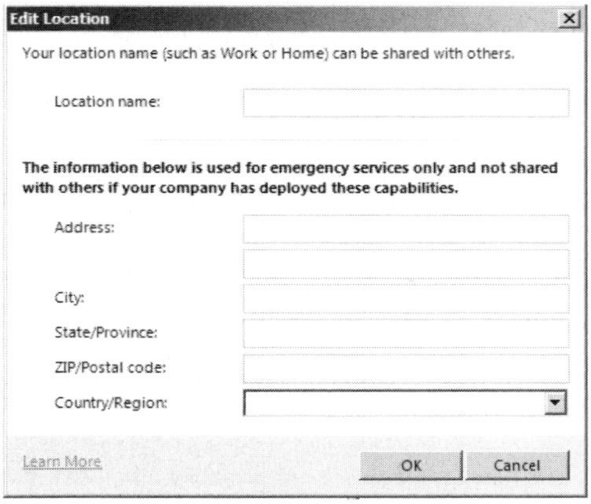

FIGURE 15.8
The custom Edit Location page

Edit Location

Your location name (such as Work or Home) can be shared with others.

Location name:

The information below is used for emergency services only and not shared with others if your company has deployed these capabilities.

Address:

City:

State/Province:

ZIP/Postal code:

Country/Region:

Learn More OK Cancel

But what happens when multiple locations have the same subnet? It's not uncommon for the same private address range (`192.168.0.0–192.168.0.255`) to be used at multiple locations—for example, the local Starbucks and McDonalds could use the same private addresses. When that happens, the custom location cache file actually stores the MAC address of the network gateway as the identifier. This ensures that each location is globally unique even if the IP address range is shared.

Although you can still define an eleventh custom location, it can only be used for the current Lync 2010 session and is not stored in the cache file.

Placing a Call

You've already seen the logs showing the exchange of information to determine the client location; Figure 15.9 shows the client feedback when placing a call.

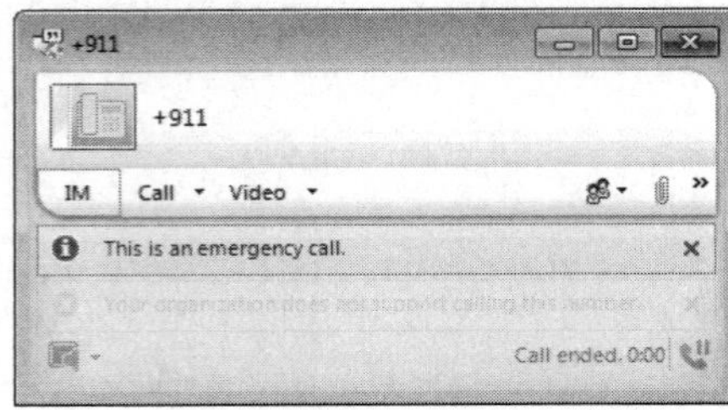

FIGURE 15.9
A client placing an emergency call

The logs capture the PIDFLO data within the SIP INVITE traffic; here is the content of this log entry:

```
Content-Type: application/pidf+xml
Content-Transfer-Encoding: 7bit
Content-ID: <sip:keith_lync@gaots.co.uk>
Content-Description: render; handling=optional
<?xml version="1.0" encoding="uft-8"?>
<presence entity="sip:keith_lync@gaots.co.uk"
 xmlns="urn:ietf:params:xml:ns:pidf">
<tuple id="0"><status><geopriv
 xmlns="urn:ietf:params:xml:ns:pidf:geopriv10">
<location-info><civisAddress
 xmlns="urn:ietf:params:xml:ns:pidf:geopriv10:civicAddr">
<RD>1 Gaots Way</RD><A3>London</A3>
<PC>NE1 2AB></PC><country>GB</country
></civicAddress></location-info>
<usage-rules><retransmission-allowed></usage-rules>
<method>Manual</method></geopriv>
<msftE911PidfExtn
  xmlsn="urn:schema:rtc.LIS.msftE911PidfExtn.2008">
<NotificationUri>sip:security@gaots.co.uk</Notification>
<ConferenceUri>sip:+112347890@gaots.co.uk</ConferenceUri>
<ConferenceMode>two way</ConferenceMode>
<LocationPolicyTagID
 xmlns="urn:schema:Rtc.Lis.LocationPolicy TagID.2008">
<subnet-tagid:1></LocationPolicyTagID>
</msftE911PidfExtn></status></tuple></presence>
```

The Bottom Line

Describe the E911 requirements for North America. Enhanced emergency services dialing provides location information to emergency services, enabling them to better respond in the event of an emergency.

Master It Is the provision of location information with emergency dialing compulsory?

Configure Lync Server 2010 to meet E911 requirements. As a viable PBX, Lync Server 2010 is required to meet the E911 requirements to provide location information data, and as such must have validated address information provided with each emergency call.

Master It Through what configuration items can location information data be delivered to the Lync 2010 client?

Understand how Location Information Services can be used by users outside North America. Although the actual requirements are only currently defined in locations in North America, beta program feedback from customers indicated that automatic location information services are extremely useful and desired worldwide.

Master It What specifically is required to enable location information services in North America, and what different requirements are in place for the rest of the world?

Chapter 16

Extended Voice Functionality

As organizations start to migrate their enterprise telephony to Microsoft Lync, they often require more functionality than is available within the core Enterprise Voice (EV) functionality. In order to fulfill the most common of these requirements, Microsoft has provided the following extended voice functions: dial-in conferencing, Response Groups, Call Park, and unassigned numbers.

For organizations that require additional functionality, a number of Independent Software Vendors (ISVs) provide applications designed for Microsoft Lync; additional details of these and other third-party applications can be found in Chapter 18, "Third-Party Integration."

In this chapter, you will learn to:

- ◆ Understand the Extended Voice Functionality
- ◆ Design and Implement Solutions Using Extended Voice Functionality

Dial-In Conferencing

For years PBXs have had the ability to create conferences. In the early days, conferences were usually limited to three people and required using a dedicated key on the phone. Most people found this type of conference hard to set up and would usually end up cutting off people when they were setting up the conference.

To provide a better solution, tools known as *conference bridges* were created. They allow participants to access their conference by calling an access number and then entering a conference ID and sometimes a passcode. These conference solutions usually come in two forms: *ad-hoc* and *scheduled*.

Ad-hoc conference bridges are often referred to as "meet-me" conference bridges, because each user has an individual conference ID and can use it when desired. Because these conferences are ad-hoc, even though users can use them when needed, there may be overall limits for the conferencing system in the number of people who can attend conference calls at any one time; these limitations can be in the form of license, hardware, or the number of available PSTN lines.

Scheduled conferences usually have to be booked, and a conference ID is assigned at the time of booking. One advantage of a scheduled conference is that resources are usually assigned to the conference, ensuring that if, for example, a conference is configured for four people from 15:00 to 17:00, then those resources will be available.

In addition to the type of conferencing bridge used, organizations have a choice of using either an on-premises system, usually integrated with their PBX, or a hosted solution. The recent trend has been for organizations to use hosted meet-me solutions. The move to hosted solutions has tended to be due to the cost of implementing on-premises solutions with organizations preferring monthly costs rather than upfront purchases.

Now that you have looked at what dial-in conferencing is, you can see how Lync handles it.

Dial-in Conferencing in Lync

In OCS 2007 R2, dial-in conferencing was a distinct feature with its own functionality, and when collaboration was required, the LiveMeeting client needed to be used. In Lync Server 2010, conferencing and collaboration have become a single feature called Online Meeting. The Online Meeting functionality removes the distinction between conferencing and collaboration, allowing all modalities to be used within a conference with a variety of access methods.

This section focuses specifically on the dial-in conferencing aspects that Online Meeting has to offer. Its approach falls within the meet-me category of conference bridges, with each allowed user (as defined by your policies) provided with their own conference ID. Dial-in conferencing provides the following functionality:

- PSTN access
- Roster of attendees
- Attendee management via roster
- Ability to secure conferences with a PIN
- Ability for Conference server to call attendees
- Meeting lobby
- DTMF codes for management
- Name recording for anonymous users
- On-Demand Recording (client side)

The last four items are new in Lync Server, and they address the limitations that prevented some organizations from migrating their dial-in conferencing facilities to OCS 2007 R2. In addition to the specific dial-in conferencing capabilities just listed, the following Online Meeting functions are also relevant:

- Scheduling via Microsoft Outlook 2010 is easy.
- Scheduling meetings via the Lync Web Scheduler allows non-Outlook users to set up meetings. You can download it at: `www.microsoft.com/download/en/details.aspx?id=3398` and install it on the Lync servers.
- Functionality can be restricted to a group of users.
- Clients can participate in meetings through a browser.

Real World Scenario

Can Dial-in Conferencing Pay for My Lync Deployment?

A number of organizations have been able to cover the costs of their entire Lync deployment purely on the basis of moving their conferencing away from a hosted solution to Microsoft Lync.

Hosted conferencing solutions may appear to be cheap initially because there are no upfront capital expenditures; however, they can often become expensive due to the costs charged by the provider. These companies often provide the accounts for free but charge per-minute, per-participant for each conference call. There can also be additional charges for recording or for toll-free numbers. Let's take a look at the cost of a conference, based on the provider charging five cents per user per minute.

A conference call with four participants for 30 minutes would cost $6.00 ($0.05 × 4 × 30). At these rates, an organization that has 10 people who perform 10 conferences a week for 52 weeks a year results in a cost of $31,200.00.

Organizations often overlook these itemized costs when they are budgeting and performing cost analysis for Lync deployments. This is probably because IT departments often do not see these costs because they are assigned to individual departments, such as Sales. Although dial-in conferencing may not pay for the entire Lync deployment, it can certainly help defray the costs.

You'll see many of these functions later in this section as you explore configuration, implementation, and client-side functionality, but for now let's look at the architectural and back-end elements.

Architecturally, there are two main items to take into consideration when planning and setting up dial-in conferencing: the Audio\Video Conferencing Service and Server and the configuration of Enterprise Voice, which is discussed in Chapter 13, "Getting Started with Voice." Within a Standard Edition deployment and the majority of Enterprise Edition deployments, this service is deployed on the same server. For organizations that are deploying Enterprise Edition and require additional capacity for conferencing, dedicated servers can be deployed—either a single, dedicated server, or a pool of servers. However, note that the Audio\Video Conferencing server pool works differently than a Lync Server pool, in that it is used only for conferencing and does not host any of the user services, and a single AV pool can be shared across multiple Lync pools. The only limitation is that there can be one only AV pool per site.

Therefore, if you take the sample deployment's three sites, each can have its own AV pool if needed. Alternatively, there can be a mix-and-match approach, with some sites having their own AV pool and others using the AV resources held on the Lync pools. This technique is used in organizations where one region doesn't use conferencing as much as others or it has fewer users, for example.

Although the AV Conferencing servers and services are the only dedicated elements, the number of components depends on the front-end servers:

Web Components These are used for the Dial-In Conferencing web page, allowing participants to look up conference access numbers and for users to set their PIN.

Conferencing Attendant Application This accepts calls from the PSTN, prompts for conference details, and then routes the call to the correct conference.

Conferencing Announcement Application This is used once the participant has joined the conference; it plays announcement to callers, and monitors and accepts DTMF tones for conference controls.

Web components also provide a Reach client option, which allows access to Online Meetings in the context of dial-in conferencing; they allow participants to specify a number for the conference bridge to call them, and they can also view the meeting in a browser. The ability for the conference bridge to call a Reach client participant can be restricted with a policy.

Although having the Lync Edge components deployed is not a requirement for dial-in conferencing, it does add another access method to conferences, and it allows federated users to access the conference the same way a user belonging to the organization would. This allows them to view the roster for the conference in the same way a user of the organization would, and to bypass any costs associated with dialing access numbers.

Before you learn at how to configure dial-in conferencing, it is worth briefly looking at the Meeting Lobby. This new Lync Server 2010 feature creates a "lobby" where users can be "parked" when they enter a meeting; the meeting presenter can then choose whether to allow them into the meeting. This provides a level of access control for the meeting. When creating the meeting, users can configure whether the lobby is to be used or not.

Configuring Dial-In Conferencing Features

Now that you know what dial-in conferencing in Lync can do, it is time to look at how it is configured. Configuration—most of it—can be performed either through the Control Panel or through PowerShell. That is, all of the required configuration to get conferencing up and running can be done through both interfaces, but PowerShell needs to be used to configure some of the more complex and custom features.

In order for dial-in conferencing to work, you need to configure the following components:

- Enterprise Voice
- Web components
- Conferencing policies
- Meeting configuration
- Access numbers
- PIN policies

Of these, all but the first two can be configured using the Control Panel as well as the related PowerShell cmdlets. For example, Figure 16.1 shows the Control Panel tab for configuring access numbers. In addition, the following optional components can be configured using PowerShell:

- Edge servers
- DTMF mappings
- Join and Leave announcements
- Conference directories

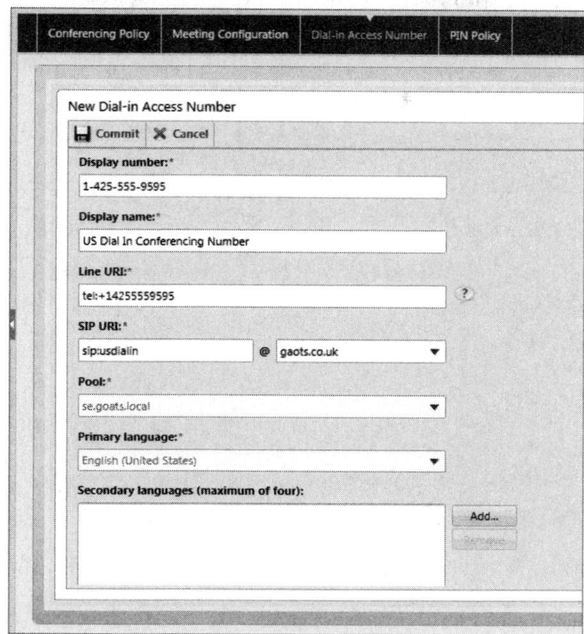

Figure 16.1 Configuring access numbers via the Control Panel

Chapter 6, "Installation," covers configuring web components and publishing them to the Internet, as well as deploying Edge servers. In addition, setting up Enterprise Voice is covered in Chapter 13, "Getting Started with Voice."

Conferencing Policies

Conferencing policies can be configured on a global, site, or user basis, depending on whether or not you require different users to have different settings. The global policy is created by default but can be modified as required.

The conferencing policy is used to control all aspects of conferencing, not just dial-in conferencing, but in this section we'll cover only the options that are either required or relevant to dial-in conferencing. In the following and similar lists throughout the chapter, only the PowerShell parameters will be listed. Options equivalent to most of the cmdlets and parameters are available through the Control Panel.

When reviewing the PowerShell cmdlets, we'll focus on the creation cmdlets. They use the verb `New`, and for each of these cmdlets there are cmdlets for changing settings (`Set`), reviewing settings (`Get`), and for deleting them (`Remove`), and although they are not explicitly discussed except as needed, they are available. `Set` and `New` cmdlets use the same parameters; the `Get` and `Remove` parameters are limited to the `Identity`.

As mentioned previously, conferencing policies can be managed either through the Control Panel (Conferencing ➢ Conferencing Policy) or through PowerShell. To create a new policy through PowerShell, the `New-CsConferencingPolicy cmdlet` is used in conjunction with the parameters outlined here:

- `Identity:` This is the policy name, which is prefixed with `site:` if the policy is a site policy rather than a user policy.

- `AllowAnonymousParticipantsInMeetings`: This allows anonymous participants.
- `AllowAnonymousUsersToDialOut`: This allows anonymous users to dial out. It is the Call Me functionality covered earlier in the section.
- `AllowConferenceRecording`: This allows the call to be recorded.
- `AllowExternalUserControl`: This allows external and anonymous users to record.
- `AllowIPAudio`: This allows audio and covers PSTN Audio as well.
- `EnableDialInConferencing`: This allows participants to call into a conference using a PSTN access number.
- `MaxMeetingSize`: This sets the maximum meeting size.

Once the policy has been created, it needs to be assigned to users. Global and site policies are assigned automatically as described in Chapter 10, "User Administration"; therefore, only user policies need to be assigned. You can do this through the Control Panel or through PowerShell using the `Grant-CsConferencingPolicy` cmdlet. For example:

```
Grant-CsConferencingPolicy -Identity "gaots\adam" -PolicyName "Std Dial In Policy"
```

This grants the `Std Dial In Policy` to the domain account with the username `adam`.

Meeting Policies

Meeting policies allow you to specify the types of meetings that can be created, and they can be created at a global, site, or pool level. They can be managed through the Control Panel (Conferencing ➢ Meeting Configuration) or through PowerShell. To create a new policy, use the `New-CsMeetingConfiguration` cmdlet.

The parameters for configuring meeting policies are as follows:

- `Identity:` Policy name
  - For site policy this needs to be prefixed with `site:`
  - For a pool policy this is be the pool FQDN prefixed with `service:UserServer:`
- `AdmitAnonymousUsersByDefault`: This parameter permits anonymous users in the meeting by default.
- `AssignedConferenceTypeByDefault`: This parameter sets the conference default type. Set it to True for meetings to be public by default. Set it to False for meetings to be private by default.
- `DesignateAsPresenter`: This parameter designates which users are automatically presenters. It can set to None, Company, or Everyone.
- `EnableAssignedConferenceType`: This parameter sets the conference type. If set to True, users can create Public or Private conferences, and setting it to False means only private meetings can be created. The only difference between them is that a private conference will use a different conference ID and access URL for each meeting.
- `PstnCallersBypassLobby`: This bypasses the lobby for PSTN users.

PINs

In order to authenticate when calling into a meeting via the PSTN, users need to set a PIN, which is used in conjunction with their phone numbers. This PIN is also used to allow users to log in to Lync IP phones. The policy for managing PIN can be configured on a global, site, or user basis.

If you are managing PIN policies using the Control Panel, they can be accessed under Conferencing ➢ PIN Policy; alternatively they can be managed through PowerShell using the `New-CsPinPolicy` cmdlet. The following options are used:

- Identity.
- Allow Common PIN Patterns (`AllowCommonPatterns`). Common patterns are defined as:
  - Containing four or more consecutive digits—for example, 781234.
  - Repeating digits—for example, 114488.
  - Matching the user's phone number or extension.
- Description.
- Maximum Logon Attempts (`MaximumLogonAttempts`).
- Minimum Password Length (`MinPasswordLength`). This is the minimum PIN length; it can be set to a minimum of 4 and a maximum of 24 digits.
- PIN History (`PINHistoryCount`). This can be set to 0 for no history and a maximum of 20.
- Days before the PIN must be changed (`PINLifetime`).

PIN lockouts work in two ways, based on the concept of *Local Logon Failures* and *Global Logon Failures*. The Local Logon Failures value is the number of failed attempts allowed within 30 minutes. If this is exceeded, the PIN is locked for 1 hour, at which time the Local Logon Failure count is reset. Global Logon Failures is the maximum number of PIN attempts allowed before the PIN is locked out and has to be unlocked by an administrator. This value is not reset when a user successfully logs in, and failed login attempts continue to be added to the Global Logon Failure counter. The counter resets only when an administrator unlocks a user's PIN.

The Local Logon Failure and Global Logon Failure values are predefined. Setting the Maximum Logon Attempts in the PIN policy will only override the Local Logon Failure value. The global lockout value cannot be modified. As shown in Table 16.1, both limits depend on the number of digits in the PIN, rather than the minimum password length specified in the policy.

TABLE 16.1: PIN Attempts

PIN LENGTH	LOCAL LOGON FAILURE LIMIT (UNLESS OVERRIDDEN)	GLOBAL LOGON FAILURE LIMIT
4	10	100
5	25	1,000
6 or more	25	5,000

The PIN policy is granted to users using the `Grant-CsPinPolicy` cmdlet.

Conference Access Numbers

Some organizations have only one access number; others have numbers covering many countries. Before you can create access numbers, you'll need to take a quick look at Enterprise Voice dial plans because the access numbers you'll need depend on them.

Dial plans are used to provide a link between users and access numbers. When a user schedules a conference, the default numbers shown in the meeting request are the ones associated with the dial plan with which the user is associated. They are also used to translate extensions to full E.164 number. When users authenticate via DTMF, this allows them to enter their extension number rather than their full DID.

In order to use a given dial plan, its dial-in conferencing region needs to be defined. You can do this when you create the dial plan or edit it; details on how to perform these actions are covered in Chapter 13. You can enter any text you wish in the dial plan region field but it should be something that external participants can understand, such as a city or country. This will be shown on the dial-in web page so that participants can look for a number other than the one specified on the invitation to the conference. It is also used in Outlook, allowing the user to select a different region and thus change the access numbers shown in their invitation.

Once the dial plans are finished, you can create the access numbers, either through the Control Panel (Conferencing ➤ Dial-In Access Number) or through PowerShell (`New-CsDialInConferencingAccessNumber`) using the following parameters:

- `PrimaryUri`: This is the contact URI, prefixed with `sip:`.
- `DisplayName`: This is the display name of the contact and how it should appear in Lync.
- `DisplayNumber`: This is how the number should be displayed in meeting requests and the dial-in web page.
- `LineURI`: This is the phone number prefixed with `tel:`.
- `Regions`: This is a comma-separated list of the regions the number is assigned to, such as `US`, and `Canada`.
- `Pool`: This is the pool with which the access number is associated.
- `PrimaryLanguage`: This is the primary language used.
- `SecondaryLanguages`: This is a comma-separated list of up to four secondary languages, such as `en-US` and `fr-CA`.

Each access number can be configured with a primary language and up to four secondary ones. This option is often used when access numbers are defined for locations multiple languages commonly spoken—for example, Montreal, Canada, where French is usually the primary language, followed by English.

A list of supported languages can be found by running this command:

```
Get-CsDialInConferencingLanguageList | Select-Object -ExpandProperty Languages
```

This command retrieves a list of the supported languages and restricts it to displaying only the language codes.

Once the access number has been created, users will be able to call it to access the conferences; they can also been seen on the Dial-In Conferencing web page, which is shown in Figure 16.2.

FIGURE 16.2
Dial-In Conferencing web page

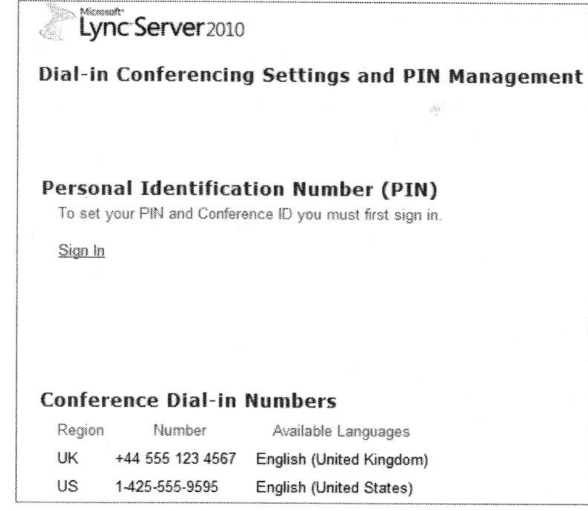

Before moving on, it is worth looking at the order in which the numbers are presented in the meeting requests and Dial-In Conferencing web page. By default, the order is alphabetical by region. If there are multiple numbers within the region, they are listed by comparing the first digit in each number. The lowest number is listed first, followed by the second lowest to the highest. If the first digit is the same, then the second number is compared. This process is continued as long as necessary to order the numbers. You may decide to reorder the numbers for a region for a number of reasons. For example, you may want a number with a higher capacity at the start of the list or a toll-free number at the end of the list. (Reordering regions isn't possible.) A specific order can be set using the `Set-CsDialInConferencingAccessNumber` cmdlet and its `Priority` and `ReorderedRegion` parameters, as in this example.

```
Set-CsDialInConferencingAccessNumber -Identity "sip:USAccessNumberToll@gaots
.co.uk" -Priority 0 -ReorderedRegion "US"
```

This will move the Toll Chargeable number to the top of the list for the U.S. region numbers.

GLOBAL ACCESS NUMBERS

Organizations often use hosted conferencing providers so that they can have global access numbers, which are usually required for organizations with a global presence. Such organizations do not need to be multinationals; many small businesses have customers in other countries.

Not having these numbers could be a potential roadblock to Lync migration conferencing for businesses that require them. Therefore, you may need to consider how to provide these numbers. Traditional PSTN providers can often provide global numbers, but setting them up is usually expensive and so is operating them.

One potential way around this is to work with a SIP trunk provider. These providers are often more competitive in their pricing for global access numbers and are often an excellent way to provide the number(s) required. While an organization may not want to move all of its PSTN access to the Cloud, this approach is a good option for conferencing. And depending on how busy the conferencing system will be, it may also mean that you won't need additional PSTN bearers from the PSTN provider.

A list of certified SIP trunking providers for Lync can be found here: `http://technet.microsoft.com/en-us/lync/gg131938#tab=4`

Additional Conferencing Configuration Options

The next three configuration items, entry and exit announcements, DTMF mappings for PSTN users, and conference directories, are not exposed through the Control Panel; they can be configured only through PowerShell.

Entry and Exit Announcements

Entry and exit announcements will be played only to people who access the bridge using the PSTN. It is assumed that announcements are not required for users who have access to the conference roster through one of the Lync clients. These settings are configured on either a global or site level. These are created using the `New-CsDialInConferencingConfiguration` cmdlet, and the following options are available:

- `Identity`, either `Global` for the global policy (only used when viewing or modifying the settings) or if creating a site policy, the site name prefixed with `site`:.
- `EnableNameRecording` specifies whether users are able to record their names when they access a conference. If it is disabled, `EntryExitAnnouncementsType` needs to be set to `ToneOnly`.
- `EntryExitAnnouncementsEnabledByDefault`
- `EntryExitAnnouncementsType` can be set to either `UseNames` or `ToneOnly`, depending on the announcement type needed.

DTMF Mappings

The next items to look at are the DTMF mappings for PSTN users that can be used during a conference call. Most of the options are limited to presenters, but two of the commands, Mute\Unmute and Private Rollcall, can be used by any participant.

These settings are configured on either a global or site level. The following options are available to create the `New-CsDialInConferencingDtmfConfiguration` cmdlet:

- Identity, either `Global` for the global policy (only used when viewing or modifying the settings) or if creating a site policy, the site name prefixed with `site`:.
- `AdmitAll`: Admit all participants who are in the lobby
- `AudienceMuteCommand`
- `CommandCharacter`: prefix for the commands, can be an * or #
- `EnableDisableAnnouncementsCommand`: Play Entry\Exit announcements
- `HelpCommand`
- `LockUnlockConferenceCommand`
- `MuteUnmuteCommand`
- `PrivateRollCallCommand`: Play rollcall to me

Digits assigned to these commands need to be unique and between 1 and 9, except for the command prefix. If you need to disable any of these settings, you can do so by setting them to `$null`.

Conference Directories

The final item to look at is the conference directory; because Lync is based on SIP URIs, you need a way to map the numeric conference IDs that are required to access a conference to the relevant SIP URI. This is where the conference directories come into play.

By default, there is a single conference directory. This lone directory is sufficient for some organizations, but for larger organizations or for those who use different conference IDs for each conference, the conference ID number can grow rather long.

In order to keep the ID at a length that people will accept—usually no more than six to seven digits—multiple conference directories can be created. A new conference directory should be created for every 999 Lync users.

To create a conference directory (`New-CsConferenceDirectory`), the following parameters must be specified:

- `Identity`: This is a unique numeric number between 1 and 999.
- `HomePool`: This is the Lync pool that hosts the Conference Directory.

Implementing Dial-in Conferencing

Now that you've looked at the capabilities of dial-in conferencing, you need to see how to implement it. In order to do this, let's work through the following scenario:

Your organization is migrating away from its current hosting provider to Lync dial-in conferencing. Dial-in numbers are required in the following countries:

- *The United States*
- *The United Kingdom*

*All users should be able to use the conference bridge. In addition, to match the current conference bridge, the Lock and Unlock Conference DTMF option needs to use *2.*

After studying the requirements statement, you see that you need to complete the following steps:

1. Create two regions, each with its own access number.
2. Modify the DTMF mappings for Lock and Unlock.

In addition to the explicit requirements just detailed, you will need to configure some other options in order for dial-in conferencing to operate. You are going to set each of them to have a global scope. Some of the settings are configured by default, but you will set them in the PowerShell commands to make sure they are configured as required.

The first thing you need to configure is the global conferencing policy:

```
Set-CsConferencingPolicy -Identity Global -AllowAnonymousUsersToDialOut $true
-AllowAnonymousParticipantsInMeetings $true -AllowConferenceRecording $true
-AllowIPAudio $true -EnableDialInConferencing $true
```

This code modifies the global conferencing policy, allowing the required settings for all users who are not affected by a site policy or have a user policy assigned.

The next item to configure is the global meeting policy:

```
Set-CsMeetingConfiguration -Identity Global -AdmitAnonymousUsersByDefault
$true -AssignedConferenceTypeByDefault $true -DesignateAsPresenter Company
-EnableAssignedConferenceType $true -PstnCallersBypassLobby $true
```

This code modifies the global meeting policy, allowing the required settings for all users who are not affected by a site policy or who have a user policy assigned.

The final policy to configure is the global PIN policy:

```
Set-CsPinPolicy -Identity Global -AllowCommonPatterns $True -MinPasswordLength 4
```

This modifies the global PIN policy, allowing common PIN patterns and shorter PIN lengths for all users who are not affected by a site policy or who have an assigned user policy.

Now you can configure the access numbers; they will be assigned to two existing dial plans:

```
New-CsDialInConferencingAccessNumber -PrimaryUri "sip:USDialIn@gaots.co.uk"
-DisplayNumber "1-425-555-9595" -DisplayName "US Dial In Number" -LineUri
"tel:+14255559595" -Pool "se01.gaots.local" -PrimaryLanguage "en-US" -Regions "US"

New-CsDialInConferencingAccessNumber -PrimaryUri "sip:UKDialIn@gaots.co.uk"
-DisplayNumber "+44 (0) 2079460836" -DisplayName "UK Dial In Number" -LineUri
"tel:+442079460836" -Pool "se01.gaots.local" -PrimaryLanguage "en-GB" -Regions
"UK"
```

These two commands create the two dial-in conferencing numbers, the first for the United States with U.S. English and the second for the United Kingdom with U.K. English. When these two commands are run, the output for the U.S. access number will be similar to the following:

```
Identity           : CN={c2052752-76c1-4f7a-81af-2ddddc90c3b5},CN=Application Con
tacts,CN=RTCService,CN=Services,CN=Configuration,DC=gaots,DC=local
PrimaryUri         : sip:USDialIn@gaots.co.uk
DisplayName        : US Dial In Number
DisplayNumber      : 1-425-555-9595
LineUri            : tel:+14255559595
PrimaryLanguage    : en-US
SecondaryLanguages : {}
Pool               : se01.gaots.local
Regions            : {US}
```

The DTMF mappings are the last things to configure; to configure them, you will need to modify the existing global policy:

```
Set-CsDialInConferencingDtmfConfiguration -Identity Global
-LockUnlockConferenceCommand 2
```

This modifies the global DTMF mapping to use 2 as the unlock code for the conference; this will affect all conferences except where the conference is hosted in a site that has a site policy assigned.

This completes the dial-in conferencing configuration. To check the configuration, run the corresponding `Get` commands to view the settings just configured.

Using Dial-In Conferencing

Now that you have implemented dial-in conferencing, you need to take a look at how users will use it. Although a conference can be accessed from virtually anywhere, here you should concentrate on how an information worker will use dial-in conferencing using Outlook and their Lync client.

Although scheduling a conference call is not a requirement for a user to use the conference bridge, Microsoft has provided an easy way to populate a meeting request in Outlook with the required information, as shown in Figure 16.3. To access this screen, go to the Calendar view and select Online Meeting or create a new Online Meeting item. You can customize these settings for a conference; by selecting Meeting Options when you create or view the meeting, you can access the following settings:

- Who can access the meeting
- Who will be a presenter
- If a different conference ID and URL should be used

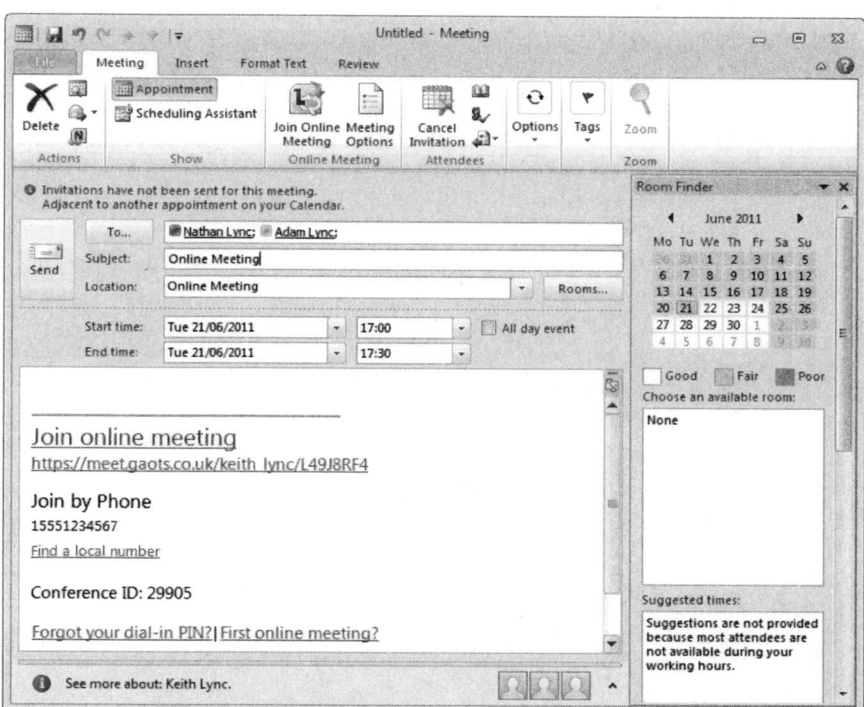

FIGURE 16.3 Scheduling a conference

Once a conference has been organized, the attendees need to be able to join it. There are a few ways to do this: they could call the access number, click on the Join link in the meeting request, or access it from the reminder for the meeting (as shown in Figure 16.4).

The last two options launch the simple join process, in which the user's default web browser starts quickly, followed by the Lync client joining the conference. If the Lync client was not installed, the Attendee client will start if it is installed; if not, by default, the Reach client will start. An administrator can configure Lync to provide a download for the Attendee client; if this has been performed, the user will be prompted to either install the client or run the Reach client. For details about how an administrator can enable this, see Chapter 4, "Client Access."

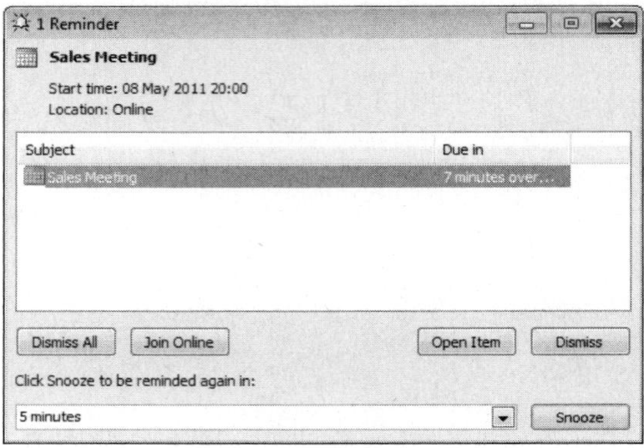

FIGURE 16.4
Joining a meeting from a reminder

Once you've joined the conference, you can see the participants, as illustrated in Figure 16.5. On this screen, you can also control the Audio settings; for example, you can escalate the conference to a video conference if video is enabled. Endpoints that do not support video will continue to access the conference using audio only.

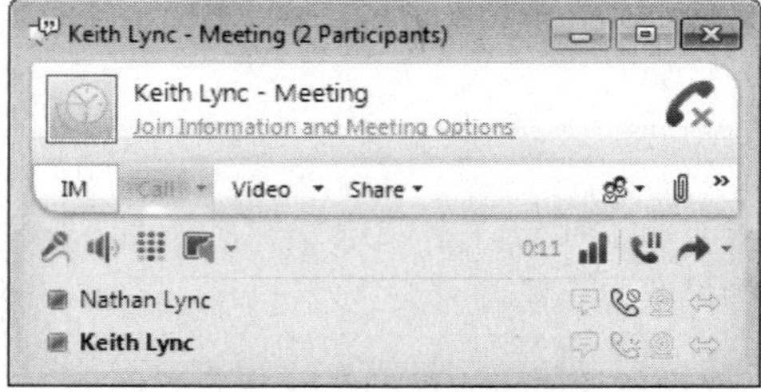

FIGURE 16.5
A conference roster

From the roster, you can also control a participant's conference options. As shown in Figure 16.6, you do this by right-clicking the participant and choosing the required option from the context menu.

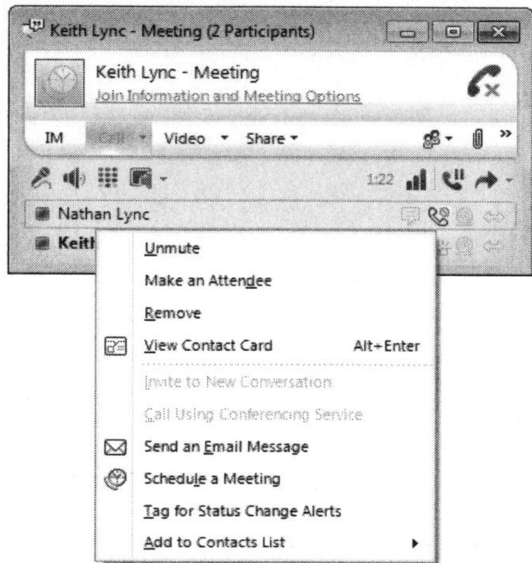

FIGURE 16.6
The Conference context menu

The final option to look at in the Lync client is inviting people to an active conference. You can do this in the following ways: by dragging and dropping someone from the buddy list into the conference, by entering their name (retrieved via the address list) or phone number (as shown in Figure 16.7), or by sending them an email with the conference details. One thing to note is that for the first two of these options, the users will be added straight to the conference. If the invited person is using Lync, they will see that they are joining a conference; however, if they are joining from a cell phone, for example, it may come as a shock!

FIGURE 16.7
Adding users to a conference

The final element is the Dial-In Conferencing web page, as shown in Figure 16.8. This interface is what users will use to configure their PIN to authenticate a conference with an access number. Additionally, this page lets participants look up more access numbers for Online Meetings.

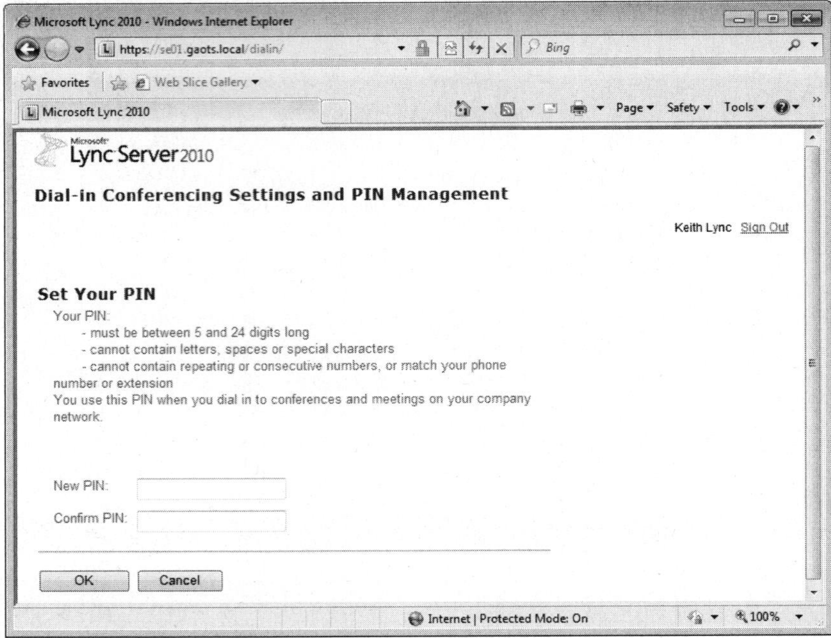

FIGURE 16.8 Setting a PIN on the Dial-In Conferencing web page

Not only can you use the Lync client, but you can manage a meeting from the Aries IP phones. On these devices, you can add people to a conference, view the attendee list, remove people, and allow access to people waiting in the lobby. If Extended Features are enabled, you will also be able to join a conference from the Calendar view.

Response Groups

Hunt groups and basic ACD (Automatic Call Distribution) are provided by most PBXs. They allow calls to be distributed between multiple users, but their functionality varies between PBXs, and the majority provide a minimum level of functionality.

Hunt groups provide the most basic form of call distribution. For each hunt group, a list of numbers to which to route calls is defined. The PBX will route each incoming call according to the distribution method defined, which is usually one of the following:

- **Serial:** Always starts at the first entry. If there is no answer or the line is busy, it tries the second number, and continues until someone answers. When the list is exhausted, it goes back to the beginning, effectively starting over.
- **Parallel:** Rings all of the numbers at the same time.
- **Round Robin:** For the first call, it starts at the first entry. If there is no answer or the line is busy, it tries the second number. If the second answers, then the next call starts at the third number. When the list is exhausted, it goes back to the beginning, effectively starting over.
- **Most Idle:** It starts at the number that has been idle the longest, and if there is no answer, it tries the next longest idle, and so on through the list.

Most PBXs allow the administrator to define the ring time on each number, along with a maximum wait time. Once the maximum wait time has been reached, calls will either be terminated or more commonly routed to a different number; this could be an overflow number or a voice mailbox.

Automatic Call Distribution (ACD) operates in a similar way to hunt groups in that calls are distributed to a range of numbers; the difference is that there tends to be more intelligence involved. With ACD, callers may be provided a DTMF-based Interactive Voice Response (IVR), allowing them to choose based on a question. The call is then usually routed to a defined hunt group.

For example, the question could be "To which department would you like to speak?" This would be followed by a list of options, such as "Press 1 for Sales, press 2 for Support, press 3 for Customer Service." The customer would then select 1, 2, or 3 and then be routed to the correct set of numbers. Once they make a selection, depending on the PBX, they may hear ringing or music on hold (MOH) until their call is answered. The announcement will usually have to be provided in a certain format, which tends to be a very basic file type. In addition, there is usually a limit to the number of ACDs that can be defined. If the organization requires more complex call routing abilities, then a contact center is usually required. In Lync, hunt groups and ACD features are incorporated into the Response Group application.

Response Groups in Lync

In order to provide hunt group and basic ACD features for organizations, Microsoft created the Response Group application and its set of cmdlets. Response Groups match the functionality found in most PBXs and exceed it to a point that they can equal some basic call center offerings, although there are limitations that prevent this feature from being classed as a call center. Response Groups exceed the following capabilities in the majority of PBXs:

- Text to speech for announcements
- Voice along with DTMF IVR options
- Ability to specify working hours
- Ability to build custom workflows

Response Groups are made up of three main components:

- **Agent Groups:** These are used to define whether the agents will need to sign in or not, the number of seconds that a call will wait for an agent to answer, the routing method, and which users are members of the group.
- **Queues:** These are used to define which agent group will handle the call, along with the Timeout and Overflow settings.
- **Workflows:** These are the initial entry points into the system. They provide the IVR functionality, which queues the call should be routed to, and other options such as working hours. In Lync as in OCS 2007 R2, there are predefined workflows. These are:
    - Hunt groups
    - Interactive, up to two levels, up to four questions per level IVR

Configuration Order

When configuring Response Groups, whether you are using the Control Panel and Response Group Web Interface or the PowerShell cmdlets, you need to create the items in a certain order. You need to define the agent groups first, followed by queues, and then the workflows. If you do not create them in the correct order, you may end up not being able to complete the configuration of an item. This results in you needing to create the prerequisite item and then starting again to configure the item.

If you are using PowerShell, note that for queues and workflows, PowerShell commands usually need to be run before the main queue and workflow commands are run, as you'll see in the following sections. Creating queues and custom workflows through PowerShell can be a complex task, and it is a task that should be carefully planned and thoroughly tested to ensure that nothing is missed. After the following summary of the configuration tools and options, we'll go through a complete implementation of a Response Group, demonstrating the most important cmdlets and parameters.

Response Group Configuration Options

Only a couple of configuration options are available at the Response Group level, and they are set on a per-pool basis. These settings are automatically created by Lync during the pool-creation process; as such, there is no "New" cmdlet. The settings can, however, be modified and viewed using `Set-CsRgsConfiguration` and `Get-CsRgsConfiguration`, respectively. The following parameters are available:

- `Identity`: The Lync Pool hosting the Response Group prefixed with `service:ApplicationServer:`
- `AgentRingbackGracePeriod`: The Ringback Grace Period is the period in which a call will not return to an agent if they declined it. This only really comes into effect when too few agents are available, and it is defined in seconds between 30 and 600.
- `DefaultMusicOnHoldFile`: The Default MoH file used when no specific MoH file is defined in the workflow.
- `DisableCallContext`: The call context consists of the details of the IVR responses, and the wait time that is shown to the agent when it answers a call using the Lync client.

`Move-CsRgsConfiguration` is used when migrating from OCS 2007 R2 to Lync; it will migrate all of the Response Groups, not just the configuration settings.

Before looking at the rest of the Response Group cmdlets, you need to see how the `Set` cmdlets work, because they operate in a slightly different way than most of the other Lync `Set` cmdlets. The difference is that the settings cannot be directly edited; instead, an instance of the settings first needs to be retrieved into a PowerShell variable, then the required updates need to be performed, and finally the instance needs to be fed into the `Set` command. Here's an example:

```
$variable = Get-CsRgsAgentGroup -Identity service:ApplicationServer:se01.gaots.
local -Name "Attendant"
$variable.RoutingMethod = "RoundRobin"
Set-CsRgsAgentGroup -Instance $variable
```

You also need to use this method when you're creating queues and workflows, because instances often need to be passed into these commands. Some of the PowerShell cmdlets are used only for populating a variable to pass into another cmdlet.

Agent Groups

Agent groups define a list of agents and their associated settings, such as call routing method and alert time. A single group can be assigned to multiple queues. Agent groups can be managed through the Control Panel (Response Groups ➤ Group) or through PowerShell. To create a new agent group, use the `New-CsRgsAgentGroup` cmdlet; the following parameters are available:

- `Parent`: This is the FQDN of the pool to host the agent group; it is prefixed with `service:ApplicationServer:`.
- `AgentAlertTime` (Ring time on Agent): This cmdlet is defined in seconds between 10 and 600.
- `AgentsByUri` (Agent List): This cmdlet is a comma-separated list of agents. Each agent should be prefixed with `sip:`.
- `Description`: This is a `description of the agent group.`
- `DistributionGroupAddress` (Distribution Group Containing Agents): This is the email address associated with the distribution group.
- `ParticipationPolicy` (Participation Type): This is set to `Formal` if the agent needs to sign in to receive calls from the Response Group, or `Informal` if they will always receive calls from the Response Group.
- `RoutingMethod`: The routing methods are:
    - Longest Idle (LongestIdle)
    - Round Robin (RoundRobin)
    - Serial
    - Parallel
    - Attendant

    Except for the Attendant routing method, all of these methods were discussed earlier in this section. As its name implies, the Attendant method is a new routing method in Lync used primarily for attendants. It operates like the Parallel method except that it ignores the user's presence state when routing a call. Normally, Response Groups will only route a call to an agent if it has a presence of Available or Inactive. When the Attendant routing method is used, the call will be routed to the agent irrespective of its presence state; the only exception to this is if the state is Do Not Disturb.

There are two ways to define which users are members of an agent group—either by defining a list of agents using their SIP URIs or by specifying a distribution group. Although specifying a distribution group can save having to specify a list of agents, you need to be aware of the following:

- Nested distribution groups will be ignored.
- Only a single distribution group can be defined.

- For the Serial and Round Robin routing methods, the calls will be routed to agents in the order listed in the distribution group. This can often cause issues when you want to use a different agent order.

When creating the agent group, you should specify only one of the two options, either `AgentsByUri` or `DistributionGroupAddress`. If you are creating a group in which you intend to use this agent group, you should store the result of the `New` command in a variable.

Queue and Workflow Preliminaries

Once the agent groups have been created, you'll need to create the queues and then the workflows. To create these elements, you will need to pass into the respective cmdlets the results of a number of other cmdlets, which define various characteristics of the queue. The elements you need to configure first are as follows:

- Prompts
- Answers
- Questions
- Call Actions

Prompts are either uploaded recordings or messages generated using Text to Speech, and they are used to read messages such as "Welcome to the Sales Department" or IVR questions. These prompts are not created in their own right; they are passed into a variable to pass into another cmdlet.

The `New-CsRgsPrompt` accepts two parameters: either `TextToSpeechPrompt`, which allows for up to 4096 characters to be specified, or an audio file, using the `AudioFilePrompt` parameter.

If you use audio files rather than TTS, they needs to be either a WAV file (`.wav`) or a Windows Media Audio file (`.wma`). WAV files need to meet the following criteria:

- 8 or 16 bits
- Linear pulse code modulation (LPCM), A-Law or mu-Law
- Mono or stereo
- 4MB or less

For Windows Media Audio files, there are no specific limitations imposed by Lync. However, you should give some consideration to the bit rate because the higher the bit rate, the greater the load is that is placed on the Lync servers.

The audio file containing the prompt is not directly uploaded; instead, the cmdlet requires a byte array representation of the file. This byte array is created using `the Get-Content` cmdlet; this array is used with the `Import-CsRgsAudioFile` cmdlet to upload the file. Here's an example:

```
$RGSPromptAF = Import-CsRgsAudioFile -Identity "service:ApplicationServer:lyncpo
ol.gaots.local" -FileName " ResGroup1FirstPrompt.wav " -Content (Get-Content C:\
RGSPrompt.wav -Encoding byte -ReadCount 0)
```

This code imports the audio file to the Lync server. It first gets a byte array of the `RGSPrompt.wav` file, which is sent to the Lync servers and saved as `ResGroup1FirstPrompt.wav`. The `FileName` specified needs to be unique and does not need to match the name of the file you are uploading. That is because you are uploading the prompt to Lync as a byte array rather than the actual file; therefore, the original name is never uploaded.

The next cmdlet you need to look at is `New-CsRgsAnswer`, which is used to specify an answer for a question. This cmdlet does not create anything, and it is used only to populate a variable. It uses these parameters:

- `Action`: This cmdlet is used with the `New-CsRgsCallAction` cmdlet to specify the action that occurs when the response is chosen.
- `DtmfResponse`: The DTMF response can either be a *,# or 0 through 9.
- `Name`: This is the name of the answer.
- `VoiceResponseList`: This is a list of voice responses this answer will match, separated by commas.

When creating the answer, either `DtmfResponse`, `VoiceResponseList`, or both must be specified.

Now that you can create both the answer and the prompt, you can create a question using the `New-CsRgsQuestion` cmdlet. Like the previous two cmdlets, this one also needs to be passed into a variable. The `New-CsRgsQuestion` cmdlet uses these parameters:

- `Prompt`: This is the question to be asked. It should be a prompt object.
- `AnswerList`: This is a comma-separated list of answers. If the question allows two answers, at least two answer objects should be specified.
- `InvalidAnswerPrompt`: This is a prompt object that will be played if an invalid answer is entered.
- `Name`: This is the name of the question.
- `NoAnswerPrompt`: This is a prompt object that will be played if no answer is entered.

When a question with associated answers has been created, you need to look at the call action. To make Response Groups even more complicated, the `New-CsRgsAnwer` cmdlet requires that a call action already be created; therefore, to get to a stage where you have a question created, you will already have had to create a call action. But a call action can also be linked to a question if required and may require a prompt to be created.

A call action can do any of the following things:

- `Terminate`: This will end the call.
- `TransferToQueue`: This allows an agent to answer the call.
- `TransferToQuestion`: This transfers to a question.
- `TransferToUri`: Transfers to a SIP URI, such as another response group, specified in the `Uri` parameter.
- `TransferToVoiceMailUri`: Transfers to the voice mailbox, specified in the `Uri` parameter.
- `TransferToPSTN`: This transfers to a PSTN number specified in the `Uri` parameter.

To create a call action, use the `New-CsRgsCallAction` cmdlet. The following parameters are available.

- `Action`: This is one of the previously specified actions.
- `Prompt`: This is a prompt to play before the action is carried out. It should be a prompt object.
- `Question`: This is required only if the Transfer to Question action is chosen and should be a question object.
- `QueueID`: This is used if Transfer to a Queue is specified. It should be the identity of the queue which was previously created. If the queue is in a variable, this is retrieved using `$variable.Identity`.
- `Uri`: This is used if Transfer to a URI or PSTN is specified. It should be prefixed with `sip:`.

You'll see examples of all of these commands in action in the section coming up shortly.

QUEUES

Queues are used to define the actions once the caller has been processed by the workflow. This could be after an option is selected on an IVR, or callers could be routed straight to a queue as soon as they call the workflow if, for example, the workflow is configured as a hunt group.

With all of the preliminaries configured, you are ready to create a queue. Unlike the last few sets of cmdlets you've looked at, the `New-CsRgsQueue` cmdlet actually creates groups. It uses the following parameters:

- `Parent:` This is the FQDN of the pool to host the agent group, prefixed with *`service:ApplicationServer:`*.
- `Name`: The is the group name.
- `AgentGroupIdList`: This is a comma-separated list of agent groups. The groups will be worked through in order; if no agent in group 1 answers, then group 2 will be tried, and so on.
- `Description:` This describes the queue.
- `OverflowAction:` This is a call action object.
- `OverflowCandidate`: The Call to Overflow can be set to `NewestCall` or `OldestCall`.
- `OverflowThreshold`: The call count to overflow can be set between 0 and 1000. When the specified number of calls is in the queue, either the oldest or newest call will overflow.
- `TimeoutAction`: This is a call action object.
- `TimeoutThreshold`: This threshold is specified in seconds between 10 and 65536. When the timeout is hit for a queued call, it will follow the timeout call action defined.

Queues can also be configured through the Control Panel. With this method, the preliminary configuration of items such as Overflow Action is not required, because they are configured at the same time as the queue, which can be accessed at Response Group ➤ Queue. Once the queues and associated aspects have been created, you can move on to workflows and the additional cmdlets required.

WORKFLOWS

Workflows are the initial entry points. They define the phone number and contact URI associated with the workflow, the questions to be presented, whether it is an IVR, and the associated queues for the call to be routed to, along with settings such as opening hours and holidays.

Workflows can be configured through PowerShell, in which case there are a number of items that need to be configured before the actual workflow is created. If configuration is performed using the Response Group Configuration Tool, then all configuration is performed when the workflow is created. The Configuration tool (Figure 16.9) can be accessed through the Control Panel (Response Group ➢ Workflow ➢ Create or edit a workflow) or through `https://poolfqdn/RgsConfig`.

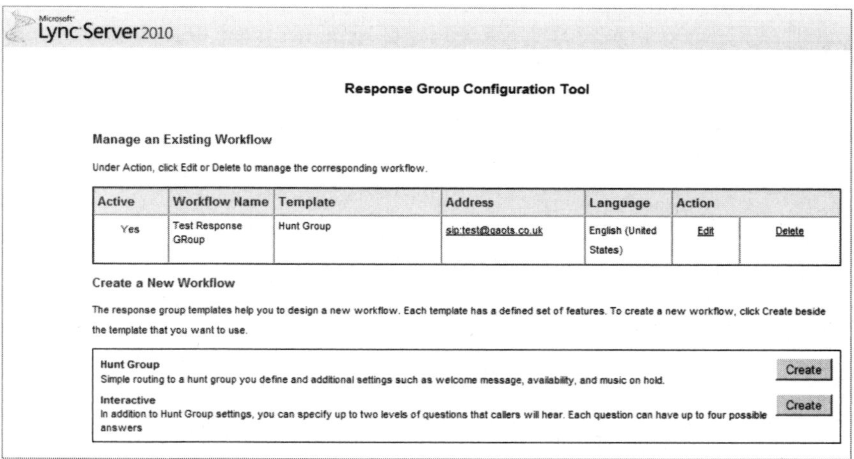

FIGURE 16.9 The Response Group Configuration Tool

The first workflow elements to define are holidays; you do that using the `New-CsRgsHoliday` cmdlet. This cmdlet does not create anything and as such needs to be passed into a variable. It lets you specify a start date and time, along with an end date and time. The following parameters are required:

- `Name`
- `StartDate`
- `EndDate`

Dates should be formatted as *MM/DD/YYYY HH:SS* `AM|PM`; for example, `12/25/2011 12:00 AM`.

When an individual holiday has been created, you need to add it to a holiday set. These are created and as such have associated `Get`, `Set`, and `Remove` cmdlets.

The `New-CsHolidaySet` cmdlet is used to create the holiday sets, which are linked to the workflows to indicate when the Response Group should be open. The following parameters are required:

- `HolidayList`: This is a comma-separated list of holiday objects.
- `Name`: This is the name of the holiday list.

- `Parent`: This is the FQDN of the pool to host the holiday set, prefixed with *`service:ApplicationServer:`*.

Now you need to define the business hours the Response Groups are open. To do that, you need to define time ranges to pass into the Hours of Business cmdlet.

Time ranges are defined using the `New-CsRgsTimeRange` cmdlet. This doesn't create anything, so its result needs to be passed into a variable. The cmdlet takes the following parameters:

- `Name:` This is the name of the time range.
- `OpenTime:` This is defined as HH:MM using a 24-hour clock.
- `CloseTime`: This is defined as HH:MM using a 24-hour clock.

If the business hours are the same for multiple days, such as Monday to Friday, only one time range needs to be defined for these hours. Next, the business hours need to be defined using the `New-CsRgsHoursOfBusiness` cmdlet. Business hours are created and, as such, have associated `Set`, `Get`, and `Remove` cmdlets. `New-CsRgsHoursOfBusiness` allows two sets of hours to be specified for each day of the week, allowing it to close for lunch, for example. This cmdlet has the following parameters:

- `Name:` This is the name of the business hours.
- `Parent:` This is the FQDN of the pool to host the business hours, prefixed with *`service:ApplicationServer:`*.
- `MondayHours 1` and `MondayHours2` through `SundayHours1` and `SundayHours2:` These are TimeRange objects.

Once all of the required objects have been created, you can finally create the workflows. Workflows link together all of the elements you've reviewed, and creating them is the final step required to complete a Response Group. They are created with `New-CsRgsWorkflow` cmdlets, using the following parameters:

- `Name:` This is the name of the workflow
- `Parent`: This is the FQDN of the pool to host the workflow, prefixed with *`service:ApplicationServer:`*.
- `PrimaryUri`: This is the SIP address of the Response Group, prefixed with `sip:`.
- `Active`: This specifies whether the workflow is active. If it is not active, calls will not be accepted.
- `Anonymous`: If this is set to True, the agent's identity will be hidden.
- `BusinessHoursID`: This is a Business Hours object.
- `CustomMusicOnHoldFile`: This is an Audio File object, which is created using the `Import-CsRgsAudiofile` cmdlet.
- `DefaultAction`: This is the default call action to use when the workflow is open; it requires a Call Action object.

- `Description`
- `DisplayNumber`
- `EnabledForFederation`
- `HolidayAction`: This is the call action to use during a holiday; it requires a Call Action object.
- `HolidaySetIdList`: This is the Holiday Set Object to use.
- `Language`: This is used to specify the language to be used for Text-to-Speech.
- `LineUri`: This is the PSTN phone number for the workflow, prefixed with `tel:`.
- `NonBusinessHoursAction:` This is the call action to use outside of business hours. It requires a Call Action object.
- `TimeZone`: This is the time zone for holidays and business hours.

As part of the Workflow creation process, an application contact is created in the configuration partition in Active Directory. The contact stores the same information the Lync-enabled user would—for example, the Display Name and Line URI. This contact is used for a number of tasks:

- When an incoming event occurs, such as a phone call, Lync will search both user and application contacts for a match. The application contact provides the application for the call to be routed to, in this case the Response Group application.
- It will be processed by the Lync Address Book Service, allowing users to search for and add the contact to their Lync contact list.

To view a list of application contacts in Lync, you can use the `Get-CsApplicationEndpoint` cmdlet.

ANONYMOUS RESPONSE GROUPS AND PRIVACY MODE

If an agent has Privacy mode enabled, the Response Group Presence Watcher can't see it, because Response Groups have no additional privileges other than a standard user when it comes to presence.

In order for Response Groups to operate when Privacy mode is enabled, the RGS Presence Watcher contact needs to be in their buddy list.

Implementing Response Groups

Now that you've looked at what you can do with Response Groups, it's time to see how you can implement them. To do this, let's work through a fairly complete, realistic scenario:

Your organization requires a Response Group to be configured for routing calls to a group of three attendants. All attendants should see all of the calls, but they should be able to specify whether they will receive calls or not. The identity of all attendants should be hidden.

In addition, the callers should be told that they are being placed in a queue and hear music on hold while waiting. Outside of business hours, calls should be routed to an Exchange mailbox, along with calls that have been waiting for longer than 5 minutes. Callers should be told they are being transferred to voice mail.

After studying the requirements statement, you determine that you need the following:

- To create an agent group
- To create a queue with overflow settings specified for callers waiting in the queue
- To create a workflow with the announcement, working hours, and agent anonymity defined

To begin, you create the agent group:

```
$AGroup = New-CsRgsAgentGroup -Parent "service:ApplicationServer:se01.gaots
.local" -AgentsByUri "sip:Attendant1@gaots.co.uk", "sip:Attendant2@gaots.co.uk",
"sip:Attendant3@gaots.co.uk" -ParticipationPolicy Formal -RoutingMethod Attendant
-Name "Attendant Group"
```

With this command, you created the agent group. It is created as a formal group, with the three specified agents and routes using the Attendant routing method to ensure that calls are presented to agents irrespective of their state (except for Do Not Disturb).

Now you need to create the prompt to transfer the caller to voice mail on timeout:

```
$TimeoutPrompt = New-CsRgsPrompt -TextToSpeechPrompt "Unfortunately all of our
operators are busy, we are transferring you to voice mail."
```

This stores the prompt in `$TimeoutPrompt`, allowing you to pass it into the next command.

Next, you need to create the call action for the timeout:

```
$TimeoutCallAction = New-CsRgsCallAction -Action TransferToVoiceMailUri -Uri
"sip:attendantMB@gaots.co.uk" -Prompt $TimeoutPrompt
```

This stores the details into `$TimeOutCallAction`. The action transfers the call to the specified voice mailbox.

Now that you have created the required objects, you can create the queue:

```
$AQueue = New-CsRgsQueue -Parent "service:ApplicationServer:se01.gaots.local"
-Name "Attendant Queue" -AgentGroupIdList $AGroup.Identity -TimeoutAction
$TimeoutCallAction -TimeoutThreshold 300
```

This creates the queue and stores the details in the `$AQueue`. It also references the agent group you created earlier; because you need the Identity value out of `$AGroup`, you specify `$AGroup.Identity`.

Now you're ready to create the objects required for the workflow. The first step is to define the time range for the business hours:

```
$TimeRange = New-CsRgsTimeRange -Name "BusinessHours" -OpenTime 08:00 -EndTime
18:00
```

This stores the time range, which is 08:00 to 18:00, in `$TimeRange`.

Now define the business hours:

```
$BusinessHours = New-CsRgsHoursOfBusiness -Name "Attendant Open Hours"
-Parent "service:ApplicationServer:se01.gaots.local" -MondayHours1 $TimeRange
-TuesdayHours1 $TimeRange -WednesdayHours1 $TimeRange -ThursdayHours1 $TimeRange
-FridayHours1 $TimeRange
```

This creates the business hours. Into this statement, you'll pass the `$TimeRange` several times, since you require the same opening hours for each day that the business is open. Because the hours aren't specified for Saturday or Sunday, it will be closed on those days.

Now you need to create the prompt to transfer the caller to voice mail outside of business hours:

```
$OBHPrompt = New-CsRgsPrompt -TextToSpeechPrompt "We are currently closed, we are
transferring you to voicemail."
```

This creates the Out of Business Hours prompt. Note that only a sort of "ghost object" is created at this point; the information is merely stored in the `$OBHPrompt` variable until the command to create the workflow is run.

Now you need to create the call action for outside of business hours:

```
$OBHCallAction = New-CsRgsCallAction -Action TransferToVoiceMailUri -Uri
"sip:attendantMB@gaots.co.uk" -Prompt $OBHPrompt
```

This creates the Out of Business Hours actions. Again, at this point, the information is merely stored in the `$OBHCallAction` variable until the workflow is created.

Now that you have created the business hours, you need to create the default call action and associated prompt:

```
$DefaultPrompt = New-CsRgsPrompt -TextToSpeechPrompt "Thanks you for calling
Contoso, please wait for an Attendant."
```

This creates the default prompt. Again, at this point, the information is merely stored in the `$DefaultPrompt` variable until the workflow is created.

Next, you need to create the call action to route to the agents:

```
$DefaultCallAction = New-CsRgsCallAction -Action TransferToQueue -QueueID
$AQueue.Identity -Prompt $DefaultPrompt
```

This creates the default call action. Again, at this point, the information is merely stored in the `$DefaultCallAction` variable for use in the next command.

Now that you've created the required objects for the workflow, you can finally create the workflow:

```
New-CsRgsWorkflow -Name "Attendants" -Parent "service:ApplicationServer:se01.
gaots.local" -PrimaryURI "sip:AttendantRGS@gaots.co.uk" -Active $true -Anonymous
$true -BusinessHoursID $BusinessHours.Identity -DefaultAction $DefaultCallAction
-DisplayNumber "1-425-555-1000"-EnabledForFederation $true -Language "en-US"
-LineURI "tel:+14255551000" -NonBusinessHoursAction $OBHCallAction
```

This creates the actual workflow. Into this workflow, you can reference the call actions created earlier. For the business hours, reference the `Identity` stored within `$BusinessHours`. The two action variables are not actually created in Lync, they are stored within the variables, so you don't need to specify a particular setting in them.

When this command is run, the output is similar to the following:

```
Identity               : service:ApplicationServer:se01.gaots.local/6876ce92-
7b33-450f-8a73-38fc7d5c1789
NonBusinessHoursAction : Prompt=We are currently closed, we are transferring you
to voicemail.
```

```
Action=TransferToVoicemailUri
Uri=sip:attendantMB@gaots.co.uk
HolidayAction             :
DefaultAction             : Prompt=Thanks you for calling please wait for an
Attendant.
                            Action=TransferToQueue
                            QueueId=dbaf6136-9386-4964-a49f-8610f0f761de
CustomMusicOnHoldFile     :
Name                      : Attendants
Description               :
PrimaryUri                : sip:AttendantRGS@gaots.co.uk
Active                    : True
Language                  : en-US
TimeZone                  : GMT Standard Time
BusinessHoursID           : service:ApplicationServer:se01.gaots.local/6f7314e7-
a88f-4f23-aa64-a9262404a050
Anonymous                 : True
DisplayNumber             : 1-425-555-1000
EnabledForFederation      : True
LineUri                   : tel:+14255551000
HolidaySetIDList          : {}
```

Now that the Response Group is configured, you can run the corresponding **Get** commands to check the configuration.

Using Response Groups

Now that you've implemented Response Groups, you need to see how network users work with them. As with dial-in conferencing and other Lync client features, admins may need to provide some level of training or support to their users. Here you are only going to look at the agent aspects of Response Groups.

If a user is assigned to a formal workflow, the first thing he or she needs to do is log into the workflow by selecting Response Group Settings from the Lync client, which then loads the web page shown in Figure 16.10. Users will be presented with the queues to which they are assigned, and they will be able to check the queues they want to sign into.

FIGURE 16.10
Signing into a queue

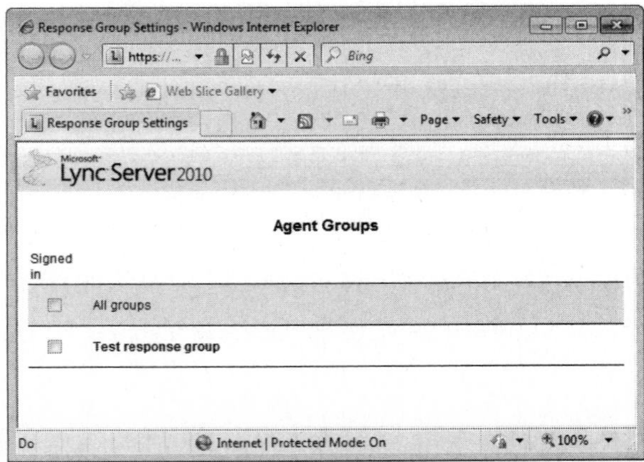

When the agent receives a call, the Toast that appears to notify the agent of the call (Figure 16.11) will contain the name of the Response Group. By receiving this information, the agent knows, for example, what greeting to use when answering the call.

FIGURE 16.11
The Toast for a Response Group

If the call is from a Response Group that uses an IVR, the agents will be presented with the IVR options that the caller selected along with their wait time, as shown in Figure 16.12.

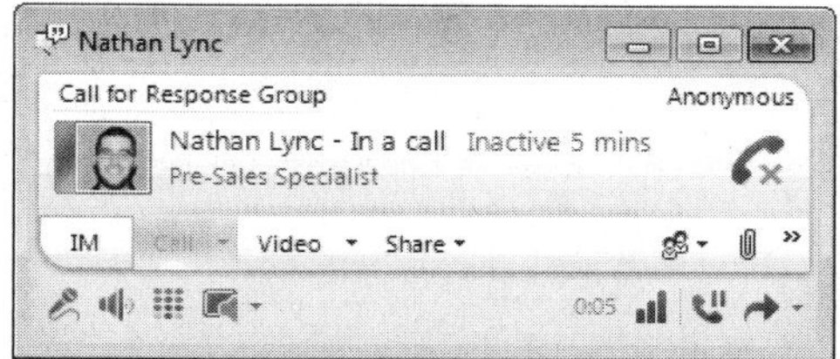

FIGURE 16.12
IVR details for a call

With this information, the agent can handle the call as required. In addition, they can introduce additional modalities, as with a normal Lync call, and they can escalate to a conference if needed. The only time this is restricted is if the Response Group that they answered the call on is configured for Agent Anonymity, in which case they cannot do any of the following:

- Share individual applications, the desktop of a single display, or the entire desktop
- Transfer files
- Use whiteboard or data collaboration
- Escalate to a conference

What happens when the agent needs to make an outbound call? For the most part making an outbound call is no different for a user configured as an agent than it is for a normal user. The only time this differs is if a user is a member of a Response Group that is configured for Agent Anonymity. In this case, as shown in Figure 16.13, the agent can choose whether they are making the call on behalf of themselves or the Response Group.

FIGURE 16.13
Choosing whether to make an anonymous outbound call

Call Park

Education, healthcare, warehousing, and retail are just a few of the organization types that take Call Park for granted. It is a feature they use every day and assume that it will be available on any PBX that they want to deploy. In order to fulfill the requirements of these organizations and others, Call Park was added as a voice application in Lync, removing a potential stumbling block for these organizations to migrate to Lync.

While you may not have heard of Call Park before, you have probably heard of it being used. If you have been in a store and heard "Call for Joe Blogs on extension 1023" over the Public Address System, they were probably referring to an incoming call for Joe Blogs that was "parked" on extension 1023. This allowed Joe Blogs to easily retrieve the call by calling 1023 from any of the store phones and be connected to the call immediately.

Why would a store use Call Park rather than, for example, having the switchboard operator put the call on hold, page Joe Blogs to call them, and then transfer the call? The new technology has emerged due to the limitations of PBXs and the way they operate. The easiest way to understand this is to look at how a call flow would operate:

1. Customer calls the store.
2. Switchboard answers.
3. Customer asks to talk to the store manager.

4. Switchboard operator places the call on hold and pages the store manager.
5. Store manager calls the operator; if the operator is busy, it could take a while for the call to be answered.
6. Operator takes a note of the number the store manager called from and hangs up.
7. Operator takes the customer off hold and transfers it to the number the store manager called from; if by sheer chance someone else has called this number before the operator managed to transfer the call, then the operator will have to wait to transfer the call.

As you can see, this is a long process and has a number of areas where issues can occur—for example, suppose the switchboard operator is busy. While that may not happen in a small retail store, in a busy hospital, the wait time could be tremendous. Some PBXs, including Lync, can shortcut part of this process by allowing calls to be *joined*, effectively removing the last two steps. However, there can be other limitations, such as the number of calls a person can put on hold at any one time.

In summary, Call Park allows a call to be parked on an extension number and retrieved by calling that extension number.

Call Park in Lync

Now that you understand what Call Park is, you need to examine how it works within Lync and the configuration options available. No separate installation is required for Call Park; it is installed as part of Lync. In order to use Call Park, you just need to configure it. You do that in the following stages:

- Voice policy configuration
- Call Park extensions
- Call Park Service configuration
- Call Park Music on Hold

In Lync, any user can retrieve a parked call by calling the extension on which it was parked. From a user standpoint, the only configuration option is whether the user can park a call. This is configured through the Voice policy assigned to the user, which was covered in Chapter 13.

Call Park Extensions

Call Park extensions are referred to in Lync as *orbits*, and they can be configured through the Control Panel or using the PowerShell. These numbers have a lot of restrictions:

- The maximum number of orbits per range is 10,000.
- The maximum number of orbits per Lync pool is 50,000.
- They cannot be Direct Inward Dial numbers (DIDs).
- They must match this regular expression:

```
([\*|#]?[1-9]\d{0,7})|([1-9]\d{0,8})
```

The first two restrictions are not likely to cause an issue, because most organizations usually require a small range of numbers to use. This range should be no larger than required; for most organizations this tends to be less than 100 extensions.

The requirement that the number not be a DID is fairly unusual for Lync, because most voice-related features require E.164 numbers to be assigned to them. A Call Park number cannot be a DID because retrieving calls from the PSTN is not supported, although retrieving calls from a PBX is supported.

The final requirement is for the number to match a specific regular expression. This breaks down as follows:

- It must start with a *, #, or the digits 1 through 9.
- If the number starts with a * or #, it must be followed by 1 through 9, followed by up to seven digits.
- If the number starts with a 1 through 9, it can be followed by up to eight digits.

Table 16.2 lists some sample orbit numbers.

TABLE 16.2: Sample Orbit Numbers

START NUMBER	END NUMBER
*1	*9
#100	#140
1000	1100
859000	859010

When assigning numbers to be orbits, you need to make sure they will not be affected by number normalizations, such as those found in the dial plans. If the number a user tries to call is converted to another number, they will be unable to retrieve the call.

This also applies to any normalizations that may be performed by a gateway linking to a PBX or by the PBX itself, if there is a requirement to retrieve calls from the PBX.

Orbits can be configured through the Lync Control Panel under Voice Features ➢ Call Park, as well as via PowerShell. From the resulting New Call Park Number Range tab, shown in Figure 16.14, they can be created, edited, and deleted. In order to create the orbit using the `New-CsCallParkOrbit` cmdlet, you specify the following:

- `Identity`: This is the orbit range name.
- `NumberRangeStart`: This is the orbit range start number.
- `NumberRangeEnd`: This is the orbit range end number.
- `CallParkService`: This is the Application server to host the orbits.

For Call Park, the application server is a Lync pool FQDN prefixed with `ApplicationServer:`. This allows you to define which pool will host the parked calls. If you will be parking a large number of calls, this could be resource intensive, because the pool needs to manage these calls and also stream Music on Hold if configured.

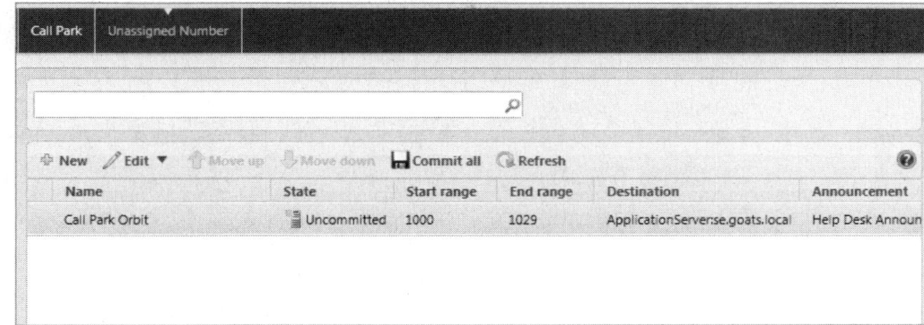

FIGURE 16.14 Creating an orbit via Call Park

MANAGING THE CALL PARK SERVICE

The Call Park service configuration can only be managed through PowerShell. There are two configuration levels: global and site. The global level will apply to all Lync sites unless a site level configuration exists. Both levels have the same configuration options; to create a new configuration, use the `New-CsCpsConfiguration` cmdlet:

- `EnableMusicOnHold:` A True or False option. This indicates whether Music on Hold (MoH) should be played. There is a default MoH file that ships with Lync; this can be replaced if required.
- `CallPickupTimeoutThreshold:` Defined as HH:MM:SS. This defines the length of time before the call recalls. This can be as little as 10 seconds or as long as 10 minutes. The default is 90 seconds.
- `MaxCallPickupAttempts:` The number of times the call will ring the person who parked the call before it will reroute to the Timeout URI. The default is 1.
- `OnTimeoutURI:` A SIP address to which the parked call will be routed if the call is not answered after the defined number of Call Pickup Attempts. The SIP URI can either be a user or a Response Group.

MUSIC ON HOLD

A custom MoH file is uploaded to the Call Park service using a dedicated PowerShell command. Only one MoH file can be used per application server; when a new file is uploaded, the existing file will be overwritten.

The file needs to be in WMA 9 format, and it is recommended that it has the following characteristics: encoded at 44kHz, 16 bit, mono, with a constant bit rate (CBR) or 32kbps.

Converting to the Recommended Format

To convert audio files to the recommended format for Music on Hold, you can use Microsoft Expression Encoder, an application that allows existing files to be encoded to the correct settings, among other things. Expression Encoder is available in a number of versions; the free version, which can convert most audio formats, can be downloaded from:

```
www.microsoft.com/download/en/details.aspx?id=24601
```

Expression Encoder is designed to do a lot more than convert audio files, so the conversion process can be confusing. The following steps will walk you through converting the file.

1. Select Transcoding Project.
2. Import the MoH file, by choosing File ➤ Import.
3. Under the Encode tab on the right-hand side of the application, expand Audio and complete the settings as shown in the following graphic.

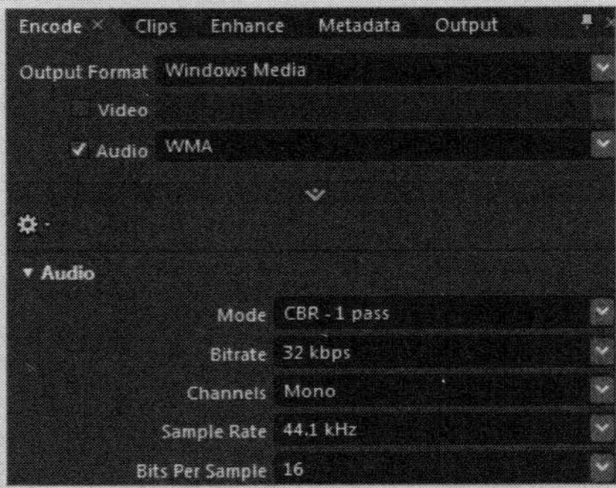

4. Select the Output location under the Output tab.
5. Encode the file by choosing File ➤ Encode.

The MoH file is not directly uploaded; instead the cmdlet requires a byte array representation of the file. This byte array is created using the `Get-Content` cmdlet, which is combined with the `Set-CsCallParkServiceMusicOnHoldFile` cmdlet to upload the file. Here's an example:

```
$MoHFile = Get-Content -ReadCount 0 -Encoding byte "C:\music_on_hold.wma"
Set-CsCallParkServiceMusicOnHoldFile -Service ApplicationServer:se01.gaots.local
-Content $MoHFile
```

These two commands create a byte array of the file `music_on_hold.wma` in the `$MoHFile` variable. Uploads it to the Lync Server and set it as the Call Park Service Music on Hold.

Implementing Call Park

Now that you know what you can and can't do with Call Park, let's look at how you can implement it. To do this, use the following scenario:

As part of the Microsoft Lync deployment, some of the staff members need access to the Call Park functionality. All other staff members should be able to retrieve calls but not park them. The staff members who should be able to park calls are the switchboard operators and the personal assistants. There should be capacity to park 30 calls at any one time; calls should recall after 30 seconds, and if they are not answered when recalled, the call should be directed to the switchboard.

After reviewing the given scenario, you determine that:

- Only the switchboard and the PA require Call Park.
- Only 30 orbits need to be set up.
- The Pickup Timeout needs to be 30 seconds.
- The Timeout URI needs to be the switchboard Response Group.
- There should be only one recall attempt.

Although Lync does not require these tasks to be completed in any particular order, you don't want to enable the users until the rest of the configuration has been completed; therefore, you should work through the list in reverse order.

The first step is to configure the Call Park service, which can only be performed via PowerShell. Since there is only a basic set-up you will configure the service at the global level rather than on a per-site basis.

```
Set-CsCpsConfiguration -Identity Global -CallPickupTimeoutThreshold 00:00:30
-OnTimeoutURI "sip:switchboard@gaots.co.uk" -MaxCallPickupAttempts 1
```

This sets the call pickup threshold, which specifies that calls reaching the timeout are routed to the switchboard after the call has rung back to the person who parked it once. This setting will apply to all users who are not covered by a site specific policy.

Once the Call Park Service is configured, you need to create the orbit numbers; although you could configure these through the Control Panel as shown earlier, you will continue to use PowerShell. Since you were not provided with specific extensions to utilize, you will use the range 1000 to 1029.

```
New-CsCallParkOrbit -Identity "CPO 1" -NumberRangeStart 1000 -NumberRangeEnd 1029
-CallParkService "se01.gaots.local"
```

This creates the Call Park orbit, with a range of 1000 to 1029, allowing 30 calls to be parked; this pool is shared across all users in the pool. Its output will be similar to the following:

```
Identity           : CPO 1
NumberRangeStart   : 1000
NumberRangeEnd     : 1029
CallParkServiceId  : ApplicationServer:se01.gaots.local
CallParkServerFqdn : se01.gaots.local
```

Almost everything is configured, but you still need to enable the users to park calls. To do this, you need to modify the Voice policies for the switchboard operators and personal assistants; because they already exist, you need to modify the existing policies:

```
Set-CsVoicePolicy -Identity Switchboard -EnableCallPark $true
Set-CsVoicePolicy -Identity PA -EnableCallPark $true
```

These two commands enable Call Park for the two Voice policies, one for PAs and the other for the switchboard.

This completes the Call Park configuration; run the corresponding `Get` commands to check the configuration.

Using Call Park

Now that you've implemented Call Park, you need to understand how network users can park and retrieve calls. Calls can be parked using the Lync client, the Attendant client, or Lync Phone Edition. These clients operate in the same way; calls are parked by transferring the call to the Parking Lot, as shown in Figure 16.15.

FIGURE 16.15
Parking a call

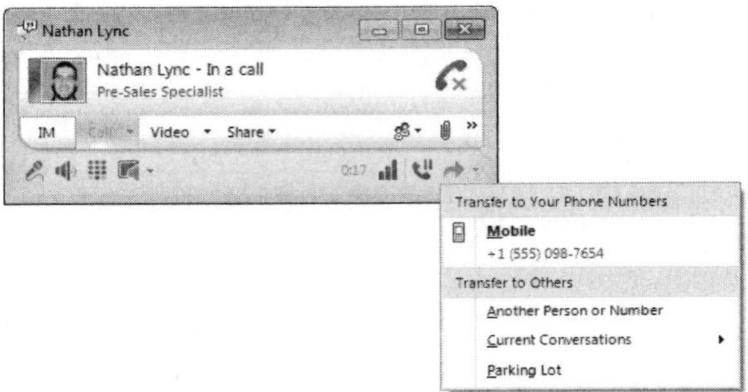

When the call is transferred, you will see that the call has been placed on hold; this notification is then replaced with the number that the call was parked on, as shown in Figure 16.16.

FIGURE 16.16
A parked call extension

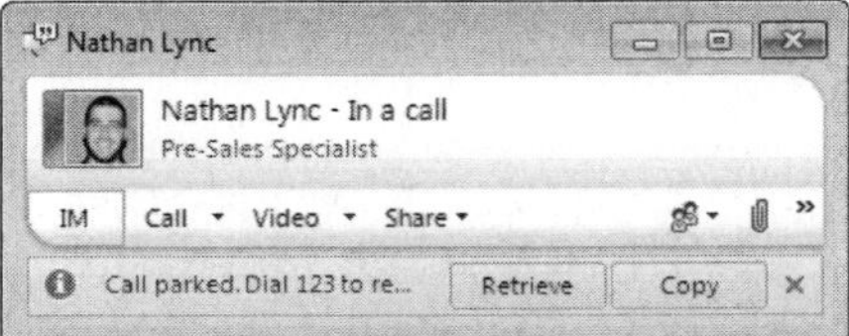

If there are no available extensions to park the call on, the user will receive a notification like the one shown in Figure 16.17. Note that the call is left on hold to ensure that caller being parked does not accidently overhear anything they shouldn't.

FIGURE 16.17
Call park failure

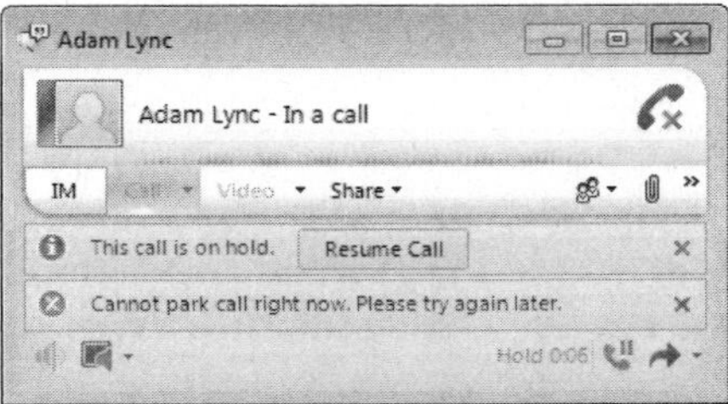

If the parked call has not been retrieved, it will recall to the user who parked the call, as shown in Figure 16.18; this is to avoid a situation where a call is never retrieved. When the recall occurs, the user will be informed that it is a recall.

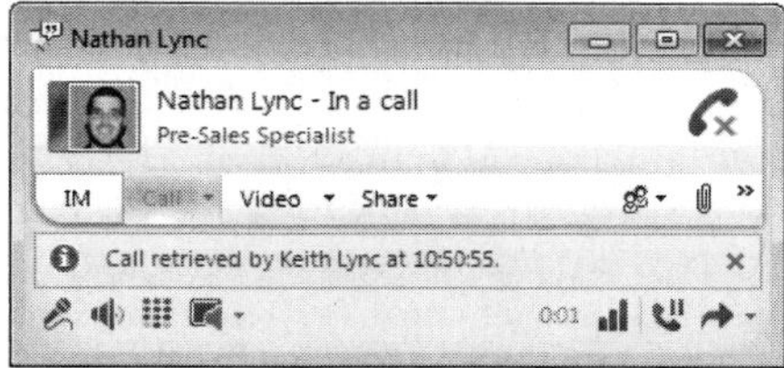

FIGURE 16.18
A call retrieved

To retrieve the call, the extension on which it was parked needs to be called. Once the call has been retrieved, it will operate like any other Lync call.

Unassigned Numbers

Organizations often have phone numbers that they do not use, for a variety of reasons. For example, they may be utilizing only part of the number range allocated to them, or staff may have left—but the organization may still receive calls to such numbers. Traditional PBXs have responded in the following ways by:

- Presenting announcements, played to the calling party, for numbers that are not allocated to a phone or service
- Allocating multiple extensions to a single phone
- Leaving phones configured with Call Forward All set to route to a different number such as an attendant

These tend to be very blunt tools, using features within the PBX for purposes for which they were not intended. Although they may do what is required, the end result may not be the best solution. For example, the first of these methods would usually result in an announcement being played, followed by the call being terminated. For some organizations, this may be satisfactory; many others would prefer the call to be transferred to an attendant. The second and third methods will have similar results for the caller, who will be expecting to speak to Joe Blogs. Instead, their call will be answered by someone completely different, which can often lead to confusion, or to the caller just hanging up.

There are also limits to the amount of extensions that can appear on a single phone, often requiring more expensive phones or expansion modules to have more extensions configured. In addition, depending on the PBX type, the more expensive the phones, the more licenses required on the PBX. There are similar issues with leaving phones configured to forward calls.

From these scenarios, you can see that there is usually no ideal way to handle unassigned numbers, although some PBXs do provide a more complete features set for this. In order to provide a better solution than most and to ensure that organizations do not lose these features if they have them, Microsoft developed the Unassigned Number functionality in Lync.

Unassigned Numbers in Lync

In Lync the Unassigned Number functionality works by defining number ranges and associated call treatments. The call treatments can send the call either to an Exchange Auto Attendant or to the Announcement Service.

The Announcement Service is used to play an announcement to the caller; the call can then be redirected to a SIP URI, voice mailbox, or telephone number. Alternatively, the call can be redirected without an announcement being played. The final option available with the Announcement Service is for it to play a busy tone to the caller. While this is better than the call just being disconnected, it does not provide any context. Using the Announcement Service allows an organization to tell the caller that a person has left the business, for example, and then redirect them to someone who can help them. For the majority of organizations, this is better than the call just being terminated after the announcement has been played.

The Announcement Service is a separate voice application within Lync, but it can be used only in conjunction with the Unassigned Number functionality. The announcements that are played to the caller can be provided either by providing an audio file or by using Text to Speech (TTS).

To TTS or Not to TTS

Text to Speech provides a quick and simple way of generating announcements, although the drawback is that they may not sound perfect; this is usually most noticeable with company and employee names. Therefore, while TTS may be usable for a proof of concept and trial deployments of Lync or for emergency announcements, many organizations prefer to use prerecorded announcements, which allow more control and remove any potential issues found with TTS.

When configuring the Unassigned Number functionality, you need to perform the basic tasks in the following order:

1. Import Announcement Service audio files.
2. Create Announcements and Exchange auto attendants.
3. Define Unassigned Number ranges.

Importing Audio Files

If you choose to use audio files rather than TTS, these audio files need to be in a specific format and must be uploaded to the Lync pool on which the unassigned numbers are defined. An audio file needs to either be a WAV file or a Windows Media Audio (WMA) file. For WAV files, the following characteristics need to be met:

- 8 or 16 bit file
- Linear pulse code modulation (LPCM), A-Law or mu-Law
- Mono or stereo
- 4MB or less

For WMA files, no specific limitations are imposed on the file by Lync. However, you should consider the bit rate, because the higher the bit rate, the greater the load placed on the Lync servers.

The announcement file is not directly uploaded; instead the cmdlet requires a byte array representation of the file. This byte array is created using the Get-Content cmdlet; this is used with the Import-CsAnnouncementFile cmdlet to upload the file. Here's an example:

```
$AnnFile = Get-Content ".\AnnouncementFile.wav" -ReadCount 0 -Encoding Byte
Import-CsAnnouncementFile -Parent ApplicationServer:se01.gaots.local -FileName
"AnnouncementFile.wav" -Content $AnnFile
```

This stores the contents of AnnouncmentFile.wav as a byte array in the $AnnFile. This is then imported using the second command and stored as AnnouncementFile.wav. The FileName specified needs to be unique and does not need to match the name of the file you are uploading.

When the file has been uploaded, the call treatments can be configured. Next, we'll discuss only the configuration of the Announcement Service, as Exchange Unified Messaging is covered in Chapter 17, "Exchange, SharePoint, and Group Chat."

Announcement Service

When using New-CsAnnouncement, there are a number of ways to create new announcements depending on what is required. Each method, of course, has different configuration options. At a minimum all announcement will use these parameters:

- Identity
- Name

The Identity is the FQDN of the Lync pool on which the announcement should be created, prefixed with ApplicationServer:. Name is the name of the announcement service.

If an announcement is created with only these settings, the caller will hear a busy tone. If you need to create an announcement using an announcement file that you have previously uploaded, you will also need to use the following:

- AudioFilePrompt

If you want to create an announcement using TTS, then in addition to Identity and Name, you need to use the following:

- Language
- TextToSpeechPrompt

For each of these three options, you can add an additional parameter, TargetURI, which will transfer the caller to the SIP URI, telephone number, or voice mailbox specified. Each of these must be specified as a SIP URI, as in the examples shown in Table 16.3.

TABLE 16.3: Transfer Options Examples

Type	Example
SIP URI	sip:joe.bloggs@gaots.co.uk
Telephone Number	sip: +14255553250;user=phone
Voice Mailbox	sip:joe.bloggs@gaots.co.uk;opaque=app:voicemail

Defining Unassigned Number Ranges

When the call treatments have been created, you can define the Unassigned Number ranges. They can be created through the Control Panel (Voice Features ➤ Unassigned Numbers) or through PowerShell; no additional configuration options are exposed through PowerShell. To create a new number range, use the `New-CsUnassignedNumber` cmdlet, which has the following options:

- `AnnouncementName`: This is the announcement name.
- `AnnouncementService`: This is the announcement service.
- `ExUMAutoAttendantPhoneNumber:` This is the Exchange Auto Attendant phone number.
- `NumberRangeStart`: This is the range start number.
- `NumberRangeEnd`: This is the range end number.
- `Priority:` This is used if number ranges overlap; if they do the announcement with the highest priority will be used.

All of these parameters are required, except `Priority`, which is required only if you have overlapping number ranges. Note that when managing Unassigned Numbers through the Control Panel, there is no priority field; instead, priorities are managed by manipulating the order of the numbers using the Move Up and Move Down options, as shown in Figure 16.19.

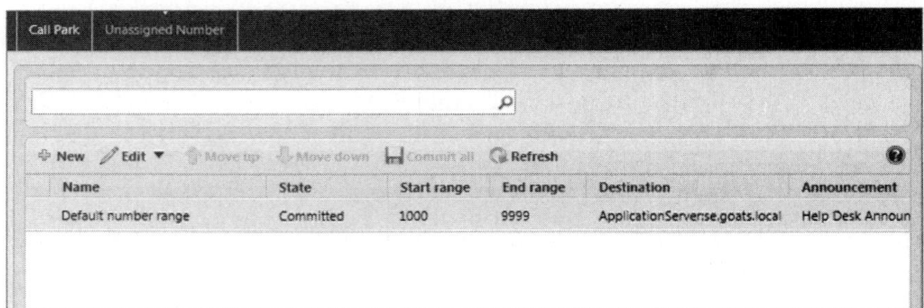

Figure 16.19 Managing unassigned numbers via Control Panel

The Announcement Service is the FQDN of the Lync pool on which the announcement should be created, prefixed with `ApplicationServer`:. If you are also using TTS, this should match the pool to which the audio file was uploaded.

The number range start and end numbers must comply with the following:

- It must match this regular expression:

  `(tel:)?(\+)?[1-9]\d{0,17}(;ext=[1-9]\d{0,9})?`
- The end number must be equal to or greater than the start number.
- The regular expression breaks down to:

- The regular expression starts with a `tel:`—although if it doesn't, it will automatically be added.
- This can then optionally have a + following it.
- This is followed by a digit, 1 to 9.
- This is followed by up to 17 digits.
- This can then be followed by `;ext=`, 1 to 9, and then up to nine additional digits if the organization uses a single DDI and an extension range.

In addition to the requirements set out by the regular expression, when the extension field is used, the start and end number must have the same number. Table 16.4 lists some examples.

TABLE 16.4: Sample Unassigned Number Ranges

START NUMBER	END NUMBER
+18500	+18600
18500	18600
+18500;ext=8000	+18500;ext=8999

Now that you have seen how unassigned numbers operate and the options for configuring them within Lync, let's look at how you can implement them.

Implementing Unassigned Numbers

Now that you know what you can do with unassigned numbers, you're ready to build a configuration based on the following scenario:

No caller should receive an unknown number response when calling into your organization. Calls to all numbers will be answered and routed as appropriate. Where there is no specific requirement, calls will be routed to an auto attendant. Calls to any numbers which used to be assigned to a sales representative will be sent to the attendants after the caller has been told they are being redirected. The sales department has its own allocated range:

Organization DDI Range: +14255551000 to +14255559999

Sales Department DDIs: +14255553250 to +14255553299

From this scenario, you determine the following:

- You need to create an unassigned number range to cover all numbers.
- You need to set up an Exchange Auto Attendant.
- You need to create an unassigned number range for the sales departments.
- You need to set up an announcement for the sales team that will play a message to any caller who dials an unused number, such as a former salesperson's number, and then redirect the call to the Attendants Response Group.

As with other configurations, you need to make sure you perform these tasks in the correct order. The Call Treatments must be set up before the Unassigned Number configuration. Configuring the Auto Attendant in Exchange is outside the scope of this book, but for this example assume it exists and has an associated phone number of +14255551010.

In Lync Server, you first need to create the announcement for the sales team. This will be performed using the Announcement Service and can only be done via PowerShell:

```
New-CsAnnouncement -Identity "ApplicationServer:se01.gaots.local" -Name "Sales
Team" -TargetURI "sip:AttendantRGS@gaots.co.uk" -TextToSpeechPrompt "Thank you
for calling a member of the sales team, please be patient while we redirect you
to an attendant" -Language "en-US"
```

This creates a new announcement using Text to Speech and routes calls to the Attendants Response Group, it will also produce an output similar to:

```
Identity           : Service:ApplicationServer:se01.gaots.local/c9780e5a-4cd2-
4bef-87d9-3a6405e73c06
Name               : Sales Team
AudioFilePrompt    :
TextToSpeechPrompt : Thank you for calling a member of the sales team, please be
patient while we redirect you to an attendant
Language           : en-US
TargetUri          : sip:AttendantRGS@gaots.co.uk
AnnouncementId     : c9780e5a-4cd2-4bef-87d9-3a6405e73c06
```

Now that you've created the announcement, you can create the unassigned numbers. Although you can do this through the Control Panel, continue to use PowerShell for the example. Because of the requirement to overlap the number ranges, you need to ensure that the `Priority` field is specified, which will allow for the sales unassigned number to supersede the organization one. Here are the final commands:

```
New-CsUnassignedNumber -Identity "All Numbers" -NumberRangeStart "+14255551000"
-NumberRangeEnd "+14255559999" -Priority 2 -ExUmAutoAttendantPhoneNumber
"+14255551010"
```

This creates an unassigned number configuration for all of the numbers the organization uses by specifying the entire number range, and it routes all calls to the Exchange Auto Attendant.

```
New-CsUnassignedNumber -Identity "Sales" -NumberRangeStart "+14255553250"
-NumberRangeEnd "+14255553299" -Priority 1 -AnnouncementService
"ApplicationServer:se01.gaots.local" -AnnouncementName "Sales Team"
```

This creates the unassigned number configuration for the sales team number range and routes them to the announcement that was created earlier, thereby producing output similar to:

```
AnnouncementServiceId   : ApplicationServer:se01.gaots.local
AnnouncementServerFqdn  : se01.gaots.local
AnnouncementName        : Sales Team
AnnouncementId          : c9780e5a-4cd2-4bef-87d9-3a6405e73c06
Identity                : Sales
```

```
NumberRangeStart       : tel:+14255553250
NumberRangeEnd         : tel:+14255553299
Priority               : 1
```

This completes the unassigned number configuration; in order to check the configuration, run the corresponding `Get` commands.

The Bottom Line

Understand the extended voice functionality. Extended voice functionality provides additional voice applications that many organizations expect a PBX to have. Understanding what these applications can and cannot do is important, so you can make the correct decisions when implementing them and know when a third-party solution is better.

Master It The manager for an internal help desk has been to a trade show and has been told he needs to have a full contact center to implement certain requirements. All he needs is to route calls to agents. He does not care about reporting or recording; he just needs to make sure that calls get to the right people. He is adamant he needs a call center because this is what the experts have told him.

Design solutions using extended voice functionality. Designing is usually seen as a boring, time-consuming task, when all you want to do is get your hands dirty and implement something. Although some of the extended voice functionality is straightforward, other elements are complex and missing the design stage could cause you problems later. Design, design, design—and implement once.

Master It You need to implement a dial-in conferencing solution globally. You need to have global dial-in numbers and support at least 100 concurrent PSTN calls to the conferencing solution.

Implement extended voice functionality. Lync's extended voice functionality is useless if you do not know how to implement it and use it to its fullest potential. To do that, you need to make sure that what you implement works and is fully tested.

Master It You have implemented Call Park but users are complaining about intermittent issues with parking calls. The complaints are coming from all user types, which is strange because not all users should be able to park calls.

Part 5

Integration

Chapter 17

Exchange, SharePoint, and Group Chat

A huge amount of communication technology is built into Lync, but it is extended even further through tight integration with external systems. You might wonder why Group Chat, which is part of Lync, is being treated as an external technology. The reason is that it was an acquisition Microsoft made a few years ago, and although it is shipped with Lync and is integrated in terms of presence and communication capabilities, it has a separate client, management interface, and server components.

The other technologies this chapter will explore are Exchange and SharePoint. Lync relies totally on Exchange to provide voice mail capabilities; not only can Lync users receive voice mail, but they also have full voice access to their mailboxes through tight integration into the Lync client. Exchange is also used to provide consolidated contacts and a store for conversation history. Lync, in turn, provides Exchange the ability to integrate presence and basic IM functionality into Outlook Web App (OWA).

Lync and SharePoint together allow intelligent communications to be integrated into business processes. At its simplest level, presence is available in SharePoint, so there is quick and easy access to contact the author of documents; at a more complex level, it is also possible to integrate presence into workflow-related decisions—for example, to route documents to the most available manager for signoff. SharePoint also provides the search capabilities to enable Lync users to search for contacts by skill set.

In this chapter, you will learn to:

- Integrate Lync with Exchange
- Integrate Lync with SharePoint
- Integrate Lync with Group Chat

Integrating Lync with Exchange

These days, it is rare not to come across an Exchange messaging platform in an organization. Exchange has become almost the de facto standard for carrying email. With its most recent versions (2007 and 2010), Exchange broadened its role, becoming part of a unified communication platform through the provision of voice mail and unified inbox capabilities. As you have seen throughout this book, Lync is a fully functional communication platform; however, it relies on the unified inbox capabilities of Exchange to store conversation history and voice mail. Because Exchange is the standard calendaring platform, Lync utilizes this information to enhance presence and give visibility to out-of-office messages. Finally, Lync can bring some of its capabilities to Exchange through the provision of presence and basic IM functionality into Outlook Web App.

DIFFERENT VERSIONS OF EXCHANGE

As you will see, Lync makes extensive use of features in newer Exchange versions, such as voice mail and web services. That said, Lync can also integrate in some ways with versions as early as Exchange 2003. Essentially, Exchange 2003 provides only the MAPI interface so it only makes available features that support MAPI. For an in-depth view of these features, see the following link:

`http://technet.microsoft.com/en-us/library/gg398806.aspx`

Because of the addition of voice mail and Exchange Web Services (EWS) capabilities, the difference between Exchange 2003 and 2007/10 support is great. However, the differences between Exchange 2007 and 2010 support are much smaller. Essentially, Exchange 2010 adds the ability to provide Message Waiting Indicator (MWI) information and also provides a contact sync feature, which allows Lync to create a personal contact in Outlook for each person on a user's Lync contacts list.

It is, of course, now possible to deploy Exchange in the Cloud using Microsoft Office 365. It is also possible for an on-premises Lync 2010 deployment to provide the following features when integrated with Exchange online:

- Calendar data and out-of-office messages
- Instant Messaging (IM) and presence interoperability in Outlook Web App
- Voice mail interoperability

For more information about configuring integration with Exchange online, see the following link:

`http://blogs.technet.com/b/nexthop/archive/2011/06/28/con"guring-on-premises-lync-server-2010-integration-with-exchange-online.aspx`

The Voice Mail Platform for Lync

The most visible integration point for Lync and Exchange is the provision of voice mail. Detailed coverage of Exchange Unified Messaging (UM) would be the subject of another book; here you will review the integration with Lync so that you can provide Lync users with voice mail. The steps you will take to enable this feature are as follows:

1. Install the Exchange UM role and ensure that the correct certificates are in place.
2. Configure the Exchange UM elements of the system (Dial Plan, Policy, and Auto Attendants).
3. Ensure that Exchange knows about Lync as a gateway.
4. Confirm that Lync dial plans are configured correctly.
5. Configure Lync to utilize Exchange UM.
6. Enable users for UM.

Installing the Exchange UM Role

The following instructions assume that the Exchange UM role is installed per best practices in your Exchange organization. If you need help to get to this point, see the following documentation:

Microsoft Exchange 2010 Deployment Documentation:

`http://technet.microsoft.com/en-us/library/dd351084.aspx`

Prerequisites for the Exchange 2010 SP1 UM server:

`http://technet.microsoft.com/en-us/library/ff742307.aspx`

Once Exchange UM is installed, you need to verify that a suitable certificate is in place to secure communication between Lync and Exchange. In the documentation, you may notice a statement that a public certificate is required. This is in some ways correct but slightly ambiguous. What is needed is a certificate from a trusted Certificate Authority (CA) rather than a self-signed certificate. This could be an internal AD-based CA that both servers trust or one from a third party (Digicert, for example). The key point is that an Exchange self-signed certificate is not going to cut it!

If you need help creating, importing, and assigning the Exchange certificate, you can find the details at this URL:

`http://technet.microsoft.com/en-us/library/dd351057.aspx`

In this case, the UM server is installed on an Exchange server with all the other Exchange roles on it as well. In order not to disrupt the certificate in place for the other services on Exchange, which may need a different subject name, you will create an Exchange certificate purely with the FQDN of the server as the subject and assign it only to the UM service.

Configuring Exchange UM

Once Exchange UM is installed and configured with the relevant certificate, you can configure the UM components of Exchange for integration with Lync. The first required piece is a new UM dial plan. The UM dial plan provides Exchange with the following information:

- The number of digits that form the extension (as discussed in Chapter 13, "Getting Started with Voice,") which in this case will be four.
- The URI type, which for communication with Lync must be SIP URI.
- The level of VoIP Security required. Choose Secured, so that both the SIP signaling traffic and the media will be encrypted. If you chose SIP Secured, only the signaling traffic would be encrypted. The other option, Unsecured, simply doesn't work—and if you are planning to deploy Lync Phone Edition, Aries Phones, you must use Secured, as in this example.

To create the UM dial plan, take the following steps:

1. Open the Exchange Management Console on your Exchange UM server, and in the left pane navigate to the Organization Configuration ➢ Unified Messaging node.
2. In the right Actions pane, click New UM Dial Plan.

3. Configure the settings as described in the previous steps (or as needed for your extension system), and as shown in Figure 17.1, and then click Next.

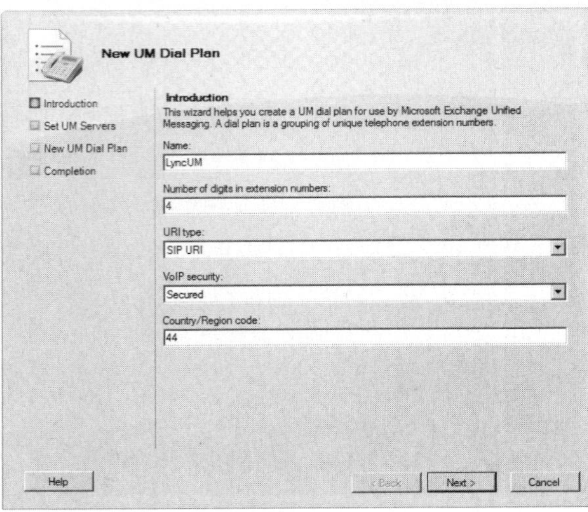

FIGURE 17.1
Configuring the Exchange UM dial plan

4. On the Set UM Servers page, click Add and select the UM servers you want to service this dial plan and then click OK and Next.
5. Review the summary information, and click New to create the dial plan.

At this point, you will have a dial plan that is assigned to the UM servers you selected. You will also have a UM Mailbox policy, named according to the dial plan; in this case, it is LyncUM Default policy. Here you configure the PIN length and other settings, as you will explore shortly.

UM STARTUP MODE

When you complete the wizard to create a new UM dial plan, you might get the following error:

```
The VoIPSecurity type of dial plan(s) 'LyncUM' does not match the UMStartupMode
of Unified Messaging server 'EXCH'. Please ensure that if the UMStartupMode of
the Unified Messaging server is TCP, the dial plan has a VoIPSecurity type of
Unsecured. If the UMStartupMode of the Unified Messaging server is TLS, the dial
plan should have a VoIPSecurity type of either SIPSecured or Secured.
```

If you get this message, it is because the server is not configured to support the security settings you set for the UM dial plan. To rectify this, use the Exchange Management Console. Navigate to the Server Configuration node and then to the Unified Messaging node. Right-click the UM server and select Properties. On the UM Settings tab, change the Startup mode to TLS and click OK. This will ensure that the server supports encrypted SIP and VoIP traffic. Also, you might have selected Dual; this would have worked, but it also would have allowed less secure nonencrypted traffic, which is not recommended. On completion, you will be warned to restart the Microsoft Exchange Unified Messaging service, which you should do.

Now that the UM service is configured and able to start securely, you should note a couple of things. First, it is worth exploring the UM Mailbox policy so that you understand the settings that are configured there. In particular, you will find that there are policies that govern the length, complexity, and age of the PIN code that is assigned to users to enable them to easily authenticate with UM via a phone device. If you are simply testing UM, you may want to ease the default of six-character complex PINs to make them simpler to remember. Obviously, if this is a production environment, you will want to make sure the required PIN is suitably secure for your organization.

Once you have made any changes to the UM Mailbox policy, you are ready to move on and configure a few other elements of UM. First, open the UM dial plan you created earlier, and on the Subscriber Access tab locate the Associated Subscriber Access Numbers section. This is where you configure the phone number that users can call to dial directly into the UM system from a telephone. It will also be the number Lync uses via a contact object you will create later in the process to route calls into the UM system. To set up a subscriber number, in the Telephone Number to Associate box enter a phone number in E.164 format—for example, **+441189091234**—and click Add and then OK. The setup will look as shown in Figure 17.2.

FIGURE 17.2
Setting up the UM Subscriber access number

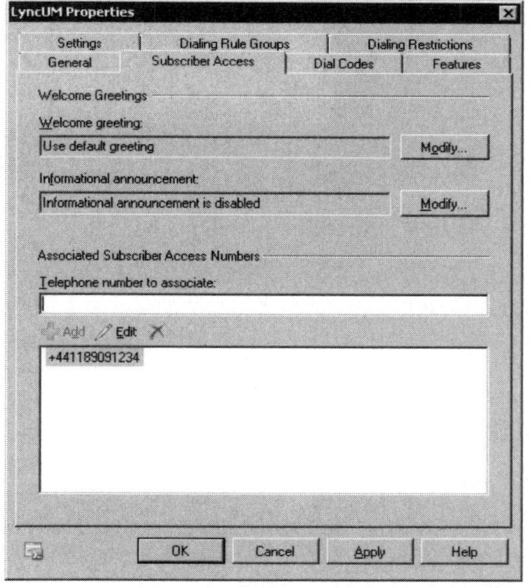

Now that you've configured the UM dial plan, the next thing you need to do is create an Auto Attendant, which is used to allow an access point for callers to be routed automatically to either a person or department. The UM Auto Attendant in Exchange is quite flexible and can be set up with personalized menus and audio recording. However, for the purpose of demonstrating Lync integration, you will simply create a basic Auto Attendant.

1. Create the Auto Attendant from the UM Auto Attendant tab by clicking New UM Auto Attendant from the right pane in the Exchange Management Console.

2. Create the Auto Attendant with a name that can be referenced, such as MainAttendant (don't use any spaces), and then make sure you assign it to the dial plan you created earlier.
3. Assign the Auto Attendant a phone number in E.164 format in the Pilot identifier list area; this will be the number that users dial to access its services.
4. Ensure that both the check boxes at the bottom of the window are checked to enable the Auto Attendant and allow it to carry out speech recognition. Finally, click New to create the Auto Attendant.

At this point, you've performed the bulk of the Exchange configuration. The next big thing to do is to introduce Exchange to Lync. This is done using a script provided with Exchange in the Exchange directory scripts folder, which when installed on the C: drive will be at `C:\Program Files\Microsoft\Exchange Server\V14\Scripts`. This script is called `ExchUCUtil.ps1` and performs the following tasks:

- Grants Lync the required permission to read Exchange UM Active Directory objects, in particular the SIP URI dial plan objects you created previously.
- Creates a UM IP gateway object for each Lync pool or for each server running Lync Standard Edition that hosts users who are enabled for Enterprise Voice.
- Creates an Exchange UM hunt group for each UM IP gateway. The hunt group pilot identifier will be the name of the dial plan associated with the corresponding UM IP gateway.

You must run this script from the Exchange Management Shell using the following command, which assumes that Exchange is installed as per default settings:

```
C:\Program Files\Microsoft\Exchange Server\V14\Scripts\ExchUCUtil.ps1
```

Once you have run the script, make sure to allow time for AD replication to occur. Once suitable time has elapsed, verify that the settings have been performed properly by running the script again, this time with a `-verify` parameter as shown here:

```
ExchUCUtil.ps1 -verify
```

This will run through and output the configuration as it stands, showing where permissions have been granted and which gateways have been created, like the following:

```
ExchUCUtil.ps1 -Verify

Using Global Catalog: GC://DC=gaots,DC=local

Configuring permissions for gaots.local\RTCUniversalServerAdmins ...
GaotsLocal: The appropriate permissions have been granted for the Office
Communications Servers and Administrators to be able to read the UM dial plan and
auto attendants container objects in Active Directory. No new permissions have
been added to the container objects.
UM DialPlan Container: The appropriate permissions have been granted for the
Office Communications Servers and Administrators to be able to read the UM
dial plan and auto attendants container objects in Active Directory. No new
permissions have been added to the container objects.
UM AutoAttendant Container: The appropriate permissions have been granted for
the Office Communications Servers and Administrators to be able to read the UM
```

```
dial plan and auto attendants container objects in Active Directory. No new
permissions have been added to the container objects.

Configuring permissions for gaots.local\RTCComponentUniversalServices ...
GaotsLocal: The appropriate permissions have been granted for the Office
Communications Servers and Administrators to be able to read the UM dial plan and
auto attendants container objects in Active Directory. No new permissions have
been added to the container objects.
UM DialPlan Container: The appropriate permissions have been granted for the
Office Communications Servers and Administrators to be able to read the UM
dial plan and auto attendants container objects in Active Directory. No new
permissions have been added to the container objects.
UM AutoAttendant Container: The appropriate permissions have been granted for
the Office Communications Servers and Administrators to be able to read the UM
dial plan and auto attendants container objects in Active Directory. No new
permissions have been added to the container objects.

Configuring UM IP Gateway objects...
Pool: lync-se01.gaots.local
A UMIPGateway already exists in Active Directory for the Office Communications
Server Pool. A new UM IP gateway wasn't created for the Pool.
IsBranchRegistrar: False
MessageWaitingIndicatorAllowed: True
OutcallsAllowed: True
WARNING: The command completed successfully but no settings of '1:1' have been
modified.
Dial plans: LyncUM

Permissions for group gaots.local\RTCUniversalServerAdmins

ObjectName                          AccessRights                    Configured
----------                          ------------                    ------
GaotsLocal                          ListChildren                      True
UM DialPlan Container               ListChildren, ReadProperty        True
UM AutoAttendant Container          ListChildren, ReadProperty        True


Permissions for group gaots.local\RTCComponentUniversalServices

ObjectName                          AccessRights                    Configured
----------                          ------------                    ------
GaotsLocal                          ListChildren                      True
UM DialPlan Container               ListChildren, ReadProperty        True
UM AutoAttendant Container          ListChildren, ReadProperty        True


PoolFqdn                            UMIPGateway                      DialPlans
--------                            -----------                      ------
lync-se01.gaots.local               1:1                              {LyncUM}
```

At this point, you're ready to move over to the Lync server and perform the configuration needed there. The Enterprise Voice is already configured and set up as shown in Chapter 13, but it is worth validating that the normalization rules on your Lync dial plans are configured to support the extension dialing configured in UM. (Remember the four-digit extension configured in the UM dial plan earlier?) You need to ensure that when someone on Lync dials the four-digit extension, Lync knows how to normalize the number to E.164 and route it correctly.

This can be validated in the Lync Server Control Panel (LSCP, or simply Control Panel). Create a new Voice Testing Routing Case and enter the last four digits of the Subscriber Access number (**1234**) in the Dialed Number to Test box. In the Expected Translation box, enter the full E.164 subscriber access number (**+441189091234**) and then run the test. If it passes, you are ready to move on. If not, go back to Chapter 13 and configure the relevant dial plan settings to cope with 4-digit dialing.

Assuming your system is set up to pass the routing test, you can move on and introduce Lync to Exchange so that it knows where to route calls that need to go to voice mail. This is done using a utility called `OcsUmUtil.exe` (yes, that should be OCS; the name hasn't changed for a while!). You can find this utility in the `C:\Program Files\Common Files\Microsoft Lync Server 2010\Support\` directory. It is used to create the contact objects in AD that Lync will use to call into Exchange UM and the Exchange Auto Attendant.

When you run the utility, you will see the window shown in Figure 17.3.

1. From the drop-down, select the relevant AD forest and then click Load Data to search the AD forest for UM dial plans.

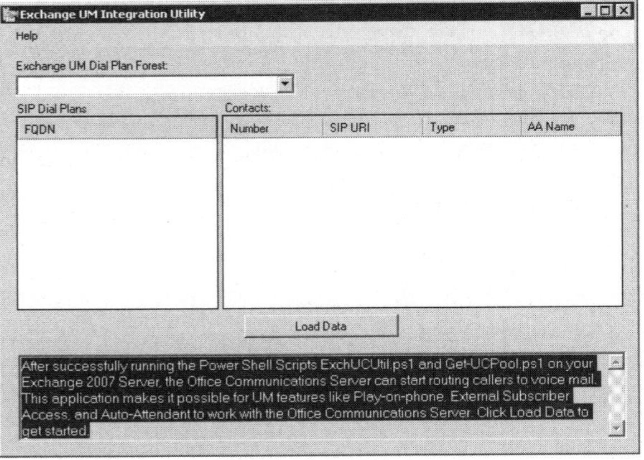

FIGURE 17.3
The OcsUmUtil opening screen

2. Once the data load has completed, you will see the dial plan on the left. Click Add to start the process of creating the Subscriber Access contact.

3. In the window that opens, select the required organizational unit (OU) in which to create the object and the name the contact. The name should be recognizable rather than something cryptic. The default settings can be used for the rest of the window. To complete the process, click OK to exit to the original window.

4. Click Add again to create a second contact, this time for the UM Auto Attendant. This time select Auto-Attendant as the contact type and then select the required OU. Give the contact a name, and then again opt for the default settings and click OK to complete.
5. Once you have created the contact objects, close the OcsUmUtil.

Now you can either wait for the Lync Address Book to update or force it, using the process described at the following URL:

`http://blog.schertz.name/2010/09/updating-the-lync-2010-address-book/`

At this point, you are ready to enable some users for Exchange UM. They should be users who are already configured for Lync Enterprise Voice as you set it up in Chapter 13. Enabling a user for UM is a simple process carried out either in the Exchange Management Console (EMC) or in Exchange Management Shell. For the first user, you'll perform the configuration using the EMC.

1. Open EMC and navigate to the Recipient Configuration ➤ Mailbox section. Locate and select the user you want to enable, in this case Test User1. In the right Actions pane, click Enable Unified Messaging.
2. In the Introduction window that opens, you will be able to select the UM Mailbox policy you configured earlier. You'll be able to indicate whether the PIN should be automatically created or you will enter one manually, as shown in Figure 17.4.

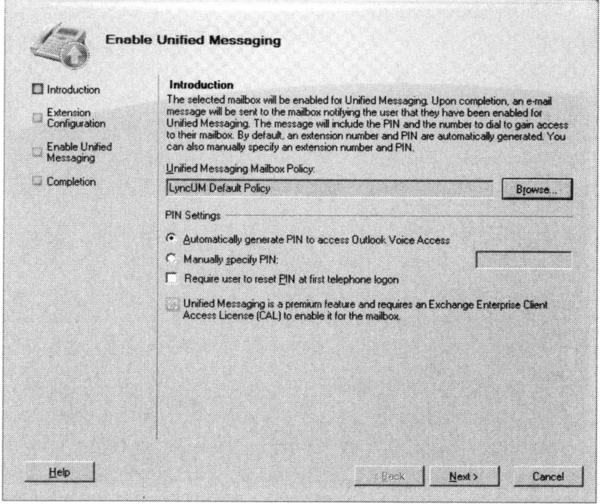

FIGURE 17.4
Selecting the UM Mailbox policy for the new UM user

3. Click Next to progress to the Extension Configuration window, where you should find that Exchange has picked up the user's telephone number and used the last four digits as specified in the UM dial plan for the extension number. You should also find that Exchange has picked up the user's Lync SIP URI and populated it in the Automatically Generated SIP Resource Identifier section.
4. Complete the wizard, and the user will be set up for UM. The user will receive a welcome email giving them a subscriber number and PIN.

If you prefer the command line, use the following command:

```
Enable-UMMailbox -Identity "Test user1" -PinExpired $false -UMMailboxPolicy
'LyncUM Default Policy' -Extensions 3333 -SIPResourceIdentifier "testuser1@gaots.
co.uk"
```

This command will enable Test User1 for UM as in the previous GUI.

Dial Plan Naming with Exchange Versions Before Exchange 2010 SP1

When working with either Exchange 2010 RTM or any flavor of Exchange 2007, you will need to ensure that you match up your dial plan names from Exchange UM and Lync, as described in the article here:

```
http://technet.microsoft.com/en-us/library/bb803622(of"ce.12).aspx
```

You will see this requirement reflected in OcsUmUtil, as the subscriber contact will show a warning red exclamation mark for any mismatch. Text in the lower pane explains the issue. When working with Exchange 2010 SP1, you can ignore the error.

At this point, you have completed the setup of UM integration with Lync. From a Lync client logged in as the user you enabled for UM, you should now see the Call Voice mail options and be able to dial into voice mail to set up your UM Mailbox with a greeting. One final thing to note is that there are additional elements that can be configured to provide an even richer voice mail solution. The primary piece of functionality here is Play on Phone, which means that instead of listening to a voice mail on your PC speakers, you can reroute it to play over a phone device. This feature is completely configured in Exchange, so if you are interested in learning more about it, you should take a look at the following link:

```
http://blogs.technet.com/b/roocs/archive/2010/12/24/exchange-um-play-on-phone-
tipps-and-tricks.aspx
```

Contacts, Free/Busy, and Other Integration

Besides the obvious element of integration just discussed in the UM section, Lync touches Exchange in a variety of other more subtle, but extremely useful ways. Like other programs that require access to Exchange data, Lync now predominantly utilizes Exchange Web Service calls to get that information. The types of information returned to Lync in this way are outlined here:

Access to Conversation History and Voice Mail Lync uses the Exchange mailbox for voice mail as previously described; however, when configured to do so, it also creates and uses the Conversation History folder in the user's Exchange mailbox. This allows a user to maintain a store of historical IM conversations, which is then searchable through normal Outlook methods. In Lync 2010, this conversation history also bubbles up into the Lync interface (the third tab in the main client) to provide information about all previous communication through Lync, including conference calls, phone calls, and of course IMs. This process of saving the conversation detail relies on the conversation window being open long enough for the conversation to be picked up and saved. It is not a server-side process; the client must perform the operation, so if the window is closed too quickly, the information is never saved.

Creation of Missed Call Notifications Through integration with Exchange UM, users will be notified in their inboxes when they miss a voice or IM conversation.

Play Back of Voice Mail Message Again through integration with Exchange UM, the Lync client can be used to play back voice mail messages through the fourth tab in the main client. These can also be accessed through Exchange directly with Outlook or OWA or by dialing into the UM server with a standard phone.

Display Free/Busy Information and Working Hours for a User As part of enhanced presence, Lync makes calls to Exchange to evaluate the logged-on user's calendar information, such as working hours, general availability and Out of Office status. Lync then publishes this information as part of the user's presence, which others can then query. Note that publishing is not triggered by someone querying a user's presence, because a Lync user cannot access another user's calendar information directly. Instead, each user publishes the information about themselves in their presence.

Display a Meeting Subject, Time, and Location Like the previous item, this is part of enhanced presence.

Display User's Out of Office Status and Note Like the previous two items, this is part of enhanced presence. Lync shows the OOF message as the user's Lync note, and publishes the information in the Lync activity feed for others who have subscribed to that user's presence.

Carry Out Exchange Contact Sync When Lync is integrated with Exchange 2010, it attempts to maintain a unified Contact Store. Each contact that is added to the Lync buddy list is also created as a personal contact in Outlook. Also, where duplicates exist an attempt is made to integrate them. This is not always 100 percent successful, so it is worth understanding a little more about the process, which is outlined in Figure 17.5.

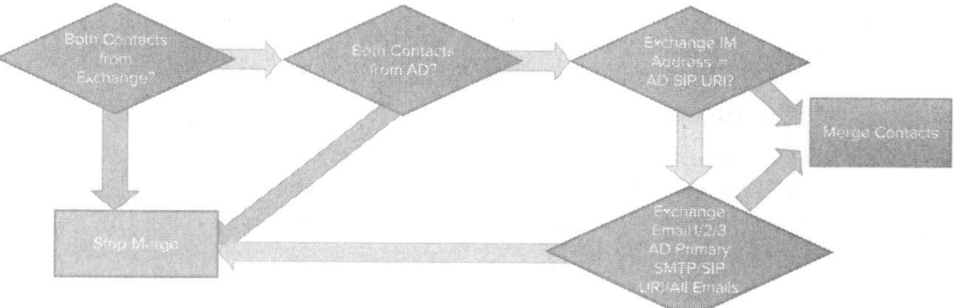

FIGURE 17.5
The Exchange Contact Sync process flow chart

The first thing you need to understand is that only contacts that are in both AD and in the Exchange (Outlook) personal contacts folder for a user can be merged. When both contacts located are in AD, those contacts are not merged because they will always be unique or they couldn't exist in AD. This is also true when both contacts are in Exchange, so they won't be merged either.

Once you understand this, then as long as the contacts are still applicable for an attempt to merge, the following fields are analyzed. For different fields, different contact locations take priority as information is taken forward to the synchronized contact:

- For the Title, Company, Department, Office, Org (e.g., Manager), Web Page (e.g., My Site), and Alias (mail nickname), the priority is given to AD, then to Lync, and then to Outlook contacts.
- For phone numbers (Work, Home, Mobile, Other), Location, Calendar Free/Busy, Presence, and IM Address (SIP URI), priority is given to Lync, then to AD, and then Outlook.
- The Display Name is taken from Outlook first, then Lync, and finally AD.
- Finally, the email address (based around the Primary Simple Mail Transfer Protocol [SMTP] Address) is referenced from Outlook, then AD, and finally Lync.

Assuming the process finds a suitable match, the new contact object with combined information is created in the Outlook contacts folder.

Search Outlook Personal Contacts for Name Lookup When you search for a user in Lync, or search the Global Address List (GAL), Lync will also search through your personal contacts in Outlook. And thanks to the Outlook social connector, it will be able to search contacts from many common social networks, such as Facebook and LinkedIn.

Where needed and/or available, Lync can fall back to using MAPI requests. More specific information about the interfaces used to access each type of data is available in the following TechNet article:

`http://technet.microsoft.com/en-us/library/gg398806.aspx`

Other areas of integration are predominantly governed by the Outlook version in use. Examples of this include the new contact card that is shown in Office 2010 and the ability to see your buddy list in the bottom-right corner of the Outlook 2010 window.

Outlook Web Access (OWA) Integration

The final piece of Exchange integration is that of providing access to Lync IM and buddy lists in OWA. This is particularly useful because in Lync there is no Communicator Web Access (CWA) server, which was used in OCS to provide IM and Presence functionality through a web browser.

The configuration required is relatively straightforward and consists of the following major steps:

- Prepare the Exchange environment with prerequisites.
- Configure required settings on the Exchange client access server.
- Ensure that Lync trusts the Exchange server.
- Test functionality as an end user.

PREREQUISITES

A handful of prerequisites must be installed on the Exchange client access servers. If you have more than one client access server, all of the servers will need these prerequisites.

First, download the Microsoft Office Communications Server 2007 R2 Web Service Provider, which contains the components you'll need to enable the basic IM and presence integration with OWA. This element can be downloaded from the following URL:

`www.microsoft.com/download/en/details.aspx?displaylang=en&id=2310`

On the download page, you may notice that, as with some of the other integration components mentioned so far in this chapter, the name refers to OCS. This is fine for use with Lync too. Another thing you may notice is that it doesn't mention support for Server 2008 R2; again, this is not a problem.

Once you have downloaded the `CWAOWASSPMain.msi` file, run it. Step through the wizard, accepting the license, and then choose a location where the installer should install to the files. Generally, something on the `C:` drive works—for example, `C:\Web Service Provider Installer Package`, which is the default. Click through the rest of the wizard and then navigate to the directory you just entered.

Once you have located the installed files in Explorer, double-click the `vcredist_x64.exe` file to install it. This will install the Visual C++ 2008 Redistributable package. Again, click through the Installation Wizard, accepting the license agreement. (If you have already installed the UM role on this Exchange server, this component will already be installed.)

At this point, it is worth outlining the system used for the following exercises. As with the other elements of integration, there is a single Exchange server with all the roles installed. Some setup elements (including the installation of the `vcredist_x64.exe` file) will differ if you have an Exchange system where the roles are broken out. These differences will be pointed out as necessary throughout the process. Again, note that if UM is installed on this server, then UCMA will already be installed.

The next component required is the Unified Communications Managed API 2.0 Redistributable, which is found in the same directory where you installed the previous files. Double-click the `UCMARedist.msi` file to kick off the installation. The installation is *silent* and doesn't indicate when it finishes! Give it a couple of minutes and then move on to the next component, which is a patch for the UCMA. The Unified Communications Managed API 2.0 Redist (64 Bit) Hotfix KB 2501720 can be downloaded here:

`www.microsoft.com/download/en/details.aspx?id=7557`

This component provides the latest updates for UCMA, which is the API used by OWA to talk to Lync and must be at version 6907.225 or later.

Now you can move on to install the web components, which are found in the original installation folder (`C:\Web Service Provider Installer Package`). Locate the `CWAOWASSP.msi` file and double-click it. This will launch the install, which again is silent.

To verify that the required software was installed, open up Control Panel and click Programs ➤ Programs and Features. In the Programs and Features window, locate the Microsoft Office Communications Server 2007 R2, Web Service, as shown in Figure 17.6.

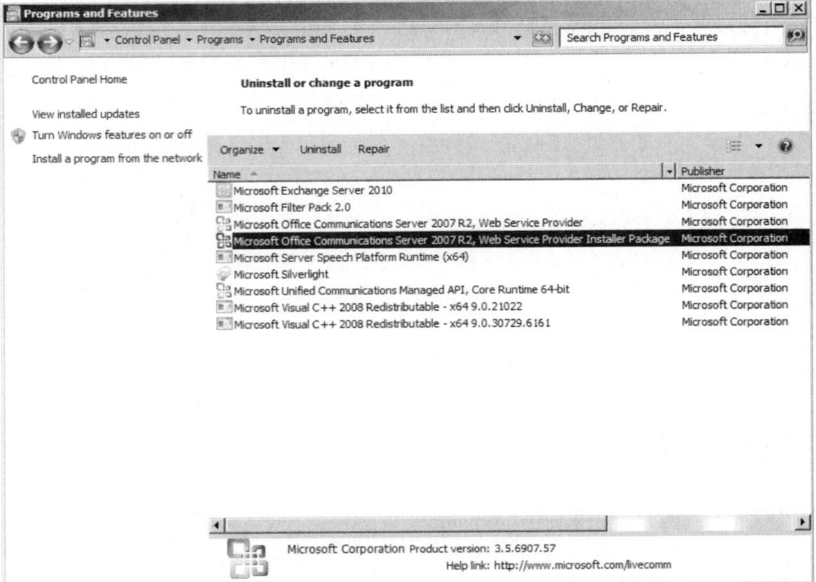

FIGURE 17.6 Checking that the web components are installed correctly

As mentioned earlier, if you click the View Installed Updates link on the Programs and Features window, you can check the installed version of the UCMA patch.

The next prerequisite is a patch for the CWAOCSSSP install. This patch can be downloaded from the following location:

```
www.microsoft.com/download/en/details.aspx?id=797
```

Once it is downloaded, install the patch. The installation is silent, so on the View Installed Updates section of the Programs and Features Control Panel, make sure that the Microsoft Office Communications Server 2007 R2 Web Service is shown as version 3.5.6907.202 or later.

Now that you've installed the prerequisites, you can configure the Exchange client access server to connect to Lync.

Configuring Exchange

For Exchange to utilize the IM and presence features of Lync, the first thing that is needed is to configure the OWA virtual directory as enabled for IM integration, to point to a specific Lync server, and to use a specific certificate for secure communication. To gather the needed information to carry out the configuration, first locate the relevant certificate using the following command:

```
Get-ExchangeCertificate | Where-Object [$_.Services -Like "*IIS*"} | Select-
Object Subject, Services, Thumbprint | Format-List
```

This command gathers all the Exchange certificates that are enabled for the IIS service and outputs the Subject, Services, and Thumbprint in a formatted list:

```
Subject     : CN=maillocal.gaots.co.uk, OU=ICT, O=Gaots, L=Croydon, S=Surrey, C=GB
Services    : IMAP, POP, IIS, SMTP
Thumbprint  : B155DE84F846DAB11762EC742F825DD8A31649F5
```

At this point, make a note of the Thumbprint and move on.

Once you have the Thumbprint, you must get the OWA virtual directory you want to configure. To do this, run the following command:

```
Get-OwaVirtualDirectory
```

This will generate a list of all OWA virtual directories, which in this environment will be the one default instance:

```
Name                       Server                     OwaVersion
----                       ------                     ----------
owa (Default Web Site)       EXCH                       Exchange2010
```

See the sidebar discussion for more information on working with multiple Exchange servers.

Assuming you have only the single virtual directory to work with, progress to the next stage, which is to enable the virtual directory for IM integration.

WORKING WITH MULTIPLE EXCHANGE SERVERS

Exchange client access is a complex subject. You could have multiple Client Access Servers (CASs), each serving a different domain. If you follow best practices, you should use the same certificate for each of your client access servers and simply export and import it to get it to a new CAS. If this is the case, the Thumbprint will remain the same even for multiple servers.

Equally, you may find that several OWA virtual directories are located when you perform `Get-OWAVirtualDirectory`. In this case, assuming they all use the same certificate, you can progress with the commands discussed in the main text to configure integration. If you want to be more specific and only work on a single virtual directory, then instead of piping the output of `Get-OwaVirtualDirectory` to the `Set-OwaVirtualDirectory` cmdlet, don't run the `Get-OwaVirtualDirectory` cmdlet and simply use the `-Identity` parameter on the `Set-OwaVirtualDirectory`.

IM integration is configured for the virtual directory using this command:

```
Get-OwaVirtualDirectory | Set-OwaVirtualDirectory -InstantMessagingType
OCS -InstantMessagingEnabled:$true -InstantMessagingCertificateThumbprint
B155DE84F846DAB11762EC742F825DD8A31649F5 -InstantMessagingServerName LyncSe01
.gaots.local
```

This will get all the OWA virtual directories, set them for OCS IM, and enable IM. It will specify the certificate to use and the Lync server with which to talk. When the command is run, there will be no output unless it errors. At this point, you must reset IIS on all servers hosting an

OWA virtual directory you have configured. If the server is in production, make sure you use the `/noforce` switch:

```
IISRESET /noforce
```

Congratulations! You have completed the Exchange configuration.

CONFIGURING LYNC

You can begin the process of ensuring that Lync trusts the Exchange client access server so that traffic can flow and presence will light up in OWA. The first stage is to create a Trusted application pool. Take the following steps:

1. Log onto the Lync server as an administrator and open the Topology Builder.
2. Download the topology, navigate to the Trusted application servers node, right-click it, and select New Trusted Application Pool.
3. In the Define The Trusted Applications Pool FQDN window that opens, enter the name of the Exchange client access server (**exch.gaots.local**, for the example), select Single Computer Pool, as shown in Figure 17.7, and then click Next.

   If you were to have multiple CA servers in an array, you would use the FQDN of the Exchange CAS Array object and select Multiple Computer Pool.
4. In the Select The Next Hop window, make sure that `Lync-Se01.gaots.local` is selected (or your own front-end pool) and click Finish.

Now you should publish the topology and then check to see whether the updates were successful.

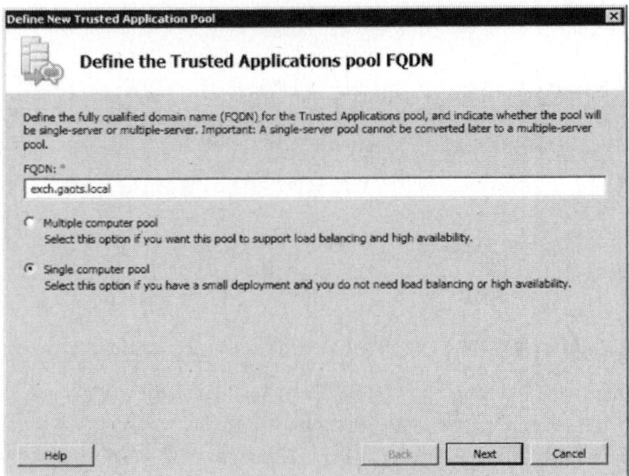

FIGURE 17.7 Configuring the FQDN for the Trusted application pool

To check that the settings applied correctly, open the Lync Management Shell and run the `Get-CsTrustedApplicationPool` command.

This will generate the following output:

```
Identity              : TrustedApplicationPool:exch.gaots.local
Registrar             : Registrar:lync-se01.gaots.local
FileStore             :
ThrottleAsServer      : True
TreatAsAuthenticated  : True
OutboundOnly          : False
RequiresReplication   : True
AudioPortStart        :
AudioPortCount        : 0
AppSharingPortStart   :
AppSharingPortCount   : 0
VideoPortStart        :
VideoPortCount        : 0
Applications          : {}
DependentServiceList  : {}
ServiceId             : 1-ExternalServer-4
SiteId                : Site:EMEA
PoolFqdn              : exch.gaots.local
Version               : 5
Role                  : TrustedApplicationPool
```

Also run the `Get-CsTrustedApplicationComputer` cmdlet to verify that you see the server FQDN you used during the creation of the Trusted application pool, as shown here:

```
Get-CsTrustedApplicationComputer
Identity : exch.gaots.local
Pool     : exch.gaots.local
Fqdn     : exch.gaots.local
```

You should be operational if your CA server also has the UM role and the UM server is configured to integrate via a SIP URI dial plan with Lync. If UM is not installed on the CAs server or is not set up as previously discussed, then you must create a Trusted application as indicated in the "If Your CAS Is Not Also Your Lync UM Server" sidebar.

If Your CAS Is Not Also Your Lync UM Server

For the examples in this chapter, the Exchange roles are all on a single server. If your CA server and UM server are not on the same box, or the UM server is not servicing Lync, then you have an additional step to take. Instead of simply creating the Trusted application pool as described in the text, you also have to create a trusted application. This is because when UM is installed, the communication required for UM already enables trust of this server; however, when only the CAS role is installed, you need to manually create that trust.

To create the trusted application, use the `New-CsTrustedApplication` cmdlet. The first thing you'll need for the application is a port on which Lync will listen. This can be any port that is not in use. We selected 5050 because it is similar to other Lync ports.

(Continued)

It is critical that nothing else use the port; to verify that, open up a Windows cmd.exe prompt as an administrator and run Netstat as follows:

```
Netstat -a | findstr 5050
```

The following output shows what it would look like if a conflict occurs because we selected a port (5070) that Lync listens on:

```
netstat -a | findstr 5070
  TCP    192.168.1.194:5070      Lync-SE01:0            LISTENING
```

When Netstat is run on the correct port, you won't see any output because there won't be any conflicts to show.

Once a suitable port is chosen, set up the trusted application as follows:

```
New-CsTrustedApplication -ApplicationId Exchange2010OWA
-TrustedApplicationPoolFqdn exch.gaots.local -Port 5050
```

This command will create an application pool with the Exchange2010OWA in the Trusted application pool set up earlier on port 5050. The ApplicationID can be any unique string, but it makes sense to use a recognizable naming convention.

When it is run, you will see the following output:

```
WARNING: The following changes must be made in order for the operation to be
complete.
Enable-CsTopology must still be run for all changes to take effect.
Identity                     : exch.gaots.local/urn:application:exchange2010owa
ComputerGruus                : {exch.gaots.local sip:exch.gaots.local@gaots.co.uk
                               ;gruu;opaque=srvr:exchange2010owa:y-
                               kadlJiL1i01PFHQWV2UQAA}
ServiceGruu                  : sip:exch.gaots.local@gaots.co.uk;gruu;opaque=srvr:
                               exchange2010owa:y-kadlJiL1i01PFHQWV2UQAA
Protocol                     : Mtls
ApplicationId                : urn:application:exchange2010owa
TrustedApplicationPoolFqdn : exch.gaots.local
Port                         : 5050
LegacyApplicationName        : exchange2010owa
```

Now all that remains is to run the `Enable-CsTopology` cmdlet as instructed, and OWA IM integration should be complete and presence will light up in OWA.

Integrating Lync with SharePoint

SharePoint 2010 is a business collaboration platform for the enterprise. SharePoint allows the creation of web portals (intranets, extranets, and websites) as a way to centralize information and applications on a corporate network. Organizations use SharePoint to connect and empower users and facilitate collaboration amongst them.

Lync 2010 and SharePoint 2010 can be integrated to give users a rich in-context collaboration experience whether SharePoint is deployed on premises or as part of Office 365 in the cloud. Lync builds on what was provided in Office Communications Server 2007 and R2, which gave users the ability to access the instant messaging (IM), enhanced presence, telephony, and the conferencing capabilities of Office Communicator from SharePoint. This basic communication functionality integration requires no complicated configuration for SharePoint or Lync Server. In this section, you will explore the available functionality and learn how to integrate Lync and SharePoint both at a simple level and in more complex scenarios. Note that as with the Exchange section, you won't learn how to configure SharePoint. You'll simply be introduced to what is needed and any Lync-specific configuration; for the other elements, you will need to see existing SharePoint documentation or your SharePoint team.

IM Presence within Sites

Lync enables presence in SharePoint sites using the same presence indicator that is displayed in the Lync 2010 client, as shown in Figure 17.8. SharePoint users can view another user's presence (based on the presence status set in their Lync client), which is displayed next to their name within a SharePoint site. They can initiate Lync communications with that user, such as sending an IM or starting a Lync audio call, so collaboration is easy and intuitive. Presence is enabled by default in SharePoint, so there is no need for any special configuration on the server side for this to work.

FIGURE 17.8
A SharePoint site showing presence indicators

A user must have Office 2003 or Office 2007 with the latest Service Pack, or Office 2010 RTM or later to view presence in SharePoint sites. This is because when Office is installed, a dynamic link library called `name.dll` is installed. It can be found at `%Program Files%\Microsoft Office\Office14` when Office 2010 is installed (lower-numbered versions refer to earlier Office versions). This `.dll` file is an ActiveX control that allows SharePoint to display a user's presence information. The ActiveX control actually leverages the Lync API to request the user's presence status so that it can be displayed within a SharePoint site. The required Lync API is installed automatically as a part of the Lync client installation. Note that when the Firefox browser is used, presence integration is not available.

Skill Search

SharePoint Search helps users in an organization find the information they need to help them in their everyday work. It provides a way to search the intranet for both content and people and to refine results by relevance. For example, you know there is a new employee named John in Finance. To find John, you could search for John in a SharePoint Search Center People search site, and all the results with John would be returned. You could further refine that search to find John in Finance. Skill Search in Lync allows you to use the search term "John Finance" and get those filtered results immediately.

People Search requires that the following service applications be available:

- Search Service application (which is explained in the following text)
- User Profile Service application, which is a shared application within SharePoint 2010 used to manage user profiles in an organization, synchronize profiles with Active Directory, and create My Sites for users
- Managed Metadata, which is used if you want to configure People Search and allow Search using a custom metadata property that is being populated into the user profiles from an external system such as a SQL or Oracle business system

People Search also requires that a Search Center site be created using the Enterprise Search Center template.

In SharePoint 2010, Search is a service application. Service applications allow more granularity and control over how Search works so that users can have a specific site collection that is associated with a specific service application. This means multiple indexes can be maintained, keeping information in separate indexes.

SharePoint 2010 Search can index all sorts of source content such as file shares, external websites (a partner's website, for example), SharePoint websites, Exchange public folders, databases, and a line of business applications (Oracle or SQL databases, product data, or customer data). This new architecture gives the user an experience that is highly efficient, effective, and personal.

With Lync 2010 and SharePoint 2010 (or SharePoint 2007) integration, one exciting and useful new feature compared to OCS 2007 or 2007 R2 is the ability to perform a skill-based search within the Lync client. For example, if you need to find a Lync expert within your organization but you don't know exactly who or what kind of expert you need, you can simply type a keyword such as **Lync** into the search bar and then click the Skill button. The client will then display anyone with Lync in their job title or listed in the profile stored in their My Site on SharePoint.

What Is My Site?

SharePoint's My Site feature provides a personal site that gives users in your organization a central location not only to store documents, links, and contacts, but also populate and keep up-to-date with appropriate information about themselves. For example, users can list their skills, which can then appear as a result in other users' searches.

Once the results are returned, you can browse through them and find someone appropriate for what you need to know and send them a quick IM with your question. Because these results come from the SharePoint skill-search component, you can add a link that opens the search results in SharePoint; you can add this at the bottom of the Lync search-results window, as shown in Figure 17.9.

FIGURE 17.9
The Lync client displays the results of Skill Search and View Results in a SharePoint link

Skill Search is not enabled in Lync by default. For this new feature to work correctly, the following components are required:

- **A full version of SharePoint:** Windows SharePoint Services (WSS) will not work with Skills Search.
- **SharePoint 2010 My Sites:** A My Site is a personal site that gives you a central location to manage and store your documents, content, links, and contacts and lets other see information about you.
- **The SharePoint User Profile service application:** This stores information about users in a central location and is where user My Sites are administered and configured.
- **A SharePoint Search Center site URL:** This is a feature introduced in Microsoft Office SharePoint Server 2007; it is a SharePoint site specifically configured for the search task. It includes certain fields, each responsible for a specific search task—for example, "people search."

In addition, you need to configure the following:

- SharePoint must be published to the Internet, so external Lync clients can access it.
- Lync Server needs to be configured with the correct Search Center URL to provide to clients. The Search Center URL is provisioned to the Lync client through in-band settings as part of the CsClientPolicy, a topic discussed in Chapter 10, "User Administration."

Lync needs to be configured to provide the relevant URLs to clients. These are the URLs of the SharePoint Search Center described in the list, which your SharePoint administrator should be able to give you. To provide this information, a client policy must be configured and applied so that the Lync clients are configured to use relevant SharePoint search URLs. To configure the client policy, you would run the following commands from the Lync Server Management Shell (LSMS):

```
Set-CsClientPolicy -SPSearchInternalURL https://<server>/_vti_bin/search.asmx
Set-CsClientPolicy -SPSearchExternalURL https://<server>/_vti_bin/search.asmx
```

With these commands, you set not only an internal URL but also an external URL so that remote users (not connected to the internal LAN) can access the Skills Search feature. If you do not specify an external URL, then upon clicking Search, users working remotely will receive an error message telling them they won't be able to search, as shown in Figure 17.10. In order to provide external access to search, the SharePoint website must be made available to users working externally.

FIGURE 17.10
The error presented to users externally if the SPSearchExternalURL is not configured

SCOPING OF POLICY

The Set-CsClientPolicy commands just discussed work on the default user policies, which are set at the global level. To target specific users or sites, review Chapter 10, which covers client policies. The policy defined in Chapter 17 will be applied to all users.

As previously mentioned and shown in Figure 17.9, there is also the option to display a link to the Search Center, entitled "Display results in SharePoint," at the bottom of the Lync client once the search has finished. The user can click this link to see the results of the search displayed in a SharePoint web page. To enable this functionality. execute the following commands in the LSMS:

```
Set-CsClientPolicy -SPSearchCenterInternalURL https://<server>/SearchCenter/
Pages/PeopleResults.aspx
Set-CsClientPolicy -SPSearchCenterExternalURL https://<server>/SearchCenter/
Pages/PeopleResults.aspx
```

Once the in-band provisioning takes effect, you will be able to conduct a Skills Search through your Lync client.

1. In the search bar, type a keyword. You will be presented with the options Name and Skill.
2. Click on Skill.

The query is sent to SharePoint, and the results are sent back to the Lync client. You can click the View Results In SharePoint link to see the search results in a SharePoint web page, as shown in Figure 17.11.

FIGURE 17.11
The People Search site in SharePoint accessed via the Lync client

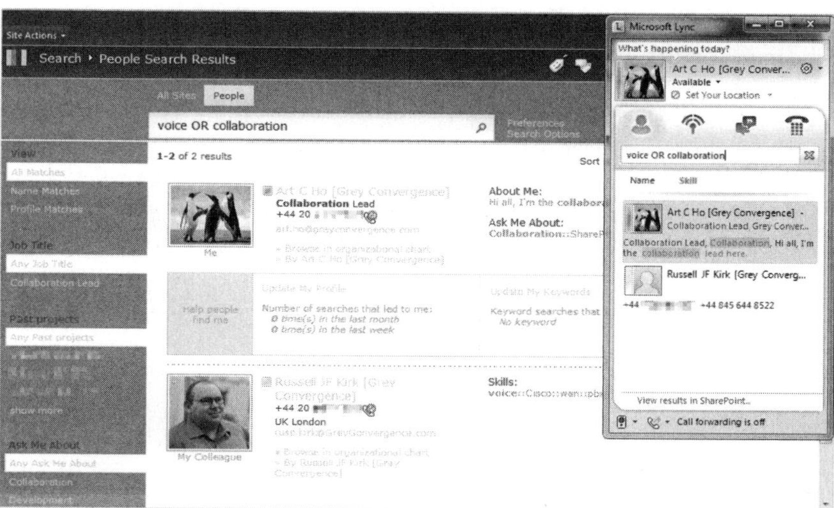

To see which URLs have been provisioned, you can use the Lync client Configuration Information tool. While holding down the Ctrl button, right-click on the Lync icon in the system tray and click Configuration Information to display the window shown in Figure 17.12. The SharePoint URLs can be seen in the Configuration Information table. This area is a handy troubleshooting tool for many Lync client configuration issues.

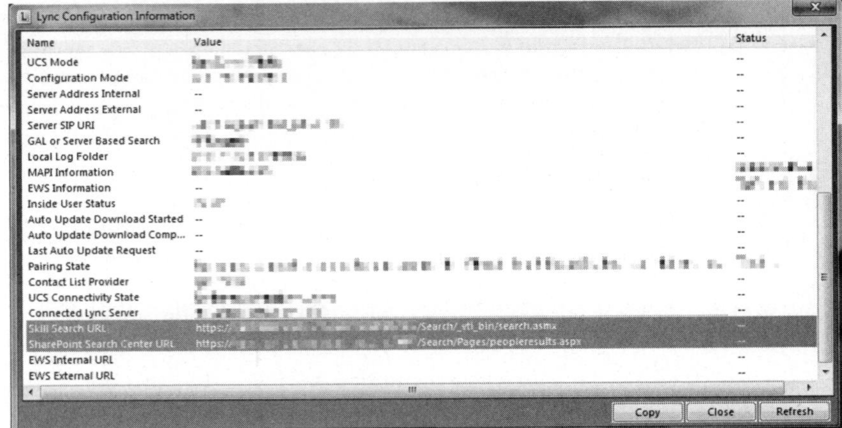

FIGURE 17.12
The Configuration Information window can be used to troubleshoot client issues

Photos

Another new feature in the Lync client that immediately stands out is its ability to display photos. Having the ability to view another person's picture is very useful in large organizations that may have many employees with the same name, or in situations where you have "met" someone on Lync and you arrange to meet face to face, a picture makes it much easier to identify them.

The photos come from either a basic web URL or from AD. They get into AD in a couple of ways. One way is to use the Exchange Management Shell cmdlet `Import-RecipientDataProperty`, but more relevantly for this section, the other way is from a SharePoint user's My Site via Active Directory integration. As with Skill Search functionality, certain components need to be set up first in order for photos to be displayed in the Lync client from SharePoint:

- SharePoint User Profile Service application and My Sites need to be set up and configured. Users must upload a photo to their My Site web page. To set up the User Profile service application, see this link:

`http://technet.microsoft.com/en-us/library/ee662538.aspx`

- SharePoint AD needs to be synchronized. SharePoint must be configured to replicate pictures from the user profile to AD. A photo is loaded through this process into the attribute named `thumbnailPhoto` on a user object within AD. Lync uses the attribute to access photos for contacts. To set up AD synchronization, follow the instructions in this link:

`http://technet.microsoft.com/en-us/library/ee721049.aspx`

- A Lync client policy must be configured. If your organization allows pictures in Lync, you can provide users with a link from within the Lync client that allows them to change their default corporate picture on their SharePoint 2010 My Site. The link can be found in the My Picture options (accessed by clicking on the photo in the Lync client), which allows the user to configure their picture without opening their My Site, instead allowing them to do it straight from the Lync client.

Once all of these components are set up and functioning correctly, a Lync client will receive pictures through in-band policies. The first two bullets cover SharePoint configuration, but the final bullet is on the Lync side. The required client policies are configured by using the `Set-CsClientPolicy` cmdlet.

The link to change the photo on My Site is not enabled by default. To add or remove it, use the following command to edit the existing global CsClientPolicy:

```
Set-CsClientPolicy -ShowSharepointPhotoEditLink $true
```

Users will be able to change their My Site picture directly through the Lync client.

One important parameter is the picture size. By default, the Lync client policy maximum size setting for pictures is 30KB, whereas in AD it is up to 40KB. To enable clients to have pictures up to 40KB, you can modify the client policy using the following command:

```
Set-CsClientPolicy -MaxPhotoSizeKb 40
```

This command will set the Lync client policy to allow photos up to 40KB in size.

Of course, you may simply decide not to allow the use of photos in Lync. To do that, you must use the `Set-CsClientPolicy` cmdlet, specifically the `DisplayPhoto` parameter. The following example uses the `PhotosFromAdOnly` setting, which specifies that only the pictures uploaded to AD from SharePoint can be shown in the Lync client. This enables the maintenance of an element of control across the organization rather than allowing linking from any website.

```
Set-CsClient -DisplayPhoto PhotosFromAdOnly
```

Once you have configured pictures, signing out and then back into Lync ensures that the client performs an Address Book web services query to the Lync server rather than possibly using cached values. Once the photo has been returned to the client, it caches it locally for 24 hours to prevent the client from unnecessarily downloading a photo it has already downloaded. After 24 hours, the client will send another query, and if the photo has changed in the SharePoint My Site and been synchronized to AD it will receive and display it.

Activity Feed and My Sites

The Activity feed in the My Site for SharePoint 2010 is a social tagging area (new in SharePoint 2010), where you can see what your colleagues are posting, if you have chosen to "follow" them. Social tagging is configured in the SharePoint User Profile service application. User social tags and notes are stored in the social tagging database, which is configured in the profile application from your SharePoint 2010 server. To create and configure the social tagging database, you will need to edit the User Profile Service application. To do this, take the following steps:

1. Go to the SharePoint 2010 Application Management section in the Central Administration website and click on Manage Service Applications.
2. In the Type column, click User Profile Service Application ➢ Properties.
3. In the resulting Edit User Profile Service Application dialog box, go to the Social Tagging Database section. In the Database Server box, enter the name of the database server where the social tagging database will be located. For the Database Name, enter the name of the database where social tags will be stored.
4. In the Social Tagging Database section, select Windows Authentication for the Database authentication option, to use Integrated Windows Authentication to connect to the social tagging database.

Lync Server also integrates out of the box with activity feeds so that you can not only see user updates and tags from your My Site, but also see a user's presence within the SharePoint Activity feed, as shown in Figure 17.13. You can also interact with them by sending an IM or initiating a Lync call, for example.

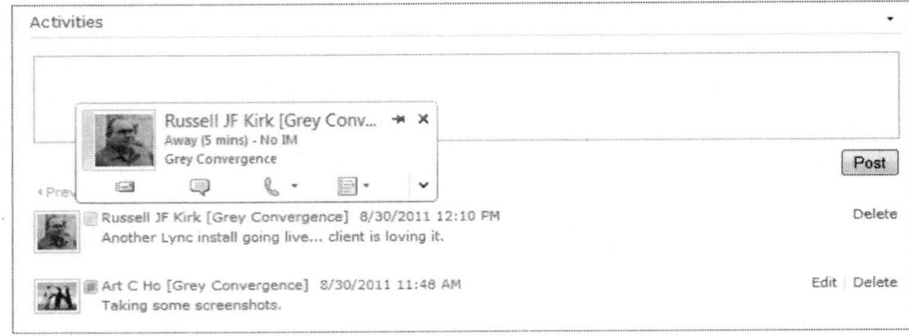

FIGURE 17.13 The SharePoint activity feed showing presence integration

By leveraging the social capabilities of SharePoint, Lync users can take full advantage of Activity Feeds and connect instantly with their colleagues.

Converting Recorded Meetings into SP Asset Libraries

Now that Lync has integrated conferencing capabilities, one new capability is to record meetings. Although these sound files can be saved to an individual's desktop machine, there is often huge benefit in sharing content, perhaps for training or catch-up purposes. With SharePoint integration, you can save and publish recorded Lync meetings to SharePoint asset libraries; this lets you quickly and efficiently share meeting content from one location with minimal effort. An organization can maintain and manage meeting recordings like other digital assets, for example, by setting retention periods on them.

To use this feature, you need to record a meeting in Lync. This can be done by simply selecting Start Recording from the menu shown in Figure 17.14.

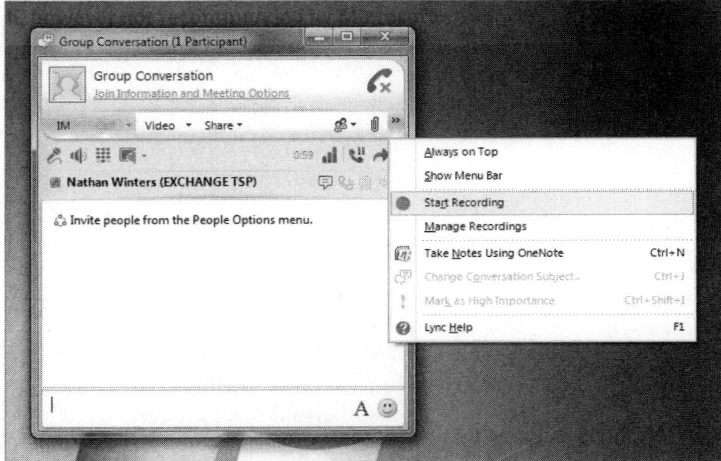

FIGURE 17.14 Record a meeting in the Lync client

Once you have recorded your Lync meeting, open the Lync Recording Manager from Start ➢ Programs ➢ Microsoft Lync. From there, you can see your Lync Recordings, as shown in Figure 17.15.

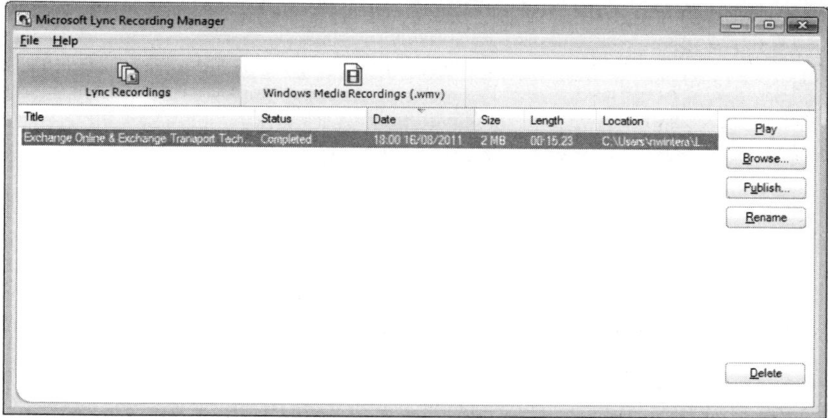

FIGURE 17.15
The Lync Recording Manager window with a saved recording

Select the recording to save up to a SharePoint asset library and click Publish. A dialog box will open where you can type in the URL to the SharePoint asset library of your choice (if you do not know the URL, simply open the SharePoint site where you want to store the recording in IE and copy and paste the URL address from the IE address bar into the dialog box). As you can see in Figure 17.16, by default the user's Lync Recordings location is shown.

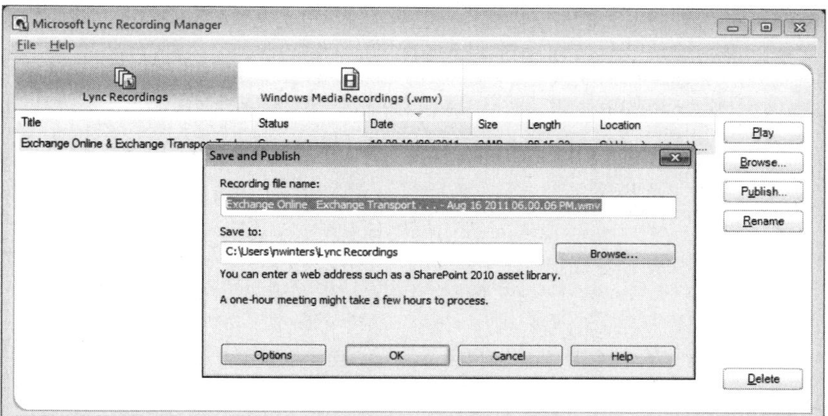

FIGURE 17.16
The Publish dialog

Business Process Communication Workflows

SharePoint 2010 and Lync 2010 together provide an extensible platform on which to build applications that are enhanced through the use of Unified Communications and collaboration technologies. Beyond the out-of-the-box integration features with SharePoint as previously discussed, businesses can use the Microsoft Unified Communications Managed API 3.0 (UCMA) to develop and deploy server-side applications hosted in IIS. The UCMA 3.0 SDK includes workflow solutions and examples that can be combined with SharePoint communication workflows to enable the standard Lync communication functionality (such as presence or clicking to IM or call) within the workflow. These workflows could include the ability to instantly contact those in an approval chain to take a decision, making the application more productive and efficient.

Using the latest UCMA 3.0 API, SharePoint workflows can be customized to add Lync-specific functions. For example, imagine you are a manager and have several employees, all of whom require expenses to be approved before being sent to the finance department. It's easy to set up an approval workflow in SharePoint using SharePoint Designer 2010 to create a codeless approval workflow, a process described at the following URL:

```
http://office.microsoft.com/en-us/sharepoint-designer-help/understand-approval-
workflows-in-sharepoint-2010-HA101857172.aspx
```

However, suppose you could further enhance the workflow with real-time communications. How could you do this? Integrating Lync and SharePoint functions allow the monitoring of unapproved expense reports as a deadline approaches. Once an employee is done filling out the expenses form, the approver could receive an instant message with the necessary information to approve or reject that expense report. To further increase efficiency, a link to the SharePoint site where the expense form is stored for approval could also be included in the instant message.

In the remainder of this section, you'll dive into how to build a basic SharePoint workflow application using a sample workflow solution that can be found once UMCA 3.0 is installed. Note that this is an example application, created to run upon user execution. In the real world, a developer would create an application as a service to run in a production environment, giving it a dedicated application server from which to run. The advantage of this is performance; UCMA applications that handle real-time collaboration media such as audio or video require a high-performing environment. That doesn't mean you can't run it on the same server that runs Lync; just be mindful of performance. In order to host the UCMA application on a dedicated server, it will need to have connectivity with the Lync server and, if it uses Mutual Transport Layer Security, a certificate the Lync server trusts.

UCMA 3.0 will need to be downloaded and then installed onto your development server. The download link can be found here:

```
www.microsoft.com/download/en/details.aspx?id=10566
```

The workflow application you are building will trigger an IM to be sent to a specified recipient, informing them that a new document has been uploaded to a SharePoint site. The trigger for the workflow is a document being saved to a SharePoint site. To build the previously described application, you'll need the following:

1. Microsoft Lync Server 2010. Create a Lync-enabled user. This user will be used by the workflow service. In this example, the user created is called SPPNotify, with a display name of SharePoint Notifications.

2. Microsoft Lync Client 2010. For testing purposes, this client will receive the instant message. Log in as the user created in step 1.

3. Microsoft Visual Studio 2008 Standard, Professional, or Team System 2008, or Microsoft Visual Studio 2010 Premium, Professional, or Ultimate. Visual Studio is a prerequisite for the UCMA 3.0 SDK.

4. UCMA 3.0 SDK, which includes the workflow API and UCMA APIs. The workflow API is used to develop the Lync functions within a business workflow solution.

5. Microsoft SharePoint 2010 Server. You need this in order to interact with UCMA 3.0. A basic SharePoint site capable of hosting a document library or document list will need to be created. This should be created from the SharePoint Central Administration console.

To get started, SharePoint 2010, Lync Server 2010, Visual Studio 2010, Professional, and UCMA 3.0 SDK are installed on the same server as a small test-only development server environment. Again, in the real world, a developer would use a dedicated development server on which to create the application. Then this application would typically be deployed onto a dedicated application server (also discussed earlier). Note that when SharePoint and Lync Server are installed onto the same server, IIS will need to be edited so that there is no conflict for port 80. SharePoint has been set to use port 8044 and Lync Server Control Panel to use port 80. These settings were modified in IIS on the server. To create this application, a sample workflow called SharePoint Sequential Workflow was used. The following steps show how the workflow was used. It can be found once UCMA 3.0 SDK is installed. For more detailed instructions on creating a Lync application server, take a look at the following link:

`http://blogs.claritycon.com/georgedurzi/2010/09/15/installing-ucma-3-0-and-creating-a-lync-server-2010-trusted-application-pool/`

The following steps outline the process of creating the workflow application:

1. Start Visual Studio. Load the `UCMASharePointWorkflow.sln` solution file into Visual Studio. You can simply locate the file and double-click it to load it. To locate the file, search for `C:\Program Files\Microsoft UCMA 3.0\SDK\Workflow\Sample Applications\UCMASharePointWorkflow.sln` in Windows Explorer.

2. Modify the `settings.settings` file. To do this, navigate to the Solutions Explorer pane on the right of the screen and expand UCMAWorkflowService. Locate `settings.settings` and double-click it to open it. Add the Lync server FQDN, the username of the user you created earlier, the password of the user, and the user domain under which the service will run.

3. This sample uses `ServerPlatformSettings` and specifies to connect using port 5060. This would work for OCS 2007 R2 but in Lync 2010, TCP (5060) is no longer supported; TLS (5061) must be used. To change this, go to `program.cs` by navigating through Solution Explorer, expanding UCMAWorkFlowService and double-clicking `program.cs`. Find the following code:

   ```
   ServerPlatformSettings platformSettings = new ServerPlatformSettings("UCMAWork
   flowService",
   Dns.GetHostEntry("localhost").HostName, 5060/*Change this to the port of
   choice.*/, null);
   ```

   Replace it with this:

   ```
   ClientPlatformSettings platformSettings = new ClientPlatformSettings("UCMAWork
   flowService", SipTransportType.Tls);
   ```

   `ServerPlatformSettings` is used along with the `ApplicationEndpoint`. Changing the code to use a `ClientPlatformSettings`, instead of `ServerPlatformSettings`, is what allows TLS to be specified.

4. To build the project, press F5 to run the UCMAWorkflowService console application. The output will show that the UCMA workflow service is ready, as in Figure 17.17.

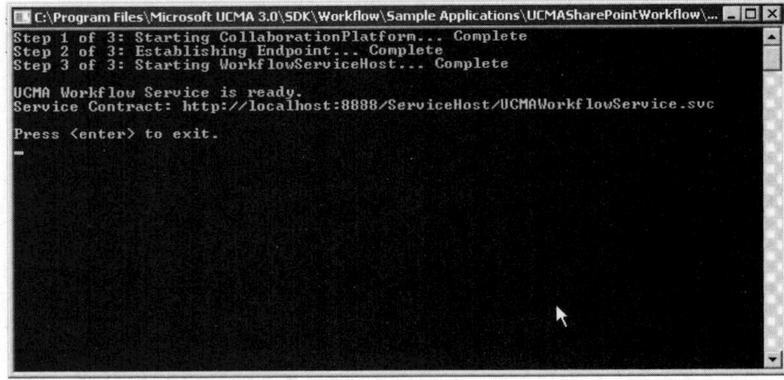

FIGURE 17.17
Running the UCMA-WorkflowService application

5. Install the `UCMAWorkFlowActivities.dll` into the global application cache (GAC) using the command `gacutil.exe /I` (path to the DLL, usually located at `C:\Program Files\Microsoft UCMA 3.0\SDK\Workflow\Sample Applications\UCMASharePointWorkflow\UCMAWorkflowActivities`).

6. Click on the `web.config` tab. Under the configuration node, copy and paste the contents of the `output.config` to the `web.config` file.

7. Create a new SharePoint sequential workflow application. To find this template, expand the workflow node in the New Project dialog box as shown in Figure 17.18.

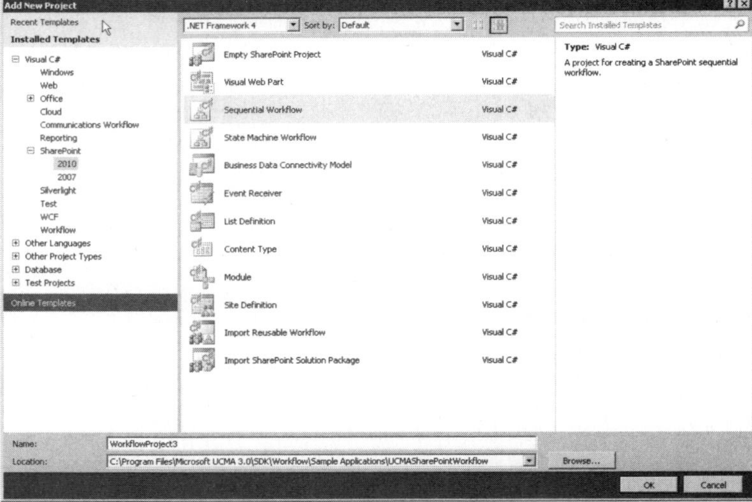

FIGURE 17.18
Creating a new sequential workflow application

8. Follow the wizard, which will ask for details including the SharePoint site name, name of the workflow, and what to associate it with, such as a document library or list. In this example, it is associated with a document library.

9. Once the wizard is completed, you will see a display like Figure 17.19.

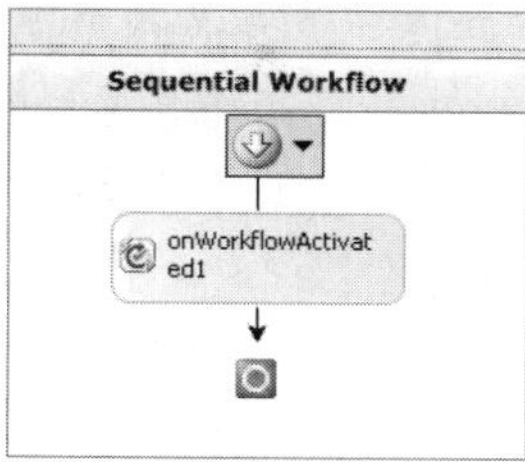

FIGURE 17.19
The beginning of the sequential workflow

10. Right-click the Visual Studio toolbox and then select Choose Items, browse to `UCMAWorkflowActivities.dll`, and click OK in the dialog box. This adds the UCMA workflow activities to the toolbox.
11. Click the toolbox and select SendInstantMessageActivity.
12. This adds the activity to the sequential workflow, as shown in Figure 17.20.

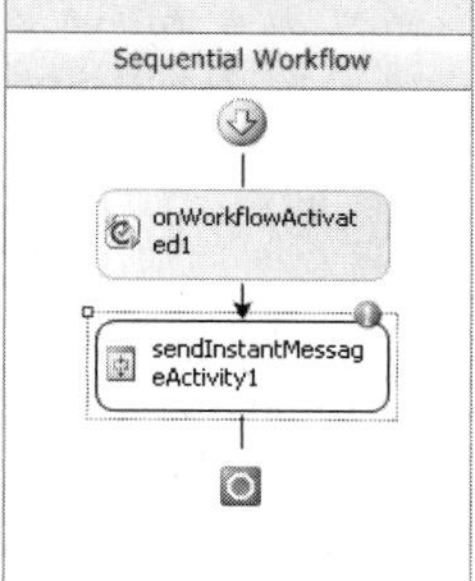

FIGURE 17.20
The workflow, with the new SendInstantMessageActivity added

13. Set the properties of the activity. In this example, you need an IM to be sent to a specific user. The IM should include text to display "a new document has arrived." To set the properties, click next to the Message attribute shown in Figure 17.21 and type the text to display in the IM. In the User attribute, specify the user to whom the IM should be sent.

FIGURE 17.21
Specifying the properties of the SendInstantMessage-Activity

14. At this point, the application is built. Now you need to start debugging the application. This is also done in Visual Studio by clicking the green start arrow on the toolbar or by pressing F5.
15. Once debugging is started, go to the SharePoint site and upload a document.
16. The logged-in Lync user will receive an IM Toast, as shown in Figure 17.22.

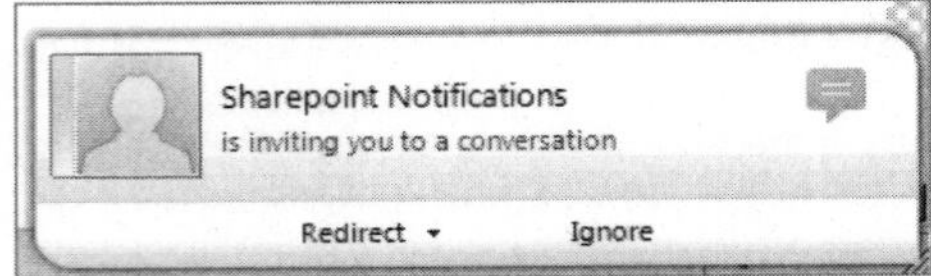

FIGURE 17.22
The IM Toast window the designated user receives when a document is uploaded

17. Click on the Toast to open the conversation. The text you specified earlier in the SendInstantMessageActivity properties will be displayed as shown in Figure 17.23.

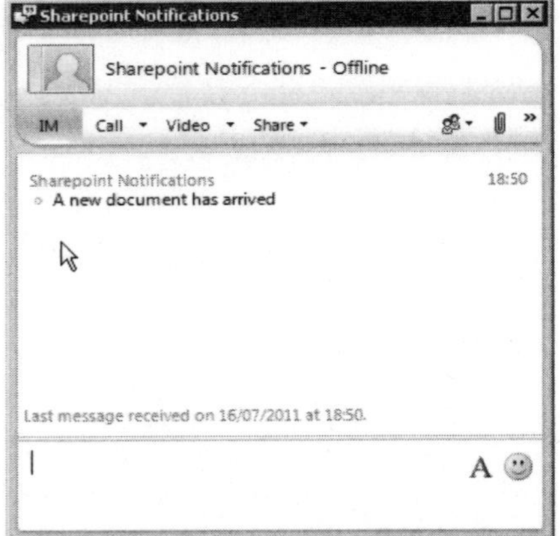

FIGURE 17.23
The opened IM conversation with custom text message

This example simply demonstrates how to create a simple workflow application. UCMA together with SharePoint can be used to create powerful applications that clearly impact business processes by enhancing them with communications, making them more efficient and collaborative.

Integrating Lync with Group Chat

Group Chat provides subject-based persistent real-time communications. In the range of communication styles, it lies somewhere between the real-time but restricted audience of an instant message and the formality of an email. It is extremely effective at distributing information rapidly to those people who are interested in it, while also making the same content available to others with a less immediate requirement. This section gives a brief overview of Group Chat and its integration with Lync; you'll also find some references for further reading.

Group Chat improves information sharing between geographically dispersed and/or cross-functional teams. By providing channels for information to be shared and without the megaphone effect of a widely circulated email, Group Chat allows fast and efficient knowledge sharing. It can be especially good at providing a means to capture the coffee machine/water cooler conversations. That is, the short bit of informal information that can be quickly shared and may be of interest among the community gathered.

While the number of channels can rapidly grow, using filters allows users to ensure they are alerted to information that is relevant to them. For example, rather than searching every single channel to see if anyone has asked for input from you, you can look at results under a default ego filter based on your name to see where you are being referenced. These benefits can be extended outside your organization using Lync federation to both Lync and public IM users. This allows you to have partner-specific channels to provide better sales and support experiences, or provide communal discussions.

All these features allow Group Chat to provide a highly efficient forum to share information in a manner that is both searchable and auditable, and it allows individual users to filter what information is relevant to them.

History of Group Chat

Group Chat was acquired by Microsoft in August 2007 through the acquisition of Chicago-based Parlano, Inc. Parlano built a product called MindAlign, which was based on Java and IRC channels. It was widely used by global financial and trading organizations to rapidly share time-sensitive information. As SIP and XMPP evolved, Parlano developed a next-generation application based on Microsoft's presence stack and using SIP as a standard protocol. While retaining much of the functionality of the IRC-based product, this new application was a fresh start, using Windows Communications Framework (WCF) and SQL Server as its foundations. Before this application was launched, Microsoft acquired Parlano and then sold off the legacy Java product to a third party to provide on-going support. Group Chat was first integrated into Office Communications Server 2007 R2.

Group Chat uses channels to organize common conversations together. A channel can also be thought of as a chat room or subject area. Depending on how you manage Group Chat, channels can be created by an administrator or by anyone. The larger the organization, the more controls you are likely to need about who can create channels and when.

The functionality offered by Group Chat is the least understood Lync feature. This is partly because it was an acquisition, rather than software developed in-house by Microsoft, but also because it is much more a business-facing project than a technical implementation. However, if you make the effort to understand how your organization works, Group Chat, like SharePoint, will reward that effort with real benefits by speeding up decision making, delivering better customer service, and improving productivity and profitability.

Group Chat is a separate server and client, which works with the Lync infrastructure. It is included as part of server licensing and within the Standard Client Access License. Therefore, if you are licensed for instant messaging and presence, you are also licensed for Group Chat.

Group Chat has three core software packages that can be downloaded from the Microsoft Download Center (`http://download.microsoft.com`) using a simple search for "Group Chat." They are

- Group Chat Server
- Group Chat Admin Tool
- Group Chat Client

There is also a Group Chat Monitoring Management Pack, for use with System Center Operations Manager (SCOM) to provide optimal management.

The server download includes the compliance server, which if required must reside on a separate server. This is discussed further in the next section. When you download the software, make sure you also obtain the latest updates and hotfixes for Group Chat from the same Microsoft download site.

Server Topology and Sizing

The Group Chat server resides behind a Lync Standard Edition server or Enterprise Edition pool. You cannot deploy Group Chat without first deploying the basics of a Lync IM and presence environment. There are four server roles that can be deployed, and all but one are mandatory:

- The Lookup server provides a well-known address, usually `OCSchat@domain.com`, and it manages load-balancing when multiple servers are used. It distributes sessions to all available Channel servers in a round-robin fashion. It is required even if only one Group Chat server is deployed.
- The Channel server provides all Group Chat channel functionality, except for file posting, which is managed through the web service.
- The web service is provided via IIS on the Group Chat server. It allows files to be uploaded and downloaded from channels.
- The Compliance server provides a route for third-party compliance tools to extract and record users' behavior within channels and submit this to an auditable store. A number of third-party compliance tools are supported; one example is Actiance, formerly Facetime.

The Lookup server, Channel server, and Web Service roles all reside on the same Group Chat server. Within your environment, there can be only a single Compliance server in each Group Chat installation, although warm-standby Compliance servers can be configured. All servers can be virtualized if required. The Compliance server must be installed on its own server. It cannot be colocated on a server running other Group Chat roles.

In addition, a SQL instance is required for Group Chat to store configuration and content. This can be its own SQL instance, or the tables can be stored in the SQL instance used by the Enterprise Edition pool. If you are installing Group Chat with a Lync Standard Edition server, you must deploy a separate SQL Server instance to support Group Chat. Use of the colocated SQL Server Express on the Standard Edition server is not supported.

Each Group Chat Channel server can support 20,000 users, and up to three servers can be pooled, giving a maximum concurrent user count of 60,000. Only one Group Chat pool is supported within an Active Directory forest, irrespective of the number of Lync Enterprise edition pools that are installed. That is, you cannot install a separate Group Chat pool against each Standard Edition or Enterprise Edition pool.

All client connections, from both the Group Chat Administration tool and Group Chat client, go via the Lync front end or Standard Edition server that Group Chat has been built behind. The Lync client does not need to be installed on the client PCs for Group Chat to be used. This is discussed further in the "User Client" section.

When there are multiple Group Chat servers, they use Windows Communications Framework over a secure TLS connection to distribute load between the servers. The load-balancing is carried out by the Lookup service. The Lookup Service must always be running, even if you have only one server, as this service provides the route to the channel server. As part of the load-balancing, when new content is posted to a channel on one Channel server, the message is rebroadcast to other participants on that Channel server via SIP and the content is forwarded to other Channel servers using WCF, who then send the content to their subscribers via SIP.

When the Compliance service is used, the Channel service uses Microsoft Message Queuing (MSMQ) to publish events to the Compliance server. The following events are captured:

- New messages/content
- File uploads and downloads
- Searches of chat history
- A user entering or exiting a channel

The Compliance server stores these events in its own database and then writes them out to files in a shared folder. This includes copies of any files that have been uploaded into channels that are stored in a separate attachments directory.

Administration Client

The channels are administered through the Group Chat Admin tool, shown in Figure 17.24. This tool allows you to configure and manage channels and their characteristics.

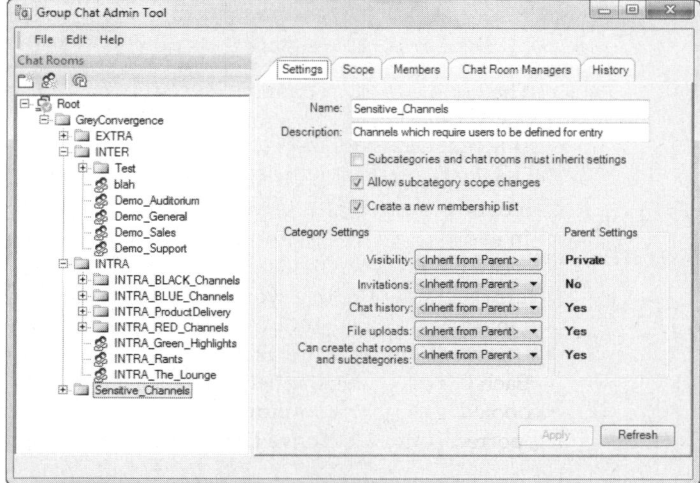

FIGURE 17.24
The Group Chat administration tool

User Client

The Group Chat client runs as its own standalone client and can be installed without the Lync client being installed; however, it is recommended to use Lync for all IM, presence, and conferencing functionality and use the Group Chat client purely for channel access.

It is possible to configure Group Chat to be the default Instant Messaging client. In this scenario, the contacts list appears and can be updated in the My Chat panel on the left side of the screen along with the channels. If Group Chat is not the default IM client, you can click on a participant name to start an IM with them, or right-click on a name to start a voice or video call, and that session will open in the Lync client.

In the recommended client deployment approach, Group Chat is not the primary IM and presence client. When that is the case, and the Lync client is running on the same machine, the Group Chat client will abide by Lync presence privacy mode. Although you can run Group Chat and the Lync client on separate machines and have Lync as the default IM and presence client, that is not a recommended approach. Figure 17.25 shows the Lync Group Chat client.

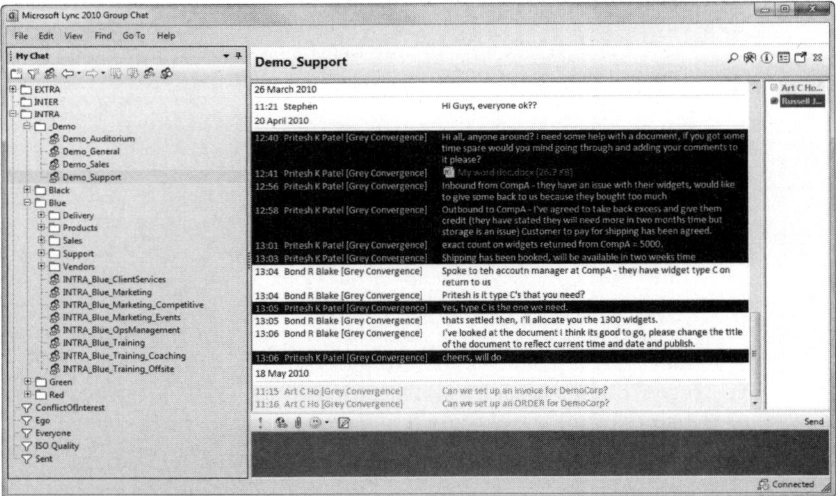

FIGURE 17.25 The Lync Group Chat client

One other consideration for the client is that of migrations. If you are moving from OCS 2007 R2 to Lync, there will be a period of coexistence, as discussed in Chapter 7, "Migration and Upgrades." Table 17.1 documents the supported combinations of server and clients for Group Chat.

TABLE 17.1: Group Chat Client and Server Compatibility in a Migration Scenario

	CLIENTS			
SERVERS	**OCS 2007 R2 WITH OCS 2007 R2 GROUP CHAT**	**OCS 2007 R2 WITH LYNC SERVER 2010 GROUP CHAT**	**LYNC SERVER 2010 WITH OCS 2007 R2 GROUP CHAT**	**LYNC SERVER 2010 WITH LYNC SERVER 2010 GROUP CHAT**
Communicator 2007 R2 with Communicator 2007 R2 Group Chat	Yes	Yes	Yes	Yes
Communicator 2007 R2 with Lync 2010 Group Chat	No	No	No	Yes
Lync 2010 with Communicator 2007 R2 Group Chat	No	No	Yes	Yes
Lync 2010 with Lync 2010 Group Chat	No	No	No	Yes

Channel Features

Organizing your chat rooms so that they are focused and relevant, while not becoming too numerous, is a careful balancing act. Normally, a hierarchical structure works well. Before commencing this task, ask around your organization for where similar structures or taxonomies already exist. If you have successfully deployed SharePoint, that experience may provide some clues, as can existing email distribution groups. Remember, however, that you may want to encourage cross-functional knowledge sharing, and a short piece of work to agree on desired business outcomes or functional requirements may be beneficial.

GROUP CHAT AT GREY CONVERGENCE

Grey Convergence is a business and technology consultancy. It uses Group Chat extensively to manage its business. Every client has three channels representing sales, delivery, and support activity. Everything that happens with each client happens within one of those channels. This provides an audit trail that is easy and quick to use and search, and it allows people who are unfamiliar with the client to quickly come up to speed. In addition, every vendor or partner has its own channel, as do specific product offerings and internal administration.

Filters are used to make content relevant. Specifically, if anyone types the words **escalate, escalation,** or **unhappy** in a channel, an alert is generated for the Quality Manager to bring their attention to the issue. In this way, the organization very easily manages its ISO 9001 Quality Standard registration and can provide an audit trail to the inspectors each year.

Group Chat supports categories to allow the grouping of channels. Categories can be nested within each other. This allows a structure to be built and allows delegated administration of both channels and categories.

You can allow all users to create channels if desired. This is best where you have a few simple rules for channel creation and people can easily identify if the channel has already been created. Some organizations also have a channel just for people to post new channel names as they are created, as a way to announce them publicly. Alternatively, you can nominate selected users to be able to create channels in a similar way that email distribution lists are managed today. It is also possible to integrate Group Chat with other applications to enable channel creation. For example, if a company uses the Customer Relationship Management (CRM) strategy, when an account record changes from prospect to active, CRM can trigger the creation of a channel just for that account, thereby automating the process.

As part of the installation, a root category is created. Settings configured on this category apply to all other categories and, therefore, rights to this category should be carefully controlled. You should minimize the number of channels created directly in root. Instead, create a subcategory, even if only one, and create your channels lower down your structure than the root.

Group Chat administration also has the concept of *scope*. You can use scope to restrict which users can access which channels. For example, in Figure 17.25, the organization described in the sidebar uses groups manually configured in the client to group channels of INTRA, EXTRA, and INTER. These groups, however, relate to categories: INTRA refers to trusted AD forest users, EXTRA includes this group and adds semitrusted partners as part of an extranet, and INTER refers to anyone in an untrusted internet community. Although these methods allow very flexible channel usage and administration, you must think through how your organization will use Group Chat because you can rapidly end up with a less than desired configuration.

Making Content Relevant

It is not uncommon to end up with a very large number of channels. As long as they have activity and aren't dormant, that is fine. Using filters, you can allow users to create alerts to notify them of content that is relevant to them, saving them the time and effort of staying up-to-date with all channels.

Figure 17.26 shows the dialog box you use to create a new filter. A number of controls are used to limit how widely this filter will be applied—for example, on all channels or a specific channel. Note that you can create simple word-matching rules or use regular expressions and create detailed pattern matches if needed.

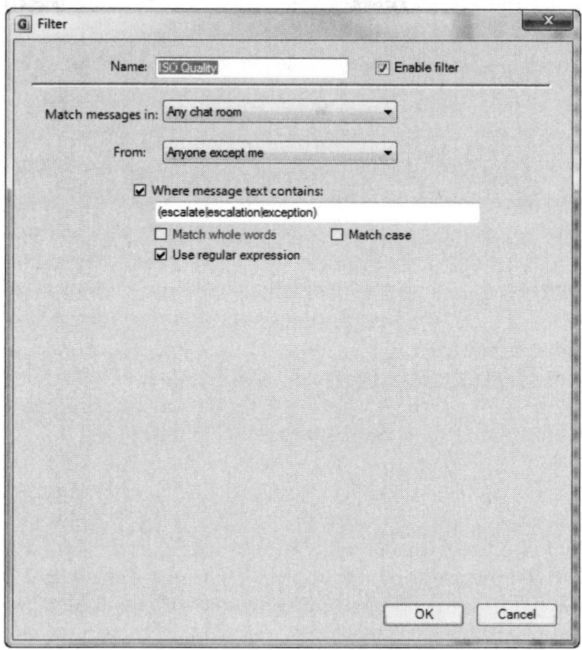

FIGURE 17.26
The Group Chat client content filter

Once you have created a filter, you can create an alert for when that filter is matched. For some results, you may choose not to be notified; all you require is a list of results when you click on the filter in the My Chat pane in the Group Chat client. You can, however, customize a number of options to draw the user's attention to a filter match, relevant to its urgency, as shown in Figure 17.27.

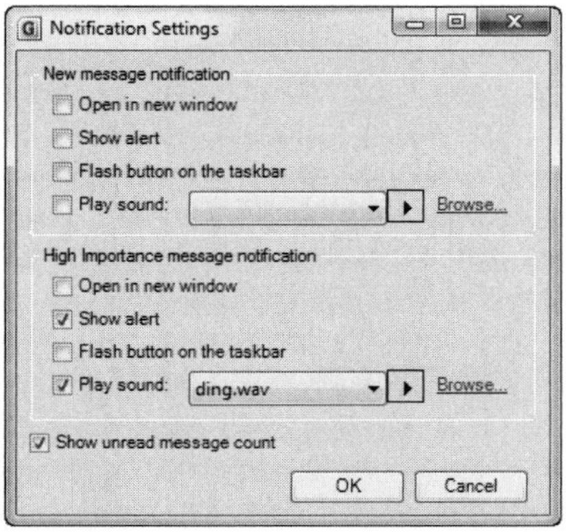

FIGURE 17.27
The Group Chat client's filter notification settings

Further Reading

You've been introduced to steps you need to take to deploy and migrate Group Chat, but you've just touched the surface of the process. For more information, here are some reading suggestions:

Microsoft Lync Server 2010 Group Chat Deployment Guide

`www.microsoft.com/download/en/details.aspx?id=9735`

Microsoft Lync Server 2010 Group Chat Administration Guide

`www.microsoft.com/download/en/details.aspx?id=6126`

The Bottom Line

Integrate Lync with Exchange. Exchange provides a wide range of functionality to Lync, and Lync helps enhance Exchange. The most important integration points are for the provision of Voice Mail, where Exchange UM is the only supported Voice Mail platform for Lync. To enhance Exchange, Lync enables building presence and basic IM capabilities directly into OWA. There are also less obvious integration points, as Lync utilizes Exchange Web Services to pull information about users' calendar entries and their contacts, providing enhanced presence information and a single view of a person as an entity with whom to communicate.

Master It You company is rolling out Lync as its telephony platform, and you will be using Exchange 2010 as your voice mail platform. You have been asked to outline the process to the Exchange administrative team.

Integrate Lync with SharePoint. SharePoint integration is both relatively simple and potentially complex! It is simple in that integrating presence capability is automatic, and it is complex in that you have the ability through application development to put together almost any piece of communication-enhanced workflow that you can think up. SharePoint integration also provides the Skill Search capability to Lync.

Master It Your organization makes extensive use of SharePoint 2010 and already has OCS 2007 R2, which has been providing presence integration. Now you are moving to Lync 2010, and you have been asked to investigate the requirements for Skill Search integration between Lync and SharePoint.

Integrate Lync with Group Chat. Group Chat is a component of Lync, but it is one which in Lync 2010 is still essentially a separate technology integrated through shared presence and communication modalities. Group Chat provides a new way of collaborating, being very specific about the information you regard as worthy of your time, through the use of careful filters. It is a great solution for those working on projects or in distributed environments perhaps even across time zones, where catching up on previous events is essential.

Master It Your company is considering deploying Group Chat as part of their Lync 2010 installation. You have been asked to understand and report back on the key Group Chat components. What would you cover?

Chapter 18

Third-Party Integration

The previous chapter discussed how Lync can be enhanced through integration with other Microsoft products; this chapter discusses how Lync can integrate with third-party systems to perform as the center of a much broader communications platform. By using the standards and protocols covered in Chapter 2, "Standards and Protocols," Lync can integrate with many systems and gateways to provide translation to other devices and systems. For example, Lync can talk directly to a SIP trunk provider for PSTN connectivity, but it can also communicate via more traditional methods using standard ISDN lines through a PSTN gateway. Likewise, Lync can integrate with existing PBX systems to provide elements of control over handsets from the PC through a technology called Remote Call Control (RCC). Lync is, of course, not limited to talking only to PBXs or the PSTN. It is perfectly capable of sitting at the center of a video conferencing system, utilizing its superb native external connectivity functionality to link hardware and software video endpoints from the likes of Radvision and Polycom. Lync's external connectivity can also be extended. While Lync can federate natively with other Microsoft communications platforms and with Internet IM clouds like AOL and Yahoo, other platforms require another type of gateway to enable communication. Microsoft provides an XMPP gateway, which translates the protocols used by Lync into the XMPP standard to enable communication with the likes of Google Talk and IBM Sametime. Finally, because Lync is a software platform, a software developer can extend and integrate applications into Lync to provide enhanced functionality that is not available by default.

In this chapter, you will learn to:

- Connect to Telephony Systems via a gateway
- Integrate with your PBX
- Use RCC to integrate with your PBX
- Deploy a Survivable Branch Appliance
- Connect to other external systems via an XMPP gateway
- Integrate with hardware video conferencing platforms
- Utilize third-party software enhancements

Connecting to Telephony Systems via a Gateway

Gateways have been referred to throughout this book, but what *is* a gateway and what does it do in the Lync environment? Fundamentally, a gateway is a hardware device from a third-party vendor that enables voice integration between your Lync deployment and other external voice elements, such as a PBX (Private Branch Exchange), the PSTN, DECT phones (digital handsets), and analog devices as represented in Figure 18.1.

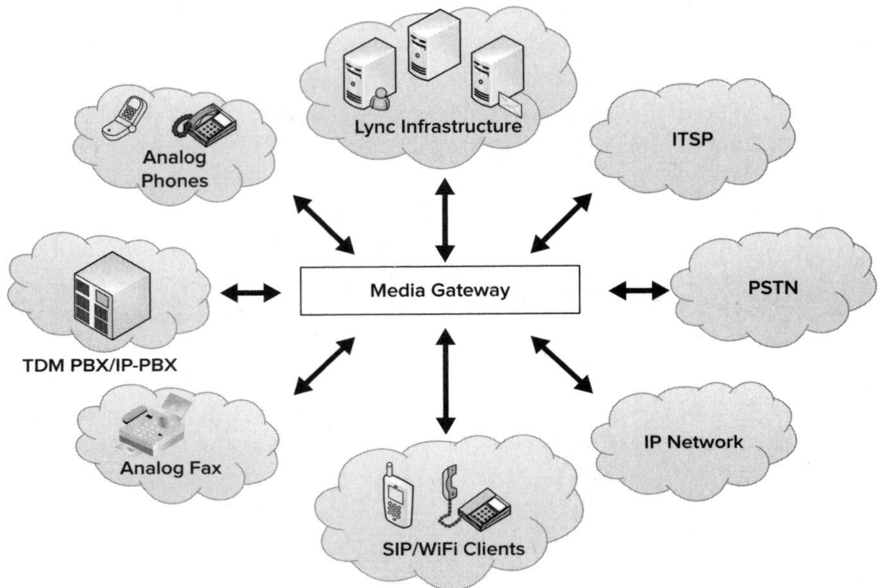

FIGURE 18.1 A Gateway connecting various voice components together

While Lync can potentially talk directly to certain PBXs or SIP trunk providers, the PBXs that support this ability are limited. Even some IP PBXs don't talk the correct variety of SIP, and SIP trunks may not be suitable to your particular environment, especially if you have a significant investment in ISDN lines. Implementing a gateway to integrate to the telephony world brings distinct benefits, including security and flexibility in manipulating traffic, which are two of the most important.

In this section, you'll explore the various benefits of using a gateway, look at some of the gateway options available in the market today, and review some of the more advanced features being implemented on the latest generation of gateways that make Lync integration and user migration easier and more robust. First though, let's take a look at some of the typical voice elements that you have to integrate with and at the challenges that lie ahead.

Public Switched Telephone Network (PSTN)

The Public Switched Telephone Network is a worldwide telephony infrastructure that is hosted and supported by various carriers in different countries all over the world. Similar to the World Wide Web, this infrastructure gives global reach and enables users to make a voice call to anywhere in the world. Figure 18.2 shows many of the typical PSTN interconnect standards and devices that exist around the world today.

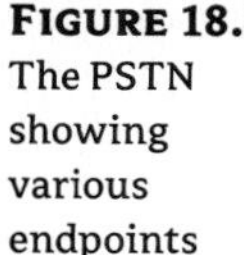

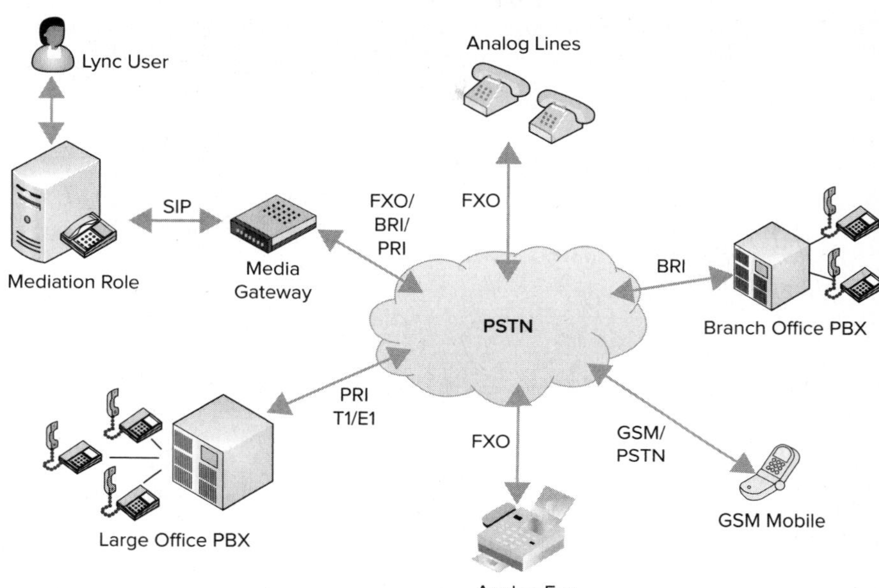

FIGURE 18.2 The PSTN showing various endpoints

In contrast to the World Wide Web, which is ultimately based on a common protocol—IP—the PSTN network has many different interfaces, protocols, and standards associated with it. This is driven by differences in local country standards, evolution of voice services over the years, and adoption of different technology by different carriers. What this means for you is that for a global Lync deployment, you may be facing a slightly different interface or protocol in each location where a connection to PSTN is required. It is in this situation that it's important for a gateway to offer a wide range of interfaces, protocols, and standards. It is also important that the gateway device is acceptance-tested (*homologated*) by the carrier in that country for direct connection to their PSTN service.

Traditional PSTN connectivity (known as *legacy PSTN*) is generally presented to an enterprise over a digital service known as ISDN (Integrated Services Digital Network) or an analog line, such as you may have at home. The digital services are presented as BRI (*Basic Rate*), which gives two voice channels and one for signaling, or PRI (*Primary Rate*), of which there are two variants—T1 and E1.

T1 is used in North America and Japan, and provides 23 channels of voice and one channel for signaling. E1 is used in Europe and Australia and is fairly widespread across the rest of the world. E1 provides 30 channels for voice and one for signaling.

Internet Telephony Service Provider (ITSP)

Another option for connecting to the PSTN network, to provide external voice services to your Lync users, is to implement a SIP trunk service from an Internet Telephony Service Provider (ITSP). A SIP trunk service is much more flexible and dynamic than the traditional PSTN services delivered by local carriers because it uses VoIP technology in much the same way that Lync does for delivering voice services over IP. In fact, some providers offer certified services that can be directly connected to your Lync infrastructure. However, these services are not available in all locations, and there are still very good reasons to consider using a gateway device between your Lync infrastructure and a Microsoft Open Interoperability Program (OIP)–certified SIP trunk service.

Microsoft OIP Certification—Open Interoperability Testing

As with any third-party device connecting into Lync, it is very important that the device interface, protocols, and features are fully tested and compliant with Lync to ensure a smooth implementation and to avoid any unexpected issues. The OIP program instigated by Microsoft ensures that any gateway or PBX equipment undergoes a full and extensive interoperability test suite before being supported and listed on the OIP web page, at this address:

`http://technet.microsoft.com/en-us/lync/gg131938`

A good SIP gateway can provide an additional layer of security and flexibility by acting as an SBC (Session Border Controller). The gateway sits on the edge of your IP network, terminating the SIP trunk service, and is able to provide stateful SIP firewall services, session management, and connection admission control. Also thanks to its location, it provides topology hiding and failover to traditional PSTN connectivity in the event of a failure or congestion on the SIP trunk.

Securing the voice traffic at the edge of your enterprise network is important. You must remember that voice traffic over IP is just like your regular Internet data. It is subject to the same security concerns and considerations that you apply to your data traffic. Various secure protocols and methods can be used to protect your voice traffic. The SBC device is key to their implementation. You'll explore these protocols in detail later, and you'll see how both the signaling and voice traffic itself can be protected against unlawful intercept or eavesdropping by unwanted parties.

Your SIP trunk will be delivered over the Internet or Virtual Private Network (VPN). The SBC will be the *voice firewall* between your SIP trunk provider and your internal Lync voice network; it will provide security and session management to make sure you don't oversubscribe your SIP trunk connection with excessive voice calls. This session management can include the ability to manage peak call periods by overflowing calls to traditional PSTN trunks when your SIP trunks are at capacity.

SIP trunk providers are growing in number and popularity right now; the flexibility and cost savings offered by some of these services are attractive, but there are differences in signaling protocols and codecs used for media encoding. This again creates a need for a flexible and capable gateway device to interface with these services; such an interface might be in parallel to your "traditional" ISDN connection as well, thereby presenting a common and known secure interface to your Lync deployment via the gateway.

Typically, an ITSP will implement the UDP protocol for signaling transport, the RTP protocol for media transport, and the G.729 codec for the media encoding itself. By contrast, a Lync Enhanced Gateway will use the TLS encrypted protocol for signaling transport, SRTP encrypted protocol for media transport, and G.711 codec for the media encoding toward the Lync Pool Mediation role, as shown in Figure 18.3.

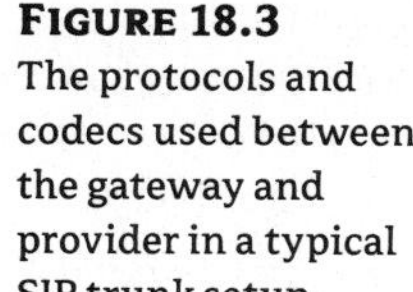

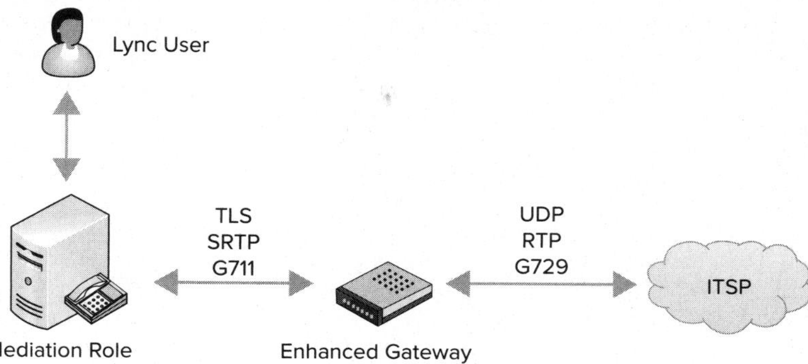

FIGURE 18.3
The protocols and codecs used between the gateway and provider in a typical SIP trunk setup

The gateway must be capable of translating between the secure and nonsecure protocols used for both signaling and media, and it must be able to transcode between the different audio codecs used on either side.

Take note of that last point; audio transcoding is becoming a key factor in today's Unified Communications (UC) telephony environment. Whereas the traditional telephony environment used in the PSTN carries the voice traffic as uncompressed audio, within the IP world it is common to encode and compress the audio data to reduce the bandwidth required to transport it end to end. With the SIP protocol, the endpoints trying to establish a voice call must agree on a common codec to use in order to transport the audio stream between them. As mentioned, many ISTP providers like to deliver the voice using the G.729 codec, which is able to compress the audio data from 64Kbps to 8Kbps while still maintaining reasonable voice quality.

Within Lync, the clients are able to support two codecs. The default used for all PC-to-PC calls is Microsoft's proprietary RTAudio codec, which is a high-fidelity wideband codec that is able to dynamically adjust the compression rate to the available bandwidth. The second codec available is G.711, which is 64Kbps voice and is comparable to uncompressed voice used on the PSTN. G.711 is used toward the gateway for calls out to the PSTN or PBX. For interfacing with Lync, the gateway must be able to transcode this G.729 audio traffic presented by the ITSP carrier to G.711 data, which is passed on toward the Lync client.

As mentioned, this direct SIP-to-SIP audio transcoding is becoming a commonplace requirement for Lync deployments where a SIP trunk connection is involved, either to an ITSP or an IP-PBX. The gateways available on the market vary greatly in their capability and capacity to perform this task. As you can imagine, this task of completely changing the voice compression technique on either side of a gateway is resource-intensive. The voice must be processed by the gateway dynamically and without introducing noticeable latency to the voice traffic. Imagine a gateway processing a few hundred calls simultaneously, each call generating hundreds of packets of audio data that require decoding and re-encoding, and you can see that audio transcoding is no trivial task. Within a gateway, this task is performed by a hardware element known as a DSP chip (Digital Signal Processor). When looking at your gateway requirements, pay particular attention to this capability. With the increasing move toward SIP trunking, this requirement is only set to grow.

Private Branch Exchange (PBX)

Another common voice element that most organizations need to interface with is the PBX. This is typically an on-premises device that delivers the existing voice capability to users; it usually hosts internal phones and fax machines and connects to the PSTN, as described previously. PBXs are proprietary; they come from an array of vendors and have different features, models, and software versions that affect their capabilities. You may have heard a PBX vendor talk about the 100-plus features that a PBX is capable of, and that a software VoIP platform cannot deliver. The question is, in any given installation, how many of those features are in fact licensed, configured, used, or even known? Maybe five or six!

Three main types of PBX technology are deployed: traditional analog/digital PBX, IP-PBX, and a combination of the two, generally known as an *I-enabled* PBX.

Traditional PBX: This describes the majority of PBX equipment deployed. It is typically very old—15 to 20 years old is not uncommon—and usually has proprietary analog or digital handsets. It is low on features.

IP PBX: Full IP VoIP PBX systems tend to be much newer and feature-rich and have VoIP endpoints, although these endpoints may run a proprietary version of the SIP protocol.

IP Enabled PBX: Some traditional PBX systems can be upgraded with an IP card to enable them to interface with VoIP platforms such as Lync. However, the SIP protocol implemented on these systems often has some proprietary SIP extensions, making interoperability and certification to Lync a challenge.

Achieving Connectivity

In order for Lync to integrate with external elements to establish a voice call, various signaling and transport protocols are involved that a gateway must be able to understand and translate. They fall under two key areas: signaling transport, which sets up the call, and media transport, which facilitates the passing of the audio stream encoded with whichever codec is being used. These areas are outlined here and shown in Figure 18.4.

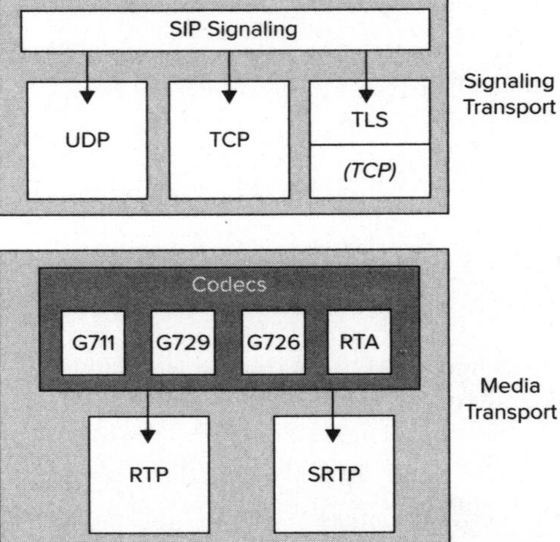

FIGURE 18.4
The connectivity components through a gateway

Signaling Transport: In order to establish a voice call, information, including the number dialed and the number of the caller, must be passed between devices. This process is known as the *call signaling*. With SIP this information can be transported using either the UDP, TCP, or secure TLS transport protocols. UDP is obviously connectionless and is often used by ITSP providers for SIP trunk signaling. It is lightweight, fast, and suited to the ITSP needs. TCP is a connection-oriented protocol that provides guaranteed data transport. Lync uses TLS for all signaling transport to avoid any unwanted data interception. TLS is based on the TCP protocol but adds a layer of encryption and security.

Media Transport: The standard protocol for transporting the voice traffic over IP is Real-Time Transport Protocol (RTP). RTP is widely used as a transport protocol for both voice and video traffic. A later extension to this protocol was the addition of security to eliminate the risk of interception and eavesdropping. Known as Secure RTP (SRTP), the endpoint devices encrypt any voice traffic within a secure payload before transmitting over the IP network. Lync employs SRTP for communication to the gateway.

Media Codec: As mentioned earlier in the ITSP section, the encoding and compression of the voice traffic element is achieved using one of the voice codecs, such as G.711, G.729, or Microsoft RTAudio. The codec used must be agreed upon by both voice endpoints during the signaling negotiations to establish the call. If no common codec is available on the devices, the call will not be established. The gateway device in your Lync deployment should be capable of changing the audio between different codecs, a process known as *transcoding*. The different gateways on the market today have different technical implementations to achieve this functionality, and they vary in capability and capacity!

SIP and ISDN Gateways

A number of gateways available on the market today are certified for Lync integration. They range from very small, low-cost analog devices to high-end data-center-type devices that can handle multiple E1 circuits, thousands of users, and high call volumes. Various vendors provide different platforms, including Dialogic, NET, Cisco, Ferrari, and Audiocodes. Again, the gateway offerings differ in interfaces, features, and capability, so be sure to research your needs carefully.

In this section, we'll take a closer look at one of the gateways available for Lync integration, the NET UX range, including the UX2000 and the new UX1000 designed for smaller office locations. The UX range is the latest gateway and Survivable Branch Appliance (SBA) platform from NET, which has been designed specifically with Lync in mind and provides a flexible and high performance way of connecting Lync to other platforms.

First, let's look at some of the models available and the typical interfaces and features that you can configure for voice integration to Lync, and then we'll review some of the GUI configuration items of the UX platform.

FEATURES

The UX2000 shown in Figure 18.5 is a higher-end modular platform allowing for growth. It allows for large volumes of direct SIP-SIP transcoded calls.

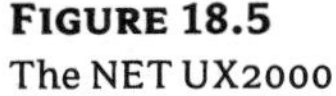

FIGURE 18.5
The NET UX2000

Courtesy of Network Equipment Technologies, www.net.com.

It provides the following features:

- ◆ Mix and match interfaces to allow the connection of digital (PRI) and analog (FXS) devices directly to the gateway. Two interface slots enable analog and digital connectivity in the same platform.
- ◆ High-capacity DSP resources that enable direct SIP-SIP transcoding of many codecs, as described in the previous section. This transcoding scales up to 600 simultaneous calls, with extremely low latency and no loss of capacity or performance.
- ◆ Call dual forking, to facilitate coexistence with your PBX. A single inbound call can be "forked" to up to eight different devices within your network.
- ◆ Router/firewall/VPN to enable SBC functionality, giving security for your voice traffic.
- ◆ Optional branch survivability with fully integrated SBA. Lync users in a branch have the ability to register directly to the gateway, providing full voice survivability in the event of a WAN outage.
- ◆ AD integration for advanced call routing, enabling smooth staged migration of users from your PBX to Lync.
- ◆ SIP trunking demark with certification. The UX2000 provides SBC security and certification against many different ITSP services.
- ◆ SIP phone registration (up to 3,000 devices). By allowing the direct registration of existing SIP phones to the gateway, the device eliminates the need for an additional registrar server. By using this feature on the gateway, SIP phones can become tightly integrated with your Lync and PBX environment.

The UX1000, shown in Figure 18.6, uses the same configuration interface and code set as its larger brother the UX2000.

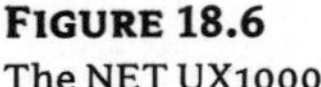

FIGURE 18.6
The NET UX1000

Courtesy of Network Equipment Technologies, www.net.com.

This similarity can make managing a solution easier when different gateway types are used. An organization can benefit from the advanced features and hardware components of the UX2000, can be used at a central office, and can provide suitable capacity and functionality with the UX1000 at small office locations. The UX1000 has the following features:

- ◆ Mixed interfaces, enabling the connectivity of analog phones (FXS), analog phone lines (FXO), and digital interfaces, both Basic Rate (BRI) and Primary Rate (PRI).
- ◆ Multipath relay (power-off bypass), enabling the use of analog phones in the event of a total power failure.
- ◆ Call dual forking, to facilitate coexistence with your PBX.

- High capacity DSP resources that enable direct SIP-to-SIP transcoding router/firewall/VPN to enable SBC functionality, giving security for your voice traffic.
- Optional Branch Survivability with fully integrated SBA, giving branch office Lync users total voice survivability.
- SIP phone registration (up to 600 devices), allowing the direct registration of existing SIP phones to the gateway.
- AD integration for advanced call routing, enabling smooth staged migration of users from an existing PBX to Lync.

Some of the advanced features now being implemented on voice gateways are specifically intended to assist in Lync deployments and migrations; one such feature is Active Directory integration, which is provided on the UX platform. This capability enables many different dynamic routing scenarios: For example, the gateway can route incoming calls to either the Lync environment or the legacy PBX, depending on whether the user's Direct Inward Dial (DID) number has been moved to Lync or not as provisioned in AD, shown in Figure 18.7. Although this may not seem hugely significant, it plays a major factor in the migration of users from the PBX to Lync, because without this feature an awful lot of manual routing table reconfiguration is needed. With AD integration on the gateway, the process is totally automated, enabling you to migrate users at your own pace and with ease.

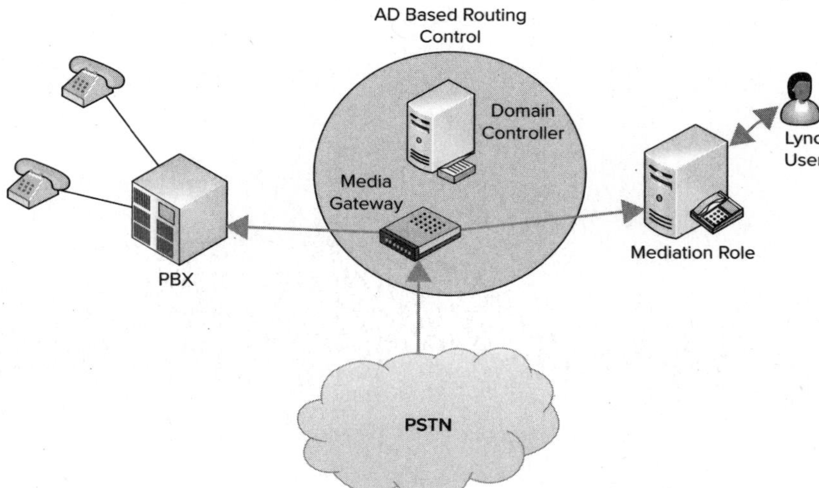

FIGURE 18.7 AD-based intelligent call routing

CONFIGURATION

Now that we've covered the main features of the gateways, let's look at some of the gateway configuration areas that pertain to Lync deployments. As you will see, the UX configuration interface is HTTPS-based and it allows wizard-style configuration, as well as full parameter configuration and manipulation. There is also a live monitor window that displays all calls, alarms, and events on the system.

By browsing to the default admin port IP address `192.168.128.2`, you can access the UX's built-in Setup Wizard screen. From there you configure the IP address that you want on the gateway, along with the DNS server, default gateway, and user credentials to log in and start your configuration. You then cable the UX into your network, and begin the configuration by browsing to the IP address just configured. From this point on the unit is secured by the credentials you have just entered.

Whether you are configuring the UX as an enhanced gateway for Lync or a full SBA branch device, the wizard will guide you through the initial configuration; it can be found under the Tasks tab at the top of the screen. The wizard creates an initial configuration that you can build upon to fulfill all of your voice routing requirements.

One core element created by the wizard is the set of signaling groups. These groups are a way to logically group and route voice traffic through the gateway, providing flexibility in the handling of different types of signaling, protocols, and codecs. They are used for both ISDN and SIP interfaces from the gateway, and they enable custom configuration of specific parameters related to the device to which it will interface. You can have multiple SIP and ISDN signaling groups, each with its own associated device (Lync front end, PBX, PSTN circuit, ITSP SIP trunk, and so on). In Figure 18.8, a SIP signaling group is configured to interface with a Lync Mediation server. The FQDN of the Lync server is the only device able to send SIP traffic into this signaling group, and it is the only configured signaling ports the UX will listen to for SIP traffic from the Lync mediation service, which in this case is TLS-secured traffic over port 5067.

FIGURE 18.8
A signaling group setup page on the UX

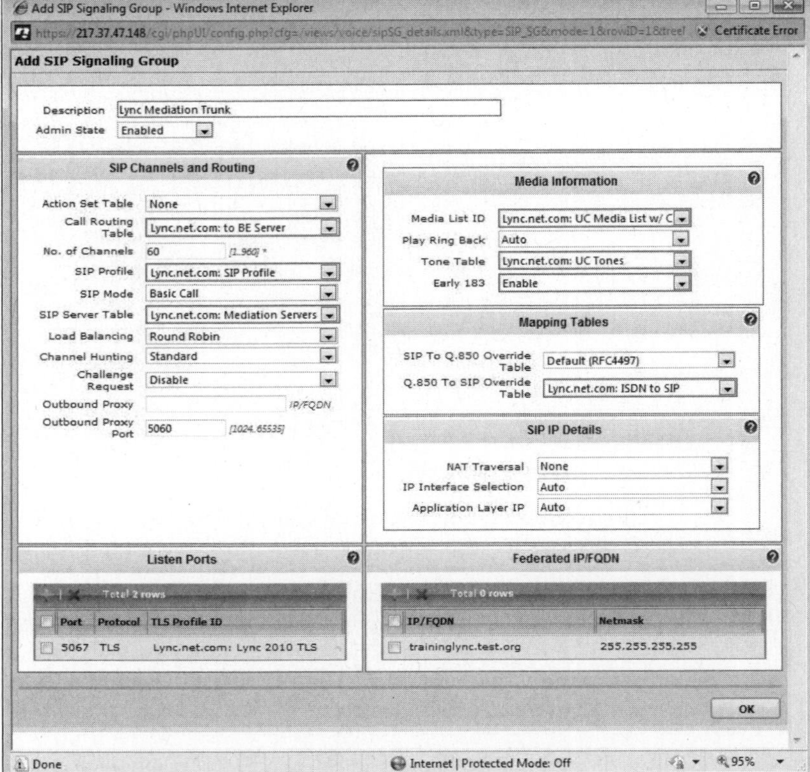

Another very common task that a gateway needs to perform is name and number manipulation; this needs to be done for the Dialed Number, Calling Number, and Diversion headers. Diversion headers are commonly used when a call goes unanswered by the end user and the PBX is sending the call to a Voice Mail server. The diversion header is used to identify for which user's extension the call was originally intended, so that the Voice Mail server can identify the correct user's mailbox to which to send the call. The recommended format to which Lync will normalize numbers as it sends calls to the gateway is E.164. Typically, a PSTN carrier will not accept the dialed or calling number if it starts with + (country code). Therefore, in the gateway it is necessary to strip off the + and replace it with a preceding zero, or maybe two zeros depending on whether it is a national or international call. Figure 18.9 shows an example in which national numbers from Lync are normalized from +1xxxxxxxxxx to 00xxxxxxxxxx.

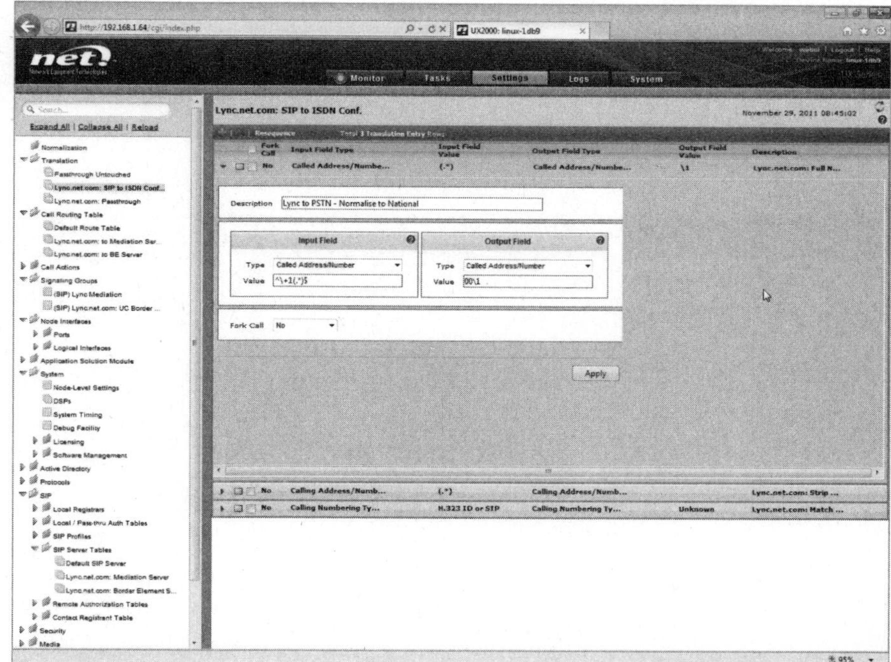

FIGURE 18.9 Number normalization in the gateway

Another common translation that many gateways will need to perform is for calls from Lync to internal PBX users. Most deployed PBX systems employ a four- or five-digit dialing plan internally; therefore, the E.164 number presented by Lync needs to be stripped down to four or five digits, but *only* for internal calls. Active Directory can again help the gateway determine what numbers are internal to that location. By using the information in Active Directory, you can see in the gateway which DID numbers are assigned to users within the enterprise; these numbers can be treated as internal, stripped down from E.164 format, and sent to the PBX. Any number that is *not* found in the AD database, therefore, does not belong to the enterprise and can be correctly formatted and sent to the PSTN for onward routing.

MONITORING

Monitoring capability is important. You need to be able to get an idea of what traffic is passing through your gateway and see the statistics of call volumes over a particular link. In Figure 18.10, you can see the live monitor aspect of the UX platform, with a call in progress from the ISDN circuit to a local SIP phone registered to the UX.

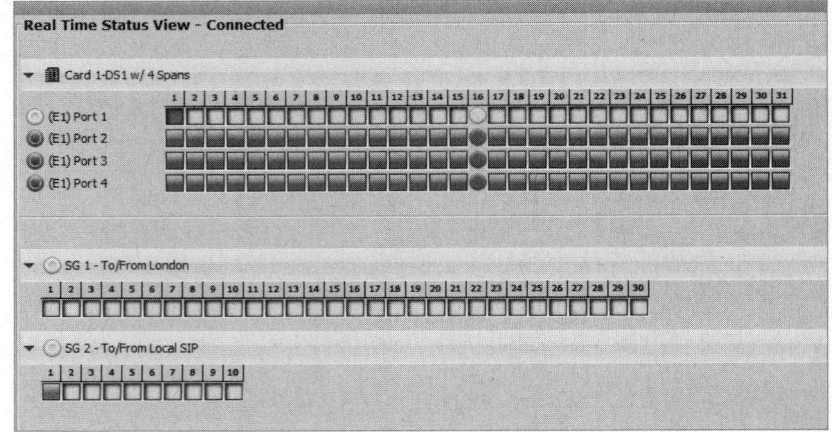

FIGURE 18.10 The monitoring capabilities of the UX

Figure 18.11 shows the statistics screen of the UX, which gives information about traffic over a particular link. You can see at a glance the current number of calls over this link and the total number of calls both inbound and outbound, including any calls rejected or refused. You can also see statistics on the SIP messages sent in and out over this link, along with any error messages; this enables you to quickly and easily diagnose issues or capacity problems on a particular link.

FIGURE 18.11
The UX Statistics page

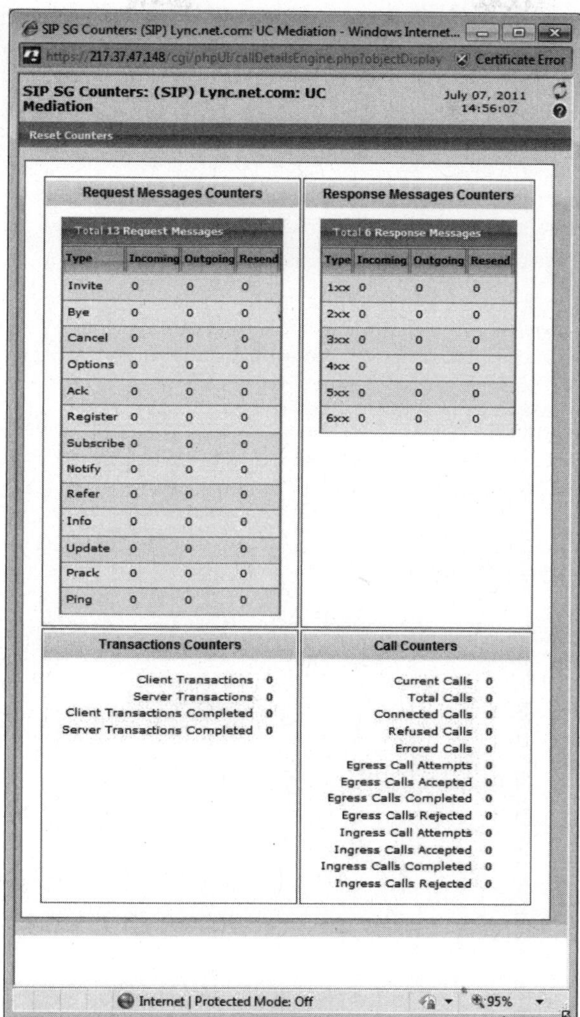

Integrating with Your PBX

Many organizations will need to enable interoperability between their legacy PBX and Lync environment. This may be for a short period during migration from a telephony platform to Lync or for an extended time as existing telephony assets are depreciated. This section will go through the different options that are available to you and offer some advice about which is best for your organization.

When you're interfacing a Lync deployment to an existing PBX infrastructure, a big challenge you'll face is the wide array of PBX devices located in different offices and the general lack of knowledge about how to configure them. Enterprises grow over time and acquire and upgrade their PBX equipment at different times in different locations. Even if all PBX equipment is supposed to be replaced with Lync Enterprise Voice, the approach may well be a staggered process across locations over a period of months.

Other aspects that will affect your integration strategy are factors such as:

- **The age of the existing telephony platform:** Consider whether the cost of the existing PBX has been written off as an asset and its capabilities.
- **The number of users and sites:** For example, a single location of one hundred people could be migrated in a single weekend, while multiple locations might be best migrated in separate phases.
- **The telephone number ranges in use:** Does everyone already have a direct-dial-inward (DDI) number, or will new numbers be required? If needed, these new numbers could be provided independent of the existing telephony platform, thus negating the need for integration.
- **The number of circuits:** The number, location, and the way in which inbound numbers are presented across the circuits will influence whether you migrate numbers gradually or you support parallel running of the PBX and Lync.

Legacy PSTN Circuits

If your telephony circuits (connections to the PSTN) are extremely old, the specific type of circuit may have been discontinued for new products and, as a result, may need to be upgraded. For example, in the United Kingdom, DASS circuits are a U.K.-specific form of ISDN that was used before Euro ISDN was standardized. It has been discontinued for new installations but can still be found in use. Although DASS circuits can be supported with some gateways, it is worth considering whether these circuits should be upgraded to ISDN Q.931 Primary Rate Interface (PRI) circuits or even replaced with SIP trunks.

A fundamental difference from the way legacy telephony has been provided is that Lync is deployed in a far more centralized manner. For example, it is customary for users to have a single identity and for there to be a single Active Directory forest across an entire organization, in contrast to the physical location boundaries that most legacy telephony deployments followed.

With Lync, a user can receive their phone calls wherever they log onto the network, including remote locations. Telephony deployments have traditionally been based on a single number provided to a single physical location, such as a desk, with little relationship to the end user beyond an entry in the phone list. More recent deployments may support hot-desking, but they often have limitations in a multiple-location organization where hot-desking may work only within a single office or country.

As part of your planning, you should make sure you fully understand the existing telephony in use. Scenarios that may need to be considered include:

Emergency phones: They are sometimes found by emergency exits. These phones automatically dial either a central security point or the local emergency services. They often can dial only a preset list of numbers and may have to be operational even when all power has been lost to the building.

Gatehouse or security barrier points: In this scenario, a handset or push-button speaker and microphone dials a predetermined number to allow access. These are often provided over long runs of copper cabling through existing duct work. Newer solutions utilize wireless Wi-Fi or mobile networks to provide similar functionality without the cabling requirements.

Elevator phones: Similar to emergency and gatehouse phones, these phones must work when no other building services are functioning, so that someone stuck in an elevator can call for assistance. They are provided over long lengths of copper cabling, which typically run from a PABX room to the roof elevator machinery room and then down the elevator shaft with the internal elevator power cables.

Rugged or explosion-proof phones: Most industrial areas require special handsets. They may need to be ruggedized, water resistant, dust resistant, have an Ingress Protection (IP) rating, designed to restrict any chance of electrical sparks (such as in grain stores or chemical plants), or any combination of these requirements.

Wireless or DECT handsets: Typically, these phones are used in large areas with only a few people, such as a warehouse, but also where users are very mobile, such as hospitals or airports.

Devices integrated with public address systems: These allow people to dial an extension and make building-wide announcements, such as fire alarm test warnings.

All these scenarios, and many more, can be supported by Lync. You need to understand your environment and know what is required from the outset. It's important so that you can plan accordingly to maximize performance. Failure to plan properly will certainly be exposed during migration and coexistence.

Integration Options

There are two basic approaches to Lync and PBX coexistence. The first is where the two platforms exist and calls are routed between them but there is no integration at a user level between them. A user can have extensions on both the PBX and Lync, but they are independent of each other.

The second is where the user's PBX phone is connected to their Lync identity and they are able to control their PBX phone from within Lync. This is called Remote Call Control (RCC) and is covered later in the chapter.

Where you logically place Lync in relation to the PBX gives you different options for call routing, as discussed next.

Lync Behind PBX

When Lync resides logically behind the PBX, all incoming and outbound calls still route via the PBX. The connection to Lync can be via an E1/J1/T1 connection from the PBX to a Lync-approved gateway and then on to Lync, or using Direct SIP. This method is the least intrusive and allows your telephony team to remain in control of the call routing. It is, therefore, normally the easiest to deploy, so it can be popular for proof-of-concept or pilot deployments.

If the PBX supports SIP IP trunks, it may be possible to connect the PBX and Lync directly using a SIP trunk across your internal network so long as it is listed as supported in the OIP. This removes the need to add any interfaces to your PBX, but not having a gateway removes a point of demarcation between the PBX and Lync. Some organizations still prefer to use a gateway with SIP trunks. For example, if your PBX is not supported, a gateway can translate between the PBX and Lync to give you a supported environment. Quite often, a demarcation device has unexpected benefits during the project, because additional functions or devices are involved in the migration and can be supported by the gateway.

SIDE-BY-SIDE

In this scenario, the existing PBX and Lync sit logically alongside each other with a gateway sitting in front of them terminating the PSTN or SIP trunks, as shown in Figure 18.12. This could be a gateway such as the NET VX or UX or, in very large environments, it may be carrier-class equipment working with SS7 signaling direct with the PSTN. The importance of this gateway is that it exists at the very edge of the voice network. This gateway allows a point of control over the call routing before the call reaches the PBX, Lync, or the PSTN. In this position, it can reroute calls intelligently using an AD lookup.

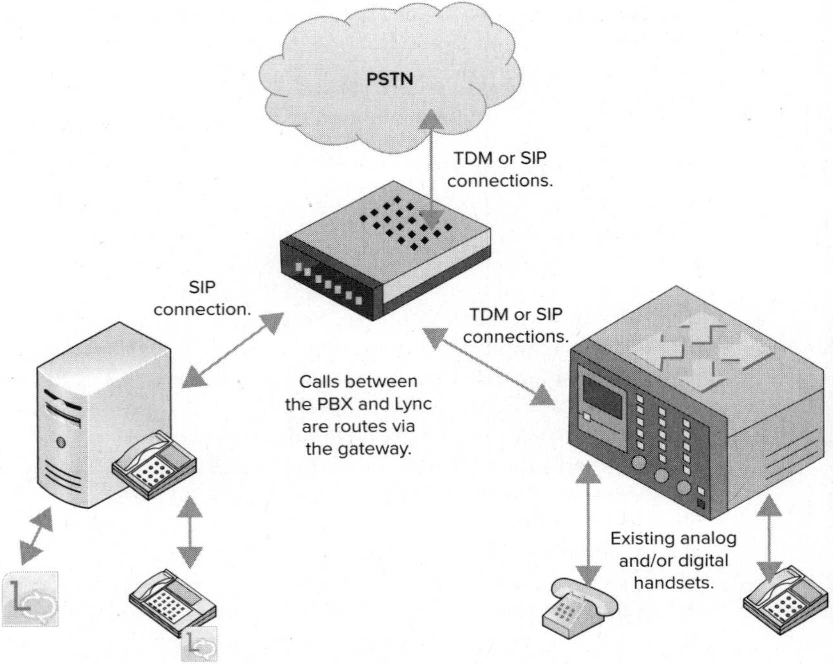

FIGURE 18.12 The side-by-side arrangement of PBX and Lync with a gateway in front

With Active Directory–based routing, the gateway constantly queries AD for relevant user configuration, usually based around the population of the msRTCSIP-Line attribute, and routes a call based on this information. If the inbound call destination is found to match the number in the msRTCSIP-Line attribute, the calls to that user are routed only to Lync. This provides for very easy migration of users and rollback if required, all from within common management tools. There is no need to change the gateway or PBX configuration to alter inbound call routing.

PBX: THE ROUTE OF LAST RESORT

Sometimes it is possible to configure the PBX to route to Lync as the route of last resort, in a similar way that IP routers are able to have a route (the default route, typically to your ISP) that says, "If I don't know where to route this address, route it to this upstream gateway for resolution." Some PBXs can be configured in a similar way, so when the phone extension is migrated to Lync and removed from the PBX, the PBX passes the call to another device to resolve. In the side-by-side scenario, the gateway resolves the routing; when Lync resides behind the PBX, then Lync resolves.

PBX BEHIND LYNC

Placing the PBX behind Lync is similar in approach to placing Lync behind the PBX, although this is rarely done because the PBX is more established within your environment. The advantage of this approach is that from day one you establish Lync as the point of control to the PSTN and you minimize any disruption from decommissioning the PBX, compared to placing Lync behind the PBX initially. However, this approach requires all the effort, and more, of a side-by-side deployment without the advantages of dual-forking. Think through your objectives carefully before adopting this method.

RECOMMENDATION AND TIPS

Wherever possible, it is generally preferable to use the side-by-side method with the gateway truncating the PSTN connections and routing calls to either Lync or PBX as needed. This involves minimal disruption initially, because the PSTN circuits can be configured to effectively pass straight through the gateway to the PBX. During migration, the side-by-side method gives the best flexibility of call routing options and when all users are migrated the PBX can be decommissioned without impacting the production environment.

Whichever logical deployment approach you choose, there are two items you need to be conscious of during the period of coexistence.

The first is link capacity and call routing. On the first day of coexistence, the majority of users will remain on the PBX and very few calls will be terminating on Lync. As your migration progresses, more calls will terminate on Lync until a point when half your traffic is on Lync and half is on the PBX. From this point on, the amount of traffic on the PBX will decline. Think of this as a set of scales with the load gradually transferring from one side to the other. As the traffic patterns change, you must make sure the connections between the systems are sized to handle the appropriate level of traffic. There will also be a certain amount of tromboning, which is acceptable as long as it is managed. *Tromboning* occurs where a call from one system, say the PBX, is transferred to the other, Lync, and then transferred back to the PBX—like a trombone going out and in again. This can happen if users divert their extensions, or sometimes it happens through misconfiguration. A certain amount of tromboning is to be expected during migration, but it must be managed so it does not become excessive. Worse still, it can lead to circular routing of calls, where a call passes back and forth between the two systems until there are no free channels or system resources to route more calls.

The second important thing to be aware of is the number of translation patterns available on the PBX. Subject to the way you deploy Lync and the specific functionality on the PBX, each extension or range of extensions will require entries on the PBX to reroute the extension number to Lync. Although this is rarely a problem early on, it can quickly become an issue as you progress through your deployment. Once it is encountered, often the only way around this is either an expensive PBX software upgrade, which is what you are trying to avoid by deploying Lync, or changing your coexistence method during your project. Note that while the number of translation patterns supported by a PBX can be found, they often get used in seemingly mystical ways, and the limit can be reached unexpectedly soon!

Using RCC to Integrate with Your PBX

Remote Call Control (RCC) allows you to control your PBX phone from the Lync client and thereby continue using your PBX as the voice transport, while using the Lync client to provide features such as click-to-call and address lookup. RCC as a feature is available with a variety of PBX systems. This section will discuss RCC in general so you may find specific features; how they behave will depend on your specific PBX and how it is configured. To begin, let's take a look at the features that RCC provides. The user can do any of the following:

- Make an outgoing call.
- Answer an incoming call; the PBX handset will generally answer in hands-free mode.
- Answer an incoming call with an instant message. (This will be available only if the calling number can be matched with an IM address in the Global Address List or in the receiving party's Lync contacts list.)
- Transfer a call.
- Forward an incoming call.
- Place a call on hold.
- Change the active call between concurrent calls, placing the nonactive call on hold.
- Answer a call while already in a call—i.e., answer a waiting call.
- Dial dual-tone multifrequency (DTMF) digits.

In addition to these features, when a call comes in, Lync will try to resolve calling numbers to names at the client using the Exchange GAL, Lync contacts list, and Outlook contacts. Entries in the Conversation History folder in Outlook for made and received calls and missed call notifications will be created if Lync is signed in when the missed call occurs.

Video and RCC

It is very important to note that when you enable Lync clients for RCC, they can no longer make video calls. In OCS 2007 R2, there was the scenario where you could make an OCS video call, but the audio portion went over the PBX voice system. With the current release (CU3) of Lync, this is not the case. You must be aware that you are losing video functionality when you deploy RCC. If you used this functionality in OCS, you can only hope that Microsoft rectifies this in the future.

A user enabled for RCC cannot be enabled for Lync Enterprise Voice. They will, however, be able to make and receive Lync PC-to-PC voice calls using the Lync client and join the audio content of a conference created by an enterprise voice user, assuming they have the relevant headset. An RCC-enabled user can also dial into a conference via their PBX handset.

To enable the Lync client to control the PBX handset, the RCC feature requires a SIP/CSTA gateway between Lync and the PBX. Computer Supported Telecommunications Applications (CSTA) is a standard managed by Ecma International. The SIP/CSTA gateway connects to Lync using TCP/IP and typically connects to the PBX using TCP/IP also. There are two main aspects to configuring Lync and RCC. The first is the configuration of the Lync backend, and the second is the configuration of the end user.

Configuring the Lync Backend

Because of the differences in how each particular vendor's SIP/CSTA gateways are configured, this section will not cover the installation of that piece of RCC. Instead, you should refer to the documentation supplied by the relevant vendor to understand how it should be configured. Once the SIP/CSTA gateway is installed, you can progress with the Lync configuration elements.

Lync must be configured to forward CSTA requests to the SIP/CSTA gateway. Each Lync pool can have its own CSTA route, and you can configure a global static route that will be used if an individual pool has not been configured. Note that the relationship of one CSTA server per Lync pool may influence your pool design based on where your PBXs are deployed and if they are from the same vendor. For example, if you have different PBXs with their own SIP/CSTA gateways in two locations, each SIP/CSTA gateway will require its own Lync pool.

The route you create can use either TCP or TLS protocols. Note that sometimes using the TLS protocol can resolve routing and trust issues, even though the gateway has been configured as trusted within Lync. Because it is also more secure as a result, this is the preferred deployment option.

If you have migrated from Office Communications Server, you must ensure that any previously entered routes or application entries for RCC are first deleted. You can use the `Get-CsStaticRoutingConfiguration` and `Get-CsTrustedApplication` PowerShell commands without any parameters to view these settings and then use the related `Remove` cmdlets to get rid of any unneeded entries.

To create a new route, you must use the `New-CsStaticRoute` PowerShell cmdlet from within the Lync Server Management Shell. The format of the command for a TCP-based route is:

```
New-CsStaticRoute -TCPRoute -Destination <gateway IP address or FQDN> -Port
<gateway SIP listening port> -MatchUri <destination domain>
```

Use the following syntax for a TLS route:

```
New-CsStaticRoute -TLSRoute -Destination <gateway FQDN> -Port <gateway SIP
listening port> -UseDefaultCertificate $true -MatchUri <destination domain>
```

The `MatchUri` parameter supports wildcards—for example, `*.mydomain.com`—to minimize the number of routes you must add. This domain name matches the domain configured for the CSTA gateway. When adding a TLS route, you must use an FQDN as the destination, while a TCP route can use either an FQDN or an IP address. Note that if you set `UseDefaultCertificate` to False, the `TLSCertIssuer` and `TLSCertSerialNumber` parameters must be specified for the certificate you are using. These parameters set the issuing CA name and the TLS certificate serial number.

When the `New-CsStaticRoute` command is issued, the default values of the following parameters shouldn't be changed: `Enabled = True`, `MatchOnlyPhoneUri = False`, and `ReplaceHostInRequestUri = False`. These parameters allow for certain complex scenarios which are unlikely to be needed when using RCC.

Once you've created the static route, a trusted application entry must be created for RCC. This entry allows Lync to use the route that was just created. To create this entry, use the `New-CsTrustedApplicationPool` cmdlet.

If the static route you created uses TCP, use the following command syntax to create the trusted application entry:

```
New-CsTrustedApplicationPool -Identity <IP address or FQDN of the SIP/CSTA
gateway> [-Registrar <Service ID or FQDN of the Registrar service>] -Site <Site
ID for the site where the trusted application pool is to be created>
```

For example:

```
New-CsTrustedApplicationPool -Identity 192.168.254.200 -Registrar lync-se01.
gaots.local -Site EMEA
```

Then add the trusted application to the pool using the `New-CsTrustedApplication` command:

```
New-CsTrustedApplication -ApplicationID <application name>
-TrustedApplicationPoolFqdn <IP address or FQDN of the SIP/CSTA gateway> -Port
<SIP gateway listening port> -EnableTcp
```

For example:

```
New-CsTrustedApplication -ApplicationID CSTAGatewayApp
-TrustedApplicationPoolFqdn 192.168.254.200 -Port 5060 -EnableTcp
```

If the static route you created uses TLS, use the following command syntax to create the trusted application entry:

```
New-CsTrustedApplicationPool -Identity <FQDN of the SIP/CSTA gateway> [-Registrar
<Service ID or FQDN of the Registrar service>] -Site <Site ID for the site where
the trusted application pool is to be created>
```

For example:

```
New-CsTrustedApplicationPool -Identity cstagw.gaots.local -Registrar lync-se01
.gaots.local -Site EMEA
```

Then add the trusted application to the pool using the `New-CsTrustedApplication` command again:

```
New-CsTrustedApplication -ApplicationID <application name>
-TrustedApplicationPoolFqdn <FQDN of the SIP/CSTA gateway> -Port <SIP gateway
listening port >
```

For example:

```
New-CsTrustedApplication -ApplicationID CSTAGatewayApp
-TrustedApplicationPoolFqdn cstagw.gaots.local -Port 5061
```

Once the trusted application is created and added to the pool, make your changes active by publishing the topology using this command:

```
Enable-CsTopology
```

If the SIP/CSTA gateway uses TCP, its IP address must be defined in Topology Builder. This is not required if the SIP/CSTA gateway uses TLS. To complete this task, start Topology Builder and download the existing topology. Once it is downloaded, expand Trusted Application Services in the site where you are configuring RCC, right-click the application pool that you created, and choose Edit Properties. Uncheck the Enable Replication Of Configuration Data To This Pool checkbox. Then choose Limit Service Usage To Selected IP Address, and in the Primary IP Address text box enter the IP address of your SIP/CSTA gateway. You must then publish these changes to the topology. To do so, click Lync Server 2010 and choose Actions and then Publish.

User Configuration

RCC can be configured using in-band provisioning policies on the server or by using client-side settings within Lync. For RCC to work, a Line Server URI and Line URI must be specified for each user. The syntax of these settings must match the syntax expected by your SIP/CSTA gateway. Check the supplied documentation for your gateway for further information.

The domain that you specify in the Line Server URI must match the domain specified in the `MatchURI` parameter in the static route you created in "Configuring the Lync Backend." The Line URI specifies the phone number assigned to the user in E.164 format with a `tel:` prefix—for example, `tel:+12121234567`. If you want to add an extension number to the Line URI, the format becomes `tel:+12121234567;ext=4567`.

To configure these settings with the Management Shell, use the `Set-CsUser` cmdlet as follows:

```
Set-CsUser –Identity <User ID> -EnterpriseVoiceEnabled $false –LineServerUri
<SIP URI of the SIP/CSTA gateway> -LineUri <TEL URI of the user>
-RemoteCallControlTelephonyEnabled $true.
```

To configure these settings in the Lync Control Panel, take the following steps:

1. Start the Lync Control Panel and choose Users.
2. Find and select the user you want to configure using the Search tool. Choose Edit ➢ Modify and then choose the Telephony section.
3. To enable Remote Call Control of the PBX phone from Lync 2010 and to allow the user to make PC-to-PC audio calls and PC-to-phone calls, click Remote Call Control. Enter the telephone number of the user in the Line URI, and in Line Server URI enter the SIP URI of the SIP/CSTA gateway.
4. If you want to enable RCC but not allow PC-to-PC calls, click Remote Call Control Only. Enter the telephone number of the user in the Line URI, and in Line Server URI enter the SIP URI of the SIP/CSTA gateway.
5. When you have completed the changes, click Commit.

Phone Number Normalization

At this point, you've configured the basics of RCC and set up a user to utilize the feature. However, there is one more important area to take into account, which will dramatically affect the usefulness of RCC. That is *number normalization*, which converts numbers Lync finds in AD or user contacts into numbers that Lync and the SIP/CSTA gateway can dial.

When a network uses Remote Call Control, phone number normalization rules are applied to inbound and outbound calls. These rules are downloaded as part of the Address Book service.

When an inbound call is received for an RCC-enabled user, the calling line ID (CLID), which is the number of the person making the call, must first be normalized to E.164 format by either the PBX or the SIP/CSTA gateway. This enables Lync to perform a reverse number lookup (RNL) on the number when the call is received against the Outlook contact list of the user receiving the call and against the GAL. If this lookup resolves a name, the name is presented within Lync rather than the calling number.

For outbound calls, the phone number normalization rules are applied before the called number is passed to the SIP/CSTA gateway.

It is generally best practice to keep all numbers within the Lync environment in E.164 format. However, reverse number lookup can rapidly become complicated, subject to the specific environment. It is sometimes necessary to configure phone normalization rules so that an alternative dial plan is maintained. This is especially true in large environments that may not have unique DDIs assigned to everyone or where routing codes are needed in conjunction with extension numbers.

Address Book Migration

If you have previously used RCC with Office Communications Server 2007 or Office Communications Server 2007 R2 and you customized the phone normalization rules, you will need to perform some manual steps as part of your migration to Lync.

1. In the root of the Address Book shared folder, find the file `Company_Phone_Number_Normalization_Rules.txt`. Copy this file to the root of the Address Book shared folder for your Lync Server 2010 pool.
2. The file will need to be edited using a text editor—for example, Notepad—to change some entries that are no longer supported with Lync. Any entry containing strings that include required whitespace or punctuation will cause normalization rules to fail, because these characters are stripped out of the string that is input to the normalization rules. If you have strings that include whitespace or punctuation, these must be modified.
3. In addition to normalization rules, if you set the `PartitionbyOU` WMI property to True to allow Address Books to be created for each OU within Active Directory, you must use the `msRTCSIP-GroupingId` Active Directory attribute on users and contacts if you want to continue grouping Address Book entries—for example, to limit the scope of Address Book searches.
4. Use the `msRTCSIP-GroupingId` attribute within a script to assign a value for each common group. For example, for each user within an OU set their `msRTCSIP-groupId` to the OU's name.

Deploying a Survivable Branch Appliance

A key feature of Lync over previous versions of OCS is the ability to deploy Remote Site Survivability so that if a WAN link back to the central Lync pool goes down, local PSTN connectivity is maintained. In order to implement such functionality, an appliance known as a Survivable Branch Appliance (SBA) must be deployed at the branch location.

Once the SBA is deployed, Lync users in the branch office will register to it as their primary registrar; they will have full Lync features provided by both the SBA and the main Lync front-end pool. In the event of a WAN outage, the Lync users remain registered to the local SBA appliance and will still have full outbound and inbound calling capability via the SBA.

The SBA combines a gateway device capable of performing media bypass, security, and all the other features associated with an enhanced Lync gateway device, with an embedded server running the Lync SBA software element. The whole idea of having a third-party appliance for this role simplifies the branch deployment, and it avoids having dedicated servers and their associated IT management and maintenance, which often become a problem in small branch locations.

As with the enhanced gateway devices, a range of vendors and appliances is available for SBAs. A list can be found on the OIP page discussed earlier in the chapter.

Preparing Lync for the SBA

The process of deploying a branch site SBA device is relatively simple. First, you must prestage the SBA in the central site. This requires the following:

- A reverse lookup must be performed on the DNS server for the SBA.
- DNS *A* records must be available for the gateway and SBA.
- The SBA should be added as a computer before the deployment, and RTCUniversalSBATechnician should be in the default group as described in the following discussion.
- A Service Principal Name needs to be applied to the SBA computer in `ADSI.edit`, as discussed shortly.
- The account used within the gateway to deploy the SBA (for example, the Administrator) should be a member of the RTCUniversalSBATechnician group.
- The SBA should be configured in the correct branch site from Lync Topology Builder and successfully published to the CMS.

To begin the configuration, make sure that DNS *A* (address) records for both the SBA and gateway IP address, resolving to their relevant FQDN, are in place.

Once the DNS records are in place, you can add the SBA into Active Directory. Make sure you do this *before* making any changes in the Lync Topology Builder.

1. Log onto a machine with the Active Directory Management Tools using an account that can create computer accounts in Active Directory.

2. Open Active Directory Users and Computers. In an organizational unit where you store computer objects, right-click and select New ➤ Computer.
3. In the window that opens, enter a name for the SBA. Note that this should be just the hostname, not the FQDN. Under User or group, click the Change button, enter **RTCUniversalSBATechnicians**, and then click OK. Click OK again to close.

After completing these steps, you need to add a service principal name (SPN) to the computer account; this is done using ADSI Edit.

To run ADSI Edit, take the following steps:

1. Click Start ➤ Run, enter **adsiedit.msc**, and then click OK. Once the program opens, right-click the root node and select Connect To.
2. Leave all the parameters at their defaults and click OK; then expand the default naming context.
3. Under the location where you created the computer object in step 1 of the previous list, locate the SBA computer account. Right-click it, select Properties, and then scroll down and highlight the servicePrincipalName. Click Edit, enter **HOST/<*SBA FQDN*>**, and click Add. Click OK twice to complete.

Now that you've created the computer account for the SBA in AD, you can move onto configuring the Lync topology.

1. Open up Topology Builder and download the topology from the CMS.
2. Under the central site where this branch site will be linked (EMEA in this case), expand the tree and drill down to the Branch Site folder. Right-click it and select New Branch Site.
3. Enter the Location of the Site for the Name and click Next. Enter a City and Country/Region, and click Next and then Finish.
4. At this stage, the Survivable Branch Appliance Wizard opens to let you configure the SBA. Enter the FQDN of the SBA (which is the host name of the computer you created plus the domain suffix) and then click Next.
5. Select the appropriate front-end pool, in this case `Lync-Se01.gaots.local`, and then click Next.
6. Select the appropriate edge server (assuming you require external connectivity for the branch users), which is `Lync-edge.gaots.local` in this case, and then click Next.
7. On the Define New Survivable Branch Appliance window, as shown in Figure 18.13, enter the FQDN of the gateway. Make sure the port is set for 5067 and the transport protocol is set for TLS, and then click Finish.
8. Once it is complete, publish the topology.

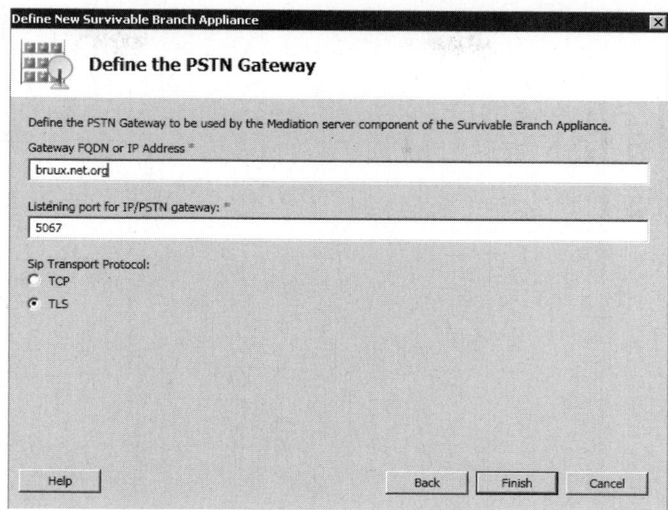

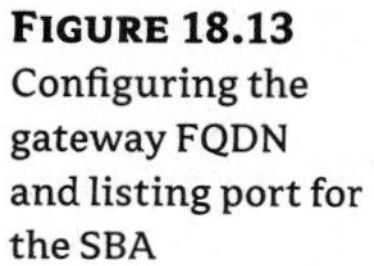
FIGURE 18.13
Configuring the gateway FQDN and listing port for the SBA

Once the main Lync topology and AD changes have been made to accommodate the new branch site, you can begin working on the SBA itself. The following general steps are required:

1. Install and physically cable the SBA at the branch site.
2. Configure an IP address for the SBA.
3. Join the domain.
4. Prepare the SBA and replicate against the front-end pool.
5. Assign the required certificates to enable security.
6. Start the services.
7. Verify the operational status.
8. Start to migrate users in the branch to the SBA.

How these steps are achieved will vary from one vendor to another, and there are key differences in how the SBA and gateway integration is done by each vendor, including the security model and deployment method employed. Figure 18.14 shows the different SBA implementation methods used by different vendors. On the left, the gateway and server are hosted in the same physical chassis, but there is no communication between the elements internally. The SBA is deployed using the standard server interface, while the gateway is configured using a separate interface. On the right, you see a fully integrated example where the embedded server and SBA software are tightly integrated to the gateway element, with a single network interface for all traffic, and a single user interface to configure the gateway and deploy the SBA. This model is highly secure and much easier to deploy in the field.

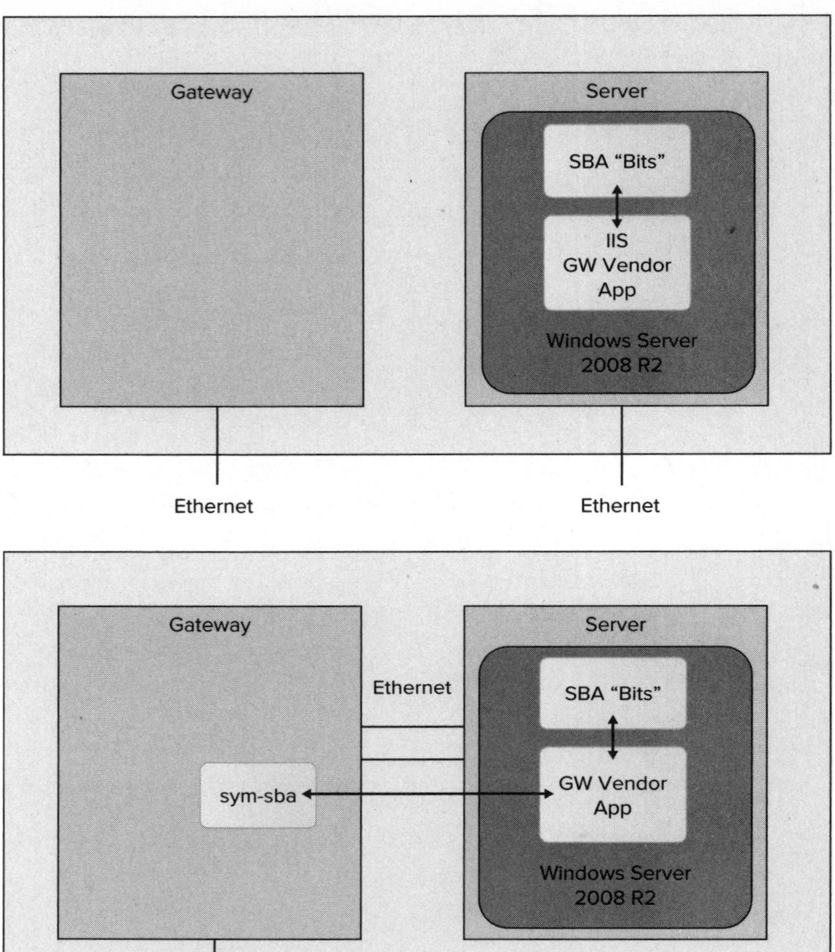

FIGURE 18.14
The different SBA security models

Let's review the UX SBA integration, which follows the true appliance high security model, giving a single user interface to perform both the gateway configuration and the SBA configuration and deployment steps.

The first step is to apply an IP address to the SBA device so that it can communicate with the Lync front-end pool. You must ensure that there is IP connectivity from the SBA to the Lync front end. Next, the SBA must be joined to the domain, using the FQDN that you have already configured in the DNS server. Both of these tasks are performed on the UX using the Deploy Survivable Branch Appliance Wizard within the main gateway GUI interface.

Once the SBA has been joined to the domain, the next step is to prepare the SBA, replicate the configuration against the front-end server, and activate the SBA device against the Lync front end. Again, ensure that there is IP connectivity between the SBA and Lync front end for this step.

Figure 18.15 shows the UX GUI interface with three simple steps to perform all of the preparation, replication, and activation of the SBA with the front-end server.

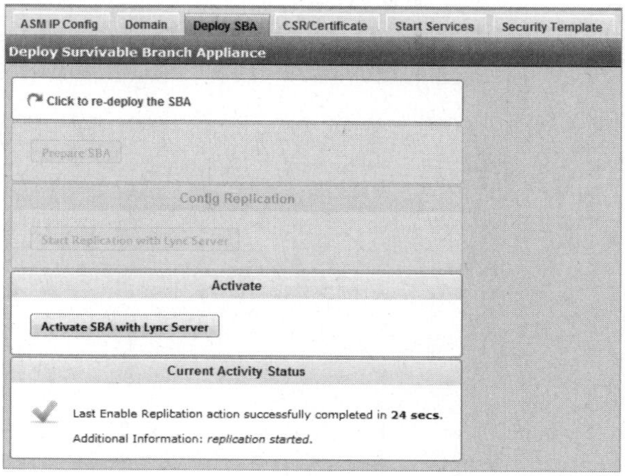

FIGURE 18.15
Deploying and activating the SBA using gateway management CLI

The next step is to configure the certificates required by the SBA to enable TLS secure signaling to the front-end server and Lync clients in the branch. Again the UX Wizard makes this task a simple process; Figure 18.16 shows the wizard screen that performs all of the certificate steps for the SBA.

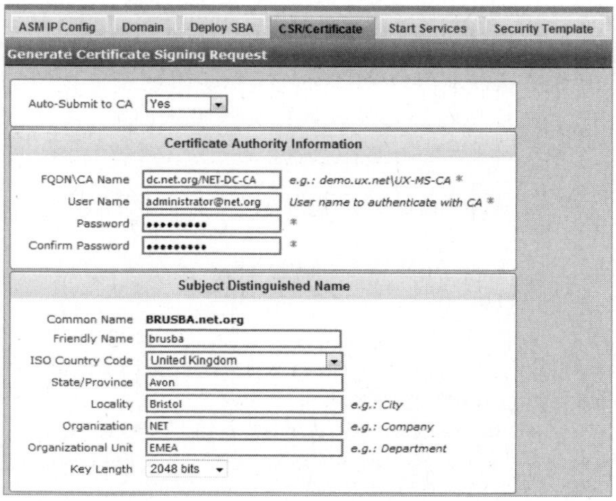

FIGURE 18.16
Configuring certificates for the SBA

Once all of the preceding steps have been completed, the SBA should be fully operational. You can easily verify the SBA processes and status from within the UX GUI interface; Figure 18.17 shows a successfully deployed and activated SBA, with all SBA processes running and showing green (highlighted).

FIGURE 18.17
Verifying SBA system status via the UX GUI

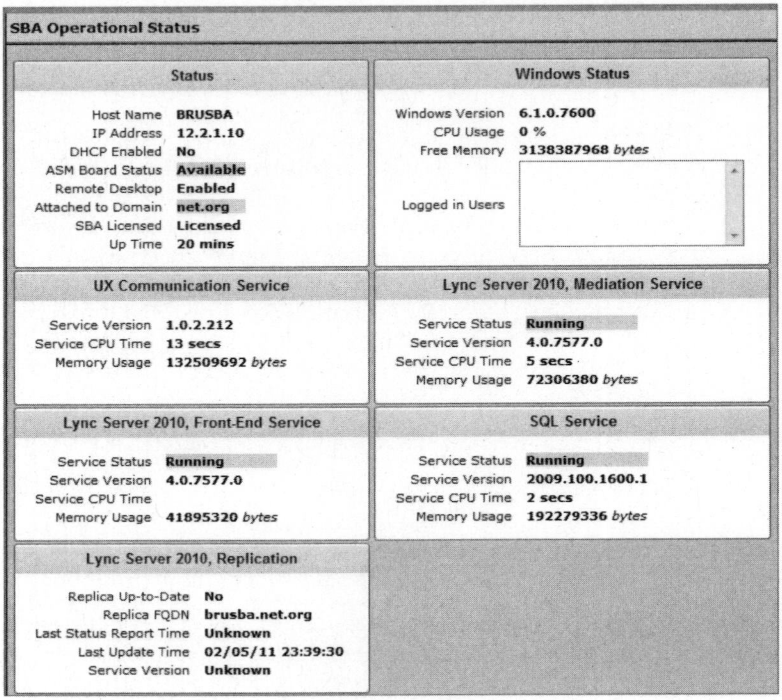

Finally, important considerations for the SBA are how updates are applied, and how a system can be factory-reset or completely reloaded should the need arise. In Figure 18.18, you can see how the UX provides both factory reset and restart functionality, and upgrade/patch ability directly to the SBA server via the Gateway GUI interface. This tight integration makes remote management and maintenance of the SBA much easier.

FIGURE 18.18
The UX SBA Reset and Upgrade options

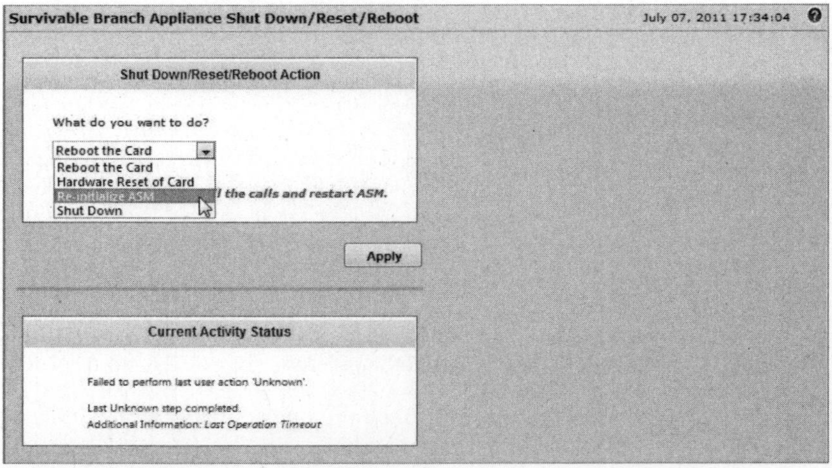

Connecting to Other External Systems via an XMPP Gateway

XMPP stands for the Extensible Messaging and Presence Protocol. Both XMPP and SIP are standards supported by the Internet Engineering Task Force (IETF). XMPP can be compared to the Session Initiation Protocol for Instant Messaging and Presence Leveraging Extensions (SIMPLE).

XMPP is used to provide presence, messaging, and collaboration features by platforms that include Cisco, Jabber, and Google. By providing the XMPP gateway, Microsoft enables interoperability with both open source and competitors' platforms. The gateway supports presence and instant messaging only. Voice, video, and desktop or application sharing are not supported.

The XMPP gateway software can be downloaded from the Microsoft download site at the following URL:

```
www.microsoft.com/download/en/details.aspx?id=8403
```

There is also a single hotfix for the gateway relating to Knowledge Base article number 2404570, which is available at this URL:

```
www.microsoft.com/download/en/details.aspx?id=12722
```

Although the name of the released version of the gateway refers to Office Communications Server 2007 R2, this version is also supported by Lync 2010.

The XMPP gateway can be used to connect to both external and internal services. For example, you may have a client or partner who uses Jabber or you may need to connect to GoogleTalk to extend Public IM Connectivity. This last scenario, connecting to GoogleTalk, is what we'll demonstrate in this section.

Configuration

The XMPP gateway connects to the external interface of the Edge server with a secure SIP connection on port 5061. It connects to the XMPP service on port 5269. You can use the same network interface card and IP address for both services to conserve address use, or use separate interfaces if required. You must make sure these ports are allowed through any firewall installed on the server, including the built-in Windows Firewall in Server 2008 or 2008 R2. Note that these changes must be done manually; unlike the other Lync components, they are not carried out automatically as part of setup.

The XMPP gateway must be installed on its own server; it cannot be collocated with the Edge or any other server role, and it is not supported for virtualization. The supported hardware specifications require a dual-core, dual CPU with 8GB of memory. However, the gateway may work adequately with lower-specification hardware if your use will be limited, depending on the number of users requiring contact with systems served by the XMPP gateway. For example, you might want to enable this functionality for completeness but with the knowledge that there will be minimal use of it.

A single XMPP gateway can support up to ten thousand Lync users, based on each identity having ten contacts requiring access through the gateway. However, the number of contacts each user has will impact the number of users supported and total system throughput.

Once you've installed the gateway, configure it by editing a text file located in the installation directory, by default `C:\Program Files\Microsoft Office Communications Server 2007 R2\XMPP Gateway`. The file to edit is named `TGWConsoleGUI.dll.config`.

Within this file, the IP address of the gateway network interface must be configured for each protocol, SIP and XMPP. The values to set are `SipIP` for the interface connecting to the Lync Edge server's external interface and `XmppIP` for the interface connecting to the XMPP service. If these values are not specified or are incorrect, the service will fail to start.

An example of the file content is shown here, where the server is configured to use the IP address `192.168.1.50`.

```
<?xml version="1.0" standalone="yes" ?>
<configuration>
<appSettings>
<add key="cultureName" value="en-US" />
<!--  Gateway IP to be used for OCS connections  -->
<add key="SipIP" value="192.168.1.50" />
<!--  Gateway IP to be used for XMPP Server connections  -->
<add key="XmppIP" value="192.168.1.50" />
</appSettings>
</configuration>
```

DNS Configuration

This section assumes that you have already configured the Edge server and that external access, federation, and Public IM are all working correctly as discussed in Chapter 6, "Installation." To add the XMPP gateway to your environment, you must create a DNS service record (SRV). The XMPP gateway requires a TCP service record and one for TLS if it is being used. For example, `_xmpp-server._tcp.gaots.local` and `_xmpp-server._tls.gaots.local` would work for the internal systems. These records should be created in the DNS domain that the gateway supports and for each XMPP domain, or namespace, that you want to support within your organization. For public IM purposes, these service records will be created in your public DNS along with your `_sipfederationtls._tcp.gaots.co.uk` record for the Lync Edge.

Configuring SIP Settings

The XMPP gateway has its own MMC snap-in that allows you to edit its settings. On the machine on which the gateway is installed, run MMC and then add the XMPP Gateway snap-in. This can be done with the following steps:

1. Click Start and enter **MMC** in the Search box. Click MMC in the returned results and then choose File ➢ Add/Remove Snap-In and choose XMPP Gateway from the list.

   After changing any settings, you will need to restart the XMPP Gateway service, either via the XMPP snap-in or via the Services Management Console.

2. Within the XMPP gateway MMC, make sure that the SIP and XMPP interfaces are correctly configured. On the left side of the console, expand XMPP Gateway and the SIP Configuration. On the right side, configure the Lync SIP domain, or namespace, to be federated with XMPP.

This will be the same namespace used by your Lync user identities. Note that the gateway can only federate with a single SIP namespace. If you have not created a service record for the domain, you can use the Host entry text box on this screen to specify the FQDN of the external interface of the Edge server.

3. You must also create and configure a certificate for the gateway to communicate with the Lync Access Edge using TLS. The certificate the XMPP gateway uses must be named after the XMPP gateways FQDN and be of the same certificate type used elsewhere by Lync components.

   When you request the certificate following the process outlined in Chapter 6 for the Forefront TMG box, client enhanced key usage (EKU) is an optional requirement, and a subject alternative name (SAN) is required only if the FQDN of the gateway and the computer name the gateway is installed on are different.

4. Once you have selected the certificate, you can then click the Validate tab within the console and confirm that connectivity to the Edge server is working.

Configuring XMPP Settings

Now you're ready to configure the XMPP settings. Take the following steps:

1. On the left side of the console, choose XMPP Configuration.

   On the right side, you must configure the XMPP domains with which you want to federate. For GoogleTalk this includes `gmail.com` and may also include country-specific domains such as `googlemail.co.uk`. Not all country-specific domains have been tested, so you should perform your initial configuration and tests with a `gmail.com` address.

2. Click Add and enter **`gmail.com`** as the domain name. The XMPP server name, username, and password can be left blank for GoogleTalk.

3. On the right side of this dialog box, choose the security setting TCP DIALBACK.

Configuring Additional Settings

Within the settings node, you can change the default timers for Connections and Sessions. These are generally best left to their default values.

Within the Connections tab, XMPP Idle Connection Timer and the XMPP Refresh Connection Timer can be changed. The Idle Connection Timer determines the idle connection time for the outgoing XMPP connection. When this value is reached, the connection to the XMPP server is closed. If you never want to close this connection (which is highly unlikely), check the Never Close Idle Connection checkbox. The XMPP Refresh Connection Timer allows you to change how often the XMPP server connection is refreshed. The Never Refresh Connection Timer checkbox allows you to make sure connections are never refreshed, which again is highly unlikely to be required.

The Sessions tab allows timers for each session and/or presence subscription to be changed. The IM/MUC Session Idle Timer specifies how long the gateway keeps a session; once this time period is reached, the gateway deletes the session. The Subscription Refresh timer can be used to minimize the load on the server. The default setting is recommended. Increasing this value will reduce server load while potentially giving users stale presence, and reducing it will increase server load while increasing presence accuracy. When this time period is reached, the presence subscription from Lync is deleted or a Subscribe refresh is initiated by XMPP, depending on which side of the gateway the subscription originated.

Remember that the XMPP service must be restarted for any changes to take effect.

Lync Edge Configuration

Any XMPP domains you want to federate with must be configured within the Lync Server Control Panel. Under External User Access, choose Federated Domains and add the XMPP domains that you have configured on the XMPP gateway. For each XMPP domain, specify the FQDN of the XMPP gateway as the Access Edge service. Once you've added all your domains, click Commit to apply your changes.

User Configuration

Support for federation and public IM must be enabled for Lync at the forest level, and individual users must be enabled for Public IM Connectivity to utilize the gateway, even if they are connecting to a system that is inside your organization, as all traffic will route via the Edge.

Lync and XMPP have different presence statuses, and the gateway maps these differences as shown in Table 18.1.

Table 18.1: Lync and XMPP Presence States

Lync	XMPP
Available	Available
Available	Free To Chat
Away	Away
Away	Extended Away
Be Right Back	Away
Busy	Do Not Disturb
Do Not Disturb	Do Not Disturb
Offline	Unavailable

Integrating with Hardware Video Conferencing Platforms

Lync provides for video conferencing natively and can accommodate sessions ranging from a peer-to-peer call to up to 250 participants in a video conference. Although this desktop video capability is useful and gaining traction in organizations, there are already many deployments of room-based and other hardware video platforms. Thankfully, Lync has the capability to integrate with these systems to provide enhanced capability. For example, not only can a hardware video endpoint dial a Lync desktop video user and hold an audio and video call, but equally a Lync user can be dialed into a conference hosted on a hardware video Multipoint Control Unit (MCU), a device to mix and distribute channels of audio and video, so as to participate in a conference that also includes those on the high-end video system in the board room. It's also possible to use the external access capabilities of Lync to allow remote or federated users to dial into conferences held on hardware systems; such systems can provide connectivity to a wide range of legacy video standards and also different ways of displaying end users, so that all video participants can be seen at once. By contrast, Lync alone shows only the active speaker and your personal video preview.

Before we dive into configuration, it is important to note that Lync can interoperate with a wide variety of video systems, including those from Polycom, Lifesize, and Radvision. In this section, we'll cover some of the points of integration with the Polycom range of devices.

Polycom devices have two main areas of integration with Lync: endpoints and conference units. They have their HDX systems, which are essentially endpoints of different scales and sizes, ranging from simple desktop video units to room-based systems. They also have telepresence systems that are fitted in an entire room to give the experience of actually sitting around a table with those at the other end of the call. Polycom also has its RMX range; these devices are video MCUs. They provide the ability to host conferences and can tie into a wide range of video systems via various protocols, including ISDN, H.323, and SIP. For more information about the devices available, see the Polycom website:

`www.polycom.co.uk`

Polycom is working very closely with Microsoft to ensure that their products integrate closely with Lync, and they are frequently adding new functionality. Two main scenarios are possible. The first is simply enabling one of the endpoint HDX devices to dial into Lync. This is a relatively straightforward process. Assuming that the device has the latest software, it is simply a case of creating an identity for it and letting it register to Lync. This identity could either be that of an end user if the system is a personal desktop video unit, or one created for a conference room if the unit is a room-based system. The second scenario we'll cover allows integration between Lync and an RMX unit so that Lync users can internally or externally participate in conferences hosted on the RMX unit.

Given the complex nature of the configuration and the fact that new versions of the Polycom software add features and occasionally change setup steps, we won't cover the step-by-step configuration here. We'll look at the Lync and HDX integration from the Lync perspective. Then you can refer to resources that will provide up-to-date and detailed information about how to configure integration between Lync and the Polycom systems.

Configuring Lync and HDX Integration

As mentioned, having a Polycom HDX system sign onto Lync is relatively straightforward. There are a couple of prerequisites that must be checked before you try, though. First, you must confirm that NTLM authentication is enabled on the registrar. This can be checked in the Lync Server Control Panel (LSCP) on the Security tab under the Registrar policy as shown in Figure 18.19.

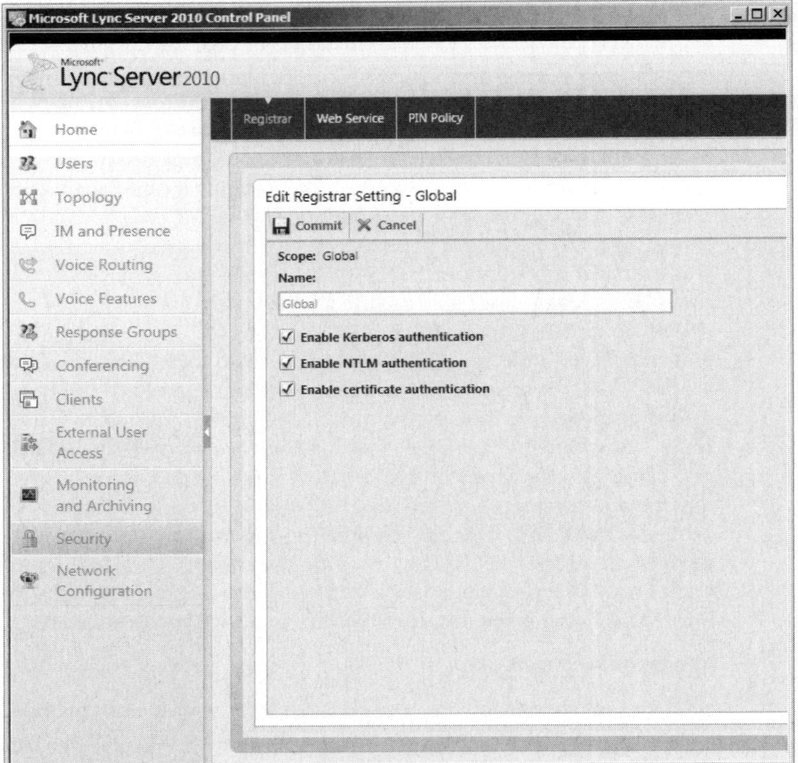

FIGURE 18.19 Checking the authentication types available on the registrar policy

As long as NTLM is enabled, you are ready to create the required users. It is, of course, possible to have any Lync user who has Enterprise Voice enabled (although it doesn't need a number assigned) log onto the HDX, so creating specific users is only needed if this is a room system that you need to specifically identify rather than a personal one.

To refresh your memory, here's the required command to enable the user for Lync and Enterprise Voice:

```
Enable-CsUser -Identity "Test User1" -RegistrarPool Lync-se01.gaots.local
-SipAddressType UserPrincipalName -PassThru | Set-CsUser - Identity "Test User1"
-EnableEnterpriseVoice $True
```

This command will enable the user Test User1 for Lync and Enterprise Voice. The user that is now enabled will fall under any relevant Lync policies, so make sure that if you need external access, you have the relevant policies in place as covered in Chapter 10, "User Administration."

The HDX systems have an Address Book, which should be populated with the entries from the Lync user's buddy list. To populate the list, log onto a PC Lync client with the Lync user and populate the list in the normal way.

Finally, you must ensure that the Lync encryption settings are configured to match those configured on the HDX. The HDX supports the Lync default settings on RequireEncryption;

however, the HDX can also be configured not to use encryption. In that case, you will need to configure Lync to accept such connections using the command:

```
Set-CsMediaConfiguration -EncryptionLevel supportencryption
```

This will allow Lync to accept unencrypted media connections.

You must follow the steps in the *Polycom Unified Communications Deployment Guide for Microsoft Environments* document at the following link to configure the HDX:

```
http://support.polycom.com/global/documents/support/setup_maintenance/products/
video/UC_Deploy_Guide_MS.pdf
```

FURTHER REFERENCE MATERIAL

Although we have limited space to discuss the connectivity options in this chapter, the following resources provide useful information about the integration of Polycom and Lync systems.

This is a Polycom website with configuration material:

```
http://support.polycom.com/PolycomService/support/us/support/strategic_partner_
solutions/microsoft_software_download.html
```

This is a direct download link for the Polycom Unified Communications Deployment Guide for Microsoft Environments document:

```
http://support.polycom.com/global/documents/support/setup_maintenance/products/
video/UC_Deploy_Guide_MS.pdf
```

Here are some other blog sites that are worth viewing:

```
http://blog.schertz.name/category/polycom/

http://mikestacy.typepad.com/mike-stacys-blog/rmx/

http://blogs.technet.com/b/meacoex/archive/2011/05/26/lync-with-polycom-rmx-
integration.aspx
```

Using Third-Party Software Enhancements

As mentioned at the beginning of this chapter, Lync provides an open platform on which organizations can build their own products and services to extend Lync's core functionality. There have long been add-ons for legacy PBX phone systems to provide capabilities such as call billing and call recording, and their availability for Lync reflects the maturity of the Lync platform for voice services. Of course, because it is a software platform, the ability to build products around Lync is vastly greater than that of legacy PBXs. As you will see from some of the options described next, many varied and useful offerings are available.

Reusing SIP Handsets

Even in deployments where headsets are the predominant form of interface with the voice system, there will often be the need for physical handsets, and where there is a large investment in handsets you may want to reuse them.

NET SmartSIP allows a range of phones to be reused with Lync, using SIP phone loads rather than its own proprietary protocols. It does this by acting as a proxy, or more specifically a SIP back-to-back user agent (B2BUA), allowing phones running third-party SIP stacks to sign into SmartSIP, which then registers the phone with Lync, acting as a broker between the phones and Lync SIP stacks, as shown in Figure 18.20. SmartSIP provides not only telephony support between the SIP handsets and Lync, but also presence status to Lync users to show when the SIP phone is registered/online or in a call.

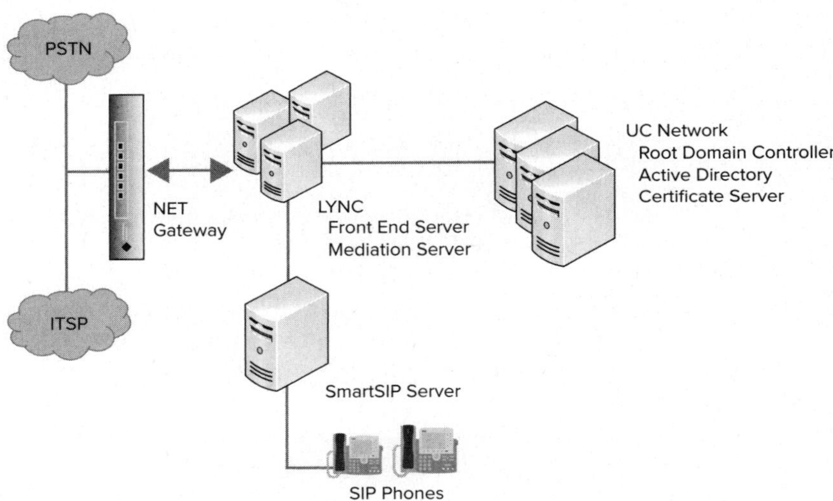

FIGURE 18.20 An overview of the SmartSIP architecture

In this way phones from Aastra, Avaya, Cisco, Linksys and Polycom can be reused with Lync. The SmartSIP server includes a TFPT server, which allows it to act as a central provisioning server. Phones can easily be correlated to a user by entering the MAC address of the phone handset within the user's AD record. As the phone registers to SmartSIP, it is automatically provisioned with all the necessary user information, and the user's presence is updated within Lync.

Call Recording

Two types of call recording are typically used: trunk-side and line-side. Trunk-side recording typically records all calls that include a participant from inside or outside the organization, both for inbound and outbound calls. Line-side recording allows calls between internal extensions, and also those external to the organization, to be recorded; this approach gives greater flexibility by allowing any call to be recorded.

Trunk-side recording equipment normally sits between the PBX and the carrier's customer premises equipment. This equipment can continue to be used with your Lync gateway. Note, however, that external calls may also exit the organization over a federated connection via the Lync Edge server role and that they may still need to be recorded subject to your organization's regulatory and compliance needs.

If you need to record line-side while using Enterprise Voice, then a third-party application is required. Using Lync APIs, the recording applications will either monitor the call or will add a call recording agent to the call, turning it into a conference, and will then record the call as shown in Figure 18.21, using the Geomant recording application.

FIGURE 18.21
Conversation with Recording server participant

If line-side recording is used a lot in your organization, you need to reflect the increased use of audio conferencing in your capacity planning.

Call Center

Lync includes basic call distribution and response group services, but they are not intended to provide a complete call or contact center solution. However, the APIs within the Lync platform allow independent software vendors to create full-featured contact center solutions.

Typical contact center products allow agents to have multiple subject skills and ratings. This can also reflect which languages an agent speaks. A contact center typically has to support a matrix of competencies, language expertise, and call routing rules; the latter can include timers to decide how long a call waits before being routed to a lower skilled agent.

Contact or call center products are deeply integrated with business processes and often have links with line-of-business applications to prepopulate information to an agent's screen.

Call center software is its own specialty, often sitting alongside a PBX running, effectively, as its PBX for the agents. Microsoft, by providing the APIs to Lync that software developers require, enables call center software to be developed with all the UC functionality of Lync, while also including call center specific functionality.

Geomant Contact Expert is one of many call center products available for Lync. When selecting your Lync call center platform, be aware of how the product performs call control. Some applications use Lync for all call control functionality, such as connections to the PSTN and signaling to make or receive a call. Others have their own call control and integrate with Lync presence separately.

Products that use Lync for call control are generally preferred, as this reduces complexity and cost, but there can be scenarios where the call center product may need to have its own call control. For example, you might need to provide call center functionality to agents, some of whom use Enterprise Voice while others use the PBX. As always, plan carefully and understand both the likely and worst-case scenarios for where call signaling and media traffic will route, paying attention to any circular routing or tromboning.

Call Billing

Call billing is a traditional PBX requirement. It provides for call costs to be calculated and then billed to internal departments. It also allows you to monitor costs and take action where required. For example, if a particular extension has very high usage, that may imply excessive personal calls or out-of-business-hours calls.

With Lync and unified communications, the environment you need to monitor includes more ways to communicate, including instant messaging and conferencing. In addition to calls to the public network, you may want to monitor usage of the entire unified communications environment. This can help show return-on-investment by reduced travel or call spend and also allow you to calculate reduced carbon footprint.

PhonEX ONE from MindCTI is an example of a call-billing platform that has been updated to reflect unified communications. It collects the raw information provided by the Lync Monitoring server role and creates easy-to-understand graphical reports of usage.

Figure 18.22 shows a sample report detailing outbound calls by carrier in the top-left panel, number of calls by device type in the top-right panel, and usage of different roles during the day across the bottom.

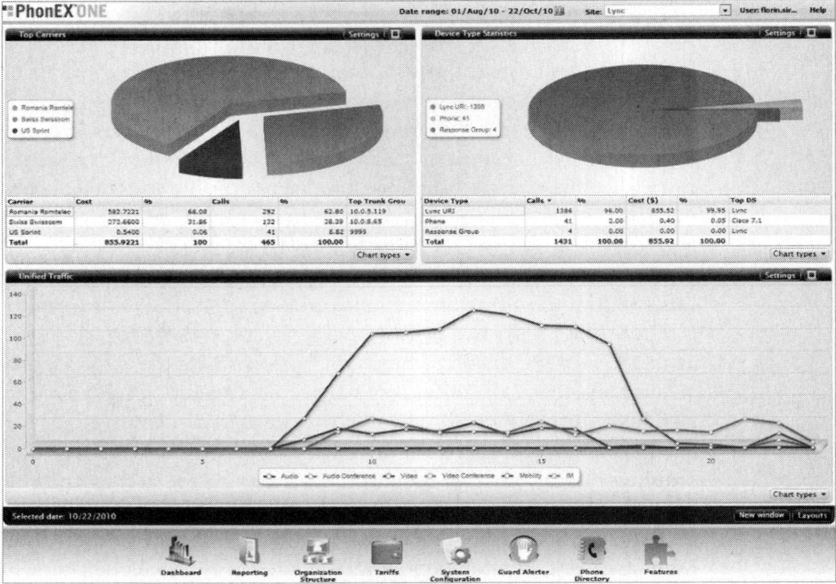

FIGURE 18.22
The MindCTI PhoneEX ONE system dashboard

Used with thought, these reports can help you plan the server hardware capacity and link capacity as you deploy. PhoneEX ONE can also connect to your existing PBX, giving you a single view of usage during your migration from a telephony platform to Lync unified communications.

Combining Presence with Location

You already have the option in the Lync client to show your location based on network mapping or an entered location. This is, however, fairly static information and is used either as information within the interface, like a status update, or for enhanced emergency services requirements such as E.911 in North America, as discussed in Chapter 15.

What if you were able to make your location real time and updated with GPS or mobile network location triangulation and integrate that with your availability? This would allow you to tightly integrate availability and location for field-based services, which would useful to a wide range of organizations, from those concerned with public safety, such as the police, to those with traveling sales staff.

Geomant Presence Suite provides such an extension, as shown in Figure 18.23, where you can see where people are across the city and their current availability.

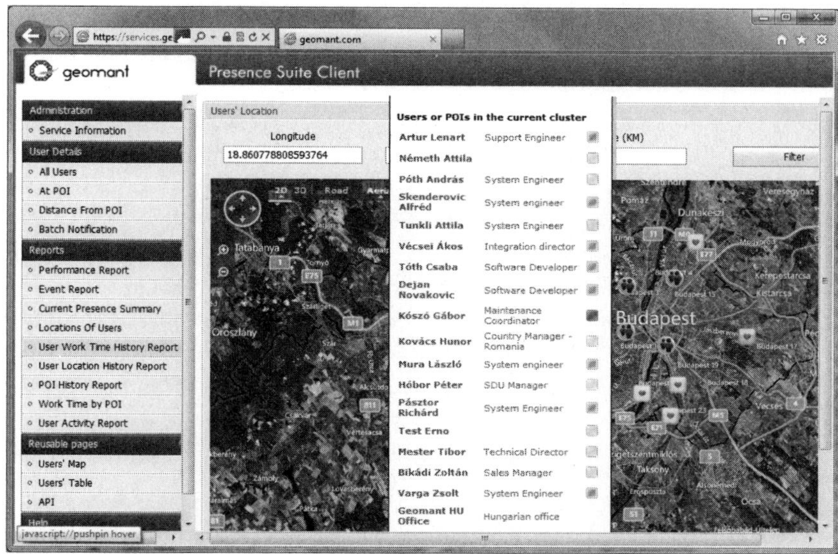

FIGURE 18.23
Geomant Presence Suite client

This information can be used by agents to make job allocation decisions or it can be extended further. For example, you could extend this for lone-worker protection, so if a field-based employee didn't change their status after the expected appointment duration they could be contacted by phone using Lync to verify they are safe and well.

Presence Suite is a great example of how Lync provides out-of-the box functionality that can then be extended to deliver significant added value using published APIs and development tools.

The Bottom Line

Connect to telephony systems using a gateway. Gateway devices enable Lync to connect to a wide range of different telephony platforms in a uniform way, providing intelligent routing and security.

Master It When connecting to telephony systems, three main components come into play. What are they?

Integrate with your PBX. Connecting Lync to telephony systems need not be hard; however, there are many areas you must consider to ensure that you make the correct deployment choices. Lync can connect directly to an ITSP or a PBX, or in both cases can utilize a gateway device to provide security, control, and intelligent routing of traffic.

Master It Your PBX is five years old and capable of being upgraded to talk to Lync directly. You want to deploy Lync for Enterprise Voice and need a way out to the PSTN. What must you consider in your decision about connecting Lync to the PSTN?

Use RCC to integrate with your PBX. Remote Call Control (RCC) allows you to use the Lync software client on your PC to control your physical phone handset from PBX vendors like Cisco, Mitel, and Avaya. It allows you to maintain your PBX as the audio transport mechanism while enhancing the functionality of the PBX with click-to-call and Address Book lookup features of the Lync software client. Each vendor has a slightly different way of hooking up Lync with their PBX, as they each provide the SIP/CSTA gateway that allows communication.

Master It You have been asked to look into why your company might use RCC. What are the key points about which you would report?

Deploy a Survivable Branch Appliance. The Lync SBA is one of the great additions that make Lync a fully viable voice platform for the enterprise. It provides the capability for branch offices to maintain the ability for PSTN breakout even if the WAN to the central Lync site is down.

Master It You have been asked to roll out an SBA to a branch location. What are the main prerequisite and deployment steps to which you should adhere?

Connect to other external systems via an XMPP gateway. The XMPP gateway provided by Microsoft as an add-on for Lync gives you the capability to connect Lync to other IM platforms, both internally (in the case of an internal Jabber or Sametime system) or externally to public clouds like Gmail. It is deployed on a separate server and interacts with Lync through the Edge server.

Master It You need to install the XMPP gateway. Where can you get it (and what is the quirk in its name)?

Integrate with hardware video conferencing platforms. Lync can integrate with several hardware video platforms to provide control and connectivity through Lync to room-based and high-quality video networks.

Master It You are trying to configure Lync integration with a Polycom HDX unit, but it won't connect. What might be causing an issue?

Utilize third-party software enhancements. As a software UC platform, Lync is infinitely extendable. This gives rise to the possibility for third-party developers to create products that enhance the native functionality in key ways, such as call recording and call billing. Equally, it enables in-house development teams to incorporate Lync communications functionality directly into line-of-business apps in your organization.

Master It Call recording is one of the available add-on applications for Lync. Name the two locations where call recording can be carried out and describe the difference this makes to the types of calls that can be recorded.

Part 6

Mobile Devices

Chapter 19

Mobile Devices

One of the aims of the Microsoft Unified Communications vision is focused on its unification, where it doesn't matter from which device you are connecting—and with the recent proliferation of mobile devices, providing a suitable client is becoming a necessity. To support mobile devices, Lync Server 2010 introduced two new services, Mobility and Autodiscover. This chapter discusses both of them.

NOTE At the time of writing, Cumulative Update 4 (CU4) is the current Lync Server 2010 release. We were fortunate to have early access to the Mobility Service update; however, as with any unreleased product, the released version may differ from the content discussed here. The Mobility Service update is a separate download and installation which has a pre-requisite of CU4.

In this chapter, you will learn to:

- Understand the differences between the Lync 2010 mobile client when installed on different types of mobile device
- Understand the planning required to implement the Mobility Service
- Understand the installation procedure for the Mobility Service update
- Understand the infrastructure changes and configuration required to implement the Mobility Service

Mobile Devices and the Unified Communications Model

As noted, mobile devices have proliferated in recent years and have become important elements in Microsoft's Unified Communications strategy. Figure 19.1 shows the integration points for mobile devices and a Lync network.

FIGURE 19.1
Integration points for Unified Communications

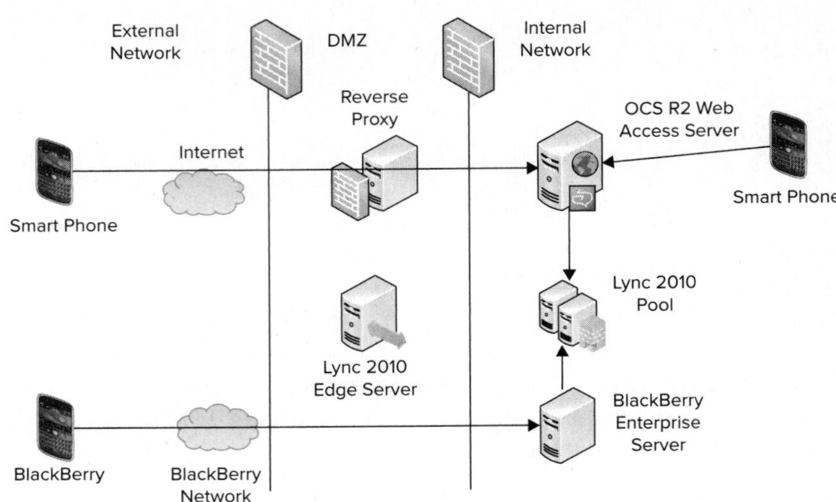

A number of clients are available to provide mobile device-based access, some of which are listed here:

- BlackBerry Messenger (requires BlackBerry Enterprise Server), provided by Research in Motion (RIM)
- iDialog (requires OCS 2007/R2 Communicator Web Access server), provided by ModalitySystems
- Xync, provided by Damaka

This chapter will focus only on the Lync 2010 mobile clients provided by Microsoft.

Understanding the Lync 2010 Mobile Client

The Lync 2010 mobile client addresses a number of user scenarios, namely:

- The user may always be connected.
- The user may want to control his or her availability.
- While available, the user needs to communicate immediately.

The expectation is that the user will always have the Lync 2010 client connected (via Wi-Fi or mobile carrier data network); however, they will typically want to control their availability—possibly only during work hours, for example.

The aim is to provide the same user experience whether the user is connected via a mobile client or the desktop client; in addition, this user experience should be transparent, whether the user is calling from the device or someone else is calling a user of the device.

In some cases, the mobile client differs depending on the hardware device used (or specifically, the hardware and OS). The specific OS versions supported are as follows:

- Windows phone 7.5 (Mango)
- Apple iPhone iOS 4+
- Apple iPad iOS 4+
- Nokia Symbian 3 SR2 1.11+
- Android 2.3+

Both on-premise and hosted environments are supported by the mobile client; however, it is important to note that in the currently released versions, the hosted offering (Office 365) does not support PSTN integration, so some device-based functionality is not available. Figure 19.2 compares the Windows Phone and iPhone login screens.

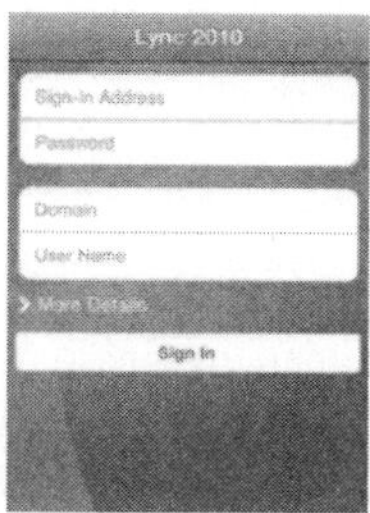

FIGURE 19.2
Windows Phone and iPhone login screens

IM, Presence, and Contact Management

In the Mobility Update, all the supported devices will provide the following features:

- Instant messaging (IM)
- Presence color and status
- Photos
- Lync contact list viewing
- Corporate directory searching
- Contact card viewing
- Multiparty instant messaging (IM)
- Distribution list expansion

Currently, the iPhone and iPad clients are capable of sending Bing map location data as an IM. This functionality is coming to Nokia devices sometime during 2012. When it is launched, contact management (adding, removing, and so on) will be available only on the Nokia mobile client—future client releases (iPhone, Windows Phone, etc.) are expected to incorporate this feature as an update.

Figure 19.3 shows the receipt of an instant message on Windows Phone and iPhone clients.

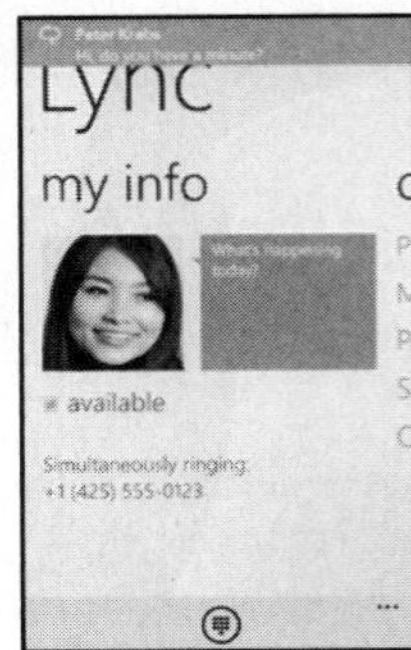

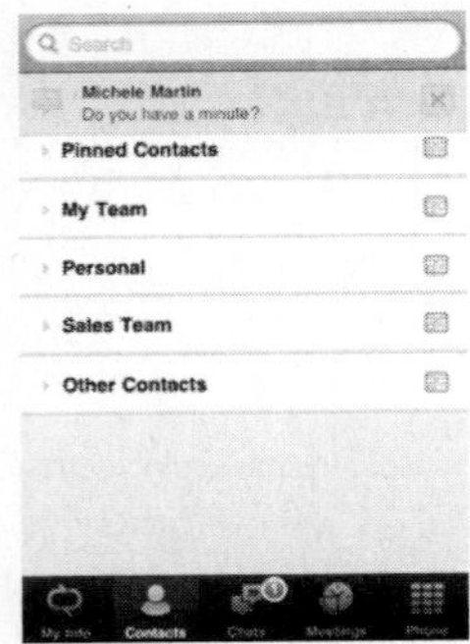

FIGURE 19.3 Receiving an IM on a Windows Phone and an iPhone

Audio Conferencing

The audio conference scenario provides the capability not only for participants to join a conference from the phone, but also for participants to request the Lync 2010 server infrastructure to call back on the mobile device number—avoiding the call charges incurred for the participant to join the call, except where charges are incurred to receive a call (such as when roaming). This functionality is available across all the clients. (On the iPad device, the callback is made to another voice device.) With the Mobility Service update, Windows Phone and Nokia will have calendar integration, allowing the join conference to be initiated from the calendar item. The Android-based devices have only a URL-based join launch, and both Apple devices provide the meeting-pane view to provide the Join button.

Making Calls

When it comes to dealing with calls, Android devices suffer badly because of technical issues when accessing the other features of the phones. An Android device currently supports only the ability to control Call Forwarding.

Like the main Lync 2010 desktop client, Apple devices support Visual Voice Mail with the use of an additional tab. However, the Windows Phone and Nokia devices will probably use the mobile Outlook client to access voice mail.

Other features supported on Windows Phone, Nokia, and Apple clients include:

- Single-Number Reach
- Dial pad
- Call from contact card
- Call from conversation window
- Call via Work

Single-Number Reach makes it unnecessary to have separate numbers for mobile and corporate use; as the name suggests, only a single number needs to be used to reach any device.

Figure 19.4 shows the screens for both the Windows Phone and the iPhone, from which the modality of the communications (for example, a call) can be selected.

FIGURE 19.4
The Windows Phone and Apple iPhone starting communications screens

The Communicator Mobile client for OCS R2 first introduced the *Call via Work* feature, which allows a user, when making a voice call, to have the server infrastructure place the call on the user's behalf and also place a call back to that user. This means that the user placing the call is not charged to place the call; instead, it is picked up by the corporate infrastructure. The Lync 2010 mobile clients support this functionality. Figure 19.5 shows how this is achieved.

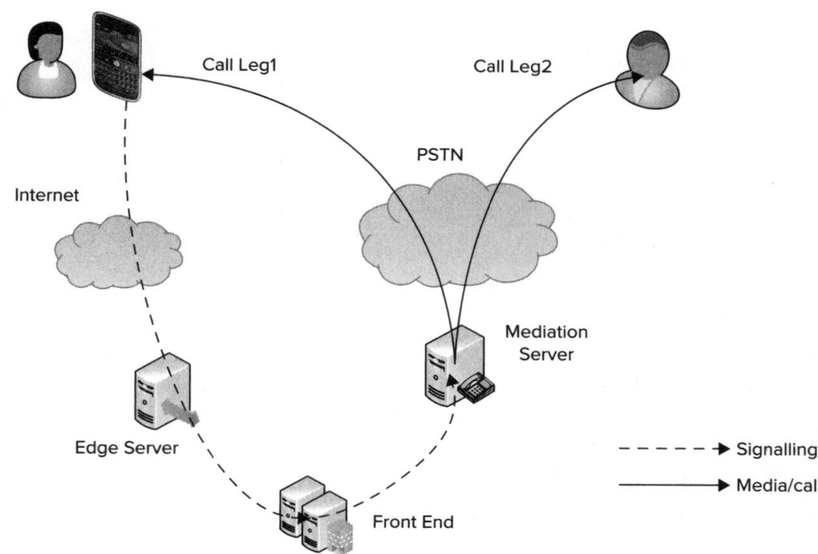

FIGURE 19.5
The call-flow architecture of the Call via Work feature

With this feature, the caller-ID displayed to the recipient is the caller-ID from the Lync 2010 Enterprise Voice account, not the caller's mobile number. This allows the use of any device (that supports the Lync 2010 mobile client) to place a call and have that call appear to originate from the user's corporate number.

FREE CALLING FROM LYNC 2010 MOBILE DEVICES

By taking advantage of the Call via Work feature in countries where only the caller pays for the call charges, a caller can make calls without incurring the mobile cost—the charge is picked up by the internal company Lync 2010 infrastructure.

As illustrated in Figure 19.5, two calls are made; both originate from the Lync 2010 infrastructure, one to the caller and one to the recipient.

Call via Work is not as beneficial in countries, such as with some calling plans in the United States, where a charge is made to receive a call; however, it can help to alleviate toll charges, because the caller will pay to receive a (typically) local call.

The Lync 2010 mobile client does not provide Voice over IP (VoIP). Like previous versions, the Lync 2010 client remains a signaling client only, with the voice calling capability provided natively via the phone device.

Comparing Device Capabilities

As mentioned previously, more and more users are utilizing a wide variety of devices both in their work lives and home lives. From an administration perspective, it is important to understand that it will be difficult to restrict individual device versions from accessing Lync 2010 functionality—if a feature is enabled, it's enabled for all devices.

Table 19.1 provides a summary of the features available for each client.

TABLE 19.1: Feature Summary per Mobile Device

FEATURE	WINDOWS PHONE 7.5	NOKIA SYMBIAN	IPHONE (IOS 4)	IPAD (IOS 4)	ANDROID 2.3+
Instant Messaging	Yes	Yes	Yes	Yes	Yes
Presence colors and status	Yes	Yes	Yes	Yes	Yes
Photos	Yes	Yes	Yes	Yes	Yes
View Lync Contact List	Yes	Yes	Yes	Yes	Yes
Search Corporate Directory	Yes	Yes	Yes	Yes	Yes
View Contact Card	Yes	Yes	Yes	Yes	Yes

FEATURE	WINDOWS PHONE 7.5	NOKIA SYMBIAN	IPHONE (IOS 4)	IPAD (IOS 4)	ANDROID 2.3+
Multipart IM	Yes	Yes	Yes	Yes	Yes
Distribution List Expansion	Yes	Yes	Yes	Yes	Yes
Send Bing Map Location Data via IM	No	No	Yes	Yes	No
Contact Management	No	Yes	No	No	No
Join Conference	Yes	Yes	Yes	Yes	Yes
Conference Callback	Yes	Yes	Yes	Yes	Yes
Conference Calendar Information	Yes	Yes	No	No	No
URL-based Join	No	No	No	No	Yes
Meeting Pane Join	No	No	Yes	Yes	No
Single-Number Reach	Yes	Yes	Yes	No	Yes
Dial Pad	Yes	Yes	Yes	No	Yes
Call from Contact Card	Yes	Yes	Yes	No	Yes
Call from Conversation Window	Yes	Yes	Yes	No	Yes
Call via Work	Yes	Yes	Yes	No	Yes
Call Forwarding Control	Yes	Yes	Yes	Yes	Yes
Visual Voice Mail	No	No	Yes	Yes	No

Planning for Mobility Services

With the introduction of the new mobile clients, the Lync Server 2010 infrastructure needs to be updated. Later in this chapter, you'll see how to install and configure these new functions; in this section, we'll take a look at the additional planning required to handle this new functionality.

Two new services are introduced for mobile devices:

- Lync Server 2010 Mobility Service
- Lync Server 2010 Autodiscover Service

The Mobility service provides the actual device functionality, which consists of IM/presence, contact management, and conferencing capabilities, as well as the voice features such as Single-Number Reach and Call via Work.

The Autodiscover service helps the user's device determine its location and locate the correct resources for web services.

The Mobility service can send push notifications to both Windows phones and iPhones when the applications are not active on the devices. The Mobility service running on the front end uses HTTPS to send the notifications to the Lync Online data center, which in turn sends the notifications to the Apple Push Notification (APN) service or the Microsoft Push Notification (MPN) service, as appropriate. Additional configuration may be needed to allow the internal servers to connect to these notification services. Figure 19.6 shows this architecture.

FIGURE 19.6
Push notification architecture

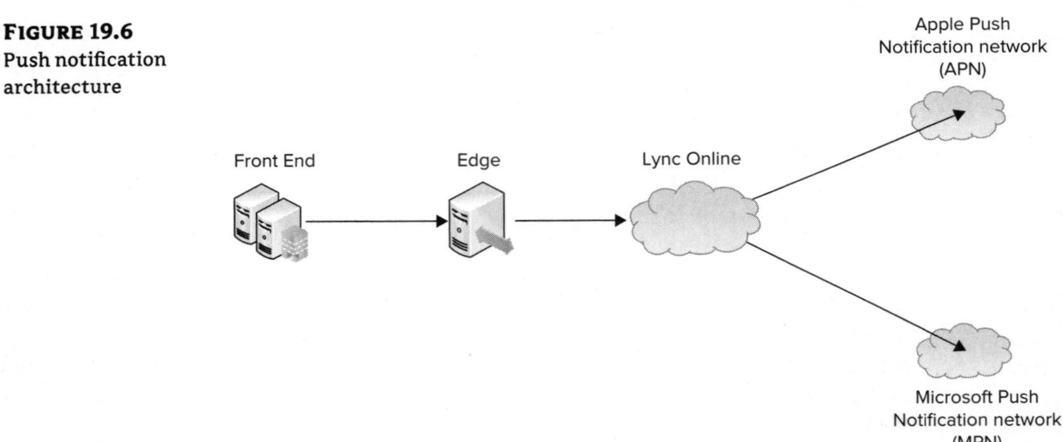

This architecture is for data update messages (SIP or IM); media traffic will continue to flow via the mobile provider network (for example, calls will be via GSM).

Android and Nokia devices do not require push notifications, as the client on these devices can run in the background (and continue to remain connected to the server).

Planning for Device Interaction

When you're planning the mobility services interaction, one major factor to consider is the external versus internal access. Almost by nature, external access is going to be enabled—otherwise, you are limiting the functionality to devices connected to the corporate wireless network. For a consistent experience, users must continue to connect to the same network point whether they are connecting on the internal wireless network or externally via 3G or a home wireless network. Ensuring that this is possible requires the user to always connect to the *external* mobility website, even when internal. This requirement only applies to the Mobility service and not to any of the other web-provided services (such as the Address Book). Figure 19.7 shows the connectivity points and data flow to provide this configuration.

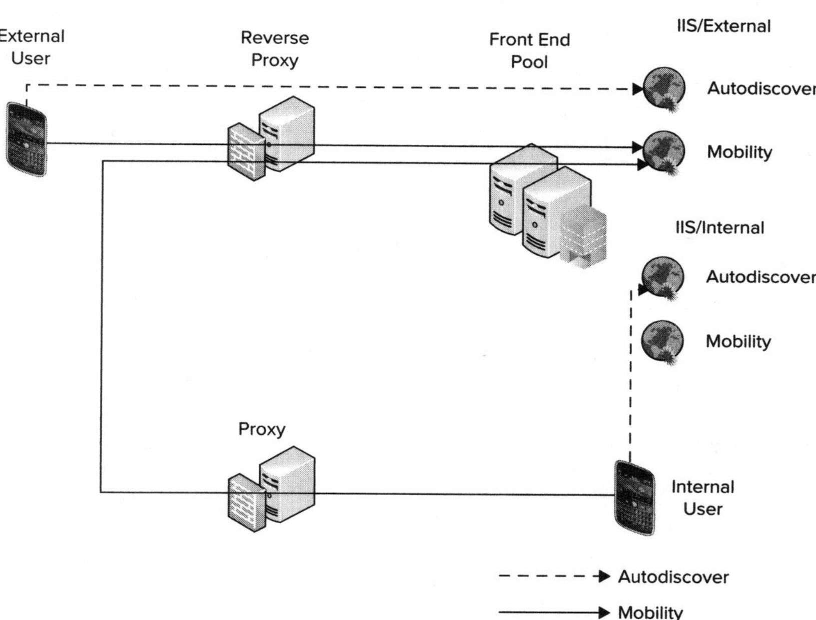

FIGURE 19.7
Autodiscover and Mobility service data flow

As shown in Figure 19.7, when internal to the corporate network, the device contacts the *internal* Autodiscover website, and this is then rerouted to the *external* web FQDN—in this case, via a Proxy server. External devices, on the other hand, connect via the reverse proxy to the *external* Autodiscover website, which will then redirect to the *external* mobility service website.

The documentation is explicit about the requirements for the topology to support the Mobility and Autodiscover services:

- The pool internal web FQDN must be distinct from the pool external FQDN.
- The internal web FQDN must resolve and be accessible only from inside the corporate network.
- The external web FQDN must resolve and be accessible only from the Internet.
- When a user is inside the corporate network, the Mobility service URL must be addressed to the external web FQDN.
- When a user is outside the corporate network, the request must go to the external web FQDN.

Planning the Web Service URLs

It is recommended to use IIS 7.5 for the Mobility Services update as the installation package sets some ASP.NET flags for performance improvements. IIS 7.5 is available with Windows Server 2008 R2. If you are using Windows Server 2008 (IIS 7.0), these settings need to be configured manually—also it's recommended to install an IIS 7.0 hotfix: `http://go.microsoft.com/fwlink/?linkid=3052&kbid=2290617`.

The Dynamic Content Compression module for IIS is required, for installation of the update; this can be installed using the following PowerShell:

```
Import-Module ServerManager
Add-WindowsFeature Web-Server, Web-Dyn-Compression
```

To make the changes for IIS 7.0, follow the steps below:

1. Open `C:\Windows\System32\inetsrv\config\applicationHost.config` using notepad.exe.
2. Search for `<Add name="CSExtMcxAppPool"` and add `CLRConfigFile="C:\Program Files\Microsoft Lync Server 2010\Web Components\Mcx\Ext\Aspnet_mcx.config"` before the closing (>).
3. Search for `<Add name="CSIntMcxAppPool"` and add `CLRConfigFile="C:\Program Files\Microsoft Lync Server 2010\Web Components\Mcx\Int\Aspnet_mcx.config"` before the closing (>).
4. Save the file and close notepad.exe.
5. Open `%SystemRoot%\Microsoft.NET\Framework64\v2.0.50727\Aspnet.config` using notepad.exe.
6. Add or replace the `<system.web>` element with that shown here:

```
<system.web>
<applicationPool maxConcurrentRequestsPerCPU="<0>" maxConcurrentThreadsPerCPU="0"
requestQueueLimit="5000"/>
</system.web>
```

7. Save the file and close notepad.exe.

When planning for the new web service URLs, you have two choices:

- Use existing web service URLs.
- Use automatic discovery of URLs.

Obviously, if this is a new installation either choice has the same effect; however, when you're upgrading, there may be some additional considerations, such as costs of certificates.

Using Existing Web Service URLs

From an administration point of view, this approach is simple and cost-effective; however, the impact is to the users, because they will have to manually configure their devices to connect.

Using Automatic Discovery of URLs

The automatic discovery approach makes the connection simple from the user's perspective, at the cost of additional administration and certificate purchase requirements.

To enable client connectivity, additional DNS records are required to map to the servers hosting the new services:

Lyncdiscoverinternal.*<SIP domain>*

Lyncdiscover.*<SIP domain>*

Both records are CNAME records, which point to the internal and external Autodiscover websites, respectively, on the pool or Director pool. You need to create both internal and external records for each SIP domain supported. Certificate updates are required to ensure that responses can be made to these new names.

A Director pool requires the following SAN entries (for the Autodiscover URL):

SAN=lyncdiscoverinternal.*<SIP domain>*

SAN=lyncdiscover.*<SIP domain>*

A front-end pool requires the following SAN entries:

SAN=lyncwebpool.*<SIP domain>*

SAN=lyncwebextpool.*<SIP domain>*

SAN=lyncdiscoverinternal.*<SIP domain>*

SAN=lyncdiscover.*<SIP domain>*

The first two entries refer to the Mobility services, and the remaining two refer to the Autodiscover services.

Finally, the Reverse Proxy Certificate needs the following additional entries:

SAN=lyncwebextpool01.*<SIP domain>*

SAN=lyncdiscover.*<SIP domain>*

Configuring the Mobility Service

In the current beta release, there are no changes to the Control Panel configuration options, and all changes to (or viewing of) the Mobility Service configuration must be performed using PowerShell.

This may change with the final release.

CONFIGURATION EXAMPLES

The code samples used in this section are valid at the time of writing; however, we are working with beta software, and configuration details may change upon final release. Please check the CU4 and Mobility Service Update release notes for specifics prior to configuring in a production environment.

For example, note the example URL, pushdf.lync.com; ***df*** often refers to "dogfood" or the testing environments used within Microsoft.

Configuring the Service

Prior to installation of the Mobility Service update, the ports which the service will use must be configured—this aspect is one which was installed as part of CU4, and therefore CU4 is required to be installed prior to configuring these service ports.

CU4 can be downloaded from here: `http://go.microsoft.com/fwlink/?LinkID=208564`.

By running the cmdlet `Get-CsService -WebServer`, you can see the new entries for the Mobility and Autodiscover services. By default, the service URLs will already be entered, and they will be:

```
https:<FQDN>/Mcx/McxService.svc
```

```
https:<FQDN>/Autodiscover/AutodiscoverService.svc
```

Additionally, `McxSipPrimaryListeningPort` and the `McxSipExternalListeningPort` are not defined yet. This is the first task, and it is conducted using the `Set-CsWebserver` cmdlet:

```
Set-CsWebServer -Identity <FQDN of the pool> -McxSipPrimaryListeningPort
<portnumber>
```

In this case, the commands will be:

```
Set-CsWebServer -Identity se.gaots.local -McxSipPrimaryListeningPort 5086
Set-CsWebServer -Identity se.gaots.local -McxSipExternalListeningPort 5087
```

Now, when the `Get-CsService -WebServer` cmdlet is rerun, the following entries will appear:

```
McxSipPrimaryListeningPort      : 5086
McxSipExternalListeningPort     : 5087
```

Once these details are configured, the topology must be enabled using the `Enable-CsTopology` cmdlet, which should complete with no errors. A log file will be created, so you can investigate any errors that are returned. Make sure you resolve any such errors before continuing.

In the beta version, warnings are written into the log file for the unrecognized component `AutodiscoverService`; this should be corrected in the final release.

Installing the Mobility Service Update

The Mobility service will provide a web-based connectivity method (rather than the SIP connection used previously) for clients. Using a web-based service provides an improved experience for mobile device users, because it allows data to be easily cached in case of network glitches.

At the time of writing, the download is a single file (`McxStandalone.msi`) and contains only the Mobility service elements. This update is a standalone installation and unlike a Cumulative Update (which includes all previous updates), has a pre-requisite of CU4 being installed. CU4 introduces code for some of the features enabled with the Mobility Service update, such as the new cmdlets and some of the new configuration items on the web services.

The Mobility Service update must be installed on every Front End server and director from which you wish to provide access to mobile devices.

The following installation instructions assume that CU4 has already been applied to the servers successfully, and the service ports have been configured (see previous section)—if both of these tasks have not been successful, the Mobility Service will not be installed.

1. Double-click the `McxStandalone.exe` file to start the installer (shown in Figure 19.8).

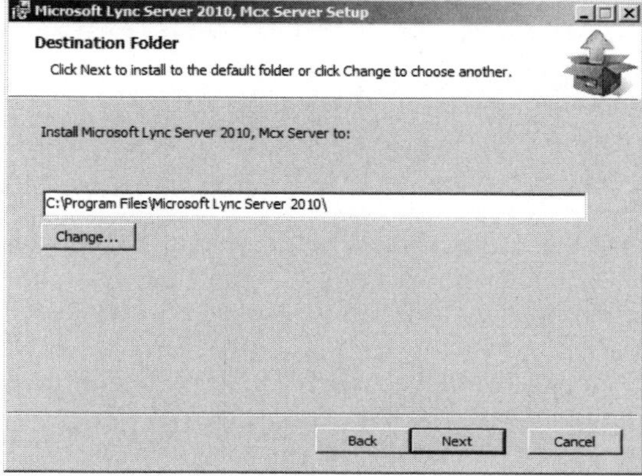

FIGURE 19.8
Run the standalone installation package.

2. The Installation Wizard will prompt you to accept the new license terms. Then you will be prompted for the location of the installation files. The default location is the same location that was used for the existing Lync Server 2010 installation. Use the default (unless you didn't use the default to install Lync Server 2010).
3. The final installation screen prompts you to click Install to begin. Then it will run through the setup. Even in a virtual environment, this takes less than a minute to install.

Once installation is complete, two new folders (`Autodiscover` and `Mcx`) are created under the Web Components folder. They contain the Int and Ext folders, representing the external and internal websites, which are shown in Figure 19.9.

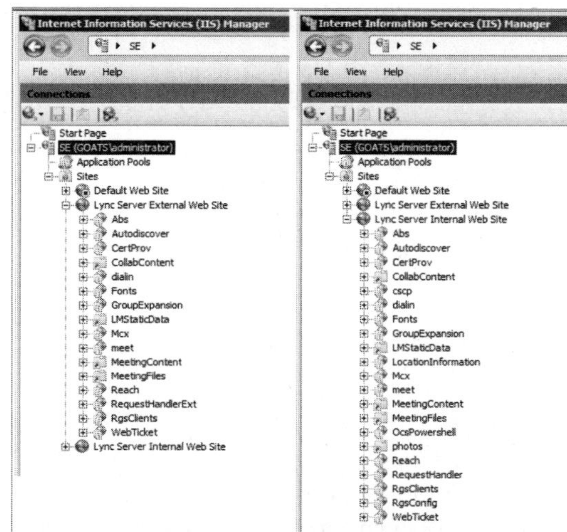

FIGURE 19.9
External (left) and internal (right) websites

The installation creates a log file in the *%TEMP%* location. In the beta version, it looks to be a random filename; however, the final release is likely to follow the standard guidelines for naming the log files and will include the date and time information in the filename.

At this stage of the beta, the installation process is extremely seamless—there is not expected to be any major changes to this upon release.

Once the Mobility Update is installed on all front-end servers in the pool, the Certificate Wizard should be rerun (on each front-end server) to request and assign the certificates containing the new SAN entries. The `Request-CSCertificate` and `Set-CSCertificate` cmdlets can be used in place of the wizard.

Remember, if the internal Front-End servers are using internal certificates (from your own PKI solution) and the mobile clients are connecting via your internal Wi-Fi network, the mobile devices must have the internal CA root certificates installed, to enable the Front-End certificates to be trusted.

Next, DNS entries for the internal and external sites need to be created, as shown in the section "Planning for Mobility Services," earlier.

Finally, the reverse proxy needs to be configured for two additional web publishing rules for the Mobility and Autodiscovery services, and its certificates need to be updated with the new FQDN details.

AN ALTERNATIVE TO UPDATING CERTIFICATES

Updating internal certificates is normally a simple and cheap process—assuming you already have an internal PKI solution.

Making changes to the externally facing public certificates can involve significant additional cost—especially if multiple SIP domains are being hosted, as each SIP domain will require additional Subject Alternative Domains (SANs).

An alternative to updating the certificates is to allow the autodiscover request to use port 80, therefore not requiring a certificate, therefore not incurring the additional cost associated with updating the certificates.

This is a supported approach, however not recommended by Microsoft.

Testing the Installation

Now that the update is installed and new certificates are assigned, you need to configure the settings. Two new Test cmdlets have been created as part of the installation:

`Test-CsMcxP2PIM`

`Test-CsMcxConference`

These cmdlets are used for testing IM and conference connectivity, specifically using the Mobility service. Now that you have deployed the update and certificates, you should be in a position to test using these cmdlets. First, test IM connectivity:

```
Test-CsMcxP2PIM -TargetFQDN se.gaots.local -SenderSipAddress sip:keith_lync@
gaots.co.uk -ReceiverSipAddress sip:nathan_lync@gaots.co.uk
```

Because you haven't provided the credentials as part of the cmdlet, you will receive a pop-up window prompt for each set of credentials.

The results should be:

```
Connecting to web service : https://se.gaots.local/webticket/webticketservce.svc
Using Machine certificate authentication
Successfully created connection proxy and website bindings
Requesting new web ticket
Sending Web-Ticket Request:
```

This will be followed by a lot of XML code, which is cut for brevity, and then, finally:

```
TargetUri   : https://se.gaots.local:443/mcx
TargetFqdn  : se.gaots.local
Result      : Success
Latency     : 00:00:00
Error       :
Diagnosis   :
```

The conference test will look like this:

```
Test-CsMcxConference -TargetFQDN se.gaots.local -OrganizerSipAddress sip:keith_
lync@gaots.co.uk -UserSipAddress sip:nathan_lync@gaots.co.uk -User2SipAddress
sip:adam_lync@gaots.co.uk
```

Again, because you have not provided the credentials as part of the cmdlet, you will receive a pop-up window prompt for each set of credentials.

The results will be similar to those previously shown, except there will be significantly more XML content because a third user account will be used in this test cmdlet. Assuming success, the final output will be:

```
TargetUri   : https://se.gaots.local:443/mcx
TargetFqdn  : se.gaots.local
Result      : Success
Latency     : 00:00:00
Error       :
Diagnosis   :
```

Configuring Push Notifications

Push notifications allow the application on the phone to be active only when there is data to be received, or when the user is specifically interacting with the application. By working with push notifications, the phone application can be active in the background (either while the screen lock is enabled or when the user is using a different application). The alternative is *application polling,* where the application is permanently active (reducing the capability of using other applications), requesting updates from the server, reducing phone battery life, and increasing the amount of data traffic used.

You need to configure a target for the initial push notification, and you'll treat this as a federated organization. Specifically, in the following commands you'll define it as a hosting provider, using the `New-CsHostingProvider` cmdlet (you can do this using the Control Panel on the External User Access ➤ Provider page, shown in Figure 19.10) and then permit federation with this provider.

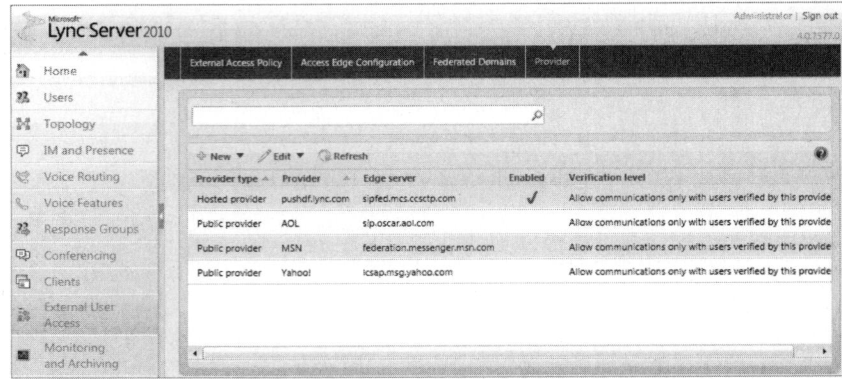

FIGURE 19.10
Adding the hosted provider via the Control Panel

```
New-CsHostingProvider -Identity "LyncOnline" -Enabled $true -ProxyFqdn "sipfed
.online.lync.com" -VerificationLevel UseSourceVerification
New-CsAllowedDomain -Identity "push.lync.com"
```

Running `Get-CsHostingProvider` after this cmdlet generates the following output:

```
Identity                    : LyncOnline
Name                        : LyncOnline
ProxyFqdn                   : sipfed.online.lync.com
VerificationLevel           : UseSourceVerification
Enabled                     : True
EnabledSharedAddressSpace : False
HostsOCSUsers               : False
IsLocal                     : False
```

By default, push notifications are disabled, but they can easily be enabled by using the `Set-CsMcxConfiguration` and `Set-CsPushNotificationConfiguration` cmdlets, as shown here:

```
Set-CsMcxConfiguration -PushNotificationProxyUri "sip:push@push.lync.com"
Set-CsPushNotificationConfiguration -EnableApplePushNotificationService $True -
EnableMicrosoftPushNotificationService $True
```

Running the `Get` commands displays the following output:

```
Get-CsMcxConfiguration
Identity                           : Global
SessionExpirationInterval          : 259200
SessionShortExpirationInterval : 3600
ExposedWebURL                      : External
PushNotificationProxyUri           : sip:push@push.lync.com

Get-CsPushNotificationConfiguration
Identity                                          : Global
```

```
EnableApplePushNotificationService      : True
EnableMicrosoftPushNotificationService : True
```

Once push notifications are defined, in order for them to take effect you need to create a new External Access policy (`New-CsExternalAccessPolicy`) or modify an existing one (`Set-CsExternalAccessPolicy`), and then apply the policy (`Grant-CsExternalAccessPolicy`) to the Mobility service trusted endpoint (created during installation). The commands look like this:

```
$McxEndpoint = Get-CsTrustedApplicationEndpoint | Where-Object { ($_.OwnerURN -eq
"urn:component:McxService") -and ($_.RegistrarPool -match "se.gaots.local") }
 Grant-CsExternalAccessPolicy "Lync Policy" -Identity $McxEndpoint.SipAddress
```

Configuring the Mobility Policy

For users to use the Mobility Service update features, they must meet two pre-requisites:

- Users must be enabled for Lync Server 2010
- Users must be enabled for Enterprise Voice

To use the *Call via Work* feature, users must also meet the following criteria:

- Users must be assigned a voice policy which allows *Simultaneous Ringing*
- Users must be assigned a mobility policy which has *EnableMobility* set to *True*

The Mobility policy acts like any other policy, so it must be configured (using `New-CsMobilityPolicy` or `Set-CsMobilityPolicy`) and applied to users (using `Grant-CsMobilityPolicy`).

First, let's look at what configuration options the policy offers by running `Get-CsMobilityPolicy`:

```
Identity           : Global
Description        :
EnableOutsideVoice : True
EnableMobility     : True
```

So, a sample policy definition might look like this:

```
New-CsMobilityPolicy -Identity "Tag:DisableOutsideVoice" -EnableOutsideVoice
$False -EnableMobilty $False
```

Once defined (using `New-CsMobilityPolicy` or `Set-CsMobilityPolicy`), the policy must be applied to users. As with any policy, use the `Grant` cmdlet:

```
Grant-CsMobilityPolicy -Identity "sip:keith_lync@gaots.co.uk" -PolicyName
"Tag:DisableOutsideVoice"
```

Now, you can look at the user settings to see the policy applied, using `Get-CsUser`:

```
Get-CsUser -Identity "sip:keith_lync@gaots.co.uk"
```

It is possible to turn off *Call via Work* and still allow mobility access; however it is not possible to disable mobility access, and allow *Call via Work*.

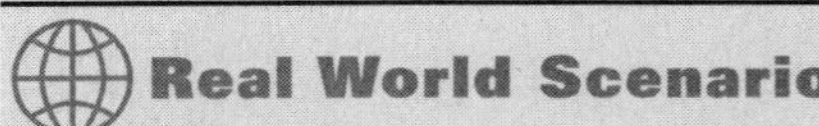

KNOWN ISSUES IN THE BETA VERSION OF MOBILITY SERVICES

At the time of writing, there are a number of known issues with the beta version of the update. Specifically, the ones we have encountered are listed here; all of them are listed in the release notes.

SERVER ISSUES

- The Certificate Wizard does not correctly populate the certificate request, so even though the wizard shows the new Subject Alternate Name (SAN) entries, the request file does not include them. To work around this, use the `Request-CSCertificate` cmdlet to generate the request using the `-AllSIPDomain` or `-DomainName` parameters; or manually add the new SAN entries to the Certificate Wizard (as well as the automatic entries).
- Users cannot use the mobile client as their first device with which to log in, because the contact management features will cause corruption within existing contacts.
- `Get-CsUser` does not report the Mobility policy applied to the user. To work around this, use:

```
$x=Get-CsUser "sip:<useruri>"; $x.MobilityPolicy
```

CLIENT ISSUES

- Off-work presence may not display in client languages other than English.
- If multiple status refreshes are conducted in a short time span, the client may receive the error: "Failed to process request. Please try again."
- The user receives a *Missed Conversation* alert when an IM conversation has been declined.
- IMs may be returned as *Delivery Failed* if the recipient does not acknowledge the notification within a minute (push notification). If the user tries to respond subsequently, they will receive an error indicating that the IM is not available.
- Photos may continue to display even if the user has selected *Do Not Show My Picture*.
- Switching between Wi-Fi and 3G may *not* connect automatically.
- The mobile number is displayed during transfer for Call via Work.
- A call forwarding alert may appear even if call forwarding is configured correctly.

The Bottom Line

Understand the mobile client features. With CU4, Microsoft provides support for some of the most popular mobile devices (phones and tablets) on the market, bringing the functionality of Lync 2010 to the mobile workforce.

Master It You have deployed the Mobility Service Update to the server infrastructure and made available the Lync 2010 mobile clients to your users. Some users report that they cannot send Bing map location information within IMs. Which client are they likely to be using?

Understand how to plan for Mobility service. In addition to providing a mobile Lync 2010 client, your organization needs to make changes to the Lync Server 2010 infrastructure and architecture. Prior to rolling out the client, these changes need to be put in place and communicated to any users using manual configuration to ensure they maintain a consistent experience and functionality.

Master It You need to make certificate changes to the front end, Directors, and Proxy servers. What additional entries are required on each certificate?

Understand the installation procedure for Mobility Services. The provision of mobility support is achieved through the upgrade of the Lync Server 2010 infrastructure to CU4 and the further application of the Mobility Service Update. As with any update, it is extremely important to follow the installation guide in the release notes, and even more so in this case as new functionality is provided.

Master It Which two websites are created on the Lync Server 2010 pool front-end servers?

Understand the infrastructure changes and configuration required for implementation of Mobility Services. Unlike CUs that implement fixes, the Mobility Service update provides new functionality, and this functionality is disabled by default, so it must be configured and enabled before users can use the new clients.

Master It Both Apple and Microsoft clients require push notification to be configured. How is this enabled through the Mobility Service Update?

Appendix A

The Bottom Line

Chapter 1: What's in Lync?

Describe the features of the client. The Lync 2010 client is designed to achieve three core goals: connect, communicate, and collaborate. This new client makes it is much easier to find people and verify identity, initiate communications (typically, with a single click), and collaborate with full-blown information sharing. Device integration and call management have been greatly simplified, removing the need to run through wizards constantly.

Master It You are assembling a new product-development team. The new product will be similar to a previously released product, and you want to ask members of the previous team for guidance. How can you find people associated with the previous product team?

Solution Use the Key Skills search feature integrated with SharePoint to return the names of the appropriate people.

Describe the features of the server. Lync Server 2010 provides most of the server roles included in Office Communications Server and introduces the Survivable Branch Appliance (or Server) to help in the high-availability scenarios. The management approach has changed through the introduction of the Topology Builder application and Role-Based Access Control to limit administrative access to defined users and scopes as required. PowerShell and Silverlight combine to provide the day-to-day administration of the environment.

Master It When deploying high availability, which of the following roles can be a primary registrar?

- Audio/Video Conferencing
- Director
- Enterprise Edition Front-End
- Standard Edition Front-End
- Survivable Branch Appliance
- Survivable Branch Server

Solution The front-end servers (Enterprise and Standard Edition) and the Survivable Branch Appliance (and Server) can be primary registrars. Only the front-end servers (Enterprise and Standard Edition) can be backup registrars.

Describe the voice features. Significant investment and development has gone into Lync Server 2010's voice feature set. The new set has allowed it to become a match for a large portion of the PBX workload and, in many cases, a viable replacement for a PBX.

New functions (such as Private Line, Call Admission Control, Call Park, E911, and Common Area Phones) provide welcome additions to the user experience. By contrast, behind-the-scenes features (such as Media Bypass, routing improvements, resiliency improvements, and analog device management) provide a more integrated and available solution for the administrator, while they help reduce the number of servers required.

Master It As the network and telephony administrator for your company, you want to invest in SIP trunks rather than legacy PBX-style PSTN connectivity using media gateways.

How should you configure media bypass and deploy mediation servers?

Solution When SIP trunks are used, separate, physical mediation servers are recommended, and media bypass should be disabled. An SIP trunk does not have a termination point to allow the client to connect directly; instead, the client will connect to the Mediation server. The client can still use G711, and the Mediation server may not be required to transcode the codec.

Chapter 2: Standards and Protocols

Understand the basics of SIP for signaling. SIP originates from an extensive background of telephony signaling. Although knowing that background is not strictly required for Lync administration, understanding how we have gotten to where we are today will help you overcome some of the challenges you'll face when integrating with legacy telephony environments.

Master It For what is a jitter buffer used?

Solution By buffering incoming data prior to playback, a jitter buffer is used to help smooth out the delay that occurs when packets are transmitted across a network.

Understand how SIP has been extended providing additional functionality for Lync Server 2010. In its plainest form, SIP provides session-based signaling; however, with some of the extensions for SIP, you can extend this session-based signaling approach to incorporate additional functionality within the SIP request itself, such as IM and presence information.

Master It Assuming a user is not yet logged in, describe the SIP requests required to log in and establish an IM session with another user.

Solution `REGISTER` — Provide the login and registration information.

`SUBSCRIBE` — Request presence information.

`NOTIFY` — Receive presence information.

`INVITE` — Initiate the session.

`ACK` — Acknowledge the `INVITE`.

`MESSAGE` — Send the instant message.

For completeness, the session should be terminated with a `BYE` request.

Identify additional protocols used by Lync Server 2010. Lync Server 2010 uses many different protocols for its various modalities as needed by the user. It can also tie many of these modalities together providing an integrated solution running on top of SIP. Microsoft has also been able to successfully (and securely) extend this functionality to the Internet.

Master It When negotiating the address to be used for an externally connected endpoint, which order is preferred for the media session?

Solution UDP direct

UDP NAT (STUN)

UDP Relay (TURN)

TCP Relay (TURN)

Chapter 3: Security

Secure External Access. Lync utilizes the Edge server and supporting components to provide external access to communications modalities. The Edge server sits in the DMZ and is a proxy between internal and external users. Many layers of security are in place to ensure that communicating externally won't cause security breaches.

Master It Describe the role the Director plays in external access. Why would you use one?

Solution The Director role sits in front of the front-end servers and carries out both authentication and redirection. When external connections are passed on to the Director through the Access Edge role, the Director acts as the point of authentication and as such will shield the front-end servers from potential DoS attacks using malformed authentication traffic. In its redirection role, the Director server will route traffic intelligently where one central site has multiple pools, thereby helping to keep the load on the front-end server to a minimum.

Understand Core Security. Lync is designed to be secure by default. It does this in many ways, not least of which is by encrypting all traffic and using certificates as part of mutual authentication of connections.

Master It In different circumstances, Lync can use four different authentication mechanisms. What are they and where are they used?

Solution Kerberos authentication is used for clients who are domain joined and inside the LAN.

NTML authentication is used for clients accessing Lync through the Edge server.

Digest authentication is used by anonymous clients participating in conferencing.

Certificate-based authentication is used in conjunction with a PIN by those signing in on IP phone devices.

Provide Security Administratively. No matter how secure a product is by design, an administrator can easily open up holes in its defenses. Lync provides many ways in which administrators can participate in tightening or relaxing security. Numerous policies are available to control users, including the clients they are allowed to use and the length and complexity of PINs. Equally, you can configure Lync to block links in IMs and prevent the transfer of files. Finally, Lync can be set up to add disclaimers to messages so that regulatory issues can be managed.

Master It You have been asked to ensure that users in the EMEA site can send only files of type `.txt` in IM messages and that any links in the messages will be prefixed with an underscore character so they must be copied into a browser manually. How would you do this?

Solution To achieve the required results, you need to use two different cmdlets. The first is the `New-CsFileTransferFilterConfiguration` cmdlet, which should be used as shown here:

```
New-CsFileTransferFilterConfiguration -Identity site:EMEA -Extensions .txt
```

This cmdlet will create a new policy assigned to the EMEA site, which will allow files with extension `.txt`.

The second cmdlet needed is `New-CsImFilterConfiguration`, which should be used as shown here:

```
New-CsImFilterConfiguration -Identity site:EMEA -Prefixes https: -Action Allow
```

Chapter 4: Clients

Understand the usage scenarios for each client. Each of the Lync clients is designed to be used for specific usage scenarios; for example, the Lync Attendee client allows external users to fully interact with an online meeting.

Master It You have been engaged by a marketing company to design and deploy Microsoft Lync; the company has 500 employees of which 100 use an Apple Mac computer. All users need to be able to use Lync, and no users can be left out.

Solution The Apple Mac users are able to use Communicator for Mac 2011, allowing them to use presence, IM, and voice. In order to participate in online meetings, they can use the Silverlight-based Lync Web App, although they are unable to share their desktop or applications.

Manage client configuration policies. In order to prevent users from using certain features, enable more niche features, and change a feature's behavior, client policies can be created. These policies can be configured globally, on a per-site basis, or on a per-user basis.

Master It Users often select Help in Lync and go to the Microsoft-hosted help pages. Your boss has asked you if they can be redirected to custom, internal help pages, so that they can provide more detailed and, in some instances, simplified information.

Solution Using Client policies, you can specify a custom help URL, so that when users go to Help in Lync they will be redirected to the website you specify. For example, if you want to redirect all users to `https://lynchelpsite/default.asp`, you could use the following PowerShell command:

```
Set-CsClientPolicy -Identity Global -CustomizedHelpUrl
"https://lynchelpsite.default.asp" -EnableEnterpriseCustomizedHelp $true
```

Configure prerequisites for IP phones. Lync IP phones are designed to be as simple as possible to deploy and receive all of their configuration settings automatically. In order for this to occur, a number of items need to be configured, such as network configuration and DHCP.

Master It You have deployed Lync IP phones, but you are unable to log in to the phones when using extension and PIN authentication; however, logging in using USB tethering works as expected.

Solution This issue usually occurs when the Lync phone cannot reach an NTP server. An indication of this is that it takes more than 30 seconds to retrieve the time during the log-in process. In a network trace, you can see the phone performing DNS queries for the NTP server, trying to connect to them, and failing.

This often occurs when the NTP DNS records weren't created and/or the NTP server is not responding. Lync will attempt to fall back to `time.windows.com`, but if the organization's firewall blocks access to UDP port 123, this will also fail.

Ensure that the DNS records are created. You should see a successful response in a network trace and verify the NTP server is working.

You can't use logging on the IP phone at this stage, because the in-band provisioning stage has not been reached to enable logging or to set the upload location.

Chapter 5: Planning Your Deployment

Use the Planning Tools available. Lync Server 2010 is an extremely complex application, even when only some of the modalities are being used. Being able to plan for capacity, not just the number of servers but also bandwidth, is extremely critical.

Master It Which of the planning toolsets would you use to determine the required bandwidth on the network?

Solution The Bandwidth Calculator

Determine when virtualization is appropriate. Unlike previous versions, Lync Server 2010 supports server virtualization across all modalities. In certain cases, this enables administrators to reduce the server footprint, giving a better "green computing" deployment.

Master It What is the typical capacity reduction expected when comparing a physical server against a virtual server?

Solution 50 percent.

Understand the prerequisites. Like most applications, Lync Server 2010 has a number of prerequisites that must be met prior to installation. These range from Active Directory requirements to individual server role requirements, both at the OS level and the component level.

Master It Which operating systems are supported for deployment of Lync Server 2010?

Solution The following systems are supported:

- Windows Server 2008 Standard (with SP2)
- Windows Server 2008 Enterprise (with SP2)

- Windows Server 2008 Datacenter (with SP2)
- Windows Server 2008 R2 Standard
- Windows Server 2008 R2 Enterprise
- Windows Server 2008 R2 Datacenter

Only the 64-bit version of the OS is supported, and if virtualization is being used, only Windows Server 2008 R2 versions are supported.

Chapter 6: Installation

Configure Windows Server for a Lync installation. Installing Lync is relatively simple, but many steps are involved. One of the most important is the preparatory work needed. If you get this wrong, it will slow down your installation and you may find that certain features will not work later down the line.

Master It Lync can be installed on several subtly different operating systems. You have been asked to lay out which OS requires the least amount of preparatory work and what the main preparatory stages are before Lync can be deployed.

Solution Lync can be installed on Windows Server 2008, 2008 R2, and 2008 R2 SP1. Windows Server 2008 R2 SP1 requires no additional patches to be installed above the standard components.

Those components are split into a few categories: the .NET Framework, the Web components, and the supporting software installed with Setup such as the Visual C++ software. Finally, for certain roles, the Windows Media Format runtime is needed as are the Active Directory remote server administration tools (RSAT-ADDS).

Prepare Active Directory for Lync installation. Like many Microsoft server applications, Lync has tight ties with AD. Lync is the first version of Microsoft's real-time communications product to start moving away from the reliance on AD, but nevertheless there are still hard requirements and preparatory steps that must be carried out, which include schema, forest, and domain prep.

Master It You are working in a large corporation with a single forest and multiple domains. You have been instructed to work with your directories team to help them understand the changes that need to be made to the schema as part of setup.

Solution Lync schema prep is run once per forest. It will create new classes and attributes and requires Schema Administrator rights to be carried out. Setup can be run from the GUI tools, which need to be run from a 64-bit server, or from the command line through PowerShell using the Lync cmdlets. If the directories team wants to maintain tight control over the installation, they can import the four .LDF files into the directory manually using the LDIFDE tool. The .LDF files are readily available to be inspected in the `\Support\schema` folder on the installation media. A great deal of detailed information about the exact changes required to AD is contained in the Lync help file.

Install your first Standard Edition server. Lync Standard Edition server is a complex environment requiring careful deployment. It has numerous prerequisites that need to be installed. Once you have completed the installation of prerequisites, setup is relatively straightforward, following a standard process.

Master It You have been tasked with installing the first Standard Edition Lync server in your network. What is one of the unique preparatory steps required for this Standard Edition, and why? Following that, what are the standard steps that setup takes?

Solution When installing the first Standard Edition server in a network, the topology needs to be published to the CMS, which first needs to be created. Because Standard Edition uses a local SQL Express deployment, you need to run Prepare First Standard Edition in the setup GUI tool to create the SQL Express instance locally, which will then allow the topology to be published and setup to continue.

The setup steps which follow are pretty standard. They are:

1. Deploy Local Configuration Store.
2. Install Lync Components.
3 Configure Certificates.
4. Start Services.
5. Install Windows Updates and the latest Lync. Cumulative Update.

Get your first users up and running. Getting the first users on Lync is slightly more involved than it first sounds. Of course, you need a couple of users with which to test. Enabling them for Lync is straightforward, especially if they already have an email address defined that matches the SIP uniform resource identifier (URI) you want the user to have. The more interesting challenge is getting the client deployed. Of course, this can be done manually, but once things scale out that won't be feasible. This leaves options to install from the command line as part of a logon script or perhaps to use the MSI installer to install via a management tool such as System Center Configuration Manager.

Master It You are rolling out the Lync client to thousands of users. How would you do this, and what are some of the considerations you need to make?

Solution Rolling out Lync to many users is possible using either a logon script with the command-line setup tool or by using the MSI file. To use the MSI, you first need to install Lync to a machine, which will leave the MSI available in the `%Program Files%\OCSetup` directory. To run Install from the MSI file requires a Registry key to be set to ensure that you understand what you are doing. That is because the MSI doesn't perform any of the prerequisite steps that the command line .exe installer does. You would only use the MSI if that is what your software deployment system requires. Otherwise, the .exe install is simpler, can be carried out silently, and gives various options to control and amend setup, such as allowing third-party apps to be integrated.

Implement external access through the Director, Edge, and Reverse Proxy servers. There are many elements that come together to provide external access. The Edge server and Reverse Proxy sit in the perimeter network and provide access to media and web components, respectively. The Director sits on the LAN and acts as a routing and security buffer between the external users and the front-end pools. The deployment of the Director follows very similar lines to the Standard Edition or front-end servers and requires similar prerequisites.

Master It You are deploying an Edge server as part of providing remote access to your network. What is different about the install compared to the Standard Edition and Director installs?

Solution The Edge server sits in the perimeter network. As such, it can't automatically pull the config from the CMS during setup. You must, therefore, export the config from the CMS to a file and import it manually as part of installing the Local Configuration Store on the Edge server. Once installation is complete, push synchronization is carried out from the CMS out to the Edge, which allows centralized management.

Understand the differences in an Enterprise Edition installation. There are many differences when working on an Enterprise deployment of Lync compared to a Standard Edition install. For example, there is the potential for a complex directory to be present, which requires close cooperation with a directories team. Another change is that SQL is installed separately from Lync and does not co-exist with the Lync server as it does with Standard Edition. Finally there is the challenge of scalability and branch offices to overcome.

Master It You have been asked to work with the database team to ensure that everything is in place for the Lync installation. What do you need to explain and how would you instruct the database team to create the databases?

Solution Lync requires both a CMS database and a general database for config and user information. Once Lync AD prep is complete, the databases can be installed from the command line. This is done using the `Install-CsDatabase` cmdlet. First, ensure that the server where the command is to be run has the following prerequisites installed:

- Lync Server 2010 `OCSCore.msi`
- SQL Server 2005 BC (`SQLServer2005_BC.msi`)
- SQL Server Native Client (`sqlncli.msi`)

Next, ensure that the PowerShell execution policy is set to RemoteSigned and then run the relevant `Install-CsDatabase` command to first install the CMS database and then later during setup to install the individual SQL stores per pool.

Chapter 7: Migration and Upgrades

Understand migration considerations. The process of migrating to Lync involves many aspects of an organization, not least of which are the end users who will have new functionality to exploit and skills to learn. It is very important to thoroughly evaluate all the phases of a migration and communicate clearly and efficiently to the staff. This is particularly true for any phase of coexistence where some users will be on Lync and others on OCS, potentially with different versions of the client in place.

Master It You have been asked to prepare a short presentation covering the key elements of the migration. List areas you would cover.

Solution When migrating to Lync, only one other version of OCS can exist in the organization. Either OCS 2007 or OCS 2007 R2 is supported, but not both. Equally, migration from LCS is not supported; instead, you must step up to OCS 2007 first. The migration is a side-by-side process where you introduce Lync into the organization and then gradually move services and users across, testing as you go. There is no direct upgrade path. It is important to fully understand the way Lync interacts with legacy components. For example, OCS clients cannot pass traffic through a Lync Mediation server; equally, Lync cannot host UCMA 2.0–based apps. These limitations must be understood and mapped out so the migration progresses smoothly. Finally, communication is critical to ensure that users understand how the migration will affect them.

Consider client pain points. During Lync migration your primary concern should be for your users. Throughout the migration users will face a changing environment. How you deal with this and control the changes both through careful process and configuration of policy will have a large impact on the successful completion of the migration.

Master It You have been asked to prepare a short presentation covering the key difficulties faced by users during migration. List the areas you would cover.

Solution The major factor in migration is client compatibility. The Lync client cannot talk to the OCS server, so where possible users should remain on Lync until the end of the migration process. This approach means that users will not be able to use Lync functionality; and in a large deployment where the start and finish are separated by months, this may not be acceptable. Therefore, rollout of the Lync client may progress before all users are off OCS. This causes challenges with coexistence. The key challenges are around policy settings. You must ensure that all OCS policies are documented and the correct Lync policies put in place so settings are maintained. Another key area of concern is that of meetings. Lync has a new meeting infrastructure both at the client functionality level and at the server level. You must ensure that users on OCS are properly trained to conduct the new Lync meeting-join experience. To help in this regard, it makes sense to roll out the Lync attendee client so that even users on the OCS client can make full use of Lync meeting features when they are invited to a Lync meeting.

Migrate to Lync Migrating to Lync is a complex set of processes that will move you from a stable OCS environment to a stable Lync environment with minimal downtime.

Master It You have been asked to lay out the steps to migrate to Lync. What are they?

Solution

1. **Prepare for the migration:** This stage includes ensuring that all documentation is up to date and that the latest patches are installed on all systems.
2. **Deploy the first Lync pool:** Here you create the Lync topology and install front-end (or Standard Edition) servers.
3. **Merge OCS and Lync Topology:** With Lync installed, you must ensure that Lync knows about the OCS organization by using the Merge 2007 or 2007 R2 Topology Wizard.
4. **Configure the first Lync pool:** At this point, you must configure the Lync pool to communicate properly with OCS, in particular the Edge and Mediation server roles.
5. **Test and migrate pilot users:** Here you move the first test users over from OCS to Lync and test coexistence functionality.

6. **Add Lync Edge and Director roles:** Introduce the Lync Edge and Director roles to give Lync its own route to the outside world.
7. **Move Lync pool from pilot to production:** This step involves migrating the remaining services required to take the Lync pool from pilot to production, including the Edge federation route, Response Group services, and Exchange UM contact objects. Once it is complete, all users are on Lync.
8. **Complete post-migration steps:** At this point all users are on Lync, so you can migrate any remaining services across to Lync such as conferencing directories, the Mediation server, and Dial-in conferencing numbers.
9. **Decommission legacy systems:** Finally, you must remove OCS from the organization and rerun the Lync Merge OCS 2007 or 2007 R2 Topology Wizard to remove OCS from the Lync topology.

Chapter 8: Introduction to PowerShell and the Lync Management Shell

Use the PowerShell command syntax. PowerShell is an easy-to-use command-line interface that provides more control over the manipulation and configuration of Lync (as well as other Microsoft and third-party products).

PowerShell cmdlets consist of a verb, indicating the process (`New`, `Enable`, `Set`, and so on) and a noun, indicating the object (`CsUser`, `CsPool`, `CsExternalAccessPolicy`, and so on).

Master It You need to enable a new user for Lync Server 2010. Which is the correct cmdlet to use?

- `Enable-CsUser`
- `Set-CsUser`
- `New-CsUser`

Solution

```
Enable-CsUser
```

Employ tips and tricks to get more out of PowerShell. PowerShell has many built-in capabilities native to PowerShell itself; extensions such as Lync provide the specifics to manage an application environment.

One of its most powerful features is the ability to pipe output from one command to another. This ability lets you easily and quickly perform repetitive tasks.

Master It You want to enable all users for Enterprise Voice. How would you do this?

Solution

```
Get-CsUser | Set-CsUser EnterpriseVoiceEnabled $True
```

Get help using PowerShell. The ability to provide detailed help information on any cmdlet, as well as use case examples, without leaving the PowerShell environment is an invaluable timesaver.

Master It You need to manipulate some pool configuration items but you can't remember which cmdlet to use. How can you identify possible cmdlets to use?

Solution

```
Get-Command *pool*
```

Understand PowerShell remoting and scripting. PowerShell provides a wealth of scripting capability, allowing relatively easy automation of everyday tasks which previously could be very complex.

Remoting extends PowerShell even further. Now you don't need to install individual administration toolsets for every application on an administrator's workstation; simply connect remotely to a PowerShell session and you can use the cmdlets.

Master It You want to administer the Lync Server 2010 configuration from your local workstation without installing any local administration tools and without using Remote Desktop. How would you connect to a remote PowerShell?

Solution

```
$session = New-PsSession -ConnectionUri https://se01.gaots.local/ocspowershell
-Authentication NegotiateWithImplicitCredential
Import-PsSession $session
```

Chapter 9: Role-Based Access Control

Use PowerShell to list the standard RBAC groups. RBAC in Lync 2010 is administered through the Lync Server Management Shell (LSMS). There are nine standard roles that ship with Lync; they provide an organization the ability to delegate administration with a reasonable degree of granularity.

Master It You are in the middle of planning your enterprise Lync deployment and have been asked by the senior architect to research the available options for administrative delegation. You have been asked to provide a list of standard RBAC roles.

Solution To list the standard roles, you would run the following PowerShell command:

```
Get-CsAdminRole | Where-Object {$_.IsStandardRole -eq $True} | fl Identity
```

Understand the permissions available to each role. There are nine RBAC roles in Lync. These roles range from granting high-level administrative access using the CsAdministrator role to read-only access with the CsViewOnlyAdministrator. To use them properly, you need to know what each role does and understand any overlaps where different roles provide the same capability.

Master It As part of an investigation into how to make the best use of RBAC, you have been asked to identify a list of cmdlets each role grants access to so that it can be analyzed to see which RBAC role best fits the way your administrative teams work.

Solution To provide a list of the cmdlets assigned to an RBAC role, use the command in the following example. It lists the cmdlets assigned to the CsArchivingAdministrator role.

```
Get-CsAdminRole -Identity CsArchivingAdministrator | Select-Object -
ExpandProperty Cmdlets | Out-File c:\csarchivingadminrolecmdlets.txt
```

Undertake planning for RBAC roles. Your implementation of RBAC roles should relate to the way your organization is set up for administration. Some organizations are centralized and others are distributed. You must understand your organizational structures and take them into account when planning RBAC roles. It is also important to follow the principle of least privilege, granting only the rights necessary for an administrator to do the job. This may mean utilizing custom roles and targeted scopes either at user OUs or Lync sites.

Master It You are in the middle of planning your enterprise Lync deployment and have been asked by the senior architect to plan the RBAC deployment in your organization. What should you consider?

Solution You must take into account many factors:

- The nature of administration in your organization, is it centralized or distributed?
- How many levels of administrators do you have; are there help-desk staff who need basic permissions, or are there a handful of senior administrators who do everything?
- Are there separate telephony teams that sit outside of the Server department but need access to maintain the telephony functions of Lync?
- Do your Lync administrators also manage Exchange? If so, how do the roles in Exchange correlate to Lync roles?
- The principle of least privilege: should you only grant administrators rights to do their job by using scopes both for site and user?

Create custom RBAC roles and assign them to administrators Lync allows the creation of custom RBAC roles. These are not as flexible as in Exchange, because you cannot grant access to specified single cmdlets. When creating a custom RBAC role, you must specify a template role from one of the nine standard roles and then set an appropriate scope.

Master It Having carried out a planning exercise, you have decided that the standard Lync roles are not adequate for your organization. Because you have a separate site supported by a separate team of junior admins who only need to manage users in one site, you need to be more specific about the areas that certain administrators can manage. How would you create an RBAC role to ensure that the junior admins don't have too many permissions?

Solution First, you would identify the relevant standard role to use as a template for the custom RBAC role. In this case, you would use the CsUserAdministrator role. Next, consider a suitable name for the role—in this case, RemoteSite-CsUserAdministrator.

Next, you would create the Universal security group in AD with the same name as the new role. Finally, you would create the actual role and while creating the role scope it to the Lync site and also to a specific OU that holds the users for the site as follows:

```
New-CsAdminRole -Template CsUserAdministrator -Identity RemoteSite-CsUser
Admin -ConfigScopes "Site:RemoteSite" -UserScopes "OU:ou=RemoteSiteUsersOU,
dc=gaots,dc=local"
```

Carry out general administration including granting and removing RBAC roles. There are few cmdlets that allow management of RBAC roles in Lync 2010 and most use the `CsAdminRole` verb. All PowerShell roles are assigned through the membership of a linked Active Directory Universal security group.

Master It A colleague who administered Lync has moved to a new role, and his replacement starts on Monday. You have been asked to ensure that the new staff member has the appropriate rights to do his job.

Solution Adding and removing RBAC roles from a user is as simple as ensuring membership in the related AD security groups. In this instance, you would first check which roles the colleague who has left was a member of using the following command:

```
Get-CsAdminRoleAssignment -Identity "Useralias"
```

Next, you would add the new administrator's user account to the relevant AD groups and remove the old administrator's account at the same time.

Report on the use of RBAC roles. Given that the purpose of RBAC is to provide people with administrative access to a system, there will always be a need to review and provide reports to management on who has what access. Reporting on RBAC takes various forms but can all be done through LMS.

Master It You have been asked to provide details on which roles have access to the APAC site and list the membership of those roles. How would you proceed?

Solution First, you would identify the roles that have access to the APAC site using the following command:

```
Get-CsAdminRole | Where-Object {$_.ConfigScopes -match "site:APAC"}
```

Next, to enable searching in AD groups, you would load the Active Directory module into PowerShell:

```
Import-Module ActiveDirectory
```

Finally, for each of the roles that the previous command returns, you would run the following command to list the membership:

```
Get-ADGroupMember -Identity Rolesfromlist | Select name
```

Chapter 10: User Administration

Search for users in the LSCP and PowerShell. Lync offers huge flexibility in what can be done to configure and control the Lync user experience. However, in order to work efficiently in Lync, being able to identify and retrieve information about different groups of users based on various criteria is critical. It is this skill which enables you to target specific groups with specific policies. As with most administration, you can search for users in both LSCP and PowerShell.

Master It You have been asked to run a report on two groups of users. How would you handle the following requests? Can you use two different types of search?

Locate all users in Marketing.

Locate all users who register to the `se01.gaots.local` pool.

Solution In PowerShell, run the following command:

```
Get-CsUser -LDAPFilter "(Department=Marketing)"
```

This will get all the marketing users enabled for Lync using an LDAP filter.

Another type of search is the standard PowerShell Filter demonstrated in the following command:

```
Get-CsUser -Filter {RegistrarPool -eq "se01.gaots.local"}
```

This command gets all users registering to the pool `se01.gaots.local`.

Perform basic user administration in the LSCP and in PowerShell. As would be expected, most basic administration can be performed in LSCP and in PowerShell. New users can be created, deleted, enabled, and disabled in both. You can, of course, also change various Lync properties—in particular, things like the SIP URI of a user and the pool to which they register. User administration is generally carried out by a user who is a member of the CsUserAdministrator RBAC role.

Master It You have been asked to enable all users, except those who are in Marketing, for Lync. How would you do this? In addition, one of your colleagues, who is a domain administrator, has asked you to make some changes to his account. What problems might you face?

Solution You first need to search for the users and then pipe the output to the `Enable-CsUser` cmdlet. Remember that until a user is enabled for Lync, you must use the `Get-CsAdUser` cmdlet to find them:

```
Get-CsAdUser -LDAPFilter "!(Department=Marketing)" | Enable-CsUser -RegistrarPool
se01.gaots.local SipAddressType EmailAddress
```

This will get all the users who are not members of the Marketing department (note the use of the ! wildcard to signify `NOT`). It then enables them for Lync on the `se01.gaots.local` pool using their email addresses for SIP URIs.

For your colleague, you can only administer domain administrator Lync users from PowerShell when you are logged on as a domain administrator yourself.

Understand Lync policies. Lync has significantly improved the policy architecture since OCS 2007 R2. Although AD Group Policy still can have a role to play in getting the Lync client up and running, Lync enforces the majority of policy through in-band provisioning. It uses SIP messages to push policy out to the client instantly and ensures that there is no requirement for domain membership. Users get a consistent experience no matter where they log on. To apply Lync policies properly, it is important to understand the new scope model, in which polices can be applied at the Global, Site, Service, and User levels and how inheritance works so that the policy closest to the user wins.

Master It You have been asked to explain to a new Lync administrator the different scopes at which a policy can be applied and how different scopes affect the identity of the policy. What would you tell her?

Solution Lync policies can apply at several levels. By default, there is a global policy that contains the default settings for each policy type. As an administrator with the CsAdministrator RBAC role, you can create policies at the Site, Service, and User level. The Identity of the policy is defined by the level at which it is assigned. For example:

```
Site:PolicyName
Registrar:se01.gaots.co.uk
```

Site and Service policies are assigned automatically when they are created, as they are specifically linked by name to a certain object. However, User policies have to be assigned. The Identity of a user policy is `Tag:`*`PolicyName`*, which is why they are sometimes called Tag policies.

Manipulate Lync policies. Lync policies are controlled and applied to users either through PowerShell or LSCP. When in the shell, your search skills are critical to ensure you can closely target relevant user groups. It is here that the piping capabilities of PowerShell are so useful. You can, of course, also apply policy through LSCP, which has a helpful Assign Policy page where you can apply applicable policies to one or many users from a single screen.

Master It You have been asked to create a new Client Policy for the APAC site. You first need to check the default settings for the policy and then customize it to limit the number of users a person can have on their contacts list to 300. How would you proceed?

Solution To see the default settings for a policy, you can always create a new policy without specifying any settings, but that would leave you with a leftover policy. Instead, a cleaner way is to use the `-InMemory` parameter as follows:

```
New-CsClientPolicy -Identity TestDefaultSettings -InMemory
```

This creates an object in memory and prints the default settings. Used in this way, it is never committed to disk.

To create the policy you require, you would use the following command:

```
New-CsClientPolicy -Identity Site:EMEA -MaximumNumberOfContacts 300
```

Choose the right policy for the job. There are a vast range of policy settings in Lync. One of the hardest things an administrator must do is understand where to make certain configurations. LSCP makes available many policy settings, but it is not always obvious which PowerShell cmdlet sets which setting, compared to what is presented in the LSCP. Equally, it is not possible to carry out all configuration through the LSCP, with some of the most wide-ranging policies only being configured through PowerShell.

Master It You have been asked to design a set of policies for your Lync organization. Where would you gather more information about specific settings?

Solution The list of cmdlets available to create Lync policies and set Lync functionality is wide, so you would use the help file to identify what each individual parameter would do. Also, searching in the help file for `cs*policy` and `cs*configuration` will bring back a raft of cmdlets to review.

Chapter 11: Archiving and Monitoring

Understand the architecture for the Archiving and Monitoring role. Although related to different aspects of the data, the Archiving and Monitoring server roles are very similar in function, and they have similar back-end requirements. This allows them to be easily colocated and share the same database.

Master it What are the names of the MSMQ queues created by the Archiving and Monitoring server roles?

Solution Archiving: lcslog

Monitoring: lcsqoeq

Monitoring: lcscdrq

Provide reporting on the data available from the Archiving and Monitoring roles. Lync Server 2010 provides a monitoring server report pack containing almost 50 reports, which focus on the QoE data. Non-Microsoft vendors provide additional report capability for the other databases and, of course, you can always write your own reports.

Master It What options are available for creating customized reports?

Solution You can connect via ODBC from any data manipulation software (such as Excel), or you can use SQL Server Report Builder to create and publish reports to the SQL Reporting Services server.

Use the capabilities in the System Center Operations Manager management pack to report on the availability of the Lync 2010 service. With the implementation of the Lync Server 2010 Monitoring Management Pack for System Center Operations Manager 2007, administrators have a consolidated approach and location for collating and monitoring system (and service) uptime.

Master it Which synthetic transactions will confirm the status of the Address Book service?

Solution `Test-CsAddressBookService`

`Test-CsAddressBookWebQuery`

Chapter 12: Troubleshooting

Confirm that the basics are in place from the infrastructure side. Lync Server 2010 relies on a range of additional infrastructure to be able to provide its functionality—such as Active Directory, SQL, DNS, Network, and so on. If any of these additional areas suffer interruptions or misconfigurations, it is extremely likely that Lync 2010 will begin to demonstrate issues also.

Master It An internal Lync 2010 client is having difficulty connecting to its home pool when using automatic configuration. Describe the flow of DNS and connection attempts made for a client on the corporate network.

Solution First automatic configuration will attempt the following DNS queries:

```
_sipinternaltal._tcp.<sip domain> (A DNS SRV record)
Sipinternal.<sip domain>
Sip.<sip domain>
```

The SRV record will return a CNAME record, which will require a further DNS lookup to return the IP address. All other requests will return the IP address of the pool.

The client will attempt to connect and register with this pool; if this is a Director pool, the client will receive a redirect to the home pool.

A further DNS lookup will be carried out due to the redirection, and the client will attempt to register with a server from this pool; if this server is not the home server itself, the final redirect will occur with the client being sent to the home server.

If the SRV record is not available, the remaining DNS records are resolved in order, with the client attempting to connect to the returned addresses.

Understand how to troubleshoot the client. The Lync 2010 client provides a lot of information in the configuration section as well as the log files to aid with troubleshooting and should not be overlooked.

Master It Where are the client log files stored?

Solution In the following folder:

```
%USER PROFILE%\Tracing
```

Know how to enable troubleshooting on the server. The Lync Server 2010 roles each have individual components that require logging and also provide performance counter objects that can be monitored.

By default, logging is not enabled on the servers, and it has a number of different levels to which it can be applied.

Master It Which tool is used to enable logging and configure the specific logging parameters on a Lync Server 2010 server?

Solution

```
OCSLOGGER.EXE
```

Called the Lync Server Logging Tool in the Lync Server 2010 programs folder.

Understand and use the troubleshooting tools available. In addition to the built-in logging functionality of Lync Server 2010, additional tools can (and should) be downloaded and installed on each of the servers to provide a better range of data, which is ready to be captured in the event of a problem.

Master It Which tool is recommended to be used for analyzing SIP logs or message traces? And where can it be found?

Solution

```
SNOOPER.EXE
```

It is part of the Lync Server 2010 Resource Kit download.

Chapter 13: Getting Started with Voice

Understand the voice capabilities. Lync Server 2010 has dramatically expanded the capabilities provided by Microsoft in the Unified Communications space to be almost on a par with enterprise PBXs (and certainly equal to, if not better, than departmental PBX offerings).

Master It Describe the benefits of media bypass.

Solution Media bypass allows the media flow to bypass the Mediation server and connect directly to the gateway or remote endpoint. This removes potential delays introduced by transcoding the media, resulting in less chance of call quality degradation. In addition, by removing this transcoding requirement from the Mediation server, it allows the Mediation server to scale up the number of concurrent calls it can handle, as well provide the capability to colocate the Mediation server on a front end, reducing the deployed server footprint.

Understand the voice architecture. With the introduction of media bypass and the support for virtualization, the architectural requirements to deploy Voice have been consolidated into a smaller server footprint, and at the same time additional functionality has been included in the product. Significant investment has been made in the high availability and resiliency deployment models.

Master It Describe the user experience when the user's home pool fails and a backup registrar has been configured.

Solution The user's clients will be disconnected from the server, and it will automatically log in to the backup registrar. This is known as Survivable mode and it provides limited functionality—the ability to make and receive voice calls, as well as the capability to search for users.

A user who has a call in progress will be able to continue this call with no impact (the client will transfer to Survivable mode seamlessly in the background).

If a user is joined to a conference hosted on the failed pool, they will lose connection to the conference and be unable to rejoin. If the conference is hosted on a different pool, they will remain connected.

Configure voice policies and routing. Aside from the architectural requirements, to enable Enterprise Voice requires configuration to be applied to users (policies) and back-end configuration to be applied to the servers (routing).

Master It What configuration joins the user configuration to the server configuration and provides the permissions to enable (or block) a call?

Solution PSTN usages are attached to both the Voice policy and the routes, and a user must have the PSTN usage as part of their Voice policy to enable them to use a route associated with the same PSTN usage.

Chapter 14: Call Admission Control

Identify Call Admission Control–capable endpoints. Before designing and configuring Call Admission Control, you need to understand where it can be applied to ensure the proper configuration is identified.

Master It You are in the process of defining a migration from OCS R2 to Lync Server 2010. Users previously reported some issues with call quality due to the capacity on the network, so Call Admission Control is required. Which user endpoints can be restricted by the Call Admission Control policy?

Solution All Lync 2010 endpoints can be restricted by the Call Admission Control policy:

- Lync 2010
- Lync 2010 Phone Edition
- Lync Server 2010 (edge, mediation, and front-end server roles)

Configure policy-based Quality of Service controls. Call Admission Control provides application-layer management of the call bandwidth; however, to truly provide this guarantee to clients, Quality of Service is required to operate on the network layer. Windows Vista introduced policy-based Quality of Service controls.

Master It You have restricted the port range to be 5000 – 5999, and you will deploy Lync 2010 to your users. An application utilized in the finance department uses the port range 5500 – 5599. How can you ensure that only the Lync 2010 traffic is prioritized on the network?

Solution Define a "Policy-based QoS" Group Policy, which specifies the port range to prioritize and sets the application to `Communicator.exe`.

Design a Call Admission Control solution. Call Admission Control can be complex in large interconnected networks. A properly designed solution will ensure two important requirements of Call Admission Control are met: user call quality is high and the network is not saturated.

Master It What special considerations should be given to an MPLS network?

Solution The MPLS cloud should be defined as a region, with each network link defined as a connection to a site. No site should be associated directly with the region. If multiple MPLS clouds are used (for example, one in Europe and one in America), then each should be a separate region, and region links (and routes) will be required too.

Configure Call Admission Control. Once designed, Call Admission Control needs to be configured and applied to the Lync 2010 servers. The servers will keep each other constantly updated as to the number of the calls and bandwidth used on the network. By using the built-in logging functionality, it is possible to capture an hourly snapshot of the state, with more detailed reporting available via the monitoring server.

Master It What needs to be defined and applied to configure Call Admission Control?

Solution

- Regions
- Sites
- Policy Profiles
- Subnets
- If multiple regions are defined, you also need Region Links and Region Routes.

Chapter 15: E911 and Location Information Services (LIS)

Describe the E911 requirements for North America. Enhanced emergency services dialing provides location information to emergency services, enabling them to better respond in the event of an emergency.

Master It Is the provision of location information with emergency dialing compulsory?

Solution Providing location information is required only in certain states in North America, and even then the requirements differ from state to state.

Configure Lync Server 2010 to meet E911 requirements. As a viable PBX, Lync Server 2010 is required to meet the E911 requirements to provide location information data, and as such must have validated address information provided with each emergency call.

Master It Through what configuration items can location information data be delivered to the Lync 2010 client?

Solution By any of the following methods:

Subnet

Switch Chassis

Switch Port

Wireless SSID

Manually

Understand how Location Information Services can be used by users outside North America. Although the actual requirements are only currently defined in locations in North America, beta program feedback from customers indicated that automatic location information services are extremely useful and desired worldwide.

Master It What specifically is required to enable location information services in North America, and what different requirements are in place for the rest of the world?

Solution Inside North America, address validation against the Master Street Address Guide provides the address validation. Outside North America, the requirement is to have installed at least Cumulative Update 1 to provide a suggested address automatically.

Chapter 16: Extended Voice Functionality

Understand the extended voice functionality. Extended voice functionality provides additional voice applications that many organizations expect a PBX to have. Understanding what these applications can and cannot do is important, so you can make the correct decisions when implementing them and know when a third-party solution is better.

Master It The manager for an internal help desk has been to a trade show and has been told he needs to have a full contact center to implement certain requirements. All he needs is to route calls to agents. He does not care about reporting or recording; he just needs to make sure that calls get to the right people. He is adamant he needs a call center because this is what the experts have told him.

Solution Response Groups can fulfill these requirements because items such as reporting and recording are not required. Although it can be difficult to dissuade people from accepting what an expert has told them, showing them what can be done is usually the best way. Find out what they need to do and create the Response Groups and show them that you can do what they want at a fraction of the cost.

Design solutions using extended voice functionality. Designing is usually seen as a boring, time-consuming task, when all you want to do is get your hands dirty and implement something. Although some of the extended voice functionality is straightforward, other elements are complex, and missing the design stage could cause you problems later. Design, design, design—and implement once.

Master It You need to implement a dial-in conferencing solution globally. You need to have global dial-in numbers and support at least 100 concurrent PSTN calls to the conferencing solution.

Solution Dial-in conferencing may seem easy. You already have Enterprise Voice deployed. You just need to add some access numbers and away you go. Usually, this is not the case. Although you may have designed for Enterprise Voice in terms of PSTN capacity and bandwidth, dial-in conferencing adds more load, in this case the requirement for 100 concurrent calls PSTN. This requires not only additional PSTN capacity but also sufficient capacity on the Mediation and Conferencing Servers.

Never assume that an existing voice design will be able to cope with additional requirements. If you are changing the dynamics of an element, in this case Enterprise Voice, you need to go back to the drawing board and update the design to cope with the new requirements.

Implement extended voice functionality. Lync's extended voice functionality is useless if you do not know how to implement it and use it to its fullest potential. To do that, you need to make sure that what you implement works and is fully tested.

Master It You have implemented Call Park but users are complaining about intermittent issues with parking calls. The complaints are coming from all user types, which is strange because not all users should be able to park calls.

Solution The first step is to determine why these users are able to park calls. To do this, you can use PowerShell to query the Voice policies to see which ones have Call Park enabled. To do that, issue the following command:

```
Get-CsVoicePolicy | select Identity, EnableCallPark | fl
```

This will return all the Voice policies and indicate if Call Park is enabled or not. In this case, the following was returned:

```
Identity       : Global
EnableCallPark : False

Identity       : Tag:Attendants
EnableCallPark : True

Identity       : Tag:IWs
EnableCallPark : True
```

From this, you can see that the IWs policy has `EnableCallPark` set to True, allowing all Information Workers to park calls. Setting this to False will prevent them from using Call Park:

```
Set-CsVoicePolicy -Identity IWs -EnableCallPark $false
```

Now only the attendants will be able to park calls. At this stage, you can wait to see if the attendants report any issues. The intermittent issue probably occurred because Call Park ran out of orbits, since it was sized only for the attendants and not for everyone.

Chapter 17: Exchange, SharePoint, and Group Chat

Integrate Lync with Exchange. Exchange provides a wide range of functionality to Lync, and Lync helps enhance Exchange. The most important integration points are for the provision of Voice Mail, where Exchange UM is the only supported Voice Mail platform for Lync. To enhance Exchange, Lync enables building presence and basic IM capabilities directly into OWA. There are also less obvious integration points, as Lync utilizes Exchange Web Services to pull information about users' calendar entries and their contacts, providing enhanced presence information and a single view of a person as an entity with whom to communicate.

Master It You company is rolling out Lync as its telephony platform, and you will be using Exchange 2010 as your voice mail platform. You have been asked to outline the process to the Exchange administrative team.

Solution Integration of Lync into Exchange UM takes the following major steps:

1. Install the Exchange UM role and ensure that the correct certificates are in place. It is important that the Exchange UM service is bound to a certificate that is trusted by Lync and has the FQDN of the Exchange UM server as its subject name.
2. Configure the Exchange UM elements of the system (dial Plan, Policy, and Auto Attendants). Exchange dial plans are used to set major configuration points such as the security of communications and the length of the phone extension number. Make sure your PIN access policy is set up suitably for your organization.
3. Ensure that Exchange knows about Lync as a gateway. You will use the `ExchUCUtil.PS1` script to set the correct permissions and to set up the Exchange VoIP gateway object to represent the Lync server.
4. Check to see that Lync dial plans are configured correctly. Lync must be able to understand the four-digit dialing setup in the Exchange dial plan.
5. Configure Lync to use Exchange UM. You will use the `OcsUmUtil.exe` application to set up the contact objects so that Lync knows how to route calls to Exchange Voice mail and Auto Attendants.
6. Enable users for UM. Each user will need to be enabled for Exchange UM through either Exchange Management Console or PowerShell.

Integrate Lync with SharePoint. SharePoint integration is both relatively simple and potentially complex! It is simple in that integrating presence capability is automatic, and it is complex in that you have the ability through application development to put together almost any piece of communication-enhanced workflow that you can think up. SharePoint integration also provides the Skill Search capability to Lync.

Master It Your organization makes extensive use of SharePoint 2010 and already has OCS 2007 R2, which has been providing presence integration. Now you are moving to Lync 2010, and you have been asked to investigate the requirements for Skill Search integration between Lync and SharePoint.

Solution SharePoint-based Skill Search is not enabled in Lync by default.

In order for this new feature to work correctly, the following components and configuration are required:

- A full version of SharePoint is required; Windows SharePoint Services (WSS) will not work with Skills Search.
- SharePoint 2010 My Sites.
- The SharePoint User Profile service application; this stores information about users in a central location and is where users' My Sites are administered and configured.
- A SharePoint Search Center site URL; a feature introduced in Microsoft Office SharePoint Server 2007, it is a SharePoint site specifically configured for the search task. It includes certain fields, each responsible for a specific search task—for example, "people search."
- SharePoint must be published to the Internet so that external Lync clients can access it.
- Lync Server needs to be configured with the correct Search Center URL to provide to clients. The Search Center URL is provisioned to the Lync client through in-band settings, as discussed in Chapter 10.

Integrate Lync with Group Chat. Group Chat is a component of Lync, but it is one which in Lync 2010 is still essentially a separate technology integrated through shared presence and communication modalities. Group Chat provides a new way of collaborating, being very specific about the information you regard as worthy of your time, through the use of careful filters. It is a great solution for those working on projects or in a distributed environment perhaps even across time zones, where catching up on previous events is essential.

Master It Your company is considering deploying Group Chat as part of their Lync 2010 installation. You have been asked to understand and report back on the key Group Chat components. What would you cover?

Solution Group Chat is provided by four server roles, all but one of which are mandatory.

- The Lookup Server provides a well-known address, usually `OCSchat@domain.com`, and manages load-balancing when multiple servers are used. It distributes sessions to all available Channel servers in a round-robin fashion. It is required even if only one Group Chat server is deployed.

- The Channel server provides all Group Chat channel functionality, except for file posting, which is managed through the web service.
- The web service is provided via IIS on the Group Chat server. It allows for files to be uploaded and downloaded from channels.
- The Compliance server provides a route for third-party compliance tools to extract and record users' behavior within channels and submit this to an auditable store. A number of third-party compliance tools are supported, one example being Actiance, formerly Facetime.

Of course, other components are used: the Group Chat Admin tool, the Group Chat client, and the Group Chat Monitoring Management Pack. The last is used with System Center Operations Manager (SCOM) to provide optimal management.

Chapter 18: Third-Party Integration

Connect to telephony systems using a gateway. Gateway devices enable Lync to connect to a wide range of different telephony platforms in a uniform way, providing intelligent routing and security.

Master It When connecting to telephony systems, three main components come into play. What are they?

Solution Signaling transport is a way of passing information about the communication between systems, such as the calling number and called number. SIP is the protocol used with Lync, which can be carried over TCP (as Lync uses) or UDP, as some SIP trunk providers use.

A media codec is the method used to encode the audio (or video) stream for transport. It is agreed to by both parties as part of the signaling traffic when the call is set up. Different systems support different codecs: Lync uses RTAudio natively, while G.711 is common on the PSTN. The gateway performs a process called transcoding, which is the process of converting audio encoded with one codec into audio encoded in another codec to help two different systems communicate.

Media transport is the process of actually getting the encoded audio from one system to another. The standard protocol for transporting the voice traffic itself over IP is Real-Time Transport Protocol (RTP). A later extension to this protocol was the addition of security to eliminate the risk of interception and eavesdropping. Known as Secure RTP, or SRTP, the endpoint devices encrypt any voice traffic within a secure payload, before transmitting over the IP network. Lync employs SRTP for communication to the gateway.

Integrate with your PBX. Connecting Lync to telephony systems need not be hard; however, there are many areas you must consider to ensure that you make the correct deployment choices. Lync can connect directly to an ITSP or a PBX, or in both cases can utilize a gateway device to provide security, control, and intelligent routing of traffic.

Master It Your PBX is five years old and capable of being upgraded to talk to Lync directly. You want to deploy Lync for Enterprise Voice and need a way out to the PSTN. What must you consider in your decision about connecting Lync to the PSTN?

Solution While your PBX could be upgraded, if you are deploying Lync for voice, it is unlikely that spending additional money on a piece of legacy hardware you plan to replace makes sense. Therefore, you have to consider either operating Lync as an entirely separate entity to the PBX with a separate numbering scheme or far more likely, utilizing a gateway to connect the two systems. You have a choice about where you position the gateway in system. Placing the gateway in front of the PBX and Lync is highly recommended; the gateway will take the place of the PBX in terminating the inbound lines. This gives the most flexibility in the way calls can be routed and means that the PBX hardly has to be reconfigured at all, leaving the gateway to intelligently route calls between the systems.

Use RCC to integrate with your PBX. Remote Call Control (RCC) allows you to use the Lync software client on your PC to control your physical phone handset from PBX vendors like Cisco, Mitel, and Avaya. It allows you to maintain your PBX as the audio transport mechanism while enhancing the functionality of the PBX with click-to-call and Address Book lookup features of the Lync software client. Each vendor has a slightly different way of hooking up Lync with their PBX, as they each provide the SIP/CSTA gateway that allows communication.

Master It You have been asked to look into why your company might use RCC. What are the key points about which you would report?

Solution RCC is useful in that it extends the capability of an existing PBX. It enables the Lync client to be used to control the phone and provides integration with the PC, for elements like name lookup, call logging, and simple by-contact (rather than number) dialing. If you have a heavily entrenched PBX system, this may be an integration point that is worth considering. However, RCC is a challenging technology to implement, given that each vendor has its own SIP/CSTA gateway. It also ties you into a legacy PBX technology, which by definition cannot provide the fully integrated experience that Lync embraced completely as a voice communication platform can provide. Finally, RCC users cannot make video calls, which is a massive limitation for some.

Deploy a Survivable Branch Appliance. The Lync SBA is one of the great additions that make Lync a fully viable voice platform for the enterprise. It provides the capability for branch offices to maintain the ability for PSTN breakout even if the WAN to the central Lync site is down.

Master It You have been asked to roll out an SBA to a branch location. What are the main prerequisite and deployment steps to which you should adhere?

Solution First, you should prestage the SBA in the central site. This requires the following steps:

1. A reverse look-up must be created on the DNS server for the SBA.
2. DNS *A* records must be available for the gateway and SBA.
3. The SBA should be added as a computer before deployment, and RTCUniversalSBATechnician should be in the default group.
4. A Service Principal Name needs to be applied to the SBA computer in `ADSI.edit`.

5. The account used within the gateway to deploy the SBA (for example, Administrator) should be a member of the RTCUniversalSBATechnician group.
6. The SBA should be configured in the correct branch site from Lync Topology Builder and successfully published to the CMS.

Once the prerequisites are met, the deployment should proceed as follows:

1. Install and physically cable the SBA at the branch site.
2. Configure an IP address for the SBA.
3. Join the domain.
4. Prepare the SBA and replicate against the front-end pool.
5. Assign the required certificates to enable security.
6. Start the services.
7. Verify the operational status.
8. Start to migrate users in the branch to the SBA.

Connect to other external systems via an XMPP gateway. The XMPP gateway provided by Microsoft as an add-on for Lync gives you the capability to connect Lync to other IM platforms, both internally (in the case of an internal Jabber or Sametime system) or externally to public clouds like Gmail. It is deployed on a separate server and interacts with Lync through the Edge server.

Master It You need to install the XMPP gateway. Where can you get it (and what is the quirk in its name)?

Solution The XMPP gateway software can be downloaded from the Microsoft download site at this URL:

```
www.microsoft.com/download/en/details.aspx?id=8403
```

There is also a single hotfix for the gateway relating to Knowledge Base article number 2404570, which is available at the following URL:

```
www.microsoft.com/download/en/details.aspx?id=12722
```

The name of the released version of the gateway refers to Office Communications Server 2007 R2, but this version is supported with Lync 2010.

Integrate with hardware video conferencing platforms. Lync can integrate with several hardware video platforms to provide control and connectivity through Lync to room-based and high-quality video networks.

Master It You are trying to configure Lync integration with a Polycom HDX unit, but it won't connect. What might be causing an issue?

Solution There are a couple of common errors when configuring the HDX platform to talk to Lync. You should double-check that the Lync user logging into the HDX for enterprise voice is enabled, and you should also check that you have matching encryption settings on both sides, so you don't have one platform requiring encryption where the other one will only send in the clear.

Utilize third-party software enhancements. As a software UC platform, Lync is infinitely extendable. This gives rise to the possibility for third-party developers to create products that enhance the native functionality in key ways, such as call recording and call billing. Equally, it enables in-house development teams to incorporate Lync communications functionality directly into line-of-business apps in your organization.

Master It Call recording is one of the available add-on applications for Lync. Name the two locations where call recording can be carried out and describe the difference this makes to the types of calls that can be recorded.

Solution Two types of call recording are typically used: trunk side and line side. Trunk-side recording typically records all calls, which include a participant from inside or outside the organization, both for inbound and outbound calls. Line-side recording allows calls between internal extensions and also those external to the organization, to be recorded, thereby giving greater flexibility by allowing any call to be recorded.

Chapter 19: Mobile Devices

Understand the mobile client features. With CU4, Microsoft provides support for some of the most popular mobile devices (phones and tablets) on the market, bringing the functionality of Lync 2010 to the mobile workforce.

Master It You have deployed the Mobility Service Update to the server infrastructure and made available the Lync 2010 mobile clients to your users. Some users report that they cannot send Bing map location information within IMs. Which client are they likely to be using?

Solution Only the clients for Apple devices (iPhone and iPad) provide support for sending Bing map information, so the users could be using any of the following:

- Windows Phone
- Android
- Nokia

Understand how to plan for Mobility service. In addition to providing a mobile Lync 2010 client, your organization needs to make changes to the Lync Server 2010 infrastructure and architecture. Prior to rolling out the client, these changes need to be put in place and communicated to any users using manual configuration to ensure they maintain a consistent experience and functionality.

Master It You need to make certificate changes to the front end, Directors, and Proxy servers. What additional entries are required on each certificate?

Solution Additional SAN entries for the Autodiscover and Mobility services are required, both for internal and external FQDNs:

`SAN=lyncdiscoverinternal.`*`<SIP domain>`* (front end, Director)

`SAN=lyncdiscover.`*`<SIP domain>`* (front end, Director, reverse proxy)

`SAN=lyncwebpool.`*`<SIP domain>`* (front end)

`SAN=lyncwebextpool.<SIP domain>` (front end, Director, reverse proxy)

Understand the installation procedure for Mobility Services. The provision of mobility support is achieved through the upgrade of the Lync Server 2010 infrastructure to CU4 and the further application of the Mobility Service Update. As with any update, it is extremely important to follow the installation guide in the release notes, and even more so in this case as new functionality is provided.

Master It Which two websites are created on the Lync Server 2010 pool front-end servers?

Solution `Autodiscover` and `Mcx` are both created on the internal and external websites.

Understand the infrastructure changes and configuration required for implementation of Mobility Services. Unlike CUs that implement fixes, the Mobility Service update provides new functionality, and this functionality is disabled by default, so it must be configured and enabled before users can use the new clients.

Master It Both Apple and Microsoft clients require push notification to be configured. How is this enabled through the Mobility Service Update?

Solution First, a new hosting provider must be configured using the `New-CsHostingProvider` cmdlet to point the Lync Server 2010 infrastructure to the Microsoft Lync Online service. Next, this Lync Online domain must be permitted access (using `New-CsAllowedDomain`). Finally, push notifications are disabled by default, so they need to be enabled using the `Set-CsMcxConfiguration` and `Set-CsPushNotificationConfiguration` cmdlets.

Any users assigned an External Access policy for mobile clients will be enabled to receive push notifications.

Appendix B

Adoption

Throughout this book, we've discussed a wide range of topics, explored details of the Lync product, and even delved into integration with third-party products. However, all this technical information is not enough to ensure that you have a successful experience with Lync.

Lync is a Unified Communications platform and, as such, has the potential to radically change a business. In particular, it changes the way people communicate. There are so many potential benefits of Unified Communications that it has become one of the top Chief Information Officer (CIO) priorities in recent years. However, unless this radical change is managed correctly within a business, it can easily cause anxiety and resentment, which hinder the implementation of the technology and slow the pace at which a business sees a return on its investment. After all, a business is simply a bunch of people who know things, and without them all you have is a shell, perhaps a brand. You need to take these people with you on your journey with Lync. This appendix aims to show you how!

Understanding the Power of UC

Unified Communications (UC) is one of the big buzz phrases in IT, rivaled only by "the Cloud" and "virtualization." It is notoriously hard to define, and people have various understandings of its meaning. For us, *unified communications* is all about providing customers—both end users and more widely the companies they work for—with the ability to work efficiently by communicating and collaborating through whatever means necessary, wherever and whenever they need to work. This communication might be either one-to-one or multiparty, either internal or across organizations. Communication should be woven tightly into an organization and integrated with the business process to drive productivity and efficiency. In that sense, UC could be thought of more as ubiquitous communication.

Of course, that utopian vision requires a fair amount of work in the background. There is the technical challenge of integrating and providing communication modalities such as voice, video, instant messaging (IM), email, voice mail, SMS, and fax, which we have covered in depth in this book. However, in many ways, the technical challenge is far simpler than changing the culture of a business, making information about people and process freely available, and changing the way people work and communicate. Any company that embarks on a Unified Communications project needs to clearly identify why they are doing so, what they must achieve, and how they will bring this change to users.

The Promise

As you can see, UC has immense power. It can allow people to communicate more efficiently than ever before, potentially saving companies millions in hard cash in several ways. For example, instead of spending money on a cents-per-minute basis with third-party conferencing services, with Lync you can bring this bridge functionality in house. In large companies, this has regularly shown savings in the order of millions or even tens of millions of dollars per year. Even in small companies of a few hundred people, it can save several thousand dollars a year, which is enough to contribute significantly to the deployment costs. Another significant savings possibility is that of travel reduction. Although we are in no way advocating stopping travel altogether, there might be chance to cut back, by perhaps sending only one person to meet a customer while the other dials in using voice and video to a meeting. Similarly, instead of senior managers all traveling to meet each other on a regular basis, some of these meetings could be held using solely Lync or Lync in conjunction with a third party like Polycom, thereby saving travel costs and time, and reducing the company's carbon footprint, which is so important these days. Other significant reductions in cost can be made through the flexibility Lync brings—for example, enabling people to work from home or from various different locations without necessarily coming into the central office all the time.

Other benefits are harder to quantify. Lync brings people together; as we've said, a business is only a bunch of people who know things working together. In that capacity, if these people cannot communicate quickly and efficiently, then you are simply not allowing them to work to their fullest potential. Enabling efficient communication can speed up business processes—for example, by allowing automated document signoff through routing to the most suitable person based on availability—and it can make resorting to voice mail a rarity, because presence makes a person's availability known. Finally, all these examples can easily be extended outside a single company to a wide ecosystem of partners and customers, allowing even wider savings and better customer service.

The Pitfalls

Unified Communications products often challenge organizational structure. Lync is no different. In fact, given that it is so successful as a true UC product bringing together IM, voice, video, and conferencing, it is perhaps even more disruptive. Traditionally, companies have had a networking team and a server team. Often there has also been a telephony team, which potentially in recent times has merged or coexisted with the networking team. Lync, of course, doesn't fit nicely into these boundaries. One of the major challenges many organizations will face is how to fit Lync into this structure. For some companies, this can stall the project to roll out Lync; other companies have to take a serious look at why they want Lync and then work out what the future looks like. In many senses that could be a combined working party or a complete restructuring, as the server team takes on board the new technology and brings in elements of the telephony and networking teams to make this work.

What is important is to be aware of the broader goal of deploying Lync and not to get bogged down in all the politics that inevitably occur as change happens within a business. Clarity of communication is important, so that people know what is happening, why it is being done, and what it means to them. Leadership is essential; projects sponsored by a strong CIO have far more chance of success than something led by a team from IT (often the server team), who inevitably end up fighting battles with networks and telecoms.

People react strongly to change, and not usually in a positive way. Of course, there are some who embrace change, but more often than not, people shy away from something different. This is simple human nature. However, in situations where you have placed your reputation on driving a successful rollout of new technology, it is something that needs significant thought to overcome. Much of the reticence can be overcome by explanation and user training.

All the elements outlined in "The Promise" earlier, when combined, offer huge potential; it is critically important that these messages are understood not just by the CIO who signs off on the project, but by the business as a whole. People need to be shown how this new technology makes their working lives easier.

Introducing Lync to Your Business

Now that we've looked at the power of UC and some of the human-related pitfalls that can befall deployments of this nature, let's move on to how best to address the rollout of Lync in your business. There are two major elements: one is to pilot Lync and the other is to ensure adequate training for users. However, there are also surrounding efforts that can be undertaken to play roles in a successful deployment.

Rolling out a new technology can be seen very much as launching a new product. As such, it is sensible to mount a marketing campaign. Many companies, for example, create posters and ads for display in prominent locations and on intranet portals. They help communicate key messages about the features of the new technology, such as the ability to create conference calls with ease; they also communicate why the business is deploying the technology, such as work flexibility and cost savings. The most successful examples of this type of campaign that we've been involved with created excitement before deployment, gradually enforced the messaging, added new information about features and functions, and highlighted where users could get support and learn more at their own pace. This type of prelaunch marketing campaign should utilize all the media types available, including items such as posters, websites, email messaging, and videos, perhaps from the CEO or other senior managers.

Lync Is More Than Just a Telephone System

Although Lync can replace a telephony system or conferencing platform, it is really important that you fight the widespread assumption that Lync is simply a replacement for whatever was previously in place. Simply put, it isn't! Yes, Lync takes over many functions provided by other communication platforms in the past; however, as we've mentioned many times, Lync is much more. It is a unified platform that allows not only communication in its own right, but communication as part of the business process.

It is absolutely essential that this mindset is positioned correctly at the highest levels of the company. This is not always a problem; sometimes people just "get it." But if your senior personnel think of Lync as "just another phone system," you will be limited, because the messages coming down from them will not be positive and will not have the changing effect that Lync can have. Be aware of this possibility and use all the resources available from Microsoft and the partner community to demonstrate the wider benefits and uses of Lync to ensure that your organization gets the most out of Lync.

Clearly not all of these and the following ideas will work for everyone, as every company is different; however, these suggestions have been tried and tested in several different scenarios and have been found to be useful.

Piloting Lync

Once you have made the decision to roll out Lync, running a pilot is essential. This may take a couple of different forms. You may find that running a proof of concept (PoC) is necessary to evaluate specific Lync features and functionality. The PoC would likely have very specific success criteria and look at only a handful of features. It would be carried out to prove that Lync can meet the stated requirements. It is important to make sure that the PoC isn't confused with a full pilot. The full pilot program should take place once the production deployment of Lync is completed. That way, people participating in the pilot would be running on the actual systems, which would be taken live if the pilot succeeds.

When starting up the main Lync pilot, the first thing to undertake is to set out the success criteria. Without this, you will never know whether you have succeeded in your aim and can continue with a Lync rollout. Success criteria can be very simple, in that you have run with Lync for two weeks across a broad range of users and received notification of issues that have been resolved. It could also be more specific, encompassing the uptime of the service and the number of minutes of voice, video, and conference calls completed. Either way, it is important to lay out these criteria and understand how you will monitor results, either through existing monitoring tools, such as System Center Operations Manager, or through Lync-specific tools, such as the Monitoring server reports, or perhaps even through your in-house help desk tool.

We have found that a pilot should take various steps. It will probably start as an evaluation by IT staff. This enables testing of all the main functionality without exposing it to the wider staff. It also enables IT to make sure they are comfortable monitoring and supporting the service and that they have hit the most common issues users are likely to experience. This is important, because part of the process of rolling out a new technology is to maintain a positive user experience. There is nothing worse than rolling out something to a wide audience too early when IT doesn't know how to support it, and when there are still major issues. Doing so causes negativity, and people won't want to use the technology, which is exactly the opposite of what is required for a successful rollout. This IT phase of the pilot is complete once any functionality issues are ironed out and the service has been running for a couple of weeks.

Of course, tech-savvy IT professionals are unlikely to use the new technology in the same way that the business users will; they can probably work around or fix most issues. Therefore, the next phase of the pilot is to broaden the scope of users. Throughout this phase, communication is key. It is very important to prepare pilot users for what they should expect, giving them clear and focused instructions, rather than bombarding them with messages that will not be read! Pilot members should be made aware of the status of the program, the way to get support, and how to give feedback. It is this feedback that will enable the project team to fully evaluate how Lync is performing for users and to tweak systems or policies as necessary to enable a wider rollout to commence.

One element of the pilot is particularly important—the choice of pilot users. The users must be chosen from various areas of the business. It is important to identify areas where different working practices are found and make sure these areas are represented. Given that Lync is a tool for communication, it often makes sense to enable a whole project team. It is, of course, also important to choose users who understand the importance of providing feedback; because without this, it is hard to gauge the status of the deployment.

Evaluation of the pilot is important. This can take several forms. You can generate reports from systems to evaluate based on your acceptance criteria, and you'll also want human input. As such, it makes sense to invite representative pilot users to a project board meeting to discuss issues and experiences. Although it may not be possible to directly quantify ease of use as a success criteria, the human feedback you get based on ease of use will help you guide the future rollout and will help you tweak the settings and policies. Furthermore, these individuals are likely to be chosen not only because they will give valuable feedback but also because they will become points of contact going forward as the technology is rolled out more widely in their areas of the business. If you like, these people will become the superusers, or champions.

Once you have properly met the criteria set out at the beginning of the pilot, you are ready to deploy more broadly. Be aware that it may take time to reach this stage, and that it is far better to spend time understanding issues, getting the support desk up to speed, and reconfiguring systems at this stage than it will be after you have rolled out more broadly. Even if you need to make significant changes, do so now. Then re-evaluate the success criteria and pilot again until you are sure that your Lync deployment is solid, fit for purpose, and meets business requirements.

Training Your Users

As with any new technology, training users is necessary if you want to ensure that the rollout is smooth and the benefits to the business are maximized. Given the type of technology Lync is, this is all the more important, as otherwise people can be left floundering and significantly slowed down. That is not to say that training needs to be extensive. Lync is a very easy to use technology; however, many people simply will have no idea of its capabilities. As part of your rollout, you can address this in many ways.

The first suggestion would be to carry out "Buzz Days." These events can take varying forms and should be carried out either during or near the Lync rollout. The general premise is that you make Lync available somewhere so people can come and play with it. These sessions can either be scheduled, whereby you identify a group of users and get them all down at once, or perhaps just set up timeslots and allow people to sign up themselves. Or you could simply set up machines with access to Lync in a common area with experts on hand so people passing can come and spend a few minutes getting the key points and having a go. The important thing with a Buzz Day is to identify the key messages you want to get across. Make sure you show people the functionality that is most important to them and then make sure they know how to back this up when they get stuck.

One thing beyond simply tasks that we believe should be covered is etiquette. Over the last ten to fifteen years people have gotten used to how email works and learned the customs associated with it, such as replying to all, using a signature, and out-of-office messages; however, Lync provides entirely new ways to communicate. Central to these is the concept of presence. It is important to discuss how you want people to use presence within your business. For example, frequently someone may be in a meeting and their presence will show as much, but they could take a quick IM. Equally, if someone doesn't want to be contacted, then they should set themselves to Do Not Disturb. A nuance to this is that people should be trained to put contacts into the relevant level of access group, so that only those who they want to be able to break through the Do Not Disturb state can do so. With all these subtle differences, it is something worth discussing as part of the pilot and then feeding into your training, so that users become accustomed to starting an IM with "Have you got a moment to talk?" rather than barging in with a direct call immediately.

It is likely that a combination of the training types previously outlined will be needed. While it will be fine for some users to come by and play with Lync, others with more specialized needs will need more extensive training. In general, this applies to two particular groups. First, those people identified as local area champions or super users should be given training. Often this will take an hour or perhaps an hour and a half, where these people are taken through Lync features in detail. They can be taught about common questions and user mistakes, which you will have picked up both from the training materials (discussed next) and also from your experiences in your pilot. Another important group is the executive assistants. This group is critical, because they have the ear of both the senior management and the wider staff in general. They also have a specific role that involves using Lync like few other people, in that they must be able to manage and make communications on behalf of others. The final group that warrants special training is the switchboard operators or receptionists. Again, they have a specific method of using Lync, usually via the Attendee Console, which provides the ability to handle and route multiple calls. Again, any loss in productivity here will be noticed quickly at high levels within the business, so this group must be given priority and have a clear method of escalation should problems occur.

Once you've conducted the training, one element that is perhaps useful is some form of accreditation. Many companies give users credit for completing training, and Lync training should be no different. This could range from online quizzes on a company portal to a specific test after the training. What you choose depends on the culture of your company, but either way, finding a method to measure capability and rewarding new education is valuable.

Training Materials

Now that we've discussed the training that should be conducted, this final section describes some of the materials already available to assist you with putting together your training.

Microsoft has put together a collection of different materials that are downloadable here:

```
www.microsoft.com/downloads/en/details.aspx?FamilyID=f01a17e2-bec0-42c7-b1ce-
fd4842ab1c91&displaylang=en
```

They are also available in online format along with a lot of useful additional material, like sample client application add-ins, here:

```
http://lync.microsoft.com/Adoption-and-Training-Kit/Pages/default.aspx
```

After downloading and extracting the 65MB ZIP file, you will find the following types of content:

QuickStarts The content enables users to get up to speed quickly with a variety of tasks including using IM and presence, using the various Lync clients, working with voice and video modalities, and sharing your desktop or programs.

ShortVideos The videos show a walkthrough of common tasks such as forwarding calls, sending an IM, and sharing your desktop, among others.

Training slides These slides provide a useful starting point for structured classroom training on topics such as conferencing and collaboration, working with delegates, working as an agent on a response group, and manning the switchboard using the Attendant Console.

WhatsNew This material is in both HTML and video format, and it highlights some of the key elements new in Lync 2010.

WorkSmarts This material covers slightly more advanced topics and is focused on developing smarter working practices, such as making presence work for you and how to schedule conferences and customize them at the same time.

CUSTOMIZING TRAINING MATERIALS

In the QuickStarts and WorkSmarts folders, the material is in HTML format and includes a folder containing style sheets and images related to the page. You have the option to customize these web pages and either publish them on an intranet or make them available to others for local download. Alternatively, they could be cut up and distributed via Word documents or inserted into regular quick-tip emails. In this way, the material can be repurposed for structured training or self-help.

Also at your disposal are a couple of resources for driving adoption. The first set of materials is aimed at helping you promote Lync and communicate with users as you move through the process of pilot and rollout of Lync. It is accessible here:

`www.microsoft.com/download/en/details.aspx?id=8737`

There are templates for posters, T-shirts, and perhaps even more usefully a variety of emails, as laid out in Table B.1.

TABLE B.1: The Template Emails Provided by the Adoption Kit

EMAIL TEMPLATE NUMBER	TIMING	SUBJECT	AUDIENCE	PURPOSE
1	1 month before rollout	Join the Microsoft Lync Rollout	All users	Build awareness and sign up users for the pilot
2a	Several weeks before rollout	Thanks for joining the Lync Pilot Rollout	Users accepted to the pilot	Notify user of acceptance to pilot
2b	Several weeks before rollout	Thanks for your interest in the Lync Rollout	Users rejected from the pilot	Notify user of rejection from pilot
3	1 week before rollout	Migration Warning	Users accepted to the pilot	Awareness of upcoming migration
4a	1 week before rollout	More Information Needed for Delegate Account	Users who will be delegates	Collect necessary information for delegate accounts
4b	Rollout day	Welcome and Installation Instructions	All users	Announcement of account migration/ installation instructions
5	Weekly after rollout	Scenario Spotlight—Highlights a common scenario each week and asks for feedback	All users	Provides a timely way to expose users to high-productivity scenarios and offers a way to collect targeted feedback

The second set of adoption materials is a custom intranet site that pulls together much of the information in the various forms previously laid out, including the HTML help pages and videos, into a website ready for deployment on the intranet in your organization. This custom site is shown in Figure B.1, and it can be downloaded at the following URL:

```
www.microsoft.com/download/en/details.aspx?id=3063
```

FIGURE B.1
The custom intranet site for assisting user adoption

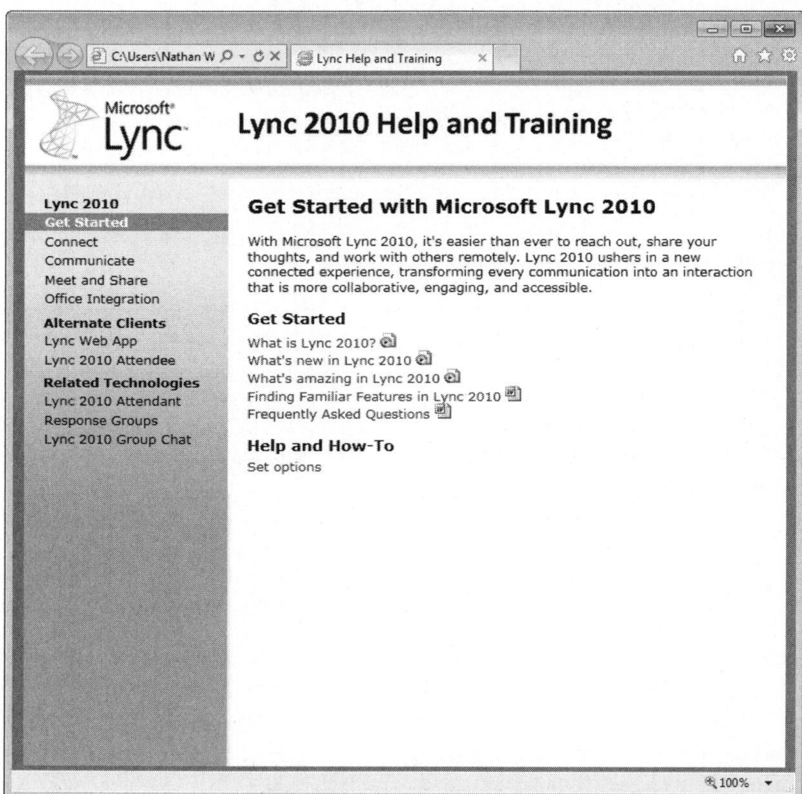

In the end, these resources are a great starting point. Likely, you will want to customize them for your company's needs. Thankfully, they were designed with that in mind!

Index

Note to the Reader: Throughout this index **boldfaced** page numbers indicate primary discussions of a topic. *Italicized* page numbers indicate illustrations.

B

E

G

H

I

N

Q

R

S

U

V